MW00778369

THE WORLDVIEW OF
THE WORD OF FAITH MOVEMENT

T&T Clark Systematic Pentecostal and Charismatic Theology

Series editors
Daniela C. Augustine
Wolfgang Vondey

THE WORLDVIEW OF
THE WORD OF FAITH MOVEMENT

Eden Redeemed

Mikael Stenhammar

LONDON • NEW YORK • OXFORD • NEW DELHI • SYDNEY

T&T CLARK
Bloomsbury Publishing Plc
50 Bedford Square, London, WC1B 3DP, UK
1385 Broadway, New York, NY 10018, USA
29 Earlsfort Terrace, Dublin 2, Ireland

BLOOMSBURY, T&T CLARK and the T&T Clark logo are trademarks
of Bloomsbury Publishing Plc

First published in Great Britain 2022
Paperback edition published 2023

Copyright © Mikael Stenhammar, 2022

Mikael Stenhammar has asserted his right under the Copyright, Designs and
Patents Act, 1988, to be identified as Author of this work.

For legal purposes the Acknowledgments on p. xiv constitute an extension of
this copyright page.

Cover design by Anna Berzovan
Cover image © naqiewei / GettyImages

All rights reserved. No part of this publication may be reproduced or transmitted
in any form or by any means, electronic or mechanical, including photocopying, recording,
or any information storage or retrieval system, without prior permission in writing
from the publishers.

Bloomsbury Publishing Plc does not have any control over, or responsibility for, any
third-party websites referred to or in this book. All internet addresses given in this
book were correct at the time of going to press. The author and publisher regret any
inconvenience caused if addresses have changed or sites have ceased to exist, but
can accept no responsibility for any such changes.

A catalogue record for this book is available from the British Library.

Library of Congress Cataloging-in-Publication Data
Names: Stenhammar, Mikael, author.
Title: The worldview of the word of faith movement: Eden redeemed / Mikael Stenhammar.
Description: London; New York: T&T Clark, 2022. | Series: T&T Clark systematic pentecostal
and charismatic theology | Includes bibliographical references and index. |
Identifiers: LCCN 2021027891 | ISBN 9780567703446 (hb) | ISBN 9780567703484
(paperback) | ISBN 9780567703453 (epdf) | ISBN 9780567703477 (ebook)
Subjects: LCSH: Faith movement (Hagin) | Christian philosophy. | Wright, N. T. (Nicholas Thomas)
Classification: LCC BR1643.5 .S74 2022 | DDC 289.9/4--dc23
LC record available at https://lccn.loc.gov/2021027891

ISBN: HB: 978-0-5677-0344-6
PB: 978-0-5677-0348-4
ePDF: 978-0-5677-0345-3
eBook: 978-0-5677-0347-7

Series: T&T Clark Systematic Pentecostal and Charismatic Theology

Typeset by Deanta Global Publishing Services, Chennai, India

To find out more about our authors and books visit www.bloomsbury.com and
sign up for our newsletters.

To Emelie.

CONTENTS

Contentsxi

FIGURES

PREFACE

My personal faith-journey within the Word of Faith movement makes the larger context of this work. In the 1990s, I joined a small Word of Faith church in Norrköping, Sweden, and then became part of the megachurch Livets Ord (aka Word of Life) in Uppsala, Sweden, pastored by Ulf Ekman. My longing for deeper knowledge led me to sit at the feet of Kenneth E. Hagin, Kenneth W. Hagin Jr., Keith Moore, and others during two years at Rhema Bible Training Center in Tulsa, Oklahoma, the United States. In my desire to spread the message, I served three years in a ministry training school in a Word of Faith megachurch in Mombasa, Kenya, led by the televangelist Wilfred Lai. The years of following and spreading the Word of Faith message enriched my faith in many ways. But the experiences also left a residue of challenging questions and concerns, which my undergraduate and postgraduate theological studies never settled. It was as if when I tried to understand the Word of Faith's *Gestalt*, its *Geist* always escaped my grasp. When returning to Kenya to start a theological school for grassroots-level church leaders and later serving as a Pentecostal pastor and Bible teacher in Sweden, the need for a holistic worldview-analysis became even more apparent. The Word of Faith is a movement too rich and complex to simply exclude or embrace. What to outsiders can look like a crude message of greed provides meaning and direction for millions of people. What to insiders look like absolute truth evidences theological flaws to outsiders. This dilemma requires a critical and therapeutic approach founded in careful analysis and discernment. For those inside the movement, I hope this study offers an opportunity for self-awareness—akin to identifying the personality you always had but never knew until taking a personality test—and hence chances for critical self-reflection, change, and growth, though that comes with growth pains. For those outside the movement, I hope this study leads to the discarding of stereotypes—though that requires humility—and provides necessary tools for the kind of cross-cultural communication needed for respectful and mutually enriching dialogue.

ACKNOWLEDGMENTS

Since this work originated as a doctoral thesis at the University of Birmingham, my sincere gratitude first goes to my supervisor Professor Wolfgang Vondey. His analytical sharpness, vast knowledge, and personal commitment have been invaluable. The wise guidance he offered throughout has sharpened the work and helped me to stay on track until my doctoral work was completed. I also want to thank Professor Allan Anderson and the rest of the staff and students at the Centre for Pentecostal and Charismatic Studies at the University of Birmingham. Being part of this academic and warm environment has been a privilege.

I also appreciate the critical questions from Dr. Daniela C. Augustine and Dr. William Atkinson during my oral defence which have further sharpened my thinking and arguments. I am particularly grateful to the editors of this series for the opportunity to publish my work and for the professional help from the team at Bloomsbury, particularly the editor Anna Turton.

My thanks also go to Dr. Keith Warrington, who directed me to the University of Birmingham and encouraged me along the way. I am also deeply grateful to Dr. Wessly Lukose, Dr. Joy Samuel, and everyone else at Transformation Church, Birmingham, for the gifts of friendship and a church home. The thoughtful input from Hein Hüpscher, Chris Anthony, and others has improved the content and sharpened my thinking. I am grateful to all friends in Linköping Pentecostal Church for their prayers and encouragement. My thanks also go to the staff and students at the Academy for Leadership and Theology in Sweden for the opportunities to present my work in seminars and lectures. I also thank Meshack Muthoka and all other friends in Logos Renewal School of Theology in Kenya for their prayers and patience while being in the "the cave" of research. My warmest thanks to Lydia Kituri for her love, prayers, and constant encouragement. Finally, my parents, Lars and Margaretha Stenhammar, are to be thanked for their unreserved love and generous support. I want to particularly recognize my daughters, Josephine and Eleanor, who are to be commended for their willingness to move to the United Kingdom and enroll in new schools and for their patience when my research kept me away. Last, but certainly not least, I thank my wife, Emelie, without whose self-giving love and support, encouragement, patience, and continuous helpful input and probing questions this project would never have become a reality. It is her hard work that has made it financially possible for me to study and write. Over and above everyone else, I acknowledge my King and Savior Jesus, "whose I am and whom I serve."

ABBREVIATIONS

COQG	*Christian Origins and the Question of God*
CC	*Counterfeit Christianity*
CIC	*Christianity in Crisis*
DG	*A Different Gospel*
FHP	*Faith, Health, and Prosperity*
FRTR	*From Rags to Riches*
FTP	*From the Pinnacle of the Temple*
HWH	*Health, Wealth, and Happiness*
ICW	*Introduction to Christian Worldview*
JDS	Jesus died spiritually
JVG	*Jesus and the Victory of God*
KJV	King James Version
MT	*The Midas Touch*
NIDPCM	*The New International Dictionary of Pentecostal and Charismatic Movements*
NKJV	New King James Version
NTE	*Naming the Elephant*
NTPG	*The New Testament and the People of God*
PFG	*Paul and the Faithfulness of God*
RR	*Righteous Riches*
RSG	*The Resurrection of the Son of God*
TV	*The Transforming Vision*

INTRODUCTION

"Word of Faith" is the descriptor of choice for the religious phenomenon also widely referred to as the "prosperity gospel" or "prosperity theology," which emphasizes that financial prosperity, physical and mental health, and overall success in life are every Christian's God-given rights. These "blessings" are attainable through faith expressed in speaking positive confessions and sowing money seeds.[1] From its roots in post–Second World War American Pentecostalism, the Word of Faith message has "emerged with surprising strength, and has had a massive impact on the life and growth of the Church around the globe."[2] While Pentecostals have been especially receptive, the message resonates with large numbers of Christians worldwide. Research data show that almost half of all self-proclaimed Christians in the United States agree with the statement that "God will grant wealth and good health to believers who have enough faith."[3] The majority of Protestants in

1. Robert Bowman, *The Word-Faith Controversy: Understanding the Health and Wealth Gospel* (Grand Rapids: Baker, 2001); Andrew Perriman ed., *Faith, Health and Prosperity: A Report on "Word of Faith" and "Positive Confession" Theologies by ACUTE (the Evangelical Alliance Commission on Unity and Truth among Evangelicals)* [FHP] (Carlisle: Paternoster, 2003); Kate Bowler, *Blessed: A History of the American Prosperity Gospel* (New York: Oxford University Press, 2013). The Pew Research Center poses the following statement to interviewees to determine adherence to Word of Faith themes: "God will grant wealth and good health to all believers who have enough faith" (Pew Research Center, "Religion in Latin America: Widespread Change in a Historically Catholic Region" (Washington: Pew Research Center, 2014), 68.

2. Valdir Steuernagel, foreword to *Prosperity Theology and the Gospel: Good News or Bad News for the Poor?* ed. J. Daniel Salinas (Peabody: Hendrickson, 2017), ix; Bowman, *Word-Faith*, 85–94; Perriman, *FHP*, 1–18; Bowler, *Blessed*, 11–40.

3. Pew Research Center, "Spirit and Power: A 10-Country Survey of Pentecostals" (Washington: Pew Research Center, 2007), 147; Bob Smietana, "Most Churchgoers Say God Wants Them to Prosper Financially," Lifeway Research, published July 31, 2018, accessed April 7, 2021, https://lifewayresearch.com/2018/07/31/most-churchgoers-say-god-wants-them-to-prosper-financially/; Lifeway Research, *Churchgoers Views–Prosperity*, published July 2018, accessed April 7, 2021, http://lifewayresearch.com/wp-content/uploads/2018/07/American-Churchgoers-Prosperity-2017.pdf; On general knowledge of the prosperity gospel in America see Pew Research Center, "What Americans Know About Religion" (Washington: Pew Research Center, 2019), 22, 32–3.

twenty Latin American countries surveyed subscribe to a form of Word of Faith emphasis, more than half of Christians in sub-Saharan Africa and 80 percent of all African Pentecostals.[4] Significant adherence to Word of Faith beliefs is also found in many Asian-Pacific countries.[5] European nations are also impacted and

4. Asonzeh Ukah, "God, Wealth, and the Spirit of Investment," in *Religious Activism in the Global Economy: Promoting, Reforming, or Resisting Neoliberal Globalization?*, ed. Sabine Dreher and Peter J. Smith (Lanham, Maryland: Rowman & Littlefield International, 2016), 73. Paul Gifford says, "it would be hard to find an African pentecostal church that is entirely untouched by the global Word of Faith movement" [Paul Gifford, "Healing in African Pentecostalism," in *Global Pentecostal and Charismatic Healing*, ed. Candy Gunther Brown (Oxford: Oxford University Press, 2011), 253]; Marius Nel, *The Prosperity Gospel in Africa: An African Pentecostal Hermeneutical Consideration* (Euguene: Wipf and Stock, 2020), Kindle edition, "Popularity of the Prosperity Message in Africa."

5. Australia [e.g., Marion Maddox, "Prosper, Consume and Be Saved," *Critical Research on Religion* 1, no. 1 (2013): 108–15]; China [e.g., Nanlai Cao, "Urban Property and Spiritual Resource: The Prosperity Gospel Phenomenon in Coastal China," in *Pentecostalism and Prosperity: The Socio-Economics of the Global Charismatic Movement*, ed. Katherine Attanasi and Amos Yong (New York: Palgrave Macmillan, 2012), 151–70]; Fiji [e.g., Karen J. Brison, "The Empire Strikes Back: Pentecostalism in Fiji," *Ethnology* 46, no. 1 (2007): 21–39]; India [e.g., Samuel, Joy T. "The Pneumatic Experiences of the Indian Neocharismatics" (Doctor of philosophy thesis, University of Birmingham, 2017); Vinay Samuel, "A Biblical Ethical Assessment of Prosperity Teaching and the Blessing Movement," in *Prosperity Theology and the Gospel: Good News or Bad News for the Poor?*, ed. J. Daniel Salinas (Peabody: Hendrickson, 2017), 77–87]; Indonesia [e.g., Juliette Koning, "Beyond the Prosperity Gospel: Moral Identity Work and Organizational Cultures in Pentecostal-Charismatic Churches in Indonesia," in *New Religiosities, Modern Capitalism, and Moral Complexities in Southeast Asia*, ed. Juliette Koning and Gwenaël Njoto-Feillard (Singapore: Palgrave Macmillan, 2017), 17–38]; Papua New Guinea [e.g., George Mombi, "Impact of the Prosperity Gospel in the Assemblies of God Churches of Papua New Guinea," *Melanesian Journal of Theology* 25, no. 1 (2009): 32–58]; Philippines [e.g., Kathrine Wiegele, *Investing in Miracles: El Shaddai and the Transformation of Popular Catholicism in the Philippines* (Honolulu: University of Hawaii, 2004); Giovanni Maltese, "An Activist-Holiness Hagin? A Case Study of Prosperity Theology in the Philippines," in *Pastures of Plenty: Tracing Religio-Scapes of Prosperity Gospel in Africa and Beyond*, ed. Andreas Heuser (Frankfurt: Peter Lang, 2015), 65–80; Erron Medina and Jayeel Cornelio, "The Prosperity Ethic: Neoliberal Christianity and the Rise of the New Prosperity Gospel in the Philippines," *Pneuma: The Journal of the Society for Pentecostal Studies* 43, no. 1 (2021): 72–93]; Singapore [e.g., Terence Chong, "Of Riches and Faith: The Prosperity Gospels of Megachurches in Singapore," in *New Religiosities, Modern Capitalism, and Moral Complexities in Southeast Asia*, ed. Juliette Koning and Gwenaël Njoto-Feillard (Singapore: Palgrave Macmillan, 2017), 147–68]; South Korea [e.g., Ron MacTavish, "Pentecostal Profits: The Prosperity Gospel in the Global South" (Master of arts thesis, University of Lethbridge, 1999)]. Generally see Joel Tejedo, "Asian Perspectives on

immigrant churches account for an influx of Word of Faith beliefs and practices.[6] The influence of the Word of Faith exceeds the religious domains and stretches into the area of politics, as some of the world's political leaders embrace its ideals.[7]

The international presence of Word of Faith themes has generated vibrant scholarly conversations, making the phenomena "one of the most talked about and most controversial strands in contemporary global Christianity."[8] Radically different theological opinions exist about the Word of Faith's nature and place in relationship to Pentecostal and evangelical Christianity. Evangelicals generally reject the Word of Faith as a syncretistic accommodation to foreign doctrine and greed, so grave that it threatens to corrupt the very foundations of the Christian faith.[9] The repertoire of Pentecostal responses is on a scale from rejection—usually following evangelical arguments—to endorsement as a legitimate contextualization

Prosperity Theology, Simplicity and Poverty," in *Prosperity Theology and the Gospel: Good News or Bad News for the Poor?* ed. J. Daniel Salinas (Peabody: Hendrickson, 2017), 136–47.

6. Eastern Europe [e.g., Daniela Augustine, "Pentecost and Prosperity in Eastern Europe: Between Sharing of Possessions and Accumulating Personal Wealth," in *Pentecostalism and Prosperity: The Socio-Economics of the Global Charismatic Movement,* ed. Katherine Attanasi and Amos Yong (New York: Palgrave Macmillan, 2012), 189–214]; Immigrant churches [e.g., Daniel Frei, "With Both Feet in the Air: The Prosperity Gospel in African Migrant Churches in Switzerland," in *Pastures of Plenty: Tracing Religio-Scapes of Prosperity Gospel in Africa and Beyond,* ed. Andreas Heuser (Frankfurt: Peter Lang, 2015), 335–70; Mika Vähäkangas, "The Prosperity Gospel in the African Diaspora: Unethical Theology or Gospel in Context?," *Exchange* 44, no. 4 (2015): 353–80; Tomas Aechtner, *Health, Wealth, and Power in an African Diaspora Church in Canada* (New York: Palgrave Macmillan, 2015); Norway [e.g., Kjell Olav Sannes, *Det Guddommeliggjorte Menneske og den Menneskeliggjorte Gud* (Oslo: Refleks-Publishing, 2005)]; Russia [e.g., Olga Zaprometova, "From Persecution to 'Prosperity,'" *Journal of the European Pentecostal Theological Association* 38, no. 2 (2018): DOI: 10.1080/18124461.2018.1423606]; Sweden [e.g., Simon Coleman, *Globalisation of Charismatic Christianity* (Cambridge: Cambridge University Press, 2000]; United Kingdom [e.g., Glyn Ackerly, "Importing Faith: The Effect of American 'Word of Faith' Culture on Contemporary English Evangelical Revivalism" (Doctor of philosophy thesis, King's College, London, 2013)].

7. E.g., John Fea, *Believe Me: The Evangelical Road to Donald Trump* (Grand Rapids: Eerdmans, 2018), 133–7.

8. Andreas Heuser, "Religio-Scapes of Prosperity Gospel: An Introduction," in *Pastures of Plenty: Tracing Religio-Scapes of Prosperity Gospel in Africa and Beyond,* ed. Andreas Heuser (Frankfurt: Peter Lang, 2015), 16; Andreas Heuser, "Prosperity Theology," in *Routledge Handbook to Pentecostal Theology,* ed. Wolfgang Vondey (London: Routledge, 2020), 410.

9. See, e.g., Daniel Salinas, ed., *Prosperity Theology and the Gospel: Good News or Bad News for the Poor?* (Peabody: Hendrickson, 2017); Deborah Mumford, "Prosperity Gospel and African American Prophetic Preaching," *Review and Expositor,* no. 109 (2012): 381.

of the gospel.[10] The powerful sentiments rouse debates. For example, the Word of Faith is characterized as heretical and destructive, its leaders as charlatans, and their followers as naïve and victims of self-interest.[11] Unfortunately, there are reasons underlying such dark portraits, yet stereotypes always fall short of accurate representations.[12] The present state of the relationship between the Word of Faith and its critics is best described as a stalemate, but there are increasing calls for discernment and dialogue.[13]

Over the past three decades, research on the Word of Faith, especially its prosperity emphasis, "has made a steep career in academic discourse."[14] Scholars direct their attention toward aspects ranging from theological, historical, anthropological, sociological, and economic interests. Despite the increasing amount of research, there remains a cluster of unanswered questions. While

10. Allan Heaton Anderson, *To the Ends of the Earth* (Oxford: Oxford University Press, 2013), 219–23; Heuser, "Prosperity Theology." See, e.g., Gordon Fee, *The Disease of the Health and Wealth Gospels* (Vancouver: Regent College Publishing, 2006); Leonard Lovett "Positive Confession Theology," in *The New International Dictionary of Pentecostal and Charismatic Movements*, ed. Stanley M. Burgess and Eduard M. Van Der Maas, rev. and exp. edn. (Grand Rapids: Zondervan, 2003), e-book edition, s.v. "Positive Confession Theology;" General Presbytery of the Assemblies of God, "The Believer and Positive Confession," *Where We Stand: The Official Position Papers of the Assemblies of God* (Springfield: Gospel Publishing House, 1994), 131–44; Terris Neuman, "Cultic Origins of Word-Faith Theology within the Charismatic Movement," *Pneuma: The Journal of the Society for Pentecostal Studies* 12, no. 1 (1990): 32–55.

11. E.g., Hank Hanegraaff, *Christianity in Crisis: 21st Century* (Nashville: Thomas Nelson, 2009), Kindle edition; Fee, *Disease*; Femi Adeleye, *Preachers of a Different Gospel* (Nairobi: WordAlive, 2011).

12. E.g., Jim Bakker, *I Was Wrong* (Nashville: Thomas Nelson, 1996); Andrew Brown, "The Prosperity Gospel Makes a Mockery of Christianity," *The Guardian*, May 29, 2013, accessed April 7, 2021, https://www.theguardian.com/commentisfree/andrewbrown/2013 /may/29/prosperity-gospel-mockery-christianity.

13. Joel Edwards, "Ethical Dimensions: Holiness and Fake Idols," in *Prosperity Theology and the Gospel: Good News or Bad News for the Poor?* ed. J. Daniel Salinas (Peabody: Hendrickson, 2017), 95–6; Russell Johnson, "The Gospel and the Prosperity Gospel: Joel Osteen's Your Best Life Now Reconsidered," *Theology* 121, no. 1 (2018): 28–34; Wonsuk Ma, "Blessing in Pentecostal Theology and Mission," in *Pentecostal Mission and Global Christianity*, ed. Wonsuk Ma, Veli-Matti Kärkkäinen and J. Kwabena Asamoah-Gyadu (Oxford: Regnum Books International, 2014), 272–91; Frank Macchia, "A Call for Careful Discernment: A Theological Response to Prosperity Preaching," in *Pentecostalism and Prosperity: The Socio-Economics of the Global Charismatic Movement*, ed. Katherine Attanasi and Amos Yong (New York: Palgrave Macmillan, 2012), 228.

14. Andreas Heuser, "Charting African Prosperity Gospel Economies," *HTS Teologiese Studies/Theological Studies* 72, no. 1 (2016): 2.

scholars express the need for an enhanced understanding of the Word of Faith,[15] few can do so from the global horizon of Philip Jenkins, who said that "comprehending the prosperity gospel might be the most pressing task for anyone trying to study the changing shape of global Christianity."[16] Though this study is not on global expressions of Christianity, Jenkins' observation points to the current knowledge gap that I want to address.

Underlying this study is the contention that in order to attain an enhanced understanding of the Word of Faith we must advance a critical stance to the current approaches. Present models have obvious merits and contribute invaluable knowledge, yet their analytical reach and explanatory power are restricted by their limited focus areas. Hence, I argue that what is needed is an inclusive image of the Word of Faith as existing foremost as a worldview. The image of the Word of Faith as a worldview requires a new and holistic model for analysis.

The argument is that the Word of Faith is not at its core a system of theological beliefs and practices or a social entity but a distinct worldview.[17] The lenses provided by biblical studies, systematic theology, history, anthropology, sociology, and economics, though irreplaceable, are insufficient on their own to do justice to the Word of Faith. Rather, the Word of Faith requires a holistic model of analysis, which is offered by worldview studies. To approach the Word of Faith as a worldview fits recent scholarship's contention that a holistic worldview approach is the most suitable method to study new religious phenomena.[18] Using worldview as a heuristic device holds the promise of a "thicker description" of the movement. By alluding to Clifford Geertz's famous phrase "thick description" (by which he called for enlarging the complexity of ethnographical research), I acknowledge the existing models' descriptions of the Word of Faith as being "thick" while arguing for using worldview to gain additional complexity and depth, hence, "thicker."[19]

"Word of Faith" as the Descriptor of Choice

Rather than using the popular alternative "prosperity gospel" in reference to the religious phenomenon under examination, the descriptor "Word of Faith" used

15. E.g., Nel, *Prosperity Gospel*, Kindle edition, "Recommendations."
16. Philip Jenkins, "The Case for prosperity," *The Christian Century*, November 19, 2010, accessed April 7, 2021, https://www.christiancentury.org/article/2010-11/case-p rosperity. See Paul Gifford, "The Complex Provenance of African Pentecostal Theology," in *Between Babel and Pentecost: Transnational Pentecostalism in Africa and Latin America*, ed. Andre Corten and Ruth Marshall-Fratani (London: Hurst, 2001), 63.
17. For definitions of "worldview," see Chapter 2.
18. André Droogers and Anton van Harskamp, eds., *Methods for the Study of Religious Change: From Religious Studies to Worldview Studies* (Sheffield: Equinox, 2014).
19. Clifford Geertz, *The Interpretation of Cultures* (New York: Basic Books, 1973). For the ongoing relevance of Geertz see Section 2.3.2.

here requires explanation and justification. Settling for which term to use faces considerable obstacles as there are no denominations, no official statement of faith, no systematic teachings, and no official body that have defining authority within the Word of Faith.[20] Much popular discourse and some scholarly work have a propensity for polemics, resulting in the pejorative terms "health and wealth," "name it and claim it," and "success theology."[21] "Prosperity gospel" and "prosperity theology" are mostly used in current academic writings, but the terms are beset with weaknesses.[22] First, the singular aspect of prosperity takes on defining power to characterize the whole. Such a reductionist approach overlooks that the Word of Faith encompasses several theological emphases, some more significant than prosperity.[23] Second, the term carries pejorative undertones and caricature adherents as motivated by a desire for mere personal profit. Third, speaking of "prosperity gospel" does not distinguish between "the evanescent, ambiguous and inconsistent nature"[24] of a prosperity mentality from the Word of Faith movement. Fourth, and perhaps most importantly, those who espouse the principal beliefs associated with the "prosperity gospel" usually reject the term as an apt description of what they believe.[25] Hence, there is a need for a precise and value-free term that

20. Simon Coleman points out the "the largely thankless task of attempting to provide a satisfactory definition and characterization of what may be seen as a movement, a network, an idiom, a theology, a heresy–or indeed not any single thing at all" [Simon Coleman, "Morality, Markets, and the Gospel of Prosperity," in *Religion and the Morality of the Market*, ed. Daromir Rudnyckyj and Filippo Osella (Cambridge: Cambridge University Press, 2017), 55–6]. See Bowler, *Blessed*, 249–62; Wilfred Asampambila Agana, *"Succeed Here and in Eternity": The Prosperity Gospel in Ghana* (Bern: Peter Lang, 2016), 30–1.

21. "Health and Wealth" (e.g., Bruce Barron, *The Health and Wealth Gospel* (Downers Grove: IVP, 1987); Roger E. Olson, *Counterfeit Christianity* [*CC*] (Nashville: Abingdon, 2015, 154–70); "Name It and Claim It" (e.g., Harvey Cox, *Fire from Heaven* (London: Casell, 1996); Stephanie Mitchem, *Name It and Claim It?: Prosperity Preaching in the Black Church* (Cleveland: Pilgrim, 2007); "Success Theology" (e.g., Anthony Barbosa da Silva, "The 'Theology of Success' Movement: A Comment," *Themelios* 12 (1986): 91). Not to mention explicitly derogatory terms, such as "Prosperity Cult," "Blab it and grab it" or "Fake it 'til you make it" [see, e.g., Marla Frederick, *Colored Television* (Stanford: Stanford University Press, 2015), 38].

22. E.g., Heuser, "Prosperity Theology." An earlier term used is "Positive Confession Theology" (e.g., Lovett, "Positive Confession Theology").

23. Bowman, *Word-Faith*, 8; Macchia, "Call for Careful Discernment," 228.

24. Amos Yong, "A Typology of Prosperity Theology," in *Pentecostalism and Prosperity: The Socio-Economics of the Global Charismatic Movement,* ed. Katherine Attanasi and Amos Yong (New York: Palgrave Macmillan, 2012), 27.

25. E.g., Susie Meister Butler, "Presents of God: The Marketing of the American Prosperity Gospel" (Doctor of philosophy thesis, University of Pittsburgh, 2014), 28–30; Bradley Koch, "Who Are the Prosperity Gospel Adherents?," *Journal of Ideology* 36 (2014): 4; Coleman, "Morality, Markets." E.g., Charisma News, "Joel Osteen: I am Not a Prosperity

takes into consideration the movement's greater theological vision and which is acceptable to stakeholders.

Instead of prosperity and health, a stronger emphasis lies arguably on the nature and practice of faith—especially speaking positive confessions—and the priority given to the Bible, or the Word.[26] These emphases have generated terms highlighting one particular aspect: for example, "Faith movement," "Word movement," "Faith-Formula," and "Positive Confession."[27] Even though many adherents would be comfortable with the first two descriptions, more preferable are terms that embrace both emphases, such as "Word-Faith," or better, "Word of Faith."[28] The term "Word of Faith" echoes the particular phraseology of Romans 10:8 in the King James version, which is a central theme of Scripture in the thought of the American Pentecostal Kenneth E. Hagin, who is widely regarded as the father of the movement.[29] "Word of Faith" is also the name of Hagin's monthly magazine, which has played a significant part during the early days of the movement.[30] The term captures the movement's emphasis on faithfulness to the Bible, the power of spoken words and the message of faith. Leading proponents also use "Word of Faith" as a self-descriptive term.[31] In contrast to the contested notion of the

Preacher," Charismanews.com, published June 9, 2014, accessed April 7, 2021, https://www.charismanews.com/us/44185-joel-osteen-i-am-not-a-prosperity-preacher.

26. Bowler, *Blessed*, 249–50.

27. D. R. McConnell, *A Different Gospel: A Bold and Revealing Look at the Biblical and Historical Basis of the Word of Faith Movement* [*DG*] (Peabody: Hendrickson, 1995), 16; Charles Farah, "A Critical Analysis: The 'Roots and Fruits' of Faith-Formula Theology," *Pneuma: The Journal of the Society for Pentecostal Studies* 3, no. 1 (Spring 1981): 6; Bowler, *Blessed*, 249–50; Lovett "Positive Confession."

28. The Swedish Word of Faith movement, founded by Ulf Ekman, named itself "*Trosrörelsen*" (Faith movement). See Coleman, *Globalisation*; Bowler, *Blessed*, 79, 250; Torbjorn Aronson, "Continuity in Charismata: Swedish Mission and the Growth of Neo-Pentecostal Churches in Russia," *Occasional Papers on Religion in Eastern Europe* 31, no. 1 (2012): 34.

29. David Edwin Harrell Jr., *All Things Are Possible: The Healing and Charismatic Revivals in Modern America* (Bloomington: Indiana University Press, 1975), 185–6; Charles Farah, *From the Pinnacle of the Temple: Faith vs. Presumption* [*FTP*] (Plainfield: Logos, 1979), 116; McConnell, *DG*, 55; Perriman, *FHP*, 1; Heuser, "Prosperity Theology," 410. To avoid confusing Kenneth E. Hagin with his son Kenneth W. Hagin Jr., I will refer to Kenneth E. Hagin as simply "Hagin" while adding Jr. in reference to the son.

30. Kate Bowler, "A Successful Calling: Women, Power, and the Rise of the American Prosperity Gospel," in *Women in Pentecostal and Charismatic Ministry: Informing Dialogue on Gender, Church, and Ministry*, ed. Margaret English de Alminana and Lois E. Olena (Leiden: Brill, 2016), 194.

31. E.g., Kenneth W. Hagin, "Back to the Basics," *Rhema.org*, accessed April 7, 2021, http://www.rhema.org/index.php?option=com_content&view=article&id=233:back-to-the-basics&catid=45:healing&Itemid=144.

prosperity gospel, "Word of Faith" provides an unbiased and inclusive descriptor that avoids the problems inherent in other terms used in the literature. Hence, I use Word of Faith in this book.

Research shows that there are many kinds of "prosperity gospels" when understood as religious movements that emphasize economic well-being.[32] My intention is not to subsume all kinds of "prosperity gospels" under "Word of Faith" but to investigate the dynamic phenomenon that explicitly or implicitly relates to its roots in early North American Pentecostalism (see the following text) that found a distinct shape in the work of Hagin, while also appearing in different forms in various historical and cultural contexts.

Word of Faith as Movement and Ethos

This book follows the common practice to speak of the Word of Faith as a movement, yet the choice to call the Word of Faith a movement needs clarification.[33] William Sims Bainbridge explains a religious movement as "a relatively organized attempt by a number of people to cause or prevent change in a religious organization or in religious aspects of life."[34] In this definition, the Word of Faith can be spoken of as a movement. In its explicit form, the Word of Faith is made up of the individuals, churches, ministries, networks, or groups which are in various ways connected (knowingly or unknowingly) with the worldview espoused by Hagin and propagate the defining beliefs and practices (explicitly or implicitly). These are mostly Pentecostal in orientation but can be found as subgroups within non-Pentecostal denominations and movements.[35] However, this understanding of the Word of Faith as movement does not fully cover the global nature and impact of the Word of Faith. Studies show that in the global manifestations of Word of Faith beliefs and practices, a complexity emerges favoring multifaceted rather than homogenic characterizations.[36] A number of those who give priority to Word

32. Bowler, *Blessed*; Yong, "Typologies." One example of non-Word of Faith prosperity gospels are the theological streams shaped largely by Norman Vincent Peale [e.g., Norman Vincent Peale, *The Power of Positive Thinking* (New York: Prentice-Hall, 1952)].

33. E.g., McConnell, *DG*.

34. William Sims Bainbridge, *The Sociology of Religious Movements* (New York: Routledge, 1997), 3.

35. E.g., The "El-Shaddai movement" within the Roman Catholic church in the Philippines (see Wiegele, *Investing in Miracles*).

36. Macchia, "Call for Careful Discernment," 230. Andreas Heuser, speaking about "prosperity gospel," addresses the significant complexities: "Prosperity Gospel cannot be reduced to a monolithic canon of ideas, ethics, or practices . . . [it] has neither developed into a consistent theology nor can it be used to label a distinctive single movement within Global Christianity. Rather, it is transformative in nature, adapting to contexts and traveling through history; its pathways are winding through local and transnational networks

of Faith convictions and practices seem not to have any known connection with Hagin and the network around him. In light of the present complex situation, it is therefore important to make a distinction between the Word of Faith as movement and ethos.

Understood as "the distinguishing character, sentiment, moral nature, or guiding beliefs of a person, group, or institution,"[37] the term "ethos" captures manifestations of the Word of Faith worldview that exist outside the distinct Word of Faith movement. The Word of Faith ethos speaks of a specific worldview orientation that grew out of the Word of Faith movement yet has life in separation from the movement and attaches itself to other theological traditions, merges with other worldviews, and can morph into numerous unique forms. Despite their different outward shapes, the Word of Faith as both movement and ethos emerge from a shared worldview.

The idea of a Word of Faith ethos detached from the movement yet related in terms of worldview is a helpful approach to the multiplicity and variety of manifestations and the puzzling fact that Word of Faith elements—for example, a prosperity emphasis and practices of speaking positive confession and sowing money seeds—are found in traditions which otherwise stand worlds apart.[38] The distinction between movement and ethos also helps in setting the parameters on the data relevant to consider here. To get to the heart of the Word of Faith phenomenon through a worldview-analysis, I include scholarly materials related to both expressions of the Word of Faith as movement and ethos. From here on I use "Word of Faith" in reference to the Word of Faith as movement, without "movement" always explicitly stated. To avoid repetitiveness, at times I substitute "Word of Faith" with "movement." However, when I speak of the Word of Faith as ethos, or as a movement in contrast to ethos, I always make that choice explicit.

The Word of Faith's Religious Context

While the Word of Faith as ethos appears in various Christian contexts not limited to any particular denomination or tradition, the immediate religious context of the Word of Faith movement is undeniably Pentecostalism. The movement arose out of American Pentecostalism and has found its strongest resonance within global Pentecostalism, making it "Pentecostalism's most prominent and controversial expression."[39] Hence, the importance of defining Pentecostalism and the basic

of churches and individuals; its messages are circulating in modern mass media and are meandering through disparate political spheres and cultural spaces" (Heuser, "Religio-Scapes," 16).

37. Merriam-Webster's Collegiate Dictionary, 11th ed., s.v. "ethos."

38. E.g., Bowler, *Blessed*, 236.

39. Anderson *To the Ends*, 219. See Bowman, *Word-Faith*, 85–94; Perriman, *FHP*, 1–18; Bowler, *Blessed*, 11–40.

forms of global Pentecostalism and how the Word of Faith movement relates to these. In what follows, definitions and typologies of Pentecostalism are considered with the aim to locate the Word of Faith's relationship to Pentecostalism. Locating the place of the Word of Faith within Pentecostalism lays the groundwork for further analysis of how the movement relates to Pentecostal distinctives.

Scholars who define Pentecostalism speak to the complexity, amorphousness, elusiveness, and bewildering aspects of this phenomenon.[40] In roughly a century, Pentecostalism has become possibly the fastest-growing religious movement in today's world, comprising around one-quarter of the population of Christians (*c.* 500–700 million people).[41] Its numerical size, wide geographical and cultural spread, diversity in beliefs and practices, and adaptive and changing nature resist delineated definitions and clean categorizations.[42] Pentecostalism is said to be "the most diverse and fragmented movement within world Christianity."[43] Positively, this is a cause of its growth. Negatively, it hinders formulating an unambiguous Pentecostal identity.[44] Two common routes in attempting to define Pentecostalism are the experiential and the theological routes. Allan Anderson, arguing for the experiential route, says that any definition of Pentecostalism "has to be inclusive enough"[45] and that "different forms of Pentecostalism will always include an emphasis on a spiritual experience."[46] Those who seek a theological definition of

40. Anderson, *To the Ends*, 4; Cox, *Fire from Heaven*, xvii; William Kay, *Pentecostalism: A Very Short Introduction* (Oxford: Oxford University Press, 2011), 7; Wolfgang Vondey, *Pentecostalism: A Guide for the Perplexed* (London: Bloomsbury, 2013), 1; Wolfgang Vondey, *Beyond Pentecostalism* (Grand Rapids: Eerdmans, 2010), 8.

41. Donald Miller, "Pentecostalism as Global Phenomenon," in *Spirit and Power: The Growth and Global Impact of Pentecostalism*, ed. Donald Miller, Kimon Sargeant and Richard Flory (New York: Oxford University Press, 2013), 9; Anderson, *To the Ends*, 1; Robert Hefner, "Gender, Piety, and Politics in the Global Pentecostal Surge" in *Global Pentecostalism in the 21st Century*, ed. Robert Hefner (Bloomington: Indiana University Press, 2013), 1.

42. "There is as yet no scholarly consensus on just where to draw Pentecostalism's borders, and there probably does not need to be, in any too-tidy sense" (Hefner, "Gender, Piety," 2).

43. Anderson, *To the Ends*, 42.

44. Ibid.

45. Allan Anderson, "Varieties, Taxonomies, and Definitions," in *Studying Global Pentecostalism: Theories and Methods*, ed. Allan Anderson, André Droogers, Michael Bergunder and Cornelis van der Laan (Berkeley: University of California Press, 2010), 27; Anderson, *To the Ends*, 9.

46. Anderson, *To the Ends*, 1, 6, 8; Allan Heaton Anderson, *An Introduction to Pentecostalism*, 2nd ed. (Cambridge: Cambridge University Press, 2014), 6; Douglas Jacobsen, *Thinking in the Spirit* (Bloomington: Indiana University Press, 2002), 3–5. See also Mark Cartledge, *Encountering the Spirit* (London: Dartmon, Longman and Todd, 2006) 19; Hefner, "Gender, Piety," 2; Alister E. McGrath, *Christianity's Dangerous Idea*

Pentecostalism argue that Pentecostal experience and spirituality express a distinct theological imaginary. Some scholars use the so-called full gospel as the defining theological narrative of Pentecostalism.[47] Others prefer the biblical metaphor of Spirit baptism in an attempt to define Pentecostalism's theological core.[48] In response to this multifaceted picture, Veli-Matti Kärkkäinen concludes, "the best thing to do is to acknowledge and live with the lack of consensus. Diversity is the hallmark of this Spirit movement."[49]

The threefold typology used in *New International Dictionary of Pentecostal and Charismatic Movements (NIDPCM)* is widely held as "the current scholarly consensus."[50] It outlines a threefold historical trajectory of development and groups. The first group is "classical Pentecostalism," which is made up of denominations with direct roots in the Azusa Street mission and revival (e.g., Assemblies of God or Foursquare Gospel). The second group comprises the "Charismatic Movements," consisting of the transdenominational movements started in mainline denominations in the 1960s with the emphasis on "life in the Spirit" and the charismata. The third is a "Neocharismatic" group which serves as a catch-all category for those who share a common pneumatic emphasis with classical Pentecostals and the Charismatic Movement yet resist the earlier classifications. Taken together, the three groups are sometimes spoken of as "Renewal" movements.[51]

In contrast to the *NIDPCM* typology, Allan Anderson presents a fourfold classification to capture the "family resemblance" among the myriad forms

(New York: HarperCollins, 2007), 424; Roger E. Olson, *The Mosaic of Christian Belief* (Downers Grove: IVP Academic, 2002), 66.

47. Donald Dayton, *Theological Roots of Pentecostalism* (Grand Rapids: Baker Academic, 1987); Wolfgang Vondey, *Pentecostal Theology: Living the Full Gospel* (London: Bloomsbury T&T Clark, 2017).

48. Frank Macchia, *Baptized in the Spirit: A Global Pentecostal Theology* (Grand Rapids: Zondervan, 2009); William Menzies and Robert Menzies, *Spirit and Power* (Grand Rapids: Zondervan, 2000).

49. Veli-Matti Kärkkäinen, "Pneumatologies in Systematic Theology," in *Studying Global Pentecostalism*, ed. Allan Anderson, André Droogers, Michael Bergunder, Cornelius Van der Laan (Berkeley: University of California Press, 2010), 232.

50. Wonsuk Ma, Veli-Matti Kärkkäinen and J. Kwabena Asamoah-Gyadu, "Pentecostalism and World Mission," in *Pentecostal Mission and Global Christianity*, ed. Wonsuk Ma, Veli-Matti Kärkkäinen and J. Kwabena Asamoah-Gyadu (Oxford: Regnum Books International, 2014), 3; Stanely Burgess, "Introduction," in *The New International Dictionary of Pentecostal and Charismatic Movements*, ed. Stanley M. Burgess and Eduard M. Van Der Maas, rev. and exp. edn. (Grand Rapids: Zondervan, 2002), e-book edition, "Introduction." See Vondey, *Pentecostal Theology*, 4.

51. Katherine Attanasi, "Introduction" in *Pentecostalism and Prosperity: The Socio-Economics of the Global Charismatic Movement*, ed. Katherine Attanasi and Amos Yong (New York: Palgrave Macmillan, 2012), 2.

of those groups with "an emphasis on the Spirit and spiritual gifts."[52] "Classical Pentecostals" is the first group made up of those who can trace their roots to early twentieth-century evangelical revival and missionary movements, especially in the Western world.[53] The second group is the "Older Church Charismatics," comprising movements within existing Christian traditions (including Roman Catholic, Anglican, Orthodox, and various Protestants branches). The third group is the "Older Independent Churches." Despite differences in theology among themselves and with other Pentecostal groups and their differing self-identification (some do not claim to be "Pentecostal"), they engage in decidedly Pentecostal practices of healing, prayer, and spiritual gifts. The fourth group is the "Neopentecostal or Neocharismatic Churches," often referred to as "Charismatic independent churches." This group comprises four subgroups: (1) "Word of Faith" (or prosperity oriented churches), (2) "Third Wave" churches, (3) "new Apostolic churches," and other different independent (4) "new churches" that are hard to categorize due to overlap with the other subgroups and Classic Pentecostals leading to large variations.

Having considered definitions of Pentecostalism and the two foremost typologies, for this project it is important to acknowledge Pentecostalism's diverse nature and that both *NIDPCM* and Anderson agree on locating the Word of Faith as a branch of Pentecostalism, more precisely a subgroup of its Neo-Pentecostal or Neo-Charismatic form.[54] That Pentecostalism forms the religious context of the Word of Faith shapes the foundation for exploring how the movement's worldview relates to Pentecostal distinctives.

Complexity and Nuance through a Worldview-Analysis

This book postulates that the Word of Faith is a worldview, and, therefore, only a worldview-analysis can add the necessary complexity and nuance to current characterizations of the movement that facilitates dialogue and "careful discernment."[55] Emerging from the claim that the Word of Faith is a worldview are three goals that I want to address in this research. My first goal is analytical. Beyond testing the validity of the argument that the Word of Faith is a worldview, I want to make a detailed examination of the Word of Faith worldview in order to understand its nature and to determine its essential features and logic. I especially

---

52. See Walter Hollenweger, *Pentecostalism: Origins and Developments Worldwide* (Peabody: Hendrickson, 1997), 1–2; Anderson, "Varieties, Taxonomies," 13, 17; Cox, *Fire from Heaven*, 120, 302.

53. Subtypes include (a) holiness, (b) finished work, (c) Oneness, and (d) Apostolic pentecostals (Anderson, "Varieties, Taxonomies," 17).

54. See also Yong, "Taxonomies;" McGrath, *Christianity's Dangerous Idea*, 434.

55. Macchia, "Call for Careful Discernment." See also Ma, "Blessing."

want to examine if the worldview carries a distinct inner logic.[56] The analytical goal is important because although scholarship often uses a somewhat unified set of beliefs and practices to define the Word of Faith, there is no consensus on what distinguishes the Word of Faith and what its identity-carrying characteristics are.

My second goal is evaluative. I want to make a careful appraisal of the Word of Faith worldview on its own merits as a Christian worldview by testing its strengths and weaknesses. This evaluative focus is an overarching concern throughout the project but comes into focus through assessing the cumulative findings of the research based on the three criteria of external fidelity, inner coherence, and openness for change.[57] These criteria are used by the worldview scholars Brian Walsh and Richard Middleton.[58] Applied to the Word of Faith, the criteria yield the following evaluative questions I want to ask: (1) Is the Word of Faith worldview consistent with reality? Leaving aside reflections on the philosophical problems surrounding definitions of "reality," it is sufficient here to speak of a fundamental division of reality as subjective interpretation and objective experience.[59] Fidelity resides in the worldview's capacity of truly offering a *world*view, in which all of life's multifaceted experiences find their place and meaning.[60] Fidelity to reality is challenged when one aspect is either absolutized or excluded by the worldview. (2) Is the Word of Faith worldview internally coherent? By this question I ask if the Word of Faith offers a coherent vision of the world or if it is fragmented or containing mutually exclusive features. (3) Is the Word of Faith worldview open to correction? This question probes the worldview's recognition of finitude and receptiveness for revision. It tests whether the Word of Faith is a worldview that has any ideological tendencies. "Ideology" is understood here to be the totalitarian function of a worldview that does not recognize its finitude and seeks to dominate all other worldviews.[61] This question is not informed by relativism, as if all worldviews are

56. N. T. Wright, *The New Testament and the People of God* [*NTPG*] (London: SPCK, 1992), 368, fn. 41. On the idea of an inner logic in the movement, see Tony Tian-Ren Lin, *Prosperity Gospel Latinos and Their American Dream* (Chapel Hill: The University of North Carolina Press, 2020), Kindle edition. See also Dayton, *Theological Roots*, 28.

57. Brian Walsh and Richard Middleton. *The Transforming Vision: Shaping a Christian World View* [*TV*] (Downers Grove: IVP, 1984), 38-9. Tawa Anderson, Michael Clark and David Naugle use the threefold evaluative criteria of: internal consistency, external consistency, and existential consistency [Tawa Anderson, Michael Clark and David Naugle *An Introduction to Christian Worldview* [[*ICW*]] (Downers Grove: Apollos, 2017), 76-89].

58. Walsh and Middleton, *TV*, 36-9.

59. On the question of reality and worldview, see Wright *NTPG*, 31-80; David Naugle, *Worldview: The History of a Concept* (Grand Rapids: Eerdmans, 2002), 260-73; James Sire, *Naming the Elephant: Worldview as a Concept* [*NTE*], 2nd ed. (Downers Grove: IVP, 2015), 70-95; Henry Lederle, *Theology with Spirit: The Future of the Pentecostal and Charismatic Movements in the 21st Century* (Tulsa: Word and Spirit, 2010), 206-11.

60. Walsh and Middleton, *TV*, 38-9.

61. Ibid.

equal in truth and value.[62] Rather, it arises out of a Christian rationality committed to altering its view of the world to fit reality and revelation and to accept correction from worldviews that give better expression to these dynamics.[63] Since the Word of Faith affects many people and presents itself as a Christian movement that offers the best possible interpretation of reality, and the present scholarly responses are ambiguous, the second evaluative goal is important.

My third goal is comparative. Given, as seen earlier, that Pentecostalism makes the larger religious context for the Word of Faith, I want to provide through this worldview-analysis the conceptual tools that make possible to measure how the Word of Faith worldview contributes and challenges Pentecostal worldview distinctives.[64] Since this work is on the worldview of the Word of Faith and not on Pentecostalism, this goal is not primary; however, the inclusion of it as a goal shapes the project in ways that make possible exploration of the relationship between the Word of Faith and Pentecostalism more fully in future studies.

The first two goals have analytical and evaluative foci and make my primary goals, as I intend the worldview-analysis to directly speak to these. The third goal is comparative and can only lay the groundwork for later studies. The worldview-analysis seeks to identify and analyze the Word of Faith's inner characteristics and logic, to evaluate the worldview's fidelity, coherence, and openness to correction, and to provide the basis for further comparative studies with Pentecostalism. Accomplishing these goals will add nuance and complexity to current characterizations of the Word of Faith. Considering that the Word of Faith is described as "one of the most widespread manifestations of Christianity on earth today"[65] and the ambivalence of present responses, it is imperative to address my three goals. My intention in this worldview approach is not to overlook the sometimes significant theological areas that have placed the Word of Faith in conflict with Pentecostalism, nor to gloss over the troubling ethical problems within parts of the Word of Faith.[66] However, in the midst of the conflicting views

---

62. See Brian Walsh and Richard Middleton, *Truth Is Stranger than It Used to Be* (Downers Grove: IVP, 1995).

63. Walsh and Middleton, *TV*, 38.

64. See James K. A. Smith, *Thinking in Tongues: Pentecostal Contributions to Christian Philosophy* (Grand Rapids: Eerdmans, 2010).

65. Christopher Wright, "Calling the Church Back to Humility, Integrity and Simplicity," in *Prosperity Theology and the Gospel: Good News or Bad News for the Poor?* ed. J. Daniel Salinas (Peabody: Hendrickson, 2017), 193.

66. "Taken together and in general, I would agree that Word of Faith teachings tend to be theologically aberrant and sub-orthodox" [Amos Yong, *In the Days of Caesar: Pentecostalism and Political Theology* (Grand Rapids: Eerdmans, 2010), 264, fn. 20]. See Lausanne Theology Working Group, "A Statement on the Prosperity Gospel," January 16, 2010, accessed April 7, 2021, https://www.lausanne.org/content/a-statement-on-the-prosperity-gospel; Nel, *Prosperity Gospel*, Kindle edition, "Essence of Neo-Pentecostalism in Africa."

that exist, it is a growing realization in Pentecostal scholarship that some Word of Faith features may be unique gifts of the Spirit that could rejuvenate not just Pentecostalism but also global Christianity.[67] Yet, it is equally observed that these features require revision to be of positive influence.[68] I want to take these challenges seriously while also recognizing the dynamic nature of worldviews that allows the possibility of change in the Word of Faith worldview that can make it enrich global pneumatic Christianity.[69]

Analyzing the Word of Faith as a Worldview

To complete the analytical, evaluative, and comparative goals, I need to perform three tasks, two initial and one dominant. The dominant task is the worldview-analysis of the Word of Faith. The initial tasks relate to the Word of Faith and worldview, respectively. The initial tasks make up Chapters 1 and 2, while the dominant task makes up Chapters 3 to 6.

The first initial task is to map the state of current research on the Word of Faith and to construct a critical taxonomy of the models of analysis used by current scholarship. Since no study has yet comprehensively surveyed the state of research on the Word of Faith, the aim is to identify the significant models of analysis used to understand the movement, what insights they generate, and how this book's worldview approach is a more suitable model to address the goals of this project and to provide the needed complexity and nuance to current characterizations of the Word of Faith. I am also concerned with testing if worldview is already used as a significant model of analysis.

The second initial task of this book relates to the theory and method of worldview. The concept of worldview needs to be discussed, defined, and justified. There is a lack of fixed points in the theory of worldview: scholarly discourse frequently uses "worldview" but the term is seldom defined, and there is no consensus in the understanding of its constitution. The ambiguity also exists in terms of method, as there exists no established model for worldview-analysis.[70] To

67. Ma, "Blessing," 273; "in the package of the PG [Prosperity Gospel], in spite of its ugly face, there may be theological elements inherent in it that beg to be liberated from abuses and stereotypical dismissal. And some of them may indeed be a unique gift of the Spirit to rejuvenate dying churches while continually fuelling the growth of global Christianity" (Ma, "Blessing," 289). See Katherine Attanasi and Amos Yong, eds., *Pentecostalism and Prosperity: The Socio-Economics of the Global Charismatic Movement* (New York: Palgrave Macmillan, 2012); Lederle, *Theology with Spirit*, 203–26.

68. Ma, "Blessing," 273, 289.

69. See Perriman, *FHP*, 235.

70. Naugle, *Worldview*; Matthew Bonzo and Michael Stevens, eds., *After Worldview: Christian Higher Education in Postmodern Worlds* (Sioux Center: Dordt College, 2009); Anderson, Clark and Naugle, *ICW*.

speak to these needs, I introduce the work of the theologian N. T. Wright, which contains a developed and holistic worldview theory and applicable model for analysis. The strengths of Wright's model are its holistic and analytical aspects. He understands worldviews to be implicit, precognitive, dynamic, and comprehensive reality-perceiving frameworks, consisting of the four interrelated elements of story, symbol, praxis, and ultimate beliefs.[71] Since little scholarly work so far interacts with Wright's worldview theory and model, the second initial task requires a close study of the literature where his theory and model are presented and applied.[72] The aim is to critically interact with Wright in order to apply his model meaningfully to the Word of Faith.

The third and dominant task is to conduct a worldview-analysis of the Word of Faith with the help of Wright's worldview-model. I intend to find whether the Word of Faith exists as a distinct worldview, consisting of Wright's elements of story, symbol, praxis, and ultimate beliefs. Hence, the dominant task is to apply each of these four elements in turn to the Word of Faith. Wright's element of story is applied to analyze the worldview's narrative dimension, the element of symbol is applied to analyze the semiotic dimension of the Word of Faith worldview, the element of praxis analyzes the worldview's practical dimension, and the element of ultimate beliefs analyzes the worldview's propositional dimension. By working through this book's initial and dominant tasks, I intend to accomplish the analytical, evaluative, and comparative goals.

The Structure of the Book

The structure of this book consists of two main parts: the first part contains the two initial tasks related to surveying the current scholarship on the Word of Faith (Chapter 1), discussing worldview theory, and presenting Wright's model for analysis (Chapter 2). The second part conducts a worldview-analysis of the Word of Faith through applying each of Wright's four elements of story (Chapter 3), symbol (Chapter 4), praxis (Chapter 5), and ultimate beliefs (Chapter 6).

Chapter 1 maps the current state of research on the Word of Faith. A taxonomy of the four key models used by scholars to understand the Word of Faith is presented: the doctrinal model, the biblical model, the historical model, and the

71. Implicit: N. T. Wright, *Paul and the Faithfulness of God* [*PFG*] (Minneapolis: Fortress Press, 2013), 26; precognitive: Wright, *NTPG*, 122; comprehensive: Wright, *NTPG*, 123, 137, 149; Wright, *PFG*, 28, 232–3; reality: Wright, *NTPG* 41, 43, 123, 137, 148; perceiving: Wright, *NTPG*, 123; frameworks: Wright, *NTPG*, 37, 43, 45. See Wright, *NTPG*, 124; N. T. Wright, *Jesus and the Victory of God* [*JVG*] (London: SPCK, 1996), 142; *PFG*, 29. See Chapter 2. On my use of "ultimate beliefs" instead of Wright's term "questions," see Sections 2.3.1 and 6.1.

72. Wright, *NTPG*; Wright, *JVG*; Wright, *The Resurrection of the Son of God* [*RSG*] (London: SPCK, 2003); Wright, *PFG*.

socioeconomical model. The chapter discusses each model's core aspects, how the model is employed in the literature and what results it generates followed by an evaluation of each model's explanatory power and how a worldview approach is better suited to address the goals and provide the needed complexity and nuance to current characterizations.

Chapter 2 focuses on worldview theory and method. Definitions of worldview and the ways the concept is appropriated by Christian worldview scholarship are first discussed followed by an overview of how current literature defines and employs worldview in studying the Word of Faith. The strengths of Wright's model are its holistic and analytical aspects that combine both views of worldview as a system of thought and a pattern of life already used on the Word of Faith. The model developed by Wright is then presented, consisting of the four elements of story, symbol, praxis, and ultimate beliefs which are applied in the remaining chapters to analyze the Word of Faith.

Chapter 3 applies Wright's element of story to analyze the narrative dimension of the Word of Faith worldview. Wright's understanding of story's function in worldviews is first explored. The element is then applied to the Word of Faith. Word of Faith discourse contains the explicit echoes of a shared plot—that I term "the Adam plot"—which, when correlated with the movement's distinctive beliefs, offers a story of five sequences (I call the story "Eden Redeemed"). These are analyzed using narrative categories and diagrams adopted from A. J. Greimas to bring out the story's inner logic, its themes, coherence, fidelity, and possible transformations. Story is first because Wright privileges story as the foundational element with which the other three elements interact.[73]

Chapter 4 analyzes the semiotic dimension of the Word of Faith worldview through Wright's element of symbol. After discussing how Wright envisages the functions of the element of symbol in worldviews and by what criteria to identify such, C. S. Peirce's semiotic theory of signs is introduced to refine and make Wright's element better applicable to the Word of Faith. Six signs emerge according to the criteria: revelation knowledge, faith, prosperity, health, optimism, and the charismatic leader. These are analyzed as semiotic signs to explicate what they signify and how they signify through the element of story in order to gain insights into the worldview of the Word of Faith

Chapter 5 applies Wright's element of praxis to the Word of Faith to analyze the practical dimension of the movement's worldview. How Wright imagines the function of praxis in worldviews and the criteria he uses to identify it are first considered. Peirce's semiotic theory is used to analyze six practices that fit Wright's criteria: speaking positive confessions, gaining revelation knowledge, sowing money seeds, manifesting prosperity, and health, following the charismatic leader and extending influence in the world. These are analyzed as signed-shaped, semiotic actions. Similar to symbol mentioned earlier, the goal is to analyze what they signify and how they signify through the context formed cumulatively by the

---

73. Wright, *NTPG*, 132; Wright, *PFG*, 456.

findings from the elements of story and symbol, focusing on what insights they provide into the Word of Faith worldview.

Chapter 6 applies Wright's element of ultimate beliefs to the Word of Faith to analyze the worldview's propositional dimension.[74] After considering how Wright envisions the propositional and presuppositional aspect of worldviews in terms of ultimate beliefs, the chapter explicates the ultimate beliefs of the Word of Faith through using Wright's five ultimate questions that speak to areas of identity, environment, evil, salvation, and, eschatology.[75] Answers are extracted from the combined findings of story, symbol, and praxis in the previous chapters and analyzed as to what their theological content and inner logic say about the Word of Faith worldview.

The conclusion summarizes the findings of the worldview-analysis and points out questions that require further research as well as new areas to explore by building on the model and findings of this work. It concludes that the argument is affirmed that the Word of Faith is a distinct worldview with a unique theological story that interrelates with a set of signs and practices which together generate a set of ultimate beliefs. The picture emerging from the study is that the Word of Faith worldview is characterized by a unique mixture of logics expressed in an instrumental use of faith made effective by words and gifts to cause a direct correspondence between present reality and Eden's perfection, imagined in ideals shaped by global consumerism. The Word of Faith worldview is tested by the criteria developed by Walsh and Middleton: the worldview's fidelity to reality, its inner coherence, and its openness to correction. Lastly, in comparison to Pentecostalism, I discuss how the Word of Faith worldview both strengthens and subverts Pentecostal distinctives.

The goal of this study is to contribute to the understanding of the Word of Faith a worldview-analysis of the movement which will demonstrate how the Word of Faith operates as a distinct worldview with its own semiotic, practical, and propositional dimensions rooted in a unique theological story. Thus, it advances a critical and therapeutic approach that challenges stereotypical and reductionist approaches to the Word of Faith while calling for a multifaceted understanding that critiques the worldview's limitations while not overlooking its potential for Pentecostalism.

74. Anderson, Clark and Naugle, *ICW*, 79 fn. 5.
75. Wright, *NTPG* 123; Wright, *RSG*, 38.

Chapter 1

MODELS FOR ANALYZING THE WORD OF FAITH

This chapter maps the state of current research on the Word of Faith and presents the four dominant models of analysis in the scholarly literature. After showing the need for and the method used to identify the dominant models, I present the four models identified: the doctrinal model, the biblical model, the historical model, and the socioeconomical model. Each model includes a discussion of its core aspects, how it is employed in the literature and its principal arguments. Closing the discussion of each model is an evaluation of the model's explanatory power and what aspects are better addressed by the worldview-model used here. Concluding this chapter is a summary of the findings as they relate to the need for a holistic worldview-analysis of the Word of Faith. This chapter contributes to the overall project by situating my research in the larger scholarly field. It shows the need for a holistic worldview-analysis that can build on the findings of the other models while providing additional complexity and nuance and so better address the analytical, evaluative, and comparative goals raised in the introduction.

1.1 Taxonomy of Models of Analysis

This chapter's task of identifying and analyzing the current models of analysis used by scholarship on the Word of Faith is important because there exists no comprehensive survey of the models used by current scholarship on the Word of Faith. By mapping the scholarly field, I can situate this work and show how it expands and complements present knowledge. For this research to address the complexities surrounding the global Word of Faith movement and the difficulties related to the phenomenon, it requires a level of conceptual precision that only comes after first assessing the present state of scholarship. Identifying and measuring the dominant models of analysis lay the essential groundwork for the dominant task of conducting the worldview-analysis.

The initial task of identifying the dominant models used by scholarship to analyze the Word of Faith requires a comprehensive survey of data. I use three criteria for data selection. First, because of the presence of the Word of Faith as movement and ethos and the variety of terms in use (see Introduction), I use an inclusive approach in the selection of data. Second, the data has to be published texts of scholarly character, that is, either an academic publication or of academically quality. Third, the data have to cover the Word of Faith's global manifestations.

The data fitting these criteria yield four distinct models, which I label "the doctrinal model," "the biblical model," "the historical model," and "the socioeconomical model."[1] As in all taxonomy, it is possible to divide the data otherwise and name the models differently while staying true to the primary sources. Yet, this categorization is itself suggested by the data without forcing a foreign pattern. The fourfold division is necessitated by each model's unique characteristics and impact on the scholarly conversations. To do justice to the complexity of the literature, the biblical and socioeconomic models are subdivided according to their specific focal points. The models are ordered in chronological order as they appear in the scholarly responses to the Word of Faith, but the description of each engages the models as a whole in their present form. The four models are separated and presented individually for clarity, while in actual usage several models are often combined.

1. Morris identifies three categories in his study: origins, key proponents, and specific theological aspects [Russell Morris, "A Biblical and Theological Analysis of Specific Tenets of Word of Faith Theology: Pastoral Implications for The Church of God" (Doctor of philosophy thesis, South African Theological Seminary, 2012), 35]; McClymond lists three types of analyses used by scholarship: biblical-theological, genealogical, and cultural historical [Michael McClymond, "Prosperity Already and Not Yet: An Eschatological Interpretation of the Health-and-Wealth Emphasis in the North American Pentecostal-Charismatic Movement," in *Perspectives in Pentecostal Eschatologies*, ed. Peter Althouse and Robby Waddell (Cambridge: James Clarke, 2012), 293–4]. See also David Reed, "The Prosperity Gospel and Money–Plundering the Devil's Den?" *Canadian Journal of Pentecostal-Charismatic Christianity* 10 (2019): 53–4; Lewis Brogdon, *The New Pentecostal Message? An Introduction to the Prosperity Movement* (Eugene: Cascade, 2015). For typologies of prosperity, see Yong, "Typology of Prosperity Theology;" Nimi Wariboko, "Pentecostal Paradigms of National Economic Prosperity in Africa," in *Pentecostalism and Prosperity: The Socio-Economics of the Global Charismatic Movement*, ed. Katherine Attanasi and Amos Yong (New York: Palgrave Macmillan, 2012), 35–62.

1.2 The Doctrinal Model

The doctrinal model is the first distinct model in the literature used to analyze the Word of Faith. This model envisions the Word of Faith as substantially a doctrinal entity, with its inner core consisting of propositional beliefs. From this image follows the method of analyzing the Word of Faith through a close study of the movement's doctrines.[2]

The demands facing the doctrinal model are substantial, from which doctrines to focus on to which primary sources to use and how to set delimitations to wider Pentecostalism.[3] These obstacles arise because the Word of Faith has no official statements of faith, no systematic treaties, and no endorsed theologians to articulate their beliefs.[4] The lack of consensus in the scholarly literature on which doctrines are essential to the movement arises because Word of Faith beliefs are expressed by a loose network of mutually independent preachers who often exchange ideas in the context of pulpit ministry.[5] The beliefs are disseminated through a discourse of an ever-growing quantity, taking the form of recorded teachings (audio and video), published materials (articles, tracts, magazines, and books), and electronic media (websites and social media). Despite these problems, three doctrines stand out in the studies as the most significant to the movement:[6] (1) an expectation

2. Some focus on general theological issues but these are not sufficient in number nor have they reached any significantly different conclusions to merit a separate model. E.g., Peter Cotterell, *Prosperity Theology* (Leicester: Religious and Theological Studies Fellowship, 1990); David Williams, "Anselm and Hagin: Ontological Argument and Prosperity Cult," *Koers* 57, no. 2 (1992): 227–39. See also Heuser, "Prosperity Theology."

3. See Tom Smail, Andrew Walker and Nigel Wright, *The Love of Power or the Power of Love: A Careful Assessment of the Problems Within the Charismatic and Word-of-Faith Movements* (Minneapolis: Bethany House, 1994), 78.

4. Agana, *Succeed Here*, 30–1.

5. Milmon Harrison, *Righteous Riches: The Word of Faith Movement in Contemporary African American Religion* [RR] (New York: Oxford University Press, 2005), 41. Debra Mumford, *Exploring Prosperity Preaching: Biblical Health, Wealth and Wisdom* (Valley Forge: Judson Press, 2012); Bowler, *Blessed*; Smail, Walker, Wright, *Power of Love*, 78; Perriman *FHP*, 16, 82; Ackerly, "Importing Faith." On "folk theology" see Joe Barnhart, "Prosperity Gospel: A New Folk Theology," in *Religious Television: Controversies and Conclusions*, ed. Robert Abelman and Stewart Hoover (Norwood: Ablex, 1990), 159; Perriman, *FHP*, 16, 100; Stanley Grenz and Roger E. Olson, *Who Needs Theology?: An Invitation to the Study of God* (Downers Grove: IVP, 1996), 27–9.

6. Barron, *Health and Wealth*, 10–11; Lederle, *Theology with Spirit*, 150–6; Dennis Hollinger, "Enjoying God Forever: An Historical/Sociological Profile of the Health and Wealth Gospel," *Trinity Journal* 9, no. 2 (1988): 131–49; Coleman, *Globalisation*; Perriman, *FHP*, 15.

of physical health,[7] (2) material prosperity as a God-given right,[8] (3) the creative power of positive confessions.[9] Several other doctrines are also examined but are less prominent in the studies compared to these three.[10]

7. Farah, *FTP*, 61–85; Fee, *Disease*, 19–35; Barron, *Health and Wealth*, 77–87; Andrew Brandon, *Health and Wealth: Does God Always Promise Prosperity* (Eastbourne: Kingsway, 1987), 47–70; McConnell, *DG*, 147–68; Hank Hanegraaff, *Christianity in Crisis* [*CIC*] (Eugene: Harvest House, 1993), 233–76; Perriman, *FHP*, 46–8, 126–35; Jones and Woodbridge, *Health, Wealth and Happiness* [*HWH*], 67–9, 107–22; Lederle, *Theology with Spirit*, 153–5; Douglas Moo, "Divine Healing in the Health and Wealth Gospel," *Trinity Journal* 9, no. 2 (1988): 191–209; Keith Warrington, "The Use of the Name (of Jesus) in Healing and Exorcism with Special Reference to the Teachings of Kenneth Hagin," *The Journal of the European Pentecostal Theological Association* 17 (1997): 16–36; Keith Warrington, "The Teaching and Praxis Concerning Supernatural Healing of British Pentecostals, of John Wimber and Kenneth Hagin in the Light of an Analysis of the Healing Ministry of Jesus as Recorded in the Gospels" (Doctor of philosophy thesis, King's College, London, 1999); Keith Warrington, "Healing and Kenneth Hagin," *Asian Journal of Pentecostal Studies* 3, no. 1 (2000): 119–38.

8. Fee, *Disease*, 7–17, 37–45; Barron, *Health and Wealth*, 88–100; McConnell, *DG*, 169–82; Hanegraaff, *CIC*, 179–231; Brandon, *Health and Wealth*, 71–100; Walter Kaiser Jr., "The Old Testament Promise of Material Blessings and the Contemporary Believer," *Trinity Journal* 9, no. 2 (1988): 151–70; Perriman, *FHP*, 48–57, 157–94; Lederle, *Theology with Spirit*, 152–3, 218–24; Harrison, *RR*, 11–12.

9. Farah, *FTP*, 123–33; Barron, *Health and Wealth*, 101–13; Brandon, *Health and Wealth*, 16–32; Perriman, *FHP*, 39–41, 143–55; James Kinnebrew, "The Charismatic Doctrine of Positive Confession: A Historical, Exegetical, and Theological Critique," (Doctor of theology thesis, Mid-America Baptist Theological Seminary, 1980); Lederle, *Theology with Spirit*, 150–3, 217–18; McConnell, *DG*, 135–8; Hanegraaff, *CIC*, 66–9; James Bjornstad, "What's Behind the Prosperity Gospel?" *Moody Monthly*, November 1986; Brandon, *Health and Wealth*, 30; Smail, Walker and Wright, *Love of Power*, 80; Dave Hunt and T. A. McMahon, *The Seduction of Christianity* (Eugene: Harvest House, 1985), 97–104; Assemblies of God, "The Believer and Positive Confession."

10. Other doctrines studied in the literature are: the nature and role of faith [Farah, *FTP*, 87–113, 205; Farah, "Critical Analysis"; Barron, *Health and Wealth*, 64–76; McConnell, *DG*, 132–46; Perriman, *FHP* 137–56; David Hunt, *Beyond Seduction: A Return to Biblical Christianity* (Eugene: Harvest House, 1987), 44–61; John MacArthur, *Charismatic Chaos* (Grand Rapids: Zondervan, 1992) 342–50; Hanegraaff, *CIC*, 59–102; Hans Johansson, ed., *Vad Ska Man Tro Egentligen? Den Modernistiska Teologin, Trosförkunnelsen och den Nya Andligheten i Biblisk Prövning* (Örebro: Libris, 1989), 82–8; Brandon, *Health and Wealth*, 33–46; Jones and Woodbridge, *HWH*, 87–9; Warrington "The Use of the Name," 28; Olson, *CT*, 157; Lederle, *Theology with Spirit*, 154–5; Femi Adeleye, *Preachers of a Different Gospel* (Nairobi: Hippobooks, 2014), 61–74]; the belief in spiritual laws, especially the universal law of divine reciprocity or "sowing and reaping" [Farah, *FTP*, 116, 135, 139, 147–8; K. L. Sarles, "Prosperity and Healing: Is It Promised to the Believer? A Theological Evaluation,"

Bibliotheca Sacra, 143 (1986): 329–52, 333, 342–3, 349; J. N. Horn, *From Rags to Riches: An Analysis of the Faith Movement and Its Relation to the Classical Pentecostal Movement* [*FRTR*] (Pretoria: University of South Africa Muckleneuk Pretoria, 1989), 92–3; Perriman, *FHP*, 33–5, 141–3; Jones and Woodbridge, *HWH*, 59–62; McConnell, *DG*, 132–46, 170–4; William DeArteaga, *Quenching the Spirit: Discover the Real Spirit Behind the Charismatic Controversy* (Lake Mary: Creation House, 1996), 188–200; Hanegraaff, *CIC*, 65–95, 73–4, 93–4, 193–209; J. Norberto Saracco, "Prosperity Theology," in *Dictionary of Mission Theology*, ed. John Corrie (Nottingham: IVP, 2007), 322–6; Hunt, *Beyond Seduction*, 44–61; Olson, *CT*, 162–3; David Downs, "Giving for Return in the Prosperity Gospel and the New Testament," in *Prosperity Theology and the Gospel: Good News or Bad News for the Poor?* ed. J. Daniel Salinas (Peabody: Hendrickson, 2017), 36–49; Daniel Maritz and Henk Stoker, "Does the Christian Worldview Provide a Place for the Law of Attraction? (Part 1): An Apologetic Evaluation of the Roots of this Doctrine," *Verbum et Ecclesia* 37, no. 1 (2016): no page numbers, accessed April 7, 2021, http://dx.doi. org/10.4102/ve.v37i1.1571; Daniel Maritz and Henk Stoker, "Does the Christian worldview provide a place for the law of attraction? (Part 2): An apologetic evaluation of the way the Bible is used in promoting this idea," *Verbum et Ecclesia* 37, no. 1 (2016): no page numbers, accessed April 7, 2021, http://dx.doi.org/10.4102/ve.v37i1.1570. Gifford credits "seed-faith theology" as the main contributor to growth of Pentecostalism in Africa [Paul Gifford, *Christianity, Development and Modernity in Africa* (London: C. Hurst & Co, 2015), 51]; the person and ministry of Jesus [Perriman, *FHP*, 105–10; Hanegraaff, *CIC*, 137–43, 186–9; MacArthur, *Charismatic Chaos*, 336–42]; the atonement and JDS (McConnell, *DG*, 114–31, 123–8; Hanegraaff, *CIC*, 145–78; Perriman, *FHP*, 22–5, 110–15; Jones and Woodbridge, *HWH*, 89–92; Brandon, *Health and Wealth*, 121–8; Johansson, *Vad Ska Man Tro*, 77–82; Smail, Walker and Wright, *Love of Power*, 80–5; Judith Matta, *The Born Again Jesus of the Word-Faith Teaching* (Bellevue: Spirit of Truth, 1987); William Atkinson, *The "Spiritual Death" of Jesus: A Pentecostal Investigation* (Leiden: Brill, 2012); William Atkinson, "Christology," in *Routledge Handbook to Pentecostal Theology*, ed. Wolfgang Vondey (London: Routledge, 2020), 217–18]; the image of God, particularly God's faith-nature and interaction with creation [Sarles, "Prosperity and Healing," 340–3; Hanegraaff, *CIC*, 86–96, 121–8; McConnell, *DG*, 140–1; MacArthur, *Charismatic Chaos*, 328–36; Farah, *FTP*, 112–13, 123–5, 139, 147–8; Perriman, *FHP*, 139–40; Jones and Woodbridge, *HWH*, 57–9; Olson, *CC*, 157; Douglas Hicks, "Prosperity, Theology, and Economy," in *Pentecostalism and Prosperity: The Socio-Economics of the Global Charismatic Movement*, ed. Katherine Attanasi and Amos Yong (New York: Palgrave Macmillan, 2012), 243; Sarles, "Prosperity and Healing," 341–2; Antonio Barbosa da Silva, *Framgångsteologin - Svärmeri eller Väckelse?* (Uppsala: Uppsala Universitet, 1988), 25; David Larsen, "The Gospel of Greed Versus the Gospel of the Grace of God," *Trinity Journal* 9, no. 2 (1988): 214]; theological anthropology, especially their trichotomist anthropology, and the human's place of dominion in the world [Bowman, *Word-Faith*, 98; Jones and Woodbridge, *HWH*, 63–4, 71; Sarles "Prosperity and Healing," 342–3; Bjornstad, "What's Behind;" Larsen, "Gospel of Greed," 213; Jimmy Swaggart, "Hyper-Faith: The New Gnosticism? Part II," *The Evangelist* 48, no. 9 (2014): 15; Farah, *FTP*, 145; Brandon, *Health and Wealth*, 101–17; Sarles, "Prosperity and Healing," 342–3; Smail,

The doctrinal model is used to substantiate three different approaches: the radical, the moderate, and the sympathetic. This division is somewhat a generalization but it is nevertheless helpful to identify the main approaches. The radical approach claims based on the doctrinal model that the Word of Faith is a heresy that bears the marks of a cult, preaching a different gospel about a different God and another Jesus.[11] In this view, the Word of Faith's chief appeal is its attraction to human egocentrism and greed.[12] The charge is justified by faulting the Word of Faith for encompassing deism, dualism, elitism, experientialism, fideism, Gnosticism, liberalism, occultism and New Age, Pelagianism, selfism, syncretism,

Walker and Wright, *Love of Power*, 77; da Silva, *Framgångsteologin*, 49, 86; Perriman, *FHP*, 45, 117–22; MacArthur, *Charismatic Chaos*, 332–3; Hanegraaff, *CIC*, 107–20; Johansson, *Vad Ska Man Tro*, 76–7; Hunt and McMahon, *The Seduction*, 80–90]; eschatology, especially the focus on the present and complete fulfilment of biblical promises [Farah, "Critical Analysis;" Moo, "Divine Healing," 198; Fee, *Disease*, 33; da Silva, *Framgångsteologin*, 92; Horn, *FRTR*, 44, 46; Hellstern, "The Me Gospel"]; the place and power of Satan and the demonic [Bowman, *Word-Faith*, 137–45; Perriman, *FHP*, 104–5; Atkinson, *Spiritual Death*, 234–5]; the believer's victory through Jesus [Farah, *FTP*, 152–7; Hanegraaff, *CIC*, 129–35; Sarles, "Prosperity and Healing," 344–6; Perriman, *FHP*, 104–5; Lederle, *Theology with Spirit*, 215].

11. Cult [McArthur, *Charismatic Chaos*, 327; McConnell, *DG*, 186, 19; Hanegraaff, *CIC*, 41–50]; different gospel [Farah, "Critical Analysis," 12; McConnell, *DG*, 51; Michael Horton, "The TV Gospel," in *The Agony of Deceit: What Some TV Preachers are Really Preaching*, ed. Michael Horton (Chicago: Moody Press, 1990), 123; J. Daniel Salinas, "Mainline Churches and Prosperity Theology in Latin America," in *Prosperity Theology and the Gospel: Good News or Bad News for the Poor?* ed. J. Daniel Salinas (Peabody: Hendrickson, 2017), 122]; a different God and another Jesus (Hanegraaff, *CIC*, 328; MacArthur, *Charismatic Chaos*, 328, 336; Salinas, "Mainline Churches," 119; Adeleye, *Preachers*, 109. E.g., "It is difficult to evaluate the health and wealth movement in soft terms. Their teaching and their claims represent blasphemy of the highest order. They demean the precious name of Christ, denying that He claimed deity, teaching that He was dragged into hell and had to be born again and then claiming that they themselves are gods. The prosperity people focus on this world and the things of this world, encouraging covetousness and worldliness. . . . To demean Christ and to exalt man to deity is heretical and blasphemous. The health and wealth movement stands outside of historic, biblical Christianity and must be rejected. *It is not* Christian" (Enns, *Moody Handbook of Theology*, 689, emphasis mine)].

12. Egocentrism [McConnell, *DG*, 170; Brandon, *Health and Wealth*, 113; Jones and Woodbridge, *HWH*, 14, 63]; greed [Larsen, "The Gospel of Greed;" Mumford, *Exploring Prosperity Preaching*, 54; Brandon, *Health and Wealth*, 88, 139; Jones and Woodbridge, *HWH*, 101; Sarles, "Prosperity and Healing," 350; Horton, "TV Gospel," 123, 128; Barnhart, "Prosperity Gospel," 162].

and triumphalism.[13] The radicals classify the Word of Faith as a "disease"[14] that spreads dangerous errors from which Christians need to be rescued.[15]

The moderate approach informed by the model is concerned with the "orthodoxy" of the Word of Faith doctrines to the point of also naming some heretical. The moderate approach is careful to avoid overstatements and caricatures and to express its concerns less polemically. It mixes the critique with self-criticism and seeks to emphasize points of agreement and areas where the Word of Faith

13. Deism [McConnell, *DG*, 44, 137, 185; MacArthur, *Charismatic Chaos*, 350; Horn, *FRTR*, 94; Perriman, *FHP*, 138]; dualism [Farah, *FTP*, 152–7; McConnell, *DG*, 44; Johansson, *Vad Ska Man Tro*, 61; Horton, "TV Gospel," 129; David Williams, *Christian Approaches to Poverty* (Lincoln: iUniverse, 2001), 231]; elitism [Farah, "Critical Analysis," 15]; experientialism [John Ankerberg and John Weldon, *The Facts on the Faith Movement* (Eugene: Harvest House, 1993), 39]; fideism [McConnell, *DG*, 103, 107; Perriman, *FHP* 96; Cotterell, *Prosperity Theology*, 24]; Gnosticism [Farah, "Critical Analysis;" da Silva, *Framgångsteologin*, 92; Neuman, "Cultic Origins of Word-Faith," 35; Olson, *CC*; McConnell, *DG*, 107–8; Horton, "TV Gospel," 128; Matta, *Born Again Jesus*]; liberalism [Farah, *FTP*, 136–7, 139; Farah, "Critical Analysis," 7; Sarles, "Prosperity and Healing," 330]; occultism and New Age [Hunt and McMahon, *The Seduction*; Sarles, "Prosperity and Healing," 345; Hanegraaff, *CIC*, 63; Ankerberg and Weldon, *The Facts*, 37–9; John Newport, *The New Age Movement and the Biblical Worldview: Conflict and Dialogue* (Grand Rapids: Eerdmans, 1998), 363–6, 391–405; Cox, *Fire from Heaven*, 276, 313]; Pelagianism [Sarles, "Prosperity and Healing," 343; Larsen, "Gospel of Greed," 219]; selfism [Larsen, "Gospel of Greed," 213; Fee, *Disease*, 15–16]; syncretism [McConnell, *DG*, 92]; triumphalism [Brandon, *Health and Wealth*, 138]. The list can be expanded: hedonism [Ankerberg and Weldon, *The Facts*, 15].

14. Fee, *Disease*.

15. Fee, *Disease*, 7; MacGregor, "Recognising and Successfully Averting;" Brandon, *Health and Wealth*, 12, 37. Writers using a radical approach include (listed in alphabetical order): Femi Adeleye [Adeleye, *Preachers*]; Andrew Brandon [Brandon, *Health and Wealth*]; Gordon Fee [Fee, *Disease*]; Hank Hanegraaff [Hanegraaff, *Christianity in Crisis 21st*]; Michael Horton [Michael Horton, "The Agony of Deceit," in *The Agony of Deceit: What Some TV Preachers are Really Preaching*, ed. Michael Horton (Chicago: Moody Press, 1990), 30; Horton, "TV Gospel," 120]; David Hunt [Hunt, *Beyond Seduction*]; David Jones [David Jones, "The Errors of the Prosperity Gospel," *9Marks Journal* 9, (2014): 34–7; Jones and Woodbridge, *HWH*]; John MacArthur [MacArthur, *Charismatic Chaos*; John MacArthur, *Strange Fire* (Nashville: Thomas Nelson, 2013)]; Daniel McConnell [McConnell, *DG*]; Justin Peters [Justin Peters, "Clouds without Water: A Biblical Critique of the Word of Faith Movement. Exposing the False Prosperity Gospel," (Edmond: Justin Peters Ministries, 2016), DVD]; John Piper [John Piper, "Prosperity Preaching: Deceitful and Deadly," *9Marks Journal* 9, (2014): 50–2]; K. L. Sarles [Sarles, "Prosperity and Healing"]; Russell Woodbridge [Russell Woodbridge, "The Prosperity Gospel in North America," in *Prosperity Theology and the Gospel: Good News or Bad News for the Poor?* ed. J. Daniel Salinas (Peabody: Hendrickson, 2017), 151–7; Jones and Woodbridge, *HWH*].

contributes to established churches and traditions.[16] The radical and the moderate approaches generally try to distinguish their critique of the Word of Faith from the rest of Pentecostalism and seek to ensure that criticisms—no matter how harsh— are not taken as anti-Pentecostal attacks.[17]

The sympathetic approach rejects the heretical charge and points to areas where the Word of Faith makes valid doctrinal contributions.[18] The argument is that several doctrines are beneficial and should be untangled from extreme and unbalanced beliefs and unethical practices. After revision, some key doctrines can help the greater Christian quest of human flourishing.[19] Tensions in Word of Faith doctrines are framed as the consequence of lack of balance by sincere yet overly zealous proponents whose primary need is advanced theological education.[20] The sympathetic approach calls for a dialogue between critics and propagators.

1.2.1 Evaluation and Remaining Questions

The doctrinal model was the first used by scholarship to analyze the Word of Faith.[21] It has arguably wielded significant formative power on the perception of the Word of Faith among evangelicals and Pentecostal scholarship (mostly classical Pentecostals).[22] But there is a notable ambiguity in the Pentecostal response to

16. Writers using a moderate approach include (listed in alphabetical order): Robert Bowman [Bowman, *Word-Faith*]; Charles Farah [Farah, *FTP*]; Andrew Perriman [Perriman, *FHP*, e.g., 217–25]. The Lausanne Movement gives room for both radical and moderate voices (Daniel Salinas, ed., *Prosperity Theology and the Gospel: Good News or Bad News for the Poor?* (Peabody: Hendrickson, 2017).

17. McConnell, *DG*, xvii–xviii; Hanegraaff, *CIC*, 47–50. Bowman, *Word-Faith*, 12, 82–4, 94; Horton, "Agony of Deceit," 12. Not so: MacArthur, *Charismatic Chaos*; MacArthur, *Strange Fire*; Hunt, *Beyond Seduction*.

18. Writers using a sympathetic approach include (listed in alphabetical order): Bruce Barron [Barron, *Health and Wealth*]; Paul King [Paul King, *Only Believe: Examining the Origin and Development of Classic and Contemporary Word of Faith Theologies* (Tulsa: Word and Spirit, 2008)]; Henry Lederle [Lederle, *Theology with Spirit*].

19. See Lederle, *Theology with Spirit*; Wonsuk Ma, "Life, Justice, and Peace in the Spirit: A Korean Pentecostal Reflection," *The Ecumenical Review* 65, no. 2 (2013): 225–43; Ma, "Blessing."

20. Barron, *Health and Wealth*, 169–70; Lederle, *Theology with Spirit*, 218–24; King, *Only Believe*; Edwards, "Ethical Dimensions;" Newport, *New Age Movement*, 404; Derek Vreeland, "Reconstructing Word of Faith Theology: A Defense, Analysis and Refinement of the Theology of the Word of Faith Movement," Paper presented at the Thirtieth Annual Meeting of the Society for Pentecostal Studies, Oral Roberts University, Tulsa, Oklahoma, March 2001.

21. Farah, *FTP*.

22. McConnell, *DG*, xiii; DeArteaga, *Quenching the Spirit*, 15; Smail, Walker, Wright, *Love of Power*; Jones and Woodbridge, *HWH*; Perriman, *FHP*; King, *Only Believe*; Ackerly,

the Word of Faith's doctrines.[23] Some Pentecostal denominations draw on the doctrinal model to openly oppose the movement, reaching conclusions similar to the moderate groups (if not the radicals). Despite strong official rejections of its key doctrines, in practice, the Word of Faith is usually accepted within global Pentecostalism.[24]

Among the benefits of the model is that it helps to prioritize by sifting doctrinal data from the sizable bulk of Word of Faith discourse and to systematize the data into manageable units. It also provides a comparative tool to study similarities and dissimilarities between Word of Faith doctrines and other theological traditions.[25] It thus contributes valuable information to better understand Word of Faith beliefs. But the model's depth of analysis is restricted by its image of the Word of Faith. That the movement's inner core should comprise propositional beliefs draws life from an overly cerebral view of faith, that is, that the heart of faith consists of ideas carried by correct doctrines.[26]

The doctrinal model runs the risk of implicitly situating itself in a position of superior knowledge, as the gatekeeper of received theology made up of better ideas. The doctrinal model's goal is to achieve "doctrinal synopticism," that is,

"Importing Faith;" Brandon, *Health and Wealth*; da Silva, *Framgångsteologin*; Johansson, *Vad Ska Man Tro*; Horn, *FRTR*; Adeleye, *Preachers*; Jimmy Swaggart, "Hyper-Faith: The New Gnosticism? Part I," *The Evangelist* 48, no. 8 (2014): 12–15; Swaggart, "Hyper-Faith," 12–15; Jimmy Swaggart, "Hyper-Faith: The New Gnosticism? Part III," *The Evangelist* 48, no. 10 (2014): 10–15; Peters, "Clouds without Water;" Michael Otieno Maura, Conrad Mbewe, Ken Mbugua, John Piper and Wayne Grudem, *Prosperity? Seeking the True Gospel* (Nairobi: Africa Christian Textbooks, 2015). The doctrinal model is arguably the underlying influence to what Peter Berger saw as "an almost universal consensus, right across the Christian theological spectrum, to the effect that the so-called prosperity gospel is an aberration" (Peter L. Berger, "'You Can Do It!' Two Cheers for the Prosperity Gospel," *Books & Culture*, September 1, 2008). Hanegraaff's rejection of Word of Faith doctrines as "horrifying," "deadly errors" that spread like "cancer" in the body of Christ has had significant influence on evangelical thinking (Hanegraaff, *CIC*, 27, 13, 11). Hanegraaff's analysis of the Word of Faith is still influential and speaks into the Lausanne movement's analysis [e.g., Femi Adeleye, "The Prosperity Gospel and Poverty: An Overview and Assessment," in *Prosperity Theology and the Gospel: Good News or Bad News for the Poor?* ed. J. Daniel Salinas (Peabody: Hendrickson, 2017), 10–11].

23. Heuser, "Prosperity Theology;" Perriman, *FHP*; Bowman, *Word-Faith*, 12, 83; Anderson, *Introduction to Pentecostalism*, 219; Fee, *Disease*; Lovett, "Positive Confession Theology;" Horn, *FRTR*; Warrington, "Teaching and Praxis;" Atkinson, *Spiritual Death*; Neuman, "Cultic Origins of Word-Faith."

24. Anderson, *To the Ends*, 219–23.

25. E.g., Bowman, *Word-Faith*, 163–4, 184–6; Perriman, *FHP,* 16.

26. Horton, "Agony of Deceit," 12–13; Walker, Wright and Smail, *Love of Power*, 73–5; Jones and Woodbridge, *HWH*, 19–20.

for the Word of Faith to conform to the *a priori* system of "orthodoxy."[27] When truth is defined as an agreement with official faith, heresy is that which creates dissonance.[28] The model can thus generate a false dichotomy, guilty of the logical fallacy of the excluded middle, which smacks of the polarized categories from a fundamentalist heritage that has influenced parts of evangelicalism and Pentecostalism.[29] On its own, the model may make users think they have done an objective analysis of the Word of Faith while in actuality only confirming the orthodoxy of their faith tradition. The doctrinal model potentially makes critical engagements with its own particular point of view, presuppositions, and biases somewhat difficult. A "dogmatic assessment"[30] easily (but not necessarily) falls prey to one-dimensional stereotypes. When locked into the binary system of truth or error, nuanced theological evaluations of the Word of Faith are hampered. The Word of Faith's doctrinal innovations or reformulations (e.g., economic dimension in its soteriology, reciprocity in giving) are then met with skepticism on the charge that novelty equals error.[31] The conclusions of scholars using the model on the Word of Faith are also reduced, illustrated by the counsel offered by the radical, moderate, and sympathetic approaches alike: the Word of Faith needs better doctrine.[32]

Operating in awareness of its inherent limitations, the doctrinal model contributes critical insights (see Chapter 6). But its image of the Word of Faith is incomplete. In terms of the goals for this book, analyzing the Word of Faith's cognitive beliefs does not penetrate to the movement's inner core. The doctrinal model cannot appreciate the Word of Faith as operating on the more elementary level of worldview. The result is a loss of explanatory power as the model does not address the narrative, semiotic, or practical dimensions related to the Word of Faith's beliefs which arguably carry greater formative and defining power over the movement than their doctrines. Questions left are if their cognitive beliefs say anything about their greater vision of reality. The model does not address if there is a fundamental narrative structure that gives broader context, coherence, and meaning to their individual beliefs and better helps to assess the Word of

---

27. See DeArteaga, *Quenching the Spirit*, 333.

28. See Alister E. McGrath, *Heresy: A History of Defending the Truth* (London: SPCK, 2009).

29. See D. A. Carson, *Exegetical Fallacies*, 2nd ed. (Grand Rapids: Baker Academic, 1996), 87–124; Roger E. Olson, *The SCM Press A–Z of Evangelical Theology* (London: SCM Press, 2005), 35–9, 77–9; Alister E. McGrath, *Evangelicalism and the Future of Christianity* (Downers Grove: InterVarsity, 1995), 143–8; Anderson, *Introduction to Pentecostalism*, 259–62; Vondey, *Beyond Pentecostalism*, 62–6.

30. Smail, Walker and Wright, *Love of Power*, 78.

31. "All that is old may not be gold, but if its new, it cannot be true" (McConnell, *DG*, 20); DeArteaga, *Quenching the Spirit*, 234.

32. E.g., Farah, *FTP*, 141; Olson, *CC*, 169.

Faith beliefs rather than merely mapping them unto a truth-heresy paradigm.[33] The doctrinal model does not resolve what the dominant characteristics of the Word of Faith are, nor can it fully identify the movement's inner logic.[34] Because the model tends to operate with a static view of truth formed by a binary system of truth or error, it is a less-reliable model to evaluate the relationship between the Word of Faith and Pentecostalism. However, the critique of the doctrinal model is not to deny the significant knowledge it provides, nor is it meant to forward a relativistic view of Christian faith as existing without any boundaries. Wright's holistic worldview-model used here makes it possible to draw the important insights generated by the model and incorporate them into a broader and more illuminating framework to address the analytical, evaluative, and comparative goals.

1.3 The Biblical Model

The biblical model is the second distinct model of analysis recognizable in the scholarly literature on the Word of Faith. This model envisions the core of the Word of Faith to lie within the domains of biblical interpretation. That is, the way to understand the Word of Faith is through the dual lens of biblical exegesis and hermeneutics. Scholars exegetically engage the Word of Faith's key pericopes and analyze the principles used in the interpretative processes. Corresponding to these dual foci, I divide the presentation of this model into exegetical and hermeneutical focus.[35]

1.3.1 Exegetical Focus

The exegetical focus of the biblical model pays attention to how the Word of Faith interprets particular biblical texts. The rationale is that the Word of Faith "is a very tight and particular system of interpretation. It is built on unique interpretations of selected key verses."[36] Studies focus on thematic and authoritative passages or

33. Beyond the narratives in Hanegraaff, *CIC*, 17–27; Brandon, *Health and Wealth*, 148–51; Perriman, *FHP,* 19–29.

34. Agana, *Succeed Here*, 30–1.

35. Though some scholars treat the concepts of biblical exegesis and biblical hermeneutics synonymously, this separation follows the understanding of exegesis focusing on the interpretation of a specific pericope while biblical hermeneutics focuses on studying the nature of the interpretive process. See Carson, *Exegetical Fallacies*, 25; Bernard Ramm, *Protestant Bible Interpretation: A Textbook on Hermeneutics, 3rd ed.* (Grand Rapids: Baker Academic, 1970), 11; Klyne Snodgrass, "Exegesis," in *Dictionary for Theological Interpretation of the Bible*, ed. Kevin Vanhoozer (Grand Rapids: Baker, 2007), 203–6.

36. Hans Lindholm and Fredrik Broshe, *Varför Är Trosförkunnelsen Farlig?* (Uppsala: EFS Förlaget, 1986), 24, my translation.

investigate the exegetical underpinnings of a particular doctrine (e.g., healing, Jesus died spiritually [JDS] or positive confession).[37] The driving concern is to measure if the Word of Faith represents valid interpretations and applications of the Bible.

A set of key Bible passages are repeatedly examined in these exegetical studies.[38] Scholars point out exegetical problems with how the Word of Faith reads several of these thematic texts and argue that the range of biblical texts is selectivity chosen and that the Word of Faith hermeneutists use obscure or difficult texts that often contain semantic or grammatical irregularities while disregarding a

37. Warrington, "Teaching and Praxis;" Atkinson, *Spiritual Death*; Kinnebrew, "Charismatic Doctrine."

38. Listed here in canonical order: Psalm 82:6 [Bowman, *Word-Faith*, 130–3; Perriman, *FHP*, 117–22]; Proverbs 18:21 [Kinnebrew, "Charismatic Doctrine," 185; Farah, *FTP*, 131]; Isaiah 53:4–5 [Kaiser, "The Old Testament Promise," 168; Farah, *FTP*, 77–85; Moo, "Divine Healing," 202–4; Nel, *Prosperity Gospel*, Kindle edition, "'Proof-Texts' of the Prosperity Message"]; Isaiah 53:9a [Atkinson, *Spiritual Death*, 104–5; Bowman, *Word-Faith*, 164–5; Perriman, *FHP*, 111; Matta, *Born Again Jesus*, 54]; Malachi 3:10 [J. Kwabena Asamoah-Gyadu, "Prosperity and Poverty in the Bible: Ghana's Experience," in *Prosperity Theology and the Gospel: Good News or Bad News for the Poor?* ed. J. Daniel Salinas (Peabody: Hendrickson, 2017), 103–6]; Mark 11:22–4 [Kinnebrew, "Charismatic Doctrine," 191, 193; Farah, *FTP*, 123–5; McConnell, *DG*, 139, 143–4; Bowman, *Word-Faith*, 107–9, 196–7; King, *Only Believe*, 179–85; Perriman, *FHP*, 84–5, 139–40; Sarles, "Theological Evaluation," 349; E. S. Morran and L. Schlemmer, *Faith for The Fearful?: An Investigation Into New Churches in The Greater Durban Area* (Durban: Centre For Applied Social Sciences University of Natal Durban, 1984), 5]; Luke 6:38 [Adeleye, *Preachers*, 88; Adeleye, "Prosperity Gospel;" Morran and Schlemmer, *Faith for the Fearful*, 5; Downs, "Giving for Return"]; John 10:10 [Judith Hill, "Theology of Prosperity," *Africa Journal of Theology* 28, no. 1 (2009): 44]; 2 Corinthians 8:9 [Abiola Mbamalu, "'Prosperity a part of the atonement': An interpretation of 2 Corinthians 8:9," *Verbum et Ecclesia* 36, no. 1 (2015): 1–8]; Cotterell, *Prosperity Theology*, 11–13; Viateur Habarurema, *Christian Generosity according to 2 Corinthians 8–9: Its Exegesis, Reception, and Interpretation Today in Dialogue with the Prosperity Gospel in Sub-Saharan Africa* (Carlisle: Langham Creative Projects, 2017); Nel, *Prosperity Gospel*, Kindle edition, "'Proof-Texts' of the Prosperity Message"]; Galatians 3:13–14a [Fee, *Disease*, 22–3; Kaiser, "The Old Testament Promise," 165–6; Asamoah-Gyadu, "Prosperity and Poverty," 107–9]; Hebrew 11:1 [Bowman, *Word-Faith*, 198–9]; 1 Peter 2:24 [Fee, *Disease*, 23–5]; 3 John 2 [Fee, *Disease*, 10; Hill, "Theology," 44; Heather Landrus, "Hearing 3 John 2 in the Voices of History," *Journal of Pentecostal Theology* 11, no. 1 (2002): 70–88; Werner, Kahl, "Prosperity-Preaching in West-Africa: An Evaluation of a Contemporary Ideology from a New Testament Perspective," *Ghana Bulletin of Theology* 2 (2007): 30–2]. Other key Scriptures less frequently studied are: Deuteronomy 8:18; Joshua 1:8; Psalms 35:27; Psalms 103:2; Malachi 3:10–11; John 14:13–14; John 15:7; Romans 4:17; Romans 5:17; Romans 10:9–10; 2 Corinthians 9:6–10; Hebrews 11:3.

bulk of opposing biblical data.[39] Word of Faith interpretations evidence lack of congruence and consistency, containing proof-texting and eisegesis.[40] The Word of Faith is particularly faulted for breaking contexts—especially overlooking the grammatical and genre contexts and not paying sufficient attention to the texts' historical-cultural settings.[41] The result is that the totality of the biblical message is at critical points overlooked and even contradicted. A common objection is that their exegetical choices are not scholarly informed, leading to novel conclusions which cannot be substantiated by exegetical research.[42] Since the model claims that the Word of Faith's unique exegetical choices are distortions because of their lack of exegetical training, it summons the Word of Faith to an advanced handling of Scripture that is true to their high bibliology.[43] In this midst of such sharp criticism, scholars using the exegetical focus seek to be fair by pointing out that many of these principles are also broken in other Pentecostal and evangelical discourse.[44]

1.3.2 Hermeneutical Focus

The biblical model's hermeneutical focus analyzes the Word of Faith's underlying presuppositions and principles that inform their exegetical choices. This model sees hermeneutics as the epicenter of the debate between the movement and its critics. The Word of Faith insists that they do not use any method of interpretation

39. Fee, *Disease*, 12; Asamoah-Gyadu, "Prosperity and Poverty," 106–13. E.g., Chong, "Of Riches and Faith," 161; Perriman, *FHP*, 84–6. E.g., cf. Bowman, *Word-Faith*, 175.

40. Keith Warrington, "Teaching and Praxis," 96–7, 99; Horn, *FRTR*, 25, 50, 99; Bowman, *Word-Faith*, 181; Debra Mumford, "Prosperity Gospel and African American Prophetic Preaching," *Review and Expositor* 109 (Summer 2012): 377; Brandon, *Health and Wealth*, 109; Henry Krabbendam, "Scripture-Twisting," in *The Agony of Deceit: What Some TV Preachers are Really Preaching*, ed. Michael Horton (Chicago: Moody Press, 1990), 64; Adeleye, "The Prosperity Gospel;" Perriman, *FHP*, 103.

41. Werner Kahl, "'Jesus Become Poor so that We Might Become Rich': A Critical Review of the Use of Biblical Reference Texts among Prosperity Preachers in Ghana," in *Pastures of Plenty: Tracing Religio-Scapes of Prosperity Gospel in Africa and Beyond*, ed. Andreas Heuser (Frankfurt: Peter Lang, 2015), 114; Bowman, *Word-Faith*, 190, 188–9; Perriman, *FHP*, 93; Farah, *FTP*; Fee, *Disease*; Brandon, *Health and Wealth*; Mumford, *Exploring Prosperity*, 25. Valdir Steuernagel and Micon Steuernagel, "Historical Overview: Cape Town and Our Mission," in *Prosperity Theology and the Gospel: Good News or Bad News for the Poor?* ed. Daniel Salinas (Peabody: Hendrickson, 2017), 57.

42. Kahl, "Jesus Became Poor," 115; Fee, *Disease*; Moo, "Divine Healing;" Kaiser, "The Old Testament Promise;" Hill, "Theology of Prosperity," 43–4.

43. Mumford, *Exploring Prosperity*, 138; Perriman, *FHP*, 233; Kahl, "Prosperity Preaching;" Fee, *Disease*; Adeleye "Prosperity Gospel," 1; Harrison, *RR*, 9.

44. E.g., Perriman, *FHP*, 103.

but only go "straight to Scripture."[45] But studies say the movement is practically "obsessed with hermeneutics,"[46] claiming to practice a superior hermeneutic while reproaching traditional Pentecostalism and evangelicalism for misreading the Bible. The Word of Faith's claim to champion serious engagements with Scripture's true meaning, turns out, ironically enough, to be their Achilles heel as they break basic hermeneutical principles and fail to align their interpretations with "the author's intended meaning"—the high standard of conservative interpretation.[47] Two hermeneutical problems are repeatedly noted:[48] the breaking of accepted evangelical principles of interpretation and underlying presuppositions that create a unique, controlling hermeneutical framework.[49] Instead of "contextual scientific exegesis,"[50] the Word of Faith practices a simplistic, reductionist, subjective, selective, and absolute hermeneutic.[51] Their hermeneutics is portrayed as being highly utilitarian in its usage of texts and displaying an impatience with theoretical reflection.[52] Some see the Word of Faith as deconstructing conservative hermeneutics because the same principles which the Word of Faith are said to break are the same they explicitly claim support their readings.[53]

45. Horn, *FRTR*, 112; da Silva, *Framgångsteologin*, 81.

46. Michael Souders, "A God of Wealth: Religion, Modernity, and the Rhetoric of the Christian Prosperity Gospel" (Doctor of philosophy thesis, University of Kansas, 2011), 68.

47. Fee, *Disease*, 8; Gordon Fee, "The 'Gospel' of Prosperity – An Alien Gospel," *The Pentecostal Evangel*, June 24 1979, 4–8; Hill, "Theology of Prosperity;" Krabbendam, "Scripture Twisting," 63–88; Salinas, "Mainline Churches," 121; "Lovett, "Positive Confession;" Asamoah-Gyadu, "Prosperity and Poverty," 107; Sarles, "Prosperity and Healing," 8. See L. William Oliverio Jr., *Theological Hermeneutics in the Classical Pentecostal Tradition: A Typological Account* (Leiden: Brill, 2012), 133–84.

48. Fee, *Disease*, 9; Barron, *Health and Wealth*, 152; da Silva, *Framgångsteologin*, 86; Horn, *FRTR*, 112; George Folarin, "Contemporary State of the Prosperity Gospel in Nigeria," *The Asia Journal of Theology* 21, no. 1 (2007): 69–95.

49. The following evaluation is representative: "Prosperity hermeneutics . . . leaves much to be desired. The method of interpreting the biblical text is highly subjective and arbitrary. Bible verses are quoted in abundance without attention to grammatical indicators, semantic nuances, or literary and historical context. The result is a set of ideas and principles based on distortion of textual meaning" [Sarles, "Theological Evaluation," 337; See Babatunde Adedibu, *Coat of Many Colours: The Origin, Growth, Distintinctivness and Contributions of Black Majority Churches of British Christianity* (Glouchester: Wisdom Summit, 2012), 152].

50. Farah, *FTP*, 138.

51. Farah, *FTP*, 233–4; Fee, *Disease*, 12; Kahl, "Jesus Became Poor," 114; da Silva, *Framgångsteologin*, 70; Perriman, *FHP*, 92; Andrew Jackson, "Prosperity Gospel and the Faith Movement," *Themelios* 15, no. 1 (1989): 17.

52. Perriman, *FHP*, 92; Harrison, *RR*, 148; Nel, *Prosperity Gospel*, Kindle edition, "The Sources of the Prosperity Message," "Hermeneutical Angle and Key of the Prosperity Gospel."

53. Souders, "God of Wealth," 100–1, 107.

Scholars seek to identify if the Word of Faith operates with an underlying hermeneutical framework which exerts interpretative control. Some studies point to how predetermined faith commitments comprise a distinct theological system that operates with its own logic within a certain reading of the salvation-historical narrative.[54] The two areas of "contractual hermeneutic" and "revelation knowledge" are held as key aspects of their hermeneutic. The Word of Faith works with a unique hermeneutic, studies claim, that approaches the Bible as a uniform, contractual document containing the detailed legal basis, universal spiritual laws, and personal promises for an abundant life.[55] Contractual hermeneutics coupled with their refusal of scholarly guidance lead to characterization of the Word of Faith as a type of fundamentalism, hermeneutical naivete, and "pseudo-scholarship."[56] Their assertion that interpretations stem from revelation knowledge—which contrasts knowledge gained through the physical senses—is hermeneutically potent as it gives the Word of Faith an "epistemic privilege."[57] Many of their original interpretations are credited to and justified by the interpreter receiving particular revelation knowledge from God.[58] Thus, revelational insights create a closed system of interpretation and an absolute hermeneutic which trumps all other forms of knowledge.[59] Researchers see a tension between the concept of revelation knowledge and the Word of Faith's commitment to the Protestant convictions of the sufficiency and authority of Scripture, short-circuiting the process of interpretation and possibly leading to idolizing the preacher, fostering

54. Perriman, *FHP* 19–29, 83, 86–7; Mumford, *Exploring Prosperity*, 138; Brandon, *Health and Wealth*, 53, 104; da Silva, *Framgångsteologin*, 83; McClymond, "Prosperity Already," 297; Hanegraaff, *CIC*, 17–27; Brandon, *Health and Wealth*, 148–51; Nel, *Prosperity Gospel*, Kindle edition, "The Sources of the Prosperity Message," "Hermeneutical Angle and Key of the Prosperity Gospel."

55. Perriman, *FHP*, 88, 90; Harrison, *RR*, 9; Johnathan Walton, "Stop Worrying and Start Sowing! A Phenomenological Account of the Ethics of 'Divine Investment'" in *Pentecostalism and Prosperity: The Socio-Economics of the Global Charismatic Movement*, ed. Katherine Attanasi and Amos Yong (New York: Palgrave McMillan, 2012), 112; Hicks, "Prosperity, Theology, and Economics," 243–4.

56. Perriman, *FHP*, 82–3, 88, 94–5; Moo, "Divine Healing," 196; Paul Gifford, "The Bible in Africa: A Novel Usage in Africa's New Churches," *Bulletin of SOAS* 71, no. 2 (2008): 214. E.g., Harrison, *RR*, 89–90.

57. Perriman, *FHP*, 82; 96–100; Warrington, "Teaching and Praxis," 83. Cf. Edwards, "Ethical Dimensions," 92–3; Souders, "God of Wealth," 86, 89. "supernatural knowledge of God and the spiritual realm revealed in the Bible . . . enables man [*sic*] to transcend the limitations of Sense Knowledge and act in faith" (McConnell, *DG*, 102).

58. Souders, "God of Wealth," 61, 86; Nel, *Prosperity Gospel*, Kindle edition, "The Sources of the Prosperity Message."

59. Souders, "God of Wealth," 61; Matta, *Born Again Jesus*; Ackerly, "Importing Faith," 307–9; Harrison, *RR*, 10; McConnell, *DG*, 71; Lindholm and Broshe, *Framgångsteologin*, 23–31.

elitism among those who are "in" and thwarting open dialogue and accountability with those who are "out."[60] Scholars also point out that the Word of Faith's hermeneutical filter, rather than coming straight from God, has worldly historical and socioeconomic sources (see Sections 1.4 and 1.5).

1.3.3 Evaluation and Remaining Questions

By measuring the movement's fidelity to the biblical texts, the model takes seriously the Word of Faith's self-understanding as a purely Bible-based "Word movement." It also engages the movement based on the shared underlying Protestant presupposition that Scriptural faithfulness is required of any legitimate Christian movement.[61] The biblical model's dual foci are valuable in bringing attention to particular exegetical choices and hermeneutical presuppositions that inform foundational Word of Faith beliefs. This model helps to identify the hierarchy of the key texts among the vast amount of Bible references in Word of Faith discourse, summarize their interpretative positions, compare their interpretations with standard readings, and make explicit what are implicit Word of Faith hermeneutical commitments.

One limiting aspect of the biblical model is its privilege of conservative evangelical exegetical and hermeneutical choices that do not acknowledge how Word of Faith interpretations at some points offer fundamental—and possible legitimate—challenges to static interpretations.[62] The biblical model's principal limitation is its image of the Word of Faith to be a set of exegetical choices and hermeneutical commitments. Its attempt to reach the core of the Word of Faith does not fully acknowledge that worldview makes up the most foundational exegetical and hermeneutical formative influence in the interpretative process.[63] The discussion of hermeneutical presuppositions comes close to an analysis of ultimate beliefs and the question of a theological narrative wielding interpretive control come close to worldview concerns. But a fuller understanding of the Word of Faith requires a holistic analysis. An underlying cause for exegetical and hermeneutical differences is what James Sire calls "worldview confusion."[64] Interpreters operate

---

60. Nel, *Prosperity Gospel*, Kindle edition, "The Sources of the Prosperity Message;" Krabbendam, "Scripture-Twisting," 86; Edwards, "Ethical Dimensions," 92–3; Perriman, *FHP*, 97–8; Lindholm and Brosche, *Varför är Framgångsteologin*, 28.

61. See Alister E. McGrath, *Christianity's Dangerous Idea: The Protestant Revolution—A History from the Sixteenth Century to the Twenty-First* (New York: HarperCollins, 2007); Warrington, *Pentecostal Theology*, 180–205.

62. E.g., Downs, "Giving for Return." See Roger E. Olson, *Reformed and Always Reforming: The Postconservative Approach to Evangelical Theology* (Grand Rapids: Baker Academic, 2007).

63. Naugle, *Worldview*, 310–21.

64. James Sire, *Scripture Twisting: 20 Ways Cults Misread the Bible* (Downers Grove: InterVarsity Press, 1980), 30.

out of different worldviews resulting in conflicting readings. Hence, only a proper understanding of the Word of Faith worldview can fully explain their hermeneutical foundational assumptions underlying the interpretations which appear foreign and nonsensical to scholarship.[65] The worldview-analysis of the Word of Faith, particularly focusing on its narrative dimension, promises to shed more light on issues that the biblical model seeks to understand.

1.4 The Historical Model

The third dominant model used within scholarly literature to analyze the Word of Faith is the historical model. It envisions the Word of Faith as substantially a historical product, a synthesis of currents and ideas which need to be identified and examined. The process of employing the historical model is not homogenous— alike to other historical studies on religious concerns.[66] The unifying factor is the model's driving theological concern: Are the theological roots of the Word of Faith within orthodox Christianity? Given the seeming novelty of distinctive Word of Faith beliefs and practices, the historic model asks if these are legitimate developments of seeds already within Christianity or if foreign elements were imported at some point. Of interest to scholars in the historical model is also to understand the movement's fountainheads and their biographies.[67]

The model espouses two leading historical narratives. The most influential and controversial is the so-called Kenyon-connection.[68] From the late 1970s, the Word of Faith gained momentum and spread across the United States and beyond. While researchers note the formative influence from personalities in the American Pentecostal healing revival, such as A. A. Allen, William Branham, and Oral Roberts, it is evident that the American freelance Pentecostal preacher Kenneth

65. See Albert Wolters, "Worldview," in *The Dictionary for Theological Interpretation of the Bible*, ed. Kevin J. Vanhoozer (Grand Rapids: Baker, 2005), 854–6.

66. See Wright, *NTPG*, 81–118.

67. Harrell, *All Things Are Possible*; Steve Brouwer, Paul Gifford and Susan Rose, *Exporting the American Gospel: Global Christian Fundamentalism* (New York: Routledge, 1996), 20–8; McClymond, "Prosperity Already;" Coleman, *Globalisation*, 40–8; J. Gordon Melton, "The Prosperity Gospel in Texas: The Case of Kenneth Copeland," Paper presented to the Forty-Seventh Annual Meeting of the Society for Pentecostal Studies, Cleveland, Tennessee, March 2018.

68. McConnell, *DG*, 77–82. It appears that Charles Farah was first to note the connection. He writes, "Most important of all influences on faith-formula theology are the works of E. W. Kenyon. Mr. Kenyon's many writings form a treasure trove which all present faith-formula teachers mine" (Farah, "Roots and Fruits," 6). Farah's student McConnell then expounded the idea of the Kenyon-connection in a master thesis in the early 1980s. He later published the book *DG* that popularized the hypothesis (see DeArteaga, *Quenching the Spirit*, 233–4; Neuman, "Cultic Origins," 52–3).

E. Hagin (1917–2003) was the principal leader and expositor.[69] Hagin's claimed divine revelations as the source for his teachings set his ministry apart as a prophet-teacher, earning him the title of the "father" of the movement.[70] The Kenyon-connection narrative radically altered this perception. The basic hypothesis held that the movement's real father was not Hagin and his supernatural visions but the somewhat obscure American Baptist E. W. Kenyon (1867–1948).[71] Kenyon had knowingly merged Christianity with New Thought metaphysics that focuses primarily on the power of the mind and its instrumental usefulness to gain health, wealth, and happiness.[72] The Word of Faith's roots were thus non-Christian, resulting in the movement being "a different gospel,"[73] a "cultic infiltration of the Pentecostal and charismatic movements."[74] Hagin contributed to this false

69. Harrell, *All Things*, 74; Horn, *FRTR*, 38, 46; Bowman, *Word-Faith*, 85–94; Bowler, *Blessed*, 77–138; Paul Gifford, "The Complex Provenance of Some Elements of African Pentecostal Theology," in *Between Babel and Pentecost; Transnational Pentecostalism in Africa and Latin America*, ed. Andre Corten and Ruth Marshall-Fratani (London: Hurst, 2001), 62–3.

70. Harrell, *All Things Are Possible*, 185–6; Farah, *FTP*, 116; McConnell, *DG*, 55–74; Dale Simmons, "Hagin: Heretic or Herald of God? A Theological and Historical Analysis of Kenneth E. Hagin's Claim to Be a Prophet" (Master of arts thesis, Oral Roberts University, 1985).

71. For biographical information on Kenyon, see Dale Simmons, "The Postbellum Pursuit of Peace, Power, and Plenty: As Seen in the Writings of Essek William Kenyon" (Doctor of philosophy thesis, Drew University, 1990); Geir Lie, "E. W. Kenyon: Cult Founder or Evangelical Minister?" *Journal of the European Pentecostal Theological Association* 16, (1996): 71–86; Geir Lie, *E. W. Kenyon: Cult Founder or Evangelical Minister* (Oslo: Refleks, 2003); Joe McIntrye, *E. W. Kenyon and His Message of Faith: The True Story* (Lake Mary: Charisma House, 1997); McConnell, *DG*, 29–54; Matta, *Born Again Jesus*, 21–34; Bowman, *Word-Faith*, 57–84; Bowler, *Blessed*, 15–21; King, *Only Believe*, 64–5; Jones and Woodbridge, *HWH*, 51–4.

72. "New Thought is made up of a cluster of thinkers and metaphysical ideas, of which three has been foundational for later developments: (1) a high anthropology (i.e., an optimistic belief in human potential); (2) reality as spiritual (i.e., the world composed of thought rather than substance); (3) the creative power of positive thoughts (i.e., humans shared in divine creative power through right thoughts)" (Bowler, *Blessed*, 13–14). See Martin Larson, *New Thought or A Modern Religious Approach: The Philosophy of Health, Happiness, and Prosperity* (New York: Philosophical Library, 1985).

73. McConnell, *DG*, 51.

74. Some scholars argue that the historical roots of the Word of Faith go further back than nineteenth-century American metaphysics to ancient Gnosticism: e.g., Matta, *Born Again Jesus*; Kent Gunnarsson, "Den Kristna Gnosticismens Återkomst: Ett Studium av Ulf Ekmans Teologi [The Return of Christian Gnosticism: An Investigation of the Theology of Ulf Ekman]" (Doctor of theology thesis, Umeå Universitet, 2004). Studies also seek to trace metaphysical influences on the Word of Faith from Ralph Waldo Emerson's philosophical

gospel by "Pentecostalising" and popularizing Kenyon's metaphysical beliefs by plagiarism—copying large sections verbatim while crediting divine revelation as the source.[75] The Kenyon-connection narrative underlies some of the strongest objections against embracing the Word of Faith.[76]

That Kenyon and not Hagin should be credited as the originator of most of the Word of Faith's distinctive beliefs is now an established point, as is Hagin's general dependency on Kenyon. Yet, when placing Kenyon within his historical and religious milieu, the Kenyon-connection becomes more complex than drawing a straight line from Kenyon's theology to metaphysical sources. A second narrative within the historical model challenges the hypothesis of a direct link between the Word of Faith and metaphysics mediated via Kenyon.[77] Studies question key aspects, such as the hypothesis' coherence, its selection, and use of sources, and why it excludes Kenyon's own religious and cultural contexts.[78] It is argued that metaphysical religious ideas (especially New Thought and Christian

---

idealism, Emmanuel Swedenborg's Neoplatonic theory of correspondence, and Helena Blavatsky's theosophical quest for uniform spiritual laws and Phineas Parkhurst Quimby's focus on the subconscious. See Bowler, *Blessed*; Ackerly, "Importing Faith;" Jones and Woodbridge, *HWH*. Especially the Word of Faith belief in spiritual laws and its relation to the eighteenth-century Swedish mystic Emmanuel Swedenborg has generated particular interest. See Simmons, "Hagin: Heretic or Herald," 88–99; DeArteaga, *Quenching the Spirit*, 188–200; Perriman, *FHP*, 68; Jones and Woodbridge, *HWH*, 28–30, 36–7; Ackerly, "Importing Faith," 103–6. For Swedenborg's general influence see W. R. Ward, *Early Evangelicalism: A Global Intellectual History 1670–1789* (Cambridge: Cambridge University Press, 2006), 40–69. See also Joanna Hill, *Spiritual Law: The Essence of Swedenborg's Divine Providence* (Santa Fe: Rock Point, 2014).

75. McConnell, *DG*, 7–11, 24; Bowman, *Word-Faith*, 38; Simmons, "Hagin: Heretic or Herald." DeArteaga says that Hagin's plagiarizing could have happened without any ill intent because of Hagin's photographic memory, lack of formal education, and the special homiletic genre of his discourse (DeArteaga, *Quenching the Spirit*, 243–5).

76. Harrison, *RR*, 6; Jones and Woodbridge, *HWH*, 55; Maura, Mbewe and Mbugua, *Prosperity*, 130; Adeleye, *Preachers of a Different*, 67; Ackerly, "Importing Faith;" Hanegraaff, *CIC*; McArthur, *Charismatic Chaos*; Hunt and McMahon, *Seduction*; Hunt, *Beyond Seduction*, 82–3; Johansson, *Vad Ska Man Tro*, 2 fn. 52; Cotterell, *Prosperity Theology*, 3; Ankerberg and Weldon, *The Facts*, 16–17; Smail, Walker, Wright, *Love of Power*, 79; Newport, *New Age Movement*, 361–6; McIntyre, *E. W. Kenyon*, 299, 306.

77. Simmons was an early voice trying to find a way between two opposite historical stands: the neglect of evangelical sources on Kenyon (McConnell, *DG*) and the neglect of New Thought influences (Barron, *Health and Wealth*). He concludes that "Kenyon's message of peace, power, and plenty was a unique hybrid created from the grafting together of various faith-cure and mind-cure sources" (Simmons, "Postbellum Pursuit," abstract) yet "it would be going too far to conclude that New Thought was *the* major contributing factor" (Simmons, "Postbellum Pursuit," 323, emphasis original).

78. Bowman, *Word-Faith*, 64–7; Perriman, *FHP*, 75.

Science) were part of the popular American religious context in the early 1900s and that Kenyon was not immune to this.[79] Like many Christians at his time, Kenyon wrestled with the biblical legitimacy of metaphysical concepts. Studies claim that Kenyon never intended to create a theological Trojan horse but to present a biblical and supernatural Christian faith that spoke to the longings that drove people to metaphysics.[80] Supporting evidence is that Kenyon throughout his ministry was welcomed among the evangelical and Pentecostal communities and associated with several of their foremost leaders.[81] Also, many of Kenyon's more controversial beliefs are not uniquely his but were espoused in the Higher-Life and the faith-cure movements and embraced by early Pentecostal leaders.[82] Sympathetic interpretations see the historical data as a vindication.[83] If others who voiced similar ideas as Kenyon are still considered theologically orthodox, there is no reason why Kenyon should be treated any differently and, in consequence, the Word of Faith as well.[84]

The two narratives in the historical model give rise to a synthesis. Studies acknowledge the two "crosscurrents"[85] of Christian renewalist movements *and* metaphysical groups in the thought of Kenyon.[86] To this is added a third formative stream consisting of a cluster of general American cultural ideals, especially pragmatism, individualism, and upward mobility.[87] The argument goes that the main bulk of Kenyon's teachings was not new in revivalist Christianity, but there

---

79. Bowler, *Blessed*, 25–6.

80. Cf. Hunt and McMahon, *Seduction*, 12–21.

81. Pentecostal leaders included: William Durham, Aimee Semple McPherson, John G. Lake and F. F. Bosworth (Bowman, *Word-Faith*, 64–7; Bowler, *Blessed*, 21).

82. King, *Only Believe*.

83. Lie, seeking to refute McConnell's "Kenyon connection," concludes: "Kenyon's historical roots seem solidly planted in an 'evangelical' tradition, namely mysticism, Brethrenism, and Higher Life/Faith-Cure (Lie, "E. W. Kenyon," 81).

84. E.g., King, *Only Believe*; Paul King and Jacques Theron, "The 'Classic Faith' Roots of the Modern 'Word of Faith' Movement," *Studia Historiae Ecclesiasticae* 32, no. 1 (2006): 309–34; McIntyre, *E. W. Kenyon*, viii.

85. Bowman, *Word-Faith*, 81.

86. "Probably all the distinctive elements of Word of Faith teaching can be found within the two broad currents of American religious experience represented by the Holiness/Faith-Cure/Pentecostal movements and the metaphysical cults. These two currents were not entirely distinct. They intermingled at places; they shared common interests; they exchanged terminology and arguments. Kenyon was perhaps the best example of that confluence" (Perriman, *FHP*, 76).

87. "We might envision the prosperity gospel as composed of three distinct though intersecting streams: pentecostalism; New Thought . . .; and an American gospel of pragmatism, individualism and upward mobility" (Bowler, *Blessed*, 11). See Grant Wacker, *Heaven Below: Early Pentecostals and American Culture* (Cambridge: Harvard University Press, 2003).

are still some original beliefs, which are the result of influences from especially New Thought categories.[88] Yet, these "Kenyonisms"[89] appear not to be incorporated uncritically and without alterations. Rather, Kenyon appropriated ideas from New Thought selectively and "evangelically."[90]

The findings of the historical model can be read as inviting self-criticism within Pentecostalism. The contextual argument interpreted in favor of Kenyon and the Word of Faith, rather than simply exculpating the Word of Faith might display a larger issue relating to Pentecostal faith. Beyond some singular individuals (such as Kenyon), it appears as if the renewal movements in America—especially Pentecostalism—were influenced by metaphysical currents of thought predominant in the society. The possibility is that what is in full bloom in the Word of Faith comes from seeds that exist within evangelicalism and especially Pentecostalism.[91] As such, the Word of Faith follows a radical trajectory in that they embrace existing ideas and push them further, often to their more or less logical conclusions. In this light, the challenge to Pentecostalism is its willingness to forward a self-critical approach to its tradition(s) to ascertain if any features are shared with the Word of Faith.[92]

1.4.1 Evaluation and Remaining Questions

The historical model helps to locate currents of thought and key personalities formative to the Word of Faith.[93] The model reveals a multifaceted picture that resists quick and categorical conclusions, calling critics and sympathizers to assess their standpoints and arguments carefully. Yet, the historical model is also limited and unable to provide the "thicker description" needed of the movement. Since this model's primary concern is the cognitive belief structure of the Word of Faith, it does not reach behind the theological beliefs for other elements that give such ideas their life, coherence, and expression. In this regard, the historical model is restricted by weaknesses similar to the doctrinal model. In the search for historical parallels between the Word of Faith and other streams of thought,

---

88. Bowler, *Blessed*, 20.

89. McConnell, *DG*, 139.

90. Bowler claims that for Kenyon, "New Thought applied the right process with the wrong theology" (Bowler, *Blessed*, 20). See Edwards, "Ethical Dimensions," 95.

91. Horn suggests that all Word of Faith teachings are one of three possibilities: radicalization, resurrection, or repetition of Pentecostal doctrines (Horn, *FRTR*, 71); "Early American pentecostalism, intersected with channels of New Thought, had absorbed a high anthropology and view of divine speech that would help shape its theology throughout the rest of the century. In the postwar years, this reedy stream of pentecostal mind-power would become a flood" (Bowler, *Blessed*, 25).

92. Bowman, *Word-Faith*, 83–4; Horn, *FRTR*.

93. E.g., Bowman, *Word-Faith*; Bowler, *Blessed*.

two methodological fallacies limit their studies. The term "parallelomania"[94] captures a fallacy taking place in both historical narratives when simple word correspondence is equated for conceptual correspondence. It leads to the fallacy of worldview confusion which surfaces when the Kenyon-connection takes historic ideas without sufficient consideration to the worldview in which they belong nor studying the worldview in which they possibly were adopted.[95]

Regarding the analytical and comparative goals raised in the introduction, to settle whether the worldview of the Word of Faith conceptually belongs within Pentecostalism and in what ways it challenges and contributes to Pentecostalism cannot be fully answered by this model. Rather than focusing on historically conditioned doctrines, a worldview approach to the movement suggests a way to reach behind the Word of Faith's beliefs to explicate the underlying worldview of the Word of Faith and provide grounds to address its identity and relationship to Pentecostalism. It will lay the groundwork to later analyze what level of correspondence exists between Pentecostalism and the Word of Faith worldview and if the Word of Faith is best understood as taking Pentecostal features on a radical trajectory.

1.5 *The Socioeconomical Model*

The fourth distinct model of analysis recognizable in the scholarly literature on the Word of Faith is the socioeconomical model. This model moves the focus from doctrinal, biblical, and historical concerns to approach the Word of Faith in terms of social and economic motivations and influences. Of the four models identified, this is the most heterogeneous and complex as it encompasses literature from various academic disciplines in pursuit of various research objectives in multiple cultural and geographical contexts. In their varied interests, it is noteworthy that the key concern in the socioeconomic model is not to measure the theological legitimacy of the Word of Faith—what to a large extent unifies the other three models. The uniting element in the socioeconomic model is not one singular method but the set of key questions researchers ask about origins (which are the socioeconomic reasons for the birth of the Word of Faith?), growth (why does the Word of Faith spread?), incentives (why do individuals join the Word of Faith?), socioeconomic profile (who joins the Word of Faith?), commitment (why do people stay in the Word of Faith despite unrealized expectations, e.g., lack of material results or pervasive sickness), and impact (what are the intended and unintended socioeconomic consequences of the Word of Faith?). These concerns overlap and singular studies often address several questions.

---

94. Samuel Sandmel, "Parallelomania," *Journal of Biblical Literature* 81 (1962): 1–13. Cf. Bowman, *Word-Faith*, 48.

95. Carson, *Exegetical Fallacies*, 103–5; Sire, *Scripture Twisting*, 127–44.

The process of employing the socioeconomic model differs from study to study depending on which particular academic disciplines inform its method. Studies in the socioeconomical model struggle more than the other models with the problems of definition and demarcation of the Word of Faith—some make little to no distinction between Pentecostalism and the Word of Faith, treating them as inseparable.[96] Because of the present ambiguity, researchers using a socioeconomic approach to the Word of Faith are often caught up in the larger ongoing complex debates regarding Pentecostalism, which shows the need for greater clarity on defining the Word of Faith.[97]

This section is divided into eight subsections to capture the themes in the literature: neoliberalism, globalization, deprivation theory, Protestant work ethic, enchanted economics, gift economy, religious identity, and social agency. These are ordered according to their dominant interests, those with economic interests first and the social interests following.

1.5.1 Neoliberalism

Neoliberalism is for some scholars the best explanatory perspective to use in relationship to the Word of Faith's origins, incentives, and impact.[98] Several studies

96. E.g., Rijk van Dijk, "The Pentecostal Gift: Ghanaian Charismatic Churches and the Moral Innocence of the Global Economy," in *Modernity on a Shoestring: Dimensions of Globalization, Consumption and Development in Africa and Beyond*, ed. Richard Fardon, Wim M. J. van Binsbergen and Rijk van Dijk (Leiden: Eidos, 1999), 71–89. See also Birgit Meyer, "Pentecostalism and Neo-Liberal Capitalism: Faith, Prosperity and Vision in African Pentecostal-Charismatic Churches," *Journal for the Study of Religion* 20, no. 2 (2007): 5–26; Olugbenga Akinabola "'I Will Make It': The Socio-Economic Consequences of the Prosperity Gospel on Christian Youth in Lagos, Nigeria," (Doctor of philosophy thesis, Trinity International University, 2012); Peter Heslam, "The Rise of Religion and the Future of Capitalism," *De Ethica* 2, no. 3 (2015): 54; Drea Fröchtling, "Between Gutter and Gucci, Boss and *Botho*: A Relocation of 'Prosperity Gospel' by Nigerian Pentecostal Christians in Soweto, South Africa," in *Pastures of Plenty: Tracing Religio-Scapes of Prosperity Gospel in Africa and Beyond*, ed. Andres Heuser (Frankfurt: Peter Lang, 2015), 326; Gerardo Marti, "The Adaptability of Pentecostalism: The Fit Between Prosperity Theology and Globalized Individualization in a Los Angeles Church," *Pneuma: The Journal of the Society for Pentecostal Studies* 34, no. 1 (2012): 5–25.

97. For an introduction and overview of sociology and Pentecostalism, see J. W. Shepperd, "Sociology of World Pentecostalism," in *The New International Dictionary of Pentecostal and Charismatic Movements*, ed. Stanley M. Burgess and Eduard M. Van Der Maas, rev. and exp. edn. (Grand Rapids: Zondervan, 2003), e-book edition, "Sociology of World Pentecostalism;" Kay, *Pentecostalism*, 281–310.

98. Neoliberalism is defined as "a theory of political economic practices that proposes that human well-being can best be advanced by liberating individual entrepreneurial freedoms and skills within an institutional framework characterized by strong private

claim that the Word of Faith is the result of and promotes the neoliberal ideals of individualism, consumerism, and entrepreneurism that have made up the core of globalized economics.[99] From a macroeconomical perspective, the teachings and economic practices of the Word of Faith affirm, uphold, and provide access to and actively integrate with the existing global capitalist order.[100] Such neoliberalization

property rights, free markets, and free trade" (David Harvey, *A Brief History of Neoliberalism* (Oxford: Oxford University Press, 2007), 2; "neoliberalism denotes a positive political-economic posture, one that is: 1 Pro-markets 2 Pro-property rights 3 Pro-growth 4 Individualistic 5 Empirical and open-minded 6 Globalist in outlook 7 Optimistic about the future 8 Focused on changing the world for the better" [Jamie Peck, "Preface: Naming Neoliberalism," in *The SAGE Handbook of Neoliberalism*, ed. Damien Cahill, Melinda Cooper, Martijn Konings and David Primrose (Los Angeles: SAGE Publishing, 2018), xxii]. See Jason Hackworth, "Religious Neoliberalism," in *The SAGE Handbook of Neoliberalism*, ed. Damien Cahill, Melinda Cooper, Martijn Konings and David Primrose (Los Angeles: SAGE Publishing, 2018), 323–34.

99. Mary V. Wrenn, "Consecrating Capitalism: The United States Prosperity Gospel and Neoliberalism," *Journal of Economic Issues* 53, no. 2 (2019): 425–32; Birgit Meyer, "Commodities and the Power of Prayer: Pentecostalist Attitudes Towards Consumption in Contemporary Ghana," *Development and Change* 29 (1998): 751–76; Meyer, "Pentecostalism," 19; Marion Maddox, "Prosper, Consume and Be Saved," *Critical Research on Religion* 1, no. 1 (2013): 108–15; Katie Rose Sullivan and Helen Delaney, "A Femininity That 'Giveth And Taketh Away': The Prosperity Gospel and Postfeminism in the Neoliberal Economy," *Human Relations* 70, no. 7 (2017): 838; Stephen Hunt, "Deprivation and Western Pentecostalism Revisited: Neo-Pentecostalism," *PentecoStudies* 1, no. 2 (2002): 16; Joel Robbins, "The Globalization of Pentecostal and Charismatic Christianity," *Annual Review of Anthropology* 33 (2004): 137; Isabelle Barker, "Charismatic Economies: Pentecostalism, Economic Restructuring, and Social Reproduction," *New Political Science* 29, no. 4 (2007): 407–27; Elsie Lewison, "Pentecostal Power and the Holy Spirit of Capitalism: Re-Imagining Modernity in the Charismatic Cosmology," *Symposia* 3, no. 1 (2011): 31–54; Erron and Cornelio, "Prosperity Ethic."

100. Andrew Chesnut, "Prosperous Prosperity: Why the Health and Wealth Gospel is Booming across the Globe," in *Pentecostalism and Prosperity: The Socio-Economics of the Global Charismatic Movement*, ed. Katherine Attanasi and Amos Yong (New York: Palgrave Macmillan, 2012), 215; Robert Hefner, "Introduction: The Unexpected Modern—Gender, Piety, and Politics in the Global Pentecostal Surge," in *Global Pentecostalism in the 21st Century*, ed. Robert Hefner (Bloomington: Indiana University Press, 2013), 20; Harvey Cox, "Pentecostalism and Global Market Culture," in *The Globalization of Pentecostalism: A Religion Made to Travel* ed. Murray Dempster, Byron Klaus and Douglas Peterson (Eugene: Wipf and Stock, 1999), 392; David Maxwell, "'Delivered from the Spirit of Poverty?': Pentecostalism, Prosperity and Modernity in Zimbabwe," *Journal of Religion in Africa* 28, no. 3 (1998): 350–73; Gerardo Marti, "'I Determine My Harvest:' Risky Careers and Spirit-Guided Prosperity in Los Angeles," in *Pentecostalism and Prosperity: The Socio-Economics of the Global Charismatic Movement*, ed. Katherine Attanasi and Amos Yong (New York:

of theology, researchers claim, resonates with and is an accommodation to the neoliberal spirit of capitalist consumption.[101] This view often echoes themes of Marxist critical economic theory, interpreting the Word of Faith as the superstructure of the economic basis.[102]

The Word of Faith is "decidedly neoliberal,"[103] this model claims, in that it espouses individualism coupled with the idea that capitalism offers everyone an equal opportunity.[104] The Word of Faith, as "a child of capitalism," is deprived of any critique of—or even desire to change—the overall economic framework.[105] This uncritical acceptance of neoliberal capitalism by the Word of Faith has created "a new kind of neoliberal twenty-first-century Christian."[106] According to the socioeconomic lens of neoliberal capitalism, wherever the Word of Faith is encountered, it operates comfortably within the system of neoliberal ideology as a Christianized version of American capitalistic ideals.[107] But some argue that making too close a connection with neoliberal economics misses the critique of global capitalism that exists within Word of Faith discourse.[108]

Palgrave Macmillan, 2012), 131; Bowler, *Blessed*, 226. See Annelin Ericksen, "Engaging with Theories of Neoliberalism and Prosperity," in *Going to Pentecost: An Experimental Approach to Studies in Pentecostalism*, ed. Annelin Eriksen, Ruy Llera Blanes and Michelle MacCarthy (New York: Berghan, 2019), 138–56.

101. Wrenn, "Consecrating Capitalism." See Rudolf von Sinner, "'Struggling with Africa': Theology of Prosperity in and from Brazil," in *Pastures of Plenty: Tracing Religio-Scapes of Prosperity Gospel in Africa and Beyond*, ed. Andreas Heuser (Frankfurt: Peter Lang, 2015), 125, 129.

102. See Horn, *FRTR*, 69–84.

103. Sullivan and Delaney, "Femininity," 841.

104. E.g., "[The Word of Faith is] a form of global capitalism that has succeeded in spiritualising the materiality of that system" [Nelus Niemandt, "The Prosperity Gospel, The Decolonisation of Theology, and the Abduction of Missionary Imagination," *Missionalia* 45, no. 3 (2017): 214]; "The Gospel of Prosperity resembles neoliberal capitalism in that it preaches limitless success endorsed by God, beginning with the elites and moving from the top down" [Joerg Rieger, "Christianity, Capitalism, and Desire," *Union Seminary Quarterly Review* 64, no. 1 (2013), 1]; Daisy Machado, "Capitalism, Immigration, and the Prosperity Gospel," *Anglican Theological Review* 92, no. 4 (2010): 729. See Jonathan L. Walton, *Watch This! The Ethics and Aesthetics of Black Televangelism* (New York: New York University Press, 2009), 206.

105. Agana, *Succeed Here*, 65; Augustine, "Pentecost and Prosperity," 191; von Sinner, "Struggling with Africa," 129; Bowler, *Blessed*, 10–40; Harrison, *RR*, 149.

106. Machado, "Capitalism, Immigration," 729. See Joerg Rieger, *No Rising Tide: Theology, Economics and the Future* (Philadelphia: Fortress, 2009), 89.

107. Harrison, *RR*, 148–52, 158; Horn, *FRTR*, 77; Mumford, *Exploring Prosperity*, 54, 75. See Hackworth, "Religious Neoliberalism."

108. Paul Freston, "Prosperity Theology: A (Largely) Sociological Assessment," in *Prosperity Theology and the Gospel: Good News or Bad News for the Poor?* ed. J. Daniel Salinas (Peabody: Hendrickson, 2017), 66–76.

Without questioning the intimate relationship between the Word of Faith and neoliberalism, some prefer to study its intended and unintended consequences. The Word of Faith encourages entrepreneurship and business activity and enables adherents to participate in the global market with moral integrity.[109] The Word of Faith also provides coping mechanisms for living with the challenges brought by a capitalist environment.[110] By "breaking with the past,"[111] Word of Faith adherents can be liberated from traditional rituals and obligations to extended family which enables them to work for the betterment of their own economic life and thus conform to the expectations of the global market.[112]

1.5.2 Globalization

Studies within the socioeconomic model often look to theories of globalization for a better understanding of the Word of Faith.[113] The global, multicultural growth of the Word of Faith and its relation to indigenous cultures and religious imaginaries can be framed on a continuum between Americanization and indigenization. On the far end, following a line of reasoning similar to that of neoliberal capitalism mentioned earlier, the Word of Faith is seen as a religious product of American culture. Locally the Word of Faith helps immigrants assimilate and integrate into American culture and provides the spiritual resources to lay hold of the American Dream.[114] On the global arena, the movement's international presence speaks to a neocolonialism of American

---

109. Dena Freeman, "The Pentecostal Ethic and the Spirit of Development," in *Pentecostalism and Development: Churches, NGOs and Social Change in Africa*, ed. Dena Freeman (London: Palgrave Macmillan, 2012), 23–4; Rijk Van Dijk, "Pentecostalism and Post-Development: Exploring Religion as a Developmental Ideology in Ghananian Migrant Communities," in *Pentecostalism and Development: Churches, NGOs and Social Change in Africa*, ed. Dena Freeman, 87–109; Birgit Meyer, "Christianity in Africa: From African Independent to Pentecostal-Charismatic Churches," *Annual Review of Anthropology* 33 (2004): 456–7; Maxwell, "Delivered;" Augustine, "Pentecost and Prosperity," 206; Marti, "I Determine My Harvest;" Bowler, *Blessed*, 234; Cao, "Urban Prosperity."

110. Cf. Marti, "I Determine My Harvest."

111. Birgit Meyer, "'Make a Complete Break with the Past.' Memory and Post-Colonial Modernity in Ghanaian Pentecostalist Discourse," *Journal of Religion in Africa* 28, no. 3 (1998): 316–49.

112. Jens Köhrsen, "Pentecostal Improvement Strategies: A Comparative Reading on African and South American Pentecostalism," in *Pastures of Plenty: Tracing Religio-Scapes of Prosperity Gospel in Africa and Beyond*, ed. Andreas Heuser (Frankfurt: Peter Lang, 2015), 56–61.

113. See Coleman, *Globalisation*, 4–5, 49–71; Bowler, *Blessed*, 229.

114. See Lin, *Prosperity Gospel*.

cultural ideals.[115] Because of a direct link with the American capitalist market values and vision of life, the phenomena of the Word of Faith found outside the United States is merely the result of "exporting the American gospel"[116] (to use the book title of an early influential study).[117] As such, the Word of Faith speaks to American political and economic hegemony.[118] Media, both in its old and new forms, play key roles in spreading "sanctified American culture" as Word of Faith televangelists "sing the recognizable songs of American cultural myths"[119] for national and global audiences.[120] The Word of Faith's global success thus lies in "the exporting of the American dream."[121]

For others, the presence of Word of Faith beliefs and practices must be explained in other terms than being "a result of the globalization of capitalism and American religious exporting."[122] It is better portrayed in terms of a transposable message carried by transnational networks to find its ultimate shape when the theology and

---

115. E.g., Brouwer, Gifford and Rose, *Exporting the American Gospel*. See Niemandt, "The Prosperity Gospel," 203–19. Cf. Coleman, "The Faith Movement." Ackerly proports that the Word of Faith movement in the United Kingdom evidences "a significant importing of American cultural ideas" (Ackerly, "Importing Faith," 314, e.g., 267, 322).

116. Brouwer, Gifford and Rose, *Exporting the American Gospel*.

117. Hunt, "Deprivation and Western Pentecostalism II," 15–18; Paul Gifford, "Prosperity: A New and Foreign Element in African Christianity," *Religion* 20 (1990): 373–88; Bowler, *Blessed*, 226–38; Stephen Hunt, "'Winning Ways': Globalisation and the Impact of the Health and Wealth Gospel," *Journal of Contemporary Religion* 15, no. 3 (2000): 332.

118. Lisa Withrow, "Success and the Prosperity Gospel: From Commodification to Transformation," *Journal of Religious Leadership* 6, no. 2 (2007): 15–41.

119. Walton, *Watch This*, 198.

120. Gifford, "Prosperity," 382; Ruth Marshall-Fratani, "Mediating the Global and Local in Nigerian Pentecostalism," in *Between Babel and Pentecost*, ed. André Corten and Ruth Marshall-Fratani (Bloomington: Indiana University Press, 2001), 82–3; Quentin J. Schultze, *Televangelism and American Culture* (Grand Rapids: Baker, 1991), 125–52; Quentin J. Schultze, "TV and Evangelism: Unequally Yoked?" in *The Agony of Deceit: What Some TV Preachers are Really Preaching*, ed. Michael Horton (Chicago: Moody Press, 1990), 185–204; Allan Anderson, "Pentecostal Approaches to Faith and Healing," *International Review of Mission* 91, no. 363 (2002): 530.

121. Paul Alexander, *Signs and Wonders: Why Pentecostalism Is the World's Fastest Growing Faith* (San Francisco: Jossey-Bass, 2009), 64; Schultze, *Televangelism*, 125–52; Lin, *Prosperity Gospel*, Kindle edition, "The Future of Prosperity Gospel Pentecostalism."

122. Freston, "Prosperity Theology," 73. See Ogbu Kalu, *African Pentecostalism: An Introduction* (Oxford: Oxford University Press, 2008), 255–63; Martin Lindhardt, "Are Blessings for Sale?: Ritual Exchange, Witchcraft Allegations, and the De-alienation of Money in Tanzanian Prosperity Ministries," in *Pastures of Plenty: Tracing Religio-Scapes of Prosperity Gospel in Africa and Beyond*, ed. Andreas Heuser (Frankfurt: Peter Lang, 2015), 321.

practices are locally adapted.[123] Any perspective should avoid overgeneralizations and must include both global and local factors that lead to a "glocal" process of Word of Faith contextualization.[124] Studies on migrants who held to Word of Faith ideals in their homeland reveal how the change of socioeconomic contexts leads to reinterpretations of core beliefs.[125] A number of anthropological studies show how Word of Faith themes are relatively flexible; as they resonate with local worldviews, they are capable of being creatively contextualized and effectively propagated by nationals using indigenous cultural and religious idiom.[126] Core Word of Faith elements are appropriated and diffused differently to fit particular contexts and have been able to connect with local, often non-Christian, religious expectations.[127]

The success of the Word of Faith message especially in Africa can thus be explained in terms of such "reconstructions and innovations" by neo-Pentecostal movements adapting to new circumstances.[128] Studies also claim that the Word of Faith does not promote total and uncritical acceptance of outside cultural elements but that the movement enters a dialectical relationship with some of the most critical concerns.[129] In the traditional African religious imagination, salvation is often understood in holistic terms that includes a material dimension, therefore making a context "rich in its capacity to re-imagine the gospel from the indigenous idiom."[130] The Word of Faith found in Africa may thus resemble the American equivalent yet has acted as a "catalyst" to create a "hybridization" that bears a distinctive "Made in Africa" signature.[131] Though acknowledged as a reality, such tendencies cause worry in some literature where the process is seen as syncretistic.[132] The indigenization and appropriation of Word of Faith

---

123. Heuser, "Charting African Prosperity," 2; Lindhardt, "Are Blessings for Sale," 321. E.g., Chong, "Of Riches and Faith."

124. Gifford, "Complex Provenance," 63; Chong, "Of Riches and Faith."

125. Fröchtling, "Between Gutter and Gucci."

126. Emmanuel Anim, "The Prosperity Gospel in Ghana and the Primal Imagination," *Pentvars Business Journal* 4, no. 2 (2010): 66–76; Karen Lauterbach, *Christianity, Wealth, and Spiritual Power in Ghana* (New York: Palgrave Macmillan, 2017).

127. Cristina Mora, "Marketing the 'Health and Wealth Gospel' Across National Borders; Evidence from Brazil and the United States," *Poetics* 36, (2008): 404–20; Coleman, *Globalisation*; Anim, "Prosperity Gospel."

128. Anderson, "Pentecostal Approaches"; Kalu, *African Pentecostalism*.

129. Folarin, "Contemporary State," 70.

130. Kalu, *African Pentecostalism*, 262. See Nel, *Prosperity Gospel*.

131. Anim, "Prosperity Gospel," 73; Robbins, "Globalization of Pentecostal," 119; Daniels, "Prosperity Gospel," 266–7.

132. E.g., The Lausanne Akropong Statement says: "[It] seems clear that there are many aspects of Prosperity Teaching that have their roots in that soil [i.e., African primal or traditional religion and its practices]. We therefore wonder if much popular Christianity is *a syncretized super-structure on an underlying worldview* that has not been radically transformed by the biblical gospel. We also wonder whether the popularity and attraction

themes outside America in especially Asia, South America, and Africa have led to a number of successful local variants and adaptions.[133] The Word of Faith is thus, true to its Pentecostal origins, also "a religion made to travel,"[134] and is now documented to make its way back to impact its American roots.[135]

1.5.3 Deprivation Theory

The socioeconomic model claims that the social origins, growth, and incentives of the Word of Faith can be fruitfully studied by drawing upon the deprivation theory used to explain the worldwide growth of early Pentecostalism.[136] According to this hypothesis, socioeconomically marginalized people are more prone to accept the Word of Faith message to compensate for their predicament and as means to procure "blessings" of economic and political power otherwise unattainable.[137] As a reactive dynamic, the message of the Word of Faith is a sort of "poor people's movement" appealing to those who "seek release from a life of socio-cultural disenfranchisement."[138]

Some voices in the literature claim that the coping mechanism of deprived people is restricted to two practices.[139] The first is exemplified by the early socioeconomically deprived Pentecostals, who declared that the material wealth and power that were already out of reach for them were of little value or even spiritually harmful. The opposite option, which others say speaks to the origin and

of Prosperity Teaching is an indication of the failure of contextualization of the gospel in Africa" (Salinas, *Prosperity Theology*, 183, my emphasis).

133. E.g., see Wiegele, *Investing in Miracles*.

134. Murray Dempster, Byron Klaus and Douglas Peterson, eds., *The Globalization of Pentecostalism: A Religion Made to Travel* (Carlisle: Regnum, 1999).

135. Bowler, *Blessed*, 230–1; Afe Adogame, "The Redeemed Christian Church of God: African Pentecostalism," in *Global Religious Movements Across Borders: Sacred Service*, ed. Stephen Cherry and Helen Rose Edbaugh (Surrey: Ashgate, 2014), 35–60.

136. Stephen Hunt, "Deprivation and Western Pentecostalism Revisited: Neo-Pentecostalism," *PentecoStudies*, 1, no. 2 (2002); Stephen Hunt, "Deprivation and Western Pentecostalism Revisited: 'Classical' Pentecostalism," *PentecoStudies* 1, no. 1 (2002): 1–29; Robert Mapes Anderson, *Vision of the Disinherited* (Oxford: Oxford University Press, 1979), 135, 228

137. Ackerly, "Importing Faith," 320; Tony Tian-Ren Lin, "The Gospel of the American Dream," *The Hedgehog Review* 15, no. 2 (Summer 2013): 38–9; Lin, *Prosperity Gospel*.

138. Hollinger, "Enjoying God Forever," 146. See Horn, *FRTR*; Lin, "Gospel;" Elda Morran, and Lawrence Schlemmer, eds., *Faith for the Fearful?: An Investigation into New Churches in the Durban Area* (Durban: Centre for Applied Social Sciences, 1984), 25; Martin "New Mutations," 115–16; Harrison, *RR*, 148–52; Berger "You Can Do It;" Alexander, *Signs and Wonders*, 25–32; Bowler, *Blessed*, 233.

139. See Hollinger, "Enjoying God Forever," 484; Horn, *FRTR*.

incentive of the Word of Faith, is to devise a system that will bring the blessings within reach of the marginalized.

Quantitative research has yet to prove the basic thesis offered by deprivation theory. For example, studies on the socioeconomic strata of Word of Faith followers in the United States have somewhat differing conclusions in terms of the role of education and income.[140] It is noted in some research that globally the attractiveness of the Word of Faith is not limited to certain social classes.[141] Though its appeal to the financially challenged is evident, the Word of Faith message promises attractive resources for those ambitious to move up in any particular socioeconomic bracket.[142]

1.5.4 Protestant Ethic

Another dominant way to frame the Word of Faith's origins, growth, and economic impact in the socioeconomic model is in terms of Max Weber's Protestant ethic.[143] The ethic inherent in especially Calvinistic Christianity (Weber's main focus group) was characterized by a strict morality code, self-discipline, rational thinking, and hard work.[144] Economic returns were to be saved or invested which

140. See Bradley Koch, "The Prosperity Gospel and Economic Prosperity: Race, Class, Giving, and Voting," (Doctor of philosophy thesis, Indiana University, 2009); Scott Schieman and Jong Hyun Jung, "'Practical Divine Influence': Socioeconomic Status and Belief in the Prosperity Gospel," *Journal for the Scientific Study of Religion* 51, no. 4 (2012): 738–56.

141. E.g., Paul Gifford, *African Christianity: Its Public Role* (Bloomington: Indiana University Press, 1998); Paul Gifford, *Ghana's New Christianity: Pentecostalism in a Globalizing African Economy* (Bloomington: Indiana University Press, 2004).

142. E.g., Simon Coleman, "The Charismatic Gift," *The Journal of the Royal Anthropological Institute* 10, no. 2 (2004): 423; Tejedo, "Asian Perspectives on Prosperity," 138. Gerardo Marti, *Hollywood Faith: Holiness, Prosperity, and Ambition in a Los Angeles Church* (Piscataway: Rutgers, 2008), 191; Marti, "The Adaptability of Pentecostalism," 24–5; Cho, "Of Riches and Faith."

143. Dana Freeman, "The Pentecostal Ethic and the Spirit of Development," in *Pentecostalism and Development: Churches, NGOs and Social Change in Africa*, ed. Dana Freeman (London: Palgrave Macmillan, 2012), 1–38; Centre for Development and Enterprise, *Under the Radar: Pentecostalism in South Africa and its Potential Social and Economic Role* (Johannesburg: The Centre for Development and Enterprise, 2008). Cf. Paul Gifford and Trad Nogueira-Godsey, "The Protestant Ethic and African Pentecostalism: A Case Study," *Journal for the Study of Religion* 24, no. 1 (2011): 5–22. Max Weber, *The Protestant Ethic and the Spirit of Capitalism* (New York: Routledge, 2001). Cf. Jacques Delacroix and Francois Nielsen, "The Beloved Myth: Protestantism and the Rise of Industrial Capitalism in Nineteenth-Century Europe," *Social Forces* 80, no. 2 (2001): 509–52.

144. Peter Berger, "Max Weber is Alive and Well, and Living in Guatemala: The Protestant Ethic Today," *The Review of Faith & International Affairs* 8, no. 4 (2010): 3–9. See

resulted in unintended economic consequences on the macro and micro levels: the birth of capitalism as an economic system and profit as a sign of individual alignment with God's will. For some, this serves as an explanatory narrative of the sociological roots of the Word of Faith.[145] Because the movement has a similar emphasis on this-worldly success and material increase as indicators of faith, the Word of Faith writes a new chapter in the Weberian story.[146] The hypothesis points toward the future economic impact of the Word of Faith: "Weber himself would not have been surprised by Protestants who have no difficulty enjoying as well as making money."[147]

The idea of material profit evidencing true faith fosters Word of Faith believers to embody the core values and ethic that Weber identified, which bring social and economic upward movement, this model says.[148] Probably not leading to wealth per se, those embodying the Protestant ethic in the Word of Faith shape will be "neo-Puritans" who will at least see a "betterment" of life.[149] The new economic power might even cause political reform. Word of Faith believers can therefore be thought of as "intentional Weberians"[150] as they "consciously intend the consequences that earlier Protestants brought about unintentionally."[151] This can be interpreted as a benefit of globalization.[152]

Other studies disagree. Given that there is some overlap between the economic practices of the Word of Faith and the Protestant ethic, the Word of Faith does not

---

Tomas Sundnes Dronen, "'Now I Dress Well. Now I Work Hard.' Pentecostalism, Prosperity, and Economic Development in Cameroon," in *Pastures of Plenty: Tracing Religio-Scapes of Prosperity Gospel in Africa and Beyond*, ed. Andreas Heuser (Frankfurt: Peter Lang, 2015), 249–54.

145. Horn, *FRTR*. Cf. Ackerly, "Importing Faith," 83–8.

146. Heuser, "Charting African Prosperity," 1; Augustine, "Pentecost and Prosperity," 205; Bowler, *Blessed*, 227.

147. Martin, "New Mutations," 117.

148. Walton, *Watch This*, 117, 137–8, 161.

149. Peter L. Berger, "Afterward," in *Global Pentecostalism in the 21st Century*, ed. Robert Hefner (Bloomington: Indiana University Press, 2013), 252–3; Eloy Nolivos, "Capitalism and Pentecostalism in Latin America: Trajectories of Prosperity and Development," in *Pentecostalism and Prosperity: The Socio-Economics of the Global Charismatic Movement*, ed. Katherine Attanasi and Amos Yong (New York: Palgrave Macmillan, 2012), 87–106; Bernice Martin, "New Mutations of the Protestant Ethic among Latin American Pentecostals," *Religion* 25 (1995): 101–17.

150. Berger, "You Can Do It," 4.

151. David Maxwell, "Social Mobility and Politics in African Pentecostal Modernity," in *Global Pentecostalism in the 21st Century*, ed. Robert Hefner (Bloomington: Indiana University Press, 2013), 95.

152. Peter L. Berger, "Globalization and Religion," *The Hedgehog Review* 4, no. 2 (2002): 7–20.

sit easily in Weber's grid.[153] Tensions are created by the Word of Faith expressing aspects of the current global capitalist economic system, such as consumption, hedonism, and the encouragement to display wealth.[154] Also, the economic logic of the Word of Faith is more enchanted than rational.[155] Such practices and beliefs stand worlds apart from Weber's thesis which especially privileged rational decisions and frugality.[156] For these scholars, the Word of Faith is "far from"[157] any Protestant ethic, perhaps even evidence of its decline.[158] Though these tensions are inherent in the early Word of Faith, yet others say, there is a movement from consumption to entrepreneurship within some Word of Faith communities. Such a revised, pragmatic Word of Faith message signifies a movement toward an ethic in the shape of Weber's hypothesis.[159]

The Protestant work ethic merged with deprivation theory informs another narrative: Pentecostals came from the lower classes of society and their work ethic made them rise out of their underprivileged predicament. The second and third generations, no longer deprived but enjoying social and economic upward movement, had to formulate a theology that does not discard wealth and possessions but resonates with their newly achieved status. As such, the Word of Faith is a radical reaction toward old paradigms and "the rationalisation of an accumulated lifestyle."[160] Or one could say that the Word of Faith is the theological consequence of the cognitive dissonance felt by Pentecostals' improved social and economic state.

153. E.g., Meyer, "Christianity in Africa," 460–1; Meyer, "Pentecostalism and Globalization," 115; Gifford, *Ghana's New Christianity*, 196; Hefner, "Unexpected Modern," 24; Freeman, "The Pentecostal Ethic;" Jon Bialecki, Naomi Haynes and Joel Robbins, "Anthropology of Christianity," *Religion Compass* 2, no. 6 (2008): 1149–50; Päivi Hasu, "World Bank & Heavenly Bank in Poverty and Prosperity: The Case of Tanzanian Faith Gospel," *Review of African Political Economy* 33, no. 110 (2006): 679–92.

154. Ari Pedro Oro and Pablo Semán, "Brazilian Pentecostalism Crosses National Borders," in *Between Babel and Pentecost: Transnational Pentecostalism in African and Latin America*, ed. André Corten and Ruth Marshall-Fratani (London: Hurst, 2001), 193; Augustine, "Pentecost and Prosperity."

155. Gifford and Nogueira-Godsey, "The Protestant Ethic," 21.

156. Hefner, "Unexpected Modern," 20–1; Akinabola, "I Will Make It," 79.

157. Gifford, "The Prosperity Theology," 99.

158. von Sinner, "Struggling with Africa," 128; Gifford, *Ghana's New Christianity*, 190; Paul Freston, "Pentecostalism in Brazil: A Brief History," *Religion* 25, no. 2 (1995): 131.

159. David D. Daniels III, "Prosperity Gospel of Entrepreneurship in Africa and Black America: A Pragmatist Christian Innovation," in *Pastures of Plenty: Tracing Religio-Scapes of Prosperity Gospel in Africa and Beyond*, ed. Andreas Heuser (Frankfurt: Peter Lang, 2015), 269. Cf. Lin, "Gospel," 41.

160. Horn, *FRTR*, 83–4.

1.5.5 Enchanted Economics

The origins and incentives of the Word of Faith, other studies say, defy materialistic interpretations—be it neoliberalism or Weberian work ethic—and must instead be captured through the lens of what can be called "enchanted economics." In its most basic form, enchanted economics seeks spiritual or "magical" avenues for and explanations to material gain.[161] Hence, scholars claim that the Word of Faith's belief in spiritual laws are a result of such enchanted view of economic causality.[162]

Two approaches within the enchanted paradigm can be seen in the literature: the cargo cult theory and the occult economics theory. Some make a connection between the Word of Faith and the Melanesian cargo cults.[163] The cargo cults arose during the Second World War as a result of the Oceanian natives' exposure to Westerners and their consumer products.[164] According to native beliefs, the desired Western consumer goods—the "cargo"—should not be sought through any cooperation with the colonialists but would simply appear in direct response to magic practices. In a similar way, the Word of Faith seeks material affluence not through the natural processes but via their own devised "magical" means. This theory, though attractive to some, still has to convince most researchers in the field.[165]

In the so-called occult economics approach, scholars envisage an intimate economic relationship between the Word of Faith and the global neoliberal market. Understood as a turn to enchantment in economical attitudes, occult economics is the irrational reaction by mostly those who are disempowered and disenfranchised to explain and harness the invisible and mysterious mechanisms of an ever-changing and often chaotic market.[166] These economic outsiders seek to make sense of and by magical means act upon the economic world which is controlled by invisible forces of globalized capitalism. The expectations of

---

161. Stephen Hunt, "Magical Moments: An Intellectualist Approach to the Neo-Pentecostal Faith Ministries," *Religion* 28, no. 3 (1998): 279; von Sinner, "Struggling with Africa," 126; Robbins, "Globalization of Pentecostal," 137; Barker, "Charismatic Economies."

162. See Wariboko, "Pentecostal Paradigms," 41.

163. See Peter L. Berger, "Afterword," in *Global Pentecostalism in the 21st Century*, ed. Robert Hefner (Bloomington: Indiana University Press, 2013), 252; Jean DeBernardi, "Epilogue," *Culture and Religion* 3, no. 1 (2002): 125; Mombi, "Impact of the Prosperity," 32–58.

164. Lamot Lindstrom, "Cargo Cults," in *International Encyclopedia of the Social & Behavioral Sciences*, 2nd rev. ed., ed. James D. Wright (London: Elsevier Science), 139–44.

165. E.g., Wiegele, *Investing in Miracles*, 14–15.

166. Jean Comaroff and John Comaroff, "Occult Economies and the Violence of Abstraction: Notes from the South African Postcolony," *American Ethnologist* 26, no. 2 (1999): 279–303.

economic miracles give hope in the midst of a market controlled by Adam Smith's invisible hand.[167]

Enchanted economics claims that in the Word of Faith "Pentecostalism meets neoliberal enterprise."[168] The result is "prosperity cults"[169] that defy conventional reason and offer their own logic to accrue money out of nothing, "wealth without production, value without effort."[170] The Word of Faith is thus part of the rise of global occult economies that make magical attitudes to economics acceptable.[171] The Word of Faith is an indication that "capitalism has an effervescent new spirit—a magical, neo-Protestant zeitgeist—welling up close to its core."[172]

Directly related to neoliberal capitalism and Protestant ethic just discussed, the Word of Faith is in the occult economics perspective a "new Protestant ethic" that promises supernatural access to the world's wealth and fosters a "sanctified consumerism" or "holy materialism."[173] Making mystic sense of economic causality lies at the root of the attractiveness and spread of the Word of Faith message.[174] Though enchanted economics can help explain the Word of Faith's initial appeal, it is critiqued for failing to address the question why it remains popular even to those who have yet to see the promise of increase materialize.[175]

1.5.6 Gift Economy

According to one group of studies, questions pertaining to the origins, incentives, commitment, and impact of the Word of Faith—rather than proposing an alignment with the global capitalist market or suggesting spiritual responses to the structural mechanisms of the economic system—merit rather "a non-capitalist re-examination."[176] In what has been described as "a second

---

167. Meyer, "Christianity in Africa," 460; Amos Yong, *In the Days of Caesar: Pentecostalism and Political Theology* (Grand Rapids: Eerdmans, 2010), 23.

168. Jean Comaroff and John Comaroff, "Millennial Capitalism: First Thoughts on a Second Subject," in *Millennial Capitalism and the Culture of Neoliberalism*, ed. Jean Comaroff and John Comaroff (Durham: Duke University Press, 2001), 23.

169. Comaroff and Comaroff, "Millennial Capitalism," 23.

170. Comaroff and Comaroff, "Millennial Capitalism," 23–4.

171. Comaroff and Comaroff, "Millennial Capitalism," 20–2; Lindhardt, "More Than Just Money," 41–67.

172. Comaroff and Comaroff, "Occult Economies," 281.

173. Bialecki, Haynes and Robbins, "Anthropology of Christianity," 1149–50; Amos Yong, *In the Days*, 19.

174. Heuser, "Charting African Prosperity," 5.

175. Jeanne Rey, "Missing Prosperity: Economies of Blessings in Ghana and the Diaspora," in *Pastures of Plenty: Tracing Religio-Scapes of Prosperity Gospel in Africa and Beyond*, ed. Andreas Heuser (Frankfurt: Peter Lang, 2015), 339–54.

176. Bialecki, Haynes and Robbins, "Anthropology of Christianity," 1150.

phase"[177] in the socioeconomic analysis of the Word of Faith, attempts are made to develop a more nuanced and multifaceted understanding, portraying the movement as having its own religiously motivated economical dynamics.[178] By using perspectives on gift-giving offered by Marcel Mauss, the Word of Faith is characterized as a "gift economy" working with its own rationality.[179] Such "gift logic" is energized by the religious motivations of the adherents who envisage themselves as partaking of a complex and multilayered gift-exchange system.[180] The practice of generous, even risky, sacrificial giving of tithes and offerings often in ritualized ways makes it possible for the believer to "vacate the commercial economy and to enter another realm"—a "religious economy."[181] In Word of Faith practice, the believer moves money "from the market sphere into more value-based and personal spheres of exchange."[182] The believer thus assumes the role of a client in a reciprocal economic relationship with the divine Patron, who is expected to respond in abundant ways, either directly or indirectly through people.[183] This new relationship formed by the gift makes the believer to interpret all good things as returns ("harvests") for the gifts ("seeds") they previously shared ("sowed").[184]

Scholars in favor of the theory of a gift economy see the Word of Faith adherents who take active part by gifting as acting as free agents by personal religious impetus. There is an "attendant transformation of the sacrificer's sense of self,"[185] resulting in an increased sense of dignity, personal agency, and empowerment.[186] In many cultural contexts, giving is an expression of power while receiving signals

177. Simon Coleman, "Prosperity Unbound? Debating the 'Sacrificial Economy'," in *The Economics of Religion: Anthropological Approaches*, ed. Lionel Obadia and Donald Wood (Bingly: Emerald, 2011), 33.

178. Coleman, "Prosperity Unbound," 23–45.

179. Coleman, "The Charismatic Gift."

180. Marcel Mauss, *The Gift: The Form and Reason for Exchange in Archaic Societies* (New York: Routledge, 2002); Yvan Droz and Yonathan Gez, "A God Trap: Seed Planting, Gift Logic, and the Prosperity Gospel," in *Pastures of Plenty: Tracing Religio-Scapes of Prosperity Gospel in Africa and Beyond*, ed. Andreas Heuser (Frankfurt: Peter Lang, 2015), 295; van Dijk, "Pentecostal Gift;" Ackerly, "Importing Faith," 271–81.

181. Droz and Gez, "God Trap," 303–4; Lindhardt, "Are Blessings for Sale," 317; Susan Harding, *The Book of Jerry Falwell: Fundamentalist Language and Politics* (Princeton: Princeton University Press, 2000), 109; Heuser, "Charting African Prosperity," 1.

182. Lindhardt, "Are Blessings for Sale," 317.

183. E.g., Wiegele, *Investing in Miracles*; Coleman, *Globalisation*.

184. E.g., Wiegele, *Investing in Miracles*.

185. Premawardhana, "Transformational Tithing," 97.

186. Frederick, *Colored Television*, 69–70; Harrison, *RR*, 27, 48; Premawardhana, "Transformational Tithing," 97–8.

submission.[187] The one acting as giver asserts his or her social status and moral standing by the gift.[188] Partaking in the Word of Faith gift economy therefore makes the acting subject "experience the power of being donor."[189] Rather than looking for a monetary return, the highest goal is rather the consolidation of a relational tie between the giver and the divine Receiver which is achieved by the gift.[190] The gift economy theory leads scholars to issue a call for refraining from representing Word of Faith adherents as acting in pursuit of egocentric material objectives or as victims of scam-artists who simply peddle the Word of Faith message to enrich themselves.[191] Despite some high-profile examples speaking in favor of such stereotypes, they generally fail to capture the complex inner workings of the gift economy, especially the vital benefits such economic practices endow on the acting self.[192]

Some studies show how partaking in the Word of Faith gift economy, beyond bringing personal benefits, can also be socially productive. In some, especially African contexts, it can help young urban believers learn the practices of gifting and trust that is part of rural culture.[193] Personal sacrifice can also generate public recognition that accelerates religious entrepreneurial ambitions and social mobility.[194] The payoffs of partaking in the gift economy for the acting self help explain the persistent problem for those studying the Word of Faith, namely why believers continue to give generously despite the lack of realized promises of prosperity.[195]

However, uncritically plotting the Word of Faith on a gift-exchange grid might lead to some complicating and challenging ideas and practices, other researchers claim. The receiver, God, could be thought of as being contracted into a certain way of acting. Giving thus takes on a dimension of control, conceived of as setting "a God-trap" where the gift switches the power relation and makes God the debtor who becomes obliged to respond.[196] The believer's relationship to God can then be envisaged in purely instrumental, impersonal, and cost/benefit ways.[197] Further,

---

187. Andrew Chesnut, *Born Again in Brazil: The Pentecostal Boom and the Pathogens of Poverty* (New Brunswick: Rutgers, 1997), 119; Freston, "Prosperity Theology," 72–3.

188. Droz and Gez, "God Trap," 303.

189. Chesnut, *Born Again in Brazil*, 119.

190. Droz and Gez, "God Trap," 320.

191. Premawardhana, "Transformational Tithing;" Coleman, "Prosperity Unbound;" Droz and Gez, "God Trap."

192. E.g., Bakker, *I Was Wrong*; Costi Hinn, *God, Greed, and the (Prosperity) Gospel* (Grand Rapids: Zondervan, 2019).

193. Naomi Haynes, "On the Potential and Problems of Pentecostal Exchange," *American Anthropologist* 115, no. 1 (2013): 85–95.

194. Heuser, "Charting African Prosperity," 5.

195. Premawardhana, "Transformational Tithing," 97; Droz och Gez, "God Trap."

196. Droz and Gez, "God Trap."

197. Lindhardt, "Are Blessings for Sale."

portraying the Word of Faith in terms of a Mauss-like gift economy leaves out one crucial aspect, namely the role of the mediator. This role is then assumed by the Word of Faith minister, who often personally benefits from the gift and therefore most adamantly promotes the practice of sowing money seeds.[198] Serious misuses of the Word of Faith's economic discourse can come—and have come—in direct consequence.[199]

The gift economy approach offers creative ways to understand some of the perplexing issues surrounding giving in the Word of Faith. Instead of simply projecting a predetermined model on the movement's practice, it seeks to identify a unique underlying logic that empowers and gives meaning to giving.

1.5.7 Religious Identity

Socioeconomic researchers are interested in the impact of the Word of Faith on the formation of religious identity, that is, how the Word of Faith shapes a person's sense of religious self. But that is difficult to ascertain with any degree of generalization, studies admit, because believers tend to engage in active filtering of the messages they hear.[200] Scholars note tensions between what is publicly taught and how it is individually appropriated.[201] That considered, some credit the Word of Faith's incentives and commitment to a new form of self that their message offers; adherents are invited to adopt a particular Word of Faith identity and habitus.[202] The emphasis on prosperity, self-development and self-actualization, agency and control over one's life generate an attractive way of identity formation, meaning-making, and acting upon the world.[203] In the present globalized, capitalist

198. Droz and Gez, "God Trap," 306–7.

199. E.g., Bakker, *I Was Wrong*; Hinn, *God, Greed*.

200. E.g., Walton, "Stop Worrying," 126; Frederick, *Colored Television*, 71; "There is a more or less official reading of the Faith Message that is espoused and encouraged in their local churches. What people say they actually do with it however, how it shapes their everyday lives, does not necessarily follow" (Harrison, *RR*, 52).

201. Hicks, "Prosperity, Theology;" Harrison, *RR*, 109–16; Vinay Samuel, "A Biblical Ethical Assessment of Prosperity Teaching and the Blessing Movement," in *Prosperity Theology and the Gospel: Good News or Bad News for the Poor?*, ed. J. Daniel Salinas (Peabody: Hendrickson, 2017), 82; Freston, "Prosperity Theology," 73–4; Bradley Koch, "Penny-Pinching for Prosperity: The Prosperity Gospel and Monetary Giving Habits," Paper presented at the Annual Meeting of the American Sociological Association, August 2010 Atlanta; Walton, "Stop Worrying."

202. Coleman, *Globalisation*; Ackerly, "Importing Faith," 302–6. On definitions of "habitus" see Karl Maton, "Habitus," in *Pierre Bourdieu: Key Concepts*, ed. Michael Grenfell (London: Routledge, 2014), 47–64.

203. Harrison, *RR*, 8–10, 26–8; Lin, "Gospel;" Lin, *Prosperity Gospel*, Kindle edition, "Action;" Chong, "Of Riches and Faith," 148; Brison, "Empire Strikes Back," 26; Kathrine Wiegele, "The Prosperity Gospel Among Filipino Catholic Charismatics," in *Pentecostalism*

economic climate, identity is commodified, and individual self-promotion and branding are requirements for many if they are to attain an amount of economic well-being. Studies argue that the Word of Faith is a winning concept as it offers means of forming an ego-affirming identity that merges market requirements with the faith ideal of being an active part in God's plan for the world.[204] Some researchers see it as arising out of the core of mythologized American conceptions of self, thus making the Word of Faith "the pentecostal twin"[205] to the American social imaginary.

The new ego-affirming identity leads, as noted earlier, in some contexts to a complete break with the traditional and social past.[206] Such "rupture" in social orientation can open new realities for the Word of Faith self, no longer limited by a collectively oriented society or burden by commitments to extended family members.[207] This form of "hyperindividualism" has the potential of bringing positive economic effects, especially for migrant believers who might otherwise have a burden to provide for relatives at home.[208] Yet, it can create social problems as individualism breaks cultural norms.[209]

Some argue that the Word of Faith operates at its core as an "ideology of socioeconomic transition"[210] that gives the adherents an overarching narrative of increase with accompanying conceptual tools to make sense of the changes they have strived to attain. For believers who experience upward movement on the ladder of social class, the identity offered by the Word of Faith helps them handle the tensions that may arise as they find themselves in new economic, social, and cultural environments.[211]

Other dimensions raised in socioeconomic studies focused on religious identity are how the Word of Faith message instills a sense of superior knowledge and divine entitlement. By learning "who they are in Christ,"[212] Word of Faith believers develop an inner confidence based on access to privileged information on how to

---

and Prosperity: The Socio-Economics of the Global Charismatic Movement, ed. Katherine Attanasi and Amos Yong (New York: Palgrave Macmillan, 2012), 179–83. See Bowler, *Blessed*, 226–38.

204. Marti, *Hollywood Faith*, 177–92; Marti, "The Adaptability," 23; Sung-Gun Kim, "The Heavenly Touch Ministry in the Age of Millennial Capitalism: A Phenomenological Perspective," *Nova Religio* 15, no. 3 (February 2012): 56.

205. Bowler, *Blessed*, 226.

206. Meyer, "Make a Complete Break," 316–49; Robbins, "Anthropology of Religion," 156–78. See Marti, "Adaptability," 22.

207. Anim, "Prosperity Gospel," 72.

208. Brouwer, Gifford and Rose, *Exporting the American Gospel*, 241; Robins, "Anthropology of Religion," 168.

209. See Frederick, *Colored Television*, 68.

210. Harrison, *RR*, 156–9.

211. E.g., Chong, "Of Riches and Faith," 159.

212. Harrison, *RR*, 8–10.

live the victorious life.[213] Some studies focus on identity formation among women. Of particular interests are what image of femininity the movement fosters and the roles of women as followers and leaders.[214] The Word of Faith generates a sense of entitlement that works as an impetus for social mobility for both men and women.[215] Yet, such "right to wealth ethos" come also with ethical downsides.[216]

Contrary to popular opinion, socioeconomic studies point out that the commitment of Word of Faith believers stems not from the actual realization of the material blessings but in drawing people into being part of the powerful process of yearning and working. For those to whom the Word of Faith's economic expectations fail to materialize, the new ways of self-identification and engaging the world are enough to make believers stay within the Word of Faith.[217] The positive feeling of hope generated by the teachings is its main strength: "[their] chief allure is simple optimism."[218]

1.5.8 Social Agency

Socioeconomic studies want to study the Word of Faith's impact on social agency and engagement in social projects, such as issues of social justice and poverty alleviation. Studies from various parts of the world paint a heterogeneous picture that resists a generalized interpretation and calls for further research.[219] What

---

213. E.g., Harrison, *RR*, 51–4.

214. E.g., Sullivan and Delaney, "A Femininity that Giveth," 836–59; Maddox, "Prosper, Consume;" Kate Bowler, *The Preacher's Wife: The Precarious Power of Evangelical Women Celebrities* (Princeton: Princeton University Press, 2019); Marla Frederick, *Between Sundays: Black Women's Everyday Struggles of Faith* (Berkeley, University of California Press, 2003); Kathleen E. Jenkins and Gerardo Martí, "Warrior Chicks: Youthful Aging in a Postfeminist Prosperity Discourse," *Journal for the Scientific Study of Religion* 51, no. 2 (2012): 241–56.

215. Mumford, *Exploring Prosperity*; Lin, "Gospel;" Brouwer, Gifford and Rose, *Exporting the American Gospel,* 28; Harrison, *RR*, 157; Sullivan and Delaney, "Femininity;" Jane Soothill, "Gender and Pentecostalism in Africa," in *Pentecostalism in Africa: Presence and Impact of Pneumatic Christianity in Postcolonial Societies,* ed. Martin Lindhart (Leiden: Brill, 2015), 194–7.

216. Samuel, "Biblical Ethical Assessment," 82–4; Joel Edwards, "Ethical Dimensions: Holiness and False Idols," in *Prosperity Theology and the Gospel: Good News or Bad News for the Poor?* ed. J. Daniel Salinas (Peabody: Hendrickson, 2017), 91.

217. Lin, "Gospel," 43.

218. Gifford, "The Bible in Africa," 219; Lin, *Prosperity Gospel,* Kindle edition, "Prosperity Gospel Pentecostalism;" Bowler, *Blessed,* 232; Kay, *Pentecostalism,* 118; Rosalee Velloso Ewell, "Can We Offer a Better Theology? Banking on the Kingdom," in *Prosperity Theology and the Gospel: Good News or Bad News for the Poor?* ed. J. Daniel Salinas (Peabody: Hendrickson, 2017), 162.

219. E.g., Donald Miller and Tetsunao Yamamori, *Global Pentecostalism: The New Face of Christian Social Engagement* (Berkeley: University of California Press, 2007), 31–4.

is found so far is that the Word of Faith relates to a diversity of perspectives on society and displays a diverse agency in socioeconomic change.[220] In some contexts, the Word of Faith is coupled with social concern and responsibility.[221] And where it has not generated such, some are hopeful that it will.[222] In other contexts, studies reveal a lack of social involvement.[223] The Word of Faith's impact on poverty alleviation is the topic of interest in some research that want to address the question if Word of Faith ideals are an impetus for hope and economic agency or rather a delusion, an opium of the oppressed. Though inconclusive, studies show that Word of Faith theology and practices often act as positive motivators for economic mobility through stewardship of material resources and nurture a culture of entrepreneurial efforts.[224]

Studies show how the Word of Faith avoids framing poverty and social inequality in structural, historical, social, and political terms, making the movement express little to no interest in developing a political theology.[225] Rather, the roots and remedies of poverty are framed in terms of individualistic efforts in response to biblical promises.[226] The Word of Faith is therefore critiqued for failing to have a social-critical voice.[227] And if greed and social irresponsibility are permitted to fill the vacuum created by the absence of the critical voice, in the extreme, it allows for a "Pentecostal kleptocracy" where a few institutional agents personally benefit from people's sacrifices to God;[228] the Word of Faith, then, turns pastors

---

220. E.g., Meyer, "Pentecostalism and Globalization," 115–16; Andreas Heuser, "Charting African Prosperity," 8.

221. E.g., Helga Dickow, *Religion and Attitudes Towards Life in South Africa: Pentecostals, Charismatics and Reborns* (Baden-Baden: Nomos, 2012); Samuel, "Biblical Ethical Assessment," 80–1.

222. E.g., Heuser, "Charting African Prosperity."

223. "It is . . . unlikely that churches emphasizing the Prosperity Gospel of health and wealth will be genuine agents of change within their communities" (Miller and Yamamori, *Global Pentecostalism*, 31). See Mumford, *Exploring Prosperity*; Gifford, *Christianity, Development and Modernity*.

224. E.g., Lovemore Togarasei, "The Pentecostal Gospel of Prosperity in African Contexts of Poverty: An Appraisal," *Exchange* 40 (2011): 336–50; Richard Burgess, *Nigeria's Christian Revolution: The Civil War Revival and Its Pentecostal Progeny (1967-2006)* (Eugene: Wipf and Stock, 2008), 238; van Dijk, "The Pentecostal Gift;" Berger, "You Can Do It;" Naomi Haynes, "Pentecostalism and the Morality of Money: Prosperity, Inequality, and Religious Sociality on the Zambian Copperbelt," *Journal of the Royal Anthropological Institute* 18, no. 1 (2012): 125.

225. E.g., Gifford, "Prosperity Theology," 97.

226. Wiegele, "The Prosperity Gospel," 185.

227. Mumford, *Exploring Prosperity*.

228. Walton, *Watch This*, 176; Heuser, "Charting African Prosperity," 5; Chidiebere Ughaerumba, "Pastorpreneurship in Southern Nigeria and Weber's Protestant Ethic:

into business-minded "prophets for profit,"[229] who seek to build business empires with the main goal of generating rent.

1.5.9 Evaluation and Remaining Questions

The eight focus areas of the socioeconomical model are beneficial in several ways. The model's foremost contribution is its multifaceted approach to the Word of Faith movement. It asks questions and offers perspectives beyond what is found in the other models. It is the model where most new studies arise which offer creative approaches that supply new knowledge. The multifaceted and at times contradictory themes paint an intricate picture of the nature of the Word of Faith phenomenon. Several themes move the understanding of the Word of Faith beyond one-dimensional stereotypes and binary continuums. The model confirms Amos Yong's assessment that the Word of Faith phenomenon is made up of "an irreducible mix of sociological, economic, political, and historical factors."[230] Also, the model shows that beyond the complexity of its nature, the Word of Faith has a multifarious impact on a variety of socioeconomic dimensions. That is, the Word of Faith impacts other dimensions of life than just the level of belief. Yet, the model also shows that such an impact is "nothing if not varied."[231]

The explanatory power of this model is enhanced by how it envisions the Word of Faith in other ways than a theological entity consisting of cognitive beliefs. It offers innovative takes on key questions, suggesting approaches that can make better sense of the Word of Faith dynamics than what the other idea-centric models have been able to generate thus far. While the other models appear to have reached the end of their ability to contribute much new knowledge, entering socioeconomic studies on the Word of Faith gives the sense of vibrant scholarly conversations that hold the promise of moving beyond the present stalemate.

However, the limits of this model are also significant. The lack of fixed points in the definition of the Word of Faith and demarcations in the movement's relationship to Pentecostalism are more obvious in this model than in the others; listening to the discussions in the socioeconomic model gives the researcher a faint sense of conceptual confusion mainly caused by the lack of defined characterizations of the Word of Faith. This ambiguity hinders consistent and enhanced analyses. The scope of this model is not primarily theological; and this comes with the benefit of innovative and expanded perspectives. Yet, as the theological movement it is,

---

Insights for National Development," *International Journal of Advanced Research* 4, no. 8 (2016): 1931–41.

229. Ukah, "Prophets for Profit: Pentecostal Authority and Fiscal Accountability among Nigerian Churches in South Africa," in *Alternative Voices: A Plurality Approach for Religious Studies*, ed. Afe Adogame, Magnus Echtler and Oliver Freiberger (Göttingen: Vandenhoek and Ruprecht, 2013), 134–59.

230. Yong, "Typology of Prosperity Theology," 16.

231. Hefner, "Unexpected Modern," 23.

the Word of Faith can never be fully understood apart from a comprehensive theological analysis. Any model that lacks the theological dimension will ultimately fail to provide a fully satisfactory characterization of the Word of Faith. Given the irreducible theological dimension of the Word of Faith, is there any way to merge the gains of the socioeconomic model with theological interests? Approaching the Word of Faith through a worldview perspective speaks to this need as it includes socioeconomic interests within the larger worldview focus inclusive of theology.

Conclusion

The four dominant models emerging from surveying current scholarship on the Word of Faith generate invaluable knowledge and enhance our understanding of the movement. But the models cannot fully address the goals set out in this book. In terms of the analytical goal, no model has yet been able to reach an accepted definition of the Word of Faith. The defining, identity-carrying characteristics of the Word of Faith remain to be more fully explored and formulated. Neither do the models provide an account of the inner logic of the Word of Faith. None of the models approach the Word of Faith holistically in terms of a worldview, and they cannot evaluate the Word of Faith worldview on its own terms. In addressing the comparative goal, the relationship between Pentecostalism and the Word of Faith has been largely shaped by the doctrinal, biblical, and historical models. Since these work with a restricted image of the Word of Faith, they fail to fully do justice to the movement. Hence, I suggest that the comparative goal is better reached through using worldview as a model of analysis. Holistic perspectives on the Word of Faith are found in the socioeconomic model, yet the theological dimension of the movement is less analyzed. Since both Pentecostalism and the Word of Faith exist as foremost religious movements, a "thicker" understanding requires a thoroughly theological analysis.

Chapter 2

WORLDVIEW AND THE WORD OF FAITH

This book seeks to add complexity and nuance to current characterizations of the Word of Faith movement by using N. T. Wright's worldview-model that speaks to the set of analytical, evaluative, and comparative goals. Before conducting a worldview-analysis, two initial tasks are required. The first task, which occupied the last chapter, was to map and assess the models used by current scholarship. The doctrinal, theological, historical, and socioeconomic models identified in the literature offer critical insights, but their explanatory capacity is constrained by working with a restricted image of the movement. A holistic worldview approach promises to overcome the four models' limitations. Using worldview as the model for analysis requires a second initial task, which occupies this chapter. Because of the uncertainties surrounding the term "worldview" and the absence of proven frameworks for interpretation, I need to clarify the term and show how it has been previously applied in studies on the Word of Faith and how the work of Wright is the suitable model to use. The strengths of Wright's model are its holistic and analytical aspects that combine views of worldview as a system of thought and as a pattern of life, and thus can draw from these views already used in studies on the Word of Faith.

I begin by examining definitions of worldview and the ways the concept of worldview is understood and appropriated by Christian worldview scholarship. The section addresses critical concerns related to the definition and understanding of worldview, noting particularly how the indexical nature of the term and the worldview-dependent definitions require a well-defined model for analyzing the Word of Faith as a worldview. The next section shows how the literature employs worldview in studying the Word of Faith as either a system of beliefs or a pattern of life. Its use is limited and is not yet a distinct model of analysis. I then present the holistic worldview-model developed by Wright. I conclude by showing how Wright's holistic and analytical model fits the needs of this project and how the four elements of his model are used in the coming chapters to analyze the narrative, semiotic, practical, and propositional dimensions of the Word of Faith worldview. The second initial task of this chapter is foundational for laying the necessary groundwork for a worldview-analysis of the Word of Faith.

2.1 Worldview in Christian Scholarship

This chapter's task of clarifying the concept and usage of worldview in Christian scholarship sets the broader context for my worldview-analysis of the Word of Faith. First, using worldview to examine the religious phenomenon of the Word of Faith follows previous usages of the concept. It is observed that the idea of "Christianity as a worldview has risen to considerable prominence in the last one hundred and fifty years."[1] Interest in worldview as an analytical framework is accredited to the growing realization of the power of a "fundamental perspective"[2] on every issue of life.[3] Hence, worldview-analysis is considered by Christian scholarship to be one of the greatest achievements of the scholarly community during the last few decades.[4] Many scholars of Christianity contribute to the growing volume of worldview literature.[5] While Pentecostal scholarship appropriates worldview, it is evangelical

---

1. David Naugle, *Worldview: The History of a Concept* (Grand Rapids: Eerdmans, 2002), 4.

2. Sire, *NTE*, 24.

3. James Olthuis, "On Worldviews," in *Stained Glass: Worldviews and Social Science,* ed. Paul Marshall, Sander Griffioen, Richard Mouw (Lanham: University Press of America, 1989), 26; Sire, *NTE*.

4. Wright, *PFG*, 24. "As a matter of fact, in the entire history of 'worldview,' no single philosophic school or religious community has given more sustained attention to or taken more advantage of this concept than Protestant evangelicals" (Naugle, *Worldview*, 31). See David Naugle, "Worldview: History, Theology, Implications," in *After Worldview: Christian Higher Education in Postmodern Worlds*, ed. J. Matthew Bonzo and Michael Stevens (Sioux Center: Dordt College Press, 2009), 5–6.

5. Listed in alphabetical order, the list includes: Craig Bartholomew [Bartholomew and Goheen, *Christian Philosophy*; Michael Goheen and Craig Bartholomew, *Living at the Crossroads: An Introduction to Christian Worldview* (Grand Rapids: Baker, 2008)]; Charles Colson [Charles Colson and Nancey Pearcy, *How Now Shall We Live* (Wheaton: Tyndale, 1999)]; Herman Dooyeweerd [Herman Dooyeweerd, *Roots of Western Culture*, trans. John Kraay (Toronto: Wedge, 1979)]; Norman Geisler [Norman Geisler and William Watkins, *Worlds Apart: A Handbook on World Views*, 2nd ed. (Eugene: Wipf and Stock, 2003)]; Michael Goheen [Goheen and Bartholomew, *Living at the Crossroads*; Craig Bartholomew and Michael Goheen, *Christian Philosophy: A Systematic and Narrative* (Grand Rapids: Baker, 2008)]; Douglas Groothuis [Douglas Groothuis, *Christian Apologetics: A Comprehensive Case for Biblical Faith* (Downers Grove: IVP, 2011)]; Paul Hiebert [*Transforming Worldviews: An Anthropological Understanding of How People Change* (Grand Rapids, Baker Academic, 2008)]; Arthur Holmes [Arthur Holms, *Contours of a World View* (Grand Rapids: Eerdmans, 1983)]; Charles Kraft [Charles Kraft, *Christianity with Power* (Ann Arbor: Servant Books, 1989); Charles Kraft, *Worldviews for Christian Witness* (Pasadena: William Carrey Library, 2008)]; Richard Middleton [Walsh and Middleton, *TV*; Richard Middleton, "A New Heaven and a New Earth: The Case for a Holistic Reading of the Biblical Story of Redemption," *Journal for Christian Theological Research* 6, no. 4 (2006):

theology that exerts dominance in worldview thinking (the foremost impetus comes from the Reformed tradition).[6] Yet, despite Christian scholarship's frequent use of worldview, its precise meaning is often unclear.[7] The worldview scholar David Naugle notes the considerable "confusion and controversy"[8] regarding the definition of worldview and cautions that it is "important to be as clear as possible

73–97; Richard Middleton, *A New Heaven and New Earth: Reclaiming Biblical Eschatology* (Grand Rapids: Baker, 2014)]; Ronald Nash [Ronald Nash, *Faith and Reason: Searching for a Rational Faith* (Grand Rapids: Zondervan, 1988); Ronald Nash, *Worldview in Conflict* (Grand Rapids: Zondervan, 1992)]; David Naugle [Naugle, *Worldview*; Anderson, Clark, Naugle, *ICW*]; Roger E. Olson [Roger E. Olson, *The Essentials of Christian Thought* (Grand Rapids: Zondervan, 2017)]; James Olthuis [Olthuis, "On Worldviews;" James Olthuis, "Where There Is Love, There Is Vision: Witnessing in/under/through Worldviews," in *After Worldview: Christian Higher Education in Postmodern Worlds,* ed. Matthew Bonzo and Michael Stevens (Sioux Center: Dordt College, 2009), 81–94]; Michael Palmer [Michael Palmer, ed., *Elements of a Christian Worldview* (Springfield: Logion, 1998)]; Nancy Pearcey [Nany Pearcy, *Total Truth: 5 Principles for Unmasking Atheism, Secularism, and Other God Substitutes* (Wheaton: Crossway, 2015); Nany Pearcy, *Finding Truth* (Colorado Springs: David Cook, 2015)]; Francis Schaeffer [Francis Shaeffer, *How Should We Then Live?,* (Wheaton: Crossway, 2005)]; James Sire [James Sire, *The Universe Next Door,* 5th ed. (Downers Grove: IVP, 2009); James Sire, *NTE*]; Ninian Smart [Ninian Smart, *The World's Religions* (Cambridge: Cambridge University Press, 1989); Ninian Smart, "The Philosophy of Worldviews—That Is, the Philosophy of Religion Transformed," *Neue Zeitschrift für Systematische Theologie und Religionsphilosophie* 23, no. 1 (1981): 212–24)]; John Stott [John Stott, *Issues Facing Christians Today,* 4th ed. (Grand Rapids: Zondervan, 2006)]; Brian Walsh [Brian Walsh, *Subversive Christianity,* 2nd ed. (Eugene: Wipf and Stock, 2014); Walsh and Middleton, *TV*; Richard Middleton and Brian Walsh, *Truth Is Stranger than It Used to Be* (Downers Grove: IVP, 1995)]; Steven Wilkens [Stephen Wilkens and Mark Sanford, *Hidden Worldviews: Eight Cultural Studies That Shape Our Lives* (Downers Gove: IVP, 2009)]; Albert Wolters [Albert Wolters, *Creation Regained,* 2nd ed. (Grand Rapids: Eerdmans, 2005)]; N. T. Wright [Wright, *NTPG*].

6. For Pentecostal uses of worldview, see, e.g., Lederle, *Theology with Spirit*; Wolfgang Vondey and Chris Green, "Between This and That: Reality and Sacramentality in the Pentecostal Worldview," *Journal of Pentecostal Theology* 19, no. 2 (2010): 243–64; Wolfgang Vondey, *Pentecostalism: A Guide for the Perplexed* (London: Bloomsbury, 2013), 29–47; Palmer, *Elements of a Christian*; Amos Yong, "To See or Not to See: A Review Essay of Michael Palmer's Elements of a Christian Worldview," *Pneuma: The Journal of the Society for Pentecostal Studies* 21, no. 2 (1991): 305–27; James K. A. Smith, *Desiring Kingdom* (Grand Rapids: Baker, 2009); James K. A. Smith, *Thinking in Tongues* (Grand Rapids: Eerdmans, 2010). For evangelical predominance see Naugle, *Worldview,* 32.

7. Worldview is thus reminiscent of Bourdieu's "habitus," which, despite its wide usage, is "anything but clear" (Maton, "Habitus," 48).

8. Naugle, *Worldview,* 32.

when encountering and employing this term."[9] The following discussion is in response to that admonition.

The basic definition of "worldview" may be stated as "a comprehensive conception or apprehension of the world especially from a specific standpoint"— used in singular or plural forms.[10] Naugle sets out worldview's primary denotation as: "a person's interpretation of reality and a basic view of life."[11] But it is a formidable challenge to reach beyond such "reasonably straightforward and relatively noncontroversial"[12] definitions of this "wildly influential"[13] yet elusive and "contentious"[14] concept.[15] Worldview has a rich and fascinating history. The etymological roots of the term stem from the German word "*Weltanschauung*" coined in eighteenth-century philosophy and soon appropriated in several languages and by many academic disciplines.[16] Current popular discourse uses worldview frequently in the context of cultural analysis and political commentary.[17] Despite its common usage, the researcher faces a significant lack of fixed points in attempting to define worldview.[18]

---

9. Ibid.

10. *Merriam-Webster's Collegiate Dictionary*, 11th ed., s.v. "worldview."

11. Naugle, *Worldview*, 260.

12. Ibid.

13. Ibid., 329.

14. Anderson, Clark, Naugle, *ICW*, 1.

15. See Bryan Sims, "Evangelical Worldview Analysis: A Critical Assessment and Proposal" (Doctor of philosophy thesis, The Southern Baptist Theological Seminary, 2006), 8–11; Hiebert, *Transforming Worldviews*, 13–25, Goheen and Bartholomew, *Living at the Crossroads*, 11–19; Sire, *NTE*, 23–69.

16. Naugle, *Worldview*, 64–6. Christian theology (e.g., Abraham Kuyper; James Orr); Cultural anthropology (e.g., Michael Kearney; Robert Redfield; Clifford Geertz; André Droogers); Linguistics (e.g., Wilhelm von Humboldt; Martin Heidegger; Hans Georg Gadamer; Benjamin Lee Whorf); Natural sciences (e.g., Michael Polanya; Thomas Kuhn; Imre Lakatos); Philosophy (e.g., Johann Gottlieb Fichte; Friedrich Schelling; Georg Hegel; Wilhelm Dilthey; Friedrich Nietzsche; Edmund Husserl; Karl Jaspers; Martin Heidegger; Donald Davidson; Ludwig Wittgenstein); Psychology (e.g., Sigmund Freud; Carl Jung); Religious studies (e.g., Ninian Smart); Sociology (e.g., Karl Mannerheim; Peter Berger).

17. Worldview can be used simply to describe an outlook on the geographical, political, and economic worlds. For example, the *Washington Post's* foreign news blog is named "Worldviews." Sire notes a cultural usage: "the term *worldview* is often used as a very general label for how people view the cultures with which their culture clashes" (Sire, *NTE*, 23, emphasis original).

18. "*Worldview* is a contentious term. Some philosophers complain that it has become an abused and misused term. Others complain that worldview is regrettably neglected and overlooked in philosophical and theological conversations. Others still insist that its use is on the rise, that it has not yet hit its heyday. Still others do not even know what the concept is all about. Finally, some assert that *worldview* is simply an unhelpful term that can be

Worldview emerges as a very fluid term; its connotational and denotational meanings are rooted in the user's understanding. The result is a "plethora of diverging and conflicting explanations of the status and function of worldviews."[19] For many, therefore, worldview is "one of those fascinating, frustrating words that catches our attention . . . its ambiguity generates a great deal of study and insight, but also much confusion and misunderstanding. There is no single definition agreed upon by all."[20] This state is visually felt by the differing ways of transcribing worldview, either as a singular word (worldview) or as a compound word, with or without a hyphen (world-view or world view).[21] Christian worldview scholarship defines worldview in a variety of ways.[22] Studies observe unity on the importance,

dispensed with altogether without any profound loss" (Anderson, Clark, Naugle, *ICW,* 1, emphasis original).

19. Olthuis, "On Worldviews," 26; Geisler and Watkins offer a riddle: "What is it that everyone has, no one can live without, every important decision in life is made with, and yet most people do not even know they have?" (Geisler and Watkins, *Worlds Apart,* 9). To which it should be added "and which no one can fully define." The discussions on the concept of worldview are similar to discussions of the concept of culture: "The goal of such discussions [on the concept of culture] should not be to arrive at one right and commonly accepted definition that will once and for all lay the issue to rest. Rather, we should stay open to diverse conceptualizations of culture, provided they are clearly explained by their proponents and make sense to others" (Michael Minkov, *Cross-Cultural Analysis* (New York: SAGE, 2013), 9.

20. Hiebert, *Transforming Worldviews,* 13, 92; Bonzo and Stevens, *After Worldview;* Naugle notes that the ambiguity lies not at the basic denotative level of the "dictionary definition of 'worldview' . . . [as] a person's interpretation of reality and a basic view of life" (Naugle, *Worldview,* 259–60). "Worldviews themselves can be complex, but the definition of worldview is fairly straightforward: a worldview consists of our beliefs and assumptions about how the world fits together" [Steven Wilkens, *Beyond Bumper Sticker Ethics* (Grand Rapids: IVP, 2011), 19]; "The word [worldview] is used in a great many areas, ranging from the natural sciences to philosophy to theology. Authors who use it often do so without concern for a proper definition, and even when definitions are given, they tend to be far from precise. More cautious authors often apologize for the vagueness of the term" [Sander Griffioen, "The Approach to Social Theory: Hazards and Benefits," in *Stained Glass: Worldviews and Social Science,* ed. Paul Marshall, Sander Griffioen, Richard Mouw (Lanham: University Press of America, 1989), 83].

21. "world view" (e.g., Holmes, *Contours;* Walsh and Middleton, *TV*); "worldview" (Middleton and Walsh, *Truth Is Stranger*).

22. Some of the most noteworthy Christian definitions of worldview are (listed in alphabetical order following the first author): "[Worldview] is more than a private personal viewpoint; it is a comprehensive life system that seeks to answer the basic questions of life . . . it is an all-encompassing way of life, applicable to all spheres of life" [David Dockery and Trevin Wax, eds., *CSB Worldview Study Bible* (Nashville: Holman Bible Publisher, 2018), Kindle edition, "Preface"]; "A worldview is a way one views the whole world. A worldview

formative influence, and universal spread of the concept but also the apparent lack of agreement concerning its precise definition and functions.[23] To meaningfully use worldview to examine the Word of Faith, I need to advance beyond the lowest common denominator.

2.1.1 *The Indexical and Worldview-Dependent Nature of Worldview Thinking*

Before worldview can fruitfully be applied to analyze the Word of Faith, its indexical nature and the worldview dependency of current definitions are critically important. Worldview can be understood in linguistic terms as an indexical word, that is, a term whose meanings vary in reference with each user.[24] (The linguistic use of "indexical" here must be held separate from my semiotic use in Chapter 4 and onward.) This explains many of the misunderstandings that

is a way of viewing or interpreting all of reality. It is an interpretive framework through which or by which one makes sense out of the data of life and the world" [Geisler and Watkins, *Worlds Apart*, 11]; "Worldview is the articulation of *the basic beliefs* embedded in a shared grand story that are rooted in a faith commitment and that gives shape and direction to the whole of our individual and corporate lives" [Goheen and Bartholomew, *Living at the Crossroads*, 23, emphasis added]; "the foundational cognitive, affective, and evaluative assumptions and frameworks a group of people makes about the nature of reality which they use to order their lives" [Hiebert, *Transforming Worldviews*, 25–6]; "a conceptual scheme by which we consciously or unconsciously place or fit everything we believe and by which we interpret and judge reality" [Nash, *Faith and Reason*, 24]; "a worldview is best understood as semiotic phenomenon, especially as a system of narrative signs that establishes a powerful framework within which people think (reason), interpret (hermeneutics), and know (epistemology)" [Naugle, *Worldview*, xix]; "A worldview (or vision of life) is a framework or set of fundamental beliefs through which we view the world and our calling and future in it" [Olthuis, "On Worldviews," 29]; "A worldview is a set of beliefs and practices that shape a person's approach to the most important (and many other) issues of life" [Palmer, *Elements of a Christian*, 24, 30]; "A worldview is a commitment, a fundamental orientation of the heart, that can be expressed as a story or in a set of presuppositions (assumptions which may be true, partially true or entirely false) which we hold (consciously or subconsciously, consistently or inconsistently) about the basic constitution of reality, and that provides the foundations on which we live and more and have our being" [Sire, *NTE*, 141]; "a worldview is a passional orientation that governs how one sees, inhabits, and engages the world" [Smith, *Thinking in Tongues*, 27]; "World views [sic] are best understood as we see them incarnated, fleshed out in actual ways of life. They are not systems of thought, like theologies or philosophies. Rather, world views are perceptual frameworks. They are ways of seeing" [Walsh and Middleton, *TV*, 17]; "the comprehensive framework of one's basic beliefs about things" [Wolters, *Creation Regained*, 2].

23. Sims, "Evangelical Worldview Analysis," 8–10.
24. *Merriam-Webster's Collegiate Dictionary*, 11th ed., s.v. "indexical."

presently surround worldview—be it inside or outside Christian scholarship.[25] Central to its indexical nature is that a person's conception of worldview is actually worldview-dependent. The paradoxical consequence is that "one's view of 'worldview' depends on one's worldview!"[26] Naugle expands on this worldview dependency:

> There simply is no impartial ground upon which to stand when attempting to develop, promote, or criticize a thesis about this concept [of worldview]. Definitions, meanings, and models about "worldview" are definitely *not* the result of presuppositionless thinking, but reflect the perspectives and interests of their originators.[27]

The indexical and worldview-dependent nature of worldview thinking makes it a complex entity that requires careful and sensitive handling. But some Christian worldview thinkers are criticized for a general over-usage of the term, misunderstandings of its meaning and even blatant misuse.[28] This situation makes James Sire—who is "arguably the most influential evangelical worldview proponent over the past two generations"[29]—to issue the following warning: "Everyone who uses the term *worldview* should simply be clear about what they are doing and how they describe what they are doing."[30] I therefore develop a definition and model for worldview-analysis in adherence to both Naugle's and Sire's cautions "to be as clear as possible."[31]

Usages of the term should also be aware of the ongoing debates among scholars about the nature and functions of worldviews. Three points of concern stand out: (1) Should worldviews be seen as either cognitive and theoretical belief systems or as precognitive and pretheoretical embodied orientations of the heart?[32] (2) Are worldviews formed by active, conscious choice, or are they unconsciously

---

25. See Anderson, Clark, Naugle, *ICW*, 1.

26. Naugle, *Worldview*, 254. See Sire, *NTE*, 43, 68, 77.

27. Naugle, *Worldview*, 254, emphasis original.

28. George Pierson "Evangelicals and Worldview Confusion," in *After Worldview: Christian Higher Education in Postmodern Worlds*, ed. J. Matthew Bonzo and Michael Stevens (Sioux Center: Dordt College Press, 2009), 5–26; Kraft, *Christianity with Power*, 79. Olson, speaks of the term "Christian worldview" as "a cliché worn out by overuse" (Olson, *Essentials of Christian Thought*, 17).

29. Anderson, Clark, Naugle, *ICW*, 13.

30. Sire, *NTE*, 68, emphasis original.

31. Naugle, *Worldview*, 32.

32. Sire, *NTE*, 91, 96–126; "For Dooyeweerd, all human endeavour stems not from worldview, but from the spiritual commitments of the heart" (Naugle, *Worldview*, 26); Albert Wolters "On the Idea of Worldview and Its Relation to Philosophy," in Marshall, Griffioen and Mouw *Stained Glass*, 14–25.

absorbed, primarily through habits?[33] (3) Is there one, singular Christian or biblical worldview or a plurality of worldviews that can be called Christian or biblical?[34] I return to these questions later in the chapter.

2.2 Worldview in Word of Faith Scholarship

Using worldview to analyze the Word of Faith is of primary interest here. In order to move beyond appropriations and definitions of worldview, the first question is how the concept is utilized by Word of Faith scholarship. However, in surveying the scholarly conversations on the Word of Faith, a simple lexical survey is insufficient since "the fact that the term [worldview] is being used does not in itself guarantee that the concept (or idea) of a worldview is present in any significant way."[35] The complexity of a survey is further increased by the fact that writers on the Word of Faith almost universally see no need for definition and often employ worldview in a self-explanatory fashion without addressing the points of concern just raised. The reader's impression of a casual and imprecise usage is heightened by the fact that worldview is very seldom included in the index or as a keyword in studies on the Word of Faith, even when it is a reoccurring, meaning-carrying concept.[36] Some studies use terms and expressions with similar meanings, or which at least intersect and overlap with worldview concerns.[37] Also, the proximity of worldview vis-à-vis culture furthers the challenge of deciding which materials should be included. The survey must also account for the additional variable of "worldviewish thinking,"[38] which entails discussions which speak to worldview concerns without using the term.[39]

33. Smith, *Desiring the Kingdom.* Cf. Edgar Lee, "The Role of the Bible in Shaping a Christian Worldview," in *Elements of a Christian Worldview*, ed. Michael Palmer (Springfield: Logion, 1998), 79–106, 80.

34. Olthuis, "Where there is Love," 85.

35. Griffioen, "Approach to Social Theory," 82.

36. E.g., Both Lin and Harrison use "worldview" without any definition or entry in the index (Lin, *Prosperity Gospel*, Kindle edition, "The Floodgates of Heaven," "The Paradoxes of Prosperity Gospel Pentecostalism;" Harrison, *RR*, e.g., 8, 14, 47, 54, 58, 65, 105).

37. Cosmology [Bowler, *Blessed*, 219; Perriman, *FHP*, 32; Hunt, "Winning Ways;" Atkinson, *Spiritual Death*, 129; Anim, "The Prosperity Gospel;" Lewison, "Pentecostal Power"]; Habitus [Coleman, *The Globalisation*, 62–5; Ackerly speaks of the enchanted worldview and enchanted habitus interchangeably (Ackerly, "Importing Faith," 303, 308); Walton "Stop Worrying"]; imaginary of the world [Meyer, "Pentecostalism, Prosperity"]; *Weltanschauung* [Lie, "Theology of E. W. Kenyon," 104].

38. Grenz and Olson, *Who Needs Theology*, 15.

39. See Naugle, *Worldview*, 13, 205.

When surveying the scholarly literature on the Word of Faith, I adopt the basic and widely accepted understanding of worldview as "the fundamental perspective from which one addresses every issue of life."[40] Using this definition as a conceptual net, the survey reveals the following observations. First, the term "worldview" and its broad context of a worldviewish thinking are present in the literature and used within all the four models examined in the previous chapter. Second, two significant worldview usages are evident and fall within two categories: worldview as a system of thought and worldview as a pattern of life. As a system of thought, worldview is understood as a set of presuppositions or a system of ultimate, cognitive beliefs. This construing of worldview has until recently been the unchallenged and predominant view among much worldview scholarship.[41] The usage of worldview as a pattern of life shifts from a cognitive emphasis to embrace embodied dimensions; worldview is conceived of as a pattern of embodied and habitual behaviors. The difference between the two ways of understanding worldview in the literature on the Word of Faith is not absolute, but in degrees, as both cognitive and embodied dimensions make up part of some studies. Third, to date, worldview is not used as a distinct model of analysis of the Word of Faith. The employment of worldview is too general to be classified as a distinct model of analysis. Rather, the concept is used to serve secondary purposes for larger arguments sustained by the existing models. What follows is a presentation and critique of the two conceptualizations of worldview (as a system of thought and a pattern of life) in the literature on the Word of Faith.

2.2.1 Worldview as a System of Thought in Word of Faith Scholarship

Studies on the Word of Faith use worldview as a system of thought for comparative and evaluative purposes. Worldview terminology highlights tensions in the Word of Faith belief system with a biblical or Christian worldview.[42] Scrutiny of the cognitive content of the Word of Faith doctrines justifies the claim that the Word of Faith diverges from a Christian worldview and that the movement paints a "distorted view of reality."[43] Worldview as a system of thought is employed to identify possible connections between the beliefs of the Word of Faith and non-Christian, religious groups (e.g., New Thought, gnostic or New Age in the West, or primal worldviews in the Global South). Based on an analysis of the movement's thought-content, the Word of Faith is characterized as a "JDS worldview," an "occult worldview," a "dualistic worldview," Gnostic worldview, the result of

---

40. "until very recently most would have accepted this vague definition" (James Sire, *NTE*, 24).

41. Sire, *NTE*, e.g., 113.

42. E.g., Newport, *New Age Movement*, 361–6, 395–417; see Brandon, *Health and Wealth*, 53; Hanegraaff, *CIC*, 130; Perriman, *FHP*, 32; Horn, *FRTR*, 93.

43. Cotterell, *Prosperity Theology*, 18–21; Maritz and Stoker, "Does the Christian Worldview." See Jones and Woodbridge, *HWH*, 35.

incorporating "a New Age monistic, pantheistic worldview" or as a Christianized version of a secular, global capitalist worldview.[44] Local appropriation of the Word of Faith's emphasis on physical and financial well-being draws from similar expectations in primal, non-Christian religious worldviews.[45] The Word of Faith's belief in the casual linkage between the spiritual and the material is also interpreted as an expression of their worldview's system of thought.[46] The Word of Faith represents a form of Christian idealism, believing that words impact the natural world. Their "idealistic" system of beliefs brings together the binary categories of the sacred and the profane.[47] The Word of Faith's affirmation of the goodness of the physical world and God's desire for humanity's material well-being, some argue, transcends a negative dualism while promoting a holistic worldview, challenging the dualistic thought of modernism and conservative evangelicalism.[48] In this reasoning, the Word of Faith represents a genuinely Pentecostal holistic system of beliefs.[49]

Approaching the Word of Faith as a worldview conceived as a system of thought has potentials as well as drawbacks.[50] On the positive side, this approach can widen the analysis from the narrow lens used in the doctrinal, biblical, and historical models to include underlying presuppositions and commitments (social, economic, etc.) that wield implicit, formative power on their entire belief system—not just on their biblical hermeneutics. This perspective can move the analysis from a piecemeal approach to a wider consideration of the sum of the Word of Faith's cognitive content. On the downside, approaching the Word of Faith from an understanding of worldview as a system of thought comes with the danger of conflating worldview with explicit theological beliefs.[51] Theology, understood as a formal system of thought, is used more or less synonymously with worldview in

44. Atkinson, *Spiritual Death*, 26; Hanegraaff, *CIC*, 81, 130; Brandon, *Health and Wealth*, 53; Perriman, *FHP*, 32; Frei, "With Both Fee in the Air," 368; Matta, *Born Again Jesus*; Maritz and Stoker, "Does the Christian Worldview" 7; Newport, *New Age Movement*, 361–6, 396–405; Niemandt, *Prosperity Gospel*, 214; Harrison, *RR*, 158; Hicks, "Prosperity Theology," 246.

45. Anim, "The Prosperity Gospel;" The Lausanne Community claims that the growth of the Word of Faith, particularly in the Global South, is the result of "a syncretised superstructure built on an underlying worldview that has not been radically transformed by the biblical gospel" (Salinas, *Prosperity Theology*, 185).

46. E.g., Nimi Wariboko, *Economics in Spirit and Truth: A Moral Philosophy of Finance* (New York: Palgrave McMillan, 2014), 95–7.

47. DeArteaga, *Quenching the Spirit*, 144; Lederle, *Theology with Spirit*, 206–11.

48. Smith, *Thinking in Tongues*, 12, 43; Alexander, *Signs and Wonders*, 73; Macchia, "Call for Careful Discernment," 225–37. See Charles Taylor, *Modern Social Imaginaries* (Durham: Duke University Press, 2004), 49. Cf. Gifford, *Christianity, Development*, e.g., 155–7.

49. Lederle, *Theology with Spirit*, 17–30; DeArteaga, *Quenching the Spirit*.

50. See Lautherbach, "Fakery and Wealth," 123.

51. See Pierson, "Evangelicals and Worldview Confusion," 31.

the literature on the Word of Faith. This application reduces the reach and usability of worldview as a concept and method for analysis of the Word of Faith. It stops at the explicit and conscious levels of meaning-making, while leaving the implicit and unconscious beliefs unexamined (not to mention the formative narrative, embodied dimensions). This problem of conflating worldview with theology is present, for example, in the claim that based on its explicit doctrinal beliefs, the Word of Faith makes a New Age worldview.[52] The claim reveals a reductionist definition of worldview that equates it with a system of expressed theological beliefs. To say that Word of Faith is a non-biblical worldview based on their doctrines is in effect the same as the charge of heresy in the doctrinal model (see Section 1.3).

In the final analysis, conflating worldview with doctrine in the discussion on the Word of Faith reduces worldview to mostly a rhetorical and polemical device, which deprives worldview of its potential usefulness and explanatory power to probe deeper into the Word of Faith. What would strengthen the approach to the Word of Faith is an expanded and holistic understanding of worldview that encompasses the cognitive, narrative, material, and embodied aspects of life. Also, moving beyond a piecemeal analysis of the Word of Faith's beliefs in search of a narrative structure would deepen the understanding of how their beliefs interconnect and form an overall worldview in the Word of Faith.

2.2.2 Worldview as a Pattern of Life in Word of Faith Scholarship

Worldview understood as a pattern of life is found in studies on economic and cultural themes in the Word of Faith. It is used to address perceived interconnections between the Word of Faith and global capitalism and consumerism; questions related to economic and consumption practices are framed in terms of worldview patterns. A recurring argument is that there are worldview-level affinities ("fits") between the neoliberal capitalist market and the practices of the Word of Faith.[53] Studies claim that the American Dream, understood in worldview terms as economic aims and practices (e.g., hopeful, material success-orientation, individualism, and consumerism), finds direct religious expression through the Word of Faith.[54] The Word of Faith can be portrayed as "a distinct worldview"

52. Newport, *New Age Movement*, 361–6, 396–405.
53. E.g., "Cosmologically, Pentecostalism's prosperity theology's assertion of this-worldly evil and salvation framed in a language of modernization and development provides a theological framework for making sense of a world of non-transparent wealth flows and massive inequality" (Lewison, "Pentecostal Power," 40).
54. Lin, *Prosperity Gospel*; Peter Mundey, "The Prosperity Gospel and the Spirit of Consumerism According to Joel Osteen," *Pneuma: The Journal of the Society for Pentecostal Studies* 39, no. 3 (2017): 318–41; Marti, "Adaptability of Pentecostalism."

that exists as a product of creatively incorporating mainstream cultural ideals and aspirations that are shaped by market forces into Pentecostalism.[55]

The effects of globalization are also studied under the rubric of worldview. Using worldviewish thinking, it is argued that the Word of Faith instills a specific global identity and embodied orientation toward the world. Such lived Word of Faith worldview can be fostered in various national, economic, and cultural milieus and is expressed bodily in a particular habitus.[56]

To study the Word of Faith as a worldview consisting of embodied patterns of behavior opens new, much-needed dimensions to the analysis of the movement. This approach challenges the assumption that Word of Faith can be fully grasped by an analysis of only its cognitive content. The habitual practices fostered in the Word of Faith make a meaning-carrying dimension that requires to be considered for a fuller treatment of the movement. However, scholarly analyses of the movement seldom develop the practices theologically. On its own, worldview as a pattern of life cannot capture the fullness of the Word of Faith as it exists—this book argues—in its core also as a theological movement. Beyond the practices of the Word of Faith, proper attention must also be given to their semiotic dimension. To identify what the core signs and symbols are within the Word of Faith would deepen the analysis because signs are noted features of worldviews.[57] As the Word of Faith is first of all a religious, faith-oriented phenomenon, any worldview-analysis requires their belief structure to be fully integrated into considerations of their embodied practices. The Word of Faith's practices and symbols have to be contrasted with their theological narrative world to locate possible enlightening connections.[58] Their theological world must not be conceived of as limited to propositional statements but enlarged to consider overarching theological narrative dimensions that interconnect with their beliefs, practices, and signs. Also, another variable important to consider is on what level of consciousness their behavior patterns operate. Recent worldview scholarship emphasizes that the influence and formative power of practices often stand in direct relation to their unconscious operations.[59]

In summary, what would strengthen a worldview approach to the Word of Faith is an inclusive understanding of worldview encompassing cognitive belief structures (propositions and narratives), embodied aspects of practices and symbols, all in direct relation to their theological beliefs. It would require an updated and well-reasoned understanding of worldview and a model that can be practically applied.

---

55. On distinct worldview, e.g., Asamoah-Gyadu, "Prosperity and Poverty," 107. See Marti, *Hollywood Faith*; Marti, "The Adaptability of Pentecostalism;" Marti, "I Determine My Harvest."

56. See Coleman, *Globalisation*, 51, 234; Ackerly, "Importing Faith."

57. Wright, *NTPG*, 122–6. See Naugle, *Worldview*, 292–7.

58. See William Kay, review of *The Globalisation of Charismatic Christianity*, by Simon Coleman, *Journal of Ecclesiastical History* 53, no. 2 (2002): 427–8.

59. Wright, *NTPG*, 122; See Smith, *Desiring the Kingdom*.

A holistic take on worldview would offer new ways to analyze the Word of Faith that would do the movement greater justice and can draw from the strengths and insights gained in the available models. No study has yet, based on an informed discussion of worldview, presented a suitable worldview-model and used it for analyzing the Word of Faith. Yet, the frequent appearance of worldview as a term and concept in studies on the Word of Faith makes the possibility of worldview emerging into a distinct model of analysis possible and thus becoming a valuable resource in the pursuit of enhanced understanding of the movement.

2.3 N. T. Wright's Worldview-Model and the Word of Faith

A holistic understanding of worldview arises from the aforementioned discussions as a promising model to analyze the Word of Faith and to add nuance and complexity to current characterizations of the movement. Hence, I introduce the worldview theory and model of analysis developed by the theologian N. T. Wright. Wright stands as a significant contemporary biblical scholar and theologian whose scholarly and popular works generate considerable interest and a variety of responses: hailed by some as "one of the most formidable figures in the world of Christian thought"[60] and with an influence sometimes compared to that of Karl Barth and C. S. Lewis,[61] others critique Wright for what they see as revisioning beliefs cherished in some Christian faith traditions.[62] Leaving comments on Wright's influence till later, of interest here is strictly his worldview theory and model for holistic worldview-analysis which he developed and applied in the series *Christian Origins and the Question of God [COQG]*.[63] There he understands worldviews to be implicit, precognitive, dynamic, and comprehensive reality-perceiving frameworks.[64] Worldviews form personal and group identity, give sense

---

60. David Van Biema, "Christians Wrong About Heaven, Says Bishop," *Time*, February 7, 2008, accessed April 7, 2021, http://content.time.com/time/world/article/0,8599,1710844,00.html.

61. Derek Vreeland, *Through the Eyes of N. T. Wright: A Reader's Guide to Paul and the Faithfulness of God* (self pub., Doctrina Press, 2015), 3; Jason Byassee, "Surprised by N.T. Wright," *Christianity Today*, April 8, 2014, accessed April 7, 2021, https://www.christianitytoday.com/ct/2014/april/surprised-by-n-t-wright.html.

62. For example, John Piper, *The Future of Justification: A Response to N. T. Wright* (Wheaton: Crossway, 2007). Cf. Tom Wright, *Justification: God's Plan and Paul's Vision* (London: SPCK, 2009).

63. Wright, *NTPG*; Wright, *JVG*; Wright, *RSG*; Wright, *PFG*.

64. Implicit: Wright, *PFG*, 26; precognitive: Wright, *NTPG*, 122; comprehensive: Wright, *NTPG*, 123, 137, 149; Wright, *PFG*, 28, 232–3; reality: Wright, *NTPG* 41, 43, 123, 137, 148; perceiving: Wright, *NTPG*, 123; frameworks: Wright, *NTPG*, 37, 43, 45. The definition shows influence from James Olthuis and Brian Walsh (see Wright, *NTPG*, 112; Wright, *PFG*, 27. See Sire, *NTE*, 57).

to experiences, generate beliefs and motivations, and direct thoughts, words, and actions.[65] Worldviews work as grids through which all experience of the world is mediated, perceived, interpreted, and organized.[66] Wright uses the metaphor of glasses/lens to highlight the perceptional, precognitive, and assumed nature of worldviews and their implicit nature and function.[67] Worldviews are thus what humans normally look *through* and not *at*.[68] Worldviews, he also suggests, are like deep, hidden foundations of a house, illustrating the invisible and irreplaceable nature of worldviews and the possibility of excavating and inspecting them.[69]

While existing as human constructions, worldviews make up the most essential aspect of human life.[70] Worldviews work on community levels while individuals have variations within parent worldviews, the so-called mindsets.[71] Important for Wright's understanding is the implicit and mostly unconscious working of worldviews.[72] That is, worldviews operate beneath the active consciousness of the adherents. Though formative power increases with the level of implicitness, Wright does not imagine causality as completely one-directional; formative power flows both from the worldview to that of expressed beliefs, words, and actions and vice versa. Worldviews exert shaping influence on the levels of basic, consequent beliefs and actions/words while these levels also, in turn, shape the worldview.

2.3.1 Wright's Worldview-Model

In *COQG*, Wright develops a model for analyzing worldviews. Worldviews consist of four interrelated elements of story, symbol, praxis, and ultimate beliefs (which Wright calls "questions").[73] These elements are organically interconnected and interpenetrate and interact with one another in multiple and intricate ways. Together story, symbol, praxis, and ultimate beliefs both constitute and express

---

65. Wright, *NTPG*, 41; *RSG*, 422; Wright, *PFG*, 232–3; Wright, *PFG*, 609; Wright, *NTPG* 124.

66. Wright, *NTPG*, 32, 38, 125, 247; Wright, *JVG*, 138; Wright, *PFG*, 29.

67. Wright, *JVG*, 138; Wright, *PFG*, 28, 34, 163, 564.

68. Wright, *PFG*, 28.

69. Wright, *NTPG*, 117, 125; Wright, *PFG*, 353.

70. Wright, *NTPG*, 43.

71. Wright, *NTPG*, 110; Wright, *PFG*, 34.

72. "Worldview elements are things we take for granted, things we do or use or see or say unreflectively because they are part of the furniture we only notice if someone has rearranged it, part of the wallpaper we only 'see' if somebody has replaced it or splashes paint on it. To change the metaphor, worldview elements, though usually out of sight, become loadbearing, like the deep, hidden foundations of a house. Shake them, and we experience a mental and emotional earthquake; remove them, and the house collapses; we don't know who we are anymore. It is almost as if we had died and woken up in a whole new world" (Wright, *PFG*, 353).

73. Wright, *NTPG*, 124; Wright, *JVG*, 142; Wright, *PFG*, 29.

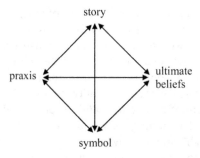

Figure 1 The four elements of Wright's worldview-model.

the particular worldview, each functioning like a two-way bridge, expressing the worldview while also offering a way to enter it.[74] We may say that Wright envisions a reciprocal relationship of the four worldview-elements (see Figure 1).[75]

The following chapters present and critically engage the elements before applying each to the Word of Faith. Before turning to this dominant task, the relevance of Wright's thinking for this project needs to be assessed, three critical concerns regarding the concept of worldview must be addressed, and the process of applying it be explained.

2.3.2 The Relevance of Wright's Worldview-Model

Four reasons support my choice of Wright to address the goals of this book. First, Wright developed the model theoretically in conversation with modern worldview scholarship, and his model meaningfully addresses the critical concerns raised earlier; worldviews, for him, encompass both belief system and embodied orientations of the heart and are formed both unconsciously

74. Wright, *NTPG*, 123.

75. Wright, *NTPG*, 124. In *JVG* the elements are in alternated places and "story" and "symbol" are in plural (Wright, *JVG*, 142; cf. Wright, *PFG*, 29). The model was developed in collaboration with Brian Walsh. Walsh's model puts the element of "praxis" as "Praxis/ Way of Life" and the element of "questions" as "Worldview/Questions" (Brian Walsh, "From housing to homemaking: Worldviews and the Shaping of Home," Paper presented at Adequate and Affordable Housing for All International Conference, University of Toronto, June 2004, 9). See Wendy Griswold, *Cultures and Societies in a Changing World*, 4th ed. (London: SAGE, 2014), 15. Beyond the core of the four worldview elements, Wright imagines two additional layers in the outworking of worldviews. It is in these layers the worldview finds increasingly practical consequences. The first layer consists of what he calls "basic beliefs" and "aims" and the second layer of "consequent beliefs" and "intentions" (Wright, *NTPG*, 110). Though these dimensions are interesting in their own right, they lie outside the scope of this thesis since they are derivative of the worldview rather than generic.

and actively by habitual actions. My reading of Wright's work in answer to the aforementioned third concern that only one worldview can be biblical or Christian is that, since worldviews are human constructions and always in a state of development and refinement—though hopefully formed in response to revelation and reason—one should allow for a variety of interpretations of the Christian or biblical view of reality. Second, Wright's holistic scope includes narrative, semiotic, practical, and propositional dimensions. It thus embraces the dual understandings of worldview noted earlier (i.e., worldview as a system of thought and worldview as a pattern of life). Third, Wright developed the model for practical, analytical purposes and consistently applied it to a variety of worldviews (e.g., in second temple Judaism, Jesus and Paul).[76] Thus, in tracing Wright's usage of the model, one learns its practical functions as well as recognizing its potential for bringing complexity and nuance to the understanding of the Word of Faith. Fourth, Wright's model is designed for a theological end. Such perspective is fitting since the Word of Faith is first and foremost a religious movement.

Wright's model and worldview thinking promise to provide the relevant and useful approach to complete this book's dominant task. Yet, three questions regarding the use of Wright to analyze the Word of Faith need to be addressed. These relate to the choice of Wright, the applicability of his model, and his conception of culture and religion. Addressing these questions is important to gain confidence that Wright's model is the appropriate one to use here. First, some readers might react to the choice of Wright as a conversation partner in this project. His background in historical and exegetical research and ecclesial service in the Church of England might raise the question if he is the most suitable source to use in the study of the distinctly contemporary Pentecostal issue of the Word of Faith. In relation to Pentecostalism, Wright's emphasis on the Spirit, precedence to Scripture, critique of traditionalism, openness to personal pneumatic experiences and the charismata, and high view of narrative all resonate with Pentecostal priorities.[77] It is not surprising, therefore, that Wright has caught the attention

---

76. He explains, "I developed the model, not a priori, but because I found myself unable to understand Jesus within the history-of-ideas models with which I started" (Wright, *JVG*, 660); See Wright, *PFG*, 474, where Wright describes his need to move from exegesis to worldview-models.

77. N. T. Wright, "The Word and the Wind: A Response," in *Pentecostal Theology and the Theological Vision of N. T. Wright*, ed. Janet Meyer Everts and Jeffrey S. Lamp (Cleveland: CPT Press, 2015), 143. See Craig Keener, *Spirit Hermeneutics: Reading Scripture in Light of Pentecost* (Grand Rapids, Eerdmans, 2016), 299. On Wright's views of the prosperity gospel see Sarah Pulliam Bailey, "'A Wake-Up Call:' British Theologian N.T. Wright on the Prosperity Gospel, Climate Change and Advent," *The Washington Post*, December 5, 2019, accessed April 7, 2021, https://www.washingtonpost.com/religion/2019/12/05/wakeup-call -british-theologian-nt-wright-prosperity-gospel-climate-change-advent/.

of Pentecostal scholarship.[78] Also, Wright's theological vision is controversial to some, and several of the most debated points arise from his application of the worldview-model to the biblical texts.[79] In reply, it is important to note that Wright's model is not dependent on the theological conclusions he draws from applying it and on his spirituality. In terms of his debated beliefs, it should be noted that in the published critiques of Wright's theology, there are, as far as I am aware, no substantial arguments directed against his worldview-model or his application of it. Rather, the worldview-model receives positive evaluations even among those critical of the theological conclusions he draws from using it.[80] My intention is strictly to apply Wright's model for a worldview-analysis of the Word of Faith. Because of this demarcation, Wright's overall theological vision and spirituality are of little consequence.

Second, using Wright's model might raise the question of its applicability since it was developed to study historical movements and figures. Though Wright uses the model for historical concerns, it can still be applied to the present phenomenon of the Word of Faith because the model itself stands apart from the particular issues which it is meant to examine. It strengthens Wright's model that he used it

---

78. Janet Meyer Everts and Jeffrey Lamp, eds., *Pentecostal Theology and the Theological Vision of N. T. Wright* (Cleveland: CPT Press, 2015); Frank Macchia, "The Spirit and God's Return to Indwell a People," in *God and the Faithfulness of Paul: A Critical Examination of the Pauline Theology of N. T. Wright*, ed. Christoph Heilig, Thomas Hewitt and Michael Bird (Minneapolis: Fortress, 2017), 632–44.

79. For example, his view of Jesus' self-understanding, eschatology, justification, and the return from exile motif. Alister E. McGrath says that some of the contents of Wright's theology "do not sit entirely easily with the settled evangelical views on matters of some importance" (Alister E. McGrath, "Reality, Symbol and History," in *Jesus and the Restoration of Israel: A Critical Assessment of N. T. Wright's Jesus and the Victory of God*, ed. Carey Newman (Downers Grove: IVP, 1999), 168. Cf. e.g., Piper, *Future of Justification*; Carey Newman ed., *Jesus and the Restoration of Israel: A Critical Assessment of N. T. Wright's Jesus and the Victory of God* (Downers Grove: IVP, 1999); Christoph Heilig, Thomas Hewitt and Michael Bird, eds., *God and the Faithfulness of Paul: A Critical Examination of the Pauline Theology of N. T. Wright* (Minneapolis: Fortress, 2017); Nicholas Perrin and Richard Hays, eds., *Jesus, Paul and the People of God: A Theological Dialogue with N. T. Wright* (London: SPCK, 2011); N. T. Wright, *The Paul Debate* (London: SPCK, 2016).

80. Sire recently assessed Wright's worldview thinking as "highly significant" and concluded that "with Wright, worldview analysis . . . is alive and well" (Sire, *NTE*, 59, 14, 56–9, 65–6, 97–8). Robert Stewart, for example, has particularly engaged Wright's hermeneutic, and while not uncritical of some of Wright's theological conclusions, says that the "use of worldview as a hermeneutical tool is to be applauded" (Robert Stewart, "N. T. Wright's Hermeneutic: Part 2 – The Historical Jesus," *Churchman* (Autumn 2003): 256; John Barclay critiques Wright's model as incomplete and the elements of symbol, praxis, and questions as "inadequate and open to challenge," yet did not develop his views (Wright, *PFG*, 28 fn.80, 108 fn.142).

fruitfully to analyze complex religious movements—and several of the worldview dynamics encountered in those studies can prove relevant for analyzing the Word of Faith.[81] Also, Wright has consistently used the model from 1992 to date, and while his continued interaction with the latest discussions in worldview theory led to slight adaptions and modifications, the fundamental composition used here has stayed intact.[82] Generally, Wright's thinking draws on the gains from the long history of Christian worldview thinking, and his contributions to worldview scholarship have recently been acknowledged.[83] Scholars positively engage his

81. A list of possible relevant worldview dynamics includes the following: how there can be new mutations within an invariable dominant worldview, as in Paul's appropriation of the Jewish belief in resurrection (Wright, *JVG*, 316; Wright, *RSG*, 372); radical revisions of older praxis, symbol, and story, as in Jesus' life and ministry (Wright, *JVG*, 201, 466, 473); how similarity of language can hide profoundly different worldviews, as in the Gospel of Thomas using "Christian language" (Wright, *NTPG*, 458; cf. Wright, *RSG*, 551 681); how Christian vocabulary can be filled with non-Christian content, as in platonic usage of "resurrection" (Wright, *RSG*, 84); how worldview stories can be told for subversive aims, as in the gospel and the Roman empire; how there can be changes of metaphor while a dominant worldview story remains intact, as in Paul's theology of the resurrection (Wright, *RSG*, 371); how foreign and powerful worldviews seek to dominate and domesticate smaller worldviews, as in Hellenization of Judaism; how new circumstances and experiences requires reinterpretation or reexpressions of a worldview, as in early Christian expectations of resurrection reimagined Jewish expectations (Wright, *RSG*, 87); how an experience requires a transformation of worldview, as in Paul's conversion experience; how symbols can be radically transformed while the story remains, as in how early Christians viewed the Jewish symbols (Wright, *NTPG*, 456); how a person can move on a spectrum of beliefs yet remain within the same worldview, as in Paul's revision of Jewish beliefs (Wright, *RSG*, 372; cf. Wright, *NTPG*, 244, 378); whether what looks like an exchange of worldview in actuality is a radical adjustment of the same, as in Paul's reframing of the Jewish worldview (Wright, *PFG*, 34); how there can be a change of literary and rhetorical style while retaining a worldview, as in some of Josephus' writings (Wright, *NTPG*, 287); how worldviews affect interpretation of Scriptures, as in a dualistic reading of New Testament passages (Wright, *RSG*, 462–3).

82. N. T. Wright, "The Challenge of Dialogue: A Partial and Preliminary Response," in *God and the Faithfulness of Paul: A Critical Examination of the Pauline Theology of N. T. Wright*, ed. Christoph Heilig, Thomas Hewitt and Michael Bird (Minneapolis: Fortress, 2017), 713.

83. "Wright's understanding of worldview is firmly based in the tradition of worldview analysis stemming from Abraham Kuyper" (Sire, *NTE*, 57). "Wright's emphasis on worldview analysis is consistent with what research in this area has brought out and therefore well founded" (Stewart, "N. T. Wright's Hermeneutic," 256). E.g., Goheen and Bartholomew, *Living at the Crossroads*, 16.

model, making their own adaptions and usage of it.[84] Applying Wright's model to analyze the Word of Faith worldview should, therefore, be seen as another creative application of it.

Third, Wright's overall worldview thinking could be criticized for reflecting what some might call overly modernistic conceptions of culture and religion.[85] Wright's model fuels expectations of finding at least some level of coherence in the worldviews under scrutiny. Hopes of finding ordered patterns can lead the researcher to look for patterns where none exist, perhaps forcing the given data into foreign images.[86] It could be argued that very few—if any—communities or individuals throughout history have had such a clean and structured worldview as Wright's worldview-model projects. These questions, therefore, need to be asked of Wright's model: Must all worldviews have integrated and compatible elements to qualify as a genuine worldview? Also, does human action by necessity flow consistently from a worldview?[87] Do not fragmented, abstracted, and mutually incompatible elements also make up "real" worldviews in their way?[88] These concerns are not foreign to Wright, who speaks to the complexity of life and how one must allow for the "real-life worldview messiness" as a critical

---

84. E.g., Mark Cartledge, *Encountering the Spirit* (London: Darton, Longman and Todd, 2006), 28–30; Michael Goheen and Craig Bartholomew, *The Drama of Scripture*, 2nd ed. (Grand Rapids: Baker Academic, 2014), 15; Goheen and Bartholomew, *Living at the Crossroads*; Brian Tabb, *Suffering in Ancient Worldview: Luke, Seneca and 4 Maccabees in Dialogue* (London: Bloomsbury, 2017); Brian Godawa, *Hollywood Worldviews*, 2nd ed. (Downers Grove: IVP, 2009), 14, 23.

85. Cf. e.g., Kathryn Tanner, *Theories of Culture* (Minneapolis: Fortress, 1997), 25–60. Wright, in explaining his critical-realism epistemology, strongly distances himself from historical positivism (Wright, *NTPG*, 31–46).

86. Richard Hays writes: "the story in Tom's [Wright] viewfinder is not exactly any of the specific stories actually told by the Evangelists; rather, it is a critically abstracted construct, the master narrative of the Bible. . . . The question that haunts many readers of *JVG* is whether Tom's synthetic construct is too clever by half, whether it obsessively forces all the evidence into the single mould of the exile and return pattern" [Richard Hays, "Knowing Jesus: Story History and the Question of Truth," in *Jesus, Paul and the People of God: A Theological Dialogue with N. T. Wright*, ed. Nicholas Perrin and Richard Hays (London: SPCK, 2011) 49, 55]. Cf. Luke Timothy Johnson, review of *The New Testament and the People of God*, by Nicholas Thomas Wright, *Journal of Biblical Literature* 113, no. 3 (1994), 536–8; Luke Timothy Johnson, "A Historiographical Response to Wright's Jesus," in *Jesus and the Restoration of Israel: A Critical Assessment of N. T. Wright's Jesus and the Victory of God*, ed. Carey Newman (Downers Grove: IVP, 1999), 206–24.

87. Johnson, "Historiographical Response," 213.

88. James Herrick, "Response to Albert Wolters," in *After Worldview: Christian Higher Education in Postmodern Worlds*, ed. J. Matthew Bonzo and Michael Stevens (Sioux Center: Dordt College Press, 2009), 116.

aspect in worldview examinations.[89] He is also open for the possibility of internal contradictions and tensions within worldviews. Moreover, Wright makes room for lived life to have the final evaluative word on what hypotheses the worldview-analysis generates. However, despite these caveats, the danger remains that the model leads the researcher to harmonize the data within the model's elements. I seek to avoid this pitfall by a close and faithful reading of multiple primary sources.

The impact of Clifford Geertz on Wright's thinking can also pose a problem to some.[90] Geertz characterized his "interpretative anthropology" as concerned with "the systems of meaning—beliefs, values, world views [*sic*], forms of feeling, styles of thought—in terms of which particular peoples construct their existence and live out their particular lives."[91] Geertz also emphasized a close connection between symbol, myth, and ritual.[92] This influence, coupled with attention to his well-known call to a "thick description," have clear and openly acknowledged resonances in Wright.[93] Some scholars express hesitations with and even rejection of Geertz's characterization of culture and religion.[94] Yet, since scholars of Pentecostalism recognize in Geertz's basic approach an ongoing significance and applicability for religious research, there are hardly any reasons why Wright's debt to Geertz should negatively influence the usage of his worldview-model in this project.[95] Overall, Wright's model for analyzing worldviews promises to be a valuable approach to analyze the Word of Faith.

89. Wright, *RSG*, 464. See Wilkens and Sanford, *Hidden Worldviews*, 15–18; Olthuis, "Where There Is Love," 87.

90. Wright, *PFG* 26, 28, 442, 1392. See Oda Wishemeyer, "N. T. Wright and Biblical Hermeneutics," in *God and the Faithfulness of Paul: A Critical Examination of the Pauline Theology of N. T. Wright*, ed. Christoph Heilig, Thomas Hewitt and Michael Bird, 82.

91. Clifford Geertz, "An Inconstant Profession: The Anthropological Life in Interesting Times," *Annual Review of Anthropology* 31 (2002): 10.

92. Geertz, *Interpretation of Cultures*, 127.

93. For example, Wright, *PFG*, 25.

94. For discussions on Geertz, cf. Kevin Schilbrack, "Religion, Models of, and Reality: Are We Through with Geertz?" *Journal of the American Academy of Religion* 73, no. 2 (2005): 429–52.

95. Amos Yong writes, "Geertz's cultural anthropology . . . can be an extremely useful, and at times even normative, tool for the theological interpretation of religious phenomena" [Amos Yong, "'Tongues,' Theology and the Social Sciences: A Pentecostal Theological Reading of Geertz's Interpretive Theory of Religion," *Cyberjournal for Pentecostal-Charismatic Research* 1 (1997), quoted in Wolfgang Vondey, "Conclusion: Christianity and Renewal – A Plea for Interdisciplinarity," in *The Holy Spirit and the Christian Life*, ed. Wolfgang Vondey (New York: Palgrave Macmillan), 218]; Wolfgang Vondey, "Conclusion: Christianity and Renewal – A Plea for Interdisciplinarity," in *The Holy Spirit and the Christian Life*, ed. Wolfgang Vondey (New York: Palgrave Macmillan), 216–25; Cox, *Market*, 256.

2.3.3 Wright and Worldview Concerns

Before applying Wright's model to the Word of Faith, scholarly concerns about the term and concept of worldview need to be addressed. The unease is for three key reasons, and I can now show how Wright responds to these concerns.[96] First, "worldview" is critiqued to be an ocularcentric term that speaks to the hegemony of vision. As such, world*view* falsely privileges sight above other critically important meaning-making aspects (e.g., sound).[97] This hegemony of vision has modernistic undertones and portrays the human agent as a rational and passive theoretical observer instead of an embodied, affective, and actively engaged participant in the process of engaging the world.[98] The second point of critique (related to the first) is that worldview leads to an overemphasis on the cognitive dimensions in the process of worldview formation. An intellectualist approach, it is argued, neglects the embodied nature of human meaning-making.[99] Third, worldview is critiqued for being used as a totalizing, one-size-fits-all term. In this view, worldview is part of a discourse of oppression that does not acknowledge how individuals and communities can differ in their view of the world.[100] The concept neglects its limitations, overlooking particularities and forces uniformity among the data. Many who adhere to a "postmodernist orientation" critique the concept of worldview for representing a singular, totalizing, and truthful representation of objective reality. "Postmoderns reject the possibility of constructing a single correct worldview and are content simply to speak of many views and, by extension, many worlds."[101] The postmodern "incredulity towards metanarratives" leads to a rejection of normative worldview talk as a discourse of power and oppression, thus conflating worldview with ideology.[102]

96. Hiebert, *Transforming Worldviews*, 15; Naugle, *Worldview*, 331–45; Goheen and Bartholomew, *Living at the Crossroads*, 19–32; Anderson, Clark, Naugle, *ICW*, 56–64.

97. See Alister E. McGrath, *Re-Imagining Nature: The Promise of a Christian Natural Theology* (Chichester: John Wiley and Sons, 2017), 57; Olthuis, "Where There Is Love," 88.

98. Hiebert, *Transforming Worldviews*, 23; Olthuis, "Where There Is Love," 88.

99. This is especially laid out in James K. A. Smith's *Cultural Liturgy* series [James K. A. Smith, *Desiring the Kingdom: Worship, Worldview and Cultural Formation* (Grand Rapids: Baker, 2009); James K. A. Smith, *Imagining the Kingdom: How Worship Works* (Grand Rapids: Baker, 2013); James K. A. Smith, *Awaiting the King* (Grand Rapids: Baker, 2017)]. Cf. Elmer John Thiessen, "Educating Our Desires for God's Kingdom," *International Journal of Christianity & Education* 14, no. 1 (2010): 47–53; Sire, *NTE*, 64–7; Anderson, Clark and Naugle, *ICW*, 58–63.

100. Hiebert, *Transforming Worldviews*, 15.

101. Grenz, *A Primer on Postmodernism*, 46. "Much of postmodernism—Derridiean deconstruction in particular—is geared to the task of enabling individuals and societies to realize that they have created their own worlds, and that there is nothing transcendent, permanent, natural, or supernatural about them" (Naugle, *Worldview*, 179).

102. Stanley Grenz, *A Primer on Postmodernism* (Grand Rapids: Eerdmans, 1996), 46. See Brian Walsh, "Transformation: Dynamic Worldview or Repressive Ideology?" *Journal*

Wright's worldview thinking addresses the critique of inherent ocularcentrism, cognitive overemphasis, and worldview as a discourse of oppression. First, Wright agrees that the term does privilege vision. However, he also admits to struggling to find a word that better describes the phenomenon of reality-perceiving frameworks.[103] Wright follows Paul Hiebert's justification for the continued usage of the term: "worldview" "is widely known and because we lack a better and more precise term."[104] So, in resonance with the pragmatic rationality of other worldview scholars, Wright chooses to "persist"[105] in using worldview. Responding to the second critique of worldview's overly cognitive emphasis, Wright claims that he developed the model to counter precisely such objections and therefore incorporated other aspects of human life, particularly the dimensions of praxis, story, and symbol.[106]

Wright's worldview thinking also carries a response to the third "postmodern concern" with the oppressive power of worldview. It should initially be noted that the indexical nature of the term demands that "worldview" is interpreted from the perspective of each user. What for postmoderns is an illegitimate usage cannot hinder Wright to define and use worldview differently. Wright's usage of worldview to probe the influence of pretheoretical commitments in human meaning-making is something which lies close to postmodern interests. Wright's understanding

---

of *Education and Christian Belief* 4, no. 2 (2000): 101–14; Olthuis, "Where There Is Love," 86; Olthuis, "On Worldviews," 34; McGrath, *Narrative Apologetics,* 43.

103. He notes that his approach does "include many dimensions of human existence other than simply theory" (Wright, *NTPG*, 123).

104. Hiebert, *Transforming Worldviews*, 15. He would as well second the Christian philosopher Albert Wolters' reference to Churchill's saying about democracy as an apology for the ongoing usage of worldview: "Democracy is the worst form of government except for all those other forms that have been tried from time to time" [quoted in Albert Wolters, "Appropriating *Weltanschauung*: On Jerusalem's Speaking the Language of Athens," in *After Worldview: Christian Higher Education in Postmodern Worlds*, ed. J. Matthew Bonzo and Michael Stevens (Sioux Center: Dordt College Press, 2009), 111].

105. Wright, "Challenge of Dialogue," 713.

106. Wright, *NTPG*, 123; Wright, *PFG*, 27–8, 28 fn. 80, 36. "This sense of a totality is part of what I have tried to indicate with the worldview-model which I and others have developed, recognizing that the word 'worldview' itself can, for some, point to a rather modern sense of 'detached ideas', but redefining it so as to bring into full and appropriately complex integration the life and tradition within which the ideas and theories mean what they mean and make the sense they make" (Wright, *PFG*, 232–3). Despite this, Wright is recently critiqued for placing an undue emphasis on the cognitive dimensions of worldview formation. Such critique is probably justified in regards to Wright's *application* of his model, but that has little effect on my present research as I only make use of the model which is holistic [Volker Rabens, "The Faithfulness of God and Its Effects on Faithful Living," in *God and the Faithfulness of Paul: A Critical Examination of the Pauline Theology of N. T. Wright*, ed. Christoph Heilig, Thomas Hewitt and Michael Bird (Minneapolis: Fortress, 2017), 568].

of worldview as a reality-perceiving framework that is formed pretheoretically and which affects all other interpretations arguably accords with postmodern sympathies rather than with modern ones. Though Wright does not directly address the power aspect of worldview, indirectly his preference for worldview thinking arises from a desire to not project any foreign worldview on the biblical texts and so free biblical studies and Jesus scholarship from different and limiting paradigms (mostly modernism) that hinder a faithful reading of the biblical texts.[107] Thus, for Wright, worldview-analysis is the very opposite of oppression; it frees the subject (e.g., a group, person, or text) to be heard from their context as well as making us appreciate and value other, perhaps contrary, perceptions of the world. Further, Wright does not see worldview-analysis as an exact science but as an ever-ongoing process within the hermeneutical circle.[108] Worldview-analysis should, therefore, never be canonized, but must always remain open for revision and refinement, even from other worldviews; "with worldview analysis there must always be a perhaps."[109] The aforementioned discussions speak to the strengths of Wright's holistic conception of worldview and his model for analysis and its relevance for studying the Word of Faith.

2.3.4 Wright's Worldview-Model Applied to the Word of Faith

I conclude, in light of the aforementioned, that worldview remains a relevant and useful concept that holds untapped potential for analyzing the Word of Faith. Adopting Wright's worldview-model promises to accomplish the book's dominant task of a holistic worldview-analysis of the movement. Wright's focus on the four elements of story, praxis, symbol, and ultimate beliefs is practically useful because it offers a way to engage the worldview of the Word of Faith holistically, investigating its narrative, semiotic, practical, and propositional dimensions. Wright's approach to worldview can also incorporate findings from the four scholarly models examined in the last chapter while also adding additional complexity and nuance since Wright transcends the limitations in these models.

In the second part of this book, I turn to apply Wright's model to the Word of Faith movement. The basic application of the model is straightforward; each of the elements identifies a distinct task. The following four chapters are dedicated individually to each of the four worldview-elements: story in Chapter 3, symbol in Chapter 4, praxis in Chapter 5, and ultimate beliefs in Chapter 6. This ordering of the elements follows Wright.[110] The chapters continue along the same three-step structure: The first step in each chapter is to critically engage Wright's conception of the element and its general function in worldviews. This is followed in the

---

107. Wright, *NTPG*, 31–46.

108. Wright, *PFG*, 24.

109. Wright, *PFG*, 555. "Worldviews and life, as everyone recognizes, are works in progress" (Anderson, Clark, Naugle, *ICW,* 216); Sire, *Universe Next Door*, 281.

110. E.g., Wright, *NTPG,* 215–338.

second step by laying out the method for applying the particular element to the Word of Faith movement. The element in the third step is applied accordingly, and the results are analyzed as to what insights they provide into the worldview of the Word of Faith and speak to the three goals set out in the Introduction.

Conclusion

The ultimate aim of this book is to reach a "thicker description" of the Word of Faith beyond that generated by the four models used by current scholarship on the movement.[111] This I seek to achieve through conducting a worldview-analysis of the Word of Faith. This chapter showed that despite "worldview" being a favored concept in Christian scholarship and used in studies on the Word of Faith, the meaning of the term is ambiguous and faces critique. Worldview's indexical character, the worldview-dependent nature of all worldview thinking as well the critique of the term as ocularcentrist, carrying a cognitive overemphasis and making a discourse of oppression, taken together require a well-defined understanding of worldview that adequately addresses these concerns. This chapter also noted two usages of worldview in studies on the Word of Faith (either worldview as a pattern of thought or worldview as a pattern of life) while to date no study employs worldview as a model to conduct a holistic worldview-analysis of the Word of Faith. The worldview theory and model for worldview-analysis found in the work of Wright meaningfully addresses the concerns raised against the use of worldview. Wright's holistic approach to worldview includes both aspects of worldview as system of thought and pattern of life, and his model's four elements allow me to study the Word of Faith's narrative, semiotic, practical, and propositional dimensions, making his worldview-model fitting to reach the analytical, evaluative, and comparative goals set for this book. In the remaining chapters, I apply in turn each of the model's four elements to the Word of Faith. I now move to the first of these, which is story.

---

111. Cf. Olthuis thinks that worldview-analysis, because of its inherent nature as a faith activity, is less "thick" than often projected (Olthuis, "Where There Is Love," 88).

Chapter 3

STORY IN THE WORD OF FAITH WORLDVIEW

Analyzing the Word of Faith through Wright's worldview-model, I mean to reach this book's analytical, evaluative, and comparative goals. Wright's fourfold model offers a holistic way to explore the worldview's narrative, semiotic, practical, and propositional dimensions and so to add complexity and nuance to current characterizations of the Word of Faith. This chapter applies Wright's element of story to identify, narrate, and analyze the narrative aspect of the Word of Faith worldview. Because story is primary in Wright's model and the findings here form the basis for the following analyses of the Word of Faith worldview, this chapter is more extensive than the others.

This chapter follows the basic division of description, application, and analysis shared with the following three chapters where I apply the other elements of Wright's model. The first section defines the key terms and explores Wright's understanding of the nature and functions of story in worldviews. In the second section I apply the element of story to the Word of Faith. I begin by showing how Word of Faith discourse contains the explicit echoes of a shared plot, which I term the "Adam plot." I then correlate the plot with the distinctive Word of Faith beliefs to narrate the hypothetical constructed story of "Eden Redeemed" and then conduct a narrative analysis of the story's five sequences, using the narrative categories adopted from A. J. Greimas. I plot the narrative entities from each of the five sequences of the story into diagrams to display their role in the story. Each of the narrative entities is then analyzed to bring out the story's inner logic, its themes, coherence, fidelity, and possible transformations. The analysis reveals, among other things, a competing prosperity narrative which recasts prosperity from means to end. I also discuss five weaknesses in the Word of Faith movement which underlie the rise of such "prosperity gospel" that makes personal prosperity the believer's objective. I conclude by recording the three most significant insights gained into the Word of Faith worldview.

3.1 Story in Worldview

This section offers the reader the essential context needed for the following tasks of identifying, narrating, and analyzing the narrative dimension of the Word of

Faith worldview. After defining key terms, I then proceed to discuss the nature and functions of Wright's element of story in worldviews. Story makes the proper starting point in applying the model because Wright privileges story and its foundational role in his model to express the worldview more explicitly than symbol, praxis, and ultimate beliefs do.[1]

3.1.1 Definition of Key Terms

I use "story," not just in reference to Wright's worldview-element but also as the chronological sequence of events, moving forward in time from a beginning, via a middle to an end.[2] "Narrative discourse" speaks of the story as narrated, that is, the means through which events are communicated.[3] This follows what is termed "a common view" among narratologists.[4] Contrary to story, narrative discourse is

---

1. Wright, *NTPG*, 132, 123; Wright, *JVG*, 142; Wright, *RSG*, 38. To what extent Wright does privilege story is discussed. See Stephen Kuhrt, *Tom Wright for Everyone* (London: SPCK), 33; Michael Goheen, "The Urgency of Reading the Bible as One Story," *Theology Today* 6, no. 4 (2008): 469–83; Timothy Senapatiratne, "A Pneumatological Addition to N. T. Wright's Hermeneutic Done in the Pentecostal Tradition," in *Pentecostal Theology and the Theological Vision of N. T. Wright*, ed. Janet Meyer Everts and Jeffrey Lamp (Cleveland: CPT Press, 2015), 46–8; cf. Wright, "Word and the Wind," 161. Wright, *NTPG*, 38–46. See also Jerome Bruner, *Actual Minds, Possible Worlds* (London: Harvard University Press, 1986), 11–43; Walter Fisher, *Human Communication as Narration* (Columbia: University of South Carolina Press, 1989), 57–84; Herbert Anderson and Edward Foley, *Mighty Stories, Dangerous Rituals* (San Francisco: Jossey-Bass, 1998), 3–19; Lee Roy Beach, *Narrative Thought* (self pub., Xlibris, 2010), 33–57; Alister E. McGrath, "Narratives of Significance," in *Theologically Engaged Anthropology*, ed. J. Dereck Lemons (Oxford: Oxford University Press, 2018), 123–39; Alister E. McGrath, *Narrative Apologetics: Sharing the Relevance, Joy, and Wonder of the Christian Faith* (Grand Rapids: BakerBooks, 2019), 9–10; Naugle writes, "Human beings, as semiotic creatures and inherent storytellers, come to grips with themselves and nature of life in the cosmos through the formation of worldviews as systems of narrative signs that form a basic outlook on life. They provide narrative answers to the fundamental questions about the realm of the divine, the nature of the cosmos, the identity of human beings, the solution to the problem of suffering and pain, and so on. Even the seemingly nonnarratival aspects of a *Weltanschauung*—its doctrinal, ethical, or ritual dimensions—can be explained by a fundamental narrative content" (Naugle, *Worldview*, 302).

2. See H. Porter Abbott, *Cambridge Introduction to Narrative* (Cambridge: Cambridge University Press, 2008), xiii, 13–27, 41, 241; H. Porter Abbott, "Story, Plot, and Narration," in *The Cambridge Companion to Narrative*, ed. David Herman, (Cambridge: Cambridge University Press, 2007), 39–51; Marie-Laure Ryan, "Toward a Definition of Narrative," in *The Cambridge Companion to Narrative*, 22–35.

3. Seymour Chatman, *Story and Discourse* (Ithaca: Cornell University Press, 1978), 19.

4. Making a story versus narrative discourse distinction is a foundational axiom in narrative criticism and one that will be followed here. Kent Puckett, "Narrative Theory's

not bound in its presentation of the order of events in chronological time nor need it cover all events but is free to reshuffle a selection of events as the creator sees fit. I use "narrative" in an inclusive sense, as the representation of events.[5] Narrative thus comprises story (events) and narrative discourse (representation). Story can be thought of as the "what" of narrative while narrative discourse represents the "how."[6] "Plot" is understood here—not as a synonym to story—but to mean the distribution of events, that is, the chain of causally connected events in the story.[7] I use "discourse" in its basic sense of referring to written and oral communication.[8] When the context so necessitates, I refer to Wright's element of story (following Wright) as "worldview-story" to distinguish the model's element from story in general.[9]

3.1.2 Nature and Functions of Worldview-Story

Story is one of the four irreducible components of all worldviews according to Wright, because "worldviews provide the stories through which human beings view reality. Narrative is the most characteristic expression of worldview, going deeper than the isolated observation or fragmented remark."[10] Stories invest events with meaning, serving key hermeneutical and epistemological functions of finding and bringing order, coherence, and sense to the fragmentary experiences

Longue Durée" in *The Cambridge Companion to Narrative Theory,* ed. Matthew Garrett, (Cambridge: Cambridge University Press, 2018), 15; Gérard Genette, *Narrative Discourse Revisited,* trans. Jane E. Lewin (Ithaca: Cornell University Press, 1988), 13; Marie-Laure Ryan, "Narrative," *Routledge Encyclopaedia of Narrative Theory,* ed. David Herman, Manferd Jahn and Marie-Laure Ryan (London: Routledge, 2005), s.v. "Narrative;" Abbott, *Cambridge Introduction to Narrative,* xiii.

    5. Ryan, "Toward a Definition of Narrative," 23. Cf. Wright, *PFG,* 462.

    6. Chatman, *Story and Discourse,* 19.

    7. Abbott, "Story, Plot, and Narration," 43–4; Abbott, *Cambridge Introduction to Narrative,* 240; Hilary Dannenberg, "Plot," in Routledge Encyclopedia of Narrative Theory, ed. David Herman, Manfred Jahn and Marie-Laure Ryan (London: Routledge, 2010), s.v. "Plot."

    8. *The Cambridge Advanced Learner's Dictionary & Thesaurus,* 4th ed. (Cambridge: Cambridge University Press, 2013), s.v. "Discourse."

    9. Wright, *NTPG,* 103, 396; Wright, *PFG,* 465. See also Naugle, *Worldview,* 302; Naugle, "Worldview: History, Theology, Implications," 21; Sire uses "master narrative" and "master story" (Sire, *NTE,* 145).

    10. Wright, *NTPG,* 123, emphasis original, 125, 132; e.g., Wright, *RSG,* 305. See Steffen, *Worldview-based Storying,* 137–60; Naugle, *Worldview;* Naugle, "Worldview: History, Theology, Implications;" Naugle, "Narrative and Life: The Central Role of Stories in Human Experience," Paper presented at Friday Symposium, Dallas Baptist University, February 5, 1999, accessed April 7, 2021, https://www3.dbu.edu/Naugle/pdf/narrative_and_life.pdf.

of reality.[11] This is why stories—rather than "unstoried ideas"[12]—are "the best way of talking about the way the world actually is."[13] Positively, they can articulate, embody, legitimate, and reinforce a worldview. In a critical function, stories have the power to challenge, modify, subvert, and even destroy the worldviews to which they relate.[14]

Wright's underlying assumption follows a standard line in worldview scholarship that sees narrative as an irreducible element in human consciousness and meaning-making.[15] For him, humans are storytelling creatures—*homo narrator*—who live within a "controlling story-world."[16] Underlying stories work as scripts by which humans structure their lives, the plays in which they see themselves as actors.[17] In this way, stories possess the power to change how people think, feel, and behave and so can alter the way the world is.[18]

The worldview-element of story must not be confused with any other type of community-shared narrative(s). The type of worldview-story speaks of a specific, overarching narrative that exists at the core of a worldview and serves certain functions.[19] A worldview-story provides its owner community with an implicit lens through which its inhabitants interpret, makes sense of and act upon

---

11. Wright, *NTPG*, 79, 38, 37, 115–16; Wright, *RSG*, 719. Theories are concerned with facts that speak about the givens of the world, while stories are "more foundational than 'facts'; the parts must be seen in the light of the whole" (Wright, *NTPG*, 83). A desire for reality becomes a quest for finding a worldview-story. This stands in contrast to a desire for "truth," which becomes a quest for facts (Hiebert, *Transforming Worldviews*, 29); "What larger narrative(s) does the sentence belong in? What worldviews do such narratives embody and reinforce? What are the universes of discourse within which this sentence, and the event it refers to, settle down and make themselves at home—and which, at the same time, they challenge and reshape from within?" (Wright, *RSG*, 720).

12. Wright, *NTPG*, 6.

13. Wright, *NTPG*, 40. See Goheen and Bartholomew, *Living at the Crossroads*, xiv. In his development of story, its importance for humans and its place in the meaning-making process, Wright draws particularly on the thought of the philosopher Alasdair MacIntyre (Wright, *NTPG*, 38, 69).

14. Wright, *NTPG*, 40, 67, 76, 116; Wright, *RSG*, 131, 409.

15. Naugle, *Worldview*, 297–303.

16. Naugle, *Worldview*, 297–303; Wright, *RSG*, 29. "Human life, then, can be seen as grounded in and constituted by the implicit and explicit stories which humans tell themselves and one another" (Wright, *NTPG*, 38, 98). See Jonathan Gottschall, *The Storytelling Animal* (New York: Mariner, 2012); McGrath, "Narratives of Significance."

17. Wright, *JVG*, 203; Wright, *PFG*, 26. Cf. Wright, *NTPG*, 140; N. T. Wright, *Scripture and the Authority of God* (New York: HarperOne, 2005). See Christian Smith, *Moral, Believing Animals* (Oxford: Oxford University Press, 2009), 63–94.

18. Wright, *NTPG*, 69; Wright, *RSG*, 131.

19. Wright, *PFG*, 456–75.

the world.[20] The worldview-story stands apart from other shared narratives by claiming the most truthful account of the world "as is" and how to improve it (the world "as if").[21] The element of story thus stands in direct relationship to the worldview-element of ultimate beliefs, because a worldview-story provides answers to the ultimate questions of life.[22] Beyond expressing the ultimate beliefs by answering life's ultimate questions, the worldview-story also gives life and meaning to the other worldview-elements of symbol and praxis.[23] It is only a story that interpenetrates the other three worldview-elements that function as a worldview-story.[24] I explore the worldview-story's relationship to symbol, praxis, and ultimate beliefs in subsequent chapters.

For Wright, only one story (at a time) can take the preeminent role over all other stories to provide the only true account of the world and answer the ultimate questions.[25] Hence, Wright uses story in reference to the worldview-element in the singular form.[26] However, to affirm the presence of a singular story at the core of worldviews is not to deny that it can be a hybrid construction or stand in conflict with other stories, only that at a specific point in time, there is only one singular story.[27] Also, to qualify as worldview-story, the story must contain all of the parts that commonly are held to be part of a story: a beginning, middle, and end of action and characters who move forward in time.[28] Though the story can have an intricate plot with a web of sequences, at its core, the story remains unified—or

20. See, e.g., Robert Wuthnow, *American Mythos* (Princeton: Princeton University Press, 2006); Walton, *Watch This*, 179–98.

21. See Wright, *NTPG*, 112; Olthuis, "On Worldviews," 29.

22. Wright, *NTPG* 123; Wright, *RSG*, 38. "To be human is to ask questions about who we are, why we are here, and what life is all about. And most often, we answer those questions using stories" (McGrath, *Narrative Apologetics*, 9).

23. Wright, *PFG*, 508, 562.

24. Wright, *NTPG*, 103, 116, 149; Wright, *PFG*, 526.

25. See McGrath, *Narrative Apologetics*, 13.

26. E.g., Wright, *NTPG*, 123. Wright refers to the element also as: "worldview-story," "worldview-narrative," "controlling story," "foundational story," and "metanarrative" (Wright, *PFG*, 535). See Wright, *JVG*, 576, 577, 591; Wright, *PFG*, 22, 33, 110; N. T. Wright, *Paul: Fresh Perspectives* (London: SPCK, 2005), 6–7; Wright's concept of "controlling stories" is derived from Nicholas Wolterstorff's concept of "control beliefs" [Nicholas Wolterstorff, *Reason within the Bounds of Religion*, 2nd ed. (Grand Rapids: Eerdmans, 1984), 67]; see Naugle, "Worldview," 21. Though Wright seldom employs the term "myth," his understanding of the element of story in worldviews coincides with how other worldview scholars define the nature and role of myth (Wright, *NTPG*, 38; Wright, *JVG*, 341, Wright, *PFG*, 456–7). See Hiebert, *Transforming Worldviews*, 66.

27. Cf. Smith, *Moral, Believing Animals*, 63–94.

28. Abbott, *Cambridge Introduction to Narrative*, 41.

looks as such to the story's owner community.[29] On a closer examination, the story can contain tensions, conflicts, gaps, and vacuums, which challenge its internal coherence and fidelity to reality and ultimately its capacity to serve as a worldview-story.[30]

Examining worldviews involves finding the worldview-story that communities and individuals (implicitly) tell one another and the world, making sure to get the plot right.[31] Hints of a worldview-story can surface in as little as one word or phrase.[32] Failure to identify an underlying worldview-story creates a vacuum that makes the researcher vulnerable to import foreign stories, which could result in a distortion of meaning.[33]

The story gains verisimilitude when it appears coherent internally and externally when there is an apparent frictionless relation to the other worldview-elements and to experiential reality, that is, the world of which the story claims interpretative privilege.[34] If the worldview-story and experience do not "fit," inhabitants of the worldview-story sense intense uneasiness—much like cognitive dissonance—that demands a responsive action to regain equilibrium: either to reinforce the story over and above experience or to allow experience to adjust the story.[35]

Wright emphasizes the implicit nature of the worldview-story. Because a worldview-story exists *behind* shared narratives and not necessarily *in* them, it requires a hypothetical construction to be explicated.[36] Identifying an overarching—but seldom fully explicitly stated—story in the narrative discourse requires creativity and "controlled and disciplined imagination, but

---

29. See Wright, *PFG*, 535; cf. Wright, *PFG*, 484–6, 489. If one subplot is taken for the main plot, it can result in a shift of worldview (Wright, *PFG*, 490).

30. See Section 3.2.6 for my definitions of these terms.

31. Wright, *PFG*, 535; cf. Wright, *PFG*, 484–6, 489–90.

32. Wright, *PFG*, 465. Commenting on Pauline theology yet with a wider application, Wright states, "What alerts us, often enough, that 'something else is going on', something we had not bargained for, is the casual remark, the throw-away line on the edge of something else, which stands as a signpost down the passage which we did not take, toward the door we never opened" (Wright, *PFG*, 467).

33. See Wright, *PFG*, 516.

34. Walsh and Middleton, *TV*, 37–8. Fisher argues that fidelity and coherence are the two main tests for a nonfictive story claiming to convey truth. He writes, "Obviously some stories are better stories than others, more coherent, more 'true' to the way people and the world are—in perceived fact and value" (Fisher, *Human Communication*, 68); see also Anderson, Clark and Naugle, *ICW*, 77–90.

35. Leon Festinger, Henry Riecken and Stanley Schachter, *When Prophecy Fails* (Minneapolis: University of Minnesota Press, 1955), 26. See Pieterse, "The Appeal of the Word of Faith Movement," 130; Ackerly, "Importing Faith," 306–7; e.g., see Bowler, *Blessed*, 175–7.

36. Wright, *PFG*, 462–3.

imagination none the less."[37] Worldview-story analysis is much like the work of historians, biographers, and journalists who search for raw data till they find enough to render a probable "narrative explanation."[38] Yet, this makes his model to be faulted by some for looking beyond explicit narratives to impose subjective expectations and thought-patterns.[39] In response, Wright argues that expressed narratives are not likely to fully express the implicit worldview-story: "we should not expect the full picture at any given moment, but we should expect that a good hypothesis about such a necessarily implicit full picture would have considerable explanatory power."[40] Wright's analysis of a worldview-story has affinities to the critique of ideologies in narratives and involves, what narrative critics call, "symptomatic interpretation."[41] In the context of this work, symptomatic interpretation entails that we decode Word of Faith narrative discourse for evidence of an overarching worldview-story which informs and shapes the explicit narratives.

3.2 Story in the Word of Faith

On the quest to identify, narrate, and analyze the narrative dimension of the Word of Faith worldview through Wright's element of story, it is essential to distinguish between story as content and narrative discourse as the expression of the content. First, granted the assumption is correct that there is a worldview-story in the Word of Faith, it means that we are unable to access the pure story on its own. Instead, since "story is always mediated (constructed) by narrative discourse,"[42] only a critical engagement with Word of Faith discourse will help us identify a worldview-story from the narrative discourse.

---

37. Wright, *NTPG*, 114.

38. Wright, *NTPG*, 109–15; Mark Bevir, "Narrative as a Form of Explanation," *Disputatio*, no. 8 (November 2000): 10–18; McGrath, *Narrative Apologetics*, 25–7.

39. "The whole quest for implicit story, whether in Paul or anyone else, is the hunt (as with Geertz, Berger and Luckman [*sic*] and others) for the signs of a *worldview*, and a worldview is precisely that which, like a pair of spectacles, you normally look *through*, not at. It is presupposed" (Wright, *PFG*, 463, emphasis original).

40. Wright, *PFG*, 535, 463, 484–6, 489–90.

41. "Decoding a text as symptomatic of the author's unconscious or unacknowledged state of mind, or of unacknowledged cultural conditions" (Abbott, *Cambridge Introduction to Narrative*, 242). See Luc Herman and Bart Vervaeck, "Ideology," in *The Cambridge Companion to Narrative*, ed. David Herman (Cambridge: Cambridge University Press, 2007); 217–30; Patrick Williams, "Ideology and Narrative," in Routledge Encyclopedia of Narrative Theory, ed. David Herman, Manfred Jahn and Marie-Laure Ryan (London: Routledge, 2005), s.v. "Ideology and Narrative."

42. Abbott, *Cambridge Introduction to Narrative*, 21.

Second, the preliminary nature of explicating the worldview-story from Word of Faith narrative discourse is an exercise that is part of the hermeneutical spiral.[43] That is, the accuracy of the initial narrative construct depends on the abilities and insights of the reader of the Word of Faith narrative discourse. Nevertheless, as the reader's abilities and insights grow through engaging the narratives, and as they are allowed to challenge and correct possible underreadings and overreadings buried in the initial story hypothesis, the construction spirals nearer and nearer the content of the expression, and the hypothetical story is thus refined and revised, though never fully perfected. The narrative of the Word of Faith worldview-story that I present in the following text as "Eden Redeemed" is ultimately a subjective and tentative construction, which remains open to reinterpretation and refinement.[44] Subsequent findings may call for reformulations, additions, or subtractions of the initial narrative. Still, the initial narrative must be constructed at some point, otherwise revised and refined versions will remain out of reach. The proposed narrative of the Word of Faith worldview-story should, therefore, be taken as a tentative construction claiming to give an authentic representation yet still being open for revision and refinement in light of better interpretations of the Word of Faith discourse. Nevertheless, as Wright explains, "what counts [in worldview-analysis] is . . . the heuristic effect, seen quite pragmatically and indeed always provisionally; as we map the landscape, are we able to explore and understand it more effectively?"[45] And as is shown, Eden Redeemed generates new insights which add complexity and nuance to understanding the Word of Faith.

3.2.1 Echoes of a Story in Word of Faith Discourse

Scholars point to evidence of an overarching theological story in the movement's discourse giving a basic narrative structure to the Word of Faith belief system.[46] The importance of a shared plot in the Word of Faith discourse is also observed in the scholarly literature.[47] However, since minimal work has been done to analyze the plot and the story, I want to develop these insights to show that in the shared

---

43. Wright, *NTPG,* 109; See Grant Osborne, *The Hermeneutical Spiral* (Downers Grove: IVP, 1991), 8.

44. See Wright, *NTPG,* 99; Abbott, *Cambridge Introduction to Narrative,* 21.

45. Wright, *PFG,* 25.

46. Atkinson, *Spiritual Death,* 9; Barron, *Health and Wealth,* 66–7; Brandon, *Health and Wealth,* 148–51; Hanegraaff, *CIC,* 18–27; Perriman, *FHP,* 19–29, 83, 115–16; "The common thread within this otherwise diverse movement is its biblical narrative" (Reed, "Prosperity Gospel," 54); "The fundamental premise of the Word-Faith doctrine is that Adam was the god of this world" (Bowman, *Word-Faith,* 141).

47. E.g., Barron, *Health and Wealth,* 66; Bowman, *Word-Faith,* 137–45; Perriman, *FHP,* 115–16; Bowler, *Blessed,* 17–18, 97; Mary Jo Weaver and David Brakke, *Introduction to Christianity,* 4th ed. (Belmont: Wadsworth, 2009), 178; McClymond, "Prosperity Already," 297, 307–8; Nathan Ivan Walton, "Blessed and Highly Favored: The Theological

basic plot lies the essentials of a larger story. I then want to narrate that story and analyze it as a story in its own right, that is, to analyze the story's internal narrative features and dynamics. In the analysis, I critically engage the story's inner structure to test its internal coherence, fidelity to reality and identify any logic carried by the story.

Engaging Word of Faith narrative discourse gives glimpses of an underlying story. These glimpses come in the form of repeated attention given to specific narrative sequences which are drawn from the general biblical storyline of creation, fall, Israel, redemption, and consummation. Such narrative doorway is provided by an openly shared plot within Word of Faith discourse. This plot contains the chain of the causally connected key events in the Word of Faith story. The basic storyline is familiar to Pentecostals and evangelicals, yet a closer study of the Word of Faith discourse reveals that the sequences are narrated in unique ways, to the extent that they become distinct to the Word of Faith.

The main sequences come, as noted, directly from the biblical storyline, yet the content has unique elements. In the Word of Faith story, Adam was created in equality with God[48] and given absolute ruling power over the whole world and blessed with prosperity and health. But Adam surrendered his authority to Satan, who took full charge of the world. Through Jesus' redemption, Satan was defeated and Adam's original position and provision were regained. Every believer can now live in the same reality as Adam did in Eden.[49] I call this Word of Faith plot "the Adam plot." The most central narrative themes of the Adam plot are absolute ruling power over the world, the blessing of prosperity and health, and the drive to increase. The Adam plot has a clear U-shaped structure with a noticeable return theme.[50]

Anthropology of the Prosperity Gospel" (Doctor of philosophy thesis, University of Virginia, 2018), 31–2; Reed, "Prosperity Gospel," 54.

48. "He [man/Adam] was created on terms of equality with God" [Kenneth E. Hagin, *Zoe: The God-Kind of Life* (Tulsa: Faith Library Publications, 1981), 36]. See Section 3.2.6.4.

49. Copeland writes: "Man [*sic*] was created to function on God's level. Adam walked on that level in the Garden of Eden; but when he disobeyed God, he fell from his position of fellowship and oneness with God. It took Jesus coming to earth as a man to reclaim the authority Adam gave over to Satan. Today, every born-again believer can live on that supernatural level through the power of the Holy Spirit" [Kenneth Copeland, *Walking in the Realm of the Miraculous* (Forth Worth: Kenneth Copeland Publications, 1980), e-book edition, "Faith in God's Love"]. See Joseph Prince. "Born Again to Have Dominion," *Daily Grace* (blog), Joseph Prince Ministries, accessed June 6, 2020, https://www.josephprince. org/blog/daily-grace-inspirations/born-again-to-have-dominion). See also McClymond, "Prosperity Already," 308.

50. The Adam plot thus fits well into the archetypal category of "comedy" used by literary theorists. Comedy is a U-shaped story "that begins in prosperity, descends into tragedy, but rises to a happy ending as obstacles to success are overcome" [Leland Ryken, *Words of Delight*, 2nd ed. (Grand Rapids: Eerdmans, 1992), 49]; see Wright, *NTPG*, 77.

The importance of the Adam plot for this book is at least threefold. First, the plot provides an explicit and unifying core to the Word of Faith. Second, the plot shows that the core in the Word of Faith is narratival.[51] Third, and for my purposes most important, the plot functions as a suitable entry point into examining a potential worldview-story in the Word of Faith. The plot offers the researcher the chance to move from what is explicitly stated to search for the more implicit worldview-story.

Scholars have previously made limited attempts to explicate a story out of Word of Faith discourse.[52] However, four significant weaknesses can be identified in some of these presentations particularly among those who belong to the radical group (see Section 1.1.2). First, the evidence is often absent that the compositions are impartial and unbiased. Rather, the constructed narratives tend to draw too much upon controversial features, abstracting singular and radical statements that are not representative of the larger movement but were rhetorically shaped to conjure homiletical pathos.[53] Second, the constructed narratives tend to be told in a condescending tone, the narrator implicitly claiming to speak for orthodoxy.[54] Third, the general category of story is held subordinate to the primacy of rational propositions and expressed doctrinal beliefs. The narrative, therefore, serves merely illustrative purposes for a larger propositional argument shaped by the doctrinal model. Fourth, the narrative's role as a worldview-story in the Word of Faith has never been explored. No work until present systematically tries to connect such a story with the movement's semiotic, practical, and propositional dimensions.

In contrast, I want to (as far as possible) give an impartial and unbiased hearing to a wider body of Word of Faith discourse to avoid focusing on a limited selection of extreme statements. I then want to narrate the story that arises out of the discourse. Through a narrative analysis I want to examine the story based on its own merits and not use an external doctrinal grid that is held *a priori* as the orthodox canon of beliefs. That is, to analyze the story's inner structure to test its internal coherence, fidelity to reality and locate what logic it nurtures. In the coming chapters, I explore how the story interrelates with the other worldview-elements of symbol, praxis and ultimate beliefs.

3.2.2 The Adam Plot in Word of Faith Discourse

The discourse of key Word of Faith proponents gives evidence to the explicit presence of a shared plot, that is, the Adam plot. This chain of causally connected key events can be narrated differently while unmistakable traits are its U-shaped

---

51. E.g., Bowman, *Word-Faith*, e.g., 219; Ben Pugh, *Bold Faith: A Closer Look at the Five Key Ideas of Charismatic Christianity* (Eugene: Wipf and Stock, 2017), 67–87.

52. E.g., Barron, *Health and Wealth*, 66–67; Brandon, *Health and Wealth*, 148–51; Hanegraaff, *CIC*, 18–27. See also Perriman, *FHP*, 19–29, 83, 115–16.

53. Bowman, *Word-Faith*, 29–30; e.g., Hanegraaff, *CIC*, 18–27. Cf. Perriman, *FHP*, 82.

54. E.g., Hanegraaff, *CIC*, 18–27.

structure and distinctive themes of ruling power and increase. Following I give citations from key international Word of Faith leaders, past and present, to show the contours and content of the Adam plot and how it is explicitly shared in the movement. Kenneth E. Hagin is first to be considered since he is widely recognized as the father of the movement and its chief storyteller.[55] His view is followed by Kenneth Copeland and John Osteen, two of the early American formative voices in the movement. These give room to four second-generation American representatives in the form of Joyce Meyer, Creflo Dollar, Andrew Wommack, and Bill Winston. Lastly is a selection of three global voices with significant impact: David Oyedepo from Nigeria, Nicolas Duncan-Williams from Ghana, and Joseph Prince from Singapore. Taken together, these ten leaders represent a large portion of the global Word of Faith movement. By providing evidence to these leaders' usage of the Adam plot, the reader will see the essential parts of the plot and its spread among the key Word of Faith proponents. The citations substantiate the claim that the basic Adam plot is explicitly stated in the worldwide Word of Faith discourse, past and present. Evidencing the presence of this shared plot supports the central task of this chapter, which is to identify and analyze the larger story to which the Adam plot is the entry point.

The list of other key Word of Faith proponents (past and present) referencing the Adam plot could be extended significantly. Surfacing in either condensed forms or spread out through larger units of discourse, the list includes most of the movement's leaders: Gloria Copeland;[56] Kenneth W. Hagin Jr.;[57] Jerry Savelle;[58]

---

55. E.g., McConnell, *DG,* 55; Coleman, *Globalisation,* 29; Hanegraaff, *Christianity in Crisis 21st,* Kindle edition, "Chapter 3;" Perriman, *FHP,* 1; Scott Billingsley, "The Midas Touch: Kenneth E. Hagin and the Prosperity Gospel" in *Recovering the Margins of American Religious History,* ed. Dwain Waldrep (Tuscaloosa: University of Alabama Press, 2012), 43–59; Jones and Woodbridge, *HWH,* 54; Heuser, "Prosperity Theology;" Cf. Bowman, *Word-Faith,* 92; Bowler, *Blessed,* 65.

56. "Since God owns everything in heaven and in earth, He could take dominion everywhere. But He has chosen to exercise that dominion through man. He gave Adam authority over the earth in the Garden of Eden. That's why Jesus had to come into the earth and become flesh. To exercise God's dominion over Satan in the earth, He had to do it as a man" [Gloria Copeland, *Living in Heaven's Blessings Now* (Tulsa: Harrisons House, 2012), e-book edition, "A Superior Kingdom"]. See also Gloria Copeland, *Blessed Beyond Measure: Experience the Extraordinary Goodness of God* (Forth Worth: Kenneth Copeland Ministries, 2004), e-book edition, "Chapter 3."

57. Kenneth W. Hagin, *Overflow: Living Above Life's Limits* (Tulsa: Rhema Bible Church, 2006), e-book edition, "The Thief Defeated."

58. "When Adam sinned, he lost his authority. But Jesus restored that authority. . . . Satan is under our feet. Authority has been restored to you" [Jerry Savelle, *Take Charge of Your Financial Destiny* (Crowley: Jerry Savelle Ministries, 1998), 13]. See Ackerly, "Importing Faith," 214–49.

Guillermo Maldonado;[59] Charles Capps;[60] Clarence McClendon;[61] Myles Munroe;[62] Ulf Ekman;[63] Uebert Angel;[64] Paula White-Cain;[65] and Enoch Adeboye.[66] Others, such as Joel and Victoria Osteen, can employ the plot in fuzzier ways, though the U-shaped structure is still evident.[67] Bill Johnson, who is not usually considered part of the Word of Faith movement, narrates believers into the Adam plot to assume the responsibility of bringing God's miraculous power into manifestation on the earth.[68] Identifying possible formative sources to the Adam plot lies beyond

59. Guillermo Maldonado, *The Kingdom of Power* (New Kensington: Whitaker House, 2013), e-book edition, "The Original Mandate of Dominion."

60. "God delegated the first authority to Adam, but Adam turned it over to Satan. Satan entered this earth illegally. But Jesus has come that we may have life. He has come to destroy and take away those things Satan perpetrated upon man. He came to restore man to his rightful authority" [Charles Capps, *Authority in Three Worlds* (Tulsa: Harrison House, 1980), e-book edition, "Legal Authority"].

61. E.g., LoveWorld Television Ministry, "Watch Your LoveWorld Praise-A-Thon with Pastor Chris & Pastor Benny Hinn Day 3," YouTube Video, 38:14, December 11, 2019, accessed June 6, 2020, https://www.youtube.com/watch?v=BW9c2DOXnwM.

62. Myles Munroe, *The Purpose and Power of Authority* (New Kensington: Whitaker House, 2011), e-book edition, "The Betrayal of Authority;" Myles Munroe, *Applying the Kingdom* (Shippensburg: Destiny Image, 2007), e-book edition, "Introduction."

63. Ulf Ekman, *Tillintetgör Djävulens Gärningar* (Uppsala: Livets Ords Förlag, 1987), 5. See Gunnarson, "Den Kristna Gnosticismens Återkomst," 98–9, 107–8; Simon Coleman, "From excess to encompassment: Repetition, recantation, and the trashing of time in Swedish Christianities," *History and Anthropology* (2018): 1477–2612.

64. Uebert Angel, *Praying for the Impossible* (n.p.: SpiritLibrary Publications, 2012), e-book edition, "The Accuser in Action."

65. Millennium Magazine, "Pastor Paula White: Taking Ownership," *Millmag.org*, published May 19, 2020, accessed April 7, 2021, https://www.millmag.org/pastor-paula-whi te-taking-ownership-2/.

66. Sam Eyoboka and Olayinka Latona, "RCCG Convention: Adeboye prepares Christians to regain dominion," *Vanguard*, August 5, 2018, accessed April 7, 2021, https:// www.vanguardngr.com/2018/08/rccg-convention-adeboye-prepares-christians-to-regain- dominion/. See Asonzeh Ukah, "The Redeemed Christian Church of God (RCCG), Nigeria. Local Identities and Global Processes in African Pentecostalism," (Doctoral dissertation, University of Bayreuth, 2003); Ukah, "God, Wealth," 83.

67. Victoria Osteen, "Keeping Dominion," *Joel and Victoria's Blog*, Joel Osteen Ministries, September 29, 2015, accessed April 7, 2021, https://www.joelosteen.com/Pages /Blog.aspx?blogid=10587.

68. "Mankind's authority to rule was forfeited when Adam ate the forbidden fruit. . . . In that one act mankind became the slave and possession of the Evil One. All that Adam owned, including the title deed to the planet with its corresponding position of rule, became part of the devil's spoil. . . . Jesus would come to reclaim all that was lost" [Bill Johnson, *When Heaven Invades Earth* (Shippensburg: Destiny Image, 2005), 30]. See

the scope of this research. However, a decisive influence is E. W. Kenyon, who gives the Adam plot explicit and repeated place in his writings.[69] Since his relation to the Word of Faith movement is a debated issue, references to Kenyon's works are only for illustrative purposes.[70]

The first direct evidence that the basic Adam plot is explicitly shared in the past and present worldwide Word of Faith discourse comes from Hagin. He returned to the Adam plot repeatedly (credits visions of Jesus as its source) and made use of the plot as the narrative lens for how the believer presently is to view and engage the world:[71]

> God created everything; then He made man, Adam, and gave him dominion over all of it. . . . In other words, Adam was the god of this world. But Adam committed high treason and sold out to Satan. Thus, Satan became the god of this world. Jesus, however, came to redeem us from Satan's power and dominion over us. . . . That means that we have dominion over our lives. . . . We are to dominate circumstances. . . . We are to rule and reign over poverty. . . . We are to rule and reign over sickness. We are to reign as kings in life by Christ Jesus, in whom we have redemption.[72]

Hagin clearly shows the plot's U-shaped narrative sequences and the themes of ruling power and increase. The Adam plot also finds multiple echoes in Kenneth

also Bill Johnson, *Release the Power of Jesus* (Shippensburg: Destiny Image, 2009), e-book edition, "Our Original Purpose." For a discussion of Bill Johnson's theology with a focus on his healing practice, see Abigail Shuttleworth, "On Earth as It Is in Heaven: A Study of The Healing Praxis of Bill Johnson" (Doctor of philosophy thesis, University of Birmingham, 2015).

69. E.g., E. W. Kenyon, *The Bible in the Light of Our Redemption* (Lynnwood, Kenyon's Gospel Publishing Society, 1989), 35; E. W. Kenyon, *The Father and His Family* (Lynnwood, Kenyon's Gospel Publishing Society, 1998), 29–43. See McConnell, *DG*, 29–54; Bowman, *Word-Faith*, 137–45.

70. See Section 1.4.

71. See Kenneth E. Hagin, *The Midas Touch: A Balanced Approach to Biblical Prosperity* [*MT*] (Tulsa: Faith Library Publications, 2000), 17–27; Kenneth E. Hagin, *Growing up Spiritually* (Tulsa: Faith Library Publications, 1976), 135; Kenneth E. Hagin, *What to Do When Faith Seems Weak and Victory Lost* (Tulsa: Faith Library Publications, 1979), 15; Kenneth E. Hagin, *Right and Wrong Thinking* (Tulsa: Faith Library Publications, 1986), 12, 23; Kenneth E. Hagin, *The Triumphant Church* (Tulsa: Faith Library Publications, 1993) 8–10; Kenneth E. Hagin, *Biblical Keys to Financial Prosperity* (Tulsa: Faith Library Publications, 1995), 46–9; Kenneth E. Hagin, *The Art of Prayer* (Tulsa: Faith Library Publications, 1992), 3.

72. Kenneth E. Hagin, *New Thresholds of Faith* (Tulsa: Faith Library Publications, 1985), 56.

Copeland—the one considered Hagin's "real successor."[73] Copeland used the plot to substantiate an exalted anthropology and a radical kenotic Christology, to motivate believers for "supernatural" living:

> Man was created to function on God's level. Adam walked on that level in the Garden of Eden; but when he disobeyed God, he fell from his position of fellowship and oneness with God. It took Jesus coming to earth as a man to reclaim the authority Adam gave over to Satan.[74]

The Adam plot's U-shape and theme of ruling power are explicit in Copeland's quote.

John Osteen—the father and formative theological influence to Joel Osteen, who some claim "is Americas most notable twenty-first century Christian minister"—employed the Adam plot to sketch the background for God having to redeem humanity:[75]

> When God created Adam, He gave him authority to rule and reign over all He had created. As long as Adam fellowshipped with God and obeyed God's commands, he kept his authority. The moment Adam sinned, he relinquished his authority to the devil. And Satan became the god of this present world system. God commanded Adam to have dominion on earth like God had in Heaven; but through Adam's disobedience, Satan became the god of this world. . . . Satan usurped man's God-given authority and seized control of the human race.[76]

Osteen narrated the theme of ruling power in the Adam plot which follows the plot's U-shaped form.

Joyce Meyer, counted as "probably the most prominent female preacher in global Pentecostalism today"[77] and formative in the Word of Faith movement, narrates the basics of the plot to motivate believers to take personal spiritual action:

> God had given Adam and Eve dominion over everything in the Garden, but when they disobeyed Him, they lost their authority and suddenly, Satan had the

---

73. Perriman, *FHP*, 3.

74. Copeland, *Walking in the Realm*, 16. See also Kenneth Copeland, *The Blessing of the Lord* (Tulsa: Harrison House, 2012); Kenneth Copeland, *Freedom from Fear* (Forth Worth: Kenneth Copeland Ministries, 1979), e-book edition, 6; Kenneth Copeland Ministries, "What Does It Mean to Be Born Again?," *Kcm.org*, accessed April 7, 2021, https://www.kcm.org/read/questions/what-does-it-mean-be-%E2%80%9Cborn-again%E2%80%9D.

75. Sinitiere, *Salvation with a Smile*, 19–59, 211.

76. John Osteen, *Unravelling the Mystery of the Blood Covenant* (Houston: John Osteen Publications, 1988), 8–9.

77. Arlene Sánchez-Walsh, *Pentecostals in America* (New York: Columbia University Press, 2018), 91; Bowler, *Preacher's Wife*, 24.

upper hand! The Lord, in His sovereignty, thankfully already had the solution in order to redeem man back to Himself—through His son, Jesus Christ.[78]

Meyer expresses the U-shaped plot and its theme of ruling power. While the other examples here only focus on Adam, it is noteworthy that Meyer includes Eve in narrating the plot.

Creflo Dollar, a significant global African American Word of Faith megachurch pastor and televangelist, expounds on the Adam plot:[79]

> When God created Adam, he gave him dominion and authority over the earth. . . . However, when Adam rebelled against God, he turned his authority to rule over to the devil. Satan then had control over everything except the throne of God. . . . Through Jesus' death and resurrection, he defeated Satan and took back our authority to rule . . . and we have been restored to our rightful place of authority.[80]

The plot's U-shaped form with its theme of ruling power is fully stated by Dollar.

The American Word of Faith Bible teacher and televangelist Andrew Wommack narrates the Adam plot for the purpose of teaching the present power status ("authority") of believers.

> When God created man, He spoke and gave them dominion—power and authority—over all the earth. . . . God placed zero qualifications on this dominion that He gave to mankind . . . the Lord never meant for man to . . . just turn it over to Satan.[81]

Wommack's statement expresses the Adam plot's theme of absolute ruling power and Adam's surrender of it to Satan. Wommack implies the completion of the U-shaped plot in the restoration of ruling power through Jesus' redemption.

The African American Word of Faith pastor and televangelist Bill Winston develops the Adam plot for his teaching on prosperity:

> When Adam sinned in the garden of Eden, he lost more than his spiritual authority in the earth; he also lost God's ability to provide for him. The earth

---

78. Joyce Meyer Ministries, "Exercise Your Authority," Joycemeyer.org, accessed April 7, 2021, https://www.joycemeyer.org/everydayanswers/ea-teachings/exercise-your-authority.

79. Mitchem, *Name It*, 76–83; Walton, *Watch This*, 145–65.

80. Creflo Dollar Ministries, "Walk in Your Authority," Creflodollar.us, accessed, April 23, 2019, http://www.creflodollar.us/creflo-dollar-walk-in-your-authority/; ByGodsGrace, "Your Spiritual Authority and Spiritual Law Pt. 2," YouTube Video, 1:25:37, October 14, 2017, accessed June 6, 2020, https://www.youtube.com/watch?v=5FwCqcd0KJI.

81. Andrew Wommack, *The Believer's Authority* (Tulsa: Harrison House, 2009), e-book edition, "No Restrictions."

became cursed, and mankind was now under the dominion of a new "overlord," Satan.[82]

Winston's quote, like Wommack's mentioned earlier, illustrates how parts of the plot can be stated while the reaming parts of restoration through Jesus and implementation by the believer are implied and developed in the larger message.

The Adam plot finds expression through the Ghanaian megachurch leader Nicolas Duncan-Williams:

> He [God] gave man authority and responsibility over the affairs of the earth. Man, therefore, became God's delegated authority and was to fully represent God's interest on the earth. Satan, through his deceptive and manipulative acts, caused man to commit high treason. Satan stole the authority and dominion that God had given to man in the beginning. Through the work of the cross, Satan has been defeated. . . . The authority Satan stole from Adam in the Garden of Eden has been recovered by Jesus Christ and has been handed over to every believer in Christ from Pentecost to the rapture.[83]

Duncan-Williams articulates the full U-shaped Adam plot with focus on ruling power given to every believer and emphasizes the role of Satan and the believer's present dominion over evil.

The Nigerian David Oyedepo, the founder of the globally influential ministry Living Faith Churches Worldwide also known as *Winner's Chapel*, uses the Adam plot to empower believers to reject mediocrity in pursuit of personal success.[84]

> He [God] put him [Adam] in the garden and made him the god of all His works. He asked him to reign, rule and exercise dominion over every living being on earth. At the end of it all Adam became the god of this world. . . . [Satan] tempted God's man and got him to sin against God. Tragedy struck and the devil took over the administration of this world. It was legally handed over to him by Adam and no one could take it except a man [Jesus].[85]

82. Bill Winston, *Imitate God and Get Results* (Oak Park: Bill Winston Ministries, 2005), 2–3, 10.

83. Nicolas Duncan-Williams, *Binding the Strong Man* (self-pub., Xulon, 2012), e-book edition, "Introduction." See also Nicolas Duncan-Williams, *Destined to Make an Impact* (Accra: Digital iNQ, 2012), e-book edition, "Chapter 1;" Nicolas Duncan-Williams, *Prayer that Moves God* (Accra: Prayer Summit Publishing, 2015), Kindle edition, "Chapter 2."

84. Gifford, "Prosperity Theology;" Gifford, *Christianity, Development*, 29–45.

85. David Oyedepo, *Born to Win* (Lagos: Dominion Publishing House, 1993), e-book edition, "The Drama at Calvary." See also David Oyedepo, *Releasing the Supernatural* (Lagos: Dominion Publishing House, 1995), e-book edition, "Chapter 1."

Oyedepo expresses the Adam plot's main sequences and in the subsequent teachings develops how the believer is to implement their regained ruling power.

The Singaporean Word of Faith megachurch pastor and global TV-profile Joseph Prince embraces the Adam plot as the broader context in which he theologizes about healing:[86]

> When God created man, He gave man authority to have dominion over everything on earth. . . . But when man sinned, he gave this authority to Satan. And when man's authority was transferred to Satan, Satan brought in diseases, poverty, strife, bitterness, pain, loss and death.[87]

The first parts of the Adam plot are expounded by Prince. Like Wommack, Winston, and Oyedepo, the remaining parts of the plot are developed in Prince's subsequent teaching.

These citations show the plot's spread among the Word of Faith movement's key leaders, past and present, inside and outside the United States. The U-shaped structure of the plot with its theme of ruling power is evident, while the citations show how either the full plot or parts of it can be explicitly narrated depending on for what reasons it is used.

3.2.3 Eden Redeemed: Narrating the Word of Faith's Story

Building on the explicitly shared Adam plot, this section narrates the fuller, underlying story in the Word of Faith worldview. Here I follow Wright's method of narrating a fuller worldview-story from an identified plot.[88] That the Adam plot hints at a larger story and thus serves as a fitting entry point into such story is suggested by how Word of Faith discourse uses the plot to undergird various

---

86. Jeaney Yip and Susan Ainsworth, "'We Aim to Provide Excellent Service to Everyone Who Comes to Church!': Marketing Mega-Churches in Singapore," *Social Compass* 60, no. 4 (2013): 503–16; Daniel Goh, "Grace, Megachurches, and the Christian Prince in Singapore," in *Pentecostal Megachurches in Southeast Asia*, ed. Terence Chong (Singapore: ISEAS Publishing, 2018), 181–206.

87. Joseph Prince, "Jesus' Authority has been Given to Us," *Daily Grace* (blog), *Joseph Prince Ministries*, no date, accessed June 6, 2020, https://www.josephprince.org/blog/d aily-grace-inspirations/jesus-authority-has-been-given-to-us; "God gave Adam and Eve dominion over this world, but the moment Adam and Eve bit into the forbidden fruit, sin and death corrupted it. Adam and Eve ceded control of this world to the devil" [Joseph Prince, *Grace Revolution* (New York: FaithWords, 2015), e-book edition, "Speak Forth Your Authority in Christ"]; Joseph Prince, *Destined to Reign* (Tulsa: Harrison House, 2010), e-book edition, "Is There Judgment for the Believer?"

88. See Wright, *PFG*, 456–537.

key beliefs, such as prosperity,[89] the believer's position of ruling ("authority"),[90] prayer,[91] healing,[92] and positive confession.[93] To narrate the story, I therefore correlate the Adam plot with the distinctive Word of Faith beliefs expressed in the movement's discourse (I reference every part of the narration from primary sources).[94] In doing this, I develop the scholarly insight that there is a narrative structure to the Word of Faith beliefs.[95] Based on this scholarly position, I argue that the defining beliefs of the Word of Faith interconnect according to the inner logic of the Adam plot—whether explicitly stated or implicitly—and that their beliefs can, therefore, be faithfully narrated in story form. The story has to be constructed, because—true to its implicit nature as worldview-story—it is never narrated in its completeness in Word of Faith discourse. Taking the Adam plot as the entry point, the fuller story is narrated using discourse from the aforementioned key Word of Faith proponents who explicitly echoes the Adam plot—Hagin is prioritized due to his unrivaled position as the movement's fountainhead.[96]

I now expand the Adam plot to a story through correlating the plot with the distinctive Word of Faith beliefs, which gives rise to five sequences that together make the essence of the story. I label the sequences (1) "Eden," (2) "The Fall," (3) "Redemption," (4) "The Church," and (5) "Heaven." I name this five-sequence story "Eden Redeemed" because the heart of the story is for God to restore humankind to their first state of blessed vocation of dominion over the world and its resources.[97] The name draws on the explicitly stated desire in the Word of Faith of a return to Eden.[98] The Eden Redeemed story contains all features necessary

---

89. E.g., Hagin, *MT*, 17–40; Copeland, *Laws of Prosperity*, 39–42.

90. E.g., Hagin, *Believer's Authority*, 19–20; Wommack, *Believer's Authority*, e-book edition, "No Restrictions."

91. E.g., Hagin, *Art of Prayer*, 3–4; Duncan-Williams, *Prayer*, Kindle edition, "Chapter 2."

92. E.g., Kenneth Hagin, *The Bible Healing Study Course* (Tulsa: Faith Library Publications, 1999), e-book edition, "Chapter 1;" Prince, "Jesus' Authority."

93. E.g., Hagin, *Believer's Authority*, 27–44; Kenneth E. Hagin, *How to Turn Your Faith Loose* (Tulsa: Faith Library Publications, 1980), e-book edition, "Chapter 2."

94. See Chapter 1 for a discussion of the distinctive beliefs.

95. Barron, *Health and Wealth*, 66–7; Brandon, *Health and Wealth*, 148–51; Hanegraaff, *CIC*, 18–27; Perriman, *FHP*, 19–29, 83, 115–16.

96. E.g., McConnell, *DG*, 55; Coleman, *Globalisation*, 29; Hanegraaff, *Christianity in Crisis 21st*, Kindle edition, "Chapter 3;" Perriman, *FHP*, 1; Billingsley, "Midas Touch;" Jones and Woodbridge, *HWH*, 54. Cf. Bowman, *Word-Faith*, 92; Bowler, *Blessed*, 65.

97. Perriman, *FHP*, 116, 118, 139; Kenneth Copeland Ministries, "The Garden of Eden Restored," YouTube Video, 23:57, December 8, 2019, accessed April 7, 2021, https://www.youtube.com/watch?v=t1QZjdvClNs.

98. "We have to get back to where Adam was before he fell" (Winston, *Imitate God*, 10); "God is returning mankind back to where we were designed to live originally, the Garden of Eden" (Bill Winston Ministries, *According to Heaven's Economy*, Bwm.org, December

to be classified as a story and, more particularly, as a functional worldview-story. As a story, following the aforementioned definition, Eden Redeemed contains a chronological sequence of events, moving forward in time from a beginning, via a middle to an end, inclusive of actions and characters.[99] In terms of worldview-story, Eden Redeemed is a faith-based, theological story which interconnects with Wright's worldview-element of ultimate beliefs, that is, the story gives answers to the five ultimate questions about life and the world.[100] Moreover, as will be probed in the following chapters, the story also dynamically interrelates with the other worldview-elements of symbol and praxis.

Before narrating Eden Redeemed, some caveats are in order. First, Eden Redeemed is my hypothetical narrative construction, yet claims to give an authentic representation of the plot and its main sequences. Because the story is created within the hermeneutical spiral, it remains open for revision and refinement (as well as the possibility of containing error) in light of better interpretations of the Word of Faith discourse. Second, since worldview-stories tend to be precognitively absorbed rather than consciously learned, I do not claim that every Word of Faith propagator or member necessarily is fully aware of every aspect of the story or has made a rational decision to accept Eden Redeemed as part of their lens for reality.[101] Third, the claim that Eden Redeemed captures the essence of the worldview-story in the Word of Faith does not mean that one must inhabit the story in full to be classified as a Word of Faith believer. Rather, the individual mindset of many who associate with the Word of Faith movement is composed of a mixture of narrative fragments absorbed from a variety of worldview-stories (which could be contradictory).[102]

2012, accessed April 7, 2021, http://lwccportal.com/ebooks/ebook/pl122012/files/assets/downloads/publication.pdf.); Copeland, "What Does It Mean;" Copeland, *Blessing of the Lord,* e-book edition, "Yoke-Destroying, Burden-Removing Power." See Perriman, *FHP,* 116, 139; Bowler, *Blessed,* 97.

99. Abbot, *Cambridge Introduction to Narrative,* 41.

100. Wright, *NTPG,* 77–80, 122–39; Middleton and Walsh, *Truth Is Stranger,* 11, 87; Naugle, *Worldview,* 297–303; Wilkens and Sanford, *Hidden Worldviews,* 17–26; Sire, *NTE,* 119–25; Klink and Lockett, *Understanding Biblical Theology,* 93–122.

101. "any given individual who is in fact under the influence of a narrative may not fully recognize all elements of its story in his or her own life. . . . That does not reduce the power of the narrative in and over their life. It is not necessary for individuals to be fully aware of or articulate about the details or variants of the historical narratives that shape their lives or to represent in their particular experience every element of the narrative story line. Most people relate to their narratives not as literary critics or analytical philosophers but as believing actors swept up in the movement of grand historical drama. Their lives are embedded within and expressive of big stories, whether or not they can recognize every detail of any version of the story in their present life" (Smith, *Moral, Believing Animals,* 72); Wilkens and Sanford, *Hidden Worldviews,* 12–13.

102. See Bob Goudzwaard, *Idols of Our Time* (Downers Grove: IVP, 1984), 56.

Only when the Adam plot with its major sequences narrated in Eden Redeemed somehow enters the inner core of a person's or group's worldview, and so merge with symbol, praxis, and ultimate beliefs, does a person fully enters the Word of Faith world.

3.2.3.1 Eden Redeemed's Five Narrative Sequences The Eden Redeemed story is my construction based on the Adam plot correlated with the distinctive beliefs of the Word of Faith movement. The narration here follows the story's five sequences, and I retain, as far as possible, the idiom of Word of Faith discourse. I intend to let the story itself be the chief carrier of meaning for its parts (following Wright); hence, I leave all discussions of particular phrases and narrative beliefs to the subsequent analysis (Section 3.2.6). This approach is also well fitting since the Word of Faith introduces some unique beliefs and interpretations that differ from conventional definitions and interpretations, thus requiring the context of the story to be explicated. It should be noted that the number of references is representative and could be significantly extended.

Sequence 1: Eden In the beginning, God used God's faith and the spiritual law of confession to speak the world into existence.[103] God also created and placed Adam in Eden, a garden which provided the blessing of prosperity and well-being in all dimensions of human life: spiritual, economic, physical, mental, and social.[104] Adam was made in God's exact image as a spirit being,[105] yet also having a soul and living in a body.[106] As a sprit being, Adam partook of God's very nature and life;

---

103. Hagin, *Exceedingly Growing Faith*, 101; Hagin, *What to Do*, 108; Hagin, *Prevailing Prayer*, 22; Oyedepo, *Born to Win*, e-book edition, "The Fight of Faith;" Creflo Dollar, *The Divine Order of Faith* (College Park: World Changers Ministries, 1993), e-book edition, "Chapter 1;" Andrew Wommack Ministries, "Power of Faith-Filled Words," *Awmi.org*, accessed April 7, 2021, https://www.awmi.net/reading/teaching-articles/power_faith/. See also Don Gossett and E. W. Kenyon, *The Power of Your Words* (New Kensington: Whitaker House, 1981), e-book edition, "Realization Follows Confession."

104. Hagin, *Biblical Keys*; Kenneth Copeland, *The Laws of Prosperity* (Fort Worth: Kenneth Copeland Ministries, 1974); Jerry Savelle, *Why God Wants You to Prosper* (Crowley: Jerry Savelle Ministries, 2014); Copeland, *Blessed Beyond Measure*, 29. See also T. L. Osborn, *The Good Life* (Tulsa: Harrison House, 1994); John Avanzini, *John Avanzini Answers Your Questions on Biblical Economics* (Tulsa: Harrison House, 1992), 117–18.

105. See Section 3.2.6.3.

106. Hagin, *Growing Up*, 65; Hagin, *Zoe*, 27, 36–7; Hagin, *New Thresholds*, 52; Kenneth E. Hagin, *Man on Three Dimensions: Volume 1 of the Spirit, Soul, and Body Series* (Tulsa: Faith Library Publications, 1979), 8, 15, 17; Kenneth E. Hagin, *Classic Sermons* (Tulsa: Faith Library Publications, 1992), 46; David Oyedepo, *Operating in the Supernatural* (Lagos: Dominion Publishing House, 2004), e-book edition, "You Are a Spirit Being;" Oyedepo, *Born to Win*, e-book edition, "Your New Status;" Charles Capps, *Authority in Three Worlds* (Tulsa: Harrison House, 1980), e-book edition, "In His Image;" Andrew Wommack, *Spirit,*

this divine equality[107] made him to operate by the same faith and spiritual laws that God used to create the world.[108] Adam's task was to rule and increase in the world for a specific time, and to accomplish this, God had delegated to him absolute physical and spiritual authority.[109]

Sequence 2: The Fall Though life in Eden was blessed, Adam followed the tempter Satan and rebelled against God. In that act of high treason, human's spiritual nature changed into sinful, satanic nature;[110] faith was replaced with fear as he became separated from God and was spiritually dead.[111] Adam surrendered his legal authority over the world to Satan, who began to reign as the god of this

---

Soul and Body (Tulsa: Harrison House, 2010), e-book edition; Guillermo Maldonado, *Supernatural Transformation* (New Kensington: Whitaker House, 2014), e-book edition, "What is the Heart?;" Winston, *Imitate God*, 3–4; Duncan-Williams, *Destined*, e-book edition, "Chapter 1: The Story of Salvation." See also Kenyon, *The Father*, 30, 45; T. D. Jakes, *Release Your Anointing: Tapping the Power of the Holy Spirit in You* (Shippensburg, Destiny Image), e-book edition, "Humankind Is Body, Soul, and Spirit."

107. "He [man/Adam] was created on terms of equality with God" [Kenneth E. Hagin, *Zoe: The God-Kind of Life* (Tulsa: Faith Library Publications, 1981), 36]. See Section 3.2.6.4.

108. Hagin, *Zoe*; Duncan-Williams, *Destined*, e-book edition, "The Story of Salvation;" Oyedepo, *Releasing the Supernatural*, e-book edition, "Introduction." See Walton, *Watch This*, 150–2.

109. Kenneth E. Hagin, *The Believer's Authority* (Tulsa: Faith Library Publications, 1984), 33; Hagin, *What to Do*, 100; Joseph Prince, *Destined to Reign* (Tulsa: Harrison House, 2010), 143–4; Kenneth Copeland, *The Laws of Prosperity* (Fort Worth: Kenneth Copeland Ministries, 1974); Savelle, *Why God Wants You to Prosper*, e-book edition, "Prosperity Isn't a Get-rich-quick Scheme." See also Kenyon, *Father*, 34, 69; Bill Johnson, *When Heaven Invades Earth* (Shippensburg: Destiny Image, 2005), 30–1; Bill Johnson, *Hosting the Presence* (Shippensburg: Destiny Image, 2012), 37.

110. "man fell from his exalted state, he was literally 'born again.' He took upon him the nature of Satan. He became one with the devil in his satanic nature of spiritual death and was thus separated from God" (Oyedepo, *Born to Win*, e-book edition, "The Drama at Calvary"); Hagin, *Man on Three Dimensions*, 29; see Section 3.2.6.2.

111. Hagin, *Growing Up*, 106; Kenneth E. Hagin, *The New Birth* (Tulsa: Faith Library Publications, 1994), 11; Hagin, *Man on Three Dimensions*, 29–30; Kenneth E. Hagin, *The Name of Jesus* (Tulsa: Faith Library Publications, 1984), e-book edition, "Chapter 3: By Inheritance;" Hagin, *Triumphant Church*, 145; Copeland, "What Does It Mean;" Guillermo Maldonado, *How to Walk in the Supernatural* (New Kensington: Whitaker House, 2013), e-book edition, "How Humanity Lost Its Spiritual Perception." "The faith force that was born into Adam when God breathed His life into him was perverted and turned into the force that we know and recognize as fear" [Kenneth Copeland, *Force of Faith* (Forth Worth: Kenneth Copeland Publications, 1983), e-book edition, "The Force of Faith"]. See also Kenyon, *Father*, 110.

world.[112] Adam and Eve were expelled from Eden, and its blessings were replaced by the curse of physical and spiritual death, sickness, and poverty.[113]

Sequence 3: Redemption God initiated a plan of redemption to regain the lost dominion over the world from Satan and restore humanity to Eden's blessings. It started with entering a covenant with Abraham, which later found its ultimate fulfillment in the sending of God's own son Jesus.[114] Though fully divine, Jesus operated on earth as a human anointed by the Spirit and in Adam's lost authority.[115] He thus exemplified how to live a life of faith, prosperity, and health.[116] In his dual death on the cross and in hell,[117] Jesus defeated Satan, physical and spiritual death, and the curse of sickness and poverty.[118] When Jesus was resurrected to new life,

112. Hagin, *Believer's Authority*, 19; Johnson, *Hosting the Presence*, 35; Wommack, *Believer's Authority*, e-book edition, "Chapter 6: God of This World;" Munroe, *Purpose and Power*. See also Kenyon, *Father*, 57, 69. See Bowman, *Word-Faith*, 141.

113. Kenneth E. Hagin, *Redeemed from Poverty, Sickness and Spiritual Death*, 2nd ed. (Tulsa: Faith Library Publications, 1983); Munroe, *Purpose and Power*, 65–90. See also Kenyon, *Father*, 29–42; Bill Johnson, *Release the Power of Jesus* (Shippensburg: Destiny Image, 2009), 43; Johnson, *Hosting the Presence*, 38.

114. Hagin, *Believer's Authority*; Hagin, *Right and Wrong Thinking*, 12; Copeland, *Walking in the Realm*, "Faith in God's Love;" Copeland, "What Does It Mean;" Copeland, *The Blessing*, e-book edition, "Tracking the Bloodline of the Blessing;" Capps, *Authority in Two Worlds*, 51–52; Osteen, *Unveiling the Mystery*, 10, 19–23; "The blessing of Abraham is extremely powerful. It started out as the blessing of Adam. It is the creative power and dominion God bestowed on man" (Kenneth Copeland, "No Poor among You," *Believer's Voice of Victory*, October 2018, 7). See also Johnson, *Hosting the Presence*, 38.

115. Prince, "Born Again to Have Dominion."

116. Hagin, *New Thresholds*, 81; Hagin, *Triumphant Church*, 10; Hagin, *MT*, 41–66; Dollar, *Divine Order*, e-book edition, "Chapter 2: You Gotta Have Faith;" Savelle, *Spirit of Might*, e-book edition, "Equipping the Church of Jesus Christ;" Oyedepo, *Anointing for Breakthrough*, e-book edition, "The 'Poor' Jesus;" Oyedepo, *Born to Win*, e-book edition, "Drama of Calvary." See also Avanzini, *Answers Your Questions*, 118–19; Johnson, *Hosting the Presence*, 174.

117. See Section 3.2.6.14.

118. Hagin, *Triumphant Church*, 145–9; Hagin, *Biblical Keys*, 18–19; Hagin, *Present Day Ministry*, 11–12; Hagin, *Name of Jesus*, e-book edition, "Chapter 3 By Inheritance;" Joyce Meyer, *The Most Important Decision You Ever Make* (Tulsa: Harrison House, 1996), 39–42; Kenneth Copeland Ministries, "Did Jesus Go to Hell?," *Kcm.com*, accessed April 7, 2021, https://www.kcm.org/de/node/7893; Oyedepo, *Born to Win*, e-book edition, "The Drama at Calvary." See also E. W. Kenyon, *What Happened from the Cross to the Throne* (Lynnwood, Kenyon's Gospel Publishing Society, 1993), 60; E. W. Kenyon, *Advanced Bible Course* (Lynnwood, Kenyon's Gospel Publishing Society, 1998), 150.

he fully restored to the church Adam's authority to rule and increase in the world and Eden's lost blessings of prosperity and health.[119]

Sequence 4: The Church Restored to Eden's authority and blessings, the church made up of all born-again believers is now to rule and increase in the world and spread the gospel of Jesus.[120] To this end, the Holy Spirit empowers the believer through spiritual gifts and provides revelation knowledge from the Bible to inspire faith and give instructions on utilizing authority and the spiritual laws of confession and sowing and reaping.[121] Prosperity and health are the rights of every believer, waiting to be realized from the spiritual realm for the ultimate purpose of bringing the gospel of Jesus to those under Satan's rulership.[122] The defeated Satan and demons are still present, working to thwart God's plan for the believer to rule and increase in the world by keeping the believer in ignorance and under the curse of poverty and sickness.[123]

Sequence 5: Heaven When the time expires on the lease of the earth that God gave Adam in Eden, Jesus will return.[124] Jesus will completely destroy Satan, judge sinful humanity, and bring the saved spirit of every born-again believer into heaven's fullness.[125]

119. Hagin, *Believer's Authority*, e.g., 11, 39; Copeland, *Blessing of the Lord*, e-book edition, "Not Just Weed-Pullers;" Munroe, *Purpose and Power*; Prince, *Destined to Reign*, e-book edition, "Destined to Reign;" Capps, *Authority in Three Worlds*, e-book edition, "Legal Authority."

120. Hagin, *Triumphant Church*.

121. Kenneth E. Hagin, *Knowing What Belongs to Us* (Tulsa: Faith Library Publications, 1989), 5; Hagin, *Growing Up*, 73; Hagin, *Triumphant Church*, 10; Copeland, *Laws of Prosperity*, 15–21; Winston, *Imitate God*, 4–5. See also Kenyon, *Father*, 199; Johnson, *When Heaven Invades*, 31.

122. Hagin, *Redeemed*; Copeland, *Giving and Receiving*; Gloria Copeland, *Harvest of Health* (Fort Worth: Kenneth Copeland Ministries, 1992); Savelle, *Why God Wants*, e-book edition, "Introduction;" Charles Capps, *Seedtime and Harvest* (England: Capps Publishing, 1988); Creflo Dollar, "The Blessings of Good Health and Long Life," *Creflodollarmin istries.org*, July 18, 2018, accessed April 7, 2021, https://www.creflodollarministries.org/Bible-Study/Articles/The-Blessings-of-Good-Health-and-Long-Life?returnUrl=%2FBible-Study%2FArticles%3Fpage%3D3; Andrew Wommack, "You Already God It!," *Awmi.org*, accessed April 7, 2021, https://www.awmi.net/reading/teaching-articles/already_got/.

123. Hagin, *Triumphant Church*, 171–250; Copeland, *Freedom from Fear*; Jerry Savelle, *If Satan Can't Steal Your Joy . . . He Can't Keep Your Goods*, rev. ed. (Tulsa: Harrison House, 2002), e-book edition; Winston, *Imitate God*.

124. Hagin, *Triumphant Church*, 8–10; Capps, *Authority*, e-book edition, "Adam's Lease on the Earth."

125. Hagin, *What to Do*, 23; Hagin, *Triumphant Church*, 10; Hagin, *Art of Prayer*, 4; Gloria Copeland, *Living in Heaven's Blessings Now* (Tulsa: Harrison House, 2012), e-book edition. See also Kenyon, *Father*, 35.

To better understand the story's inner structure, that is, how key entities, characters, events, and themes narrative relate to one another and what logic that nurtures, I conduct a narrative analysis.

3.2.4 *Narrative Analysis of Eden Redeemed*

So far, I have identified the Adam plot in Word of Faith discourse and narrated the story of Eden Redeemed by correlating the plot with the movement's distinctive beliefs. The third and last objective of this chapter remains, which is to conduct a narrative analysis of the story. After introducing the model used for narrative analysis, I plot the five sequences of Eden Redeemed in narrative diagrams to visibly show their structure, key entities, and their relationships. This is followed by an analysis of each of the narrative entities to reveal the story's themes, internal coherence, fidelity to reality, and possible transformations. The narrative analysis allows me to present the beliefs of the Word of Faith in a storied form as opposed to a propositional form and thus shapes a much-needed careful and sensitive reading in the pursuit of a better understanding of the worldview and its inner logic. The analysis also facilitates the application of Wright's other worldview-elements of praxis, symbol, and ultimate beliefs to the Word of Faith in the coming chapters.

To analyze Eden Redeemed, I follow Wright's method in analyzing worldview-stories through the categories for narrative analysis developed by A. J. Greimas.[126] A combination of how Wright and Richard Middleton use Greimas is employed here because together it makes Greimas' original diagram more accessible and useful for my purposes of visibly showing the inner structure of the story and to analyze it.[127] Structuralism, in which Greimas constructed his so-called actantial approach, has declined after the 1970s, and I do not mean to draw from or engage this semiotic theory.[128] Neither do I (like Wright) claim that Greimas' method embraces all narratives, only that it promises to bring out aspects of the Word of Faith worldview-story that otherwise would be hard to spot.[129] Greimas' graphic depiction continues to be used by narratologists and theologians, who

126. Robin Parry, "Narrative Criticism," in *The Dictionary for Theological Interpretation of the Bible*, ed. Kevin J. Vanhoozer (Grand Rapids: Baker, 2005), 528–31; Patrick O'Neill, "Narrative Structure," *Routledge Encyclopaedia of Narrative Theory*, ed. David Herman, Manferd Jahn and Marie-Laure Ryan (London: Routledge, 2005), s.v. "Narrative Structure;" David Herman, "Actant," *Routledge Encyclopaedia of Narrative Theory*, ed. David Herman, Manferd Jahn and Marie-Laure Ryan (London: Routledge, 2005), s.v. "Actant."

127. Wright, *NTPG*, 69–76; N. T. Wright, *The Climax of the Covenant: Christ and the Law in Pauline Theology* (Minneapolis: Fortress Press, 1993), 204–14; Middleton, *New Heaven*, 57–73. See also Richard Hays, *The Faith of Jesus Christ*, 2nd ed. (Grand Rapids: Eerdmans, 2002), 82–117.

128. See Brue Ellis Benson, "Structuralism," in *The Dictionary for Theological Interpretation of the Bible*, ed. Kevin J. Vanhoozer (Grand Rapids: Baker, 2005), 772.

129. Wright, *NTPG*, 70; Wright, *Climax*, 204. See Hays, *Faith of Jesus*, 82–3.

use adaptions of Greimas' approach as a "heuristic tool" (without adopting a structuralist paradigm), especially for examining and graphically depict the biblical story and assessing its narrative trajectory.[130]

Greimas' narrative categories pay special attention to the sending of agents to accomplish tasks, assisted by helpers and combated by opponents. Greimas' approach is beneficial in that it makes vague elements visible, sifting away details to highlight the basic narrative structure with its key entities, characters, events, and themes.[131] Another benefit of the diagrams is that they can reveal twists in the story, the existence of parallel sequences, and the possibility of morphed sequences as well as showing tensions, conflicts, gaps, and vacuums (for my usage of these terms, see the following text).

Greimas' model uses the following narrative categories: the "Sender," who is the initiator of the action and who commissions the "Agent" to perform the "Task" for the benefit of the "Receiver." The Agent is prevented by personal or impersonal forces called the "Opponents." To assist the Agent to achieve the Task is one or more "Helpers."[132] I capitalize the names of the narrative categories to highlight their distinctive use in Greimas' model. His narrative categories are directly applicable to explicate Eden Redeemed with its U-shaped plot. Especially the sharp division between what functions as Helper contra Opponent explicates Eden Redeemed's categorical approach of classifying areas of human experience in the polarized categories of either/or.

A typical and basic story, according to Greimas' model, can be divided into three moments, with possible subdivisions.[133] The initial sequence is where the problem is set up or created, with a hero or heroine called to solve the hard or almost impossible Task. The topical sequence is where the central character(s) tries to solve the problem and finally is able to do so. The final sequence is where the initial Task is finally completed. Eden Redeemed lends itself to be divided into the following sequences: the initial sequences are Eden and The Fall; the topical sequences are Redemption and The Church; the final sequence is Heaven. Figure 2 shows the order of the five sequences of Eden Redeemed in diagram format.

There are two particular dimensions to the Word of Faith story that Greimas' model fails to capture, namely setting (or storyworld) and how time is portrayed in the story. Setting and time are crucial parts of all stories, and especially in

---

130. Parry, "Narrative Criticism;" Middleton, *New Heaven*, 57–73. See Joel R. White, "N. T. Wright's Narrative Approach," in *God and the Faithfulness of Paul: A Critical Examination of the Pauline Theology of N. T. Wright*, ed. Christoph Heilig, Thomas Hewitt and Michael Bird (Minneapolis: Fortress, 2017), 181–204.

131. Wright, *NTPG*, 70; Parry, "Narrative Criticism," 531–2.

132. Wright, *NTPG*, 69–76; Middleton, *New Heaven*, 57–73; Parry, "Narrative Criticism;" O'neill, "Narrative Structure."

133. Wright, *NTPG*, 69–76.

Initial Sequences		Topical Sequences		Final Sequence
Eden	The Fall	Redemption	The Church	Heaven

Figure 2 The five sequences of Eden Redeemed.

Eden Redeemed. Both dimensions are discussed in Chapter 6 when analyzing the ultimate questions of "Where are we?" (Section 6.2.2) and "What time is it?" (Section 6.2.5).

3.2.5 Eden Redeemed in Narrative Diagrams

To visibly display the inner structure of Eden Redeemed, I now plot each sequence in the order they appear in the story into the narrative diagram adapted from Greimas through Wright and Middleton. The diagrams help to identify and analyze the key entities, characters, events, and themes. Preceding each diagram is a brief synopsis of the narrative sequence using Greimas' narrative categories. The arrows in the diagrams indicate a narrative relation. That is, they show the role and direction of the narrative category toward the indicated category in the progression of the sequence. The dotted line in the diagrams visualizes the disruptive force of the Opponents. The synopsis and the diagrams form the basis for the analysis of the narrative categories.

Initial Sequence 1: Eden In the first initial sequence of Eden, God sends Adam as the Agent with the Task to rule and increase in the world. As Helpers, Adam has divine equality, faith, authority, spiritual laws, and the double blessing of prosperity and health. But Adam gives up his authority to the Opponent Satan, and Adam loses his place in Eden. Figure 3 illustrates how the narrative entities of the Initial Sequence 1 fit into the narrative categories of the model for narrative analysis and how the entities relate one to another as shown by the arrows.

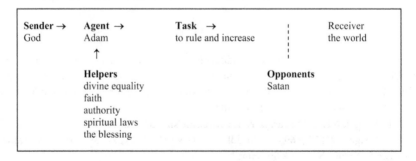

Figure 3 Narrative diagram of the Initial Sequence 1: Eden.

Initial Sequence 2: The Fall In the second initial sequence of The Fall, Adam is dead spiritually, and his former rulership over the world is lost to Satan. Satan is now the acting Agent, ruling the world through the Helpers of authority and the curse of poverty, sickness, and spiritual death. God takes the place of an Opponent, who begins to implement a plan of redemption. Figure 4 shows how the narrative entities of the Initial Sequence 2 are classified and related in the succession of the narrative (highlighted by the arrows), according to the narrative categories provided by the model for analysis. The brackets under Sender signify the currently empty space, since the story does not specify a Sender.

Topical Sequence 1: Redemption Redemption is the first of the two topical sequences. There God sends Jesus with the Task to redeem Adam's lost authority. As Helpers, Jesus has divine equality, the anointing of the Holy Spirit, faith, spiritual laws, the blessing of prosperity and health, and dual death. Opponents are Satan and the curse of spiritual death, sickness, and poverty. Through his dual death, Jesus successfully defeats the Opponents and accomplishes the Task of redemption. Figure 5 plots the narrative entities of the Topical Sequence 1 in the narrative categories of the model for analysis.

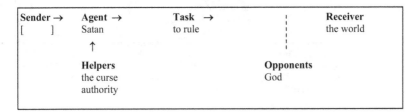

Figure 4 Narrative diagram of the Initial Sequence 2: The Fall.

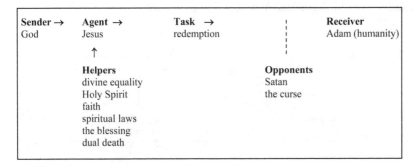

Figure 5 Narrative diagram of the Topical Sequence 1: Redemption.

Topical Sequence 2: The Church In the second topical sequence of The Church, the Agent comprises the church made up of every born-again believer. The church's Task is to rule and increase in the world and share the news of spiritual salvation. As Helpers the church is aided by divine equality, the revelation knowledge, faith, spiritual laws, authority, God, Jesus, the Holy Spirit, and the blessing of prosperity and health. The Opponents against the church fulfilling the Task are the defeated but still present Satan and the curse of spiritual death, poverty, sickness, and ignorance. Figure 6 visibly shows the place of the narrative entities of the Topical Sequence 2 as they are listed under the narrative categories of the model for analysis, and the arrows bring out their relations. The brackets under Sender signify the currently empty space, since the story does not specify a Sender.

Final Sequence: Heaven In the final sequence of Heaven, God acts again as the Sender of Jesus, who is tasked to bring the spirit of the born-again believers to heaven. Satan and the curse are finally destroyed. Figure 7 demonstrates how the narrative entities of the final sequence fit into the narrative categories of the model for analysis and their relationships as indicated by the arrows. The brackets under Helpers signify an empty space since the story does not specify any Helpers for this sequence.

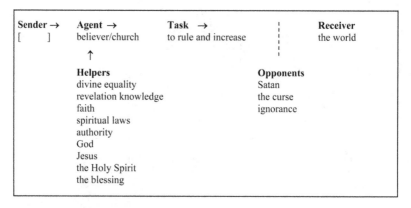

Figure 6 Narrative diagram of the Topical Sequence 2: The Church.

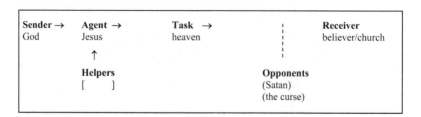

Figure 7 Narrative diagram of the final sequence: Heaven.

With the overall aim of letting the Word of Faith story be heard as a story in its own right, I plotted the five sequences of the Eden Redeemed story in narrative diagrams. I now turn to analyze the content of the diagrams.

3.2.6 Analysis of the Narrative Entities

To better understand the story's structure, this section offers an analysis of the content of each of Greimas' narrative categories (Sender, Agent, Task, etc.) as set out in the aforementioned diagrams. I refer to the content of the narrative categories (God, Adam, blessing, etc.) inclusively as "entities."[134] The analysis aims to bring out narrative themes, gaps, tensions, conflicts, vacuums, and weaknesses in the story. Also, because a worldview-story by nature is dynamic and evolving, I discuss signs for potential transformation. A driving question is what makes Eden Redeemed a distinct story and to analytically engage the story in order to evaluate its internal coherence and fidelity to reality and to identify if it carries a certain logic. Since one of the goals is for my research to provide tools for comparative analyses between the Word of Faith and Pentecostalism, a selected number of theological cruxes in the story are noted as they present particular challenges for the coherence and fidelity of the story and as such directly impact the relationship between the Word of Faith movement and the wider Pentecostal community. The overall aim of the analysis is to allow Eden Redeemed to speak as a story in its own right. A fair hearing is particularly important due to the amount of sharp critique voiced against some of the Word of Faith doctrinal positions.[135] Understanding the inner working of Eden Redeemed is essential in order to analyze the other three worldview-elements of praxis, symbol, and ultimate beliefs as they interrelate the story.

I list and discuss the narrative entities found under the categories in the five sequences in the above diagrams. The discussion is organized following the progression of the storyline, that is, the entities follow their appearance in the sequences of the story. The reason why the discussion is arranged following the entities rather than the narrative categories is that that order brings out better the inner structure of the story. Since some of the same entities appear in different narrative categories during the various sequences of the story (e.g., God is Sender in Eden but Helper in The Church), the clarity of the presentation is enhanced by following the entities. Some entities are for the same reason grouped into one heading (e.g., the Task of redemption and heaven are both discussed under the entity of Jesus; the entity of ignorance is included under the entity of revelation knowledge), and some of the opposite entities are also grouped together (the curse of poverty and sickness are included in their opposite blessings of prosperity and health). Of critical interest is to identify any tensions, conflicts, gaps, or vacuums in the narrative that require to be addressed for enhanced coherence and fidelity of the story.

---

134. This leaves out particular distinctions between character and event. See Abbott, *Cambridge Introduction to Narrative*, 232.

135. See Section 1.2.

I use "theme" to speak of a subject that is repeatedly occurring in the story. I use "tension" for lack of coherence within the story and "conflict" for lack of coherence between the story and experienced reality. "Gap speaks of areas arising in the story but that are unaddressed by the story, while 'vacuum' speaks of areas arising from human experience that are unaddressed by the story."[136] I use "fidelity" to speak of the story's capacity to give a truthful representation of experienced reality, that is, to function as a satisfying worldview-story. I use "competing narrative" for a narrative that largely overlaps with Eden Redeemed yet seeks to morph a key aspect of its storyline significantly and "subversive narrative" to speak of a narrative that stands in opposition to the present worldview-story.[137] In applying Wright's elements, I want to identify if the Word of Faith worldview carries a distinct "logic," by which I mean a rationale that arises out of the worldview-elements.[138]

It should be noted that individuals within the Word of Faith movement may narrate the story with personal emphases which are not captured here. For example, some proponents give a privileged place to other Helpers in their narration of The Church sequence. Examples are the emphasis on the need of being connected to a specially anointed man or woman of God to get prosperity and healing or the importance of personal entrepreneurship to realize prosperity.[139] Though arguably not presently part of the larger shared Eden Redeemed, they might soon take a place in the story.[140] Yet, as merely additional Helpers, they do not bring any tangible alteration to the Adam plot nor to the original Task. Neither do such Helpers significantly impact the relationship between the existing Helpers.

Because the majority of primary sources are referenced in the narration of aforementioned Eden Redeemed, the following analysis does not repeat the same. New primary sources are noted only when they offer important additions, while secondary sources are referenced at critical points to support various interpretations.

3.2.6.1 God: Sender, Opponent, and Helper The way God is narrated in Eden Redeemed is resonant with the traditional Christian belief in a personal, triune

---

136. Cf. Abbott, *Cambridge Introduction to Narrative*, 234, 242.

137. See Wright, *NTPG*, 40–1.

138. E.g., see Dayton, *Theological Roots*, 28.

139. Nel, *Prosperity Gospel*, Kindle edition, "Unique Element of African Prosperity;" Gifford, "Prosperity Theology," 83–100; Gifford, *Christianity, Development and Modernity*, 39–44; Bowler, *Blessed*, 144–6, 166. For fame as Helper, see Marti, *Hollywood Faith*, 190. For anointing as Helper see Asamoah–Gyadu, *Contemporary Pentecostal Christianity*, 121–44.

140. J. Kwabena Asamoah-Gyadu argues that, in narrative categories, prophets make a new set of Helpers as believers seek their guidance when the lofty promises of health and wealth have failed to materialize: "Independent prophetic ministries that specialise in diagnosing spiritual problems have arisen across Sub-Saharan Africa, and have invented new interventionist rites and rituals to deal with the fallout of the prosperity gospel" (J. Kwabena Asamoah-Gyadu, "Christianity in Sub-Saharan Africa," in *Christianity in Sub-Saharan Africa*, ed. Kenneth R. Ross, J. Kwabena Asamoah-Gyadu and Todd M. Johnson (Edinburgh: Edinburgh University Press, 2017), 36.

being of Father, Son, and Holy Spirit.[141] Following the conventional usage in Word of Faith discourse, "God" is used here to speak of the first person of the Trinity, God the Father. God fulfills the roles of Sender, Opponent, and Helper in different sequences of the story. As the Sender in Eden, God creates everything and gives Adam the Task of ruling the world.[142] God's narrative role shifts in The Fall to become Opponent to Satan with the goal of restoring authority over the world back to humanity. God fulfills the new role of Opponent by the help of covenants (e.g., Noah, Abraham) that finally birthed Redemption.[143] In Redemption, God can once more act as Sender, and so dispatches the Son who is the Agent with the Task to win back the power over the world from Satan.[144] In the sequence of The Church, God's place in the story changes dramatically; as God accomplished redemption through Jesus, God now takes up the passive role of a Helper, available to support the Agent to fulfill the Task of ruling and increasing.[145] Yet, in the final sequence of Heaven, God once more assumes the role of Sender when God sends Jesus, who is tasked to bring the church to heaven.

The way God is narrated in Eden Redeemed generates a significant narrative gap. God's shifting roles in the story mean that in Topical Sequence 2—where Eden Redeemed currently places us—God's role is as Helper to the Agent. The gap consists of the fact that this sequence has no active Sender; that is, God is not fulfilling the role of Sender.[146] Wright notes that such gaps—what he calls

---

141. See Alister E. McGrath, *Christian Theology: An Introduction,* 5th ed. (Chichester: Wiley-Blackwell, 2011), 234–64. E.g., Kenneth E. Hagin, *Don't Blame God* (Tulsa: Faith Library Publications, 179), e-book edition, "Chapter 1;" Kenneth E. Hagin, *The Healing Anointing* (Tulsa: Faith Library Publications, 1997), 9, 11; Andrew Wommack. "The Holy Spirit," *Awmi.org,* accessed April 7, 2021, https://www.awmi.net/reading/teaching-articles/holy_spirit/. See also Atkinson, *Spiritual Death,* 25; Bowman, *Word-Faith,* 148. Cf. Jones and Woodbridge, *HWH,* 57–9.

142. "[God] made His man Adam and He said, 'Adam, I give you dominion over all the work of my hands.' (That's over the earth and everything). 'You dominate.' Or, in other words, 'I am making you the god of this world. You run it'" (Hagin, *What to Do,* 15); "God literally gave the earth to mankind. The Creator gave us the power and authority to rule over this earth as if we were the creator" (Wommack, *Believer's Authority,* e-book edition, "Chapter 6." See Bowman, *Word-Faith,* 137–45.

143. Copeland, "No Poor among You," 7–8; Oyedepo, *Born to Win,* e-book edition, "Born Winner."

144. Wommack, *Believer's Authority,* e-book edition, "Chapter 7." See Perriman, *FHP,* 21.

145. "The power of God is passive until faith is exercised" [Kenneth E. Hagin, *The Human Spirit: Volume 2 of the Spirit, Soul, and Body Series,* 2nd ed. (Tulsa: Faith Library Publications, 1985), 14]; "God can only intervene as Christians seek His face and ask Him to move" (Hagin, *Art of Prayer,* 200); "The truth is, you don't need the Lord to do anything for you. He's already done His part" (Wommack. "You Already God It!").

146. "a concept of faith that is not only pragmatic, but mechanistic: no active divine participation seems to be needed for man to draw blessings from the spiritual realm into

narrative "blanks"—"may hide significant implications . . . blanks in stories are usually pregnant."[147] The present blank under Sender in Topical Sequence 2 (signified by the empty bracketed space in Figure 6) gives the proper context to two characteristics of the Word of Faith that puzzle scholars. First, it explains how Word of Faith discourse often contains, somewhat paradoxical to their emphasis on faith's unlimited possibilities, strong assertions of God's limitations to realize God's will on the earth.[148] Second, God's passive role means God is currently not ruling the world as God is dependent on human cooperation through their use of faith and authority.[149] Eden Redeemed's passive narration of God stands in stark contrast to how God is narrated in Pentecostal narratives and underlies the critique which categorizes the Word of Faith's characterization of God with that found in deistic and semi-Pelagian narratives.[150]

Significantly, grace is not listed as a key Helper in Eden Redeemed even though the theme of grace is reoccurring and somewhat controversial in Word of Faith discourse.[151] The basic description of grace in the Word of Faith is as a characteristic of God, consisting of God's "unearned, unmerited and undeserved favor"[152] by which God makes Godself and the other Helpers available to the

---

the physical world by the power of faith alone. God's role seems limited to an automatic response to man's confession of faith" [Malgorzata Pasicka, "Mundane Transcendence? Conceptualisations of Faith in Prosperity Theology," in *Cognitve Linguistics in Action: From Theory to Application and Back*, ed. Elzbieta Tabakowska and Michal Choinski and Lukas Wiraszka (Berlin: De Gruyter Mouton, 2010), 372–4, 382]; Farah, "Roots," 9.

147. Wright, *NTPG*, 76.

148. "God is not ruling the world. He is not ruling on the earth" (Hagin, *Art of Prayer*, 3); Hagin, *Believer's Authority*, 30; Hagin, *Exceedingly Growing*, 23; Hagin, *The Human Spirit*, 25; Jerry Savelle, *Victory and Success are Yours* (Tulsa: Harrison House, 1982) e-book edition, "How It All Works." See Nel, *Prosperity Gospel*, Kindle edition, "View of God."

149. Hagin, *Man on Three Dimensions*, 12; Hagin, *What to Do*, 11; Hagin, *Believer's Authority*, 27, 37, 48; Winston, *Imitate God*, 30; Wommack, "You've Already Got It." See also Kenyon, *Father*, 199. Cf. "Man [sic] becomes the chief actor in the drama of his own redemption; the gospel of God is rewritten as the gospel of man" (Brandon, *Health and Wealth*, 102). E.g., "It is in your control. It is up to you. It all depends on you, not on God. Whatever happens to us happens because of us. Whether we fail or succeed, whether we are prosperous or poor, it's all up to us, not up to God" (Lin, *Prosperity Gospel*, Kindle edition, "Get Ready for the Harvest!"). See Section 6.2.2.2.

150. For deism, see McConnell, *DG*, 44, 137, 185; MacArthur, *Charismatic Chaos*, 350; Horn, *FRTR*, 94; Perriman, *FHP*, 138; MacGregor, "Recognising and Successfully Averting;" Nel, *Prosperity Gospel*, Kindle edition, "View of God." For semi-Pelagianism see Sarles, "Prosperity and Healing," 343; Larsen, "The Gospel of Greed," 219.

151. See Michael L. Brown, *Hyper-Grace: Exposing the Dangers of the Modern Grace Message* (Lake Mary: Charisma House, 2014).

152. Andrew Wommack Ministries, "Living in the Balance of Grace and Truth," *Awmi .org*, accessed April 7, 2021, https://www.awmi.net/reading/teaching-articles/living-in-the -balance-of-grace-and-faith/.

Agent through Jesus' finished work.[153] That is, grace was God's motivation or Helper in Redemption, but grace plays no active part in The Church sequence. Though this is a synchronic and not a diachronic analysis of Eden Redeemed, one historical point highlights the dynamic nature of worldview-stories. Grace was largely absent in early Word of Faith discourse, meaning that its role did not qualify it to have a distinct part of the story.[154] From the early 2000s, however, grace became an emphasis in some Word of Faith discourse. Beyond being a way to explain God's motivation in redemption as formerly done or simply extending the list of Helpers, the way grace is sometimes characterized has the potential of becoming a competing narrative which alters the story itself in a radical way by narrating God as Sender. Some current Word of Faith discourse places grace in a prevenient role in the sequence of The Church, thus allowing grace to morph the story by moving God from passive Helper to active Sender.[155] A recasting of God from Helper to Sender would have significant consequences for the Eden Redeemed story itself, and the worldview with its related practices, symbols, and ultimate beliefs. If grace is allowed formative influence on Eden Redeemed, it will make that story more compatible with Pentecostal narrations of God as Sender. However, at present, Word of Faith discourse continues to objectify and instrumentalize grace, thus turning it into just another Helper.

3.2.6.2 Adam and Believer: Agent, Receiver, and Opponent Adam and the believer make up the human Agents in the sequences of Eden and The Church, respectively. To accomplish the Task of ruling and increasing, the Agent has several Helpers. How the Word of Faith imagines the human constitution is of particular weight in understanding the inner structure of the story and how the Helpers function in relation to the human Agent. The Word of Faith conviction that Adam was created with a trichotomist constitution—as a spirit, who has a soul and lives in a body—is

153. Prince, *Destined to Reign*; Prince, *Grace Revolution* (New York: FaithWords, 2015); Joseph Prince Ministries, "God's Grace Is Unmerited," *Daily Grace* (blog), *Joseph Prince Ministries*, accessed June 6, 2020, https://www.josephprince.org/blog/daily-grace-inspirati ons/gods-grace-is-unmerited; Wommack, "Living in the Balance;" Creflo Dollar, "2018 Grace Life Conference (Session 1)," *Creflodollarministries.org*, July 9, 2018, accessed April 7, 2021, https://www.creflodollarministries.org/Bible-Study/Study-Notes/2018-Grace-Life -Conference-Session-1?returnUrl=%2FBible-Study%2FStudy-Notes%3Fpage%3D3; "I'm a grace teacher. I emphasize what God *has* done for us" (Andrew Wommack, *You've Already Got It!: So Quit Trying to Get It* (Tulsa: Harrison House, 2006), e-book edition, 44, emphasis added.

154. Prince, *Destined to Reign*, 271–2.

155. E.g., see Joseph Prince, *The Power of Right Believing* (New York: FaithWords, 2013), 321.

more than a doctrinal tenant but a distinctive of the entire story.[156] The spirit-nature of Adam means that he shared in the very nature and life of God (divine equality) and therefore could access the same Helpers available to God, that is, faith and spiritual laws.[157] Yet, Adam's trichotomist nature was corrupted in The Fall, and so access to the Helpers were lost. Adam's spiritual nature changed from partaking of God's nature to partaking of sinful, satanic nature.[158] Jesus' dual death makes the believer to be born again in their spirit, to become fully righteous, with their sinful, satanic nature eradicated.[159] The new status makes the believer able to partake of the very life and nature of God, with full access to the Helpers available to realize the Task of ruling and increasing.[160]

The relationship between the divine Sender and human Agent in the story makes a narrative theme that is best described in terms of a transactional or instrumental relationship grounded in a divine-human exchange.[161] God's role as Helper while absent as Sender in The Church sequence is an indication and a natural consequence of this narrative theme. God has no transaction to make

156. Andrew Wommack, "Spirit, Soul and Body," *Awmi.org*, accessed April 7, 2021, https://www.awmi.net/reading/teaching-articles/spirit-soul-and-body/; Oyedepo, *Born to Win*, e-book edition, "Your New Status." Bowman sees trichotomy as giving structure to the whole of the Word of Faith belief system (Bowman, *Word-Faith*, 98). See also Atkinson, *Spiritual Death*, 253.

157. "Understanding your divine nature, that you are in the class of God is the way to the release of the supernatural" (Oyedepo, *Releasing the Supernatural*, e-book edition, "Introduction"). See Perriman, *FHP*, 20.

158. "When he [Adam] sinned, he didn't cease to existing as a spirit being, but his spirit became separated from God and the nature of the devil came into his spirit. He became a spiritual child of the devil" (Hagin, *Man on Three Dimensions*, 29); "The Word-Faith teachers universally agree that when Adam fell, he forfeited God's nature with which he had been endowed in his 'spirit being' and took within himself instead the nature of his new god, Satan" (Bowman, *Word-Faith*, 145).

159. Kenneth Copeland, *Your Rightstanding with God* (Tulsa: Harrison House, 1983), e-book edition.

160. "Christ took away our old sin-nature and gave us the life and nature of God" (Hagin, *Present-Day Ministry*, 6; Hagin, *Zoe*; Hagin, *Knowing What Belongs to Us*, 8; Hagin, *The Human Spirit*, 2; Copeland, *The Force of Righteousness* (Tulsa: Harrison House, 2015), e-book edition.

161. To probe further into the theme of a transactional God-human relationship in the story, Martin Buber's distinction between "I-Thou" and "I-It" relationships is helpful. I-It speaks of the relationship between a subject and an object (what he calls "experience"). I-Thou speaks of the interpersonal relationship between two subjects (what he calls "encounter"). In Buber's terms, the Eden Redeemed story leans toward an I-It relationship between the human Agent and God. See Asher Biemann ed., *The Martin Buber Reader* (New York: Palgrave Macmillan, 2002), 181–8.

during this sequence and therefore assumes the role of an instrumental Helper.[162] When the Task to rule and increase through Helpers is coupled with the theme of a transactional and instrumental God-human relationship, a pragmatic logic emerges.[163] This pragmatic logic makes the story, in a broader perspective, to absorb other entities as practical Helpers for the Agent to successfully accomplish the Task of ruling and increasing. Prayer, praise, and love are examples of entities which become objectified as usable instruments through the story's pragmatic logic.[164]

In the sequence of The Church, it is the human Agent who occupies center stage and generates the actions;[165] God is active only in response to the Agent's faith-claims.[166] A central objective in the story is, therefore, for the Agent to activate God as Helper.[167] The proactive role which such instrumental relationship affords radically empowers human agency.[168] Eden Redeemed thus ascribes the human Agent an exceedingly high profile, constituting a narrative theme which can rightly be characterized as "ego-affirming."[169]

162. Wommack, "You've Already Got It." See Jones and Woodbridge, *HWH*, 63–4.

163. E.g., "It's not a matter of trying to get God to move in your life; it's a matter of you moving over into agreement with Him and receiving what He has already provided" (Wommack, "You Already Got It"). See also Hagin, *Growing Up*, 91; Hagin, *Prevailing Prayer*, 1. See Harrison, *RR*, 32; Pasicka, "Mundane Transcendence," 379.

164. E.g., Hagin, *Love*, 183; Hagin, *Prevailing Prayer*, 13, 16; Gloria Copeland, *Love: The Secret of Your Success* (Fort Worth: Kenneth Copeland Ministries, 1985); Kenneth W. Hagin, *The Untapped Power of Praise* (Tulsa: Faith Library Publications, 1990); Andrew Wommack, "Effects of Praise," *Awmi.org*, accessed April 7, 2021, https://www.awmi.net/reading/teaching-articles/effects_praise/. See also Paul Yonggi Cho, *The Fourth Dimension: Volume 2* (South Plainfield: Bridge, 1983), 181. Since the human Agent is thought of first and foremost as a spirit being, the believer's relationship to his/her body (thought of as the spirit's "earth-suit") and soul (defined as mind, will, and emotions) is also easily conceived of in impersonal categories and objectified. E.g., see Kenneth E. Hagin, *A Commonsense Guide to Fasting* (Tulsa: Faith Library Publications, 1981), 25; Hagin, *Growing up*, 115–26.

165. See, e.g., Frederick, *Colored Television*, 42.

166. "it is when you take your place and begin to assume your rights and privileges that God begins to respond to you" [Kenneth E. Hagin, *Your Faith in God Will Work* (Tulsa: Faith Library Publications, 1991), e-book edition, "Chapter 3"]; Kenneth W. Hagin Jr., *It's Your Move* (Tulsa: Faith Library Publications, 1994), 6; Kenneth E. Hagin, *God's Word* (Tulsa: Faith Library Publications, 1996), 16; Wommack, *Believer's Authority*, e-book edition, "Exceedingly Abundantly Above."

167. Or to "get God to work" (Hagin, *Exceedingly Growing Faith*, 102).

168. "The autonomy the faith-teachers afford to people who are allegedly able to exercise faith and speak things into existence without the Holy Spirit commissioning them to do so on a particular occasion goes hand in hand with their overall exaggeration of the human ontological status" (Hejzlar, *Two Paradigms*, 199); Harrison, *RR*, 22–8.

169. Marti, *Hollywood Faith*, 177–92; Marti, "The Adaptability," 23.

3.2.6.3 Authority to Rule and Increase: Task and Helper Adam's original Task in the story was to rule and increase in the world.[170] Because this Task directly relates to the Helper of authority, the entities of rule, increase, and authority are discussed together. Authority is narrated as God's delegated power that entitles its holder the right and ability to rule and increase in the world.[171] This mandate for dominion meant an absolute, forensic transaction—a "lease"[172]—in which God submitted to Adam power over all dimensions of creation (physical and spiritual) for a specific period of time.[173] Authority follows the U-shaped plot: Adam's authority was lost to Satan in The Fall who ruled the earth till authority was redeemed by Jesus to be realized by the born-again believer. The essence of the Task in The Church sequence is for the believer to rule and increase by manifesting the blessed life of Eden and to bring spiritual salvation to humanity.[174]

The Task encompasses personal and global dimensions. In the Agent's world, Eden is manifested when authority is exercised over Satan and the curse, captured by the metaphor of victory.[175] The reality of Eden's life now is evidenced in financial abundance, achieving success, self-realization by maximizing one's potential, bodily health and fitness, physical beauty, longevity, mental tranquility, and overall happiness.[176] The global dimension progresses out of the Agent's personal

170. "The theme of 'dominion' . . . [is] the operating religious paradigm" (Asamoah-Gyadu, "God Is Big," 1).

171. E.g., Hagin, *Believer's Authority*, 7, 19. A certain, literal reading of "dominion" in the KJV (Hebrew *rāḏāh*) in Genesis 1:26 informs how the Task is narrated. See, e.g., Wommack comments: "God literally gave the earth to mankind. The Creator gave us the power and authority to rule over this earth as if we were the creator. We weren't the Creator, but that's how much dominion He gave us" (Wommack, *Believer's Authority*, e-book edition, "God of This World").

172. Hagin, *Triumphant Church*, 8–10.

173. Capps, *Authority in Three Worlds*, e-book edition, "Adam's Lease on the Earth;" Hagin, *What to Do*, 15; Hagin, *Triumphant Church*, 8–9, 165; Copeland, *The Blessing*, e-book edition, "The Day God Retired." See Bowman, *Word-Faith*, 142–3. Cf. "The Creator appoints human beings as stewards and gardeners but, as it were, retains title to the earth" (Cox, *Market*, 20).

174. Rom. 5:17 KJV. E.g., Hagin, *Believer's Authority*, 39; Hagin, *MT*, 68–9; Oyedepo, *Anointing for Breakthrough*, e-book edition, "Chapter 10."

175. Hagin writes, "we must use our God-given authority to enforce Satan's defeat and enjoy the blessings of God that we have in Christ, including financial prosperity" (Hagin, *MT*, 22–3). For the metaphor of victory, see, e.g., Kenneth W. Hagin Jr., *God's Victory Plan* (Tulsa: Faith Library Publications, 1994); Kenneth W. Hagin Jr., *You Can Make It* (Tulsa: Faith Library Publications, 2009); Jerry Savelle, *Turning Your Adversary into Victory* (Tulsa: Harrison House, 1994); Oyedepo, *Born to Win*. See Bowler, *Blessed*, 178–225.

176. E.g., see Kenneth E. Hagin, *El Shaddai: The God Who Is More Than Enough* (Tulsa: Faith Library Publications 2010), e-book edition; Kenneth W. Hagin, *Creating the World You Want to See* (Tulsa: Rhema Bible Church, 2011), e-book edition, see chapters 4 and 5.

appropriation of Eden, enabling him/her to reach the world with the gospel.[177] An intimate connection between the blessing of prosperity and the Task is thus at the heart of Eden Redeemed. It is a troubled relationship which is investigated further in the following text. The Task also gives rise to the narrative theme of power and a rationality of constant and unending growth that are discussed in Chapters 4 and 5.

There are three aspects to authority worth mentioning. First, the amount of authority utilized by the Agent effectively sets limits on both the action of Satan and God. Satan, demons, and the curse have to obey the believer speaking in authority while God—because He is not Sender in the sequence—is unable to act on earth without the Agent first making use of the authority.[178] Second, "the name of Jesus" functions as an activation formula for the release of authority in The Church sequence.[179] The use of Jesus' name is shaped by the transactional and pragmatic logic discussed earlier, where the name is abstracted from a personal relationship to function in formulaic terms. Third, because the authority encompasses God's holy angels, the Agent can commission angels to bring into manifestation other Helpers, such as prosperity.[180]

The fidelity of the story is challenged by a significant vacuum (when human experience is unaddressed by the story) in the relation between the Task and role of authority in the story and the outside world, that is, shared social reality. The narrative vacuum is seen in its emphasis on the function of spiritual authority to fend off Satan and the curse for the believer to enjoy and share the blessings of Eden. What the Task could further entail is not explored.[181] Questions such as if ruling the world has bearing on larger issues in the world of social justice, racism, poverty reduction, the environment, consumerism, nationalism, and the like lie outside Eden Redeemed.[182] The narrative vacuum where social and political dimensions are left unaddressed makes Eden Redeemed limited to provide a comprehensive story and makes it vulnerable to be influenced by other narratives that speak to these issues (e.g., a narrative of global consumerism).[183]

---

177. Kenneth Copeland, *Blessed to be a Blessing* (Tulsa: Harrison House, 2013), e-book edition.

178. Hagin, *Believer's Authority*, 37.

179. Hagin, *Believer's Authority*, 4, 10; Oyedepo, *Operating in the Supernatural*, e-book edition, "The Name of Jesus."

180. Hagin *Biblical Keys*, 58–60; Charles Capps, *Angels—Ministering Spirits* (England: Charles Capps Ministries, n.d.). Creflo Dollar Ministries, "Angel Power Confession," *Cre flodollarministries.org*, January 18, 2016, accessed April 7, 2021, https://creflodollarminis tries.org/Daily-Confessions/Angel-Power-Confession. See Harrison, *RR*, 111.

181. Perriman, *FHP*, 123.

182. See Chapter 1. See also Brad Christerson and Richard Flory, *The Rise of Network Christianity: How Independent Leaders Are Changing the Religious Landscape* (Oxford: Oxford University Press, 2017), 135–40.

183. See Section 1.5.

3.2.6.4 Divine Equality: Helper Divine equality is a significant Helper to Agents in several narrative sequences. Divine equality speaks of how Adam was created in "God's class"[184] of beings and so shared God's nature and life in his spirit.[185] An often-used metaphor for divine equality in Word of Faith discourse is "righteousness."[186] Divine equality does not mean that Adam was divine, for he retained his creaturely nature.[187] Divine equality makes the same U-type journey of lost-redeemed-regained as the other Helpers given Adam in Eden. It began with God taking something of Godself, which is spirit, and putting it into Adam, thus making him partake of the very life and nature of God.[188] Adam could, therefore, access the realm of God and operate by the same Helpers that God uses.[189] With divine equality lost in The Fall, Adam has no access to any of the Helpers. Jesus used divine equality (which for him as the Son of God was different in quantity but not in quality) and so exemplified how the believer should live by the same aid.[190] Divine equality forms the believer's new identity and entitles him/her to the other Helpers, especially the blessing of prosperity and health.[191] The role of divine equality in the story sheds light on how Word of Faith discourse speaks of health and prosperity as the entitled rights of every believer waiting to be claimed by faith.[192]

3.2.6.5 Faith: Helper In its essence, faith is the spiritual, creative force, dimension, or reality by which God operates.[193] Faith is narrated as Helper to God in creating

---

184. "He made us the same class of being that He is Himself" (Hagin, *Zoe*, 36–7).

185. "God took something of Himself, which was spirit, the life of God, and put it into man" (Hagin, *Zoe*, 37).

186. Oyedepo, *Born to Win*, e-book edition, "Your New Status."

187. Hagin, *Human Spirit*, 9. See Perriman, *FHP*, 117, 121; Bowman, *Word-Faith*, 129–30.

188. Hagin, *Exceedingly Growing*, 32; Oyedepo, *Born to Win*, e-book edition, "Your New Status."

189. Hagin, *Human Spirit*, 9; Winston, *Imitate God*, 39; Oyedepo, *Born to Win*, e-book edition, "Your New Status."

190. Prince, "Born Again to Have Dominion."

191. "Your spirit and His Spirit intermarried, merged, and became one to create a totally new person. That's why God's mirror reflects you as righteous, holy, and pure. The makeup of your born-again spirit is identical to Jesus Himself!" (Wommack, *Spirit, Soul,* e-book edition, "Fix Your Gaze"); "You have His nature, His life, His spirit, His faith, His love. Everything about Him has been made available to you through the new creation" (Oyedepo, *Born to Win*, e-book edition, "Your New Status").

192. "I'm totally righteous and holy. . . . This entitles me to everything God is and has" (Wommack, "Spirit Soul and Body"). Cf. Edwards, "Ethical Dimensions," 91.

193. Kenneth E. Hagin, *What Faith Is* (Tulsa: Faith Library Publications, 1983); Hagin, *New Thresholds*; Hagin, *The Real Faith* (Tulsa: Faith Library Publications, 1985); Copeland, *Force of Faith*; Jerry Savelle, *The Nature of Faith* (Crowley: Jerry Savelle Ministries, 2012);

the world.[194] Because Adam was created as a spirit being and so shared divine equality, he is entrusted with a measure of "the God-kind of faith"[195] as his Helper to rule.[196] In The Fall, however, Adam lost access to faith since he lost divine equality. In Redemption, Jesus coming in full divine equality completes his Task by the help of faith.[197] The believer regains divine equality and hence possesses a measure of the God-kind of faith again.[198] The key role of faith in Topical Sequence 2 is that faith is the operational environment and power that makes the other Helpers to function correctly.

A brief comment on the setting of the story is beneficial at this point (for more, see Section 6.2.2). To better grasp the role of faith in Eden Redeemed, it is critical to understand that Word of Faith divides reality into two dimensions: the spiritual, unseen, eternal, and supernatural realm, on the one hand, and the physical, natural, passing, and seen realm on the other.[199] It is helpful to think of the spiritual realm as the "really-real"[200] world and the physical realm as the "lesser-real" world.[201] Since God in Word of Faith discourse is a spirit being, God only lives and acts in the spiritual world.[202] To gain access to God, one must enter the spiritual realm, which Adam could do since he was created first of all as a spirit being. But Adam lost access to the spiritual dimension in The Fall, and in consequence, his access to God was blocked.[203] The rebirth of the human spirit in salvation restored access to the really real. The believer's Task requires him/her to operate in the spiritual realm, which is done through faith. The Helpers are available in the spiritual world and faith is the force that sees and grasps ("claims") them from the spiritual

Dollar, *Divine Order*; Joyce Meyer, *Jesus: Name Above All Names* (New York: Warner, 2000), e-book edition, "Faith as a Force." See also E. W. Kenyon, *Two Kinds of Faith* (Lynnwood, Kenyon's Gospel Publishing Society, 1989). Bowman, *Word-Faith*, 105–14.

194. "God used His faith to create the world" (Winston, *Imitate God*, 36). See Bowman, *Word-Faith*, 193–203.

195. Hagin, *New Thresholds*, 80–4.

196. See also David Yonggi Cho, *Fourth Dimension* (Alucha: Bridge-Logos), e-book edition, 16; Chris Oyakhilome, *How to Make Your Faith Work* (Essex: LoveWorld, 2005), e-book edition, "Chapter 5."

197. Kenneth E. Hagin, *Bible Faith Study Course* (Tulsa: Faith Library Publications, 1991), e-book edition, "Chapter 18;" Dollar, *Divine Order*, e-book edition, "Chapter 2;" Copeland, *Force of Faith*, e-book edition, "The Force of Faith."

198. Wommack, "Power of Faith-Filled Words;" Oyedepo, *Born to Win*, e-book edition, "The Fight of Faith."

199. Copeland, *Force of Faith*; Duncan-Williams, *Destined*, e-book edition, "Chapter 1."

200. See Sire, *NTE*, 20.

201. Hagin, *Man on Three Dimensions*, 11; Hagin, *Exceedingly Growing*, 32; Copeland, *Force of Faith*, e-book edition, "A Message from Kenneth Copeland." See Gunnarson, "Kristna Gnosticismens Återkomst," 96–8.

202. Wommack, "You've Already Got It."

203. Maldonado, *How to Walk*, 31.

world and so brings them into physical manifestation.[204] For example, by faith the believer channels the blessing of prosperity and health into manifestation in the lesser-real world.[205] The individual believer has the responsibility of making faith grow through "feeding" faith on revelation knowledge and exercising faith by channeling Helpers into the physical world.[206] The role faith plays in Eden Redeemed follows the larger impersonal and transactional narrative themes and the pragmatic logic; faith is narrated as an object that the Agent should use as an instrument.[207] As an impersonal Helper, when used rightly by the Agent, faith realizes the other Helpers.[208]

The dual division of reality into either spiritual realm or physical realm nurtures a certain logic of polarized categories. An integral part of the inner structure of Eden Redeemed is that it offers only dually opposite, either-or categories as Helper *or* Opponent. The polarized logic effectively excludes nuance and paradox. It generates the logic that any consonance between the Helpers available in the spiritual world and the lack of their manifestations in the physical world can only testify to the Agent's lack of using faith.[209]

3.2.6.6 Spiritual Laws: Helper   God used spiritual laws as a Helper (similar to faith) to create the world. Adam was granted access to operate by the same spiritual laws in Eden. Jesus was also helped by them to accomplish redemption, and the believer must likewise operate by the spiritual laws to rule and increase.[210] God still relies on these spiritual laws and the human Agent have to do the same.[211]

---

204. Copeland, *Laws of Prosperity*, 16; Hagin, *Believer's Authority*, 5; Hagin, *Biblical Keys*, 68, 49, 167; Hagin, *Prevailing Prayer*, 1, 3, 7; Prince, *Destined to Reign*, 282. See also Johnson, *When Heaven Invades*, 43.

205. "your faith will bring into manifestation what God has provided for you in His great plan of redemption" (Hagin, *Biblical Keys*, 68); Hagin, *New Thresholds*, 50; Oyedepo, *Operating in the Supernatural*, e-book edition, "Chapter 4: The Name of Jesus." See also Johnson, *When Heaven Invades*, 43; "Faith reaches over into the spiritual realm and draws what God has already supplied, out into the physical realm" (Wommack, *You've Already*, 56).

206. Hagin, *Exceedingly Growing Faith*, 99; Copeland, *Force of Faith*, e-book edition, "Chapter 1;" "The Word of God causes the same kind of faith to be dealt to our hearts that God used to speak the universe into existence. Faith is given or imparted to us through the Word. Hearing the Word brings faith" (Hagin, *Bible Faith Study Course*, e-book edition, "Faith is a Gift of God").

207. Meyer, "Pentecostalism and Neo-Liberal Capitalism," 15; Bowler, *Blessed*, 79.

208. Hagin, *Prevailing Prayer*, 63.

209. Wommack, *Believer's Authority*, e-book edition, "I'm the Problem." See Harrison, *RR*, 60–1.

210. Kenneth Copeland, *Giving and Receiving* (Fort Worth: Kenneth Copeland Ministries, 1987), 5–8; Wommack, "Power of Faith-Filled Words."

211. Hagin, *MT*, xiii.

Foundational to spiritual laws is the presupposition that the spiritual world operates analogous to the physical world (see Section 6.2.2).[212] Since there are physical laws that govern the physical creation (e.g., the law of gravity), there must consequently be spiritual laws that govern the spiritual world.[213] These spiritual laws, akin to their physical counterparts, are immutable, absolute, and universal and affect everyone's life, whether the person is cognitively aware of their existence or not.[214] Two spiritual laws stand out in the story: the law of confession and the law of sowing and reaping.[215] The spiritual law of confession guarantees that words spoken by faith generate creative power to accomplish what was spoken.[216] In creation, God uses this law when God spoke the world into existence.[217] Jesus used confession to accomplish redemption, and the believer can only rule by the same law of confession.[218] Confession is directly related to faith, as it is only through the law of confession that faith effectively can manifest other Helpers.[219] The spiritual law of sowing and reaping is also a prominent Helper to the Agent. This law guarantees the reciprocity of every action, in equal form and in parallel or larger volume.[220] All dimensions of the Agent's life are affected by sowing and

---

212. See Hagin, *Biblical Keys*, 115, 118–19; Copeland, *Laws of Prosperity,* 15–21. Cf. Perriman, *FHP*, 141.

213. Capps, *Seedtime and Harvest*, e-book edition, "Spiritual Law Works."

214. Hagin, *Biblical Keys*, 118–19. See Coleman, *Globalisation,* 188.

215. The Word of Faith story offers no restriction on the possibility of there being other laws beyond these two, and there are suggestions of other laws, e.g., the law of contact and transmission where God's healing power is transmitted from an anointed minister to the sick upon physical touch (Kenneth E. Hagin, *Seven Things You Should Know About Divine Healing* (Tulsa: Faith Library Publications, 1979), 51. Hagin also speaks of "the law of sin and death" (Hagin, *Biblical Keys*, 3). For "the law of sacrifice," see Nel, *Prosperity Gospel*, Kindle edition, "View of God." On laws, see Maritz and Stoker, "Does the Christian Worldview 1;" Maritz and Stoker, "Does the Christian Worldview 2."

216. Kenneth E. Hagin, *In Him* (Tulsa: Faith Library Publications, 1983), 9; Hagin, *Words* (Tulsa: Faith Library Publications, 1979), 12, 25; Hagin, *Exceedingly Growing*, 79; Joyce Meyer, *Change Your Words, Change Your Life* (New York: FaithWords, 2012), e-book edition, "Chapter 1: The Impact of Words;" Oyedepo, *Born to Win*, e-book edition, "Address the Situation."

217. Charles Capps, *Faith and Confession: How to Activate the Power of God in Your Life* (England: Capps Publishing, 1987), 28–30.

218. Wommack, "Power of Faith-Filled Words."

219. Kenneth E. Hagin, *Must Christians Suffer?* (Tulsa: Faith Library Publications, 1982), 31; Hagin, *In Him*, 1; Hagin, *Welcome to God's Family* (Tulsa: Faith Library Publications, 2003), 100; Meyer, *Change Your Words*, 32; See also E. W. Kenyon and Don Gossett, *The Power of Your Words* (New Kensington: Whitaker, 1981).

220. Hagin, *Biblical Keys*, 115; Copeland, *Walking in the Realm*, 54.

reaping. For prosperity to materialize, it requires that financial "seeds" of tithes and offerings are first "sown."[221]

Spiritual laws relate to the theme of an impersonal and instrumental relationship as the relationship between the Agent and the Helper flows through an impersonal transaction. This causes a narrative tension between spiritual laws and grace. Grace is understood, to repeat, as God's "unearned, unmerited and undeserved favor"[222] through which God sent Jesus to work redemption without humanity ever having deserved such treatment. Grace thus leads to free giftings by God before any action of the Agent. However, the narrative role of spiritual laws, and especially that of sowing and reaping, undermines grace by the law's demand of initial, adequate corresponding action prior to a return.[223] This incompatibility between unmerited grace and merited reward leaves the Eden Redeemed with a notable and unresolved narrative tension.[224]

There is a narrative gap when it comes to the origin and role of spiritual laws in relation to God. The gap leaves Word of Faith discourse to embrace two mutually exclusive positions. Either spiritual laws are narrated as part of God's creation, being external representations of God's character and word.[225] The term "law" is then used metaphorically as a moral principle of God. Or spiritual laws are narrated as eternal, seemingly preexistent to and ordering God's actions in the world.[226] "Law" is then used in its direct and absolute sense. The former option of law as metaphor appears to be a commonly shared position among other early Pentecostals and evangelicals.[227] The latter option of law as absolute, on the contrary, appears to connect with non-Christian metaphysical narratives, especially that of New Thought.[228] The preexistence and sovereignty of God as well as God creating the world *ex nihilo* are for Pentecostals irreducible parts of their theological narrative, which stand in direct tension to God's action being channeled and limited by

221. See Copeland, *Giving and Receiving*; Capps, *Seedtime and Harvest*; Hagin, *Biblical Keys*, 112. See also John Avanzini, *Powerful Principles of Increase* (Tulsa: Harrison House, 1989), 29–43. See Bowler, *Blessed*, 236.

222. Wommack, "Living in the Balance."

223. E.g., "God wanted to bless you, but He couldn't because you hadn't invested anything" (Hagin, *Biblical Keys*, 112). See also Gifford, *Ghana's New Christianity*, 62; Gifford, *Christianity, Politics*, 155.

224. See Lin, *Prosperity Gospel*, Kindle edition, "The Dream of Meritocracy."

225. DeArteaga, *Quenching the Spirit*, 188–200; 256–7; King, *Only Believe*, 143–51. E.g., Hagin, *MT*.

226. McConnell, *DG*, 132–46; e.g., Wommack, *Believers Authority*, e-book edition, "Exceeding Abundantly Above."

227. King, *Only Believe*, 143–51.

228. Bowler, *Blessed*, 11–40; Bowman, *Word-Faith*, 43–55. See also Chapter 1.

eternal spiritual laws.[229] The narrative gap caused by spiritual laws challenges the coherence of Eden Redeemed.[230]

3.2.6.7 The Curse: Opponent and Helper "The curse" is a collective term for poverty, sickness, and spiritual death. It also includes fear, worry, low self-esteem, and failure.[231] The curse is Satan's Helper to rule the world in The Fall and in the parallel sequence (see Section 3.2.6.11). The curse is also a chief Opponent against Jesus in Redemption, and for the believer to fulfill the Task in The Church sequence. Jesus defeated the curse, thus setting the believer free to rule over all its aspects.

The curse makes up the full results of Adam's lost blessing and rulership and is best understood as the reversal of the provision and position of Eden. Spiritual death is taken to be the result of the change of nature that took place in Adam when he surrendered to Satan and satanic nature entered the human spirit.[232] All human sin and evil, and physical and eternal death, are the direct results of spiritual death.

3.2.6.8 Health and Sickness: Helper and Opponent The blessing of health comprises perfect health to the body and mind resulting in longevity.[233] These dimensions of health are the natural results of the Agent's participation in God's life through divine equality. Health follows the U-shaped journey: Adam had access to health in Eden, it was replaced by the curse in The Fall, yet restored by Jesus in Redemption and now to be enjoyed in full by every believer.[234] Health is present in the spiritual realm waiting to be realized in the physical realm

229. E.g., see Timothy Munyon, "The Creation of the Universe and Humankind," in *Systematic Theology*, rev. ed., ed. Stanley Horton (Springfield: Logion, 2007), 215–54. Cf. "God did not create out of nothing. He created everything with faith. Even though you can't see it, the Bible calls faith a substance" [Kenneth Copeland Twitter post, August 28, 2018, 4:30 a.m., accessed April 7, 2021, https://twitter.com/copelandnetwork/status/1034402 721200304128?lang=en].

230. See Section 6.2.2.

231. Joyce Meyer, *In Pursuit of Peace* (New York: Warner Faith, 2004), e-book edition; Joyce Meyer, *How to Succeed at Being Yourself* (New York: Warner Faith, 1999), e-book edition; Kenneth W. Hagin Jr., *How to Live Worry Free* (Tulsa: Faith Library Publications, 1996); Kenneth E. Hagin, *The New Birth* (Tulsa: Faith Library Publications, 1975), 31.

232. Hagin, *Redeemed*, e-book edition, "Chapter 3."

233. Hagin, *El Shaddai*, e-book edition, "Chapter 3;" Gloria Copeland, *Don't Buy the Lie* (Forth Worth: Kenneth Copeland Publications, 2013); Gloria Copeland, *Live Long Finish Strong* (New York: FaithWords, 2010); Keith Moore, *God's Will to Heal* (Branson: Moore Life Ministries, 2013).

234. Kenneth E. Hagin, *Healing Belongs to Us* (Tulsa: Faith Library Publications, 1981); Hagin, *In Him*, 21; Kenneth E. Hagin, *Classical Sermons*, (Tulsa: Faith Library Publications, 1992), 21; Hagin, *Must Christians Suffer*, 2, 23; T. L. Osborn, *Healing the Sick* (Tulsa: Harrison House, 1992).

through faith.[235] Health is an irreplaceable Helper for the Agent to fulfill the Task, while the curse of sickness is an Opponent to rule and increase that must be overcome.[236]

Analyzing Eden Redeemed shows how health introduces a narrative gap that leads to a narrative conflict. The gap is made visible by the limited option of assigning sickness as only a cursed Opponent (and consequently health as exclusively a blessed Helper), closing any possibility of sickness functioning as a Helper in some circumstances.[237] This gap leads to conflicts between the story and lived reality when sickness and disease enter the human experience. In accord with polarized logic, the option of categorizing sickness as a possible Helper is effectively closed out. Experiences of prolonged sickness cause conflict as reality and story fail to comply.[238] Prolonged sickness demands someone inhabiting Eden Redeemed to force the story over and above experienced reality, leading to either denial of reality or discouragement. Prolonged sickness can also lead to questioning the story's ability to explain the world, that is, to truly function as a worldview-story. Either option reveals a gap that leads to an unresolved narrative conflict which challenges the story's capacity to give a truthful representation of experienced reality.[239] The gap and conflict caused by the role of health undermine the story's fidelity.

3.2.6.9 Prosperity and Poverty: Helper and Opponent The blessing God first bestowed on Adam in Eden consists of the dual Helpers of health and prosperity.[240] Though prosperity often takes on wider significance in Word of Faith discourse (see Section 4.3.3), I use the term here in the limited sense of economic and

---

235. Hagin, *Seven Things*, 11, 21; Dollar, "The Blessing."

236. "We need to understand that since God's greater purpose is for man to have dominion on earth, it would include the lesser blessings such as health and provision" (Prince, "Born Again").

237. "there is no mystery at all about life. It is simple. . . . Satan is the one who brings sickness and disease . . . it is very easy and simple to see that when you incline your ears to what God says in His Word" (Hagin, *God's Word*, 19).

238. E.g., Billy-Joe Daugherty's public struggle with cancer and Eddie Long's death despite public confessions of health. See Adrianne Gaines, "Billy Joe Daugherty Dies at 57," *Charisma Magazine*, November 23, 2009, accessed April 7, 2021, https://www.charisma mag.com/site-archives/570-news/featured-news/8133-billy-joe-daugherty-dies-at-57; Charisma News, "Bishop Eddie Long Dead at 63," charismanews.com, accessed April 7, 2021, https://www.charismanews.com/us/62407-bishop-eddie-long-dead-at-63.

239. There are tensions within the Word of Faith movement on how to define the blessing of health, as either just physical healing for the body or including inner healing of the spirit. See Joseph Williams, *Spirit Cure: A History of Pentecostal Healing* (Oxford: Oxford University Press, 2013), 98–121.

240. Bowler, *Blessed*, 78.

material prosperity as "abundant provision."[241] The interest in prosperity by scholarship invites some extended reflections on prosperity's narrative role in Eden Redeemed. Misunderstandings regarding the role of prosperity exist inside and outside the Word of Faith movement. The most significant insight explored further in the following text is how a recasting of prosperity within the movement leads to a morphed, competing prosperity narrative.[242]

God gifted Adam the blessing of prosperity in Eden, which meant an abundant supply for all dimensions of human life: material, physical, and spiritual.[243] God's abundant material provision served as a Helper for Adam to rule and increase.[244] Adam had the right to access prosperity since he partook through divine equality in the abundant life of God. Yet, the prosperity was forfeited by Adam in The Fall. Caught in the story's U-turn, prosperity was replaced by the curse of poverty. In Redemption, Jesus defeated poverty and gave the believer the right to access the original abundance of Eden. Prosperity is thus available for every believer in the spiritual world, waiting to be claimed by faith and brought into manifestation by the help of the law of sowing and reaping and positive confession.[245]

It is important for interpreters of the Word of Faith to understand prosperity's role as Helper. Prosperity's ultimate purpose in Eden Redeemed is to complete the Task of ruling, increasing, and spreading the gospel in the world.[246] In The Church sequence, this means to manifest the life of Eden

241. Hagin, *Biblical Keys*, 30. See Ma, "Blessing;" Wonsuk Ma, "David Yonggi Cho's Theology of Blessing: Basis, Legitimacy, and Limitations," *Evangelical Review of Theology* 35, no. 2 (2011): 140–59.

242. See Introduction and Chapter 1.

243. Hagin, *Prevailing Prayer*, 3; Hagin, *MT*, 1–2; Copeland, *Blessed Beyond Measure*, e-book edition, "Chapter 3: Tracking God's Goodness Through the Bible."

244. Hagin, *Biblical Keys*, 1; "Adam was, without a doubt, the richest man that ever lived. He was so rich that he actually had legal control of every asset on planet earth" (John Avanzini, *Rich God, Poor God* [Tulsa: Abel Press, 2001], 33).

245. Hagin, *New Thresholds*, 56–7; Kenneth E. Hagin, *Obedience in Finances* (Tulsa: Faith Library Publications, 1983), 2; Copeland, *Laws of Prosperity*; Andrew Wommack, *Financial Stewardship: Experience the Freedom of Turning Your Finances Over to God* (Tulsa: Harrison House, 2012), e-book edition. A special "anointing" for prosperity, claimed by especially David Oyedepo, can also function as a Helper, yet not so widespread as to be included in Eden Redeemed (see Gifford, *Christianity, Development and Modernity*, 29–45).

246. E.g., Marti, *Hollywood Faith*, 123. Milmon Harrison renders the following reply of one Word of Faith member he interviewed to the question of the reason for prosperity: "it's not just having enough or barely enough for yourself, it's the stage where you can be a blessing to others . . . I was praying 'God, make me a channel of your blessings. Make me a channel to other people. So we can reach this world with the gospel of Christ.' And I believe because of it I'm blessed, and I will be blessed even more—you'll hear it on the TV one day! (She laughs)" (Harrison, *RR*, 69).

and bring spiritual salvation to humanity.[247] Because the believer's prosperity reveals God's loving character, reigning and increasing requires prosperity. Only a prosperous Agent can fully manifest the life of Eden and reach the whole world with salvation.[248]

The curse of poverty and its connected mindset of lack—"poverty-mentality"— entered as an Opponent in The Fall.[249] Satan uses these to oppose the Agent to fulfill the God-given Task.[250] Poverty disqualifies the Agent from fulfilling the Task.[251] Put differently, a poor Christian does not manifest the life of Eden completely because their meager financial abilities limit the impact of the gospel in the world. The rationality that "more money results in more ministry"[252] makes the opposite equally true: less money results in less ministry.[253] Thus, the proposal in Word of Faith discourse that selfishness consists of *not* seeking prosperity makes perfect narrative sense according to Eden Redeemed, while in the context of other theological narratives it sounds paradoxical.[254]

Tracing the narrative role of prosperity leads to the important recognition of an innate degree of self-serving within the story. Once the Agent uses prosperity to fulfill the Task of ruling and increasing, the Receiver is by necessity inclusive of the self-same Agent.[255] The rationale is that as long as the Agent primarily uses prosperity as Helper,

247. Agana, *Succeed Here*, 225. See, e.g., Hagin, *MT*, 68–72; Hagin, *Obedience in Finances*, 32; Copeland, *Blessed to Be*; Winston, *Imitate God*, i; Wommack, *Financial Stewardship*, e-book edition, "Prosperity Isn't Selfish."

248. Oyedepo, *Releasing the Supernatural*, e-book edition, "Chapter 3: Recreated for Distinction." See Marti, *Hollywood Faith*, 157, 170; Walton, *Watch This*, 156. "The purpose or reason for prosperity. . . to have enough so that one can be a blessing to others—is one of the most important and overlooked points about the teaching on prosperity" (Harrison, *RR*, 69).

249. Copeland. *Blessed to Be*, e-book edition, "Chapter 1: A Blessing or a Curse?." Hence, the repeated phrase in Word of Faith discourse that "poverty is a curse" must be understood as arising out of a story rather than being a simple propositional statement about the moral nature of poverty (e.g., Hagin, *Redeemed*).

250. Hagin, *Believer's Authority*, 40–1; Hagin, *MT*, 72.

251. Hagin, *Biblical Keys*, 19, 23; Hagin, *Classical Sermons*, 71; Hagin, *Obedience*, 32; Hagin, *Classical Sermons*, 31, 71. See Olson, *CC*, 161.

252. Hagin, *MT*, 86.

253. "the Church as a whole has been hoodwinked by the devil . . . he knew if the Church prospered, Christians would send the message of salvation around the world. But if he could slip up on their blind side and make them believe they shouldn't have any of 'this world's goods,' they wouldn't prosper and therefore wouldn't evangelize" [Kenneth E. Hagin, *A Better Covenant* (Tulsa: Faith Library Publications, 2013), e-book edition, "Chapter 1"]. See also Hagin, *MT*, 86–9.

254. E.g., Copeland, *Blessed to be a Blessing*, e-book edition, "Where Is Your Trust?;" Wommack, *Financial Stewardship*, e-book edition, "Chapter 6: Prosperity Isn't Selfish." See Gifford "Prosperity Preaching," 87; Perriman, *FHP*, 55.

255. "As Christians, we can expect to be blessed and to prosper if we seek prosperity as a means to help accomplish God's will and purpose [i.e., world evangelism]" (Hagin, *MT*, 71);

the Agent is justified as a partial Receiver. This degree of self-serving easily empowers the recasting of prosperity's narrative role that is explored in the following text.

3.2.6.10 The World: Receiver The world—that is, the earth and its inhabitants—is the Receiver when Adam fulfills his Task of ruling and increasing (in the sequence of Eden), also when Satan operates in the usurped dominion (The Fall), and when the believer rules again (The Church). The role of the world in the story generates a notable narrative tension. In the final sequence, Jesus brings the church from earth to heaven and the world is replaced by the church as Receiver. According to Greimas' model, the final sequence is where the Task set out in the first initial sequence should finally find its solution and be completed.[256] However, in the Word of Faith narrative, the world, which was meant to be the final Receiver of Adam's dominion, disappears from the final sequence. Word of Faith discourse follows dispensationalist eschatology in believing that the world will be destroyed in the parousia.[257] Such an abrupt ending—that has no narrative connection with the problem set out in the initial sequences—speaks to a level of incompleteness in the story. The role of the world in Eden Redeemed limits a sense of closure and questions the story's inner coherence.[258] The lack of closure breeds a narrative tension regarding whether it is the initial or final sequences that should be primary. Emphasizing the final sequence with its spiritual focus reduces physical creation and human embodiment to a long parenthesis in a story of spirit beings and spiritual salvation.[259] Such spirit-focus ultimately questions the integrity of the earthly and material focus of the Adam plot. An emphasis on the initial sequence's primacy on creation would require a harmonizing of the final sequence to include physical creation as Receiver in some sense. Such an ending would agree with the Adam plot and so better fit the story's sequences, not to mention the biblical story with its holistic view of salvation as including the renewal of physical creation.[260] At present, there is little evidence of an altered final sequence developing in that direction. However, the dynamic nature of worldview-stories opens for the possibility of the story transforming. The present narrative tension caused by the lack of closure in the final sequence illustrates how Eden Redeemed need not be consistent nor fully harmonized to function as a worldview-story. But the conflict between the initial and final sequences challenges its inner coherence.

Kenneth E. Hagin, *Jesus the Open Door* (Tulsa: Faith Library Publications, 1996), 143–56. See also Marti, *Hollywood Faith,* 155, 175, 179.

256. Wright, *NTPG*, 71.

257. Middleton, *New Heaven,* 300–3.

258. "When a narrative ends in such a way as to satisfy the expectations and answer the questions that it has raised, it is said to close, or to have closure" (Abbott, *Cambridge Introduction to Narrative,* 230).

259. This spiritual emphasis explains in part the charges of Gnosticism that have repeatedly been leveled at the Word of Faith. Matta, *Born Again Jesus*; Ackerly, "Importing Faith," 307–9; Harrison, *RR*, 10. See also Chapter 1.

260. Middleton, *New Heaven,* 21–34.

3.2.6.11 Satan: Opponent and Agent Satan makes the chief Opponent in the story.[261] This personified evil is characterized as one of God's holy angels who rebelled and fell.[262] In Eden, Satan deceived Adam to surrender his authority, thus making Satan to assume the role of Agent to rule the world in the following sequence.[263] To accomplish this Task, Satan uses several Helpers: demonic spirits, ignorance, but particularly powerful is the curse of poverty, sickness, and spiritual death.[264] Yet, in Redemption, Jesus conquered Satan and all Satan's Helpers, restoring to the believer their lost authority. While Satan is defeated in principle—which brings an end to the sequence of The Fall—Satan remains an active Agent, ruling over the part of the world that has, because of their fallen nature or ignorance, not appropriated the Helpers.[265]

The defeated yet present Satan in the story introduces an opposite, parallel mirror-sequence to that of The Church. Every born-again believer is meant to be an Agent to the world in The Church sequence. The believers who are not enlightened by revelation knowledge, however, though technically belonging to The Church sequence, are bound by their ignorance and unbelief to live in the parallel sequence.

Figure 8 illustrates how the parallel sequence to Topical Sequence 2 looks when plotted in the narrative categories of the model used for the narrative analysis.

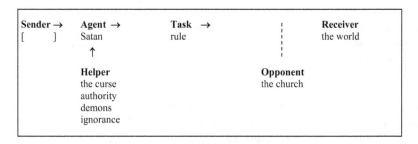

Figure 8 Narrative diagram of the parallel sequence to Topical Sequence 2.

---

261. E.g., Oyedepo, *Born to Win*; Hagin, *Triumphant Church*. Other names used Word of Faith discourse include "the devil;" "the Evil One;" "Enemy."

262. Hagin, *Triumphant Church*, 1–20; Wommack, *Believer's Authority*, e-book, "Unconditional Authority."

263. Hagin, *Growing Up*, 135; Hagin, *Art of Prayer*, 3–4. See Bowman, *Word-Faith*, 137–45.

264. Hagin, *Don't Blame God*, e-book edition, "Chapter 2."

265. Hagin, *Exceedingly Growing Faith*, 25; Kenneth E. Hagin, *The Origin and Operation of Demons* (Tulsa: Faith Library Publications, 1983), e-book edition, "Chapter 1: The Origins of Demons."

The Word of Faith movement's mission is, therefore, to bring believers out from life within the parallel sequence into an experiential reality of The Church sequence (see Section 6.2.4.2).[266]

3.2.6.12 Jesus: Agent and Helper The roles of Jesus differ in the story's progression. In Redemption, Jesus is the Agent sent by God to restore Adam's authority in the world.[267] In The Church sequence, Jesus assumes the role of Helper to the human Agent. In the last sequence of Heaven, Jesus is again the Agent whose Task it is to bring the church to heaven. In Topical Sequence 1, Jesus is sent by God to the earth as a human being, to accomplish redemption. Jesus completed the Task as a Spirit-anointed human Agent and not as the unique Son of God he is ontologically.[268] According to the rationale of the story, Jesus had to get a physical body to operate on the earth and so be able to redeem authority from Satan.[269] Jesus completed this Task by using the Helpers of divine equality, faith, spiritual laws, dual death, and the Holy Spirit. In The Church sequence, Jesus assumes the new role of passive Helper to the believer. Jesus' Task in the final sequence of bringing the church to heaven is seldom expounded upon in Word of Faith discourse. Rather, the narrative emphasis is on realizing heaven's blessings in the present (i.e., Topical Sequence 2), thus leaving the narration of the final sequence undeveloped (see Section 3.2.5).

Jesus' role in the story takes on three expressions worth noting. First, his life sets the supreme example for every believer to embody in full.[270] Since the believer shares the same set of Helpers available to Jesus, there is no reason the believer cannot live

---

266. See Walton, "Blessed and Highly Favored," 148.

267. Hagin, *Believer's Authority*; Wommack, *Believer's Authority*.

268. "Jesus was and is the Son of God. But Jesus was not ministering as the Son of God. He was ministering as a mere man anointed by the Holy Ghost!" (Hagin, *Healing Anointing*, 9); Hagin, *Biblical Keys*, 48. Hence the strong kenotic emphasis in Word of Faith discourse (see Chapter 1). Oyedepo, *Born to Win*, e-book edition, "Drama of Calvary." See Bowman, *Word-Faith*, 148. The way Jesus is narrated in Word of Faith discourse does not fully resonate with Pentecostal and evangelical theology. Eden Redeemed narrates Jesus in a way that de-emphasizes the incarnation and the hypostatic union in which Jesus stands as the only unique and incomparable son of God. Such view coupled with the exalted anthropology in Eden Redeemed makes the story to blur the distinction between the Creator and creation, that for most other Christians are central to their theological narratives (see, e.g., Bowler, *Blessed*, 11–40; Jones and Woodbridge, *HWH*, 59–64, esp. 61).

269. "It all comes back to this issue of authority being given to physical human beings. God didn't have a physical human body, so He wasn't free to just operate unrestricted on this earth. He had to become a man. Jesus—the Word made flesh, the God-Man—had to become a physical person so that He could have authority on this earth" (Wommack, *Believer's Authority*, e-book edition, "Chapter 6").

270. Hagin, *Healing Anointing*, 13.

as Jesus did. Second, in his role as Helper, Jesus is standing by in the spiritual realm, ready to act in the physical realm when the Agent appropriates him by faith.[271] The rationale of the story is that Jesus, as the head of the church, must act in sync with his body, the church. This head-body connection means that Jesus is unable to exercise power in the physical realm unless his body (the church) utilizes its authority.[272] Third, the name of Jesus functions as a formula to activate God's power. Jesus' name asserts authority over Satan and the curse.[273] If the believer does not speak Jesus' name and properly use faith, Jesus cannot act in the world.[274]

3.2.6.13 The Holy Spirit: Helper, Sender? The Holy Spirit makes another valuable Helper in the story. In Redemption, the Spirit is Jesus' key Helper to accomplish his Task of restoring human authority.[275] As a Spirit-anointed human, Jesus exemplifies how all Agents in the following sequence of The Church are dependent on the pneumatic Helper to fulfill their Task.[276] The story carries the rationale that the believer cannot rule and increase without pneumatic empowerment.[277] The Spirit as Helper in The Church sequence thus creates an expectancy on the charismata and other Pentecostal expressions, such as glossolalia, personal Spirit-guidance, exorcism, prophecies, and various other pneumatic experiences (e.g., holy laughter, falling under the Spirit's power, Spirit-empowered running and dancing).[278] It is important to note how the Spirit's role in the topical sequences makes Eden Redeemed Pentecostal in character. Any other theological story containing the themes of prosperity and health but fails to assign the Spirit a distinctive Pentecostal role cannot be properly thought of as Word of Faith.[279] Non-Pentecostal prosperity stories may have close affinities to—or even be morphed versions of—Eden Redeemed, but in the final analysis should be thought of as separate because of this distinct pneumatic emphasis.

---

271. Hagin, *Believer's Authority*, 30, 37.

272. Hagin, *Believer's Authority*, 27–31. See Perriman, *FHP*, 25.

273. Hagin, *The Name of Jesus*.

274. Hagin recounts that in one of his visions Jesus repeatedly emphasized his total reliance of human action and inability to act in separation. E.g., "If you [Hagin] hadn't done something about that [an evil spirit], I [Jesus] couldn't have" (Hagin, *Believer's Authority*, 30); Hagin, *Present Day Ministry*, 9; Hagin, *Triumphant Church*, 168.

275. Hagin, *Healing Anointing*, 9–13.

276. Kenneth E. Hagin, *A Fresh Anointing* (Tulsa: Faith Library Publications, 1989), 23–32; Kenneth E. Hagin, *How to Be Led by the Spirit* (Tulsa: Faith Library Publications, 1993).

277. Cf. Perriman, *FHP*, 116.

278. E.g., Kenneth E. Hagin, *Concerning Spiritual Gifts* (Tulsa: Faith Library Publications, 1986); Hagin, *Why Tongues?* (Tulsa: Faith Library Publications, 2001); Hagin, *Why Do People Fall Under the Power?* (Tulsa: Faith Library Publications, 1981).

279. E.g., Norman Vincent Peale's message of positive thinking and prosperity. Also cf. Mari, *Hollywood Faith*, 119–20.

Nonetheless, Word of Faith discourse contains a tension regarding the role of the Spirit: the Spirit is assigned the passive role of Helper in The Church sequence *and* a degree of personal sovereignty. This tension comes out in how Word of Faith discourse provides two distinct methods to realize the blessing of prosperity and health. The first method in which prosperity and health can manifest is through the direct intervention of the Holy Spirit. The Word of Faith portrays the Spirit as moving "as He wills," the pneumatic operations cannot be controlled, manipulated, or predicted.[280] Such expectancy for the Spirit's sovereign inbreaking stands in broad agreement with other Pentecostal narratives, which place the Agent in a mood of waiting ("tarrying") on the Spirit to act as Sender.[281] This characterization of the role of the Spirit is shared with Pentecostal narratives and is not unique to the Word of Faith. However, what Eden Redeemed adds is a unique twist in the tale, namely a second method of activating the Helpers that is detached from the sovereign move of the Spirit.[282] If the Holy Spirit does not manifest the Helpers— if the Pentecostal side of the story of the Spirit as Sender fails—the Agent can always use faith (working in correlation with spiritual laws and authority) to manifest health and prosperity.[283] Since faith is absolute and unfailing when used rightly, it is the Agent's responsibility to learn the rules that govern faith and so be ready to put faith into action if, for any reason, the unpredictable Spirit does not "manifest," that is, fails as Sender.[284] The tension resides in the relation of the Spirit with the Agent. If the first method places the Spirit as Sender (albeit in an unpredictable way), the second method radically subordinates the Spirit to the Agent and makes the manifestations of prosperity and health predictable.[285] What degree of sovereignty Word of Faith discourse awards with one hand to the Spirit in the Pentecostal emphasis of the Spirit's work it takes away with the other when radically subordinating the Spirit as Helper to the Agent.[286]

---

280. 1 Cor. 12:11. E.g., Hagin, *Biblical Keys*, 116; Hagin, *Concerning Spiritual Gifts*, 64.

281. Guy Duffield and Nathaniel Van Cleave, *Foundations of Pentecostal Theology* (Los Angeles: LIFE, 1987), 317–20. See the phraseology of Luke 24:49 KJV.

282. Hejzlar, *Two Paradigms*, 199.

283. Hagin, *God's Word*, 2; Hagin, *Healing Belongs*, 1–8; Kenneth Copeland, *Dream Big, Talk Big* (Forth Worth: Kenneth Copeland Ministries, 2012). See Perriman, *FHP*, 116.

284. Hagin, *The Human Spirit*, 20.

285. "He [the Holy Spirit] can help us *only* as we respond to Him" (Hagin, *The Human Spirit*, 14, emphasis added).

286. The formula for sowing and reaping, Wariboko says, "casts the Spirit as predictable and the Spirit's movements as normally distributed. So here we have a tension: the dynamic, unpredictable Spirit is ostensibly captured in the investment bottle of the prosperity preachers as predictable, linear, and well behaved. The Spirit in the bottle is one with clipped sovereignty. There is no surprise in the faith equation . . . [revealing] a pneumatology that presents the Spirit as a wind (pneuma) that does not really move to where it wishes to go" (Wariboko, *Economics*, 97). This explains how some voice charges of deism or Pelagianism against the Word of Faith (see Section 3.2.6.1 and Chapter 1).

Eden Redeemed offers the Agent a power boost to act autonomously and proactively to fulfill the Task.[287] This highlights the narrative theme of human proactivity. A passive approach in fulfilling the Task of ruling and increasing is effectively censured in the story while the new method to activate God's power through faith is privileged. The new way of faith lies within the Agent's control.[288] The question arising from a Pentecostal perspective is if such a way of storying the subordinate relationship of the Spirit to the Agent in actuality makes a narrative that "quench[es] the Spirit"[289] by effectively demoting the free and sovereign role of the Spirit.[290] Such a shift of roles speaks to a lack of trust granted the Spirit by Eden Redeemed, which makes it less Pentecostal than it might first appear.[291] On a constructive note, the story can become more Pentecostally aligned by assigning the sending role to the Spirit in The Church sequence and so subordinating the Agent and all Helpers to the Spirit's sovereign will. Assigning the Spirit such a new role in the story would open new vistas for mutually enriching dialogues between the Word of Faith and other Pentecostal groups, which before have felt estranged from one another, partly due to the Word of Faith's lack of emphasis on the Spirit's sovereignty.[292]

3.2.6.14 Dual Death: Helper In Redemption, Jesus used dual death as Helper to conquer the Opponents of Satan and the curse. On the cross Jesus took in himself the spiritual nature of Satan, was separated from God the Father, and after being spiritually dead in hell for three days, he rose again (was "born again") to new life. In dying a dual death, Jesus defeated Satan, sin, and death and freed humans from the satanic nature in their spirits.[293] Only through such total identification and substitution could the sin-nature be destroyed and human spirits be free from satanic nature and sin and be born again into divine equality.[294] It is clear from Eden Redeemed that this highly controversial, so-called Jesus died spiritually (JDS) belief must be understood in light of the whole story and not as a separate, free-standing

287. "The manifestations of the Holy Spirit are as He wills; we can't make them happen. But whether there is a manifestation of the Holy Spirit or not, we always have the Word to act upon." (Hagin, *Biblical Keys*, 116).

288. It is this unique method that probably lies behind Kate Bowler's observation that, what she calls the prosperity gospel, is a theodicy-theology, in the sense that it has arisen to speak to the problem of human suffering [Kate Bowler, *Everything Happens for a Reason* (New York: Random House, 2018), xiii].

289. 1 Thess. 5:19 KJV.

290. Macchia, "Call for Careful Discernment," 235; Perriman, *FHP*, 116. "The church is under the reign of the Spirit, not the reverse" [Clark Pinnock, *Flame of Love: A Theology of the Holy Spirit* (Grand Rapids: IVP Academic, 1996), 131].

291. See Wariboko, *Economics*, 94–5.

292. See Introduction.

293. Andrew Wommack, "The War Is Over," *awmi.org*, accessed April 7, 2021, https://www.awmi.net/reading/teaching-articles/war_over/; See Perriman, *FHP*, 22–5.

294. Hagin, *Present Day Ministry*, 13.

atonement doctrine or exegetical choice.[295] JDS is nourished and carried by the overarching story. JDS has roots within the Eden sequence and is getting its impetus and logic from the heart of the story, as Jesus' spiritual death becomes the answer to the spiritual death of Adam.[296] Rejecting JDS on a propositional level without altering the story (as some have tried in the Word of Faith) leads to conflicts with the overall storyline.[297] The only way to narrate the atonement without contradicting how Pentecostals tend to read the biblical texts—which JDS does—is first to alter the initial sequences, which set out the problem, that is, Adam's trichotomist nature and spiritual union with Satan, to which Jesus' dual death becomes the solution according to the rationale of the story.[298] Chapter 6 discusses some of the problems JDS poses for Pentecostal theology.

3.2.6.15 Revelation Knowledge and Ignorance: Helper and Opponent Another irreplaceable Helper to the Agent in The Church sequence is revelation knowledge.[299] It speaks of a certain function of the Bible in the story. The biblical texts become a Helper for the believer when the Bible becomes a medium of revelation knowledge through the illuminating work of the Holy Spirit.[300] On their own are the biblical texts only capable of giving knowledge to the senses ("sense knowledge"). The Bible does not, therefore, make a significant Helper.[301] The real Helper is the revelation knowledge gained through the Bible. Such insights can be given directly to a believer through the Spirit's illumination but are mostly channeled through especially "anointed" ministers.[302]

Revelation knowledge interconnects with the other Helper of faith; revelation knowledge forms the sphere in which faith is operative.[303] The believer can only use faith within the limits of their knowledge.[304] The rationale of Eden Redeemed is that

---

295. See Atkinson, *Spiritual Death*.

296. E.g., Oyedepo, *Born to Win*, e-book edition, "Drama of Calvary."

297. E.g., Hobart Freeman. See McConnell, *DG*, 129.

298. Hagin, *Redeemed*, e-book edition, "Chapter 3: Redemption from the Curse." See Atkinson, *Spiritual Death*.

299. Perriman, *FHP*, 30–3.

300. Kenneth Hagin Jr., *Another Look at Faith* (Tulsa: Faith Library Publications, 1996), e-book edition, "Faith Is a Spiritual Force;" Oyedepo, *Born to Win*, e-book edition, "Release Your Faith."

301. Hence, theological education and scholarship is commonly held in low esteem in Word of Faith discourse as academic studies transmit merely sense knowledge (e.g., Maldonado, *Kingdom of Power*, e-book edition, "The Outpouring of the Holy Spirit;" Duncan-Williams, *Destined*, e-book edition, "Emancipation Proclamation").

302. See See Sections 4.3.1; 4.3.6.

303. Often phrased as "promises," "keys," "steps," "principles," and "laws." Meyer, *Change Your Words*, e-book edition, "Chapter 5: What Do You Want in the Future?."

304. Hagin, *Right and Wrong Thinking*, 1. See also Osborn, *Healing the Sick*, 72; F. F. Bosworth, *Christ the Healer* (Grand Rapids: Revell, 1973), 40.

the believer's completion of the Task hinges on getting the right kind of knowledge. Without revelation knowledge leading to faith, the other Helpers are blocked and the Task will remain unfinished.[305] Because the Agent is reliant on revelation knowledge to activate and strengthen ("feed") faith, ignorance—understood as a lack of revelation knowledge—makes a forceful Opponent in the story.[306] Ignorance can only be overcome by gaining revelation knowledge.[307] Hence, Word of Faith sets out on the pedagogical mission of spreading revelation knowledge.

3.2.7 *The Competing Prosperity Narrative*

Having analyzed the narrative entities and their relationships in Eden Redeemed, the entity of prosperity merits further discussion because of its prominence in scholarly conversations on the Word of Faith.[308] Here I explore further the observation that a reimagination of prosperity's role from Helper to Task leads to a competing narrative. I also note five underlying weaknesses which facilitate such a recasting of prosperity.

In which narrative category prosperity is imagined challenges the movement from within. The critically important insight made visible by the aforementioned narrative diagrams is that prosperity in Eden Redeemed is a Helper for the Agent to complete the Task.[309] Prosperity's role is to empower the believer to rule and increase and so bring spiritual salvation to humanity.[310] Prosperity is not the Agent's Task in The Church sequence, and Eden Redeemed does not place prosperity as the goal of the story. That said, there is a competing narrative in the Word of

305. Hagin, *God's Word*, 39.

306. Hagin, *Biblical Keys*, 54, 56; Hagin, *Right and Wrong Thinking*, 1; Hagin, *Growing Up*, 90. Wommack, *Spirit, Soul and Body*, 24–6; Oyedepo, *Born to Win*, e-book edition, "Get Hold of the Word;" Duncan-Williams, *Destined*, e-book edition, "Success Mindedness."

307. Oyedepo, *Operating in the Supernatural*, e-book edition, "Chapter 4."

308. See Introduction.

309. Hagin is explicit on this point: "prosperity is a means to an end" (Hagin, *MT*, 68–9, 71–2, 232); Copeland, *Laws Prosperity*, 21. See Kenyon, *Advanced Bible Course*, 59; Brian Houston, *How to Maximize Your Life* (Castle Hill: Hillsong Music, 2013), 106, 145. See also Marti, *Hollywood Faith*, 123, 126–7, 179, 184; Coleman, *Globalisation*, 188; McClymond, "Prosperity Already," 296; "The purpose of wealth is philanthropic" (Sarles, "Prosperity and Healing," 333); Reed, "Prosperity Gospel," 61; Vreeland, "Reconstructing Word of Faith," 18, 19; "Prosperity preaching aims to help the body of Christ claim the full promises of the gospel so as to become better able to affect the world powerfully for Christ" (Macchia, "Call for Careful Discernment," 228); Eriksen, "Engaging with Theories," 147.

310. Kenneth E. Hagin, *Where Do We Go from Here?* (Tulsa: Faith Library Publications, 1988), 23–4; Hagin, *MT*, 69; Savelle, *The Spirit of Might*, e-book edition, "Introduction;" Wommack, *Financial Stewardship*, e-book edition, "Hidden Treasure," "Seek First the Kingdom of God." "Prosperity is missional, not a *quid pro quo*" (Reed, "Prosperity Gospel," 61, emphasis original).

Faith movement, which recasts prosperity's narrative role from Helper to Task. This competing narrative morphs the original Task of the Adam plot of ruling and increasing into the limited experience of personal prosperity. The competing prosperity narrative transforms the Task from "being a blessing" to "be blessed."[311] One major consequence of recasting prosperity is that the Receiver contracts from the world to the Agent. Moving prosperity from Helper to Task thus usurps the original story, becoming self-serving to the Agent.

A sequence where the Agent's Task is to prosper and the Receiver is the self-same Agent shapes a competing narrative in the movement. Figure 9 plots the entities of the competing prosperity narrative sequence into the narrative categories of the model used for narrative analysis.

It is important to observe that this competing prosperity narrative is not part of a separate story that challenges the Word of Faith from the outside. Rather, as a competing narrative, it arises from changes within the story, and its difference from Eden Redeemed must thus be read on a scale of degrees and not in absolutes. This narrative can rightly be called a "prosperity gospel," even when all narrative entities of Eden Redeemed are left intact.

3.2.7.1 Weaknesses Enabling the Competing Prosperity Narrative There are weaknesses in the Word of Faith which enable the recasting of prosperity from Helper to Task (with the corresponding narrowing of the Receiver from the world to the Agent). As long as these weaknesses are left unaddressed, the "prosperity gospel" will exist as a competing narrative and fragmenting force challenging the worldview's coherence. Five weaknesses stand out. First, Word of Faith discourse is unaware of prosperity's narrative dimension, apart from

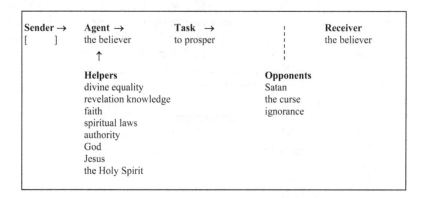

Figure 9 Narrative diagram of the competing prosperity narrative sequence.

---

311. Hagin, *Obedience in Finances,* 32. See Bowler, *Blessed,* 235; "Prosperity gradually became an end in itself" (Horn, *FRTR,* 38).

the prevalent and explicitly narrated Adam plot. Instead of as a narratival entity, prosperity is approached as a detached, storyless doctrinal belief (or "truth").[312] Such storyless conception of prosperity leads to the two-step process I call "commodification of prosperity."[313] In the first step, prosperity is extracted from its home in the Eden Redeemed story and treated as a storyless entity or commodity. Since a doctrine arguably does not—indeed cannot—exist as a storyless entity, prosperity by necessity in the following step either is incorporated into an existing narrative (e.g., global consumerism) or shapes the new prosperity narrative.[314]

A second weakness is a narrative gap that exists in the story's rendering of the Task to increase. Eden Redeemed does not develop what increase fully entails and therefore leaves room for the influence from outside narratives. Because of this gap, the Task is easily taken into other narratives, which read increase in strictly economic terms and carry their own logic, for example, that increase is to be quantified by the standard of perpetual economic growth as in the narrative of neoliberal consumerism.[315] When the Agent realizes prosperity, such quantifiable economic growth is easily placed in a morphed narrative where personal increase is interpreted as equal to the fulfillment of the original Task to increase.

Third, the relationship between the Agent and prosperity in Eden Redeemed has a narrative gap in that the story offers no restriction to the Agent's pursuit of prosperity. Prosperity is narrated as a spiritual reality to be realized by faith, which positions the Agent in an active relationship toward the Helper. Any passivity in the Agent's pursuit of prosperity is effectively censured by the story as the corruptive influence of Satan, poverty-mentality, and ignorance. Fully in line with the narrative theme of growth, the story thus presses the Agent to resist such Opponents and strive to appropriate prosperity. It is in this active pursuit of prosperity that Eden Redeemed contains a narrative gap challenging its coherence; no limits are set on the amount of prosperity the Agent should pursue. The only dynamic that can curb prosperity to finally seize the role of the story's Task is its global focus on bringing blessings to the nations (i.e., the spiritual salvation of humanity). When that Task loses its primary emphasis, the competing prosperity narrative naturally emerges.

Fourth, there exists another narrative gap regarding the story's lack of limitations set on the believer's self. This gap is seen in the complex and intermingled relationship of the self in the categories of the Agent, the Task, and

312. E.g., Wommack, *Financial Stewardship*.

313. I draw from Vincent Miller in my understanding of the process of commodification as basically extracting an element from its narrative home, for either consumption or insertion into a foreign narrative [Vincent Miller, *Consuming Religion* (New York: Continuum, 2003)].

314. See Green, "Narrative Theology;" Olson, *Reformed and Always Reforming*, 153–82.

315. See Peck, "Naming Neoliberalism," xxii–iv.

the Receiver.[316] Eden Redeemed envisions prosperity as the Agent's Helper for the Task of ruling and increasing in the world, which includes the Agent as a partial receiver.[317] Though the story makes clear that the ultimate purpose of prosperity is to complete the Task of blessing the larger world, the emphasis in much of Word of Faith discourse is placed on prosperity's benefit to the individual.[318] It is arguably the Agent's gain which occupies the greatest focus in Word of Faith prosperity discourse.[319] Eden Redeemed thus motivates self to be in active pursuit of prosperity that puts self on the receiving end. Since Eden Redeemed declares the inner core of the self—the human spirit—to be restored into divine equality with the sinful nature eradicated, the self is encouraged to be realized within the parameters of the story.[320] Apart from repeated warnings of greed and encouragements to generosity in Word of Faith discourse,[321] there is little within the story itself that in actuality critiques, much less resists, any ambitions of the Agent's self to recast prosperity to be entirely self-directed.

Finally, the place of prosperity in Eden Redeemed as only a Helper makes a narrative conflict regarding human experience in the world, not to mention the biblical story to which the Word of Faith claims fidelity and to be its best representation. Human experience and biblical theology reveal with unpleasant clarity not just prosperity's potential for empowerment but also prosperity's destructive power.[322] It is not only poverty that can be an Opponent for the Agent to fulfill the Task; even prosperity can make a forceful Opponent. This dual and paradoxical role of prosperity, as being potentially Helper *and* Opponent, is overlooked in Eden Redeemed. The logic of polarized categories makes the Word

316. See also Marti, *Hollywood Faith,* 155, 175, 179.

317. E.g., "When we give, we're planting financial seed which THE BLESSING of the LORD can multiply into a financial harvest that will break us out of poverty, prosper us and make us a BLESSING to the world!" (Copeland, "No Poor," 6, emphasis original).

318. "There is a sense in which we *do* give to get. But we don't give *just* to get. The 'getting' is not our main motive" (Hagin, *Biblical Keys,* 161, emphasis original). See Wommack, *Financial Stewardship,* e-book edition, "Prosperity Isn't Selfish;" Hagin, *Growing Up,* 34–41.

319. E.g., Hagin's "manifesto" on prosperity, *Biblical Keys to Financial Prosperity,* only has sporadic references to the ultimate goal of prosperity as the salvation for humanity (e.g., Hagin, *Biblical Keys,* 23, 158). Hagin's book *Redeemed from Poverty, Sickness and Spiritual Death* has virtually no reference to the world as ultimate Receiver, while the focus lies on the Agent's benefit of prosperity. See Coleman, *Globalisation,* 188.

320. Wommack, "Spirit, Soul and Body."

321. "It must also be stated that several prosperity teachers have emphasized that believers should guard against the love for money. Money may never become a goal in itself" (Nel, *Prosperity Gospel,* Kindle edition, "View of God").

322. E.g., Richard Foster, *Money, Sex and Power* (London: Hodder and Stoughton, 2009); Ben Witherington, *Jesus and Money* (London: SPCK, 2010); Craig Blomberg, *Neither Poverty nor Riches* (Downers Grove, IVP, 1999); Scott Gustafson, *At the Altar of Wall Street* (Grand Rapids: Eerdmans, 2015), 108–41; Cox, *Market.*

of Faith to overlook the Janus-faced nature of prosperity, which gives rise to a banal treatment of prosperity that enables it to usurp the most prominent narrative role. Prosperity thus ends up through the commodification process to compete with the original story that gave birth to it.

3.2.7.2 Consequences of the Competing Prosperity Narrative The competing "prosperity gospel" narrative exerts an influence both inside and outside the Word of Faith movement. A misreading of prosperity as the story's Task leads to sharp conflicts within the movement and to misjudgments by outsiders. As for misinterpretations, when the competing prosperity narrative is taken as the authentic representation of the Word of Faith story, it generates the common descriptions of Word of Faith believers as greedy and obsessed with their own material increase, using God as an instrument for personal gain.[323] Misreading the Word of Faith story leads to critiques that equate the Word of Faith with neoliberal capitalism or classify the movement as a spiritualized version of the American Dream. This narrative analysis shows that such critiques, though expressed in scholarly and popular works, ultimately do not engage the complexities of Eden Redeemed. But misreading the narrative role of prosperity is not only a problem to outside critics; the competing narrative is an internal problem for the Word of Faith movement.[324]

Hagin reacted at a late point in life against what he saw as misuses of his faith and prosperity message.[325] His position as "father" of the Word of Faith movement makes his response particularly important.[326] To address the most central problems brought on by the recasting of prosperity, he wrote the book *The Midas Touch: A Balanced Approach to Biblical Prosperity* (*MT*).[327] Hagin's argument is best read as describing the consequences of the competing prosperity narrative: "getting rich is the main focus; God's main interest is your material well-being; material gain shows godliness; preachers should teach more about money than any other subject."[328] To counter these undesired consequences, Hagin repeatedly questioned the ultimate motivation among those who seek prosperity, whether financial increase is for selfish gain or world evangelism.[329] His answer was to make a case for "biblical prosperity" as the golden mean between the two ditches of "poverty mentality" on one hand and, what is best called, a "prosperity gospel" on the other.[330] The

323. E.g., Hanegraaff, *CIC*.

324. Ma argues that the first component in "a proper theological 're-visioning'" of the Word of Faith is a "repositioning 'prosperity' from its place as an end of Christian aspiration to a means to fulfilling God-given mandate, or mission" (Ma, "Blessing," 290).

325. Lee Grady, *The Holy Spirit Is Not for Sale* (Grand Rapids: Chosen, 2010), 157.

326. Bowler, *Blessed*, 45.

327. Hagin, *MT*.

328. Hagin, *MT*, 184.

329. E.g., Hagin, *MT*, 69. See Hagin, *Jesus*, 143; Hagin, *Classic Sermons*, 71.

330. Hagin, *MT*, 40.

way forward, Hagin argued, was to apply common sense and balance in biblical interpretation (i.e., the usage of basic principles of hermeneutics).[331] Though he presented prosperity as a rational doctrine that exists in the dimension of propositional truth and facts, Hagin explicitly used the Adam plot to give context to his otherwise rationally based arguments.[332] Such use of the Adam plot—beyond strengthening the claim of this chapter that the Adam plot makes the center of the worldview-story—shows that Hagin, at this point, conceived prosperity's narrative role as a Helper and not as the Task in the original plot.[333] The book shows, paradoxically it may seem, yet true to the unconscious and implicit nature of worldview-stories, that apart from the Adam plot, Hagin was largely unaware of the narrative shape of the Word of Faith belief system and the underling Eden Redeemed story with its logic that shapes the role of prosperity. Neither does Hagin show signs of being aware of the inherent weaknesses in the story that facilitates the competing narrative. Because of his lack of narrative-awareness, Hagin's attempt to rely on mostly logical arguments and principles of biblical hermeneutics to rein in prosperity from overtaking the Task is rather sterile and was consequently ignored in principle by several of the key leaders in the movement.[334] Once prosperity is recast as Task, no set of theological ideas or exegetical expositions can alter its new and dominant role. Subverting the competing "prosperity gospel" requires a coherent and robust narrative, yet the weaknesses noted in Eden Redeemed make it unfit to offer such a narrative.[335] It is ironic that while Hagin attempted to distance himself from the morphed prosperity narrative, it arose as an unintended consequence of the Eden Redeemed story, the global impact of which Hagin had facilitated. The book reveals Hagin's inability to identify, much less to address, the story's inherent weaknesses which empower the undesired recasting of prosperity from Helper to Task. *MT*, though celebrated by some as a balanced approach to prosperity, instead stands as an ironic monument of the power of worldview-story over ideas, and of humans as (among other things) *homo narrator*, who tells stories to make sense of the world.[336] Such worldview-stories are dynamic and can take new shapes which early exponents never desired or foresaw.

Conclusion

In performing the task of conducting a worldview-analysis of the Word of Faith through Wright's worldview-model, this chapter applied his element of story. The

331. Hagin, *MT*, 25–9, 184, 204; See Souders, "God of Wealth," 61–119.

332. Hagin, *MT*, 25–9, 184, 204.

333. See Hagin, *Biblical Keys*, 45–68.

334. Grady, *The Holy Spirit*, 157; Bowler, *Blessed*, 138–9.

335. See Wright, *NTPG*, 65–9.

336. See Naugle, *Worldview*, 297–303; Fisher, *Human Communication*, 62; McGrath, *Narrative Apologetics*, 9–10.

findings generate four critical insights into the Word of Faith worldview that speak to the analytical, evaluative, and comparative goals of this book. First, the Adam plot and the story of Eden Redeemed evidence that the Word of Faith worldview contains a storied core. Entities such as prosperity thus operate according to a narrative pattern and require to be interpreted within its controlling worldview-story.[337] The storied core in the Word of Faith generates a sense of coherence in the movement.[338] Second, though the Eden Redeemed story is relatively coherent, it is challenged by the competing "prosperity gospel" narrative that recasts prosperity from Helper to Task. The narrative arises because of internal weaknesses in Eden Redeemed. Coherence is also challenged by the lack of closure in the final sequence that does not resolve the problem set out in the initial sequence of their worldview-story. Third, the chapter reveals how Eden Redeemed nurtures a pragmatic logic and polarized logic. The pragmatic logic makes the Word of Faith objectify and use as instruments entities such as grace or faith to fulfill their narrative Task. The polarized logic leads the Word of Faith to categorize entities in the binary categories of either/or Helper or Opponent. Since the polarized logic of Eden Redeemed excludes nuanced approaches to prosperity/poverty and health/sickness, the worldview's fidelity is challenged. Fourth, in relation to Pentecostalism, the passive and reactive narration of the Spirit in relationship to the believer and the causal power of spiritual laws place the story in tension with Pentecostal convictions regarding the freedom and sovereign work of the Spirit.

The insights gained in this chapter are developed further in relation to the findings of the coming chapters. What follows in the next three chapters is to relate the Eden Redeemed story with the remaining elements of the model for worldview-analysis, namely symbol (Chapter 4), praxis (Chapter 5), and ultimate beliefs (Chapter 6).

---

337. Cf. Lauterbach, "Fakery and Wealth."

338. This is arguably one reason underlying Bowman's comment: "We must never lose sight of the fact that many persons do, after all, find in the Word-Faith doctrine a convincing and coherent message" (Bowman, *Word-Faith*, 30). See also Walton, "Stop Worrying," 127; Brandon, *Health and Wealth,* 53, 104.

Chapter 4

SYMBOL IN THE WORD OF FAITH WORLDVIEW

The dominant task of this book is to conduct a worldview-analysis of the Word of Faith through Wright's fourfold model to add nuance and complexity to current characterizations of the movement. Having completed the two initial tasks of identifying the scholarly models of analysis and clarifying worldview as a concept and method, the last chapter analyzed the narrative dimension of the Word of Faith worldview through Wright's element of story. Here I analyze the semiotic dimension of the Word of Faith worldview through Wright's element of symbol. I follow Wright's early usage of the model that starts with story and continues on with symbol.[1]

Identifying the key semiotic processes in the Word of Faith is important as they make an integral and irreducible part of the Word of Faith worldview. I begin by discussing Wright's element of symbol and how he envisions its nature and functions in worldviews. To refine and make Wright's element more usable for the Word of Faith, I introduce C. S. Peirce's semiotic theory of signs. Peircean understanding of the three components of the sign and his threefold taxonomy integrates with Wright's overall worldview thinking and offers a way to apply his element of symbol to investigate Word of Faith semiosis. I then discuss how semiosis takes place in the Word of Faith worldview and list eight criteria to identify "worldview-signs" in the Word of Faith discourse. In the next section, I present and analyze six signs which fit the criteria of functioning as worldview-signs: revelation knowledge, faith, prosperity, health, optimism, and the charismatic leader. In closing, I discuss three of the most critical insights that this semiotic analysis provides into the Word of Faith worldview.

4.1 Analyzing the Semiotic Dimension of Worldview

Wright's emphasis lies less on defining a category of symbol than on its function in worldviews.[2] He is particularly interested in how worldviews find tangible

---

1. Wright, *NTPG*, 224–32.
2. Andrew McGowman, "Ecclesiology as Ethnology," in *God and the Faithfulness of Paul: A Critical Examination of the Pauline Theology of N. T. Wright*, ed. Christoph Heilig, Thomas Hewitt and Michael Bird (Minneapolis: Fortress, 2017), 584–5.

expressions and what he calls "symbols" or "worldview-symbols" are "things which bring the worldview into visibility," entities which can encapsulate, embody, and express worldviews.[3] Wright emphasizes predominantly but not exclusively the material dimension of symbols as the "visible reminders of a worldview"[4] and the "everyday things that carry more than everyday meanings"[5] which express the worldview.[6] Artifacts, songs, cultural events, social realities, certain actions, and keywords all exemplify Wrightian symbols that can point beyond themselves to a worldview.[7] Worldview-symbols form the basis for knowledge of and orientation in the world; symbols provide a set of lenses to see the world and empower the worldview adherents to structure and direct their lives.[8] Symbols function in Wright as powerful social and cultural boundary markers, giving fixed points that signify whether a person is an insider or an outsider. Challenging worldview-symbols consequently evokes strong and deep-seated responses, such as anger or fear.[9]

For a symbol to qualify as a worldview-symbol, it must relate to the other worldview-elements to which it is organically connected.[10] Since Wright sees symbols as encoded, material anchors of the other worldview-elements, he aims to read the symbols for the meaning they carry. The worldview-symbol's meaning is contextually and dynamically construed from the interpretative context formed by the other worldview-elements of story, praxis, and ultimate beliefs—with story forming the foundational part.[11] Symbols give the "sense of living within a large and powerful narrative,"[12] giving the worldview-element of story particular importance in understanding symbols.[13] The process of interpreting worldview-symbols consists of identifying and explicating the relationship between the symbol and the nexus of story, praxis, and ultimate beliefs.[14] When interpreting a symbol, it is important to keep in mind that its meaning is neither innate nor static. Since the symbols' relationship to the other worldview-elements is dynamic,

---

3. Wright, *NTPG*, 123; Wright, *JVG*, 369; Wright, *PFG*, 396; Wright, "Challenge of Dialogue," 713.

4. Wright, *NTPG*, 124.

5. Wright, *PFG*, 353.

6. E.g., Wright, *PFG*, 396.

7. Wright, *NTPG*, 112, 123–4, 133, 224; Wright, *JVG*, 554; Wright, *PFG*, 26, 233, 352–3, 383; Wright, "Challenge of Dialogue," 713.

8. Wright, *PFG*, 454; Wright, *NTPG*, 130, 133. "Symbols provide the interpretative grid through which humans perceive both how the world is and how they might act within it: they provide a vision *of* reality and a vision *for* it" (Wright, *NTPG*, 112, italics original).

9. Wright, *NTPG*, 124, 232; Wright, *PFG*, 1138; Wright, *JVG*, 369.

10. Wright, *PFG*, 353; Wright, *NTPG*, 224, 230, 369; Wright, *PFG*, 353.

11. E.g., Wright, *JVG*, 614–15.

12. Wright, *PFG*, 345.

13. Wright, *NTPG*, 123, 224; Wright, *PFG*, 345, 728, 856.

14. See Wright, *PFG*, 297.

the meaning of symbols can be "rethought, reworked and revised."[15] A worldview-symbol that drifts away from the other worldview-elements loses its original meaning and either takes on new meanings and functions not originally intended or simply loses its meaning.[16]

Since Wright's work yields no specific method to identify and analyze worldview-symbols, the element benefits from a methodological supplement to be applied to the Word of Faith. Because the semiotic nature of symbols is open to the use of basic semiotic categories, I employ the semiotic theory of C. S. Peirce to clarify and apply Wright's element of worldview-symbol.[17] Peirce offers a general theory of signs that, as I will show, easily integrates with Wright's view of symbol. Peircean semiotics sharpens the model's use of symbol and provides a valuable method to analyze the semiotic dimension of the Word of Faith worldview.[18]

Given that the term "symbol" is polyvalent, it requires interpretation within the context of each user (alike to the indexical nature of "worldview"). Wright's conception of worldview-symbol stands apart from the concept of a theological or religious symbol, while having an affinity with the general category of "material culture" or the "material dimension" of worldviews used in worldview literature.[19] Clifford Geertz's definition of symbol is particularly formative for Wright: "any object, act, event, quality, or relation which serves as a vehicle for a conception [i.e., meaning]."[20] In applying Wright's model, it is noteworthy that Geertz's definition of symbol corresponds to, and is largely replaceable with, the definition of sign in Peircean semiotics. This similarity to the sign theory of Peirce is something Geertz

15. Wright, PFG, 365. See Wright, JVG, 443.

16. Wright, JVG, 443, 506, 615; Wright, PFG, 562, 365; Wright, NTPG, 230.

17. See Andrew Robinson, God and the World of Signs (Leiden: Brill, 2010), 118.

18. My need to first develop the concept of symbol to be used on the Word of Faith resembles the need scholars have to develop Bourdieu's "habitus" before it can be fully utilized (e.g., Maton, "Habitus").

19. E.g., Paul Tillich, "The Religious Symbol," Daedalus 87, no. 3 (1958): 3–21; Langdon Gilkey, "Symbols, Meaning, and the Divine Presence," Theological Studies 35, no. 2 (1974): 249–67; Louis-Marie Chauvet, The Sacrament, trans. Madeleine Beumont (Collegeville: Liturgical Press, 2001), Kindle edition, 69–96; Jeff Pool, God's Wounds (Eugene: Pickwick, 2009), 36–41; Vondey, Pentecostal Theology, 283. See Winfred Nöth, Handbook of Semiotics (Bloomington: Indiana University Press, 1990), 381–4; Hiebert, Transforming Worldviews, 81; Smart, World's Religions, 7. See, e.g., Walsh, "From Housing to Homemaking."

20. Geertz, Interpretation of Cultures, 91; Wright, PFG, 27–8. See Janet Hoskins, "Symbolism in Anthropology," in International Encyclopedia of the Social and Behavioral Sciences, ed. James D. Wright (Oxford: Elsevier, 2015), 860–5; Birgit Meyer, "Religious Sensations: Why Media, Aesthetics and Power Matter in the Study of Contemporary Religion" (presentation, Vrije Universiteit, Amsterdam, 2006), 19.

also acknowledged.[21] Though Wright does not explicitly engage semiotic theory, his conception of symbol and the process of interpretation and dependency on Geertz speak to a fundamental underlying agreement with Peircean sign theory.[22] This unforced agreement between Wright's theory of worldview-symbol and Peircean semiotics is recognized in the literature.[23] Wright's conception of worldview-symbol can, therefore, be categorized with no alteration of meaning as a semiotic sign in Peircean terms and thus fruitfully be explored as a process of semiosis in this project.[24]

4.1.2 C. S. Peirce's Model of the Sign

The two fountainheads in the modern development of the study of signs are Ferdinand de Saussure and C. S. Peirce.[25] The semiotic theory of de Saussure revolutionized the study of linguistic signs and provided the catalyst for the development of structuralism.[26] Regardless, Peircean "semiotics"—in contrast to Saussure's "semiology"—is better fitted to apply Wright's category of worldview-symbol to the Word of Faith. Without getting into semiotic complexities and controversies, Peircean semiotics expands the conception of signs beyond Saussure's dominant interest in linguistic signs to include objects similar to Wright's worldview interests.[27] Also, Peirce's triadic conception of the sign and how it means fit Wright's understanding of how symbols function in worldviews rather than Saussure's dyadic conception of the sign.

Peirce's conception of signs and how they signify has secured considerable attention and gained extensive adherence among semioticians. Peircean semiotics

---

21. Arun Micheelsen, "'I Don't Do Systems': An Interview with Clifford Geertz," *Method & Theory in the Study of Religion* 14, no. 1 (2002): 2–20.

22. For Wright's use of Peirce's theory of abduction see Wright, *PFG*, XVIII; Theresa Heilig and Christoph Heilig, "Historical Methodology," in *God and the Faithfulness of Paul: A Critical Examination of the Pauline Theology of N. T. Wright*, ed. Christoph Heilig, Thomas Hewitt and Michael Bird (Minneapolis: Fortress, 2017), 115–50.

23. Robinson, *God and the World*, 111–19.

24. Naugle says that "to examine the nature and function of worldview *sub specie semiotica*" is "wise" and "entirely appropriate" (Naugle, "Worldview, History, Theology," 21, emphasis original; Naugle, *Worldview*, 292). See also Hiebert, *Transforming Worldviews*, 81–2.

25. Nöth, *Handbook of Semiotics*, 11–76. For an introduction to semiotics, see Thomas Sebeok, *Signs: An Introduction to Semiotics,* 2nd ed. (Toronto: University of Toronto Press, 2001).

26. Carol Sanders, ed., *The Cambridge Companion to Saussure* (Cambridge: Cambridge University Press, 2004); Nöth, *Handbook of Semiotics*, 56–63.

27. Nöth, *Handbook of Semiotics*, 42–3.

is welcomed as a "viable working account of all semiosis"[28] and therefore "has become the 'gold standard' in semiotics."[29] Theologians and religious scholars employ Peirce's model of the sign and threefold taxonomy to explore areas of theological beliefs and practices.[30] Hence, his semiotic theory serves to apply Wright's element of symbol to the Word of Faith. In turning to Peircean semiotics, I do not intend to engage Pierce's thought beyond what is needed to refine and apply the semiotic dimension of Wright's worldview-model to the Word of Faith.

Fundamental for Peirce is that a sign is "something which stands to somebody for something [its object] in some respect or capacity."[31] Signs can be anything in the realms of material objects, audible sounds, visual stimuli, smells, and felt touches.[32] Peirce understood the sign to be the unity, formed by what is represented, how it is represented, and how it is interpreted.[33] A Peircean sign is not an entity in itself but consists of the relationship between the three elements. Peirce claims that a sign always comprises a dynamic, triadic relationship between three interrelated elements: (1) the sign-vehicle, (2) the object, and (3) the interpretant.[34] The sign-vehicle speaks of the elements of the sign responsible for signification, that is, the particular dimensions of the sign which represents something else.[35] The object is that which the sign-vehicle represents.[36] The interpretant is the element that brings the other two elements of sign-vehicle and object together to create a meaningful relationship between them. The interpretant translates the signifying relationship between the sign-vehicle and the sign-object and is partly anticipated by the sign-

---

28. Graham Hughes, *Worship as Meaning* (Cambridge: Cambridge University Press, 2010), 124.

29. Robert Yelle, "The Peircean Icon and the Study of Religion: A Brief Overview," *Material Religion* 12, no. 2 (2016): 243. See McGrath, *Re-Imagining Nature*, 94.

30. Amos Yong, *Spirit-Word-Community* (Eugene: Wipf and Stock, 2002); Robinson, *God and the World*; Hughes, *Worship as Meaning*; McGrath, *Re-Imagining Nature*; Robbie Goh, "Hillsong and 'Megachurch' Practice: Semiotics, Spatial Logic and the Embodiment of Contemporary Evangelical Protestantism," *Material Religion* 4, no 3 (2008): 284–304. For relation to worldview studies, see Naugle, *Worldview*, 295.

31. C. S. Peirce quoted in Nöth, *Handbook of Semiotics*, 42. See also McGrath, *Re-Imagining Nature*, 95; David Chandler, *Semiotics*, 2nd ed. (London: Routledge, 2007), 29. Also "a sign is something by knowing which we know something more" [C. S. Peirce quoted in Jørgen Johansen and Svend Larsen, *Signs in Use*, trans. Dinda L. Gorleé and John Irons (London: Routledge, 2010), 25].

32. Floyd Merrell, "Charles Sanders Peirce's Concept of the Sign," in *The Routledge Companion to Semiotics and Linguistics*, ed. Paul Cobley (London: Routledge, 2001), 34.

33. Chandler, *Semiotics*, 29.

34. Nöth, *Handbook of Semiotics*, 42; Johansen and Larsen, *Signs in Use*, 26–7; Chandler, *Semiotics*, 29–33; Hughes, *Worship as Meaning* 121–2.

35. Chandler, *Semiotics*, 29; Nöth, *Handbook of Semiotics*, 42; Hughes, *Worship as Meaning*, 122.

36. Chandler, *Semiotics*, 29; Nöth, *Handbook of Semiotics*, 42–3.

producer and partly supplied by the sign-receiver.[37] All the three elements of sign-vehicle, object, and interpretant are essential to qualify as a sign.[38]

4.1.2.1 The Threefold Taxonomy of Signs Based on his triadic model of the sign, Peirce developed a taxonomy as "the most fundamental" division of how semiosis is affected by the relationship between the sign-vehicle and the object.[39] The sign-vehicle's relationship to its object makes it either an icon-sign, an index-sign, or a symbol-sign.[40] Understanding how a sign relates to its object in either of these three moods elucidates aspects of the Word of Faith worldview's logic which otherwise is difficult to analyze (see the following text).

Iconic signs signify by "having a certain property in common."[41] They represent by perceived commonality, a resemblance between the sign-vehicle's qualities to that of the object.[42] Maps, photographs, and scale models are examples of icon-signs which signify through likeness.[43] The second form of sign is the indexical signs. An index-sign "represents an object by virtue of its connection with it."[44] Index-signs signify by some actual, physical, or imagined causal connection with the thing signified.[45] Indices can also signify by directing attention directly to the object.[46] Examples of indexical signs are smoke, footprints, medical symptoms, and measuring instruments (e.g., weathercock).[47] The third category of signs is the symbolic. Peirce explains symbolic signs as: "The symbol is connected with its object by virtue of the idea of the symbol-using mind, without which no such connection would exist."[48] Symbolic signs thus signify the object by convention, that is, "a habit, disposition, or other effective general rule that it will be so

37. Nöth, *Handbook of Semiotics*, 42–4; Hughes, *Worship as Meaning*, 122, 138, 185; Merrell, "Charles Sanders Peirce," 30. Cf. Roy Rappaport, *Ritual and Religion in the Making of Humanity* (Cambridge: Cambridge University Press, 1999), 61.

38. Chandler, *Semiotics*, 29; Nöth, *Handbook of Semiotics*, 42.

39. T. L. Short, "The Development of Peirce's Theory of Signs," in *The Cambridge Companion to Peirce*, ed. Cheryl Misak (Cambridge: Cambridge University Press, 2009), 214–22; Chandler, *Semiotics*, 36–44.

40. Nöth, *Handbook of Semiotics*, 44–5. See also Yong, *Spirit, Word, Community*, 157.

41. C. S. Peirce quoted in Hughes, *Worship as Meaning*, 140. See Yelle, "The Peircean Icon," 241–3.

42. Short, "Development of Peirce's Theory," 215; Chandler, *Semiotics*, 40; Johansen and Larsen, *Signs in Use*, 36–43.

43. Short, "Development of Peirce's Theory," 215; Hughes, *Worship as Meaning*, 139; Chandler, *Semiotics*, 36–37; Merrell, "Charles Sanders Peirce," 37–8.

44. Quoted in Hughes, *Worship as Meaning*, 140; Johansen and Larsen, *Signs in Use*, 32–6.

45. Chandler, *Semiotics*, 42–4; Merrell, "Charles Sanders Peirce," 31.

46. Rappaport, *Ritual and Religion*, 59.

47. Hughes, *Worship as Meaning*, 141; Chandler, *Semiotics*, 37.

48. Quoted in Hughes, *Worship as Meaning*, 141.

interpreted."[49] Language, national flags, and traffic lights exemplify symbolic signs since they signify by a received rule of interpretation.[50]

The threefold relationship between the sign-vehicle and the object as iconic, indexical, or symbolic is never exclusive but only speaks of the predominant quality of the sign.[51] One sign can function as an index and icon at the same time in various degrees, for example, a megachurch can be an index-sign of God's presence and an iconic sign of God's greatness.[52] Signs may also change how they mean over time, as when an index-sign shifts to a symbolic sign.[53]

4.1.2.2 The Key Role of the Interpretant Another dimension of Peirce's semiotics that informs my application of Wright's symbol to the Word of Faith is how a sign's meaning is not inherent in the sign-vehicle but arises out of the dynamics of the triadic sign relationship (i.e., between the sign-vehicle, the object, and the interpretant). The interpretant is Peirce's most original and distinguishing contribution to semiotic theory. Because the sign-recipient is deeply involved in the sign's meaning through the interpretant, the meaning intended by the sign-producer is not necessarily the meaning taken by the sign-recipient.[54] To clarify the key role of the interpretant, Peircean semiotics differentiates between the "intentional interpretant" and the "effectual interpretant," that is, between what interpretant the sign-receiver intended ("intentional interpretant") and what interpretant the sign-receiver uses ("effectual interpretant").[55]

In a situation when the intentional interpretant differs from the effectual interpretants, the sign-vehicle ends up signifying an object which the sign-recipient receives but which is different from the object intended by the sign-producer. The object intended by the sign-producer is called the "immediate object," and the object which the sign-recipient receives is the so-called "dynamic object."[56] The goal for a successful semiosis is sufficient correspondence between the intentional and the effectual interpretants. "Successful semiosis, a meaningful transaction of

---

49. Johansen and Larsen, *Signs in Use,* 43.

50. Hughes, *Worship as Meaning,* 142–2; Short, "Development of Peirce's Theory," 221; Chandler, *Semiotics,* 36.

51. Hughes, *Worship as Meaning,* 139; Chandler, *Semiotics,* 44. E.g., the word "this" can be symbol and index at the same time (Rappaport, *Ritual and Religion,* 67).

52. Johansen and Larsen, *Signs in Use,* 51. E.g., map (Chandler, *Semiotics,* 44) or Holy Communion (Yong, *Spirit-Word-Community,* Kindle edition, 216); Goh, "Hillsong and Megachurch," 296. See also Chandler, *Semiotics,* 45.

53. E.g., "a Rolls-Royce is an index of wealth because one must be wealthy to own one, but social usage has led to its becoming a conventional symbol of wealth" (Chandler, *Semiotics,* 45). See Rappaport, *Ritual and Religion,* 55–6.

54. Hence Peirce writes: "it seems a strange thing ... that a sign should leave its interpreter to supply a part of its meaning" (C. S. Peirce quoted in Hughes, *Worship as Meaning,* 118).

55. Hughes, *Worship as Meaning,* 144–7.

56. Ibid.

meaning, therefore depends upon the ability of both [sign-] producer and [sign-] recipient to bring their respective interpretants sufficiently close for their mutual satisfaction."[57]

The task for this chapter is to analyze the semiotic dimension of the Word of Faith worldview through Wright's element of symbol refined by Peirce's model and taxonomy. I will show how Peirce's triadic model integrates and complements Wright's overall conception of symbol and facilitates a semiotic analysis of the Word of Faith worldview. The element of symbol captures how worldviews are expressed semiotically through particular signs.

4.2 Studying Worldview-Signs in the Word of Faith

The role of signs in the Word of Faith is discussed by scholarship but a semiotic study of signs within the context of Wright's worldview-model has not been carried out.[58] My study, therefore, promises additional insights by revealing how semiosis exists at the heart of the movement.

The semiotic theory introduced earlier helps to apply Wright's element of symbol to the Word of Faith in three ways.[59] First, Peircean semiotics brings terminological clarification. Because Wright's element is essentially a semiotic analysis of signs, "sign" is the preferable term since symbol is only a subcategory of the larger semiotic category of signs.[60] This distinction helps to accurately categorize and analyze the signs within the Word of Faith. I retain Wright's terminology of "symbol" to refer to this element of the fourfold worldview-model. I use the terms "symbol-sign," "semiotic symbol," or "symbolic sign" when I specifically reference

57. Ibid., 185.

58. E.g., Coleman notes the key role of signs in the Word of Faith: "Faith 'culture' is embodied and diffused not only in narratives, but also in a coherent system of visual, material and embodied aesthetics" (Coleman, *Globalisation*, 144); Winslow, "Imaged Other;" J. Kwabena Asamoah-Gyadu, *Sighs and Signs of the Spirit: Ghanaian Perspective on Pentecostalism and Renewal in Africa* (Oxford: Regnum, 2015), 31–46.

59. The analysis of the semiotic dimension of worldviews used here has affinities with what Keane calls "semiotic ideology" [Webb Keane, "On Semiotic Ideology," *Signs and Society* 6, no. 1 (2018): 64–87]. Semiotic ideology is defined as "people's underlying assumptions about what signs are, what functions signs do or do not serve, and what consequences they might or might not produce" (Keane, "Semiotic Ideology," 65). This "semiotic reflexivity" draws on assumptions and presuppositions which fundamentally are part of worldviews, e.g., "assumptions about the nature of the world, the kinds of being that inhabit it, and the kinds of causes and effects with which they are involved" (Keane, "Semiotic Ideology," 66–8).

60. See Robinson, *God and the World*, 118. "What in popular usage are called 'symbols' would be regarded by semioticians as 'signs' of some kind but many of them would not technically be classified as purely 'symbolic'" (Chandler, *Semiotics*, 38).

the Peircean symbolic subcategory of signs. The term "worldview-sign" is used for any sign (symbolic, iconic, or indexical), which meaning arises in relation to the other worldview-elements of the Word of Faith worldview (story, praxis, and ultimate beliefs).

Second, Peircean semiotics clarifies the intentional interpretant in Word of Faith semiosis. A worldview-symbol for Wright is in semiotic terms an interpreted sign in its complete sense. Peirce's triad highlights how interpretants partly construct and mediate a sign's meaning.[61] The interpretant specifies in which signifying relation the sign-vehicle stands to the object.[62] Since the interpretant mediates the sign-vehicle to the object to generate meaning, in semiotic terms, the intentional interpretant in Wright's element of symbol consists primarily of the element of story together with praxis and ultimate beliefs.[63] However, since I have thus far explored only the worldview-story of the Word of Faith (Chapter 3), the intentional interpretant in the following analysis of Word of Faith semiosis must be limited to the Eden Redeemed story.

Third, Peircean semiotics clarifies the relation between the elements of symbol and praxis in Wright's model. It is rightly observed that all ritual practices ("praxis" in Wright) are ultimately signs, yet it is important to note that all signs are not rituals.[64] Hence, this chapter focuses on the nonritual signs in the Word of Faith, leaving the ritual signs for the next chapter. To phrase it in another way: worldview-signs in this chapter are those which signify through the interpretant of Eden Redeemed without the sign-vehicle demanding any elaborate embodied action.

Wright's worldview-element of symbol applied through Peircean semiotics defines the quest for worldview-signs in the Word of Faith. The task is to identify nonritual sign-vehicles that through the intentional interpretant of Eden Redeemed signify objects that ultimately interconnect with story, praxis, and ultimate beliefs. Since I have only analyzed the worldview-story so far, exploring how the signs interconnect with praxis and ultimate beliefs must wait until the following chapters.

4.2.1 Identifying Worldview-Signs in the Word of Faith

Peircean semiotics provides the framework to analyze the worldview-signs of the Word of Faith. What remains is to settle the method for identifying which signs to analyze from the host of signs in the Word of Faith discourse. Wright's criterion for a worldview-sign is its interconnection with the other worldview-elements, but his application of the worldview-model does not yield a fully applicable method that can be applied to identify worldview-signs in the

---

61. Hughes, *Worship as Meaning*, 128, 185.

62. Hughes, *Worship as Meaning*, 138.

63. Wright, *PFG*, 353; Wright, *NTPG*, 230, 369, 224.

64. Bernard Cook and Gary Macy, *Christian Symbol and Practice* (Oxford: Oxford University Press, 2005), 14.

Word of Faith. It is unresolved what criteria are determinative for locating a worldview-sign apart from interconnection with the other worldview-elements. The worldview scholar Tom Steffen uses a list of criteria to identify what he calls "master symbols," which is useful here.[65] Though the criteria were composed within the context of ethnographic studies, they fit Wright's understanding of worldviews and the element of symbol. For Steffen, an entity may function as what we call a worldview-sign based on fulfilling (at least one) of the following indicators:

> (1) The natives tell us that X is culturally important. (2) The natives seem positively or negatively aroused about X, rather than indifferent. (3) X comes up in many different contexts . . . (myth, ritual, art, formal rhetoric, etc.). (4) There is greater cultural elaboration surrounding X. . . . (5) There are greater cultural restrictions surrounding X, either in sheer number of rules, or severity of sanctions regarding its misuse.[66]

I use these criteria in addition to two additional criteria to identify worldview-signs in the Word of Faith. The first additional condition is Wright's emphasis (aforementioned) on the interpenetration of the element of symbol with the other three elements of story, praxis, and ultimate beliefs. A worldview-sign is thus one that stands in direct relation with the other worldview-elements. The second criterion is that the sign attracts significant focus among scholarship on the Word of Faith movement. An indicator of a sign functioning as a worldview-sign is arguably that it draws attention (as seen in the criteria just listed); thus, special attention by scholarship to a certain sign would indicate a possible worldview-sign. All these criteria together give shape to a conceptual eight-point grid that I use in the following section to identify which signs in the Word of Faith to analyze: (1) the sign has a central place in scholarly discussions of the movement; (2) the sign occupies an expressed privileged position among the Word of Faith community; (3) the sign is affectively charged for the Word of Faith adherents; (4) the sign signifies for the Word of Faith for an extended period; (5) the sign reappears in several contexts; (6) the sign's meaning is expanded upon in Word of Faith discourse; (7) the sign's role and use are closely monitored by the movement; (8) the sign exists in direct relation with the worldview-elements of story. I now turn to analyze signs in the Word of Faith that fit these criteria.

---

65. Steffen, *Worldview-based Storying*, Kindle edition, "Making a Case for Symbol." The list is adapted from Sherry Ortner, "On Key Symbols," *American Anthropologist* 75, no. 5 (1973): 1338–46.

66. Steffen, *Worldview-based Storying*, Kindle edition, "Symbol Signifies the Significant;" Ortner, "On Key Symbols," 1338–46.

4.3 Worldview-Signs in the Word of Faith

Six signs that fulfill the eight requirements to be categorized as worldview-signs emerge from examining the Word of Faith discourse and the scholarly literature on the movement. These signs are revelation knowledge, faith, prosperity, health, optimism, and the charismatic leader. How each sign fulfills the criteria is presented in the following text. The sequence of the signs follows their individual relationship and roles in the movement. The strategic roles of revelation knowledge and faith in the Word of Faith discourse give them priority here. Since revelation knowledge is said to set the limits for faith, I start with revelation knowledge followed by faith.[67] After this, I turn to the interrelated set of prosperity, health, and optimism. The unity among these three consists of their semiotic function as indexes in the Word of Faith worldview. I discuss the charismatic leader last because all the other signs cluster around this sign.

Since I follow Wright's model, which places worldview-story as the foundational intentional interpretant of any worldview-sign, my analysis of each sign begins by defining the sign-vehicle and then discussing the sign's immediate object through the worldview-story of Eden Redeemed. After reading the sign through the intentional interpretant, I note how the sign signifies as an iconic, indexical, or symbolic sign. I continue by discussing other signs in the Word of Faith which function in a supportive role to the worldview-sign. These, what I call "supportive signs," are signs that signify the particular worldview-sign within the Word of Faith. I divide the supportive signs into three groups: material signs, that is, sign-vehicles consisting of material or bodily elements; narrative signs, that is, sign-vehicles which are narratival in constitution; linguistic signs, that is, sign-vehicles consisting of singular words, phrases, and metaphors. All ritual signs, that is, embodied and enacted sign-vehicles, are left to the next chapter. This division of the supportive signs helps to clarify the discussion and gives structure to an otherwise assorted mix of signs in the movement. In the second part of each sign, I explore what the sign reveals about the Word of Faith worldview and how that addresses the analytical, evaluative, and comparative goals.

4.3.1 Revelation Knowledge

Revelation knowledge is a sign in the Word of Faith discourse which fulfills all the criteria of a worldview-sign.[68] Its foundational role as the basis for faith in the

---

67. Hagin, *Right and Wrong*, 1. See also Osborn, *Healing the Sick*, 72; Bosworth, *Christ the Healer*, 40.

68. (1) Revelation knowledge holds the attention in scholarly studies [Nel, *Prosperity Gospel*, Kindle edition, "The Sources of the Prosperity Message;" Harrison, *RR*, 88–93; Perriman, *FHP*, 30–3, 96–100; McConnell, *DG*, 101–13; Ackerly; "Importing Faith;" Gunnarsson, "Kristna Gnosticismens Återkomst"]; (2) revelation knowledge has an expressed privileged position in the Word of Faith community [e.g., Hagin, *Growing Up*,

Word of Faith makes it the suitable starting point here. The sign-vehicle is made up of the words and concepts of "revelation" and "knowledge." Knowledge here must not be thought of as any kind of knowledge but as the specific type of illuminated, spiritual knowledge.[69] There is an important epistemological distinction in the Word of Faith between the knowledge gained through the senses, called "sense knowledge," and the knowledge gained by spiritual illumination, called "revelation knowledge."[70] The latter is the particular knowledge that comes directly from God through revelation. It is inaccessible through the common usage of the mind; revelation knowledge can only be gained when the human spirit is enabled by spiritual illumination.[71] Because such insights disclose how "God and the spiritual world 'works,'"[72] revelation knowledge is of absolute necessity to fulfill the Task to rule and increase.[73]

Revelation knowledge's immediate object can be identified through the interpretant of Eden Redeemed. The Church sequence of the story narrates how God through Jesus already brought the believer back to the state of Eden's position and blessing, making revelation knowledge all that is needed to enter this fullness.[74] Revelation knowledge realizes Eden for the believer by first opening the believer's eyes to the realities of the really real spiritual realm and then instructing the believer how to manifest these in the present by faith. Revelation knowledge thus signifies "supernatural knowledge of God and the spiritual realm revealed in the Bible."[75] In short, revelation knowledge's immediate object is the really real spiritual realm. Using the narrative categories from Chapter 3, the really real world

81–101; Harrison, *RR*, 90]; (3) revelation knowledge is affectively charged for Word of Faith adherents [e.g., Harrison, *RR*, 30]; (4) revelation knowledge has signified during an extended period of time [McConnell, *DG*, 101–13]; (5) revelation knowledge surfaces in a variety of contexts [e.g., sermons, books, songs]; (6) the meaning of revelation knowledge is expanded upon [e.g., Hagin, *Right and Wrong*]; (7) the role and use of revelation knowledge is closely monitored by the movement [e.g., Harrison, *RR*, 88]; (8) revelation knowledge has a direct relation with the element of story (see Section 4.3.1).

69. See Section 3.2.6.15.

70. Hagin, *Growing Up*, 107–9; Andrew Wommack, "Revelation Knowledge," *Awmi.net*, accessed April 7, 2021, https://www.awmi.net/reading/teaching-articles/revelation_kn owledge/.

71. Perriman, *FHP*, 30.

72. Ibid.; See Wommack, "Revelation Knowledge."

73. Harrison, *RR*, 32; Perriman, *FHP*, 30; See Wommack, "Revelation Knowledge."

74. Hagin, *Growing Up*, 90.

75. McConnell defines revelation knowledge as "that supernatural knowledge of God and the spiritual realm revealed in the Bible, particularly Paul's epistles, which enables man [*sic*] to transcend the limitations of Sense Knowledge and act in faith" (McConnell, *DG*, 102); Matta, *Born Again Jesus*, 10. See Kenneth Copeland Ministries, "How to Receive Revelation Knowledge," *Kcm.org*, accessed April 7, 2021, https://www.kcm.org/real-help/ spiritual-growth/learn/how-receive-revelation-knowledge.

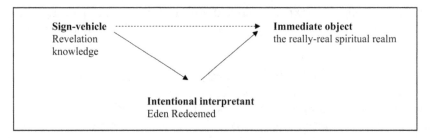

Figure 10 Revelation knowledge signifying as a Peircean sign.

is the realm where all Helpers are available for the Agent to fulfill the Task of ruling and increasing.

Figure 10 plots revelation knowledge along the terms of Peirce's semiotic model of signs.[76] This visual illustration indicates the semiosis of revelation knowledge and reveals the relation between the elements of the sign-vehicle, the intentional interpretant, and the immediate object. The dotted arrow illustrates the sign-producer's envisioned direction of the sign-vehicle to its object, while the lined arrows illustrate the actual process of signification through the interpretant. This diagram is representative of the semiosis of all signs analyzed in this chapter and is, therefore, not repeated.

Having identified revelation knowledge's immediate object, the question remains what kind of relationship the sign-vehicle has with its object (iconic, indexical, or symbolic). Word of Faith discourse repeatedly underscores the possibility to attain perfect and complete knowledge of God and the spiritual realm.[77] Hence, the sign of revelation knowledge stands for the really real in terms of resemblance. The relationship between the sign-vehicle and the object makes revelation knowledge function iconically in the Word of Faith movement.

Supportive signs of revelation knowledge include the material sign of the Bible in book form (often well used and annotated) or as an image (e.g., in logotypes for ministries and churches).[78] Linguistic signs include "Word," "identity," "knowing who you are in Christ," "truth," and "rhema."[79] Since revelation knowledge forms

76. The illustration is an adaption from Hughes (Hughes, *Worship as Meaning*, 146–7).

77. See Gunnarson, "Kristna Gnosticismens Återkomst," 96–8.

78. "In so-called Word churches . . . a well-worn, even ragged Bible marked throughout with pens, highlighting markers, and with its covers falling off signified that the owner used it regularly and was assumed to be very spiritual. By the same token, the newer a Bible looked (especially if it really were not actually new), the stronger the assumption that the person rarely used it and was less spiritual" (Harrison, *RR*, 30); Coleman, *Globalisation*, 125.

79. "Bible" and "Word" are common in church and ministry names, titles of books, and programs (e.g., *Rhema Bible Church*; *Word of Life*). Asamoah-Gyadu, *Contemporary Pentecostal*, 161. For Rhema, see King, *Only Believe*, 203–12; for Truth, see, e.g., Coleman, *Globalisation*, 157.

the basis for faith, all signs that signify faith also in a derived sense signify revelation knowledge, especially prosperity, health, and optimism. These are considered in the following text.

4.3.1.1 The Semiosis of Revelation Knowledge The iconic nature of the knowledge-sign ascribes direct resemblance between the sign-vehicle and its object. In the worldview of the Word of Faith, it is possible to have perfect knowledge of the really real spiritual realm. The expectancy is of absolute knowledge of the spiritual realm and of God's actions in the world.[80] It is the iconic function of revelation knowledge that makes the movement to reject the theological categories of mystery and paradox as acknowledgments of God's sovereignty and limits to human knowledge of God.[81] Any restriction set on the human understanding of God's actions is interpreted as indicators of the lack of revelation knowledge.[82] This iconic view of revelation knowledge makes a polarized approach to the complexities of human experience and effectively dismantles mystery in theology, and so challenges the fidelity of the worldview. In terms of evaluating the worldview's openness to correction, the semiosis of revelation knowledge explains the movement's confidence in their convictions and reluctance to change despite strong criticism.[83] Revelation knowledge's iconic function in the Word of Faith worldview is investigated further in the following chapters.

The semiosis of revelation knowledge makes clear how a particular epistemology is at work in the Word of Faith worldview.[84] This "spirit-epistemology" gives spiritual knowledge the ultimate role in the movement (see Section 6.2.4.2). The Word of Faith's reality is divided into dual categories: the really real dimension of the spiritual realm and the lesser-real, physical world.[85] Word of Faith discourse grants absolute authority to the spiritual realm over and above the natural, physical realm. This sharp division made between the spiritual and physical realms shows how the Word of Faith's "world view [sic] is based on a dualistic epistemology."[86]

---

80. McConnell, *DG*, 105.

81. Farah, *FTP*, 135–6, 152–7.

82. E.g., ending a prayer for healing with "thy will be done" is firmly rejected (Hagin, *Key to Scriptural Haling*, 8–11). See Matta, *Born Again Jesus*, 137.

83. Brandon *Health and Wealth*, 69; Art Lindsley, "Settling for Mud Pies," in *The Agony of Deceit: What Some TV Preachers are Really Preaching*, ed. Michael Horton (Chicago: Moody Press, 1990), 57.

84. Harrison, *RR*, 10; "One of the key distinctives of Prosperity Gospel communities is fundamentally epistemological. They believe they have received the unique knowledge that leads to prosperity and they intend to spread this message to other believers" (Walton, "Blessed and Highly Favored," 148).

85. See Section 3.2.6.6.

86. Horn, *FRTR*, 93. See Perriman, *FHP*, 34; Mumford, *Exploring Prosperity*, 40; Hanegraaff, *CIC*, 130. E.g., Kenneth E. Hagin, *I Believe in Visions* (Tulsa: Faith Library Publications, 1984).

The believer with illumination of how the spirit realm operates stands beyond all other Christians as such revelation knowledge trumps any insight gained through the senses.

Revelation knowledge is ultimately attained by spiritual illumination, either mediated through the biblical texts or directly received.[87] The biblical texts make a primary source of revelation knowledge.[88] Hence the emphasis on the Bible—or the Word—in the movement. However, the Bible is also supplemented with personal experiences, for example visions, dreams, and prophecies.[89] The semiosis of revelation knowledge explains the otherwise contradictory messages in Word of Faith discourse, which, on the one hand, ascribes total authority to the Bible in the formation of beliefs, while at the same time privileging personal, spiritual experiences. The semiotic logic that stipulates that revelation knowledge is necessary to realize the blessed life of Eden challenges the worldview's inner coherence. Instead of following their method of going straight to the Bible, the function of revelation knowledge gives hermeneutical priority to an extra-biblical framework largely formed by spiritual experiences.[90] The iconic emphasis on (obscure) knowledge's saving power gives rise to the critique that the Word of Faith has (neo)gnostic tendencies.[91]

4.3.2 Faith

Faith is another sign that fulfills all requirements to be considered a worldview-sign.[92] The sign-vehicle is the word and concept of faith. Since faith is arguably

---

87. Perriman, *FHP,* 30.

88. E.g., Hagin, "Bible Faith Study Guide," e-book edition, "Chapter 17."

89. E.g., Hagin, *I Believe in Visions.*

90. Perriman, *FHP,* 83–4; Horn, *FRTR,* 112; Warrington, "Teaching and Praxis," 83. See also Chapter 1.

91. Nel, *Prosperity Gospel,* Kindle edition, "Prosperity Theology's View of Christ and Humankind;" Gunnarsson, "Kristna Gnosticismens Återkomst;" Matta, *Born Again Jesus;* McConnell, *DG,* 110; Ackerly, "Importing Faith," 88–93, 307–9, 317, 322–3; DeArteaga, *Quenching the Spirit,* 228, 236–7; Harrison, *RR,* 10. "What we believe is a result of our thinking. If we think wrong, we will believe wrong. If our believing is wrong, our confession will be wrong. . . . It all hinges on our thinking!" (Hagin, *Right and Wrong,* 1).

92. (1) Faith is a central focus in the scholarly literature on the movement [Farah, *FTP,* 87–113, 125–32, 205; Farah, "Critical Analysis;" Barron, *Health and Wealth,* 64–76; McConnell, *DG,* 132–46; Perriman, *FHP,* 137–55; Hunt, *Beyond Seduction,* 44–61; MacArthur, *Charismatic Chaos* 342–50; Hanegraaff, *CIC,* 59–102; Johansson, *Vad Ska Man Tro,* 82–8; Brandon, *Health and Wealth,* 33–46; Jones and Woodbridge, *HWH,* 87–9; Warrington "The Use of the Name," 28; Olson, *CC,* 157; Lederle, *Theology with Spirit,* 154–5; Bowman, *Word-Faith,* 105–14; Bowler, *Blessed,* 41–76; King, *Only Believe*]; (2) faith has an expressed privileged position in the Word of Faith community (Bowler, *Blessed,* 41–86, e.g., part of the self-descriptive term for the movement; all literature on faith); (3) faith is

the most significant sign in the Word of Faith, it merits an expanded discussion here. (I discussed revelation knowledge prior to faith because faith is derivative of revelation knowledge in Word of Faith discourse).

Analyzing the semiosis of faith is complex because faith is used in the Word of Faith discourse to signify (at least) three objects through two distinct interpretants. A close study of the semiosis of faith contributes critical knowledge. The same sign-vehicle of faith signifies (1) power to accomplish God's will (the faith of God), (2) personal trust in God (faith in God), and (3) faith in the Bible (the Word). The complexity is increased by another intentional interpretant apart from Eden Redeemed at work within the Word of Faith discourse. This second interpretant can best be described as a general Pentecostal theological narrative made up of the basic Pentecostal narrative convictions.[93] This interpretant is thus not unique to the Word of Faith but is held in common with the larger Pentecostal world in which Word of Faith is part (see Introduction). The three usages of faith (faith of God, faith in God, faith in the Word) and the dual interpretants (Eden Redeemed, a Pentecostal narrative) are important to discuss to clarify their role in faith semiosis and so avoid reductionist readings of the Word of Faith.

When faith functions as a worldview-sign, it has the Word of Faith worldview-story as the intentional interpretant. Eden Redeemed narrates faith as part of God's nature and a force through which God operates and creates.[94] The story says that Adam partook of God's faith—"the God-kind of faith."[95] Through the faith

affectively charged for Word of Faith adherents (e.g., the argument that Word of Faith has restored the original teaching on faith that was lost to Christianity); (4) faith has signified during an extended period of time (Bowler, *Blessed*, 41–76); (5) faith surfaces in a variety of contexts (e.g., in sermons, "confessions," songs, films and personal narratives); (6) the meaning of faith is expanded upon (e.g., the countless homilies and lectures, written and oral on faith); (7) the role and use of faith is closely monitored by the movement (e.g., the detailed formulas and taxonomies of faith in e.g., Hagin, *New Thresholds*, 10; Andrew Wommack Ministries, "Faith of God," *Awmi.net*, accessed April 7, 2021, https://www.awm i.net/reading/teaching-articles/faith_god/); (8) faith has a direct relation with the element of story (see Section 3.2.6.5).

93. For Pentecostal narrative convictions see, e.g., Dayton, *Theological Roots*; Vondey, *Pentecostal Theology*.

94. Bowman, *Word-Faith*, 105–6. E.g., "God is a faith God, and He operates on the principle of faith. We are faith children because we are begotten of God, and we are to live by faith. We receive from God by faith" (Hagin, *Two Kinds of Faith*, 29); "God is a faith being" (Copeland, *Force of Faith*, e-book edition, "You Have Faith"); Copeland, *Laws of Prosperity*, 15.

95. Kenneth Copeland Ministries, "How to Develop the God Kind of Faith," *Kcm. org*, accessed April 7, 2021, https://blog.kcm.org/develop-god-kind-of-faith/; Christine Miller and Nathan Carlin, "Joel Osteen as Cultural Selfobject: Meeting the Needs of the Group Self and Its Individual Members in and from the Largest Church in America," *Pastoral Psychology* 59 (2010): 33. The Word of Faith's interpretation of Mark 11:22 raises

of God, Adam could manifest God's will on the earth.[96] Since Eden Redeemed narrates God as having and operating by faith, the immediate object of faith must be other than trust in the person of God, because it makes little sense to imagine God having faith in Godself.[97] Therefore, when Eden Redeemed is the intentional interpretant, the immediate object of faith is best understood as power.[98] Or more fully: power to realize God's will.[99] This God-kind of faith is the power or force that enables both God and the human agent; the faith of God realizes God's own intentions and empowers the believer to "operate the same way God operates."[100]

the grammatical question of how the Greek genitive phrase *echete pistin theou* should be translated. Should God (*theou*) be understood as either an objective genitive—faith that has God as its object—or subjective genitive—faith that God as the subject has? The Word of Faith argues for the second usage. Exegetical studies, however, speak to an objective interpretation: "Contextually . . . it is best to see *theou* as an objective genitive and render the verse, as virtually all versions do, 'Have faith in God'" (Kinnebrew, "Charismatic Doctrine," 193).

96. Bowman, *Word-Faith*, 106. E.g., "God is a faith God. . . . God made man [*sic*] a faith man, because man belongs to God's class. A faith man lives in the creative realm of God" (Hagin, *Zoe*, 38); Hagin, *Bible Faith*, e-book edition, "Chapter 18;" Miller and Carlin, "Joel Osteen," 33. See Kenneth Copeland Ministries, "How to Develop the God Kind of Faith," *Kcm.org*, accessed April 7, 2021, https://blog.kcm.org/develop-god-kind-of-faith/.

97. E.g., "God had faith that His own words would come to pass [in creating the world]" (Hagin, *Your Faith in God*, e-book edition, "Chapter 1"); Hagin, *Real Faith*, 29. See Bowman, *Word-Faith*, 105–14, Perriman, *FHP*, 139–40; Miller and Carlin, "Joel Osteen," 33.

98. "Believers conceptualize faith as a causal agent, a power that actualizes events and objects in the real world. Faith acts as a force that reaches through the boundaries of materiality and into the spiritual realm, as if plucking objects from there and drawing them back into space and time" (Bowler, *Blessed*, 141, 45); Kate Bowler, "Blessed Bodies: Prosperity as Healing within the African-American Faith Movement," in *Global Pentecostal and Charismatic Healing*, ed. Candy Gunther Brown (New York: Oxford University Press, 2010), 87; Smail, Walker and Wright, *Love of Power*, 80; "faith is not merely a theocentric act of the will in which one exercises simple trust in God; rather, it is an anthropocentric spiritual force one directs toward God" (Morris, "Biblical and Theological," 250); Meyer, "Pentecostalism and Neo-Liberal Capitalism," 15; Pasicka, "Mundane Transcendence," 382.

99. Perriman defines the Word of Faith view of faith as "the power by which the work of God is done in the universe" (Perriman, *FHP*, 39). See Bowler, "Blessed Bodies," 87; Bowler, *Blessed*, 147.

100. Hagin, *Bible Faith Study Guide*, e-book edition, "Chapter 18;" Sarles, "Prosperity and Healing," 347–8; Winston, *Imitate God*, i; Kenneth Copeland, *How You Call It Is How It Will Be* (Forth Worth: Kenneth Copeland Publications, 2010), e-book edition, "Paddling Upstream;" "The Lord has given us everything we need, including all the faith we need. We just need to acknowledge what we have and begin to learn the laws that govern the operation of God's faith" (Wommack, "Faith of God").

The relationship between the sign-vehicle of faith and the immediate object of power to realize God's will is best categorized as conventional as it is mediated through special revelation knowledge. Faith thus signifies by a received rule of interpretation. Faith functions primarily as a symbolic sign in the Word of Faith worldview.[101]

The most significant supportive signs to faith as power are the three worldview-signs of prosperity, health, and optimism (see the following text). Revelation knowledge also signifies faith.[102] Beyond these, faith as power is signified by measurable, perpetual growth:[103] increase in the impact and influence of one's ministry and personal life, quantified in church attendance, buildings, new converts, nations reached, products sold, number of viewers, and positions of influence in society and business.[104] Among the linguistic signs stands "faith" which is used in various contexts, for example in church names ("Living Faith Churches Worldwide") and logotypes (Rhema ministries' "Faith Shield"). Other linguistic signs include "authority," "dominion," "command," "decree," "believe [for something]," and "stand [in faith for something]."[105] "Victory" is also a common linguistic sign used in homilies, personal communication, church and ministry names, titles to books, TV programs, and so on.[106] Beyond the Pentecostal signification of Jesus' victory over sin, death, and Satan, victory signifies in the Word of Faith semiosis especially their belief in Jesus' defeat of the curse of sickness and poverty.[107] Victory thus means the end result of the faith of God; that Eden's life is restored here and now, realized especially in prosperity and health.[108] Faith

101. It is "a modified conception of faith that differed in important respects from the type of faith promoted by early believers" (Williams, *Spirit Cure*, 112). See Matta, *Born Again Jesus*, xiii, xvi.

102. "Faith teachers . . . measure faith by the type and amount of knowledge one has" (McConnell, *DG*, 110).

103. "synonyms for growth: expand, extend, enlarge, increase, multiply, impact, influence, abundance, advancement, fruitfulness, success, prosperity" (Maddox, "Growth Churches," 149).

104. Bowler, *Blessed*, 101; J. Kwabena Asamoah-Gyadu, "God Is Big in Africa: Pentecostal Mega Churches and a Changing Religious Landscape," *Material Religion* (2019): no page numbers, DOI:10.1080/17432200.2019.1590012; Maddox, "Growth Churches;" See Goh, "Hillsong and Megachurch; "the burden of their [Jim and Tammy Bakker's] gospel was it always had to be proven in an endless cycle of bigger and better" (Bowler, *Blessed*, 109, 25).

105. See, e.g., Harrison, *RR*, 64, 71; Pasicka, "Mundane Transcendence," 373.

106. Bowler, *Blessed*, 7, 178–25; Gifford, "Healing in African Pentecostalism," 251–64.

107. E.g., Prince, *Unmerited Favor* (Lake Mary: Charisma House, 2011), 25.

108. "Real faith will always end in victory" (Hagin, *Staying Positive*, 160, 28, 130); Oyedepo, *Born to Win*; Kenneth Copeland, *The Winning Attitude* (Forth Worth: Kenneth Copeland Publications, 1982), e-book edition. See Harrison, *RR*, 9.

as power is signified by mechanical metaphors: "the switch of faith,"[109] "activate faith,"[110] and "release faith."[111] Word of Faith discourse also contains an almost endless number of narrative signs of faith, in the form of testimony and personal anecdotes which attest to the efficient functions of faith as power to realize God's will to work prosperity and health.[112]

The sign-vehicle of faith stands for another object in the Word of Faith discourse. This object is signified through the second interpretant of a general Pentecostal narrative rather than the Eden Redeemed story. Instead of power (faith of God) or faith in the Bible, faith signifies here personal trust in the triune God, that is, faith *in* God.[113] The signification of faith as personal trust is not unique to the Word of Faith but shared with all who embrace an interpretant similar to the Pentecostal.[114] Hence, faith as trust in God does not fit the requirements for a worldview-sign in the Word of Faith (faith functions as a worldview-sign only when the sign-producer intends Eden Redeemed as the interpretant). Yet, this is included here because it is imperative to understand the dual semiosis of faith through two different interpretants to avoid reductionist analyses (see the following text). I also discuss the consequences of the difference between faith of God and faith in God in the following chapters.

Faith signifies through Eden Redeemed also a third object: faith in the Word. However, it is a mistake to assume that this usage of faith stands for a typical Pentecostal high bibliology.[115] Though the Word of Faith embraces a high view of the Bible's inspiration and authority, this particular meaning of faith means trusting in the biblical texts to be the literal spoken, living words of God and so able to channel God's faith and blessings.[116] The Bible thus becomes the object of faith in a unique sense beyond a high bibliology. The biblical texts are the source

109. Hagin, *Bible Healing*, e-book edition, "The Switch of Faith;" Wommack, *You Already Got It*, 55–6.

110. Hagin, *Faith Study Guide*, e-book edition, "Chapter 10," "Chapter 19."

111. Kenneth E. Hagin, *How to Turn Your Faith Loose* (Tulsa: Faith Library Publications, 1980); see Pasicka, "Mundane Transcendence," 377–84.

112. E.g., Prince, *Grace Revolution*.

113. E.g., Hagin, *Why Tongues*, 20–2; Hagin, *What to Do*, 33, 36; Dollar, *Divine Order*, e-book edition, "So What Is Faith?."

114. Keith Warrington, *Healing and Suffering: Biblical and Pastoral Reflections* (Carlisle: Paternoster Press, 2005), 35.

115. See Scott Ellington, "Pentecostalism and the Authority of Scripture," *Journal of Pentecostal Theology* 9 (1996): 16–38; Vondey, *Beyond Pentecostalism*, 47–77.

116. Wommack, *You Already Got It*, 160–1; Vreeland, "Reconstructing Word of Faith," 10; "The relationship between God and the Bible is described in almost pantheistic terms. God and God's word is one; the presence of the word is God" (Nel, *Prosperity Gospel*, Kindle edition, "View of God").

through which the believer accesses God's faith, prosperity, and health.[117] The most important supportive sign which signifies this particular trust in the Bible is the linguistic sign "the Word."[118] The Word is used frequently in Word of Faith discourse, in the movement's self-description ("Word of Faith;" "Word churches;" "Word believers"), and in names of churches and ministries ("Living Word;" "Ever Increasing Word").[119] Narrative signs take the form of stories and testimonies of how the Bible itself has produced miracles ("the Word worked").[120]

4.3.2.2 The Semiosis of Faith Recognizing the complexities in the semiosis of faith within Word of Faith discourse is critical for a better understanding of the movement's worldview. That faith can signify an impersonal object in the Word of Faith is noted by scholarship previously, but a full semiotic analysis of the faith-sign has not been done.[121] When the sign-producer has Eden Redeemed as the intentional interpretant, one of faith's intended objects is power to realize God's will.[122] This is the underlying semiotic understanding that explains why Word of Faith discourse claims that "God is a faith God"[123] and that believers have a share of "God's faith"[124] and exhorts them to "having faith in your faith."[125] The semiosis of faith sheds light on why faith is objectified in the Word of Faith and why the movement encourages an instrumental approach to faith (see next chapter).[126]

---

117. "God's Word has creative power because His words are spirit and they are life . . . All of God's blessings are contained in His Word!" (Hagin, *God's Word*, 2, 23); "The Word of God brings life. . . . The Word of God produces health. . . . The Word of God begets prosperity. . . . God's Word sown in the heart of man brings forth life, joy, peace, abundance, and health" (Savelle, *If Satan Can't Steal Your Joy*, e-book edition, "The Great Pretender").

118. Harrison, *RR*, 39.

119. See Introduction.

120. E.g., "the Word protected us. . . . The Word worked–as it always does–for our good" (Copeland, *Live Long*, e-book edition, "For Our Own Good").

121. See Pasicka, "Mundane Transcendence;" Lovett's contrast "fides quae" with "fides qua" (Lovett, "Positive Confession,"); Sarles, "Prosperity and Healing," 348; Horton, "TV Gospel," 146.

122. See Perriman, *FHP*, 139.

123. Hagin, *Zoe*, 38; "God is a faith Being" (Wommack, *You Already Got It*, 163).

124. Kenneth Copeland, "Have God's Faith," YouTube Video, 22:00, Posted by Kenneth Copeland Ministries, November 28, 2015, accessed April 7, 2021, https://www.youtube.com /watch?v=pAA-4My0FRk.

125. Kenneth E. Hagin, *Having Faith in Your Faith* (Tulsa: Faith Library Publications, 1980); Capps, *Faith That Will Work*, e-book edition, "Fear is Faith in Reverse." See Jones and Woodbridge, *HWH*, 87–9.

126. Pasicka, "Mundane Transcendence," 382. The Word of Faith "make[s] faith in principle an infallible means of getting spiritual results" (Perriman, *FHP*, 196, 137). E.g., Charles Capps, *Faith that Will Work for You* (England: Charles Capps Publishing, 1999); Hagin, *Growing Up*, 92. See Meyer, "Pentecostalism and Neo-Liberal Capitalism," 15; Olson, *CC*, 163.

There is also a direct relationship between the semiosis of faith as power and the absence of God as Sender in The Church sequence of Eden Redeemed.[127] Since the believer has restored access to the same faith by which God operates, the burden of acting lies on the believer.

When Eden Redeemed is the intentional interpretant, key distinctions between the Bible and God are blurred.[128] There is a confluence of God and the Bible in faith semiosis which makes Word of Faith discourse ascribe personal, divine attributes to the biblical texts.[129] The Bible becomes the source and energy of faith and the access point to prosperity and health, resulting in a certain spiritual approach to the Bible.[130] Hence, the affirmation that "faith in God is faith in His Word"[131] and the

127. "a concept of faith that is not only pragmatic, but mechanistic: no active divine participation seems to be needed for man to draw blessings from the spiritual realm into the physical world by the power of faith alone. God's role seems limited to an automatic response to man's confession of faith" (Pasicka, "Mundane Transcendence," 372–3).

128. "When faith in the word of God comes alive in you, you tap into the virtue that the word carries, causing you to become what the word says" (Oyedepo, *Operating*, e-book edition, "The Word of God"); "God and His WORD are One, not because we say so, but because He said so. He has made it clear that we cannot separate Him from His WORD. Just as He never changes, His WORD never changes. They are both the same–yesterday, today and forever. What's more, God's WORD is as powerful as He is" (Kenneth Copeland, "Young, Strong, Blessed," *Believer's Voice of Victory,* June 2014, 19); "In order to know God and what to expect from Him, we must know His Word–because they are one" (Meyer, *Change Your Words*, e-book edition, "Chapter 3"). See also "The Word of God is God! God is His Word and His Word is Him" (Dag Stewart-Mill, *Steps to the Anointing*, Kindle edition, "Steps 7: Listen to the Word of God." See Scott A. Ellington, "Scripture: Finding One's Place in God's Story," in *Routledge Handbook to Pentecostal Theology*, ed. Wolfgang Vondey (London: Routledge, 2020), 68–70; Matta, *Born Again Jesus*, 121.

129. "We can make contact with God through the Word, for God is the Word. This Word of God is a God-breathed, God-inspired, God-indwelt message" (Hagin, *The Key to Scriptural Healing*, 29); Hagin, *God's Word,* 11, 23–30; "When you are in the presence of the Word of God, you are in the presence of God Himself" (Copeland, *Laws of Prosperity*, 37). See Swaggart, "Hyper-Faith II," 14; Swaggart, "Hyper-Faith III," 10.

130. "The Word of God causes the same kind of faith to be dealt to our hearts that God used to speak the universe into existence. Faith is given or imparted to us through the Word. Hearing the Word brings faith" (Hagin, *Bible Faith*, e-book edition, "Faith Is a Gift from God"); "faith in the word of God brings you into the same realm with God!" (Oyedepo, *Operating*, e-book edition, "Only Believe!"); "[the Bible] literally carries within it the power to make those promises become a reality in your life" (Copeland, *Blessed to Be a Blessing*, e-book edition, "Chapter 3"); "All a man needs to live a prosperous life and enjoy good success is contained in the Word of God" (Oyedepo, *Making Maximum Impact*, e-book edition, "Chapter 3"); Copeland, *Live Long, Finish Strong*, e-book edition, "Chapter 4;" Capps, *Faith That Will*.

131. Hagin, *What to Do,* 33.

crediting of the Word for blessings received ("the Word works").[132] This particular semiosis of faith makes the Bible to be objectified and used instrumentally in the movement as the way in which God's faith and blessings are channeled to the believer.[133]

An observation of weight arising from analyzing the sign of faith is the second intentional interpretant of a general Pentecostal narrative at work apart from Eden Redeemed. The semiotic shift in the faith-sign between faith of God and faith in God is the result of the sign-vehicle signifying through two separate interpretants in the Word of Faith discourse.[134] Research into the Word of Faith must make certain to not overlook the dual interpretants, because the two significations are mixed in Word of Faith discourse and often appear in close proximity, making differentiation difficult. Studies on the Word of Faith easily commit the semiotic error of assuming that identical sign-vehicles signify the same object. A necessary question when encountering the faith-sign in Word of Faith discourse is, therefore, if it signifies the faith of God (power), faith in God (trust), or faith in the Word. Studies that recognize just one or two of these significations end up with a superficial analysis of the movement. When faith is read as only signifying impersonal power, the Word of Faith is treated as a foreign movement—a "cult"— in relation to the wider Pentecostal communities. Yet, arguing that the Word of Faith movement is heretical based on the impersonal object of faith is unsatisfying since it fails to account for the object of personal trust in many of its usages of faith.[135] But arguing that the movement is simply a continuation of historic renewal Christianity is equally unsatisfying because it interprets faith as always signifying personal trust in God. Options of the Word of Faith either as a metaphysical cult or as the heir of the baton of renewal Christianity are reductions, each overlooking the dual semiosis of faith.[136] The argument that the Word of Faith movement brings "balance" to Christianity with an emphasis on a "positive" and "active" Christian

---

132. Hagin. *Bible Faith,* e-book edition, "How Faith Comes;" Hagin, *Exceedingly Growing,* 51; Hagin, *God's Irresistible,* 1.

133. "From cover to cover it [the Bible] contains God's faith-filled words, specifically empowered to produce whatever you need in your life. When you pick up your Bible, you hold in your hands the seeds to produce finances, healing, salvation of your loved ones, a sound mind, restoration of your marriage, or anything else you could possibly need" (Dollar, *Divine Order,* e-book edition, "Chapter 2").

134. "You may be thinking, 'Everybody knows what faith is. It means belief or trust.' Of course, that's part of it. But real faith involves so much more than that" (Dollar, *Divine Order,* e-book edition, "Chapter 2").

135. E.g., McConnell, *DG;* Horton, "TV Gospel;" Hanegraaff, *CIC;* Jeff Kluttz, *Apostasy! The Word-Faith Doctrinal Deception* (self pub. Returningking.com, 2011), Kindle edition, "Chapter 6."

136. See Chapter 1.

faith over and above a "cynic" and "passive" faith exemplifies a superficial analysis that neglects faith's differing objects.[137]

4.3.3 Prosperity

Prosperity is the third sign in the Word of Faith that fulfills the requirements as a worldview-sign. I expand the analysis here because of its complexity and scholarly interest in prosperity. The semiosis of prosperity in the Word of Faith is, like faith, also complicated. The reason is that there is no consensus definition of prosperity in the movement, making prosperity to be used fluidly by propagators and differently appropriated by believers.[138] Word of Faith discourse uses prosperity in both a direct and in an expanded sense. The direct sense speaks of material, economic prosperity and the expanded sense adds spiritual, social, physical, and mental dimensions of success and wellness.[139] Since the expanded dimensions of prosperity are discussed under the signs of health and optimism in the following text, prosperity is used here in the direct economic sense. But there is even a lack of consensus in the Word of Faith discourse on how to define prosperity's economic dimension. Prosperity stands for wealth, "excess or abundance" to some, while for others it stands for a full supply and "lack of need."[140] Prosperity is thus understood on the continuum from absolute wealth to relative provision. Absolute prosperity signifies that every believer should have riches quantifiable on a global

137. E.g., King, *Only Believe*, 103–15. Vreeland's attempt to reconstruct Hagin's emphasis on faith fails to recognize the dual interpretants in the semiosis of faith (Vreeland, "Reconstructing Word of Faith," 12–14). Historical comparisons between "classical" and "contemporary" teachings on faith have yet also to pay sufficient attention to the complexities in the faith semiosis.

138. "Prosperity, as constructed in the minds of most believers, is not a fixed and absolute condition, based solely in the acquisition of material goods. Its meaning is neither static nor stationary. Thus, there is a social logic among followers of the prosperity gospel that causes the theology to hold saliency in people's lives even as the reality of social stagnation sets in. Prosperity's condition as a 'moving target' allows for this type of commitment" (Frederick, *Colored Television*, 71).

139. "The theology of 'that all may go well with you' [3 John 2] is comprehensive and totalizing in conception; practitioners describe prosperity as material advancement, success, and promotion in worldly affairs" (Ukah, "God, Wealth," 77). E.g., Copeland, *Laws of Prosperity*, 9–13.

140. Walton, "Blessed and Highly Favored," 120. E.g., see Maxwell, "Social Mobility." Copeland writes, "True prosperity is the ability to use God's power to meet the needs of mankind in any realm of life. This covers much more than just finances, politics and society. Money is not the only degree of prosperity. You can have all the money in the world and still be poverty-stricken spiritually, mentally and physically" (Copeland, *Laws of Prosperity*, e-book edition, "Chapter 1").

scale, regardless of their economic context.[141] Relative prosperity means rather that the believer enjoys provision for their economic needs (with an excess to share) comparative to their particular economic context.[142] What is important in the present analysis of the semiosis of prosperity is not the term's precise definition but to analyze the sign of prosperity as a whole (i.e., all the sign's parts). Prosperity fulfills the eight criteria for being a worldview-sign in the Word of Faith.[143]

Following Wright's worldview-model, a worldview-sign signifies through the interrelated worldview-story. Since Eden Redeemed makes the worldview-story of the Word of Faith, its role is as intentional interpretant in the semiosis of prosperity. According to the narrative of Eden Redeemed, prosperity was God's creative intention for humanity in Eden. Nevertheless, Adam forfeited prosperity in The Fall, and prosperity was replaced with the curse of poverty. In turn, Jesus defeated the curse and restored access to prosperity. Hence, the believer has now the right to live in prosperity and can claim it through the faith of God.[144] Eden Redeemed narrates God to already having done everything for the believer to realize prosperity in the present life; the believer and not God is the proactive

---

141. Gifford, *Ghana's New Christianity*, 53–6.

142. Hagin, *Biblical Keys*; "Prosperity is relative" (Hagin, *MT*, 199). Cf. "'Relative prosperity' . . . blends the material, spiritual, and social motivations and outcomes of giving in a way that allows the giver to consistently offer his or her seed-faith gifts amid incongruent social realities. The instability and malleability of the concept of prosperity is central to its longevity. Without this fluidity of meaning, such a theology could not sustain itself" (Frederick, *Colored Television*, 71).

143. (1) prosperity is a specific focus in the scholarly conversations (e.g., Coleman, *Globalisation*, 187–8; Bowler, *Blessed*, 77–138); (2) prosperity enjoys a privileged position within Word of Faith discourse (e.g., it makes a popular descriptor of the movement, as in "prosperity gospel" and "health and wealth" [Harrison, *RR*, 51]); (3) prosperity is affectively charged for the Word of Faith adherents (e.g., the language used in Faith discourse to classify prosperity as an unreserved "blessing" and poverty as a "curse" ([Hagin, *Redeemed*]); (4) prosperity has signified for the Word of Faith since the movement's inception (Bowler, *Blessed*, 72–138); (5) prosperity reappears in several contexts (e.g., songs and music videos, church names, bumper stickers, themes of conventions, book and sermon titles, slogans ([Bowler, *Blessed*, 97, 135; Gifford, *Ghana's New Christianity*, 44–5; Simbarashe Gukurume, "Singing Positivity: Prosperity Gospel in the Musical Discourse of Popular Youth Hip-Hop Gospel in Zimbabwe," *Muziki* 14, no. 2 (2017): 36–54; Sinitiere, *Salvation with a Smile*, 195]); (6) the meaning of prosperity is expanded upon (e.g., the ever-expanding list of published materials, sermons and books, on the subject); (7) prosperity's role and functions are closely monitored by the movement (see discourse aimed at countering misunderstandings by outsiders and misuse by insiders, e.g., Hagin, *MT*); (8) prosperity stands in direct relation to the Eden Redeemed worldview-story (see Sections 3.2.6.9; 3.2.7; Hagin, *Biblical Keys*, 1; Savelle, *Why God Wants You to Prosper*, e-book edition, "Chapter 1").

144. Perriman, *FHP*, 196. See, e.g., Gloria Copeland, *God's Will Is Prosperity* (Forth Worth: Kenneth Copeland Ministries, 1978), e-book edition, "Chapter 1."

subject in manifesting prosperity, that is, the believer uses faith to bring prosperity from its existence in the spiritual realm into material reality.[145] The emphasis placed on the believer does not negate the Word of Faith's strong expectancy of God's personal and continuous interventions, only that God's actions are in response to the believer's faith.[146] The sign-vehicle of prosperity thus signifies through Eden Redeemed the immediate object of faith. More particularly, prosperity signifies the financial aspect of faith: that God's economic purposes for humans to rule and increase are fulfilled by the believer's faith.[147]

Eden Redeemed narrates how fixed and causal spiritual laws govern prosperity and that such laws function without failure when rightly applied.[148] Spiritual laws make the relationship between prosperity and faith causative and mechanical. This relationship makes prosperity to serve as an index-sign.[149] That is, in the Word of Faith worldview, prosperity signifies faith in a direct, mechanical, and causal way.

145. "It [God's promise] is already real in the spirit realm. But we want it to become real in this physical realm where we live in the flesh" (Hagin, *In Him,* 11); "Faith reaches over into the spiritual realm and draws what God has already supplied, out into the physical realm" (Wommack, *You've Already,* 56).

146. "the worldview of these [Prosperity Gospel] believers teaches them that everything happens because God is working for their good *as a result of their faithfulness*" (Lin, *Prosperity Gospel,* Kindle edition, "The Renewing of Their Minds," emphasis added).

147. Copeland, *God's Will,* e-book edition, "Chapter 1." See Harrison, *RR,* 66–7; Gifford, *Ghana's New Christianity,* 50; Perriman, *FHP,* 51.

148. "God has set forth principles, laws, rules, requirements, and conditions, which if observed and carried out, will result in a life of prosperity and pleasures" (Savelle, *Why God Wants,* e-book edition, "Prosperity Isn't A Get-Rich-Quick"); "I am persuaded that no one succeeds by chance, no one makes things happen by accident" (Oyedepo, *Making Maximum Impact,* e-book edition, "Chapter 3"). See Harrison, *RR,* 32, 100; Coleman, *Globalisation,* 188–9.

149. "Physical and material well-being . . . become an index of successful commitment to the Faith" (Coleman, *Globalisation,* 151); "The car [Mercedes or Cadillac] and the [vanity] license plates become yet another way of confessing and testifying (signifying) prosperity and making the direct conceptual linkage between one's faith and one's possession of the status symbol" (Harrison, *RR,* 78, 100); Heuser, "Religio-Scapes," 16, 20. "Big Faith = Big Consumer Lifestyle: New Homes, New Clothes, and Swimming Pools" (Mundey, "Osteen," 326). See also Bowler, "Blessed Bodies," 83; Walton, "Blessed and Highly Favored," 144; Meyer, "Pentecostalism and Neo-Liberal Capitalism," 19; Chong, "Of Riches and Faith," 161; Walton, *Watch This,* 95; Agana, *Succeed Here,* 198; Rey "Missing Prosperity," 348–9; e.g., "if you'll continually honor and obey God and His Word, it [prosperity] *will* come" (Hagin, *Biblical Keys,* introduction, emphasis original); "When you are living by faith—the faith of God—you will be on top, and if you are not on top, or moving toward the top, then you are not living by faith" (Fred K. C. Price, *Faith, Foolishness or Presumption* (Tulsa: Harrison House, 1979), 10; Copeland, *Laws of Prosperity,* 14.

There is a cluster of supportive signs within the Word of Faith that signify prosperity. The most central material signs consist of money (e.g., high salaries, large offerings, and big budgets);[150] consumer goods and services (e.g., designer clothes, electronics, watches and jewelry, expensive hotels, and luxurious foods);[151] and other assets (e.g., cars, airplanes, mansions, church buildings, and technology).[152] Narrative signs of prosperity often take the form of rags-to-riches stories and testimonies of wealth and consumption.[153] Word of Faith discourse uses Jesus' earthly life as a sign of prosperity, arguing that he had a splendid house, costly clothing, and handled large sums of money.[154] The numerous linguistic signs meaning prosperity in Word of Faith discourse include "harvest," "progress . . . breakthrough, success, achievement, destiny, favour, dominion, blessing, excellence, elevation, promotion, increase, expansion, plenty, open doors, triumph, finances, overflow, abundance, newness, fulfilment, victory, power, possession."[155] Several of these signs are further explored in Chapter 5 in relation to the worldview-element of praxis.

4.3.3.1 The Semiosis of Prosperity Prosperity's function as an index of faith is one of the most significant and unique features of the Word of Faith. Prosperity

150. Frederick, *Colored Television*, 31–59; Shayne Lee, *T. D. Jakes: America's New Preacher* (New York: New York University Press, 2005), 103; Asamoah-Gyadu, "God Is Big."

151. Bowler, *Blessed*, 28, 94–5, 106, 120, 134–5; Harrison, *RR*, 12, 75, 78; Walton, *Watch This*, 158; Coleman, *Globalisation*, 150; Lee, *T. D. Jakes*, 109–10; "contemporary notions of designers clothes and other conspicuous symbols of material success are turned back and used as a lens through which to understand and redefine God's promises to give the believer a life of abundance" (Harrison, *RR*, 12); Meyer, "Pentecostalism and Neo-Liberal Capitalism," 17; Maltese, "Activist-Holiness Kenneth Hagin," 77.

152. Bowler, *Blessed*, 135–6; Harrison, *RR*, 43; Coleman, *Globalisation*, 153–4; Lee, *Jakes*, 109–10; Asamoah-Gyadu, "God Is Big," 1; Heuser, "Religio-Scapes," 19; "The sign of progress in prosperity is the successful acquisition of things and the display of this wealth to others. Many television ministers who align themselves with this doctrine sport expensive suits, luxury cars, extravagant homes, and elaborate, well-furnished sanctuaries" (Frederick, *Between Sundays*, 150). See also Steven Félix-Jäger, "Material Visions of the Good Life," *Pneuma: The Journal of the Society for Pentecostal Studies* 41, no. 2 (2019): 279–90.

153. Lin, *Prosperity Gospel*, Kindle edition, "La Predicacíon (The Preaching);" Frederick, *Colored Television*, 31–59; Bowler, *Blessed*, 135–6; Gifford, "Prosperity," 376; Walton, "Blessed and Highly Favored," 137–8; Maltese "Activist-Holiness Kenneth Hagin," 77.

154. E.g., Hagin, *MT*, 41–66; Oyedepo, *Anointing for Breakthrough*, e-book edition, "The 'Poor' Jesus;" Avanzini, *Answers Your Questions*, 118–19. See Harrison, *RR*, 12; Bowler, *Blessed*, 91; Perriman, *FHP*, 175–6; Mumford, *Exploring Prosperity*, 47–8; Lee, *T. D. Jakes*, 109. Though Word of Faith rejects the notion of Jesus being economically poor, the extent of his prosperity varies from having his needs "abundantly" met to being wealthy.

155. Gifford, *Ghana's New Christianity*, 46; Asamoah-Gyadu, "God Is Big," 1; Bowler, *Blessed*, 191; Heuser, "Religio-Scapes," 16.

as an index-sign makes "a core canon"[156] in their worldview.[157] The Pew Research Center used the indexical role of prosperity as their central identifying aspect in surveying the global spread of Word of Faith convictions.[158] The question posed to the interviewees to determine their level of adherence to Word of Faith beliefs was: "God will grant material prosperity to all believers who have enough faith."[159] This question poses an indexical, cause-and-effect relationship between prosperity and faith as the determining factor of Word of Faith commitment.[160]

Placing prosperity in an indexical relation to faith is controversial, triggering much of the critique against the movement and confusion within the movement.[161] Word of Faith semiosis offers a radical resignification of prosperity compared to Pentecostalism previously (e.g., wealth is released from its negative

156. Heuser, "Religo-Scapes," 22.

157. To ascribe a cause-and-effect relation between Christian faith and prosperity is not new from a historical perspective. For example, central in Weber's thesis on the Protestant work ethic is the argument that Christians translated prosperity indexically to faith (David W. Miller, "Wealth Creation as Integrated with Faith" (presentation, Muslim, Christian, and Jewish Views on the Creation of Wealth, Notre Dame, April 23–24, 2007), 5–6. Yet, in analyzing the indexical role of prosperity, it is important to differentiate between the dual semiosis of the faith-sign within Word of Faith discourse.

158. See Heuser, "Religo-Scapes," 22.

159. Pew Research, *Spirit and Power*, 10, 30.

160. See Lausanne, "Cape Town Commitment," II-E-5. Asamoah-Gyadu defines "prosperity gospel" as "the popular teaching that material things and wellbeing constitute the only sure indicators of God's favour" (Asamoah-Gyadu, *Contemporary Pentecostal Christianity,* 106).

161. "we deny as unbiblical the teaching that spiritual welfare can be measured in terms of material welfare, or that wealth is always a sign of God's blessing" (Lausanne, "Cape Town Commitment," II-E-5). Souders writes: "The particular danger of the CPG [Christian Prosperity Gospel] to orthodox Christianity lies in its deconstructive use of the signs and techniques of the evangelical tradition and its redeployment of those very signs and techniques for its own purposes and perspectives—purposes more consonant with the materialist desires of a diverse audience" (Souders, "God of Wealth," 90). James K. A. Smith warns: "But how many of us are still quite comfortable with more 'low grade' (or 'soft sell') versions of a prosperity gospel? For instance, how many of us buy into a logic that assumes if a Christian is wealthy, he or she has been 'blessed' by God—as if material prosperity was a kind of magic, rather than the product of often unjust systems? While many of us might be quick to loudly denounce the 'heresy' of the prosperity gospel, we're quite comfortable with affirming the good of affluence. But isn't that just a prosperity gospel without the glam?" [James K. A. Smith, "Abundance for All," *Catapult* 8, no. 10 (2009), accessed April 7, 2021, http://www.catapultmagazine.com/life-abundant/feature/abundance-for-all/.]. See Macchia, "Call for Careful Discernment," 235–6; Perriman, *FHP*, 116, 198.

connotations of "mammon" to be renegotiated to stand for blessings).[162] Scholarly critiques regard the indexical relation between prosperity and faith as a serious misinterpretation that, in semiotic terms, is caused by an intentional interpretant other than a Christian narrative.[163] The suggestions as to which interpretant underlies the indexical semiosis differ, falling within the range of socioeconomic interpretants (e.g., neoliberal consumer capitalism, the American Dream, and Weberian work ethic) and metaphysical interpretants (e.g., New Thought or occult economics).[164] Precision in these discussions is reduced by not fully accounting for the interpretant the sign-producers themselves intended (i.e., Eden Redeemed).[165] That Eden Redeemed is the intentional interpretant in the semiosis of prosperity is not to deny any formative influences from socioeconomic or metaphysical narratives on Eden Redeemed, only that identifying such influences must be of secondary concern. A "thicker description" of prosperity only begins once the intentional interpretant is identified and satisfactorily examined (what this book wants to provide). Eden Redeemed must be analyzed as a story in its own right (i.e., based on its internal narrative dynamics) and its shaping power on the semiosis of prosperity be fully investigated. When critics overlook Eden Redeemed as the intentional interpretant, and so translate prosperity through another effectual interpretant, it leads to a dynamic object (e.g., greed) that is other than the immediate object. Such semiotic misunderstanding, though prevalently expressed, is regrettable because it fails in offering an accurate representation of the Word of Faith.[166] Awareness of the semiosis of prosperity will enable dialogue with the movement and sharpen investigations on the role of prosperity in global Christianity. The complexity of the semiotic process of prosperity shows that before comparisons can be made between various occurrences of prosperity in differing global contexts, each sign-producer's intentional interpretant must first be properly analyzed.[167]

162. "The ingenuity of Pentecostal prosperity theology is evident in the most striking resignification of 'mammon' into financial blessing" (Heuser, "Charting African Prosperity," 3).

163. Harvey Cox, "Pentecostalism and Global Market Culture," in *The Globalization of Pentecostalism: A Religion Made to Travel*, ed. Murray Dempster, Byron Klaus and Douglas Peterson (Eugene: Wipf and Stock, 1999), 392; Kaiser Jr., "The Old Testament promise," 162.

164. See Sections 1.4; 1.5.

165. Hagin clearly intended the Adam plot and its expanded story as the interpretant of prosperity: "I couldn't do justice to a study on prosperity without explaining the great Bible truth of redemption" (Hagin, *Biblical Keys*, 1); Savelle, *Why God Wants*, e-book edition, "Prosperity is a Redemptive Truth;" Gloria Copeland, *God's Will Is Prosperity*, e-book edition, "chapter 1." See also Bowler, *Blessed*, 96–7.

166. E.g., Savelle, *Why God Wants*, e-book edition, "Things Follow the Seeker."

167. On the use of various interpretants, see, e.g., Walton, *Watch This*, 81. Not paying sufficient attention to the role of intentional interpretants is a common weakness in some suggested typologies of prosperity.

Though Eden Redeemed holds to an indexical interpretation of prosperity, Word of Faith discourse exhibits ambivalence on the semiosis of prosperity. In similarity to the tension regarding the narrative role of prosperity discussed in the last chapter, the Word of Faith embraces two opposite accounts of the semiosis of prosperity. On the one hand, as noted, Word of Faith discourse places prosperity in an indexical relationship to faith, thus making prosperity a sign of the believer's faith. Yet, in other instances, prosperity is interpreted as another kind of index-sign, this time not of faith but of satanic allegiance or even as a sign that must be interpreted based on the unique and individual context in which it occurs, that is, prosperity as a symbolic sign.[168]

The paradoxical readings of prosperity come out in Hagin's work. At the end of his life, he showed uneasiness with an indexical and absolute reading of prosperity, causing him to distance himself from an interpretant that always places prosperity in a causative relation to faith.[169] In contrast, Hagin suggested that prosperity must at times be understood as an arbitrary sign that signifies by convention.[170] In semiotic terms, Hagin argued for reading prosperity as a symbolic sign rather than indexical; that the sign-vehicle of prosperity does not always signify the identical object of faith, nor that semiosis is achieved by cause and effect; the interpretant must be extracted from the unique context of each sign-vehicle.[171] This is an obvious adjustment in the semiosis of prosperity that arises out of Eden Redeemed, the story which Hagin originally shaped to a significant extent. Hagin's uneasiness in late life with an indexical reading of prosperity

---

168. See Perriman, *FHP,* 50. E.g., Copeland, *Blessed,* e-book edition, "The Fool's Dozen;" Meyer, "Pentecostalism and Neo-Liberal Capitalism," 17–19; see also Birgit Meyer, "'Delivered from the Powers of Darkness': Confessions of Satanic Riches in Christian Ghana," *Africa: Journal of the International African Institute* 65, no. 2 (1995): 236–55; Simon Coleman and Martin Lindhardt, "Prosperity and Wealth," in *The Routledge Handbook of Economic Theology,* ed. Stefan Schwarzkopf (London: Routledge, 2020), Kindle edition.

169. Consider how Hagin addresses the rhetorical question if prosperity is always indexical, or in his phraseology "is financial prosperity a sign of spirituality?": "One teaching supposes that financial prosperity is a sure sign of spirituality. This teaching suggests that throughout the Bible, God has rewarded faith and holiness with material blessings. The implication is that if a person is not experiencing financial abundance, there must be a spiritual deficit in his [sic] life. . . . This is the same kind of abuse as telling a person who has not received healing for a sickness or disease that evidently he [sic] just doesn't have enough faith" (Hagin, *MT,* 137). See also Bakker, *I Was Wrong,* 539, 541.

170. "material wealth can be connected to the blessings of God or it can be totally disconnected from the blessings of God. Certainly, financial prosperity is not an infallible gauge of a person's spirituality. . . . It simply is not true that everyone who has faith for prosperity will live in a palace, drive a luxurious car, and dress in expensive, designer-label clothes" (Hagin, *MT,* 199).

171. See, e.g., Sondra Wheeler, *Wealth as Peril and Obligation* (Grand Rapids: Eerdmans, 1995); Witherington, *Jesus and Money.*

stands apart from his earlier discourse where he claimed in absolute terms that "godliness [i.e., faith] is profitable"[172] and that faith brings results (e.g., prosperity) every time.[173] In addressing this problem, Hagin affirmed that the sign-vehicle of prosperity can signify through other interpretants and that the objects can also differ. In suggesting such symbolic understanding of prosperity, Hagin drew on a Pentecostal interpretant rather than on Eden Redeemed. Yet, he failed to address the root cause, which is that prosperity functions indexically to faith because of the Eden Redeemed story. As long as Eden Redeemed remains the worldview-story of the Word of Faith, prosperity will function indexically to faith, resisting a symbolic interpretation.[174]

A word must be said about prosperity's opposite, that is, poverty, as it is directly affected by the semiosis of prosperity.[175] When Eden Redeemed is the interpretant, poverty signifies that the agent is not living by faith; instead of fulfilling their Task of ruling and increasing on the earth, poverty shows that the believer has unbelief and is dominated by Satan and the curse.[176] Also, because of the indexical function of prosperity in the Word of Faith worldview, interpretations of poverty as standing for objects of virtue (e.g., humility, godliness, sacrifice, or a God-given test) are rejected as the result of replacing the "true" and "biblical" interpretant for a foreign and misleading interpretant shaped by "dead religion," "poverty mentality" or satanic deception.[177] Since faith is signified by prosperity, poverty—including

---

172. Kenneth E. Hagin, *Godliness is Profitable* (Tulsa: Faith Library Publications, 1982).

173. Hagin, "Faith Brings Results," Rhema.org, Accessed April 7, 2021, https://www.rhema.org/index.php?option=com_content&view=article&id=1026:faith-brings-results&catid=46&Itemid=141; Hagin, *Seven Things*, 19. Hagin has repeatedly placed prosperity as an index-sign to faith, e.g., "We as Christians need not suffer financial setbacks; we need not be captive to poverty or sickness! God has provided healing and prosperity for His children if they will obey His commandments" (Hagin, *New Thresholds*, 57). See Bowler, *Blessed*, 137–8.

174. Cf. da Silva, *Framgångsteologin,* 83.

175. See Perriman, *FHP,* 52.

176. Hagin, *New Thresholds*, 56–7; Hagin, *Human Spirit*, 12; Duncan-Williams, *Destined to Make,* e-book edition, "Wrong Concepts." E.g., "if we are experiencing any kind of failure or defeat in our lives, including being trapped in financial bondage, we are the ones who are responsible. If we are not prospering, if we are not successful, the fault is neither with God nor with the Word of God" (Savelle, *Why God Wants,* e-book edition, "Why God's People Are in Financial Bondage"); Bakker writes, "I admit, in the past I had used this verse [Deut. 8:1–18] to make it sound as though it was God's will to make everyone wealthy and if any of His people were poor, it was probably due to lack of faith or not applying the biblical 'formulas' correctly" (Bakker, *I Was Wrong,* 539, 541). See also Harrison, *RR,* 60.

177. Hagin, *Keys*; Copeland, *Blessed,* e-book edition, "A Blessing or a Curse?." See Perriman, *FHP,* 51; Gifford, *Ghana's New Christianity,* 46; Chong, "Of Riches and Faith," 154; "sacrificial poverty is not a virtue since it denies everything that Christ has won through his death, that is, prosperity for the born-again believers" (Hasu, "World Bank," 684).

failure to display signs of prosperity—has destructive effects on the believer's self-perception and social status in the Word of Faith community.[178] In the worldview where prosperity is indexical to faith, poverty is a self-made curse.[179] The semiosis of prosperity underlies the often-voiced concern that Word of Faith discourse victimizes the poor.[180]

4.3.4 Health

I use the sign-vehicle of "health," following its use in the Word of Faith, in an inclusive sense of both physical and psychological (emotional and mental) dimensions.[181] Health "prize as normal or standard the able-bodied, physically fit, emotionally balanced, and physiologically healthy Christian body."[182] All eight criteria for worldview-signs are found in how health is used in Word of Faith discourse.[183] Though health occupies a central place in the Word of Faith, since

178. E.g., "If individuals are not prospering, it is assumed to be their own fault in some way . . . they may be in sin, lacking faith, or they may simply be ignorant" (Harrison, RR, 70); Hasu, "World Bank," 686; Mumford, Exploring Prosperity, 66.

179. Oyedepo says, "Poverty is a proof of unrighteousness! [. . .] Poverty is a curse and self-made (. . .) It comes largely as a result of a willful act of disobedience to the law of abundance by the believers" (David Oyedepo quoted in Gifford, "Prosperity Theology," 87).

180. Lin, Prosperity Gospel, Kindle edition, "The Paradoxes of Prosperity Gospel Pentecostalism;" Harrison, RR, 70; Mumford, Exploring Prosperity, 43; Michael Biehl, "To Prosper and to Be Blessed: Prosperity, Wealth and 'Life in Abundance' in Ecumenical Debate," in Pastures of Plenty: Tracing Religio-Scapes of Prosperity Gospel in Africa and Beyond, ed. Andreas Heuser (Frankfurt: Peter Lang, 2015) 145; Fee, Disease, 8–9; Bakker, I Was Wrong, 541. See Walton, "Blessed and Highly Favored."

181. Bowler, Blessed, 140.

182. Sinitiere, Salvation, 90. See Lynne Gerber, "Fat Christians and Fit Elites: Negotiating Class and Status in Evangelical Christian Weight-Loss Culture," American Quarterly 64, no. 1 (March 2012): 61–84.

183. (1) Health is a specific focus in the scholarly conversations (Farah, FTP, 61–85; Fee, The Disease, 19–35; Barron, Health and Wealth, 77–87; Brandon, Health and Wealth, 47–70; McConnell, DG, 147–68; Hanegraaff, CIC, 233–76; Perriman, FHP, 46–8, 126–35; Jones and Woodbridge, HWH, 67–9, 107–22; Lederle, Theology with Spirit, 153–5; Moo, "Divine Healing," 191–209; Warrington, "The Use of the Name;" Warrington, "Teaching and Praxis;" Warrington, "Healing and Kenneth Hagin;" Bowler, Blessed, 139–77; Bowler, "Blessed Bodies;" (2) Word of Faith discourse gives health a privileged position (healing is a significant part of sermons, teachings, and practices. See Bowler, "Blessed Bodies"); (3) health is affectively charged in Word of Faith discourse (e.g., Hagin, Seven Things); (4) health has signified for the Word of Faith from the movement's early days (Bowler, Blessed, 139–77); (5) health surfaces in multiple contexts (e.g., sermons, songs, private conversations; Bowler, "Blessed Bodies," 96); (6) the meaning of health is expounded in Word of Faith discourse (e.g., Hagin, Bible Healing); (7) the place and use of health is closely monitored by

the semiotic dynamics of health mirror that of prosperity (see the following text), I keep my comments brief in this section to avoid repetitiveness.

Eden Redeemed makes the intentional interpretant of health. The semiosis of health, like prosperity, follows the U-shaped storyline of Eden Redeemed: God provided full divine health to Adam in Eden, health was lost to Satan in The Fall but restored through Jesus in Redemption and awaits to be claimed by the believer's use of the faith of God.[184] Signified through this interpretant, health's immediate object—like prosperity—is faith. More expanded, health signifies how God's goodness and creational intention of sharing God's life and wholeness with humans is fulfilled by the believer's correct usage of the faith of God.[185] Health signifies how the agent is living the life of Eden now by ruling over Satan and the curse while "tapping" into the life of God and claiming one's entitled right to health by faith.[186] Through the agent's faith, health shows that God's will is accomplished in the body.[187]

The relationship between the sign-vehicle of health and the immediate object of faith is direct, mechanical, and causal. Health, like prosperity, functions, therefore, as an indexical sign in the Word of Faith worldview.[188] The Eden Redeemed story establishes that health is, without exception, God's will and that Jesus has already provided health for every believer; all that remains is for the agent to claim health by faith.[189] Health thus indexes faith through the interpretant of Eden Redeemed.[190]

the movement (Williams, *Spirit Cure*, 116–21); (8) health is intimately connected with Eden Redeemed worldview-story (see Section 3.2.6.8).

184. See Chapter 3.

185. Copeland, *Live Long*, e-book edition, "Chapter 9."

186. Hagin, *Seven Things*, 15, 54; Copeland, *Harvest of Health*; Hagin Jr., *Staying Positive*, 61. Dollar speaks of his battle with cancer as: "I was defeating cancer from trying to steal my healing" (Creflo Dollar, "Sunday Service," YouTube Video, 2:30:16 (1:13), Creflo Dollar Ministries, May 12, 2019, accessed June 6, 2020, https://www.youtube.com/watch?v=W8U 5YuGAZZI).

187. Hagin, *Keys to Scriptural Healing*, 6; Bowler, *Blessed*.

188. Coleman notes that "a healthy, strong body" acts "as an index of faith" (Coleman, *Globalisation*, 147, 151). "For the Word of Faith movement, healing is not a sovereign miracle bestowed by a merciful God. Healing is a cause-and-effect formula that works every time the Christian applies it in 'faith'" (Newport, *New Age Movement*, 365); Arlene Sanchez-Walsh, "Santidad, Salvación, Sanidad, Liberación: The Word of Faith Movement among Twenty-First-Century Latina/o Pentecostals," in *Global Pentecostal and Charismatic Healing*, ed. Candy Gunter Brown (Oxford: Oxford University Press, 2011), 162; Bowler, "Blessed Bodies," 84.

189. Hagin, *Healing Belongs*; Creflo Dollar, "Abundant Health on All Levels," *Creflod ollarministries.org*, January 23, 2019, accessed April 7, 2021, https://www.creflodollarm inistries.org/Bible-Study/Articles/Abundant-Health-on-All-Levels?returnUrl=%2FBible-S tudy%2FArticles%2FBe%2520Healed.

190. Walton, "Blessed and Highly Favored," 144; Walton, *Watch This*, 95; Bowler, *Blessed*, 141; Simon Coleman, "Why Health and Wealth? Dimensions of Prosperity among

The material signs of physical health include a perfectly healthy, strong, and attractive body, signified by fitness, vitality, youthfulness, hygiene, sex-appeal, and longevity.[191] Happiness, good self-esteem, self-confidence, and self-control signify mental health. Narrative signs of health consist of testimonies of how long one has been in perfect physical and mental health and stories of miraculous physical and emotional healings.[192] Linguistic signs of health include "divine health," "life," "strength," "wholeness," "healing," "prosper in body and soul," and "peace."[193]

4.3.4.1 The Semiosis of Health The Word of Faith imagines an uncomplicated relation between health and the correct usage of faith.[194] However, the semiosis of health as an indexical sign affects the worldview's fidelity, coherence, and challenges a Pentecostal emphasis on the necessity of divine healing embracing the paradox of human experience. That health signifies faith through an interpretant consisting of absolute spiritual laws relativizes God's sovereignty and mystery in divine healing.[195] As such, the fidelity of the worldview is contested as it does not acknowledge the paradox in human experience. The indexical nature of health also generates tensions with a theology of God's sovereignty and Word of Faith portraits of God's power as free and absolute.[196] Pentecostal readings claim that the relation between health and faith must not be thought of as mechanical and absolute, but a discourse on healing should include an aspect of mystery as God's actions cannot be fully predicted or understood.[197] In semiotic terms, a symbolic reading

Swedish Charismatics," in *Global Pentecostal and Charismatic Healing*, ed. Candy Gunter Brown (Oxford: Oxford University Press, 2011), 49; Williams, *Spirit Cure*, 15–16; "Healing has become, along with wealth, a sign of the amount of faith in the believer" (Matta, *Born Again Jesus*, 120).

191. Williams, *Spirit Cure*, 122–56, 132; Bowler, *Blessed*, 149; Winslow, "Imaged Other;" Jenkins and Marti, "Warrior Chicks." See Copeland, "Young, Strong, Blessed."

192. Coleman, "Why Health and Wealth," 53; Bowler, "Blessed Bodies," 88; Bowler, *Blessed*, 141. E.g., Hagin, *Bible Healing*, e-book edition, "My Testimony of Healing;" Hagin also narrates, "For more than sixty-five years I haven't even had a headache. I've walked in health" (Hagin, *Bible Healing*, e-book edition, "God Was Israel's Healer"); Andrew Wommack, "It's Not a Faith Problem, It's Your Unbelief," YouTube Video, 1:18, Living Word Christian Center, July 27, 2016, accessed April 7, 2021, https://www.youtube.com/watch?v=lq6YjjxUY5s.

193. See Bowler, *Blessed*, 138–77.

194. E.g., Hagin, *Bible Healing*, e-book edition, "The Switch of Faith."

195. Faith discourse rejects praying "if it be your [God's] will" in relation to healing (e.g., Hagin, *Bible Healing*, e-book edition, "Road Block Number Two"). See Matta, *Born Again Jesus*, 137; Moo, "Healing," 208.

196. Farah, *FTP*, 74; Fee, *Disease*, 34; Joe Magliato, *The Wallstreet Gospel* (Eugene: Harvest House, 1981), 97; Brandon, *Health and Wealth*, 47–70.

197. General Presbytery of the Assemblies of God, "Divine Healing: An Integral Part of the Gospel," in *Where We Stand: The Official Position Papers of the Assemblies of God*

of healing and health over and above the Word of Faith's indexical signification would increase the worldview's fidelity and coherence as such is more true to life and to their image of God as free and powerful. Allowing a conventional and unique interpretation of healing and health would also fit a Pentecostal emphasis on paradox and the limits to human knowledge of God's actions.

The indexical semiosis of health carries a particular view of suffering.[198] Though Word of Faith discourse gives multiple reasons for an unproductive faith (e.g., disobedience, lack of knowledge, demonic activity), ultimately the agent—not God nor any power outside of the believer—carries the full responsibility for a "faith failure."[199] It follows from the semiotic logic that a lack of health indexes that "something is wrong with that [sick] person's faith."[200] Suffering has no virtuous facet in the semiosis of health.[201] As long as Eden Redeemed is the intentional interpretant, health's indexical function places the responsibility for prolonged suffering on the sick.[202] As the indexical interpretation of prosperity victimizes the poor, the semiosis of health equally victimizes the sick.[203]

The indexical reading of health is not uncomplicated in Word of Faith discourse. Hagin reacted late in life also against the pastoral consequences of the semiosis of health, claiming that to blame the sick for lack of faith amounted to "abuse."[204] Again,

---

(Springfield: Gospel Publishing House, 1994), 54. See Warrington, *Healing and Suffering*; Moo, "Healing."

198. E.g., Sánchez Walsh, "Santidad, Salvación," 164; Perriman, *FHP*, 202.

199. Mumford, *Exploring Prosperity*, 87; Perriman, *FHP*, 47; Wiegele, *Investing in Miracles*, 21; Kenneth Copeland Ministries, "Why Do Bad Things Happen?," *Kcm.com*, accessed April 7, 2021, https://www.kcm.org/real-help/spiritual-growth/learn/why-do-bad -things-happen; Wommack "It's Not Faith;"

200. Tammy Williams, "Is There a Doctor in the House?," in *Practicing Theology*, ed. Miroslav Volf and Dorothy Bass (Grand Rapids: Eerdmans, 2002), 109–10; Mumford, *Exploring Prosperity*, 93, 82, 87; Perriman, *FHP*, 42, 61, 202; See, e.g., Joseph Prince, *Healing and Wholeness through the Holy Communion* (Singapore: Joseph Prince Teaching Resources, 2006), 12; Hagin, *Exceedingly Growing*, 51. See Perriman, *FHP*, 61. Example of reasons are: the devil, lack of patience, inadequate faith, failure to tithe, personal sin, negative confessions (Agana, *Succeed Here*, 207; Perriman, *FHP*, 42–3, Mumford, *Exploring Prosperity*, 43). Agana, *Succeed Here*, 198, 208; Farah, *FTP*, 159; Wrenn argues that this personal fault-finding is parallel to the logic of neoliberalism, both movements "overascribe agency to the individual" (Wrenn, "Consecrating Capitalism," 429). See, e.g., John Avanzini, *It Is Not Working, Brother John* (Tulsa: Harrison House, 1992).

201. Wiegele, *Investing in Miracles*, 22.

202. "the GHW [Gospel of Health and Wealth] necessarily, logically blames the victims of illness and poverty for their conditions. . . . The logic is ironclad, even if most promoters of the GHW are reluctant to follow it" (Olson, *CC*, 161). See Bowler, "Blessed Bodies," 96–8; Wiegele, *Investing in Miracles*, 21.

203. E.g., Harrison, *RR*, 60–1; See Ma, "Blessing," 277–8, 290; Farah, *FTP*, 158–61.

204. Hagin, *MT*, 137.

this goes contrary to how he at a younger age pressed an indexical relationship between health and faith through the Eden Redeemed interpretant.[205] As seen in Hagin's previous reactions to prosperity, though he pointed out weaknesses and suggested some theological changes, he never addressed Eden Redeemed and its semiotic logic. Because it is this story that wields the shaping power in Word of Faith semiosis, as long as it remains the worldview-story of the Word of Faith, the indexical semiosis of prosperity and health—no matter its negative pastoral consequences—stands unchallenged. Hagin's reactions illustrate that his hesitation with indexical semiosis arises in contrast to a Pentecostal narrative as interpretant. Hagin shows how one can indwell a worldview without either being fully aware of it or in agreement with all its consequences. Also, Hagin's usage of both Eden Redeemed as interpretant and a Pentecostal interpretant illustrates how a person's mindset can be made up of a mixture of different and contradictory interpretants and how the mindset can alter over time.

4.3.5 Optimism

The sign-vehicle of optimism consists of a positive mental attitude and outlook on life, hopeful confident expectations, happiness, a joyful state, energy, and enthusiasm.[206] Optimism fits all the eight requirements for being a worldview-sign in the Word of Faith worldview.[207]

---

205. E.g., Hagin at a younger age said: "As soon as I can get people to . . . start believing, they are healed immediately" (Hagin, *What Faith Is*, 6).

206. Perriman, *FHP*, 219; Bowler, *Blessed*, 193; Coleman, *Globalisation*, 150.

207. (1) optimism is noted in scholarship on the movement [Walton, "Blessed," 184–7; Lin, *Prosperity Gospel*, kindle edition, "Prosperity Gospel Pentecostalism;" Lin, "Gospel," 42; Coleman, *Globalisation*, 138, 150; Harrison, *RR*, 24; Mitchem, *Name It*, 81; Perriman, *FHP*, 219; Gifford, "The Bible in Africa," 219; Walton, *Watch This*, 109; Bowler, *Blessed*, 232; Kay, *Pentecostalism*, 118; Ewell, "Can We Offer," 162; N. M. Hobson, J. J. Kim and G. MacDonald, "A Camel Through the Eye of a Needle: The Influence of the Prosperity Gospel on Financial Risk-Taking, Optimistic Bias, and Positive Emotion," *Psychology of Religion and Spirituality* (2018), Accessed April 7, 2021, https://doi.org/10.1037/rel0000235; Barbara Ehrenreich, *Bright Sided: How Positive Thinking Is Undermining America* (New York: Picador, 2010), 123–46; Wrenn, "Consecrating Capitalism"]; (2) Word of Faith discourse gives optimism a privileged position [e.g., Kenneth W. Hagin, *Staying Positive in a Negative World* (Tulsa: Faith Library Publications, 2003); Savelle, *If Satan Can't Steal*]; (3) optimism is affectively charged for the Word of Faith adherents ["The more positive you and I become, the more we will be in the flow of God. God is certainly positive, and to flow with Him, we must also be positive" (Joyce Meyer, *Battlefield of the Mind* (New York: Warner Faith, 1995), e-book edition, "The Force of Hope")]; (4) optimism has signified during a considerable time (Bowler, *Blessed*, 41–76); (5) optimism reappears in manifold contexts (e.g., in private and public speech and in praxis); (6) the meaning of optimism is elaborated (e.g., Hagin, *Staying*

Optimism signifies through the Word of Faith worldview-story. Hence, the optimism of the Word of Faith is this-worldly and should not be confused with a Pentecostal eschatological optimism, which places hopeful expectations in the parousia of "the soon-coming King" (see Section 6.2.5).[208] The Church sequence of Eden Redeemed locates the believer in a world where Satan, sin, and the curse of poverty and sickness are presently defeated and no power can withstand the believer's progress. The blessing of prosperity and health has already been provided in the spiritual realm, waiting to be realized through using the God-kind of faith. Through faith the believer enters the spiritual realm where there are no limits to what can be achieved in the here and now; success is inevitable for the believer who practices the faith of God.[209]

Optimism signifies in the Word of Faith worldview the immediate object of faith.[210] Particularly, optimism stands for how the believer uses the God-kind of faith to connect with the spiritual realm and keeping themselves pure from any influences of the devil, circumstances, and the flesh.[211] The believer's confident expectation of good evidences that they are living out of the really real spiritual realm, where every promise of God is a present reality and positive outcomes are certain. When Eden Redeemed is the interpretant, optimism relates to the object of faith in a causal way; optimism rises when the God-kind of faith is active.[212] Optimism thus functions, alike to prosperity and health, as an index-sign of faith in the Word of Faith.[213]

Positive)]; (7) and optimism's place is closely monitored by the movement (Harrison, *RR*, 11); (8) optimism relates directly with the Word of Faith worldview-story (see Chapter 3).

208. See McClymond, "Prosperity Already."

209. "a theology that promotes the inevitability of success . . . this optimism stems from a theological conviction that one is chosen by God for material favor" (Walton, "Blessed and Highly Favored," 168).

210. "When you are really walking by faith, there is joy" [Joyce Meyer, *Expect a Move of God in Your Life* (New York: Warner Books, 1996), e-book edition, "Waiting on God Brings Deliverance"]; Andrew Wommack Ministries, "Staying Positive in a Negative World," *Awmi.net*, accessed April 7, 2021, https://www.awmi.net/reading/teaching-article s/stay_positive/.

211. Jerry Savelle, *A Right Mental Attitude* (Tulsa: Harrison House, 1993), e-book edition, "Two Avenues—Faith and Fear;" Oyedepo, *Anointing for Breakthrough*, e-book edition, "Two Weapons for Conquering;" Hagin Jr., *Staying Positive*, I, 86–7, 104; "Believing keeps your heart full of joy" (Joyce Meyer, *Enjoying Where You Are on the Way to Where You Are Going* (New York: FaithWords, 2012), e-book edition, "Believers Are Supposed to Believe"); Hagin, *New Thresholds*, e-book edition, "How Do We Get Faith?."

212. E.g., "Joy . . . is always present where there is belief" (Meyer, *Enjoying Where You Are*, e-book edition, "Joy and Peace Are Found in Believing").

213. "faith is joyful. You can tell when you are operating in true faith, because you will have joy rising up out of your spirit" (Savelle, *Force of Joy*, e-book edition, "Chapter 3").

There is a cluster of supportive signs that stand for this emphasis on the positive. Material and bodily signs of optimism include attitudes of happiness, boldness, humor, confidence, good self-esteem, and expectancy. A joyful habitus or persona, indicated by laughter and smile, is a noteworthy bodily sign of optimism.[214] Linguistic signs of optimism include "joy," "peace," "positive," "hope," and "rest."[215] Narrative signs include personal testimonies of living with joy and enjoyment, without depression, fear, and worries and stories of personal challenges—often economic- or health-related—that ended in positive solutions.[216]

4.3.5.1 The Semiosis of Optimism The semiosis of optimism makes the Word of Faith worldview to be one of "exuberant hope and unbridled optimism."[217] Optimism is grounded in the possibilities of faith. The indexical, cause-and-effect relationship between faith and the blessing of prosperity and health makes the desired results guaranteed when the faith of God is properly used. The indexical function of faith fosters the confident expectation of "upward trajectories"[218] for every true believer within the Word of Faith. It is possible to predict a positive future in this world as long as the believer continues to operate in faith by an optimistic attitude.[219]

Because of optimism's embodied and visible nature, it serves as a particularly powerful index-sign of the believer's faith.[220] Financial lack and sickness can often be hidden from public sight while optimism is directly evident in the believer's habitus. The Word of Faith worldview, which privileges polarized categories, leaves no middle ground when it comes to optimism: either the believer expresses positive

214. "Spiritually, if you don't smile, you are defeated, because the secret of strength is in your rejoicing" (Oyedepo, *Anointing for Breakthrough*, e-book edition, "Give Thanks and Sing Praises"); Meyer, *Enjoying Where You Are*, e-book edition, "Joy Defined;" Savelle, *If Satan Can't Steal*, e-book edition, "First the Word, then Affliction, then Joy." E.g., Harrison, *RR*, 53.

215. E.g., Savelle, *The Force of Joy*; Hagin Jr., *Staying Positive*, 29; Osteen, *Wake up*.

216. E.g., Hagin, *Prevailing Prayer*, 9–12; Savelle, *If Satan Can't Steal Your Joy*; Hagin, *Staying Positive*.

217. "The constant allusions to God as supplier and copious scripture references to health, wealth, and sowing reveal a world of exuberant hope and unbridled optimism" (Walton, "Stop Worrying," 108); "Performing happiness and the expectation of positive tomorrows became a staple of Sunday mornings, and many of these churches (particularly those with more immediatist views about the relationship between positive affect and results) were among the happiest I have ever attended" (Bowler, "Daily Grind," 631).

218. Walton, "Blessed and Highly Favored," 184.

219. "Their metaphors and language rested on potentiality and perseverance for the not-yet-future." (Bowler, "Daily Grind," 631).

220. Coleman, *Globalisation*, 134. "if we are believing the Word of God, we should have a positive mental attitude" (Hagin, *Overflow*, e-book edition, "Chapter 3").

confidence or they express the opposite. Conflicting attitudes to optimism—fear, negativity, discouragement, worry, and pessimism—signify a lack of faith.[221]

Underlying the emphasis on optimism is a motivation by anxiety.[222] Believers are motivated to express optimism by the anxiety that *if* they fail to do so, fear will take optimism's place and so invite the destructive power of Satan. As faith stands for power, so also does fear; fear is a power that activates Satan to bring destruction.[223] Fear is storied in the Word of Faith as faith's opposite.[224] Faith or fear are in Word of Faith discourse both put within the control of the individual believer. So, it is up to each believer to choose faith or fear, yet what they chose is determinative for one's future.

Since the semiosis of optimism signifies the Word of Faith's unique understanding of faith, it is a mistake to interpret the positive energy of the Word of Faith movement simply as standing for a more joyful, energetic type of faith in contrast to "the apathy and negativism that dominates the Christian mind-set."[225] Such reading overlooks the complexities in the objects of faith; the optimism of the Word of Faith signifies first of all the possibilities of the faith of God.

4.3.6 *The Charismatic Leader*

The last worldview-sign to discuss is what I term the "charismatic leader."[226] The sign-vehicle consists of individuals who are considered by the Word of Faith community to be particularly gifted and empowered by the Holy Spirit and who display the signs of revelation knowledge, prosperity, health, and optimism in higher degrees than regular believers. "Charismatic" means here the Pentecostal theological understanding of an "anointed" person—the "man of God" or the "woman of God" who is particularly gifted and empowered by the Holy Spirit.[227]

---

221. "Pessimism is the opposite of faith" (Hagin, *Staying Positive*, 45, 84); Meyer, *Enjoy Where You Are*, e-book edition, "'What's the Matter with Me?';" Hagin, *Classic Sermons*, e-book edition, "A New Creation;" Joyce Meyer, *Victory in Your Mind, Mouth, Moods & Attitudes* (Fenton: Joyce Meyer Ministries, 2013), e-book edition, 19.

222. See Lin, *Prosperity Gospel*, Kindle edition, "Trading Fear for Hope."

223. "Fear activates Satan the way faith activates God" (Copeland, *The Force of Faith*, e-book edition, "The Force of Faith").

224. "The faith force that was born into Adam when God breathed His life into him was perverted and turned into the force that we know and recognize as fear" (Copeland, *Force of Faith*, e-book edition, "The Force of Faith").

225. Perriman, *FHP,* 219.

226. Asamoah-Gyadu speaks of the "iconic charismatic leaders" (Asamoah-Gyadu, *Contemporary Pentecostal Christianity,* 80. Terms used in the literature include "charismatic leader" (Coleman, *Globalisation,* 135); "the charismatic teacher of revelation" (Edwards, "Ethical Dimensions," 92).

227. Edwards, "Ethical Dimensions," 92; Walton, "Blessed and Highly Favored," 130. See Kenneth E. Hagin, *Understanding the Anointing* (Tulsa: Faith Library Publications, 1983).

Research data shows that the charismatic leader fits all the eight criteria to be examined as a worldview-sign in the Word of Faith.[228]

Eden Redeemed stories Adam as the perfected human who lived in an abundance of provision and health and exercised royal dominion in the world.[229] His position of blessed authority was lost to Satan in The Fall but fully restored by Jesus. The believer can now access and manifest Adam's life through the faith of God. It is this narrative that forms the intentional interpretant of the charismatic leader sign in the Word of Faith worldview. The charismatic leader signifies that believers *are* back to the realities of Eden with access to its blessings and Task of ruling and increasing.[230]

The charismatic leader ultimately signifies faith. The relationship between the sign-vehicle of the anointed man or woman of God and the object of faith is in terms of correspondence; the leader shows the veracity of faith by resemblance, as their life mirrors Eden's realities. The leader thus functions as an iconic sign in

---

228. (1) the leader is an often-mentioned element in scholarly studies [Lin, "Prosperity Gospel;" Edwards, "Ethical Dimensions," 92; Bowler, *Blessed*, 255; virtually all scholarly studies on Word of Faith theology centers on a group of key leaders in the movement (e.g., Hagin, Copeland et. al.)]; (2) the leader has an expressed privileged position in the Word of Faith community [C. B. Peter, "The Church's Response to Poverty: A Jungian Appraisal of the 'Prosperity Gospel' Phenomenon," *Ogbomoso Journal of Theology* 14, (2009): 141–2; Edwards, "Ethical Dimensions," 92; McConnell, *DG*, 111; e.g., Coleman, *Globalisation*, 120, 184; Lin, *Prosperity Gospel*, Kindle edition, "The Meeting Place;" "The movement is captivated by the ideal of the man of God who has erased from his mind all fear and doubt, who speaks, prays, commands with supreme confidence in the efficiency of the law of faith, at whose words the demons flee, sickness disappears, and wealth accumulates" (Perriman, *FHP*, 1, 45)]; (3) the leader is affectively charged for the Word of Faith adherents [e.g., Lin, *Prosperity Gospel*, Kindle edition, "Studying Pentecostals," "The Meeting Place;" Harrison, *RR*, 28; Gifford, "Prosperity Theology," 83; Sanchez-Walsh, "Santidad, Salvación," 157; Ackerly, "Importing Faith," 302]; (4) the leader has signified during an extended period of time [Bowman, *Word-Faith*, 85–94]; (5) the leader-sign surfaces in a variety of contexts [e.g., spoken and written discourse, images and testimonies]; (6) the meaning of the leader is expanded upon [Kenneth E. Hagin, *The Ministry Gifts* (Tulsa: Faith Library Publications, 1981)]; (7) the role and use of the sign is closely monitored by the movement [e.g., Hanegraaff, *Christianity in Crisis 21st*, Kindle edition, "Appendix A;" Perriman, *FHP*, 33]; (8) the charismatic leader has a direct relation with the elements of story [see Chapter 3].

229. See Chapter 3.

230. "The wealth of the evangelist was the clearest possible sign that the laws of divine prosperity worked" (Perriman, *FHP*, 65); "the specially anointed individual provides the function of symbolising that which those assembled at the meeting aspire to be" (Hunt, "Dramatising," 79).

the Word of Faith worldview.[231] As the icon of prelapsarian Adam, the charismatic leader is "the living embodiment of faith in action."[232]

All the previously discussed worldview-signs cluster in various ways around the charismatic leader. Revelation knowledge signifies the charismatic leader, as the man or woman of God stands as a reservoir of revelation knowledge, evidenced by larger amounts of knowledge or having new knowledge in comparison with the followers.[233] The indexical signs of faith—prosperity, health, and optimism— serve as the most important material signs of the charismatic leader.[234] Prosperity signifies the charismatic leader by consumer goods and services, assets and narratives of wealth and consumption.[235] The level of prosperity experienced by the charismatic leader's followers also signifies the charismatic leader.[236] Health is signified through vitality, strength, beauty, and bodily fitness, which are material signs of the charismatic leader. Narratives of personal health and healing speak to the charismatic leader, as well as testimonies of health by the charismatic leader's adherents.[237] The charismatic leader is also signified by their follower's happiness, positive energy, and hope. Size, understood as "a tangible, quantifiable indication of spiritual success and influence,"[238] is another sign of the charismatic leader.[239] Size of fame and influence is signified by images of enormous crowds, photos with celebrities, security staff, and so on and by narrative statistics (number of church members, followers on social media, viewers of one's programs, books sold,

231. Walton, *Watch This*, 200, 207; Bowler, *Blessed*, 77, 134; Edwards, "Ethical Dimensions," 92; Peter, "Church's Response," 141–2; Winslow, "Imaged Other," 262.

232. Walton, *Watch This*, 200. "Leaders proved to be the most powerful demonstrators of divine wealth, and the living testimony and continued revelation of successful prosperity teachers presented an idealized portrait of what it meant to live victoriously. Their chauffeured cars and private jets served as tangible reminders of their blessedness" (Bowler, *Blessed*, 134).

233. Edwards, "Ethical Dimensions," 92. E.g., see Lin, *Prosperity Gospel*, Kindle edition, "Get Ready for the Harvest!"

234. Perriman, *FHP,* 32.

235. E.g., designer clothes, jewellery, technology, five-star hotels, houses, cars, and jet airplanes. See Meyer, "Pentecostalism and Neo-Liberal Capitalism," 6; Oyedepo owns four private jets (Gifford, "Prosperity Theology," 86). As Bowler notes, "Pastors found that parishioners wanted leaders who looked and preached like an ambassador for unrelenting progress" (Bowler, *Blessed*, 118, see also 134, 136–7; Walton, *Watch This*, 207; Gifford, *Ghana's New Christianity*, 66–8; Copeland, *Blessed*, e-book edition, "The Gospel to the Poor."

236. Meyer, "Pentecostalism and Neo-Liberal Capitalism," 16.

237. Bowler, "Blessed Bodies," 88. E.g., Hagin writes, "I have not had one sick day in 45 years. I did not say that the devil hadn't attacked me. But before the day is out, I am healed" (Hagin, *Name of Jesus*, e-book edition, "Chapter 21").

238. Coleman, *Globalisation*, 154.

239. Goh, "Hillsong and Megachurch," 296–7; Coleman, *Globalisation*, 154, 185.

offerings gathered, size of staff, number of nations visited, building projects, etc.).[240] Signs of size also include the material signs of the globe, world maps, eagle, and flags and the linguistic signs such as "international" and "worldwide."[241] Linguistic signs supporting the charismatic leader semiosis are titles, for example, "anointed," "man/woman of God," "ambassador," reverend, bishop, "dad," prophet, apostle, teacher, and doctor.[242] TV and media make powerful signs of the charismatic leader for especially two reasons.[243] First, media technologies speak of size because of the (potentially) significant larger reach and number of listeners. Second, media distribute iconic images and sounds of the leader, which directly strengthen the semiosis of the charismatic leader as an icon of faith.[244]

4.3.6.1 The Semiosis of the Charismatic Leader The logic generated by the semiosis of the charismatic leader answers some otherwise difficult problems, for example why the lavish wealth of some of the most prominent Word of Faith preachers is not detrimental to the impact of their message, nor poses a real problem for most followers—even among those who are materially disadvantaged.[245] From the semiotic logic follows that the clearer the indices of faith the Word of Faith leader manifests, the better the leader is. The leader's amount of revelation knowledge, prosperity, health, and optimism determine the extent the members will consider him or her a true leader. Word of Faith leaders deem their calling to display indexical signs of faith (see Chapter 5).[246] Iconic logic thus explains why Word

---

240. Coleman, *Globalisation*, 185; Walton, *Watch This,* 7, 200; Asamoah-Gyadu, "God Is Big," 1; Mitchem, *Name It,* 77; Agana, *Succeed Here*, 209–11.

241. Walton, *Watch This,* 96, 146; Mitchem, *Name It,* 78; Bowler, *Blessed,* 255; Asamoah-Gyadu, "God Is Big," 1; Asamoah-Gyadu, *Sighs and Signs,* 31–46; Agana, *Succeed Here,* 211; Walton, "Blessed and Highly Favored," 102.

242. Frederick, *Colored Television,* 52; Walton, *Watch This,* 158; Adeleye, *Preachers,* 43–4.

243. Walton, *Watch This,* 4.

244. Frederick, *Colored Television,* 58; Coleman, *Globalisation,* 166–86, 207; Walton, *Watch This,* 5; Commenting on TV's semiotic power to make a sign-vehicle signify an object which is not genuine, Richard Dortch writes in relation to Jim Bakker and the PTL scandal: "A person whose lifestyle and character are questionable can suddenly receive unmerited prominence from one well-placed television appearance. Frail, weak, ordinary people appear strong and powerful. Most are perceived as something they are not" [Richard Dortch, *Integrity: How I Lost It and My Journey Back* (Green Forest: New Leaf Press, 1991), 40].

245. Asamoah-Gyadu, "Prosperity and Poverty," 103. E.g., Oyedepo's wealth (Gifford, "Prosperity Theology," 86); Edward Luce, "A Preacher for Trump's America: Joel Osteen and the Prosperity Gospel," *Financial Times Magazine Life & Arts,* April 18, 2019, accessed April 7, 2021, https://www.ft.com/content/3990ce66-60a6-11e9-b285-3acd5d43599e.

246. E.g., Duncan-Williams "I believe that God has raised me as a leader and as an example to my generation to demonstrate His goodness, mercy and prosperity" (Duncan-

of Faith leaders unselfconsciously speak and display the beauty standards of the secular market as wealth and physical attractiveness increase the leader's impact and following.[247] Jonathan Walton's observations of how prosperity signifies the charismatic leader in the context of televangelism are applicable to other contexts: "the preacher's aesthetic symbols of prosperity serve as an authoritative source. As the living embodiment of faith in action, these dynamic personalities are able to authenticate the worldview that they promote."[248]

The iconic function of the charismatic leader instills hope because they make embodied proof that "faith works."[249] When prosperity, health, and optimism are visible in the charismatic leader's life, "the subconscious message is that 'this pattern has worked for us, it will work for you too.'"[250] The way to attain to Eden's life is to align one's life with the charismatic leader whose life already evidences its reality.[251] As the icon of faith, the charismatic leader functions as the hero in the Word of Faith worldview.[252] The semiosis of the charismatic leader thus sheds light on why Word of Faith leaders hold a very high level of influence in their community

Williams, e-book edition, "That You May Prosper"); Fred K. C. Price: "The Bible says that He [Jesus] has left us an example that we should follow His steps. That's the reason why I drive a Rolls Royce. I'm following Jesus' steps" (Fred K. C. Price quoted in Hanegraaff, *Christianity in Crisis 21st,* Kindle edition, "Cultural Conformity"); Rey, "Missing Prosperity," 352.

247. Winslow, "Imaged Other."

248. Walton, *Watch This*, 200. "Leaders proved to be the most powerful demonstrators of divine wealth, and the living testimony and continued revelation of successful prosperity teachers presented an idealized portrait of what it meant to live victoriously. Their chauffeured cars and private jets served as tangible reminders of their blessedness" (Bowler, *Blessed*, 134).

249. "Pastors' health, wealth, and charmed lives serve as the bedrock of their ministries, as they offer themselves as living examples of how prosperity theology works" (Bowler, *Blessed Bodies*, fn.3); Bowler, "Successful Calling," 185; Walton, *Watch This*, 164–5; Harrison, *RR*, 39. E.g., Gifford, "Prosperity Theology," 88.

250. "The sign of progress in prosperity is the successful acquisition of things and the display of this wealth to others. Many television ministers who align themselves with this doctrine sport expensive suits, luxury cars, extravagant homes, and elaborate, well-furnished sanctuaries. The subconscious message is that 'this pattern has worked for us, it will work for you too'" (Frederick, *Between Sundays*, 150); "particularly the preachers, set an awe inspiring example of the success of what they are preaching by driving late-model luxury cars, owning large homes, and boasting expensive wardrobes" (Farah, "Roots," 18); "Brother Mike's own life has long been used as evidence for the validity of the prosperity gospel" (Wiegele, "Prosperity Gospel," 177).

251. Perriman, *FHP*, 234.

252. Peter, "Church's Response," 141–2, 144.

and arouse intense loyalty among their followers.[253] Their iconic position makes it, however, "all too easy for the image of the prosperous, high-profile, charismatic leader to replace Christ as the object of adulation and imitation."[254] The iconic logic also places inordinate expectations on the movement's leaders. A direct consequence of the semiosis of the charismatic leader is that any known financial or health-challenge in a leader is detrimental to gaining or keeping influence in the movement.[255] Sickness, poverty, or depression signal failure to personally realize Eden in the now and effectively disqualify a person from being a leader.

Overall, the charismatic leader is not favored by God beyond other believers; rather, they are the pioneers who evidence through their lives what faith can do for anyone who dares to use the God-kind of faith in the same way the leader does.[256] The semiosis of the charismatic leader generates the expressed expectation that every believer should—by following their charismatic leader—eventually become an icon of faith.[257] That is, the believer who faithfully follows their charismatic leader is on the trajectory of their lives also corresponding to the realities of Eden's prosperity, health, and happiness.[258]

Conclusion

This chapter set out to analyze the semiotic dimension of the Word of Faith worldview by using the element of symbol in Wright's worldview-model through Peircean semiotic theory. The six signs of revelation knowledge, faith, prosperity, health, optimism, and the charismatic leader fulfill the requirements for worldview-signs in the Word of Faith. The semiotic analyses of these signs

253. Edwards, "Ethical Dimensions," 91–4; Walton, *Watch This*, 6; Lin, *Prosperity Gospel*, Kindle edition, "Studying Pentecostals." See also Frederick's usage of "the religious dandy" which she defines as "the charismatic figure of success and possibility" (Frederick, *Colored Television*, 31–59, 54. See Perriman, *FHP*, 31–2; Hunt, "Dramatising," 79.

254. Perriman, *FHP*, 234; Kalu, *African Pentecostalism*, 112.

255. "If you do not prosper, the world will not listen to your wisdom when you share the Gospel. A few may hear your testimony, even if you are poor. However, many, many more will listen to your testimony if you are prosperous" [John Avanzini and Larry Huggins, *Prosperity: The Choice Is Yours* (self-pub., The Commonwealth of Christ Embassy Press, n.d.), "Money Is Not Evil"].

256. Hagin, *Your Faith*, e-book edition, "Chapter 2: God Has No Favorites." Cf. Gifford, "Prosperity Theology."

257. Coleman, *Globalisation*, 150, 138; Bowler, *Blessed*, 141. The iconic logic underlies the following episode: "One day in chapel [at Oral Roberts University] a well-known African American Pentecostal GHW [Gospel of Health and Wealth] pastor, televangelist, and author spoke about God's 'promise' to reward positive faith. . . . He shouted, 'You can't be a witness of Jesus from a wheelchair!'" (Olson, *CC*, 155).

258. Coleman, "Why Health and Wealth," 56–7.

generate three particularly critical insights into the worldview of the Word of Faith: the predominance of iconic expectations, the privilege of indexical logic, and its semiotic complexities. Each insight requires some expansion.

First, the semiotic analysis discloses the predominance of iconic expectations. The Word of Faith's iconic logic expects a resembling relationship between the sign and the object, which forms expectancies of this-worldly perfection within their worldview. The semiosis of revelation knowledge makes the Word of Faith to expect absolute knowledge of the spiritual realm. Iconic logic also sets the expectations on the charismatic leader to mirror the realities of faith as a perfect representation of the prelapsarian Adam.[259] Yet, the space allowed God's sovereignty and human weakness is effectively limited by iconicity; the theological categories of mystery and paradox—expressions of a symbolic logic—are deconstructed in the Word of Faith.[260] Instead, iconic logic breeds a "bold faith," characterized by an exuberant confidence that expects the realization of the abundant life of Eden in the now while being impatient with human limitations and frailty.[261] Iconic logic shapes the Word of Faith's expectations of present perfection.

Second, the semiotic analysis shows how the Word of Faith worldview is privileging indexical semiosis.[262] The worldview-story of Eden Redeemed places prosperity, health, and optimism in a cause-and-effect relationship to faith. Considerable attention is given to signs that make faith "palpable"[263] and the indexical logic generates an "immediate expectation of faith producing tangible material results."[264] Since the indexical signs are empirically verifiable, they provide evidential proof of faith's veracity.[265] The indexical signs also seek to make human experience understandable, predictable, and absolute and can, therefore, motivate human agency and provide a sense of meaning in a highly complex and

259. See Perriman, *FHP,* 202.

260. Farah, *FTP,* 135–6, 152–7.

261. Pugh, *Bold Faith.*

262. Bowler, *Blessed,* 7. In semiotic terms, both Weber's Protestant work-ethic and the American Dream can be understood as privileging indexical logic, which places material success in a causative relation to hard work and moral virtue (see, e.g., Walton, *Watch This,* 180). The classical Pentecostal movement has an equal privileging of index-signs, especially the initial physical evidence doctrine which places glossolalia in an indexical relation to Spirit baptism. It could also be argued that the healing semiosis of the Word of Faith follows the semiotic logic of the classical Pentecostal doctrine of healing in the atonement (see Perriman, *FHP,* 61).

263. "the [Word of Faith] movement envisions faith as palpable. This faith is measured in the wallet, in one's personal finances, and in the body, in one's personal health, making material reality the measure of the success of immaterial faith" (Bowler, "Blessed Bodies," 83).

264. Sanchez-Walsh, "Santidad, Salvación," 158.

265. See ibid.

arbitrary world.[266] However, the Word of Faith's indexical semiosis simplifies the complexities of human experience, lead to a quantifiable spirituality and can easily generate a culture of censuring where faith is measured and monitored—causing blame to follow suffering when the desired end is not reached.[267] The indexical logic places the believer rather than God in the position of proactivity. As the initiator of the process, the believer is in control while God's role is passive and reactive. In contrast to an indexical interpretation of prosperity, health, and optimism, a robust case can be made that these function rather as symbolic signs in a biblically shaped worldview—an insight which appears to have dawned on Hagin late in life.[268] Regardless, the Word of Faith worldview is characterized by indexical semiosis.[269]

Third, the semiosis of faith and prosperity illustrates the complexities of the Word of Faith worldview that resist homogenizing and reductionism. It is important to observe the radical resignification of certain signs in Word of Faith discourse (e.g., faith signifying faith of God), while at the same time acknowledging the prevailing presence of a Pentecostal narrative in Word of Faith semiosis.[270] The different semiosis of identical sign-vehicles and the use of different interpretants

266. Due to the deductive logic at work in index-signs, they carry within "them the highest degree of logical force" and are "least open to controversy or interpretative difference" (Hughes, *Worship as Meaning*, 143).

267. "the saints expected that their faith would be measured in their bodies" (Bowler, "Blessed Bodies," 98, 96–9); "One's physical and financial condition is thus intimately tied to—and can provide evidence concerning—the state of one's faith" (Sanchez-Walsh, "Santidad, Salvación," 162); "the logic of the GHW [Gospel of Health and Wealth] forces the blame back on the person suffering" (Olson, *CC*, 162); "the physical body and spiritual state can be judged" (Coleman, *Globalisation*, 151, 155); Walton, *Watch This*, 95; *The Cape Town Commitment* says that "we deny as unbiblical the teaching that spiritual welfare can be measured in terms of material welfare, or that wealth is always a sign of God's blessing" (Lausanne, "Cape Town Commitment," II-E-5); See Matta, *Born Again Jesus*, 137.

268. Hagin, *MT*. "Wealth and prosperity can be a blessing from God, but they can also be Satan's temptation" (Perriman, *FHP*, 240); Anderson, *To the Ends*, 222; Anderson, *Introduction to Pentecostalism*, 218; da Silva, *Framgångsteologin*, 63, 83. "Suffering and dying is the way by which the world is changed" [N. T. Wright, *The Day the Revolution Began* (London: SPCK, 2016, 368]. For arguments on a symbolic interpretation of prosperity see Wheeler, *Wealth as Peril*; Witherington, *Jesus and Money*.

269. Bowler, *Blessed*, 7; Bowler, "Blessed Bodies," 83.

270. Perriman, *FHP*, 17. "a modified conception of faith that differed in important respects from the type of faith promoted by early believers" (Williams, *Spirit Cure*, 112); critique in Matta, *Born Again Jesus*, xiii, xvi. "The particular danger of the CPG [Christian Prosperity Gospel] to orthodox Christianity lies in its deconstructive use of the signs and techniques of the evangelical tradition and its redeployment of those very signs and techniques for its own purposes and perspectives–purposes more consonant with the materialist desires of a diverse audience" (Souders, *God of Wealth*, 90).

in the Word of Faith defy simple approaches and conclusions. The semiotic complexity explains the "puzzling mix of the familiar and the unfamiliar"[271] that persons from non–Word of Faith backgrounds experience in contact with Word of Faith discourse. Yet, attributing semiotic differences in the Word of Faith vis-à-vis Pentecostalism to matters of rhetoric or theological emphases is an unsatisfactory way to homogenize them. The other option of letting the semiosis of a select number of signs (e.g., faith and revelation knowledge) define the Word of Faith is equally unsatisfactory. Interpretations of Word of Faith discourse that show sensitivity to the sign-producer's intentional interpretant and immediate object will generate a multifaceted and complex picture of the movement. As I continue to pursue such a "thicker description," the next chapter analyzes the practical dimension of the Word of Faith worldview through Wright's element of praxis.

271. Perriman, *FHP,* 17.

Chapter 5

PRAXIS IN THE WORD OF FAITH WORLDVIEW

This research claims that the Word of Faith is best approached as a distinct worldview and that a worldview-analysis answers to the need for additional complexity and nuance in understanding the movement and is better suited than other models to speak to this book's analytical, evaluative, and comparative goals, that is, to understand the Word of Faith worldview's essential features, inner logic, to test its strengths and weaknesses, and to compare its relationship with Pentecostal distinctives. The dominant task of conducting a worldview-analysis required the two initial tasks of mapping the current scholarly landscape and clarifying the concept and method of worldview. I use Wright's model which consists of the four elements of story, symbol, praxis, and ultimate beliefs. The previous two chapters applied the worldview-elements of story (Chapter 3) to analyze the narrative dimension of the Word of Faith worldview and the element of symbol (Chapter 4) to analyze its semiotic dimension. Wright's element of praxis is the focus here, while the element of ultimate beliefs is left until the following chapter (Chapter 6). Practices, according to Wright, make an irreducible part of worldviews, reflecting and contributing to their shape. Applying the element of praxis to the Word of Faith offers, therefore, vital insights into the practical dimension of the movement's worldview.

In the first section, I discuss Wright's conception of praxis, its nature, and its functions in worldviews and his threefold criteria to identify praxis. This is followed by presenting how praxis is best imagined as a sign-shaped action and hence fruitfully analyzed through the Peircean semiotics used in the last chapter. In the next section, Wright's element of praxis is applied to the Word of Faith through Peircean semiotics. I then present and analyze six sign-shaped actions, which fit Wright's criteria for praxis: speaking positive confessions, gaining revelation knowledge, sowing money seeds, manifesting prosperity and health, following the charismatic leader, and extending influence in the world. I conclude with discussing three critical insights that arise from the chapter and which offer insights into the Word of Faith worldview and speak to this book's goals.

5.1 Praxis in Worldview

I begin the examination of the Word of Faith worldview's practical dimension using the element of praxis by first considering Wright's understanding of how praxis functions in worldviews and by what criteria he identifies praxis. I then note how praxis is best understood in semiotic terms as sign-shaped actions. Hence, I show that the Peircean semiotic categories introduced in the last chapter provide the necessary framework for analyzing praxis in the Word of Faith.

5.1.1 Wright's Element of Praxis

The term "praxis," by which Wright refers to the practical element of his worldview-model, has a rich history in philosophy.[1] Wright uses the term in a broad sense in his worldview thinking, speaking of an action or a pattern of behavior which stands in a unique, functional relationship to the worldview through interrelating with the other worldview-elements of story, symbol, and ultimate beliefs.[2] Praxis is a realm of human action that communicates worldview-level meaning through "practical and physical expression."[3] Strictly speaking, all human practices arise within the context of worldviews, but Wright categorizes only those actions that reflect the worldview as praxis. Praxis thus makes a certain "mode of being-in-the-world,"[4] which gives the worldview bodily and acted shape by dramatizing the element of story, performing the element of symbol, and embodying the ultimate beliefs.[5]

An action that practically manifests the other worldview-elements of story, symbol, and ultimate beliefs constitutes Wright's praxis. A large variety of actions can thus be counted as praxis. Wright includes symbolic and nonsymbolic actions (i.e., everyday, purpose-oriented actions) and uses a variety of terms in reference

---

1. Ranging back to Aristotle's notion of a goal-oriented action, to later be used by Kant to speak of the application of a theory and especially by Marx, who used praxis to (among other aspects) emphasize authentic human action. See Simon Blackburn, *Oxford Dictionary of Philosophy* (Oxford: Oxford University Press, 1996), 298.

2. "the real shape of someone's worldview can often be seen in the sort of actions they perform, particularly if the actions are so instinctive or habitual as to be taken for granted" (Wright, *NTPG*, 124).

3. "How did the worldview of the apostle Paul come into practical and physical expression in a way which would form a key part of worldview-praxis?" (Wright, *PFG*, 417, 411).

4. Wright, *NTPG*, 133.

5. Wright, *NTPG*, 124, 133, 232; Wright, *JVG*, 142; Wright, *PFG*, 29, 439. Wright's emphasis on praxis as exhibiting worldviews draws upon Walsh and Middleton, who said: "If we want to understand what people see, or how well people see, we need to watch how they walk" (Walsh and Middleton, *TV*, 1).

to the content of praxis, such as "action," "behaviour," and "practice."[6] Actions that typically are classified as "rituals" (understood as "special, non-ordinary behaviour") are also included though the formal definitions and discussions common in ritual studies do not play any significant part.[7] Praxis makes the larger category that includes but cannot be reduced to ritual. Wright's list of early Christian praxis exemplifies the possible variety of actions that can be part of this worldview-element: water baptism, Eucharist, missions, money-sharing, prayer, acts of justice, and peacemaking.[8] Nonaction, what Wright calls "negative praxis,"[9] is also counted as praxis. Negative praxis is an action the worldview adherents do *not* perform, which the dominant culture or another significant group otherwise expect.[10] Undergoing persecution and martyrdom are two examples of negative praxis.[11]

A basic premise for Wright is that worldview makes the underlying, generative context of praxis.[12] Because of praxis's interconnection with the worldview, praxis also functions (like the other worldview-elements) as a window into the underlying worldview.[13] In fact, a praxis-type action illuminates the agent's level of commitment to the related worldview and serves as a reliable worldview indicator because practices "may offer a truer account"[14] of a worldview than the agent's stories or propositional statements.[15]

6. E.g., Wright, *NTPG*, 124, 134, 361, 363. See Ann-Christine Hornborg, *Ritualer: Teorier och Tillämpning* (Lund: Studentlitteratur, 2005), 17; Coleman, *Globalisation*, 134.

7. Wright, *NTPG*, 112, 361; Wright, *PFG*, 411, 418. See Paul Bradshaw and John Melloh, eds., *Foundations in Ritual Studies* (London: SPCK, 2007), 11; Grimes, *Craft of Ritual*, 185–210; Hornborg, *Ritualer*, 11–22. For ritual studies see Cathrine Bell, *Ritual Theory, Ritual Practice* (Oxford: Oxford University Press, 1992); Cathrine Bell, *Ritual* (Oxford: Oxford University Press, 1997); Grimes, *The Craft*; Barry Stephenson, *Ritual: A Very Short Introduction* (Oxford: Oxford University Press, 2015).

8. Wright, *NTPG*, 128, 361, 364; Wright, *RSG*, 274, 578; Wright, *PFG*, 401. Sabbath, food laws, and circumcision are held by Wright as key Jewish praxis (Wright, *NTPG*, 124, 364; Wright, *RSG*, 580).

9. Wright, *NTPG*, 364.

10. Wright, *NTPG*, 361, 363–4; See also Wright, *PFG*, 434.

11. Wright, NTPG, 363–4; Wright, *PFG*, 434.

12. Wright, *NTPG*, 133–4; *RSG*, 274.

13. Wright, *NTPG*, 134; See Bell, *Ritual Theory*, 25–9.

14. Wright, *NTPG*, 128.

15. Wright, *NTPG*, 41, 124, 128; Wright, *RSG*, 578; Wright, *JVG*, 296. See Anderson and Foley, *Mighty Stories*, 28. See also Rappaport, *Ritual and Religion*. "Humans live in overlapping worlds, and, as individuals or groups, they may well tell themselves different and overlapping, but also competing stories. In addition, the stories that are explicitly told by a group or individual may well be consciously or unconsciously deceitful, and will require checking in light of actual praxis and of a wider symbolic universe. What someone habitually *does*, and the symbols around which they order their lives, are at least as reliable

Praxis operates mostly on the subconscious level of human intentionality. In describing praxis as "a habit of the heart," Wright emphasizes how praxis consists of actions and patterns of behavior that adherents of a worldview "do habitually, characteristically, and usually unreflectively," in a "taken-for-granted" manner that has become "second nature."[16] That the agent operates mostly in an unreflected manner does not, however, negate that actions which function as praxis can initially be consciously learned or adopted.[17]

Wright envisions the relation between thinking and action as fundamentally reflexive, and deliberately included the element of praxis in his model for worldview-analysis to avoid an otherwise overly cognitive conceptualization of worldviews.[18] This dimension in Wright's worldview-model evades polarizing acting and thinking,[19] which is a particularly welcome corrective to the overrational conceptualizations of worldviews present in some schools of worldview theory.[20] A thought-action dichotomy leads to a reduction of practice to rational meaning as if worldviews are systems of thought simply expressed in human action.[21] For Wright, actions do not just have the power to communicate a worldview; they wield dynamic and transforming power over worldviews.[22] Wright's understanding of praxis should not be read as an overly deterministic view of human behavior, as if practices merely reflect the worldview—and so deny conscious motives and individual goals.[23] The focus on human action enlarges Wright's worldview concept beyond the common understanding

an index to their worldview as the stories they 'officially' tell" (Wright, *NTPG*, 40–41, emphasis original).

16. Wright, *NTPG*, 124, 361; Wright, *PFG*, 417, 448, 450; Wright, *RSG*, 578; Wright, *JVG*, 37, 148, 448; N. T. Wright, *After You Believe: Why Christian Character Matters* (New York: HarperCollins, 2010). See Robert Bellah et al. eds., *Habits of the Heart* (Berkeley: University of California Press, 1996).

17. Wright, *JVG*, 169; Wright, *PFG*, 453. See also Wright, *After You Believe*.

18. Wright, *PFG*, 27. See also Rabens, "The Faithfulness of God," 568.

19. Mark J. Cartledge, "Text–Community–Spirit: The Challenges posed by Pentecostal Theological Method to Evangelical Theology," in *Spirit and Scripture: Exploring a Pneumatic Hermeneutic*," ed. Kevin L. Spawn and Archie T. Wright (London: T&T Clark, 2012), 139.

20. Wright, *PFG*, 27–8. See Stephenson, *Ritual*, 3.

21. See Smith, *Desiring the Kingdom*. Despite the dialectic dimension in Wright's model, it lies beyond this thesis to explore to what extent Wright is vulnerable for the type of critique raised against views of ritual as communication and symbolic actions privileging an ethnocentric view of the primacy of thought over action and neglecting the subversive and creative dimension of ritual.

22. Wright, *PFG*, 417; Wright, *JVG*, 245. See Bradshaw and Melloh, *Foundations*, 12; Thomas Csordas, "Ritualization of Life," in *Practicing the Faith: The Ritual Life of Pentecostal-Charismatic Christians*, ed. Martin Lindhardt (New York: Berghahn Books, 2011), 129.

23. See Walton, "Stop Worrying," 122.

of worldviews as rational systems of thought to embrace the role of practices in shaping and communicating worldviews.[24] Praxis is thus one of his most significant contributions to worldview thinking.

Wright employs three criteria for identifying when an action can be categorized as praxis. First, the action is habitual and characteristic.[25] That is, the practice is regularly performed and indicative of the person's or group's unique identity. Second, the action is mostly unreflected and takes place on the level of assumption. That is, praxis comprises actions that are "second nature"[26] and "taken for granted;"[27] once established, they do not need conscious motivation or justification to be habitually done. Third, the final and most important criterion is that the action must stand in a symbiotic relationship to the other worldview-elements. An action that fully integrates with and expresses practically and physically the worldview-elements of story, symbol, and ultimate beliefs (arising out of the same worldview) makes a praxis.[28] Though all four elements interrelate, story has a privileged place in Wright.[29] In short, praxis is for Wright an inclusive category for characteristic, habitual, and mostly unreflected actions which stand in a reflexive relationship to the underlying worldview and integrates with the other worldview-elements, where story has the predominant part.[30]

Wright's conception of the worldview-element of praxis and his threefold criteria to identify such provides a useful way to analyze Word of Faith practices. Particularly, Wright's element of praxis enlarges the focus in worldview-analysis from the common focus on propositional content to offer a holistic model of analysis which accommodates the pragmatic logic of the movement.[31]

5.1.2 Praxis as a Sign-Shaped Action Applied to the Word of Faith

Having noted the usefulness of the worldview-element of praxis to explore the dimension of human practices in the Word of Faith, Wright's general threefold criteria to identify praxis invite additional input to further define and sharpen the application of praxis to analyze the Word of Faith worldview. The Peircean semiotics introduced in Chapter 3 provides such a necessary framework. The previous chapter showed how Peircean semiotics integrates with Wright's

24. See Smith, *Desiring the Kingdom*, 63–71.

25. Wright, *NTPG*, 112; Wright, *PFG*, 417, 448, 450; Wright, *RSG*, 578; Wright, *JVG*, 37, 448.

26. Wright, *NTPG*, 361.

27. Wright, *NTPG*, 361–2.

28. Wright, *NTPG*, 124, 128; Wright, *PFG*, 411, 417.

29. Wright, *NTPG*, 132.

30. Wright, *NTPG*, 361, 365. I use "praxis" and "worldview-praxis" following Wright in reference to the actions that function as this worldview-element.

31. Harrison, *RR*, 31–2; Heuser, "Charting African Prosperity," 3.

worldview thinking in general and strengthens the application of his element of symbol to the Word of Faith. This chapter continues this semiotic approach because it captures Wright's understanding of praxis and provides a model that is directly applicable in this study. The semiotic approach to praxis accommodates Wright's focus on the communicative function of praxis, is able to explicate the inner logic of how praxis integrates with the other worldview-elements, and caters for the close relationship between symbol and praxis in Wright.[32] Peircean semiotics has been used to analyze religious practices in other studies, including practices in Word of Faith megachurches.[33] These studies show that analyzing practices semiotically as sign-shaped actions is a fruitful way of gaining insights into the worldview of religious movements such as the Word of Faith.

The Peircean semiotics used in the last chapter to apply the worldview-element of symbol is therefore fruitful in applying the element of praxis to the Word of Faith. An action categorized as praxis in Wright's model is best approached as a sign-shaped action, or as a "semiotic practice."[34] Wright's praxis functions as sign-shaped actions, made up in their essence of the three elements of the sign: sign-vehicle, interpretant, and object (see Section 4.1.2). As a sign-shaped action, the practice itself makes the sign-vehicle that signifies an object through the interpretant, both interpretant and object correlate with the worldview.

Analyzing praxis as comprising the three elements of Peirce's sign allows me to examine the actions' inner logic. Yet, accessing how praxis fully functions as a semiotic practice in the Word of Faith worldview is not possible without looking to the ultimate beliefs which will be discussed in the following chapter. Since the elements of story and symbol have been covered so far, the analysis is limited to the worldview-story I refer to as "Eden Redeemed" from Chapter 3 and the six worldview-signs from Chapter 4 (revelation knowledge, faith, prosperity, health, optimism, and the charismatic leader). Figure 11 graphically depicts praxis as a sign-shaped action and the process of signification in the context of the Word of Faith worldview. The dotted arrow illustrates the sign-producer's envisioned direction of the sign-vehicle to its immediate object in the semiotic process, while the lined arrows illustrate the actual process of signification through the intentional interpretant.

---

32. See Wright, *NTPG*, 124, 229, 359; Wright, *PFG*, 385, 403; Wright, *JVG*, 168.

33. Hughes, *Worship as Meaning*; Goh, "Hillsong and Megachurch;" Rappaport, *Ritual and Religion*; Joel Robbins, "Ritual Communication and Linguistic Ideology," *Current Anthropology* 42, no. 5 (December 2001): 591–614; Jens Kreinath, "Semiotics," in *Theorizing Rituals: Issues, Topics, Approaches, Concepts*, ed. Jens Kreinath, Jan Snoek and Michael Stausberg (Leiden: Brill, 2006), 429–70; S. J. Tambiah, *A Peformative Approach to Ritual* (Oxford: Oxford University Press, 1979).

34. Goh, "Hillsong and Megachurch," 300.

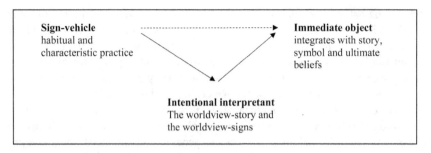

Figure 11 Praxis as a sign-shaped action.

Following the diagram, what remains is to identify and describe sign-vehicles in the Word of Faith that consist of habitual and characteristic practices (often unreflected and operating on the level of assumption) and what object they signify through the intentional interpretant of their worldview-story and worldview-signs.

5.2 Praxis in the Word of Faith

Because of the pragmatic nature of the Word of Faith movement, Wright's element of praxis is a particularly fitting line of study. Practices play a significant role in the movement's self-understanding and studies show how the movement cherishes a strong pragmatic emphasis.[35] Theological studies of the Word of Faith which use the doctrinal and biblical models include some characteristic practices (e.g., positive confession and sowing money seeds) but often privilege the movement's propositional aspects. Analyses of practices are mostly left to the domain of the social sciences.[36] It is, however, a mistake to privilege the propositional dimension above practices thinking that Word of Faith theology is only—or at least best—carried by the movement's doctrinal beliefs. A thorough theological understanding of the Word of Faith requires that sufficient attention is given to the movement's worldview-praxis.

A close study of Word of Faith discourse and relevant scholarly materials yields six practices that fit Wright's threefold category of worldview-praxis as characteristic, habitual, and mostly unreflected actions which interrelate with the other worldview-elements: speaking positive confessions, gaining revelation knowledge, sowing money seeds, manifesting prosperity and health, following the charismatic leader, and extending influence in the world.[37] The practices are labeled descriptively of

35. E.g., Lin, *Prosperity Gospel*, Kindle edition, "A Different Kind of Conversion." See Heuser, "Charting African Prosperity," 3.

36. See McConnell, *DG*, 163; Marti, *Hollywood Faith*, 124–5. See also Joel Robbins, "World Christianity and the Reorganization of Disciplines," in *Theologically Engaged Anthropology*, ed. J. Derrick Lemons (Oxford: Oxford University Press, 2018), 226–43.

37. A recent example of how these six practices emerge as the central practices in the Word of Faith, though he does not use the same terms or divide them into as strict categories as I do,

the action's nature, and their order correlates with their sequential appearance in
the Eden Redeemed story (e.g., beginning with confession as the primal action in
creation and gaining revelation knowledge of the spiritual world as the prerequisite
for sowing financial seeds which in turn serves to manifest prosperity and health).
I analyze each practice as a sign-shaped action, first by describing the sign-vehicle,
that is, the action in embodied performance, followed by a semiotic description of
how the action signifies its immediate object through the intentional interpretant of
the Word of Faith elements of story and symbol. Closing each section is a discussion
of how the semiotic analysis of the practice generates an enhanced understanding
of the inner logic of Word of Faith worldview. Extra attention is given to the two
practices of speaking positive confessions and manifesting prosperity and health
due to the widespread scholarly interest in those practices and because both reveal
particularly important aspects of the Word of Faith worldview.[38]

5.2.1 Speaking Positive Confessions

Speaking positive confessions is a practice which I also refer to as "confession"
and "confessing." Scholarship holds this practice as definitive of the Word of Faith
movement.[39] The centrality of the practice gives rise to the descriptors of the
whole movement as "Word of Faith," "rhema," "positive confession," or "name it
and claim it" and to a variety of signifiers for the action itself: "speak," "declare,"
"affirm," "demand," "command," and "decree."[40]

is Walton: Speaking positive confessions (Walton, "Blessed and Highly Favored," 113, 122–3);
gaining revelation knowledge (Walton, "Blessed and Highly Favored," 147–9); sowing seeds
(Walton, "Blessed and Highly Favored," 113–15); manifesting prosperity (Walton, "Blessed
and Highly Favored," 103–4); following the charismatic leader (Walton, "Blessed and Highly
Favored," 130–3); extending influence (Walton, "Blessed and Highly Favored," 116–17, 136–8).

38. The Word of Faith naturally encompasses a wide range of practices, most of which
are shared with other Pentecostals. However, I do not include them here as they are not
unique for the Word of Faith movement and fall outside Wright's criteria for worldview-
praxis. Agana argues that prayer is the most significant practice. However, as all Pentecostals
generally pray, it is the particular practice of speaking positive confession which makes their
prayers to take a different shape (Agana, *Succeed Here*). See also Ma, "Blessing," 279–81.

39. Farah, *FTP*, 123–33; Barron, *Health and Wealth*, 101–13; Brandon, *Health and
Wealth*, 16–32; Perriman, *FHP*, 39–41, 143–55; Kinnebrew, "Charismatic Doctrine;"
Lederle, *Theology with Spirit*, 150–3, 217–18; McConnell, *DG*, 135–8; Hanegraaff, *CIC*,
66–9; Bjornstad, "What's Behind;" Smail, Walker, Wright, *Love of Power*, 80; Hunt and
McMahon, *Seduction of Christianity*, 97–104.

40. Bowler, *Blessed*, 65–6. Other referents are "Confess it and possess it;" "you can have
what you say" or the derogatory "blab it and grab it" (King, *Only Believe*, 321; Hanegraaff,
Christianity in Crisis 21st, Kindle Edition, "Formula of Faith;" Bowman, *Word-Faith*, 199;
Coleman, *Globalisation*, 131; Lovett, "Positive Confession." The Lausanne community uses
the following definition: "We define prosperity gospel as the teaching that believers have a

The sign-vehicle consists of uttering words of desired, positive future states *as if* they were already-present realities.[41] Positive confession is a distinct practice from the confession of sins in traditional Christianity and must be held separate from a denial of empirical circumstance (as when a sick person says "I am not sick").[42] Speaking positive confessions means, rather than a denial of a present state, that the agent declares "those things which do not exist as though they did"[43] (as when a sick person says "I am well"). Certain formulas and biblical promises which verbalize the agent's desire make up the confession.[44] Positive confessions tend to be repetitive and are uttered or sung in a variety of settings, from liturgical to nonliturgical contexts, in group and private contexts.[45]

The practice of speaking positive confessions fits Wright's criteria for being a worldview-praxis: it is a habitual, characteristic, practice within the Word of Faith which signifies through the intentional interpretant made up of the

---

right to the blessings of health and wealth and that they can obtain these blessings through positive confessions of faith and the 'sowing of seeds' through the faithful payments of tithes and offerings" (Salinas, *Prosperity Theology*, 182); Bowler, *Blessed*, 125; Hagin Jr., *Create the World*, e-book edition, "Chapter 9;" Coleman, *Globalisation*, 193; Agana, *Succeed Here*, 191.

41. Vondey, *Pentecostalism*, 102. Kinnebrew offers a fuller definition: "the confident vocalization, by either a Christian or an unbeliever, of God's words (as they are found in Scripture) or of one's own inherently powerful words with a view toward increasing one's faith or improving one's circumstances" (Kinnebrew, "Charismatic Doctrine," 53).

42. Barron, *Health and Wealth*, 9; Harrison, *RR*, 55. E.g., see Hagin, *Words*; Hagin, *Exceedingly Growing*, 20; Meyer, *Change Your Words*, e-book edition, "So Choose Your Food." Cf. McConnell, *DG*, 163–5.

43. Romans 4:17 NKJV.

44. E.g., "Money cometh!" (Leroy Thomson, *Money Cometh! to the Body of Christ* (Darrow: Ever Increasing Word Ministries, 1997). See Agana, *Succeed Here*, 190–1; Bowler, *Blessed*, 128; Walton, "Stop Worrying," 115–16; Jones and Woodbridge, *HWH*, 61. The number of formulas is boundless as long as it agrees with how the movement interprets the Bible. See, e.g., Creflo Dollar, "Concerning Total Life Prosperity," *Creflodollarministries.org*, January 18, 2016, accessed April 7, 2021, https://www.creflodollarministries.org/Daily-Confessions/Concerning-Total-Life-Prosperity?returnUrl=%2FDaily-Confessions.

45. Coleman, *Globalisation*, 131; Harrison, *RR*, 57. E.g., "I was not talking to a human person when I made these confessions. I was usually home alone and merely spoke them out into the atmosphere as an act of faith" (Meyer, *Change Your Words*, e-book edition, "Chapter 5"). Positive confession stands in some tension with a chief characteristic of much other Word of Faith language, namely spontaneity. The prevalence of preformulated confessions in church and private settings challenge the *ex tempore* expectancy of religious language within the movement and an otherwise widespread hesitancy toward written and standardized language as being a "religious" hindrance to the spontaneity of the Holy Spirit [see Martin Lindhardt, "Introduction," in *Practicing the Faith: The Ritual Life of Pentecostal-Charismatic Christians*, ed. Martin Lindhardt (New York: Berghahn, 2011), 4–5].

worldview-elements of story and symbol.[46] The sign-vehicle of speaking positive confessions signifies through the intentional interpretant the immediate object that the agent has returned to the reality of Eden. Confession makes the agent unbound by the limitations of this world and shows that the agent is actively using the authority to rule the world that God delegated to Adam.[47] As such, positive confession functions as an index-sign, showing in a direct way that the believer appropriates Eden's realities in the now.

There is another aspect to the indexicality of confession. Roy Rappaport uses the sign theory of Peirce for semiotic analyses of confessional practices, and his work offers an important insight that elucidates the logic of positive confession. Rappaport shows that an index-sign also "refers to the Object it denotes by being really affected by the Object,"[48] thus making an indexical performance not limited to representative significations alone but open to standing in a causative relationship to its object.[49] It is helpful to understand confession in this light. Positive confessions function indexically—not just as representing the agent's return to Eden—but in making the sign-vehicle of the spoken word and its fulfillment "absolutely inseparable."[50] This causal link is explored in the following text.

The practice of positive confession interrelates with the heart of the Eden Redeemed story and gives embodied expression to a cluster of worldview-signs. Positive confession integrates with the Eden Redeemed story's narrative Task of ruling and increasing in the world.[51] In positive confession, the agent performs their

---

46. Salinas, *Prosperity Theology,* 182; Heuser, "Religio-Scapes," 16; Harrison, *RR,* 10–1, 55, 63–5; Bowler, *Blessed,* 65–6; Coleman, *Globalisation,* 117–42; McConnell, *DG,* 135–8; Barron, *Health and Wealth,* 101–13; Jones and Woodbridge, *HWH,* 59–62; Walton, *Watch This,* 153–5; Walton, "Stop Worrying," 111–12; Maltese, "Activist–Holiness," 71–3; Vondey, *Pentecostalism,* 102; Asamoah-Gyadu, *Sighs and Signs,* 75–83.

47. E.g., "You always get and have in your life what you believe for and say" [Hagin, *You can Have What You Say* (Tulsa: Faith Library Publications, 1988), 5]; Hagin, *Believer's Authority,* 7, 19; Joseph Prince Ministries, "Declare God's Word Over Your Situation," *Josephprince.org,* accessed June 6, 2020, https://www.josephprince.org/blog/daily-grace -inspirations/declare-gods-word-over-your-situation; Andrew Wommack Ministries, "Power of Faith-Filled Words," *Awmi.net.,* accessed April 7, 2021, https://www.awmi.net/ reading/teaching-articles/power_faith/. See Bowman, *Word-Faith,* 73.

48. Rappaport, *Ritual and Religion,* 59.

49. Rappaport, *Ritual and Religion,* 14, 54, 55, 57, 59.

50. Rappaport, *Ritual and Religion,* 67.

51. "This is the way Adam was to have dominion in the beginning. God told Adam to have dominion . . . How was Adam going to subdue the elephant? He would have to do it with his faith. There was not much he could do about it physically. He had to do it with his faith and the power of words. He had to operate in dominion by his faith. He had to operate the way God operated. He was in His likeness" (Capps, *Seedtime and Harvest,* e-book edition, "Dominion with Words").

equality with the God who spoke the universe into existence in "the archetypal act of positive confession"[52] and equality with Jesus who also used faith-filled words to accomplish redemption.[53] Other key narrative entities apart from equality with God and authority are also expressed in the practice of confession: the entities of faith and the law of confession fuse in the practice of positive confession. Faith is narrated in Eden Redeemed as requiring a "release" to be effective, and the law of confession guarantees that spoken words generate power.[54] Thus, the power of faith becomes operative through speaking.[55] The confession of "faith filled words" serves the dual capacity of strengthening the agent's faith and "unleashing" the force of the faith of God to cause the desired outcome to materialize.[56] Revelation knowledge is also signified in the practice. Confessing something which the natural senses do not affirm to be real shows that the confessing agent is living out of the really real spiritual realm and is not limited by the lesser-real world of sense knowledge.[57] Further, optimism finds its most distinct embodiment in the practice of positive confession. Since words carry creative power, the agent must only speak of positive conditions. Speaking of negative outcomes—that is, words of sickness, poverty, fear, and failure—be it present experience or anticipated future states, are classified as "negative confessions," which should be completely avoided as they stand in contradiction to faith and optimism.[58] Negative confessions show that the agent does not live in the reality of Eden. The refusal to speak of anything undesirable functions as Wright's negative praxis (see the following text).

52. Perriman, *FHP*, 39.

53. Henry Knight III, "God's Faithfulness and God's Freedom: A Comparison of Contemporary Theologies of Healing," *Journal of Pentecostal Theology* 2 (1999): 67. See, e.g., Capps, *Faith and Confession*, 28–30; Hagin, *Words*.

54. Hagin, *In Him*, 9; Hagin, *Words*, 12, 25; Hagin, *Exceedingly Growing*, 79; Meyer, *Change your Words,* e-book edition, "Chapter 1;" Oyedepo, *Born to Win,* e-book edition, "Address the Situation."

55. Perriman, *FHP*, 39; Bowler, *Blessed*, 66. See, e.g., "There is no faith without confession. Confession is faith's way of expressing itself" (Hagin, *Turn Your Faith*, e-book edition, "Chapter 3"); "When we speak God's words, we release His power" (Hagin Jr., *Create the World*, e-book edition, "Chapter 9"); "Faith is always expressed in WORDS. Faith must be released in WORDS through your mouth" (Hagin, *Words*, 30, emphasis original); Hagin, *Must Christians Suffer*, 31; Hagin, *In Him*, 1; Hagin, *Welcome*, 100; Meyer, *Change Your Words*, 32.

56. Bowler, *Blessed*, 66; Walton, *Watch This*, 153–5; Walton, "Stop Worrying," 112; Gifford "Prosperity Theology," 85.

57. Hanna Rosin, "Did Christianity Cause the Crash?," *The Atlantic,* December, 2009, accessed April 7, 2021, https://www.theatlantic.com/magazine/archive/2009/12/did-christianity-cause-the-crash/307764/.

58. Gifford "Prosperity Theology," 85; Barron, *Health and Wealth*, 10. E.g., Hagin, *Words*, 7, 21; Alexander, *Signs and Wonders*, 62.

A note should be made about positive thinking which is also a widespread practice in the Word of Faith.[59] Positive thinking is not included here as a separate practice because it is arguably inclusive in positive confession; positive thoughts must, it is believed, be expressed through positive confessions to be effective.[60] A distinctive mark of the Word of Faith is the expression of positive thoughts in positive words.[61]

5.2.1.1 Analysis of Speaking Positive Confessions The causative dimension of indexicality shown by Rappaport generates a logic in the Word of Faith that "you can have what you say."[62] "In 'positive confessions', words come to create the very reality which they purport to describe."[63] Human language is thus transferred in the practice from the sphere of the symbolic to that of indexicality. As such, positive confession has some affinities with speech-act theory.[64] Nonetheless, positive confession brings the indexical nature of human speech to significantly greater heights by bringing all human speech into the realm of limitless possibilities—a sphere Christianity previously reserved for God's speech alone.[65] Positive confession entails little less than a semiotic revolution of religious language, arising out of the Word of Faith worldview that favors indexicality over the symbolic as well as privileging human proactivity and an "exalted" anthropology (see Section 6.2.1.3). The causative power of words makes one of the worldview's chief characteristics.

Positive confession is critiqued in the literature as a harmful form of idealism. Because the practice resists empirical experience as mere "sense knowledge" which must be overruled by revelation knowledge put into spoken words, confession

59. Bowler, *Blessed*.
60. Hagin, *How to Turn*.
61. Olson, *CC*, 156; Heuser, "Prosperity Theology."
62. Hagin, *You Can Have*. See Gifford, *Ghana's New Christianity*, 52.
63. Coleman, *Globalisation*, 131.
64. See J. L. Austin, *How to Do Things with Words* (Oxford: Clarendon Press, 1962); John Searle, *Speech Acts* (Cambridge: Cambridge University Press, 1969); "Ritual Use of the Bible in African Pentecostalism," in *Practicing the Faith: The Ritual Life of Pentecostal-Charismatic Christians*, ed. Martin Lindhardt (New York: Berghahn, 2011), 180.
65. "you can talk as a man at the same time talk as a god and creation and everything exists even Satan and his . . . demonic powers have to obey you like it obeyed Jesus" (Leroy Thomson, "I AM a Commander Over Unlimited Prosperity #PR19," YouTube Video, 0:20:19, LeroyThomson TV, November 7, 2019, accessed June 6, 2020, https://www.you tube.com/watch?v=W_sPgQmzdow.); "The Word of God is my guarantee that I can speak as God speaks and call into existence everything that I need to succeed. I take authority over sickness, disease, poverty and insufficiency, and I rule as a king in life!" (Creflo Dollar Ministries, "Becoming Established in Righteousness," *Creflodollarministries.org*, accessed April 7, 2021, https://www.creflodollarministries.org/Daily-Confessions/Becoming-Esta blished-in-Righteousness?returnUrl=%2FDaily-Confessions).

makes an "irresponsible flight from reality."[66] Positive confession has, in some cases, resulted in excessive suffering and personal tragedy. There are testimonies of sick people who have died prematurely after confessing their healing, even refusing medicine and medical treatments because that would negate their positive confession.[67] Others, empowered by positive confession, entered into economic ventures but ended up in bankruptcy.[68] Without diminishing such tragic consequences, it is important to acknowledge that in positive confession the Word of Faith explores to what degree words carry power in a Pentecostally enchanted world.[69] Extending a critical approach to the Eden Redeemed narrative framework in which the practice takes place, the basic performance of the power of words in human life and Christian spirituality should not be too quickly dismissed as harmful idealism. Rather, the practice should be seen as an invitation to Pentecostal scholarship to further explore a holistic spirituality which gives place to human thoughts and words in a Spirit-filled worldview.

Positive confession is also criticized for having close affinities with magic or occult, non-Christian practices, thus making the practice "one of the worst seductions ever."[70] Others refute such unreserved rejection of confession as based on a limited, outsider perspective.[71] These opposing views arise out of an inherent ambiguity in the practice which challenges the coherence of the worldview. Confession operates by a "quasi-mechanical function of words"[72] but the imagined dynamic "is not *necessarily* a power detached from the person of God."[73] The equivocality noted in the quote relates to two most pressing questions. The first is about the source of the power imagined being activated by confession and the second concerning the agent's role in relation to God. Word of Faith discourse is unclear; at times it credits the power to the spiritual law of confession that infuses spoken words with creative power and at other times to the person of God.[74] The ambiguity related to the source of power exists within the narrative rationale of Eden Redeemed. Chapter 3 noted how the story contains a narrative gap regarding the nature and origin of spiritual laws and their relationship to God.[75] God's role

66. McConnell, *DG*, 104–5; Adeleye, "Prosperity Gospel and Poverty," 15.

67. Farah, *FTP*, 52–4, 121–3; Bowler, *Blessed*, 161; Barron, *Health and Wealth*, 14–34. Cf. Lin, *Prosperity Gospel*, Kindle edition, "Action."

68. Farah, *FTP*, 198–9; Rosin, "Did Christianity;" Cf. Coleman, "Prosperity Unbound." E.g., Lin, *Prosperity Gospel,* Kindle edition, "Faith."

69. See Asamoah-Gyadu, *Sighs and Signs*, 75–83.

70. E.g., Brandon, *Health and Wealth*, 30; Hunt, *Beyond Seduction*, 32–4; Olson defines "magick" (as distinguished from "magic" as the illusionary tricks of entertainment) as "manipulating reality through paranormal means" (Olson, *CC*, 162).

71. Harrison, *RR*, 58.

72. Perriman, *FHP*, 41.

73. Perriman, *FHP*, 41, emphasis added.

74. Hagin, *Words*, 2–3.

75. See Section 3.2.6.6.

in the present narrative sequence—as either active (as Sender) or passive (as Helper)—is also unclear in the story.[76] These narrative gaps affect how the agent imagines their role and the source of power initiated by confession. The semiotic shift of the objects signified in the semiosis of faith—from faith in God to faith of God (see Section 4)—energizes the instrumental approach to faith embodied in confession; the practice of speaking positive outcomes performs an objectified faith. Evaluating the source of confession's power is a matter of nuance and degree; the complexity is not solved by assigning God as the source of the confessed words' power. The question then turns to God's limited freedom in the response to confession. As Roger E. Olson points out, in the Word of Faith "the power that brings health and wealth to the person is God's, but the means of accessing that power is the individual's."[77] That is, by the believer operating by spiritual law, God is compelled to act in response. Thus, it is God's power which is activated by confession, yet God's power is at the command of the believer. When confession is imagined to "make" God act, it is an attempt to gain power over God and so manipulate God to fulfill the confession. As such, acting according to spiritual laws sets a "God-trap" (explored in the following text).[78]

The causative dimension of confession generates what Wright calls "negative praxis" (somewhat ironically termed), that is, refraining from speaking of anything negative, such as sickness, lack, fear, and failure.[79] Hence, there is a considerable hesitation within the Word of Faith to verbalize experiences of suffering and failure because negative confessions glorifies Satan and carry creative power to accomplish what is spoken.[80] For example, by saying "I am catching the flu," the person will get sick or acknowledging that "I am worried about my economy" will make matters worse. Because negative confessions also carry causative power, self-monitoring, and careful editing processes to filter speech of negative words are part of Word of Faith practices.[81] Language, whether found in private or public discourse, oral or written, is closely monitored to identify negative confessions of defeat and failure and to substitute such with proclamations of victory and success.[82] This

---

76. See Section 3.2.6.1.

77. Olson, *CC*, 156.

78. Droz and Gez, "God Trap."

79. Wright, *NTPG*, 361, 363–4; See also Wright, *PFG*, 434.

80. Gifford, *Ghana's New Christianity*, 52; Gifford, "Prosperity Theology," 85; Magliato, *Wall Street Gospel*, 107; Coleman, *Globalisation*, 131; Bowler, *Blessed*, 143; Harrison, *RR*, 64; Barron, *Health and Wealth*, 10; McConnell, *DG*. Creative power is restricted by some to words that are spoken by faith (e.g., Wommack, "Power of Faith-Filled Words").

81. Kate Bowler, "Daily Grind: The Spiritual Workday of the American Prosperity Gospel," *Journal of Cultural Economy* 8, no. 5 (2015): 631. E.g., "I never talk discouragement. I never talk worry. I never talk defeat" (Hagin, *Words*, 23).

82. E.g., "some of the churches refuse to use the phrase 'for better, for worse' in the marriage ceremony, preferring 'for better and better'" (Gifford, *Ghana's New Christianity*, 52).

word-censuring leads believers to edit published texts (e.g., song lyrics), altering common idioms, censoring private conversations, and creating neologisms.[83] The negative praxis is problematic in that it stifles honesty and vulnerability in personal communication and limits the width of human experience that can be voiced in prayer and conversation.[84] A conflict in the believer is introduced by the praxis, that is, whether to voice experienced reality or rather to speak of that which is in line with the worldview. This conflict poses a problem for the worldview's fidelity. The censuring of speech and texts also reveals an ideological tendency in the Word of Faith worldview in that it forces itself upon other ways of viewing and living in the world.

The indexical power of confession places the practice in tension with the traditional Christian views of prayer, thus creating a tension between the Word of Faith and Pentecostal understandings of prayer.[85] Even though semantically the terms "confession" and "prayer" can be interchanged in Word of Faith discourse, the practices must not be held as identical. Confessions are imagined to carry creative power in themselves (regardless of the power is imagined to come from a spiritual law or from God), while "prayer is asking God to do something; it recognizes God's sovereignty alongside God's power."[86] Confessions do not require any outside recipient or God's personal, free, and direct intervention to be effective.[87] Confession thus absorbs the practice of prayer when the believer has a promise from God, making prayer to be "understood not as asking for, but as demanding for. Prayer [in the Word of Faith] is less a plea or petition than a claim of one's rights."[88] Positive confession thus relativizes prayer in certain cases. For example, the Word of Faith refuses petitionary prayer for sick people once they have been ministered to by positive confession.[89] Similar to the aforementioned comments, without diminishing the theological and pastoral problems posed by positive confession, the practice raises the important question what functions—if any—declarative utterances have in Pentecostal spirituality? It is an area that Pentecostal scholarship needs to further explore.

---

83. Walton, *Watch This*, 94, 152–3; Harrison, *RR*, 64. Examples of idioms avoided are "I'm tickled to death" or "I'm dying to know" (Magliato, *Wall Street Gospel*, 108). E.g., see Wommack, *You've Already*, 1–2.

84. Harrison, *RR*, 118; Coleman, *Globalisation*, 193; Gifford, "Prosperity Theology," 96.

85. Perriman, *FHP*, 145–8; Olson, *CC*, 162–3.

86. Olson, *CC*, 162; Harrison, *RR*, 57; Nel, *Prosperity Gospel*, Kindle edition, "View of God." On prayer see, e.g., Warrington, *Pentecostal Theology*, 214–19; Warrington, *Healing and Suffering*, 46; Stanley Grenz, *Prayer: The Cry for the Kingdom* (Grand Rapids: Eerdmans, 2005).

87. Vreeland, "Reconstructing," 15.

88. Agana, *Succeed Here*, 191; Harrison, *RR*, 55. See, e.g., Hagin, *Words*.

89. Williams, "Is There a Doctor," 110; Sanchez-Walsh, "Santidad, Salvación," 155.

5.2.2 Gaining Revelation Knowledge

The second practice of gaining revelation knowledge functions as a worldview-praxis in the Word of Faith, according to Wright's threefold criteria listed earlier.[90] Gaining revelation knowledge means to actively increase one's amount of illumination of the really real spiritual realm. Revelation knowledge primarily consists of focusing on God and how the spiritual world operates, particularly in relation to the believer's true identity.[91] In the epistemology of the Word of Faith, revelation knowledge transcends the mere sense knowledge of the physical world;[92] It exceeds the capacity of the mind and can only be received by the human spirit. The human spirit—created in equality with God and made perfect in the new birth—is meant to, illuminated by revelation knowledge, govern the mind and feelings (soul), since they are "unreliable guides to what is really true."[93]

The sign-vehicle in the semiotic practice of gaining revelation knowledge takes three distinct forms: Bible study, spiritual experiences, and institution building. Bible study forms a central part of Word of Faith liturgy. This is so because the primary method to gain revelation knowledge is by hearing God's Word through one's spirit.[94] Homilies are typically longer and with a didactic emphasis focusing on the exposition of Bible passages—with an eye to details—that appears to support Word of Faith convictions.[95] The expectancy is for the sermon to mediate revelation knowledge and parishioners often actively participate by vocal approval, following in their own Bibles and by note-taking.[96] In private spiritualty, repetitive exposure to the Bible is paramount: the believer memorizes Bible passages and "meditates" on them, that is, pondering a certain verse for a prolonged time to gain revelation knowledge.[97] The believer also consumes religious media in the form of books, published materials, television, radio, social media, and internet broadcasts[98]—intently and repeatedly consume the same teaching until they "get

---

90. Gaining revelation knowledge is a habitual, characteristic, practice within the Word of Faith, which signifies through the intentional interpretant made up of the worldview-elements of story and symbol. See Harrison, *RR*, 8–9; Perriman, *FHP*, 96–7; Bowman, *Word-Faith*, 97–104; McConnell, *DG*, 101–13.

91. Harrison, *RR*, 8–9; Walton, *Watch This*, 94–5.

92. See Chapters 3, 4, and 6.

93. Bowman, *Word-Faith*, 98.

94. Wommack, *You Already Got It*, 160, 173; Hagin, *Bible Faith*, e-book edition, "Chapter 1."

95. Walton, *Watch This*, 156–7; Souders, "God of Wealth," 111; Bowler, *Blessed*, 120; Gifford, "Ritual Use."

96. Bowler, *Blessed*, 120; Harrison, *RR*, 30; Lin, *Prosperity Gospel*, Kindle edition, "Get Ready for the Harvest!"

97. Perriman, *FHP*, 36. E.g., Kenneth Copeland Ministries, "How to Meditate on the Word of God," *Kcm.org*, accessed April 7, 2021, https://www.kcm.org/real-help/spiritual-growth/learn/how-meditate-the-word-god.

98. E.g., Lin, *Prosperity Gospel*, Kindle edition, "The American Dream."

the revelation"[99] in the message. The Word of Faith tends to reject engagement with biblical scholarship and academic theological education as mere "sense knowledge" that is, at best, unproductive or, at worst, obscuring true spiritual revelation.[100] Supernatural experiences also make part of gaining revelation knowledge. Illumination comes through personal encounters with Jesus, visions of angels, and the performance of spiritual gifts, especially prophecy.[101] Part of the practice is for believers to narrate their revelations, whether received privately or through a charismatic leader.[102] Gaining revelation knowledge also fosters institution building. The movement runs media outlets, publishing houses, and numerous training schools and programs meant to give access to revelation knowledge. Bible schools train Word of Faith ministers in the principles of faith, while niche knowledge is offered to the sick through healing schools, entrepreneurs in business programs, and the spiritually desiring through prophetic schools.[103]

The intentional interpretant consists primarily of a combination of the signs of faith and knowledge within the narrative thrust of Eden Redeemed. The immediate object signified by revelation knowledge is the empowering of the agent to perform equality with God and so transcend the limitations of sense knowledge and the barriers of Satan's power, progressing into the restored blessings of the realized life of Eden. Revelation knowledge is meant to give a perfect representation of the spiritual realm and thus functions iconically in the Word of Faith worldview.

5.2.2.1 Analysis of Gaining Revelation Knowledge Analyzing the practice of gaining revelation knowledge shows how iconic logic generates a resolute confidence in how the Word of Faith sees the world, a privileging of spiritual insights that challenges a Pentecostal commitment to biblical authority while confirming their worldview, carries a fragmented view of human nature, and promotes individualistic and passive approaches to social problems. These aspects are examined now.

Word of Faith semiosis links revelation knowledge iconically to the really real world (as seen in Chapter 4), that is, that revelation knowledge of the spiritual realm signifies by correspondence. The iconic function of revelation knowledge in the Word of Faith worldview awards such illuminated insights with a level of truth and authority that cannot be surpassed and makes the believer to have total confidence in their illuminated world while practicing a robust hermeneutic of suspicion toward all traditional Christian beliefs and interpretations.[104]

---

99. Gifford, *Ghana's New Christianity*, 49; Walton, *Watch This*; Frederick, *Between Sundays*.

100. Harrison, *RR*, 9–10.

101. Perriman, *FHP*, 96–7.

102. E.g., Harrison, *RR*, 111–12.

103. E.g., Daniels, "Prosperity Gospel," 269–73; Walton, "Blessed and Highly Favored," 86; Ukah, "God, Wealth," 81.

104. E.g., Perriman, *FHP*.

The commitment of Word of Faith adherents to revelation knowledge causes them to be taken up in a process of reification of their worldview, which means that they strategically limit their exposure to materials which endorse their view of reality—that "feed" their faith—and filter theological intake that opposes what they have known by revelation knowledge.[105] An anti-intellectual stance is noted as Word of Faith training schools are often "tightly-controlled, exclusivist, and strongly doctrinaire."[106] The limited number of themes and biblical texts studied easily forms a canon within the canon.[107] Because of the hesitation to academic, theological scholarship, and the primacy awarded the humans spirit above the mind, a large quantity of the new knowledge produced by Word of Faith teachers falls within the category of "pseudoscholarship."[108] This assessment is not to deny that the Word of Faith advances some legitimate insights and challenges dated and static readings of the biblical texts, but that by favoring the autodidactic and anecdotal over scholarly engagement with the Bible and theology the movement is vulnerable to misrepresent the biblical texts and commit theological inconsistencies which challenge the worldview's coherence and tarnish their legitimate contributions and impact.[109]

The practice of gaining revelation knowledge speaks to how the Word of Faith worldview privileges correct, spiritual information gained by subjective experience. The full appropriation of the biblical "contract" makes prior revelation knowledge necessary, privileging revelation knowledge above the biblical texts. The effectiveness of the agent's faith to activate the Helpers (e.g., prosperity, health, authority) is narrated in *Eden Redeemed* to correlate with the agent's amount of revelation knowledge, thus making right understanding the sine quo non for the agent to complete the narrative Task of ruling and increasing: "It is on the basis of their knowing . . . that they expect to be blessed as abundantly as they do."[110]

Word of Faith discourse emphasizes that all spiritually gained insights must be grounded in the Bible. But atomistic (as opposed to contextual) and eisegetical (as opposed to exegetical) handling of biblical texts invite new interpretations, some of which run contrary to the range of possible interpretations based on biblical hermeneutics.[111] The "contractual" approach to the Bible (see Section 1.3) follows their view of revelation knowledge as it uses the Bible as the source of iconic knowledge to establish the spiritual principles and laws which stipulate the believer's rights and privileges.[112] The unsurpassed authority awarded to

---

105. See Naugle, *Worldview*, 178–80, 331–9; Mitchem, *Name It*, 69; Perriman, *FHP*, 233.

106. Perriman, *FHP*, 233.

107. Gifford, *Ghana's New Christianity*, 75 fn. 46.

108. Perriman, *FHP*, 82.

109. E.g., Downs, "Giving for Return."

110. Harrison, *RR*, 10.

111. See Section 1.3.

112. E.g., Harrison, *RR*, 9; Perriman, *FHP*, 88.

revelation knowledge challenges Pentecostal commitments to biblical authority because revelation knowledge privileges subjective spiritual experiences above Scripture.[113] It also makes the Word of Faith movement vulnerable to the influence from narratives and practices which subvert Pentecostal distinctives, for example, New Thought metaphysics and market consumerism (see Section 5.2.4.1).

The revelation knowledge is of a spiritual quality which cannot be gained through the mind or the body.[114] Since revelation knowledge is received by the human spirit, the human spirit stands in a polarized position toward the mind in the epistemological pursuit of correct insights.[115] The practice of gaining revelation knowledge compartmentalizes the human nature and furthers a fragmented anthropology (further explored in Chapter 6).

The Word of Faith's practice of gaining revelation knowledge implicitly fosters an individualistic and passive approach to ills that are social or systemic in nature and that often require to be addressed by group action.[116] Eden Redeemed narrates poverty as a spiritual problem that revelation knowledge overcomes.[117] Therefore, the "answer to poverty is to teach people to build up their faith and be aware of biblical promises."[118] The response of gaining revelation knowledge thus weakens initiatives for social and political action and offers no challenge to socioeconomic status quo as long as the system favors the Word of Faith worldview (see Section 5.2.6.1).[119]

---

113. See Warrington, *Pentecostal Theology*, 180–205.

114. Bowman, *Word-Faith*, 98; Gifford, *Ghana's New Christianity*, 71; Mitchem, *Name It*, 69; Perriman, *FHP*, 233.

115. Perriman, *FHP*, 96; Bowman, *Word-Faith*, 98–104.

116. Wrenn, "Consecrating Capitalism;" Mumford, *Exploring Prosperity*; "With its emphasis upon material gain, there is little critique of systems that perpetuate poverty. Instead, poverty is at worst seen as a demonic spirit that must be cast off by positive confession. According to prosperity doctrines, financial wealth is a promise of God to all believers. However, wealth is attained not through a reordering of unjust society, but rather through an abundance of faith. 'Name it and claim it' prosperity teachings abound, wherein the force of positive affirmation from your lips determines whether or not you will receive this blessing of wealth. Such teachings reflect the immediate triumph of individualism. Those with enough faith will triumph; those without will be left behind. Prosperity ministers do not teach that unjust systems do not exist. Rather, they teach that the believer will 'find favor' within the system, advancing by God's intervention through job situations that would inevitably hinder others" (Frederick, *Between Sundays*, 150, 139).

117. Frederick, *Between Sundays*, 150; Walton "Stop Worrying," 119; Wrenn, "Consecrating Capitalism," 426.

118. Lee, *T. D. Jakes*, 103; Mumford, *Exploring Prosperity*, 120; Walton, "Blessed and Highly Favored," 143.

119. "Instead of advocating protest marches, voting drives, and other forms of activism familiar to black church movements, word churches teach members that poverty is a curse of the devil and that the power to transform their oppression resides within their ability

5.2.3 *Sowing Money Seeds*

The semiotic practice in the Word of Faith of sowing money seeds consists of the sign-vehicle of the agent giving away money or material objects with an articulated expectation of "reaping" a future "harvest" of return in this life.[120] The practice fulfills Wright's conditions for being interpreted as a worldview-praxis.[121] I refer to it also as "sowing" or "sowing and reaping."

Sowing money seeds is a spiritually directed action ultimately aimed at God, while the earthly receiver can either be an individual (often a wo/man of God) or a religious institution (church or ministry).[122] The earthly recipient must make "good ground" to guarantee an ample harvest.[123] The practice of sowing remains consistent in all the Word of Faith's various modes of giving (e.g., tithing, love offerings, first fruit, and personal gifts), while the seed can take other forms than monetary (e.g., jewelry, cars, houses, airplanes, electronics, and air tickets).[124] Sowing takes place within liturgical settings (church service, prayer meeting) or in private contexts, such as watching televangelism and giving to friends.[125] The time to sow is often the peak of a Word of Faith service or broadcast: a short, motivational homily usually precedes the scheduled time of sowing, and the actor

---

to appropriate their faith and take their rightful place in the kingdom of God. Prosperity theology's answer to poverty is to teach people to build up their faith and be aware of biblical promises" (Lee, *T. D. Jakes*, 103); Mumford, *Exploring Prosperity*; Walton, *Watch This*. See Wariboko, "Pentecostal Paradigms," 37; Wrenn, "Consecrating Capitalism."

120. Harrison, *RR*, 70.

121. Sowing money seeds is a habitual, characteristic practice within the Word of Faith, which signifies through the intentional interpretant made up of the worldview-elements of story and symbol. See Wariboko, *Economics,* 87–104; Alexander, *Signs and Wonders,* 61; Droz and Gez, "A God Trap;" Downs, "Giving for Return;" Harrison, *RR*, 96; Salinas, *Prosperity Theology,* 182; Heuser, "Religio-Scapes," 16; Coleman, "Prosperity Unbound;" Rey, "Missing Prosperity;" Perriman, *FHP*; Bowler, *Blessed*. See "[R]eligious giving is part of a much larger cluster of beliefs and cultural assumptions and, for this reason, cannot be separated from how people think about their work, money, and materialism, any more than it can be cut off from beliefs about God, spirituality, and stewardship. This is because religious giving has important symbolic qualities. It dramatizes commitment and withdrawal, expenditure and sacrifice, what it means to be a spiritual person, and what a good religious organization should be" [Robert Wuthnow, *God and Mammon in America* (New York: The Free Press, 1994), 249].

122. Harrison, *RR*, 70, 72.

123. Haynes, "Potential and Problems," 88–90; Augustine, "Pentecost and Prosperity," 204–5.

124. Lee, *T. D. Jakes*, 112; Asamoah-Gyadu, *Contemporary Pentecostal Christianity*, 83, 86–7, 91; Bowler, *Blessed*, 130. Whether tithing should technically be considered a seed or the preparation for sowing seed lies beyond this thesis to discuss.

125. E.g., Lin, *Prosperity Gospel*, Kindle edition, "La Oportunidad de Prosperar;" Coleman, *Globalisation*, 202.

is regularly encouraged to display the gift by either lifting, weaving, or bringing it to the front while expressing joy and expectation through dancing, clapping, or smiling.[126] Spontaneous sowing is initiated by the agent in services, such as placing seed on the platform while the preacher is speaking.[127] The agent is encouraged during the act of sowing to practice positive confession, claiming prosperity and declaring needs met and desires fulfilled.[128] In the act of "naming" the seed, the giver confesses what specific harvest the seed is meant to produce.[129] At times, givers are instructed what exact amount to sow for the seed to generate a specific harvest (e.g., $240 for a twenty-four-hour blessing).[130] In church services, givers can be divided into different groups to receive prayer according to the amount they sow.[131] Once the seed is sown, the agent looks to God for a return (some a hundred times multiplied).[132] The return can come in a variety of forms, such as "money, jobs, promotions, health, children."[133] Even though the action carries potential in some contexts to be socially productive by forming social ties, the earthly receiver is not expected to return the gift.[134]

The sign-vehicle of giving money signifies through the intentional interpretant of the Eden Redeemed story. The practice of sowing is intimately related to the

---

126. E.g., Marti, *Hollywood Faith*, 123; Marti, "You Determine," 141; Walton, "Stop Worrying," 113–14; Lindhardt, "Are Blessings for Sale," 317–18; Bowler, *Blessed*, 128–9; Agana, *Succeed Here*, 192–3, 216–19; Lee, *T. D. Jakes*, 104, 112; Asamoah-Gyadu, *Contemporary Pentecostal*, 91; Coleman and Lindhardt, "Prosperity and Wealth."

127. Walton, "Stop Worrying," 114.

128. Walton, "Blessed and Highly Favored," 180; Bowler, *Blessed*, 128–9; Lindhart, "Are Blessings for Sale," 318; Heuser, "Religio-Scapes," 20. For the confession issued by Rhema Bible Church see Bowler, *Blessed*, 129.

129. Bowler, *Blessed*, 98–9; Asamoah-Gyadu, *Contemporary Pentecostal Christianity*, 90; Perriman, *FHP*, 53. E.g., Gifford, "Ritual Use," 192.

130. J. Kwabena Asamoah-Gyadu, "Did Jesus Wear Designer Robes?" *Lausanne.org*, November 1, 2019, accessed April 7, 2021, https://www.lausanne.org/content/did-jesus-we ar-designer-robes. E.g., Mike Murdock, *The Craziest Thing God Ever Told Me* (Fort Worth: The Wisdom Center, 2002).

131. E.g., Agana, *Succeed Here*, 218–19.

132. E.g., see Copeland, *Laws of Prosperity*, e-book edition, "Chapter 2;" The promises of thirty-, sixty-, or hundredfold harvests on money seeds sown are criticized also within the movement (see Hagin, *MT*, 146–50).

133. Asamoah-Gyadu, *Contemporary Pentecostal*, 81, 83; Walton, "Stop Worrying," 118; Marti, "I Determine," 140; Agana, *Succeed Here*, 224. The return expected is sometimes realistic in terms of the socioeconomic context of the agent (e.g., John Cox, "The prosperity gospel in anthropology and theology: the case of fast money schemes in Papua New Guinea," *St Mark's Review* 2, no. 244 (June 2018): 94.

134. Coleman, *Globalisation*, 194–5, 202, 204; Haynes, "Potential and Problems;" Premawardhana, "Transformational Tithing." See Joel Robbins, "Pentecostal Networks and the Spirit of Globalization," *Social Analysis* 53, no. 1 (Spring 2009): 55–66.

believer's narrative Task of ruling and increasing in the world. The immediate object is that the agent performs both their equality with God (who also uses the spiritual law of sowing and reaping) and their Task. By sowing, the giver becomes an active agent who performs the restored life of Eden.[135] The harvest of prosperity is the increase which every agent is tasked to manifest.

Behind the practice "lies a far-reaching and quite radical understanding of how the economy of the kingdom of God might work."[136] Sowing stands in a symbiotic relationship with the Eden Redeemed story, which narrates how there is an absolute and causal spiritual law of sowing and reaping by which God and the spiritual world function. When this law is rightly applied, it guarantees that money sowed will generate a harvest to the giver.[137] In the act of giving, the agent performs their divine equality since God also operates according to the same law of sowing and reaping.[138] Sowing money also signifies how the agent possesses revelation knowledge of how the spiritual world operates by spiritual law.

The practice functions indexically in the Word of Faith. Sowing stands in a causative relationship to the harvest of prosperity through the law of sowing and reaping. Sowing seeds also indirectly relates to the indexical semiosis of prosperity, as financial increase only comes by first sowing: prosperity index that seed has been sown, while financial poverty index the lack of seed sown.[139]

5.2.3.1 Analysis of Sowing Money Seeds Analyzing the Word of Faith practice of sowing money seeds brings out its complex role in the Word of Faith worldview. Sowing brings positive benefits to the agent and the movement, while its indexical logic draws on market logic, victimizes the poor, and challenges traditional concepts of giving and the nature of God. These issues are considered in turn.

The practice of sowing money seeds is "the bedrock"[140] of the Word of Faith movement, making it "the new liturgy"[141] with "sacramental implications."[142] The practice generates sizable sums of money that help churches operate large ministries and stay independent from outside support, and, therefore, is held as

135. See Chesnut, "Prosperous Prosperity," 219.

136. Perriman, *FHP*, 53.

137. Harrison, *RR*, 32, 100; Coleman, *Globalisation*, 188–9. E.g., Savelle, *Why God Wants*, e-book edition, "Prosperity Isn't A Get-Rich-Quick Scheme;" Oyedepo, *Making Maximum Impact*, e-book edition, "Chapter 3."

138. Chapter 3.

139. Rey, "Missing Prosperity," 339–40; Gifford, "Prosperity Theology," 87; Gifford, *Ghana's New Christianity*, 64. E.g., see Haynes, "Potential and Problems," 88.

140. Sarles, "Prosperity and Healing," 349.

141. Bowler, *Blessed*, 128.

142. Asamoah-Gyadu, *Contemporary Pentecostal*, 80; Asamoah-Gyadu, "Prosperity and Poverty," 103.

the underlying "motor"[143] that enables the explosive growth of Pentecostalism, especially in Africa.[144] Sowing is also said to engender hope and empower personal agency.[145] Some see it as a subversive act, a way to free oneself from the globalized market to become part of an alternative, charismatic gift economy.[146]

The expected return, though guaranteed, may take time to materialize. There is a noticeable difference of expectation in Word of Faith discourse and practice regarding how the harvest comes. Some expect the harvest to spring directly, in a miraculous way from the spiritual realm while others imagine physical causality, with the harvest coming indirectly through the believer's entrepreneurship and wise stewardship.[147] The variation does not alter the practice nor the underlying story but generates significantly different orientations while waiting for the harvest. The time lag between sowing and reaping carries the potential of a "greater moral economy of blessings"[148] that challenges the practices of market consumerism, such as attitudes of trustful waiting and delayed gratification.

Despite its benefits, sowing seeds is "among the more controversial and contested aspects"[149] of the Word of Faith movement. One reason is that it performs a significant semiotic transformation of money (noted in Chapter 4), where wealth is resignified from a negative object ("mammon") to a positive one ("blessing").[150] Sowing seed is a performance of the goodness of material wealth, as it acts out a positive expectation of prosperity. But the indexical relation between personal success and giving reveals an oppressive side in the worldview. When the relationship between sowing and reaping is understood in indexical terms, the poor are effectively (often expressively) blamed as suffering because of their lack of giving. J. Kwabena Asamoah-Gyadu notes, "in contemporary [Word of Faith] Pentecostal discourse, need, lack, misfortune, affliction, and poverty are constantly linked to lack of faithfulness in tithing and freewill offerings."[151]

---

143. "This 'seed-faith' theology is not an incidental or optional extra to Africa's Pentecostalism, but has been indispensable, for this has been the motor that has powered this entire explosion" (Gifford, *Pentecostalism and Modernity*, 51).

144. Asamoah-Gyadu, "Prosperity and Poverty," 102; Heuser, "Charting African Prosperity," 9.

145. Chesnut, "Prosperous Prosperity," 219; Marti, *Hollywood Faith*, 141, 177–92; Marti, "The Adaptability," 23; Premawardhana, "Transformational Tithing;" Heuser, "Charting African Prosperity," 5; see Section 1.5.

146. See Section 1.5.6. Coleman, "Prosperity Unbound;" Heuser, "Charting African Prosperity," 4–6.

147. Marti, *Hollywood Faith*; Gifford, *Christianity, Development*, 48; Asamoah-Gyadu, "Prosperity and Poverty," 106–7.

148. Rey, "Missing Prosperity," 342.

149. Walton, "Stop Worrying," 112.

150. Heuser, "Charting African Prosperity," 3.

151. Asamoah-Gyadu, *Contemporary Pentecostal*, 89; Gifford, "Prosperity Theology," 87; Gifford, *Ghana's New Christianity*, 64. E.g., see Haynes, "Potential and Problems," 88.

The reciprocal expectation in the practice can be critiqued for being manipulative and self-serving, thus undermining the true nature of Christian giving.[152] The underlying rationale of "giving to get" can be seen as a market-driven accommodation to egocentric profit that appeals to human self-interest to a degree that exceeds that of Adam Smith's analogy of the baker and the butcher.[153] The Word of Faith commonly uses the business metaphors of investment and return to speak of the practice of sowing.[154] Sowing is therefore critiqued by some as a modern-day equivalent to Tezel's sale of indulgences during the Reformation, worthy of only oxymoronic descriptors: "divine investment,"[155] "contractual giving,"[156] "transactional-giving,"[157] and "interested giving."[158] To support the critique stand various examples of Word of Faith leaders who have grown personally wealthy as a result of congregants sowing money into their ministries in the hope of a multiplied harvest.[159]

A nuanced argument is made that an amount of self-interest in giving should not by default disqualify the practice.[160] In fact, the argument goes, the basic idea of interested giving, or giving for a return, is sanctioned by the biblical texts as a more authentic Christian attitude to giving than critics acknowledge.[161] Sowing should, however, rightly be critiqued, not for this basic motivation but on two other distinct points: the identity of the immediate recipients and the harvest expected. The practice causes givers to sow into individuals and institutions

152. Hunt, *Beyond Seduction*, 67; Perriman, *FHP*, 54; Asamoah-Gyadu, *Contemporary Pentecostal*, 95. Cf. McIntyre's discussion of contingent actions which include an amount of selfishness [Eve Poole, *Buying God: Consumerism and Theology* (London: SPCK, 2018), 102].

153. "It is not from the benevolence of the butcher, the brewer, or the baker that we expect our dinner, but from their regard to their own interest" [Adam Smith, *The Wealth of Nations Books I–III* (London: Penguin, [1776] 1999), 119]. See Augustine, "Pentecost and Prosperity," 192–3; Wariboko, *Pentecostal Paradigms*, 40.

154. Harrison, *RR*, 70–1.

155. Walton, "Stop Worrying."

156. Walton, "Stop Worrying," 112.

157. Asamoah-Gyadu, *Contemporary Pentecostal*, 80.

158. Downs, "Giving for Return," 36. For the analogy to Tezel see Gifford "Prosperity Theology," 98; Barnhart, "Prosperity Gospel," 162.

159. E.g., Katharine Wiegele, "Politics, Education, and Civic Participation: Catholic Charismatic Modernities in the Philippines," in *Global Pentecostalism in the 21st Century*, ed. Robert Hefner (Bloomington: Indiana University Press, 2013), 225.

160. Downs, "Giving for Return."

161. "My hunch is that on this point, the prosperity gospel actually has something to teach the Church, perhaps especially Protestants—for proponents of the prosperity gospel may be more sensitively attuned to the connection between giving and reward than many evangelicals" (Downs, "Giving for Return," 48); Asamoah-Gyadu, *Contemporary Pentecostal*, 80.

who are judged as "good ground" often based on their present prosperity rather than—and following the biblical imperative—to the marginalized and poor.[162] The expected return of personal prosperity in this life also misses the biblical emphasis on communal participation, common flourishing, and ultimately eschatological rewards.[163]

Given that to criticize sowing as just an expression of greed is one-dimensional, the practice does operate by a logic following globalized consumer capitalism, what I call "market logic" (see Section 5.2.4.1).[164] Consumerism is characterized by the rationale that anything the world has to offer functions as commodities for the individual's consumption.[165] Such "what's in it for me?" attitude and profit-seeking find performed expression in sowing money seeds.[166] Thus, giving as sowing and investing differs from how giving traditionally is imagined among Pentecostals through the metaphor of sacrifice.[167] Following the theme of polarized categories in the Word of Faith worldview, the seed has replaced the image of sacrifice. Yet, a biblically informed perspective on giving is arguably found in the paradoxical tension of seed and sacrifice. The market's inherent individualism is also performed in the practice, in that each agent carries the responsibility to sow and reap, while communal and structural contexts are considered either of secondary importance or entirely irrelevant.[168] Since sowing operates according to spiritual laws rather than the "worldly principles" of socioeconomics, the practice hinders prophetic critique of existing oppressive socioeconomic structures that do not contradict the Word of Faith worldview.[169]

162. Augustine, "Pentecost and Prosperity," 205.

163. Downs, "Giving for Return," 48.

164. Cox, "Pentecostalism and Global Market," 393.

165. "a consumerist paradigm ends up making an idol of the self as the center of the universe, and thus construes all of the world's 'goods' (both the fruit of nature and culture) as if they were there *for me*" [James K. A. Smith, *The Devil Reads Derrida and Other Essays on the University, the Church, Politics and the Arts* (Grand Rapids: Eerdmans, 2009), 41, emphasis original].

166. See Ukah, "God of Wealth," 77.

167. See Asamoah-Gyadu, *Contemporary Pentecostal*, 79–104.

168. Marti: "I determine My Harvest;" Augustine, "Pentecost and Prosperity;" Gifford comments on Oyedepo: "It is in no way a political theology. Oyedepo is simply not interested in the wider world" (Gifford, "Prosperity Theology," 97); Wrenn, "Consecrating Capitalism."

169. Ukah, "God, Wealth," 73. Walton makes the following important observation: "This reality does not mean that the Prosperity Gospel does not have a response to systemic injustice. Instead, this response is pedagogical rather than political. In other words, the social responsibility of adherents is to prioritize teaching others about the sufficiency of spiritual laws and piety rather than prioritizing the critique of systemic structures" (Walton, "Blessed and Highly Favored," 68); Wrenn, "Consecrating Capitalism."

Sowing brings incoherence into how the Word of Faith images God in relation to spiritual laws and the concept of grace. Sowing—like confession—embodies the gap of how to imagine God's action in relation to spiritual laws. The crux consists of ascribing the source for the effecting power triggered by sowing: Does the power stem from an impersonal spiritual law or from God?[170] The practice of sowing leaves this question unresolved. The general difficulty with impersonal spiritual laws in Eden Redeemed finds performative expression in the action: If a harvest comes automatically through spiritual law, what part, if any, does a personal relationship with God play? And what is ultimately to be credited for the harvest: God or the spiritual law? When spiritual law is imagined as the source of the harvest, faith and God are reduced to a formula that guarantees results,[171] making God and prosperity to be commodities of the worldview.[172]

The idea that a gift must be prior to God's blessing undermines the Christian representation of God's unmerited grace by which God is believed to act freely in love prior to any human merit.[173] The logic of quid pro quo contains a "veiled threat:"[174] you cannot reap if you have not sown.[175] Sowing consequently stands in tension with how Pentecostals commonly understand God's grace as "unmerited favor."[176] The tension is also unresolved in the Eden Redeemed story. Chapter 3 noted the gap regarding God's grace and sovereignty and spiritual laws. Sowing does not resolve this; the vacuum inherent in the practice only further entrenches the gap. The practice of sowing is, therefore, rightly critiqued for setting a "God-trap."[177] That is, sowing asserts control over God in that the practice binds God to an obligatory response.[178] The practice breeds "an illusion of control"[179]

---

170. King seeks to solve the problem by saying: "The law of sowing and reaping is a general principle, not a legalistic formula that implicitly denies God's control and authority" (King, *Only Believe*, 261).

171. See Farah, "Critical Analysis."

172. Lindhardt, "Are Blessings for Sale," 311; Macchia, "Call for Careful Discernment," 234–5; "Commodification in the most literal form is clear in the (age-old) promises of healings or blessings in return for seed money" (Miller, *Consuming Religion*, 78). I draw from Vincent Miller in my understanding of the process of commodification as basically extracting an element from its narrative home, for either consumption or insertion into a foreign narrative (Miller, *Consuming Religion*).

173. Sarles, "Prosperity and Healing," 349. See Bialecki, Haynes and Robbins, "Anthropology of Christianity," 1150.

174. Bowler, *Blessed*, 133.

175. Asamoah-Gyadu, *Contemporary Pentecostal*, 91; Bowler, *Blessed*, 133; Gifford, *Christianity*, 155.

176. Stanley Horton ed., *Systematic Theology*, rev. ed. (Springfield: Logion Press, 2007), 644.

177. Droz and Gez, "God Trap."

178. Wiegele, "Prosperity Gospel," 176.

179. Macchia, "Call for Careful Discernment," 235.

that goes contrary to "true faith and as such is not the life of the Spirit."[180] Since the giver is the acting Agent who initiates the divine-human transaction, God's role is restricted to the narrative categories of responding Helper rather than prevenient Sender.[181]

5.2.4 Manifesting Prosperity and Health

The fourth practice of manifesting health and prosperity fits Wright's criteria for being a worldview-praxis in the Word of Faith.[182] The sign-vehicle consists of demonstrating visible evidence of economic success, healthiness, and physical beauty through storytelling, commodity, and bodily displays, giving and the so-called corresponding action,[183] each of which is briefly described here.[184] The agent manifests prosperity and health by sharing stories in public and private.[185] Word of Faith sermons and personal communication are saturated by narratives of health and prosperity. The attainment of goods and rags-to-riches stories are celebrated as are narratives of miraculous healings—particularly cherished are those involving the financial increase and healing of a charismatic leader.[186] Testimonies and "praise reports" (e.g., the purchase of a house or car, a new job or promotion, or debt cancelation) narrate prosperity in liturgical settings.[187] The practice also entails commodity display through parading one's possessions,

---

180. Macchia, "Call for Careful Discernment," 235.

181. Sowing thus stands in tension with Frank Macchia's call that the Word of Faith must show care "to respect the sovereignty and freedom of the Holy Spirit" (Macchia, "Call for Careful Discernment," 235).

182. Manifesting prosperity and health is a habitual, characteristic practice within the Word of Faith which signifies through the intentional interpretant made up of the worldview-elements of story and symbol. See Bowler, *Blessed*, 77–138; Augustine, "Pentecost and Prosperity," 203; Frederick, *Between Sundays*, 150; Walton, "Blessed and Highly Favored," 103–4; Winslow, "Imaged Other."

183. Perriman, *FHP*, 41.

184. Bowler, *Blessed*, 98; Augustine, "Pentecost and Prosperity," 203.

185. "By ritually talking about the world in particular ways, people become co-constructors of the specific social reality they are part of" (Lindhart, "Introduction," 21).

186. Bowler, *Blessed*, 128–9; Miller and Carlin, "Joel Osteen," 31; Gifford, *Ghana's New Christianity*, 53–5; Ebenezer Obadare, "'Raising righteous billionaires': The Prosperity Gospel Reconsidered," *HTS Teologiese Studies/Theological Studies* 72, no. 4 (2016): 6.

187. Agana, *Succeed Here*, 198; Bowler, *Blessed*, 128; Obadare, "Raising Righteous Billionaires," 4; "By being personal and stereotypical at the same time, testimonies integrate individual biographies within a shared story of the religious community and implicitly express a commitment to its values and worldviews" (Lindhart, "Introduction," 14). See Gifford, "Ritual Use," 188.

especially expensive luxury goods.[188] In church services, TV studios, social media, and personal life, the agent performs their attained degree of prosperity by displaying consumer goods and exhibit physical and emotional health through their body.[189] Physical beauty, in the form of a well-toned, attractive, and youthful body, functions as a significant and powerful sign-vehicle.[190] Bodily health is manifested through attention to physical appearance, cosmetic surgery, dieting, exercise routines, and the pursuit of weight-loss.[191] Expressions of optimism display emotional health.[192] Manifesting health carries the negative practice of skepticism toward medical science, causing some to reject needed medical treatments, deny the danger of viruses, and dismiss vaccinations.[193] For them, medical assistance is understood in the narrative categories of Chapter 3 as Opponents in the quest for Eden's promise of health. Sowing money seeds also manifests prosperity.[194] Lavish gifts to a leader or to a church or ministry display one's economic well-being, as the amount given is often announced and

---

188. Walton, "Blessed and Highly Favored," 103–4. E.g., Lin, *Prosperity Gospel*, Kindle edition, "The Meeting Place;" Hinn, *God, Greed*, 58.

189. Bowler, *Blessed*, 106–7; Williams, *Spirit Cure*, 15–16; Sinitiere, *Salvation*, 88–95.

190. Maddox, "Prosper, Consume;" Jenkins and Marti, "Warrior Chicks," 246; See Gerber, "Fat Christians."

191. Maddox, "Prosper, Consume," 110; Walton, *Watch This*, 207; Shayne Lee and Phillip Luke Sinitiere, *Holy Mavericks: Evangelical Innovators and the Spiritual Marketplace* (New York: New York University Press, 2009), 121; Frederick, *Colored Television*, 51; Coleman, *Globalisation*, 164; Williams, *Spirit Cure*, 5–6, 128–9. E.g., Cynthia Mcfadden and Mary Marsh, "How Joyce Meyer Built a Worldwide Following," *ABC News*, April 13, 2010, accessed April 7, 2021, https://abcnews.go.com/Nightline/joyce-meyer-transparent-evangelist/story?id=10355887.

192. Savelle, *Right Mental Attitude*, e-book edition, "Two Avenues–Faith and Fear;" Oyedepo, *Anointing for Breakthrough*, e-book edition, "Two Weapons for Conquering;" Hagin Jr., *Staying Positive*, I, 86–7, 104; "Believing keeps your heart full of joy" (Meyer, *Enjoying Where You Are*, e-book edition, "Believers Are Supposed to Believe"); Hagin, *New Thresholds*, e-book edition, "How Do We Get Faith?"

193. Marwa Eltagouri, "A Televangelist's Flu-season Advice: 'Inoculate Yourself with the Word of God,'" *The Washington Post*, February 6, 2018, accessed April 7, 2021, https://www.washingtonpost.com/news/acts-of-faith/wp/2018/02/06/televangelist-suggests-alternate-flu-shot-inoculate-yourself-with-the-word-of-god/. For a study on how Word of Faith beliefs shape a social response to Covid-19 in the United States, see Paul Djupe and Ryan Burge, "The Prosperity Gospel of Coronavirus Response," *Politics and Religion* (2020): 1–22. See also J. Kwabena Asamoah-Gyadu, *Christianity and Faith in the COVID-19 Era: Lockdown Periods from Hosanna to Pentecost* (Accra: Step Publishers, 2020), Kindle edition, "Chapter 9: Charismatics and Coronavirus;" Asonzeh Ukah, "Prosperity, Prophecy and the Covid-19 Pandemic: The Healing Economy of African Pentecostalism," *Pneuma: The Journal of the Society for Pentecostal Studies* 42, no. 3–4 (2020): 430–59.

194. Giving as an action to index wealth, see Rappaport, *Ritual and Religion*, 56–7.

celebrated.[195] In the practice of "corresponding action,"[196] the agent behaves "as if their prayers had already come true,"[197] that is, speaking and acting according to their desired state and not according to their present experience.[198] Such "acting in faith" includes "risk taking in the name of constant progress,"[199] for example moving the body as though not sick, acting prosperous by purchasing a too-expensive home, giving beyond their means, taking insecure loans, engaging in Ponzi schemes, and, in extreme cases, terminating a needed medical treatment.[200]

Manifesting prosperity and health draws signifying power from the intentional interpretant of the Eden Redeemed story and the signs of prosperity and health. The predominant quality of the practice is indexical while also functioning in a secondary way as an iconic sign.[201] This follows Peirce's understanding of how signs are not exclusively categorized in one of the threefold categories, but that one sign can function in various degrees as icon, index, and symbol.[202] As an indexical practice, the story places the agent back in the spiritual state of Eden with full access to prosperity and health as an already-present spiritual reality. The display of such blessings functions as a cause-and-effect sign that the agent is successful in living out the Task of ruling and increasing.[203] Performing prosperity reveals how the agent's life is not bound by a poverty mentality, the system of the fallen world, or ruled by Satan. The consumption of especially luxury commodities shows that the agent has reached a level beyond meeting mere needs to live in the "world of more-than-enough."[204]

195. Perriman, *FHP*, 41. E.g., Melanie Henry, "Wealth Without Toil," *Believer's Voice of Victory*, September 2019, 12–17, accessed April 7, 2021, https://www.kcm.org/magazines/wealth-without-toil.

196. Perriman, *FHP*, 41.

197. Bowler, "Daily Grind," 631.

198. Gifford "Prosperity Theology," 86, 96; Olson, *CC*, 160.

199. Coleman, *Globalisation*, 195.

200. Mumford, *Exploring Prosperity*, 42–3; Coleman, *Globalisation*, 193; Peter, "The Church's," 141; Perriman, *FHP*, 41; Augustine, "Pentecost and Prosperity," 204; Cox, "Prosperity Gospel," 96; Frederick, *Between Sundays*, 147.

201. Walton, *Watch This*, 207. "The popularization of tithes in Africa developed when Pentecostals started making direct connections between tithes and offerings, on one hand, and material blessings in health and wealth, on the other" (Asamoah-Gyadu, *Contemporary Pentecostal*, 84, 89).

202. Hughes, *Worship as Meaning*, 139. See Section 4.1.2.

203. Bowler, *Blessed*, 78. Weber's work ethic also draws from an indexical reading of prosperity; the immediate object signified through the interpretant of Calvinism, Weber argued, was that of election for salvation. It is an indexical logic applied to prosperity that unities Word of Faith with the protestant work ethic.

204. Mundey, "Prosperity Gospel," 326, 332; Rey, "Missing Prosperity," 349; Bowler, *Blessed*, 137.

The iconic signification of the practice resides in how the agent evidences a direct resemblance with the abundant life of the really real spiritual realm; prosperity, health, and beauty glorify God as they mirror God's goodness, plan of salvation, and Satan's defeat.[205] Iconic logic expects the perfect representation of Eden by the believer in this life. The level of attained iconic resemblance between the believer and Eden's perfection decides the believer's fulfillment of their Task.[206]

Displaying prosperity and health takes on evangelistic and apologetic overtones; the agent shows God's goodness as well as proving that the Word of Faith message works.[207] Iconic logic fosters "envy evangelism:"[208] believers "should be such examples of His [God's] goodness—so blessed, so prosperous, so generous, so full of joy—that other people want what we [the believers] have."[209] Word of Faith Christians thus engage in the consumption of goods and services and celebrate physical health and beauty to show Eden's perfect life through indexical and iconic logic.[210]

5.2.4.1 Analysis of Manifesting Prosperity and Health Requiring extra attention is how manifesting prosperity and health interrelates with globalized capitalism, as the practice expresses consumerism, individual agency, market-shaped aesthetic ideals and desires. This is a pressing task due to the increasing body of scholarship which argues that global capitalism carries all the necessary marks to be considered a religion in its own right.[211] "The Market [*sic*]," as Harvey Cox calls late modern

---

205. "prosperity in all its forms is a sign of God's blessing and should be displayed to the glory and honour of God. Hence enjoyment of riches and acknowledgment of success in the public domain bring glory to God, who is the ultimate source. Besides it also serves a missionary and evangelical purpose for the good course of the Gospel. It is a source of encouragement and example for non-believers to embrace the Christian faith and accept Jesus as their personal lord and saviour. And for those who already believe, it is a source of hope, motivation and encouragement to take their faith more seriously and to remain resolute" (Agana, *Succeed Here*, 212).

206. Olson, *CC*, 155.

207. Maddox, "Prosper, Consume," 110; Mundey, "Prosperity Gospel," 330, 332; "The unabashed display of one's personal wealth is considered an authenticating witness of God's existence, his [*sic*] providential care in the life of the believers, and the validity of the prosperity principles and practices" (Augustine, "Pentecost and Prosperity," 203).

208. Maddox, "Prosper, Consume," 110

209. Joel Osteen and Victoria Osteen, *Wake Up to Hope Devotional* (New York: FaithWords, 2016), 135. "A styled home, honed figure, elaborate grooming, lavish wardrobe and unmatched sex life stimulate one's unsaved friends' envy and, hopefully, their interest in Jesus, to whom all this is credited" (Maddox, "Prosper, Consume," 110). See Jenkins and Marti, "Warrior Chicks," 249–50.

210. See Mundey, "Prosperity Gospel," 325; Bowler, *Preacher's Wife*, 192–236.

211. Cox, *Market*, 6; Robert Nelson, "Economics and Environmentalism: Belief System at Odds," *The Independent Review* 17, no. 1 (Summer 2012): 5–17; Gustafson, *Altar of*

global capitalism, makes "a powerful and all-encompassing worldview, a vision of reality that pulls everything into its orbit and that should therefore be recognized as a kind of religion."[212] The market offers a different image of the world than what is found in Christianity.[213] Its practices relate to a worldview that is "the main rival of Christian faith today."[214] To criticize any correlation between Word of Faith practices and those of the market, as this book does, is ultimately a theological critique and not a social, political, or economic ditto because performing the market is in Christian terminology a form of idolatry. The confluence of the Word of Faith practices and the market challenges the coherence of the Word of Faith worldview, which portrays itself as the real Christian faith and alternative to the systems of the fallen world.

5.2.4.1.1 Consumerism and Individual Agency The Word of Faith practice of manifesting prosperity and health draws upon consumerism and shapes believers' identity as consumers.[215] Most central to consumerism is not—as often thought—crude materialism, understood as the acquisition of more things with accompanied sensual pleasure and trust.[216] Less-nuanced critiques of the Word of Faith miss that the movement renounces such hedonistic materialism.[217] While blatant materialism can be found among Word of Faith individuals, the connection between consumerism and the Word of Faith lies also on the deeper level of consumerism's ultimate promise: namely, the possibility of attaining immaterial objects (e.g., identity, personal transformation, happiness, health, love, and status) through consuming material commodities.[218] "The central proposal of the

---

Wallstreet; Mark Clavier, *Rescuing the Church from Consumerism* (London: SPCK, 2013), xiii, 3, 27; John Kavanaugh, *Following Christ in a Consumer Society* (Maryknoll: Orbis, 2006), 38. "Consumer culture offers a powerful cosmology, maybe the only cosmology that is able to act as a common referent all across the globe" [Adam Arvidsson, "Christianity and Consumer Culture," *Sociologica* 3 (2014): 3].

212. Cox, *Market*, 6, 8.

213. Kavanaugh, *Following Christ*, 38.

214. Cox, "Pentecostalism and Global Market," 388; Pope Francis, *Evangelii Gaudium: The Joy of the Gospel* (Vatican: Vatican Press, 2013), 47–4.

215. Maddox, "Prosper, Consume;" Arvidsson, "Christianity and Consumer Culture." See Heuser, "Charting African Prosperity," 4.

216. Arvidsson, "Christianity and Consumer Culture," 8. Consumerism is about "disacquiring as much as possessing," about losing interest in stuff as much as wanting them (see Miller, *Consuming Religion*, 114).

217. E.g., "God is not seeking a greedy, selfish, get-all-we-can people; He is seeking a peculiar people, a royal people, a people who have set their minds on pursuing Him and not on things" (Savelle, *Why God Wants*, e-book edition, "Chapter 9"); Copeland, *Blessed*, e-book edition, "Chapter 3;" Hagin, *MT*. E.g., Hanegraaff, *CIC*; Larsen, "Gospel of Greed."

218. Peter Sedgwick, *The Market Economy and Christian Ethics* (Cambridge: Cambridge University Press, 1999), 82–150; "the driver [of consumerism] is self-

religion of consumption is the belief in the transformative potential of consumer goods."[219] So in buying (often branded) products, the consumer ultimately seeks to consume, not the item itself, but the meaning which the commodity represents and its potential for personal metamorphosis.[220] But it is a deceptive promise, because in performing consumerism, the ultimate transformation is that of the "consumers into commodities"[221]—a dehumanizing process that hinders true human flourishing.[222] The aspect of "commodity fetishism"[223] and transformation by consumption inform Word of Faith logic, because it is only through consuming goods and services that the believer's true identity as ruler is fully realized.[224]

Consumption functions as "a religiously legitimated practice"[225] in the Word of Faith.[226] Beyond merely expressing consumerism, inherent in manifesting prosperity and health is its formative power of shaping consumerist practices: The Word of Faith frames consumption as "not merely permissible but as a religious duty."[227] By encouraging conspicuous consumption and "conspicuous displays of wealth,"[228] the Word of Faith makes consumption an essential part of the believer's

identity and not consumption, which is a mere means to that end" (Poole, *Buying God*, 98); "Commodities become vehicles of individual expression, even the self-definition of identity" [Charles Taylor, *A Secular Age* (Cambridge: Belknap Press, 2007), 483, 473–504]; Arvidsson, "Christianity and Consumer Culture," 1–11; Zygmunt Bauman, *Consuming Life* (Cambridge: Polity, 2007), 111; Rieger, *No Rising*, 101; Clavier, *Rescuing the Church*, 1–18.

219. Arvidsson, "Christianity and Consumer Culture," 3.

220. E.g., "The new car, for instance, is not simply about a desire for a new toy or a better and more reliable means of transportation, but about intangible things like feelings of security, power, and happiness" [Rieger, "Christianity, Capitalism, and Desire," 8]; Gauthier, Woodhead and Martikainen, "Introduction: Consumerism as the Ethos of Consumer Society," in *Religion in Consumer Society: Brands, Consumers and Markets*, ed. François Gauthier and Tuomas Martikainen (London: Routledge, 2013), 10, 14; Tom Beaudoin, *Consuming Faith* (Lanham: Sheed and Ward, 2003), 9.

221. Bauman, *Consuming Life*, 12.

222. Bauman, *Consuming Life*, 12, 57, 67; Maddox, "Prosper, Consume," 109–10. See Kavanaugh, *Following Christ*, 3–24; Katja Rakow, "Religious Branding and the Quest to Meet Consumer Needs," in *Religion and the Marketplace in the United States*, ed. Jan Stievermann, Philip Goff and Detlef Junker (Oxford: Oxford University Press, 2015), 218–19, 229.

223. Rieger, *No Rising*, 89.

224. Walton, *Watch This*, 207; Kavanaugh, *Following Christ*, 32–6; Arvidsson, "Christianity and Consumer Culture," 4; "Prosperity Gospel audiences are encouraged to buy the newest, the latest, and the best to maintain their identity" (Winslow, "Imaged Other," 254, 267).

225. Meyer, "Pentecostalism and Neo-Liberal Capitalism," 17.

226. Meyer, "Pentecostalism and Neo-Liberal Capitalism," 14, 17, 19; Winslow, "Imaged Other," 254, 267.

227. Maddox, "Prosper, Consume," 109; Winslow, "Imaged Other," 267.

228. Harrison, *RR*, 75.

Task.[229] In fact, ruling the world is signified by consuming the world.[230] To resist the consumption practices formed by market-shaped desires is not a neutral option in the movement; nonconformity to the market is judged as "poverty mentality" and a "defeated mindset."[231] In relation to the competing prosperity narrative discussed in Chapter 3, which places prosperity as the end (Task) rather than the means (Helper), it is noteworthy that the practice of manifesting prosperity and health has within itself no boundaries to protect prosperity from shifting its narrative role. Rather, in consumerism, prosperity's narrative role is easily recast as the goal.[232]

By conceding to consumerism, the Word of Faith embraces the dominant economic ideals and practices.[233] The individualism that correlates with the market (noted in sowing money seeds) is also performed in the practice of manifesting prosperity and health.[234] Word of Faith discourse "overascribe[s] agency to the individual"[235] and so "place happiness and contentment solely within the agency

229. "contemporary notions of designer clothes and other conspicuous symbols of material success are turned back and used as a lens through which to understand and to redefine God's promises to give the believer a life of abundance" (Harrison, *RR*, 12); Bowler, *Blessed*, 136; Hinn, *God, Greed*; Anderson, *To the Ends*, 221–2; Maddox, "Prosper, Consume."

230. A. J. Swoboda, "Posterity or Prosperity? Critiquing and Refiguring Prosperity Theologies in an Ecological Age," *Pneuma: The Journal of the Society for Pentecostal Studies* 37, no. 3 (2015): 397–8.

231. Mundey, "Prosperity Gospel," 326, 332; Winslow, "Imaged Other," 262; Maddox, "Prosper, Consume," 113.

232. Hagin's attempt in *MT* to curb the growth of the competing narrative by doctrinal adjustments was largely unsuccessful. One reason for his lack of impact is arguably that he did not significantly address prosperity practices (neither among his followers nor in his own life); practice spoke louder than doctrine (Bowler, *Blessed*, 138–9; Grady, *The Holy Spirit*, 157).

233. Walton, *Watch This*, 207: "The number of advertisements for ministerial conferences with images of mansions in the background, television broadcasts that prominently display luxury goods, and even church Web sites that feature high-end automobiles as the dominant visual focal point imply that economic empowerment is not about real wealth creation but rather about conspicuous consumption, hyperconsumerism, and commodity fetishism" (Gauthier, Woodhead and Martikainen, "Consumerism as the Ethos," 2); Williams, *Spirit Cure*, 10; Rieger, "Christianity, Capitalism;" Maddox, "Prosper, Consume;" Thorsten Veblen, *Theory of the Leisure Class* (New York: Penguin, 1995). Cf. Sedgwick, *Market*, 82–150.

234. Wrenn, "Consecrating Capitalism;" Gauthier, Woodhead and Martikainen, "Consumerism as the Ethos;" Harrison, *RR*, 149; Frederick, *Between Sundays*, 139, 150.

235. Wrenn, "Consecrating Capitalism," 429.

of an individual."[236] The "exalted" anthropology (see Section 6.2.1.3) of the Word of Faith, which sees inner self—the spirit of the born-again believer—as totally righteous and good, silences self-critique and easily merges with the positive view of self's desire within consumerism and is a fit with neoliberalism's narrative of human agency.[237]

5.2.4.1.2 Market-shaped Aesthetic Ideals and Desires Manifesting prosperity and health speaks to how iconic logic forms Word of Faith aesthetics. The expectations of realizing a "like-like" resemblance between the believer and the spiritual world fuels the ideal of the believer as the perfect representation. The Word of Faith is "a faith meant to be read onto a believer's perfected body and life."[238] The movement's culture of "excellence" is a result of iconic logic.[239] The iconic aesthetics within the Word of Faith generates an extremely high ideal and considerable pressure; to simply have "an average, ordinary life"[240] and to look plain is to miss the mark of the believer's high calling of ruling, increasing, and so attract people to God.[241] For those who aspire status in the movement, yet cannot manifest genuine wealth, health, and attractiveness, the pull is great to manufacture signs.[242]

236. Rakow, "Religious Branding," 229; Wrenn, "Consecrating Capitalism;" Walton, *Watch This*.

237. Wrenn, "Consecrating Capitalism;" Catherine Brekus, "The Perils of Prosperity," in *American Christianities*, ed. Catherine Brekus and Clark Glipin (Chapel Hill: The University of North Carolina Press, 2011), 283; Rieger, *No Rising*, 21; Smith, *Wealth of Nations*. See Poole, *Buying God*; Clavier, *Rescuing the Church*; Gauthier, Woodhead, Martikainen, "Consumerism as Ethos," 8.

238. Bowler, *Preacher's Wife*, 208.

239. Bowler, *Blessed*, 191–2; Yip and Ainsworth, "We Aim to Provide;" Walton, "Blessed and Highly Favored," 103–4.

240. "God doesn't want you to live to an average, ordinary life. . . . Father, thank You for equipping me and choosing me to be Your ambassador on this earth. I choose to live an extraordinary life, not just an average life" (Osteen and Osteen, *Wake Up*, 6, 55; see Bowler, *Blessed*, 191).

241. Winslow, "Imaged Other," 260–1; Bowler, *Preacher's Wife*, 207–12; Maddox, "Consume, Prosper," 112. "Osteen believes that one way of keeping God in 'first place' in one's life is by dressing nicely. Because the body is God's temple, Osteen believes it should be adored in a God-honoring way, which for him includes regularly purchasing new clothing and keeping up with the latest styles" (Mundey, "Prosperity Gospel," 328); Sinitiere, *Salvation with a Smile*, 88.

242. "When expectations regarding the efficacy of faith and the availability of material blessings and physical healing are raised to such a great height, pastors and evangelists will find themselves under pressure to make faith work, to create the *appearance* of success, and to conceal failure" (Perriman, *FHP*, 233 emphasis original). This method is called "fake it till you make it," but used not just among leaders. See, e.g., Frederick, *Colored Television* 38; Hagin, *MT*, 194–5.

The prevalence of cosmetic surgery and attention to body image among Word of Faith leaders can be explained in the light of iconic logic; only a perfect body can fully represent the perfect God.[243]

Word of Faith discourse is conflicted on aesthetics, which challenges the worldview's coherence.[244] Though Word of Faith leaders verbally critique the market-formed beauty regimes and explicitly confront the pressures they assert over believers, at the same time the success of many also comes from embodying the same aesthetic images.[245] Word of Faith aesthetics uses the market logic shaped by the entertainment and the hyper-sexualized advertisement industries, which operate with a commodified, consumer image of human identity as its interpretant for what characteristics in the believer signify beautiful and attractive.[246] The Word

---

243. Winslow, "Imaged Other," 260–1; Joyce Meyer explained her facelift with iconic logic: "I want to look my best for God" (Bowler, *Preacher's Wife*, 209); The same iconic logic is at work healing, where only a healthy body can represent the perfect world of the spirit (Moore, *God's Will to Heal*, 276–7). Such iconic logic explains how an American Word of Faith leader could say that "You can't be a witness for Jesus from a wheelchair" (Olson, *CC*, 155).

244. "Though White often challenges contemporary notions of beauty and their residual pressures on women, her success also comes from embodying them. Her television program invites celebrity guests like the bestselling author and wellness expert Jordan Rubin and fitness guru Donna Richardson to discuss diet tips and how to achieve a well-toned look. Her Satisfied Woman Retreat offers the services of beauty consultants who give makeovers and other tips to accentuate women's aesthetic appeal. Since becoming a celebrity preacher, White has reinvented her image with extensive plastic surgery, modish hairstyles, perfectly manicured nails, chic silk suits, fitted dresses, and a leaner size 4 figure, all in contrast to photos and videos from earlier years. She often reveals details about her workout regimen and eating habits that help her stay in shape, and she encourages women to enhance their sex appeal to their husbands. By appearing on television in stylish outfits and form-fitting suits, White constructs a new, trendy prototype for the female televangelist" (Lee and Sinitiere, *Holy Mavericks*, 121).

245. Lee and Sinitiere, *Holy Mavericks*, 121; Winslow, "Imaged Other." This lack of congruence is especially visible in Joel and Victoria Osteen. Their affirmation that "Always remember, you have been made in the image of Almighty God. God did not make any mistakes. You are the perfect size. You have the right personality, the right gifts, the right looks and the right skin color" stands in stark contrast to their performance of commercialized Market aesthetics, in the form of cosmetic surgery, church-sponsored fashion shows, and images of the perfected, commodified body (Osteen and Osteen, *Wake Up*, 52, 157); Sinitiere, *Salvation with a Smile*, 88–95; Bowler, *Preacher's Wife*, 207; Jenkins and Marti, "Warrior Chicks," 246.

246. Winslow, "Imaged Other," 259, 267; "The theological tradition with the greatest emphasis on physical beauty was undoubtedly the prosperity gospel, and its strong influence on 40 percent of megachurches with over ten thousand members gave megaministry much of its reputation for setting the entertainment industry's standard of beauty" (Bowler, *Preacher's Wife*, 208).

of Faith's aesthetics performed in the display of prosperity and health is not only an accommodation to market-shaped standards of physical beauty. Rather, the Word of Faith has come to act as a player at the forefront, developing, propelling, and capitalizing on market aesthetics. Leaders in the movement wear the latest line of clothing and create fashion brands, model the standards of the culturally desired body image, and offer workout routines while being recognized as fashion and fitness examples by non-Christian actors.[247] In fact, performance of market aesthetics is a Word of Faith distinctive in relation to many other Christian ministers.[248] Yet, drawing on market aesthetics challenges the coherence of the worldview because, in Jonathan Walton's words, "the Word of Faith movement is informed by the same 'world system' it castigates."[249] Understanding how the dominant aesthetic values are created by market forces while the market serves as a functional religion means that the fulfillment of the beauty ideals of consumerist culture in the Word of Faith movement is not a theologically neutral activity.

Consumerist society's criteria for beauty are inherently unequal because they require a consumerist lifestyle with a significant investment of money and time only available to the privileged.[250] As such, they challenge deeply held Pentecostal practices and beliefs. The foundational criteria of participation in the Spirit for involvement in Pentecostal ministry (expanded on later) is effectively relativized by privileging market aesthetics.[251] Classical Pentecostalism has reacted strongly to the reshaping of traditional Pentecostal attitudes toward consumption, self-promotion, elitism, beauty, and sexuality by the practice of manifesting prosperity and health.[252] Christian unity is thwarted by "promoting visible economic inequality through the display of consumer goods."[253] Iconic logic's high expectations also limit transparency about one's personal trials or failures, cultivating hero-myths about charismatic leaders in whom Eden's ideal is supposedly personified.[254] Apart from iconic logic,

247. Yip and Ainsworth, "We Aim to Provide," 509; Maddox, "Consume, Prosper;" Sinitiere, *Salvation*, 88–95; Bowler, *Preacher's Wife*; Lee and Sinitiere, *Holy Mavericks*; Gina Meeks, "Hillsong NYC's Carl Lentz Dubbed 'Apostle of Cool' By Secular Men's Mag," *Charisma News*, September 26, 2013, accessed April 7, 2021, https://www.charismanews.com/us/41154-hillsong-nyc-s-carl-lentz-dubbed-apostle-of-cool-by-secular-men-s-mag.

248. Harrison, *RR*, 41.

249. Walton, "Stop Worrying," 109. See Chesnut, "Prosperous Prosperity," 215.

250. Sinitiere, *Salvation*, 91; Winslow, "Imagined Other," 254.

251. See, e.g., Kalu, *African Pentecostalism*, 113; Cox, "Pentecostalism and Global Market," 394; Joel Robbins, "The Obvious Aspects of Pentecostalism: Ritual and Pentecostal Globalization," in *Practicing the Faith*, ed. Martin Lindhardt (New York, Berghahn, 2011), 56.

252. Yong, *Days of Caesar*, 263; Maddox, "Prosper, Consume," 111; Bowler, *Blessed*, 107.

253. Haynes, "Pentecostalism and Morality," 135; Walton, "Blessed and Highly Favored," 144.

254. See Section 4.3.6.

displaying the market's standard of beauty on church stages, in television studios, and in images draws from an indexical logic that uses beauty in a cause-and-effect way to signify one's place of successfully ruling the world.[255]

At the heart of the Word of Faith's consumerism and aesthetics lie accommodation to, disseminating of, and a capitalization on the desires formed by the market.[256] Instead of offering a prophetic critique of market-inspired desires (especially by the advertising industry), the practice of manifesting prosperity and health sanctions "insatiability of desire" as part of God's will and plan.[257] Desire is not reshaped in the light of real human need, in the good of community and creation, and ultimately toward God and God's eschatological kingdom. Taking an eschatological perspective, manifesting prosperity instills the habit formed by "a society of consumers"[258] of being dissatisfied with one's present life while looking for the fulfillment of all desires in the present.[259] The practice thus stands in sharp tension to the passion for the Spirit that characterizes much of Pentecostalism.[260] Word of Faith practices' correlation with the market hinders the movement to provide the church with "an alternative *telos*—another set of desires—that can contribute to the healing of the world"[261] and so fails to offer "a critical theology of culture"[262] and a theology of creation.[263] Milmon Harrison concludes, "the Faith Message [*sic*] encourages individuals to be successful *within* the existing

255. "These standards of beauty were also declarations of triumph: by putting outwardly beautiful women on stage, or in front of the camera, or on a magazine cover, evangelicals and pentecostals were asserting that theirs was a faith for successful people" (Bowler, *Preacher's Wife*, 197). Bowler notes that beauty is for the American megachurch wife, many of whom are within the Word of Faith movement, "one of the most important markers of success" (Bowler, *Preacher's Wife*, 202; Bowler, "Successful Calling," 192). For relation between power and body image, see Gerber, "Fat Christians."

256. Rieger, *No Rising*, 89–121; Wariboko, "Pentecostal Paradigms," 40; Wariboko, *Economics*, 100–1; Alexander, *Signs and Wonders*, 69. See also Smith, *Desiring the Kingdom*.

257. Yong, *Days of Caesar*, 312–14; Rieger, *No Rising*, 90, 98, 100–1, 115; Rieger, "Christianity, Capitalism and Desire;" Mundey, "Prosperity Gospel," 332; Bauman, *Consuming Life*, 31, 47.

258. "The society of consumers derives its animus and momentum from the dissatisfaction it expertly produces itself" (Bauman, *Consuming Life*, 48, 47).

259. Augustine, "Pentecost and Prosperity," 205; Mundey, "Prosperity Gospel," 340; William Cavanaugh, *Being Consumed: Economics and Christian Desire* (Grand Rapids: Eerdmans, 2008), 35; Poole, *Buying God*, 85.

260. Lee Roy Martin, "Longing for God," *Journal of Pentecostal Theology* 22, no. 1 (2013): 54–76; Steven J. Land, *Pentecostal Spirituality: A Passion for the Kingdom* (Sheffield: Sheffield Academic Press, 1993). See Poole, *Buying God*, 99–101.

261. Yong, *Days of Caesar*, 294.

262. Cox, "Pentecostalism and Global Market," 387.

263. Yong, *Days of Caesar*, 294; Cox, "Pentecostalism and Global Market;" Kavanaugh, *Following Christ*, 36; Swoboda, "Prosperity or Posterity."

economic and social system rather than seeking to overthrow it or necessarily to reform it to any great degree."[264] That manifesting prosperity and health relies on the existing system opposes the movement's self-understanding of embodying the original Christian alternative to the fallen system of this world. In conforming to, affirming of, and capitalizing on consumerist and aesthetical regimes, the Word of Faith does not "offer a subversive, counternarrative" to the market.[265] No prophetic word is carried by the practice of manifesting prosperity and health that unmasks structural injustices, challenges the ultimate values, and confronts the powers that be.[266] As such, the Word of Faith does not help "Pentecostalism . . . to do more than merely embrace the cultural and economic horizons of global capitalized culture."[267] Thus, the Word of Faith is "haunted by their own successful message and subverted by the very forces they built upon."[268] The practice of manifesting prosperity and health limits the Word of Faith's imagination from painting the world subjunctively, that is, "as if" free from the dominance of the market.

5.2.5 Following the Charismatic Leader

In the practice of following the charismatic leader, the sign-vehicle consists of performing the sign of the charismatic leader discussed in Chapter 4. In short, the believer gives personal allegiance to an "anointed" or charismatically gifted wo/man of God in the Word of Faith movement.[269] The practice of following the charismatic leader fulfills Wright's criteria for a worldview-praxis.[270]

264. Harrison, *RR*, 149, emphasis original. "Prosperity ministers do not teach that unjust systems do not exist. Rather, they teach that the believer will 'find favor' within the system, advancing by God's intervention through job situations that would inevitably hinder others" (Frederick, *Between Sundays*, 150); Niemandt, "Prosperity Gospel," 214.

265. "In [Joel] Osteen's discourse, the potential for Christianity to attack the market is neutralized and transformed into commodity-driven fetishism where his audience has moral permission, if not divine responsibility, to consume and display the symbols of capitalist, market-driven success" (Winslow, "Imaged Other," 267).

266. "Thus rather than the convergence we so often witness between Pentecostalism and prosperity—between the 'full gospel' and big business—we ought to expect a certain confluence between 'Marx and the Holy Ghost'" (Smith, *Thinking in Tongues*, 46).

267. Shane Clifton, "Pentecostal Approaches to Economics," in *The Oxford Handbook of Christianity and Economics*, ed. Paul Oslington (Oxford: Oxford University Press, 2014), 277.

268. Meyer, "Pentecostalism and Neo-Liberal," 23.

269. Lin, *Prosperity Gospel*, Kindle edition, "La Predicacíon (The Preaching);" Walton, "Blessed and Highly Favored," 130. "In Pentecostal/charismatic discourse, anointing is usually a metaphor for the presence of power" (Asamoah-Gyadu, *Contemporary Pentecostal*, 121).

270. Following the Charismatic leader is a habitual, characteristic practice within the Word of Faith, which signifies through the intentional interpretant made up of the

The practice means either a direct following through membership in the leader's church or an indirect following by partnership in their ministry and ongoing consumption of the leader's media productions. Personal sacrifice is part of following the charismatic leader: attending multiple meetings weekly, offering extensive volunteer work in the church or ministry, and sowing money to the church or ministry and to the charismatic leader and their family.[271] It is not only believers who practice following a charismatic leader, even leaders who are less influential in the movement enter submissive relationships to senior, stronger charismatic leaders.[272] An unparalleled degree of formative influence is awarded the charismatic leader over the follower's beliefs, actions, and aesthetics; the leader's appearance, tastes, and body language tend to be imitated by the agent; the leader is referenced in submissive, paternal terms, and their image is placed in prominent places in churches, homes, and publications.[273]

Following the charismatic leader is a semiotic practice that signifies its object through the immediate interpretant of the worldview-elements of story and symbol. The Adam plot's representation of Adam as a solitary individual granted by God absolute power over all creation shapes the ideal and narrative for leaders in the movement. The last chapter highlighted the iconic relation between the charismatic leader and faith, making the leader to embody the blessed life of Eden.[274] The semiotic logic carried in the practice of following the charismatic leader is that the world iconically resembled in the leader can be "tapped into" by practicing a loyal following of the self-same leader.[275] The practice of following the charismatic leader is thus a performance of the charismatic leader sign, intending to empower the agent to realize for themselves the same blessed life of Eden evidenced in the leader.

worldview-elements of story and symbol. See Walton, "Blessed and Highly Favored," 130–3; Ukah, "Redeemed Christian Church," 170–2; Brandon, *Health and Wealth*, 136–7; Peter, "Church's Response," 141–2; Obadare, "Raising Righteous Billionaires," 4–5; Gifford, *Christianity, Politics*, 185–8.

271. Harrison, *RR*, 100–1; Rey, "Missing Prosperity," 340; Gifford, "Prosperity Theology," 88; Frederick, *Colored Television*, 37; Lin, *Prosperity Gospel*, Kindle edition, "Sunday Worship."

272. E.g., Bowler, "Successful Calling," 197–8.

273. Harrison, *RR*, 109; Chesnut, "Prosperous Prosperity," 216; Ukah, "The Redeemed Christian Church," 83, 170–2, 211–12; Bowler, "Successful Calling," 197–8; Harrison, *RR*, 28.

274. Walton, *Watch This*, 172.

275. Sánchez-Walsh, *Pentecostals*, 67–8; Walton, "Blessed and Highly Favored," 130–3; Gifford, *Ghana's New Christianity*, 55. "In the eyes of the congregation, Pastor Gielis's personal wealth and success confirm that he is a blessed man. During his sermons, he often refers to his house, his job, and his salary as signs of God's blessing, and he encourages believers to 'take hold of their promise' like he did" (Lin, *Prosperity Gospel*, Kindle edition, "La Predicacíon (The Preaching)."

5.2.5.1 Analysis of Following the Charismatic Leader The practice of following the charismatic leader gives insights into how iconic logic generates the leaders' high status in the movement, that is, the practice draws on branding, and how power and the flow of blessings are imaged in a vertical matrix that challenges Pentecostal commitments to the "prophethood of all believers"[276] and preference to the poor.

The iconic logic which looks to the leader to represent Eden now generates a culture of celebrity and elitism, inspiring personality cults and "preacher worship."[277] The iconic status of the leader sanctions a highly self-referential rhetorical practice among Word of Faith propagators.[278] The status of the charismatic leader is furthered by the claim in Word of Faith discourse that revelation knowledge is transmitted through the charismatic leaders who are "ordained and anointed by God for the express purpose of restoring these neglected and misunderstood teachings of the church."[279] The charismatic leader is also anointed to impart other spiritual gifts which the agent requires, thus making the leader "someone you need if you are to realize the scriptural promises in a similar way."[280]

The promises of a return to Eden with realized health and wealth in the now may sound as illusionary rhetoric, thus generating anxiety in the followers who look for evidence of the message's fidelity. The charismatic leaders enter as the "proof-producers,"[281] their own lives confirming that the world actually is as

276. Roger Stronstad, *The Prophethood of All Believers* (Irving: ICI University Press, 1998).

277. McConnell, *DG*, 111; "whatever the motives and intentions of the particular minister may be, it is all too easy for the image to replace Christ as the object of adulation and imitation" (Perriman, *FHP*, 234); "the new pastor engages in personality cult, and flaunts his person, wealth, and status" (Kalu, *African Pentecostalism*, 112).

278. Gifford, *Ghana's New Christianity*, 53, 55; Gifford, "Prosperity Theology," 85; Anderson, *To the Ends*, 221–2. E.g., Lin, *Prosperity Gospel*, Kindle edition, "La Predicacíon (The Preaching)."

279. Perriman, *FHP*, 32. E.g., McConnell, *DG*, 101–13; Harrison, *RR*, 10, 111. Two particular roles in the movement are nurtured by this primacy awarded revelation knowledge, namely that of teacher and prophet (Perriman, *FHP*, 32. Walton, *Watch This*, 156–7; Lee, *T. D. Jakes*, 102). The teacher seeks to access revelation knowledge through a close study of Bible texts—meant to engage the human spirit rather than an academic pursuit of the mind. The prophet seeks to access revelation knowledge through spiritual experiences and inspiration. The most successful Word of Faith leaders arguably are able to perform both roles (e.g., Hagin, Copeland, and Oyedepo are held as prophet-teachers). "Herein lies the genius of Hagin: his followers believe him to be a mystical seer and a biblical scholar at the same time" (McConnell, *DG*, 61); Souders, "God of Wealth," 111; Bowman, *Word-Faith*, 98. E.g., "I believe that Kenneth Copeland is the greatest prophet on earth today" (Henry, "Wealth Without Toil," 14).

280. Gifford, "Ritual Use," 188; Gifford, *Christianity, Politics*, 129–33.

281. Bowler, *Blessed*, 134.

they characterize it.[282] The success displayed by the charismatic leader—beyond indexing the leader's faith—transforms the leader into an icon of the prosperous life available for everyone.[283] That is, the leaders are "the living embodiment of faith in action"[284] as their lives iconically show the reality of the worldview they promote. Following "the big man of the big god"[285] thus generates comfort and hope for the believer. Comfort in that the world makes sense and hope that the same level of prosperity will one day be realized for oneself; the underlying rationale is that "if it [prosperity] happened to him, it can happen to me."[286] Comfort is offered not just to the needy, the middle class is also relieved of angst, as the context formed by the prosperous leader creates "an avenue for the upward mobile middle class to express conspicuous consumption and wealth consolidation without moral awkwardness or embarrassment."[287]

The practice of following the charismatic leader—like displaying prosperity and health mentioned earlier—draws on the logic of market practices. One point not yet discussed is that following the charismatic leader builds on how consumers become loyal to a certain commercial brand.[288] In the Word of Faith practice, the charismatic leader functions as the branded commodity, while the followers make the consumers. The charismatic leader is approached as a commodity that needs to be branded, packaged, distributed, and marketed to attract maximum interest, positive response, and prolonged loyalty from the consumers.[289] Studies show how the practices of commodifying, branding, and marketing are deliberately employed

282. Obadare, "Raising Righteous Billionaires," 5.

283. "As embodiments of prosperity, prosperity pastors offered tangible reminders of God's goodness and the abundant provisions in store for all who believed" (Bowler, *Blessed*, 134); Kalu, *African Pentecostalism*, 112; Gifford "Prosperity Theology."

284. Walton, *Watch This*, 200.

285. Kalu, *African Pentecostalism*, 115.

286. Gifford, *Ghana's New Christianity*, 64; "The subconscious message is that 'this pattern has worked for us, it will work for you too'" (Frederick, *Colored Television*, 150); Perriman, *FHP*, 234; Lin, *Prosperity Gospel*, Kindle edition, "The American Dream."

287. Chong, "Of Riches and Faith," 159; "One of the great problems with the prosperity gospel is that it removes any lingering guilt about being a conspicuous consumer and indeed aids the process of increasing spiritual deafness to the cries of the poor" (Witherington, *Jesus and Money*, 144).

288. "Branding is a commercial process of storytelling that gives consumers something to think and feel about a commodity that goes beyond its physical attributes and that attaches those associations to a brand name" (Rakow, "Religious Branding," 218); David Burns and Jeffrey Fawcett, "The Role of Brands in a Consumer Culture," *Journal of Biblical Integration in Business* 15, no. 2 (2012): 28–42; Adam Arvidsson, "Brands: A Critical Perspective," *Journal of Consumer Culture* 5, no. 2 (2005): 235–58. See also Naomi Klein, *No Logo* (New York: Picador, 2002).

289. In the Nigerian RCCG, Enoch Adeboye functions as the brand: "We have a brand; Daddy Adeboye is our brand and he sells our products more than any other brand in the

within the Word of Faith movement to gain a larger and more devoted following of their leaders.[290] There is, however, a lack of critical analysis of what unintended consequences on the overall gospel message such practices might carry.[291]

The practice of following the charismatic leader correlates with how the Adam plot imagines human and spiritual power relations in a vertical matrix. Word of Faith leaders form top-down, hierarchical, and independent structures—free from denominational or other forms of oversight—and expect a high degree of loyalty from their followers while offering little power, accountability, and transparency in return.[292] Their image of power follows that of the market's hierarchical business structures. The charismatic leader's high status as the "hero figure"[293] demands an equally high level of integrity and ethical standards. But numerous examples from the movement evidence the opposite.[294] Critical voices from within and outside the movement are often either ignored or threatened to silence with the justification that "touch not the Lord's anointed."[295] Due to the intimate connection between the leader and the Word of Faith worldview forged by the leader's iconic function, if the charismatic leader fails to meet the high expectations they enthused, the followers experience a disconcerting crisis.

Eden Redeemed carries the vertical logic that God's blessings start with the leader to later "trickle down" to the followers.[296] This logic should not be understood as the leader's material prosperity being shared among the followers, but rather as a spiritual law and expectancy directed toward God. This logic generates the circular practice of giving money to the already-prosperous charismatic leader.[297] Such personal giving is understood as sowing seeds into "good ground," as the

market today. He is a brand of God" (Ukah, "God, Wealth," 83); Sinitiere, *Salvation with a Smile*, 122.

290. Paula McGee, "The Wal-Martization of African American Religion: T. D. Jakes and Woman Thou Art Loosed," (Doctor of philosophy thesis, Claremont Graduate University, 2012); Rakow, "Religious Branding;" Miller, *Consuming Religion*.

291. E.g., Miller, *Consuming Religion*, 82.

292. E.g., Walton, "Blessed and Highly Favored," 136; Uka, "Redeemed Christian Church;" Yip and Ainsworth, "We Aim to Provide," 513; Bowler, *Preacher's Wife*, 226; Maddox, "Growth Churches," 152; Nel, *Prosperity Gospel*, Kindle edition, "Chapter 1: Introduction," "Recommendations." See also Christerson and Flory, *Network Christianity*, 48–73.

293. Peter, "Church's Response," 141–2.

294. Peter, "Church's Response," 141–2; Perriman, *FHP*, 233–4; Bakker, *I Was Wrong*; Hinn, *God, Greed*.

295. See Ps. 105:15 KJV; Hinn, *God, Greed*, 77–9; Perriman, *FHP*, 97–8; Hunt, *Beyond Seduction*, 39–41; Nel, *Prosperity Gospel*, Kindle edition, "The Sources of the Prosperity Message."

296. Rieger, "Christianity, Capitalism and Desire," 1; Gifford, *Ghana's New Christianity*, 50.

297. Edwards, "Ethical Dimensions," 93.

leader and their family make particularly fertile soil for the seed to be multiplied (see Section 5.2.3).[298] The more prosperity a leader manifests as signs of being good ground, the more believers will sow seeds into their ministry.[299] This spiral of sowing into good ground generates a dramatic material increase for the charismatic leader, which becomes evidence to the fidelity of the message and the leader's status, leading to a self-perpetuation of the practice.

The Word of Faith operates with an iconic logic that makes the charismatic leader's status increase by manifesting material abundance, health, and beauty on a scale higher than the common believer.[300] A positive benefit is how these signs are gender inclusive, making it easier for women to arise as Word of Faith leaders.[301] But the differentiation of the leader from the followers in the Word of Faith corresponds with the market's bias for the powerful, rich, famous, and beautiful.[302] It furthers a logic that subverts a Pentecostal "bias for the poor"[303] that holds how God's power is working foremost from below, among communities of "*me onta*, those who 'are not', the despised and foolish of the world."[304]

The practice thus challenges how Pentecostals generally imagine that only prerequisites for participating in pneumatic ministry is Spirit empowerment. The phrase "the prophethood of all believers"[305] summarizes the common Pentecostal expectation that every believer equally carries an anointing by the Spirit, which makes them fit for participation in charismatic practices; "the clergy has no monopoly on ritual"[306] in such a view. Yet, the practice of aligning oneself to a charismatic leader operates with hierarchical views of power and God's blessings. The Word of Faith is thus on a "nonegalitarian trajectory"[307] that challenges the

298. Augustine, "Pentecost and Prosperity," 204–5; Haynes, "Potential and Problems," 88–9; Harrison, *RR*, 100. E.g., Hinn, *God, Greed*, 53.

299. Resembling the functions of a self-vindicating Ponzi scheme (see, e.g., Cox, "Prosperity Gospel").

300. Coleman, *Globalisation*, 185. For the role of charisma, see, e.g., Haynes, "Potential and Problems." See Section 4.3.6.

301. See Bowler, "Successful Calling," 184, 198. See also Section 6.2.2.3.

302. See Rieger, *No Rising Tide*; Joerg Rieger, *Jesus vs. Caesar: For People Tired of Serving the Wrong God* (Nashville: Abingdon, 2018). See Ukah, "God, Wealth."

303. Smith, *Thinking in Tongues*, 45. See Amos Yong, *The Spirit Poured Out on All Flesh: Pentecostalism and the Possibility of Global Theology* (Grand Rapids: Baker, 2005), 93.

304. Smith, *Thinking in Tongues*, 45. Rieger, *Jesus vs. Caesar*, 73–92; Perriman, *FHP*, 173–4. Hence the Word of Faith stands in sharp contrast to liberation theology (Chesnut, "Prosperous Prosperity," 216). E.g., Kenyan Word of Faith megachurch pastor Wilfred Lai preached, "I refuse to be a pastor of people that are going nowhere, of sick people. I refuse to pastor you when you are sickly, that's not where you belong. I refuse to be a pastor of poor people" (quoted in Gifford, *Christianity, Politics*, 130).

305. Stronstad, *Prophethood*.

306. Robbins, "Obvious Aspect," 56.

307. Gifford, "Ritual Use," 188.

Pentecostal belief in the prophethood of all believers.[308] Their view of power can also lure Word of Faith believers to give allegiance to nonreligious leaders, such as political and business "strongmen," whose actions resonate with a vertical power matrix while lacking the moral standards Pentecostals traditionally have held as imperative for leaders.[309]

5.2.6 Extending Influence

Extending influence in the world is the last practice to examine here. The sign-vehicle comprises performing an "expansive agency"[310] by increasing the believers' and their institution's (church or ministry) sphere of influence and status level in the Christian and non-Christian worlds.[311] All Wright's criteria for determining a worldview-praxis are fulfilled in the practice of extending influence.[312]

The practice typically takes the form of a large variety of actions. Here I consider constructing buildings, networking, for-profit businesses, media, educational projects, giving, spiritual warfare, and body display.[313] Large building projects most visibly perform extended influence—megachurches are especially common in the movement.[314] The building's size and its construction budget

---

308. Gifford, *Christianity, Politics*, 185–8. See, e.g., Haynes, "Potential and Problems," 89.

309. E.g., Fea, *Believe Me*, 33–4; John McCauley, "Africa's New Big Man Rule? Pentecostalism and Patronage in Ghana," *African Affairs* 112, no. 446 (January 2013): 1–21; John McCauley, "Pentecostals and Politics: Redefining Big Man Rule in Africa," in *Pentecostalism in Africa: Presence and Impact of Pneumatic Christianity in Postcolonial Societies*, ed. Martin Lindhardt (Leiden: Brill, 2014), 322–44; Joerg Rieger, "Divine Power, Donald Trump, and How the 2016 Presidential Elections Challenge Common Religious Assumptions," *Huffpost*, October 18, 2016, accessed April 7, 2021, https://www.huffpost .com/entry/divine-power-donald-trump_b_12488082.

310. Coleman, *Globalisation*, 187.

311. J. Kwabena Asamoah-Gyadu, "Pentecostalism and the Transformation of the African Christian Landscape," in *Pentecostalism in Africa: Presence and Impact of Pneumatic Christianity in Postcolonial Societies*, ed. Martin Lindhardt (Leiden: Brill, 2014), 110. See also Christerson and Flory, *Network Christianity*, 66–70.

312. Extending influence is a habitual, characteristic practice within the Word of Faith, which signifies through the intentional interpretant made up of the worldview-elements of story and symbol. See Kate Bowler and Wen Reagan, "Bigger, Better, Louder: The Prosperity Gospel's Impact on Contemporary Christian Worship," *Religion and American Culture* 24, no. 2 (2014): 199; Kalu, *African Pentecostalism*, 112; Asamoah-Gyadu, "God Is Big;" Marti, "I Determine," 140.

313. Loudness in prayer, singing, and preaching can make an aspect of the praxis: "loudness is a mark of victory, dominion and authority" (Agana, *Succeed Here*, 191).

314. Bowler, *Blessed*, 239–48; Maddox, "Prosper, Consume," 108–15; Maddox, "Growth Churches;" Goh, "Hillsong and Megachurch," 284–304.

tend to be visionary rather than reflective of the current financial situation, necessitating "a step of faith"[315] in expectation of future growth. Networking is a key aspect of the movement's extension into the world, taking the shape of international alliances and partnerships, joint conferences, and global travel.[316] The practice also includes seeking to increase one's fame and status in the world, often by courting the favor of personalities with significant political influence, economic power, or social capital (e.g., entertainment or sports celebrities).[317] An entrepreneurial motivation follows extending influence in the world; churches and ministries venture into for-profit businesses (e.g., hotels, shopping malls, banks, and gyms), and individuals seek entrepreneurial opportunities.[318] The techniques of the market are employed, such as branding and marketing for self-promotion and attracting attention to generate a larger following and greater profits.[319] All the significant Word of Faith ministries and personalities engage old and new media: broadcasting on radio, television, and online and publishing in various formats (e.g., books, magazines, and newsletters).[320] Several Word of Faith books have become international bestsellers.[321] Technologically driven worship music production, performance, and marketing are part of media practices, including

315. Coleman, *Globalisation*, 195.

316. Bowler, *Blessed*, 258–9; Heuser, "Charting African Prosperity," 3; E. Z. M Gbote and S. T. Kgatla, "Prosperity Gospel: A Missiological Assessment," *HTS Teologiese Studies/ Theological Studies* 70, no. 1 (2014).

317. Lin, *Prosperity Gospel*, Kindle edition, "Prosperity Gospel Pentecostalism;" Marti, *Hollywood Faith*; Marti, "I Determine;" Walton, *Watch This*, 200; Agana, *Succeed Here*, 210; Goh, "Hillsong and Megachurch," 300; Fea, *Believe Me*, 133–7; Heuser, "Religio-Scapes," 19.

318. Gifford, *Christianity, Politics*, 151; Gifford, *Christianity, Development*, 48; Gifford, *Ghana's New Christianity*, 53; Miranda Klaver, "Pentecostal Pastorpreneurs and the Global Circulation of Authoritative Aesthetic Styles," *Culture and Religion* 16, no. 2 (2015): 146–59; "In addition to its emphasis on material things as indicative of God's favor in the life of the Christian, the ability to develop a mega business, a mega bank account, a mega residential property, and (for the leaders in particular), to grow a mega ministry, church and media empire, have become some of the most important indicators of the workings of the prosperity gospel" (Asamoah-Gyadu, "God Is Big," 1); Bowler, *Blessed*, 170; Yip and Ainsworth, "We Aim to Provide;" Lin, *Prosperity Gospel*. See Maltese, "Activist-Holiness Hagin." See also Hinn, *God, Greed*, 56.

319. Chong, "Of Riches and Faith," 149; Miller and Carlin, "Joel Osteen."

320. Walton, *Watch This;* Bowler and Reagan, "Bigger, Better," 194; "media production (DVDs, books, devotionals, mobile apps) improves and extends a leader's authority and standing among his or her followers and the larger Pentecostal public" (Ukah, "God, Wealth," 78, 77).

321. Kalu, *African Pentecostalism*, 111–14; Lin, *Prosperity Gospel*, Kindle edition, "The Genesis of Pentecostalism;" Gifford, *Ghana's New Christianity*, 54; Lee, *T. D. Jakes*, 2.

ventures into the movie industry.[322] Extending influence also consists of engaging in educational endeavors, ranging from religious education in weekend-seminars, Bible schools, and theological colleges to nonreligious education in kindergarten to university level.[323] The Word of Faith agent practices generous giving to perform influence extension, and money and commodities become mediums through which their status and power are extended in the world.[324] Displaying a body that exemplifies the market-shaped aesthetics is another way to extend power into the world.[325] Extending influence is not just set toward the material world but also toward the spiritual world: spiritual warfare functions to extend influence in the spiritual realm.[326] Precisely how such warfare is waged against Satan and satanic strongholds differs within the movement, from dramatic deliverance services, loud authoritative commands, and prayers directed against Satan to limited and composed expressions by positive confessions of Satan's defeat.[327]

Extending influence in the world draws its semiotic signification through the intentional interpretant made up of Eden Redeemed's narrative thrust of ruling and increasing and the key signs of faith and prosperity. In the expansive agency, the believer fulfills the narrative Task assigned by the "expansive God"[328] of ruling and increasing in the world with God's delegated authority.[329] The implementation of Adam's lost authority that Jesus regained from Satan rests entirely on the believer's correct usage of faith and prosperity.[330] Hence, the agent is tasked to rule and increase and thereby extend their influence in the territories occupied by Satan. By using faith, the agent becomes "unbound in God"[331] to overcome demonic opposition and extend the really real spiritual world in the material realm and so display the prosperous and blessed life of Eden. The practice of extending influence signifies that the believer is fulfilling their Task assigned by God to rule and increase in the world.

5.2.6.1 Analysis of Extending Influence The practice of extending influence reveals critical aspects of the Word of Faith worldview. Discussed here are the presence

322. Lee, *T. D. Jakes*, 2; Bowler and Reagan, "Bigger, Better;" Asamoah-Gyadu, "God Is Big," 1.

323. Coleman, *Globalisation*, 92–2; Bowler, *Blessed*, 223; Ukah, "Redeemed Christian Church;" Nel, *Prosperity Gospel*, Kindle edition, "A New Form of Marketing and Financing." See Section 6.2.4.

324. Coleman, *Globalisation*, 190, 202; Marti, "I Determine," 141.

325. See Gerber "Fat Christians."

326. See Lindhart, "Introduction," 15–19.

327. Chesnut, "Prosperous Prosperity," 221; Meyer, "Make a Complete Break." See, e.g., Hagin, *Triumphant Church*; Oyedepo, *Born to Win*.

328. Coleman, *Globalisation*, 187.

329. Kalu, *African Pentecostalism*, 112. See Section 3.2.6.3.

330. See Chapter 3.

331. Coleman, *Globalisation*, 190.

of the market's quantifiable hermeneutic, areas where iconic logic challenges Pentecostalism, how the medium of television breeds social accommodation, the movement's social and political involvement, and the significant role of Satan. I discuss these to add complexity and nuance to characterizations of the movement and speak to this book's analytical, evaluative, and comparative goals.

Extending influence is a semiotic practice grounded in iconic logic, which holds that a sign-vehicle must be grand to signify God. Practicing such iconic logic is well characterized as "performing the mega,"[332] because the agent acts out the rationale that "if something is for God . . . it has to be big."[333] The interpretant used to determine if a sign-vehicle is "big" is this-worldly, as it is shaped by the quantifiable hermeneutic of the market.[334] Though theologically based in Eden Redeemed, the rationale of the "bigger and better"[335] fits the market's "growthism"—the emphasis on perpetual, computable growth as the highest good and ultimate task.[336] Performing a quantifiable hermeneutic shows a logic "infected by the pathology of the Market [sic] logic, which celebrates 'growth' above all else."[337]

The "mega mindset,"[338] formed by expecting a like-like relationship between the sign-vehicle and God's greatness, stands in tension to Pentecostalism's desire of faithfulness to the biblical narrative and early attitudes toward greatness and ambition. First, the mega mindset subverts the repeated Scriptural warnings not to confuse size with significance, the emphasis being on God's pleasure in using what appears as weak and insignificant sign-vehicles to signify God's glory.[339] Second, the rationale of the early Pentecostals was that "the proof that God was with them was that they were so small and so despised."[340] The Word of Faith's iconic logic thus subverts Pentecostal distinctives that hold what appears as weak and insignificant in the eyes of the world can be both beautiful and powerful in God's

332. Goh, "Hillsong and Megachurch," 295.

333. Asamoah-Gyadu, "God Is Big," 1.

334. Maddox, "Growth Churches."

335. Bowler and Reagan, "Bigger Better," 199.

336. Robert Nelson, "The Secular Religion of Progress," *The New Atlantis* 39 (Summer 2013): 48–9; Gauthier, Woodhead, Martikainen, "Consumerism as Ethos," 21; Jean Comaroff and John Comaroff, "Privatizing the Millennium: New Protestant Ethics and the Spirits of Capitalism in Africa, and Elsewhere," *Africa Spectrum* 35, no. 3 (2000): 293–312; Rey, "Missing Prosperity," 341; Maddox, "Growth Churches;" Swoboda, "Prosperity or Posterity."

337. Cox, "Pentecostalism and Global Market," 393; Robert Nelson, "Economics as Religion," in *Economics and Religion: Are They Distinct?* ed. Geoffrey Brennan and A.M.C. Waterman (New York: Springer, 1994), 227–36; Maddox, "Growth Churches."

338. Asamoah-Gyadu, "God Is Big," 1.

339. E.g., see Gordon Fee, *The First Epistle to the Corinthians* (Grand Rapids: Eerdmans, 1987), 78–84.

340. Cox, *Fire from Heaven*, 273.

eyes.[341] Third, the mega mindset invites the Word of Faith agent to think big and to embrace personal ambition as part of one's divine assignment.[342] Differences are muddled between ambitions arising from one's own desires vis-à-vis desires for God's kingdom. The expanding agency places the agent in a constant effort to supersede one's present state, fostering discontent with current levels of influence (be it great or small) and easily cultivates non-Christian positions (conflict and competition with those who potentially threaten one's status, envy of those who succeed at a faster pace, or contempt for those who fail to increase). Fourth, the practice of extending influence in the world speaks of a vertical image of power in the Word of Faith. Seeking influence in the world by gaining personal wealth and fame (by courting politicians, business leaders, and entertainment celebrities) testifies to a vertical view of the flow of power as working from the top-down. In such hierarchical imagination, the believer can only fulfill their Task by being on top of the world.[343] The potential in Word of Faith practice to disclose and deconstruct oppressive power structures within their religious context and outside society is therefore significantly restricted. Fifth, the Word of Faith practice engages early Pentecostalism's emphasis on reaching out into the whole physical world.[344] However, the iconic logic inevitably advances a quantifiable hermeneutic that uses a this-worldly interpretant to determine what qualifies as big enough to stand in a "like-like" relationship to God.[345] This logic contrasts early Pentecostal emphasis on holiness and ascetical inclinations, which often favored a withdrawal from the standards of "the world."[346]

The Word of Faith uses television broadcasts to extend influence in the world—probably more than any other Christian group.[347] Television and media technologies extend their influence as such mediums "authenticate their existence in the minds of the rest of society."[348] Television studios also can create an

341. Smith, *Thinking*, 44–6; Cox, *Market*, 128.

342. "Within this worldview, there is nothing too big for them to dream or for God to deliver to the faithful" (Harrison, *RR*, 65); Asamoah-Gyadu, "God Is Big," 1; Perriman, *FHP*, 41; Coleman, *Globalisation*, 190; Marti, *Hollywood Faith*, 4.

343. A vertical image of power underlies views that the sick and poor cannot be a good witness of God's kingdom (e.g., see Olson, *CC*, 155).

344. Vondey, *Pentecostalism*, 105; Heuser, "Religio-Scapes," 20. E.g., Harrison, *RR*, 66; Anderson, *To the Ends*.

345. Cf. Cox, *Fire from Heaven*, 273.

346. Anderson, *Introduction to Pentecostalism*, 292.

347. See D. J. Hedges, "Television," in *The New International Dictionary of Pentecostal and Charismatic Movements*, ed. Stanley M. Burgess and Eduard M. Van Der Maas, rev. and exp. edn. (Grand Rapids: Zondervan, 2003), e-book edition, "Television;" "the prosperity theology is moored to the upbeat mood and glitz of television for nurture, expression, representation, and propagation" (Kalu, *African Pentecostalism*, 110).

348. Schultze, *Televangelism*, 195; Coleman, *Globalisation*, 179; Kalu, *African Pentecostalism*, 108.

appealing, artificially created image which serves to validate the Word of Faith worldview.[349] Nonetheless, the Word of Faith engages media technology with little critical thought of how these media challenge their identity and accommodate to the dominant society.[350] Researchers argue that the dynamics of the television medium requires a level of accommodation to the dominant cultural narrative themes and aesthetics to be successful.[351] To attract and maintain a maximum audience, the worldview(s) of the dominant culture must find some amount of affirmation in the television broadcast. In semiotic terms, the Word of Faith has to make use of the dominant interpretants. So, in their pursuit of growing influence, the Word of Faith's television performance can cause the movement to reinforce "the very social systems that they believe themselves to be dismantling."[352] Further, it is a repeated argument in the scholarly literature that television ministry was formative to the practice of sowing money seeds.[353] It is highly likely, therefore, that the practice of television empowers the competing narrative of prosperity, which recasts prosperity as the Task. Gaining money thus shifts from Helper to Task when the medium of television requires significant financial resources; "prosperity gradually became an end in itself."[354]

The practice of extending influence in the world raises questions of the Word of Faith's social and political involvement. Their social agency is caught in the narrative vacuum that exists regarding the Word of Faith agent and the outside world (see Chapter 3). The story's Task for believers to rule the world does not develop a rationale for social action in the world. Because of this underlying ambiguity regarding the believer's responsibilities toward society, social involvement of the Word of Faith generates a multifaceted picture.[355] In some instances, Word

349. Walton, *Watch This*, 15, 172, 174, 232–3; "the stories and images in books and videos construct the enchanted worldview that attracts people to these ministries" (Ackerly, "Importing Faith," 301); Peter, "Church's Response," 143.

350. "TV is not a 'neutral' communications medium; its message is always shaped by the technology and by those who use it" (Schultze, "TV and Evangelism," 186); Schultze, *Televangelism*, 125–52; Walton, *Watch This*. E.g., see Dorch, *Integrity*.

351. Schultze, *Televangelism*, 137; Walton, *Watch This*.

352. Walton, *Watch This*, 17.

353. Barron, *Health and Wealth*, 63; Barnhart, "Prosperity Gospel," 162; Harrison, *RR*, 96; Horn, *FRTR*, 35, 38; Walton, *Watch This*: 64; Frederick, *Colored Television*, 53–4; Hollinger, "Enjoying God," 148; "More often than not, high pressure fund-raising methods were a product of desperation, not greed. The financial pressures on the evangelists who aspired to national reputations were enormous" (Harrell, *All Things*, 105). Horn writes, "From the outset prosperity teaching was closely linked to fundraising efforts" (Horn, *FRTR*, 35).

354. Horn, *FRTR*, 38. Cf. Yong's comment, "Neither poverty nor riches for their own sake are the will of God" (Yong, *Days of Caesar*, 315).

355. See Section 1.5.8. Heuser, "Charting African Prosperity;" Vondey, *Pentecostalism*, 89–110; Mumford, *Exploring Prosperity*, 115–16; Kate Bower, "Here's Why People Hate Joel

of Faith groups engage in social transformation: from collective action in large-scale, ambitious social projects (poverty relief, medical aid, education, etc.) to small-scale, individual action (e.g., personal giving). The significant level of altruism expressed in many Word of Faith groups has caught the attention of scholars, especially as the practice challenges the common stereotype of greed as the ultimate motivation in the movement.[356] However, social involvement has yet to become a shared practice in the whole movement as it is downplayed by other Word of Faith groups.[357] Eden Redeemed ascribes the underlying sources of social ills to the spiritual realm, therefore concluding that spiritual treatments are what is first required in the form of sharing revelation knowledge or spiritual warfare.[358] Yet, practicing active social involvement fits as part of extending influence in the world. Performing social agency strengthens Eden Redeemed's Task for believers to rule the world, and so subverts the competing prosperity narrative's egocentric agenda. Though social action is not yet part of the Word of Faith worldview, an increasing number of Word of Faith groups engage in some form of social involvement.[359] Such social actions could alter the worldview-story and the other worldview-elements and so become part of Word of Faith worldview-praxis. This future possibility shows how the Word of Faith worldview is, like all worldviews, in a state of flux.[360]

The Word of Faith movement is often faulted for a laissez-faire attitude and lack of critique of oppressing political and economic structures.[361] The movement can be thought of in apolitical terms, as a group concerned only with private, spiritual progress. However, the practice of extending influence in the world also encompasses political dimensions, even though that is not always noticeable.[362] One reason why the Word of Faith is often politically invisible is that their political engagement lies dormant if their worldview can be expressed unhinderedly within the governing political, economic, and social structures. Hence, Word of Faith practices often appear politically neutral in a neoliberal context. But that should not be interpreted as an inherent apolitical attitude. In contexts where the Word of Faith worldview is threatened or actively pressed by political structures

Osteen," *The Washington Post*, August 29, 2017, accessed April 7, 2021, https://www.was hingtonpost.com/news/acts-of-faith/wp/2017/08/29/heres-why-people-hate-joel-osteen/.

356. Togaresi, "The Pentecostal Gospel of Prosperity."

357. Heuser, "Charting African Prosperity;" Vondey, *Pentecostalism,* 103.

358. Mumford, *Exploring Prosperity,* 120; Hefner, "Introduction," 23.

359. See Heuser, "Prosperity Theology;" Heuser, "Charting African Prosperity."

360. Wright, *PFG,* 555; "Worldviews and life, as everyone recognizes, are works in progress" (Anderson, Clark and Naugle, *ICW,* 216); Sire, *Universe Next Door*, 281. See Bowler, "Successful Calling," 194.

361. E.g., Walton, *Watch This*; Frederick, *Between Sundays*, 152.

362. E.g., Nel, *Prosperity Gospel*, Kindle edition, "Popularity of the Prosperity Message in Africa."

to conform to other patterns, the movement easily turns to political action.[363] The political motivation inherent in the practice of extending influence in the world is evidenced by the direct involvement of some Word of Faith leaders in national and international politics.[364] Indirectly, the movement's political involvement is seen by political references in homilies (e.g., critique or praise of various political policies), members' participation in national politics, and by endorsement and cooperation with political candidates.

Since the Word of Faith worldview-story affirms Satan's total influence and control over the earth, extending influence generates a significant focus on Satan and the practice of spiritual warfare.[365] The believer is urged into action by the narrative rationale that the world is dominated by Satan while Jesus—though having won the complete victory—is passively waiting for the believer to do the implementation.[366] The Word of Faith worldview places the believer in constant conflict with Satan and evil forces, which will prevail if the believer does not practice faith properly (see Section 6.2.3). This need for correctly implemented faith to be victorious over Satan can easily generate spiritual performance anxiety within the Word of Faith movement.[367]

Conclusion

Wright's worldview-element of praxis applied through Peircean semiotics to the Word of Faith movement generated six practices analyzed as signed-shaped, semiotic actions. From the cumulative insights gained by these analyses, three types of rationalities in the Word of Faith worldview stand out: the iconic logic, indexical logic, and market logic. Closing this chapter, I consider how each of the three offers additional complexity and nuance to our understanding the movement's worldview and speak to the analytical, evaluative, and comparative goals set out for this book.

First, iconic logic is formative in the Word of Faith worldview—expressed in the practices of gaining revelation knowledge, manifesting prosperity and health, following the charismatic leader, and extending influence in the world. Because iconicity represents by resemblance, iconic logic shapes the ideal of the believer as the perfect representation of life in Eden. Practices shaped by iconic logic also hold grand promises: by engaging in iconic practices, the perfection of the spiritual world enters the realm of present possibility. Iconic logic speaks to the Word of

---

363. Coleman, *Globalisation*, 213–15; Fea, *Believe Me*, 133–7. The political topics are not always shared: Yong, *Spirit Poured Out*, 65–6.

364. Coleman, *Globalisation*, 213–14; Wiegele, "Prosperity Gospel," 173; Wrenn, "Consecrating Capitalism," 426; Fea, *Believe Me*.

365. See Chapters 3 and 6.

366. Hagin, *Believer's Authority*.

367. See Warrington, "Teaching and Praxis," 88.

Faith's desire to transcend creatureliness by overcoming the limits of creation and human shortcomings in finances, health, beauty, knowledge, and power. Practicing iconic logic thus makes a forceful answer to the Word of Faith's deep dissatisfaction with the world as is and their longing for the full realization of the really real, spiritual world in the here and now.

Second, indexical logic makes the Word of Faith worldview privilege practices that carry causal power.[368] Making positive confessions and sowing money seeds operate by such cause-and-effect logic. Positive confession upgrades human speech from the realm of the symbolic to that of indexicality, making the believer's confessions equal in power to God's creative utterances. Sowing places giving in an indexical relation to economic increase through the spiritual law of sowing and reaping, thus putting the guaranteed harvest at the control of the believer.[369] Indexical practices speak to the Word of Faith longing for believers to operate on God's level. Such functional divine equality makes the believer able to realize God's perfect world at their own initiative. Practices formed by indexical logic offer practical solutions—for example, "if you have a need, plant a seed"[370]—aimed at problems that in other paradigms lay outside of the believer's control (e.g., unjust economic structures).[371] Indexical practices provide a sense of control and predictability as they perform a straightforward, cause-and-effect logic that answers puzzling experiences (e.g., sickness came because of confessing negative but healing comes by speaking positive confessions) and offer a sense of predictability to human life (e.g., sowing guarantees a financial harvest).[372] Indexical practices bring out human agency in the fulfillment of the Task of ruling and increasing.

Third, the Word of Faith worldview embodies logic from the functional religion of the market.[373] The rationalities underlying globalized consumer capitalism find performative expressions in the movement's practices: a vertical power matrix, a quantifiable hermeneutic, profit-seeking, consumerism, branding, commodification, and commodity fetishism. The logic of the market shapes the aesthetic ideals and desires and the overascribed individual agency

368. The centrality awarded indexical semiosis led Farah to call the Word of Faith an "act-consequence theology" (Farah, *FTP*, 144).

369. "Seed" is a very powerful metaphor that carries indexical logic.

370. Alexander, *Signs and Wonders*, 61.

371. Walton, "Stop Worrying."

372. Wariboko, *Economics*, 94–5; "negative confession is also, we must realize, an unassailable device to explain why in fact you are not healed. The whole issue is presented by Faith teachers almost as a (bogus) syllogism of Aristotelian logic: Premise One: Those who confess that they are healed will be healed. Premise Two: Those who do not confess their healing will stay sick. Conclusion: Therefore all those who are not healed have made negative confession" (Smail, Walker and Wright, *Love of Power*, 80).

373. Cox, *Market*.

within the Word of Faith.[374] There is a fit between market logic and the Word of Faith's iconic and indexical worldview. Iconic logic encourages the believer to realize the perfect spiritual world in the now, while indexical logic provides the means to do so through cause-and-effect acts. This follows the market's promise of the perfect life now (iconic logic) through the consumption of commodities (indexical logic). Market logic also fits the Word of Faith view that consuming the world indexes ruling the world.[375] Thus, the Word of Faith worldview-praxis "promote and even sacralize the false values of the Market [*sic*]."[376] This confluence between the Word of Faith and the market is first of theological weight because worldwide consumerism takes on the properties of a functional and competing religion.[377] As long as the logic of "the religion of the market"[378] is accommodated, spread, and capitalized on through the Word of Faith practices, the movement fails to offer a critique of the powers that be and present a prophetic image of the world "as if" free from the dominion of globalized consumer capitalism which relativizes all other values apart from itself.[379]

The insights gained from analyzing the practical dimensions of the Word of Faith have further theological consequences which are explored in the final chapter. There I analyze the worldview's propositional dimension by applying ultimate beliefs, the last of Wright's four elements to constitute the movement's worldview.

---

374. See Wrenn, "Consecrating Capitalism;" Maddox, "Prosper, Consume."

375. See Smith, *The Devil Reads*, 40–1.

376. Cox, "Pentecostalism and Global Market," 392.

377. Cox, *Market*.

378. Richard Foltz, "The Religion of the Market: Reflections on a Decade of Discussion," *Worldviews* 11 (2007): 135–54.

379. Market logic relatives all other values: "Markets, after all, render merely irrational many of the concerns we put at the center of our existence, concerns like art, justice, love, friendship, democracy, even worship itself. Within the closed system of economic logic, individuals have no principles, only preferences: a taste for freedom cannot be distinguished from a taste for french fries" [Bethany Moreton, *To Serve God and Wal-Mart: The Making of Christian Free Enterprise* (Cambridge: Harvard University Press, 2009), 271]. Market logic is formed in Christian theological terms by an idolatrous worldview shaped by "money-theism" rather than monotheism (Rieger, *No Rising*, viii); Foltz, "Religion of the Market," 148.

Chapter 6

ULTIMATE BELIEFS IN THE WORD OF FAITH

The additional complexity and nuance needed for a "thicker description" of the Word of Faith movement require, I contend in this study, the lens offered by worldview studies. Wright's fourfold model for worldview-analysis is particularly well suited because of its holistic scope. His model allows for an analysis of the Word of Faith's narrative dimension through the element of story (Chapter 3), its semiotic dimension through the element of symbol (Chapter 4), and the practical dimension through the element of praxis (Chapter 5). What remains is to apply the fourth and last element of Wright's model. The element of ultimate beliefs offers an analysis of the propositional and presuppositional dimension of the Word of Faith worldview. Wright argues that every worldview contains propositional content in the form of ultimate beliefs which can be articulated by letting a set of five questions be answered from the context formed by the other three worldview-elements. This chapter analyzes the theological presuppositions contained in the Word of Faith's ultimate beliefs as they are expressed in the answers to Wright's questions.

In the first section, I explain how Wright envisions the nature and function of the element of ultimate beliefs in worldviews and his method of using five ultimate questions. In the next section, I let the combined findings of the previous three chapters answer each of Wright's ultimate questions which speak to the Word of Faith's identity, their perception of the environment, their problem description, how they define the remedy, and how they view time.[1] After presenting the question and the concise answer emerging from the findings of the past chapters, I analyze the answers' theological content and inner logic to gain additional insights into the Word of Faith worldview and to speak to the analytical, evaluative, and comparative goals set out in the introduction. In closing the chapter, I bring out four insights gained from the analysis of ultimate beliefs which address the Word of Faith worldview's characteristics, essential parts, identity-carrying features, and inner logic.

The overall task of analyzing the ultimate beliefs of the Word of Faith is important, not least because it completes my application of Wright's fourfold worldview-model but also because this analysis adds additional theological analysis to the

---

1. Wright, *NTPG*, 123; Wright, *JVG*, 467; Wright, *RSG*, 38; Wright, *PFG*, 33.

narrative, semiotic, and practical studies of the previous chapters. This chapter draws upon work done in the doctrinal and biblical models (see Chapter 1), yet the lens of worldview offers additional depth in the understanding of the Word of Faith belief system as it draws on the other elements of the worldview previously examined.

6.1 Ultimate Beliefs in Worldview

This chapter is occupied with how the Word of Faith worldview addresses the ultimate issues of life. Worldviews, for Wright, are implicit, precognitive, dynamic, and comprehensive reality-perceiving frameworks.[2] Worldviews generate propositional and presuppositional content in the form of ultimate beliefs.[3] These deep-rooted convictions are (as the name suggests) beliefs from which basic and consequent beliefs are derivative.[4] Wright means that ultimate beliefs are part of the worldview's answer to the ultimate questions of human life.[5] Here Wright's approach corresponds to a commonly shared view among Christian worldview scholars that human life is largely carried out in the interrogative mode, thus making worldviews to provide implicit answers to universally shared ultimate questions, that is, key "questions of belief" that are elementary and determinative to human existence.[6] If (what is thought to be) a worldview does not provide such

---

2. Wright, *NTPG*, 37, 43, 45, 122–3, 137, 148–9; Wright, *PFG*, 26, 28, 232–3.

3. Wright, *NTPG*, 122; Wright, *PFG*, 29, 33. On the echo of Paul Tillich's "ultimate concern," see Wright, *NTPG*, 122; Paul Tillich, *Ultimate Concern* (London: SCM, 1965). "A proposition is a meaningful linguistic construct that makes a truth claim. That is, a proposition is a sentence, fragment, or paragraph, in verbal, written, or demonstrative form, claiming to represent reality" (Anderson, Clark and Naugle, *ICW*, 79 fn. 5).

4. See Chapter 2.

5. Wright, *NTPG*, 123.

6. James Olthuis, echoing Paul Tillich, calls these "ultimate beliefs" (Olthuis, "On Worldviews," 29). Walsh and Middleton, *TV*, 35; Middleton and Walsh, *Truth Is Stranger*, 11; Naugle, *Worldview*, 83; Sire, *NTE*, 113; Wright, *NTPG*, 123, 243; Wright, *JVG*, 142; Wright, *RSG*, 713; Hiebert, *Transforming Worldviews*, 29. Sire lists seven questions: "(1) What is prime reality—the really real? (2) What is the nature of external reality, that is, the world around us? (3) What is a human being? (4) What happens to persons at death? (5) Why is it possible to know anything at all? (6) How do we know what is right and wrong? (7) What is the meaning of human history?" (Sire, *NTE*, 20–1); Olthuis provides another list: "A worldview gives fundamental, seminal answers to the ultimate questions: Who are we? Where are we? What are we to do? What is good and what is evil? Where are we going?" (Olthuis, "On Worldviews," 31); Anderson, Clark and Naugle list four questions: "Four core worldview questions are . . . the heart of every individual and corporate worldview. (1) What is our nature? (2) What is our world? (3) What is our problem? (4) What is our end?" (Anderson, Clark and Naugle, *ICW*, 3, 18–21).

answers, it is not a complete worldview—because all worldviews per definition address the ultimate issues of life.[7] Wright's element follows what appears to be the most common method for analyzing worldviews, namely that of probing the worldview under investigation for answers to a set of existential questions.[8] However, much of worldview thinking prioritize cognitive content, making worldviews to be essentially systems of thought and fundamentally products of the mind. Wright's expanded definition of worldview includes other aspects as equally formative to worldviews, while retaining the element of ultimate beliefs to allow studying propositional content. In applying this element, the intellectual shape of the Word of Faith worldview can be extracted and articulated.

Suggesting no changes to the content and function of the worldview-element that Wright calls "questions," I refer to it as "ultimate beliefs" because it better captures the elements' instrumental purpose, fills a pedagogical role in highlighting its constitution, and elucidates its logical connection with the corresponding "basic beliefs" and "consequent beliefs" of Wright's larger model.[9] Ultimate beliefs is a terminology in line with Wright's thinking and carries the benefit of accentuating his model's close affinity with the majority of other Christian worldview thinkers who consider ultimate beliefs as an (if not the) integral part of worldviews.[10]

To probe the propositional and presuppositional dimension of worldviews, Wright employs five ultimate questions to which each worldview implicitly carries

7. Walsh and Middleton, *TV*.

8. Sire, *NTE*, 113–17. E.g., "worldview can be understood in the singular form, as a human capacity to raise and answer life's ultimate questions" [André Droogers, "The World of Worldviews," in *Methods for the Study of Religious Change: From Religious Studies to Worldview Studies*, ed. André Drooger and Anton van Harskamp (Sheffield: Equinox, 2014), 21–4].

9. Taken from Olthuis, "On Worldviews," 29. Or perhaps the neologism "ultimates" in short could match the other one-word elements in Wright's model. Walsh and Middleton call their four questions "ultimate questions" (Walsh and Middleton, *TV*, 35). See Section 2.3.

10. Wright can speak of the element "questions" as "questions of belief" (Wright, *RSG*, 713) and substitute "questions" for "belief" in listing the worldview-elements: "praxis, narrative, symbol and belief" (Wright, *RSG*, 725). E.g., "In its simplest terms, a worldview is *a set of beliefs* about the most important issues in life" (Nash, *Worldviews in Conflict*, 16, emphasis added); "worldview will be defined as 'the comprehensive *framework of one's basic beliefs* about things" (Wolters, *Creation Regained*, 2, emphasis added); "A worldview (or vision of life) is *a framework or set of fundamental beliefs* through which we view the world and our calling and future in it" (Olthuis, "On Worldviews," 29, emphasis added); "Worldview is the articulation of *the basic beliefs* embedded in a shared grand story that are rooted in a faith commitment and that gives shape and direction to the whole of our individual and corporate lives" (Goheen and Bartholomew, *Living at the Crossroads*, 23, emphasis added); Anderson, Clark and Naugle, *ICW*, 43–6.

the answers.[11] These worldview-questions speak to identity, perception of the environment, a problem description, defining the remedy, and what is the current position in that process.[12] They make it possible to identify the answers which operate on a subconscious worldview-level and "determine human existence."[13] The ultimate questions are:

(1) "Who are we?"
(2) "Where are we?"
(3) "What is wrong?"
(4) "What is the solution?"
(5) "What time is it?"[14]

Every worldview, Wright argues, implicitly speaks to each of these queries.[15] The sum of the answers constitutes the basic propositional content of the worldview. By answering these questions, worldviews provide "the presuppositions which enable people to make sense of everything else."[16] Since the answers are implicit,

---

11. The questions are adapted from Walsh and Middleton, with two significant alterations. They are in first-person plural instead of the original first-person singular. Wright added the fifth question. Reasons being that it helps to provide the deeper structures of certain worldviews (in his case, especially Jewish and Christian worldviews), otherwise accounts risk to collapse them into timelessness (Wright, *JVG*, 443). In *PFG*, Wright introduces a new set of more general questions which he uses in parallel to the aforementioned. The so-called "six honest serving men" that Rudyard Kipling formulated as central in his thought and that "taught him all he knew." These key questions are: What, Why, When, How, Where, and Who (Wright, *PFG*, 26, 538). Through these questions, one is able to "probe down to the bedrock of the worldview and mindset" (Wright, *PFG*, 454). This is how he envisions the connection between the two set of questions: Who are we? Where are we? What is wrong? What is the solution? (= How?) What time is it? (=When). Kipling's "Why?" question is not covered in the previous set. In pressing the "Why?" question "the answers go back and back to more and more basic answers" (Wright, *PFG*, 27). It is at this point that many worldviews enter the level of theology to address such ultimate questions.

12. Wright, *NTPG*, 123; Wright, *JVG*, 467; Wright, *RSG*, 38; Wright, *PFG*, 33.

13. Wright, *NTPG*, 123.

14. Wright, *NTPG* 123; Wright, *RSG*, 38. The first four questions are taken from Walsh and Middleton, *TV*, 35. See Middleton and Walsh, *Truth Is Stranger*, 11. The four questions are used by other scholars, e.g., Christopher Wright, *The Mission of God* (Downers Grove: IVP Academic, 2006); Kenneth J. Archer, *The Gospel Revisited: Towards a Pentecostal Theology of Worship and Witness* (Euguene: Pickwick, 2011), 39. The fifth question is a unique addition by Wright, appearing first in *RSG* (p.38). Wright's five questions are also used by other scholars, e.g., Wolters, *Creation Regained*, 127; Goheen and Bartholomew, *Drama of Scripture*, 15.

15. Wright, *NTPG*, 243; Wright, *JVG*, 564, 576; Wright, *PFG*, 33, 177.

16. Wright, *PFG*, 33.

the ultimate beliefs are not (necessarily) held consciously by the worldview adherents.[17] Studying the ultimate questions must, therefore, not be confused with a group's articulated theological or philosophical system of thought. Rather, all theoretical thinking is based on the answers assigned to the ultimate questions.[18]

Wright probes the elements of story, symbol, and praxis for the answers they as an entity supply to each question.[19] Though the worldview-story plays a privileged part (as always in Wright), in the final analysis, it is the integration of story, symbol, and praxis that make up the context from which to extract the answers.[20] The data is then presented as answers to each question in narrative form. It is important to recognize that the questions carry an essential narrative structure, making them answerable in narrative form rather than in isolated propositions.[21]

Appearing as the odd one out, scholars have either excluded ultimate beliefs from Wright's model or extracted it for independent use.[22] But such use misses the interconnectedness and the irreducibility of the four elements in Wright's

17. Walsh and Middleton, *TV*, 35.

18. Walsh and Middleton, *TV*, 35.

19. Wright, *PFG*, 562–3. For examples of how Wright uses the questions to probe the Pharisaic worldview see Wright, *PFG*, 177–9; Paul's worldview see Wright, *PFG*, 538–71; Jesus' worldview see Wright, *JVG*, 443–74.

20. Wright summarizes "This, then, is how 'worldviews' work. Story, praxis and symbol generate and sustain a set of implicit answers to the five questions" (Wright, *PFG*, 33).

21. See Wright, *NTPG*, 123; Wright, *JVG*, 142, 576; Wright, *RSG*, 38; Middleton and Walsh, *Truth Is Stranger*, 212. "Human beings, as semiotic creatures and inherent storytellers, come to grips with themselves and nature of life in the cosmos through the formation of worldviews as systems of narrative signs that form a basic outlook on life. They provide narrative answers to the fundamental questions about the realm of the divine, the nature of the cosmos, the identity of human beings, the solution to the problem of suffering and pain, and so on. Even the seemingly nonnarratival aspects of a *Weltanschauung*—its doctrinal, ethical, or ritual dimensions—can be explained by a fundamental narrative content" (Naugle, *Worldview*, 302). Bartholomew and Goheen follows Wright's overall thinking and say: "Embedded in all grand stories are fundamental beliefs about the world and answers to questions of ultimate significance: What is life all about? Who are we? What kind of world do we live in? What's wrong with the world? How can it be fixed? the answer to these great questions are not philosophical concepts; they are beliefs, often not clearly articulated, embedded firmly in the particular grand story we hold. They achieve coherence precisely because are merely elements of a single, unified vision of the world that arises from that story" (Bartholomew and Goheen, *Christian Philosophy*, 16); "Worldviews answer ultimate questions that are at the heart of human life, in terms of a grounding and directing narrative or myth that is encoded in symbols and embodied in a way of life, or praxis" (Walsh, "From Housing to Homemaking," 9).

22. Cartledge excludes questions in his adaption of the model (Cartledge, *Encountering the Spirit*, 30). Wolters reduces Wright's worldview thinking to only the questions (Wolters, "Worldview," 855).

thinking. Hence, I make sure in the application of the model to the Word of Faith that each of the four elements plays its distinctive part.

I used Wright's other elements to analyze the narrative, semiotic, and practical dimensions of the Word of Faith worldview. The element of ultimate beliefs now turns our attention to its propositional and presuppositional aspect.[23] Since ultimate beliefs are based on faith commitments, every type of worldview is theological in their essence.[24] Thus, this chapter will speak to the theology of the Word of Faith as the content of their ultimate beliefs. Considering the ultimate beliefs of the Word of Faith is important for two key reasons. First, only after applying this element is the worldview-analysis of the Word of Faith complete. Second, this element allows using the findings of the doctrinal and biblical models while offering additional complexity and nuance to an analysis of the Word of Faith belief system.[25]

6.2 Ultimate Beliefs in the Word of Faith

Wright argues that every worldview contains propositional and presuppositional content. This content takes the form of ultimate beliefs, which can be articulated by letting a set of five ultimate questions be answered from the context formed by the other three worldview-elements. From this follows that the story, symbol, and praxis of the Word of Faith analyzed in the previous chapters will supply answers to these ultimate questions. To articulate the answers, I direct each of the five questions in the order Wright lists them toward the collective findings of the previous three chapters.

While each worldview-element is important to consider, following Wright, I give the worldview-story a privileged position.[26] Each section starts with a brief description of the logic of the question and the purpose for which I use it in relation to the Word of Faith. This is followed by a compressed answer in narrative format written in the first-person plural, also following Wright.[27] It is important to point out that the answers are reflective of the particularities of the Word of Faith worldview alone, thus leaving out any part that is shared with broader Pentecostalism.[28] Following the answer, I turn to analyze its content from a theological perspective to gain better insights in its inner logic and the underlying worldview, insights which address the analytical, evaluative, and comparative goals of this book. I bring in the larger context of Pentecostalism—the theological world in which Word of Faith mainly finds itself—when their beliefs stand in significant

---

23. Wright, *NTPG*, 122; Wright, *PFG*, 29, 33.

24. "worldviews . . . are profoundly theological" (Wright, *NTPG*, 122, 126–31); "world views [*sic*] are founded on ultimate faith commitments" (Walsh and Middleton, *TV*, 35).

25. See Sections 1.3; 1.4.

26. Wright, *NTPG*, 123, 132; Wright, *JVG*, 142; Wright, *RSG*, 38.

27. Wright, *PFG*, 234. Also Walsh and Middleton, *TV*, 36.

28. See Chapter 2.

tension and when highlighting that brings out a particularity in the Word of Faith belief system. Also, since the Word of Faith's expressed intention is to be biblically faithful—they profile themselves as the true "Word movement"—following the evaluative goal of testing the inner coherence of the worldview necessitates to point out when their theological convictions do not match their objective.[29] Much scholarly work examines Word of Faith doctrines, so this chapter does not repeat what has been done.[30] Rather, by the help of the other worldview-elements studied in the previous chapters, I want to identify the presuppositions and underlying logic which find expression in their belief system.

My analysis in each section draws from the types of logic that emerge out of the Word of Faith's story and semiotic system and the discussion of the influence of market logic. To recapitulate, by pragmatic logic I speak of the tendency in the Word of Faith worldview to objectify and instrumentalize, and I use polarized logic for how the worldview favors two opposed categories (both are noted in the narrative structure of Eden Redeemed). By iconic logic, I refer to the rationality which arises out of seeking to relate sign-vehicles to their object by a direct "like-like" resemblance. Indexical logic speaks of an approach that is formed by ascribing a cause-and-effect link between the sign-vehicle and the object. A rationality formed by symbolic logic opts rather for unique and conventional relations between the sign-vehicle and the object. I use market logic to speak of rationality shaped by globalized capitalist consumerism, particularly the monetized and commodified worldview.[31] In the following I examine the theological presuppositions of the Word of Faith expressed in their answers to Wright's five ultimate questions.

6.2.1 *The Word of Faith Identity: Who Are We?*

The first of Wright's five worldview-questions speaks to the ultimate belief of the Word of Faith identity. I use the question to probe how the Word of Faith worldview understands the believer's nature and position in the world.[32] The Word of Faith's answer to the question "Who are we?" that emerges from the cumulative findings of the other three chapters may be stated as: *we are God's very children, called to rule the world by faith through our entitled prosperity and health.* This answer emerges from the initial sequence of the Eden Redeemed worldview-story, where the believer's divine equality and Task of increasing and ruling are narrated. The believers' identity and Task find expression in all the worldview-signs. The answer is performed in various ways through all the worldview-praxis. The theological

---

29. Harrison, *RR*, 109–10.

30. See Section 1.2.

31. For "Market logic" see Cox, "Pentecostalism and Global Market," 393.

32. Walsh and Middleton, *TV*, 35. This is important because the worldview which gives rise to the answer shapes the adherent's "identity by constituting the telos of our being-in-the-world" (Smith, *Thinking in Tongues*, 28).

content of this answer is now analyzed to gain insights into the propositional and presuppositional dimensions of the Word of Faith worldview.

6.2.1.1 Pneumacentric Ontology The worldview-question of identity in the Word of Faith brings the focus to the core of the movement's theology.[33] This question requires, therefore, a more thorough discussion than the others. Ontological concerns, in the sense of discerning the true nature of things, are foundational to the Word of Faith.[34] Ontology informs the movement's quest to lay bare the ultimate nature of God, human beings, faith, health, prosperity, and the world. Especially formative to their view of human nature is the belief that the really real is spiritual (pneumatic) and that this dimension is always most important.[35] I speak of this belief as "pneumacentric ontology." The Greek noun transliterated "pneuma" is not in reference here to the Holy Spirit but to the metaphysical essence that is distinct from the material, physical world in Word of Faith belief. To differentiate between spirit as essence and the Holy Spirit, I refer to the former in lower case, while capitalize "Spirit" in reference to the latter. Word of Faith belief in the spiritual heart of ultimate reality informs not only their anthropology but also their theology proper and their cosmology (see Section 6.2.2).

The Word of Faith's theological anthropology is formed by pneumacentric ontology, while finding expression through an iconic logic that seeks to relate the sign-vehicle to its object by a direct like-like resemblance. Because God is believed to be spirit in essence, the human representing God must, by consequence of iconic logic, also be essentially a spirit being.[36] "Pneumacentric anthropology" describes this belief that humans "are spirit beings."[37] Iconic logic shapes their interpretation of Adam as the sign-vehicle, which stands for God as the immediate object in the direct, corresponding relationship of an icon-sign.[38] The Word of Faith holds that the first human (together with all humans afterward) was created as a spirit being in likeness with God who is spirit in essence.[39]

33. Harrison, *RR*, 166; Jones and Woodbridge, *HWH*, 40–2.

34. See Walton, "Blessed," 31, 37.

35. Hagin, *Man on Three Dimensions*, 11; Hagin, *Exceedingly Growing*, 32; Copeland, *Force of Faith*, e-book edition, "A Message from Kenneth Copeland." See also Christerson and Flory, *Network Christianity*, 137.

36. John 4:24a "God is a Spirit" (KJV).

37. "Who are you? If you are born again, then you are a spirit being inhabiting a human body" (Oyedepo, *Operating*, e-book edition, "You Are a Spirit Being"); Andrew Wommack, "Spirit, Soul and Body," *Awmi.org*, accessed April 7, 2021, https://www.awmi.net/reading/teaching-articles/spirit-soul-and-body/; See Atkinson, *Spiritual Death*, 27–8, 253.

38. "the logic . . . could equally be applied the other way round: since humanity is made in God's image, and that humanity is self-evidently physical in nature, then this must imply some physicality in God's being" [William Atkinson, "Spirit, Soul and Body: The Trichotomy of Kenyon, Hagin and Copeland," *Refleks* 5, no. 1 (2006): 3].

39. See Section 3.4.2.2.

6.2.1.2 Trichotomist Anthropology Imagining humans to be fundamentally spirit beings generates, in turn, a particular radical trichotomist conception of human nature, expressed in Word of Faith discourse as: "man [*sic*] is a spirit, who possesses a soul, and lives in a body."[40] Such trichotomist anthropology, formulated within a larger pneumacentric ontological worldview, is foundational to Word of Faith theology.[41] Understanding this theological conviction enables a greater understanding of their broader theological system.

The Word of Faith divides the human spirit, soul, and body into absolute and separate compartments, privileging the human spirit as the real person, dividing and subordinating the soul and the bodily dimensions of the human being under the spirit.[42] The resulting reduction of the human nature follows the worldview's polarized logic that favors opposed and mutually exclusive positions.[43] This polarization is evident in how the Word of Faith portrays how the believer can only access the really real spiritual realm by faith arising from the human spirit. The faith of God is a spiritual, supernatural entity within the human spirit of the born-again believer that is contrasted with natural, human faith, which arises out of the believer's soul.[44] It is only the faith of the human spirit that can access the spiritual realm and connect with God. Human feelings and thoughts stemming from the body and soul are, therefore, unreliable guides and at worst even deceptive.[45]

---

40. Atkinson, "Spirit, Soul," 98. E.g., Joyce Meyer, "Strong in Spirit," Joycemeyer.org, accessed April 7, 2021, https://joycemeyer.org/everydayanswers/ea-teachings/strong-in-spirit; Creflo Dollar Ministries. "How to Experience Real Life Transformation Part 3," *Creflodollar.us.*, accessed April 7, 2021, https://www.creflodollarministries.org/Bible-Study/Study-Notes/How-to-Experience-Real-Life-Transformation-Part-3; Maldonado, *How to Walk*, 128; Andrew Wommack, "Spirit, Soul and Body," *Awmi.net*, accessed April 7, 2021, https://www.awmi.net/reading/teaching-articles/spirit-soul-and-body/; Oyedepo, *Born to Win*, e-book edition, "Your New Status." Joel Osteen slightly revises it: "You have a spirit which is the part of you that lives for eternity, you have a soul and live in a body while you're here on earth" (Osteen, *Wake Up*, 100). Though it might look like a move toward a holistic anthropology, any holism is simply in the rhetorical phraseology. The pneumacentric ontology is clearly present.

41. "the most basic theological presupposition of the entire Word-Faith movement" (Bowman, *Word-Faith*, 98); Chris Anthony, "The theological structure of Word of Faith," (Paper presented at the Center for Charismatic and Pentecostal Studies, Birmingham, United Kingdom, January 2018).

42. McConnell, *DG*, 104; Atkinson, *Spiritual Death*, 130–2; Atkinson, "Spirit, Soul;" Lindholm and Broshe, *Framgångsteologin*, 32–6.

43. See Section 3.4.2.5.

44. Ibid.

45. Kenneth Copeland Ministries, "Your Feelings are Lying to You," 22:11. Posted by Kenneth Copeland Ministries, February 3, 2020, KCM.com, accessed April 7, 2021, https://www.youtube.com/watch?v=4YjjXDm-QqY.

However, the Word of Faith's pneumacentric anthropology does not, as one could think, result in the neglect of body and soul. Rather, as seen in Chapter 5, the body is allowed an important role through health, physical development through exercise and healthy diet, and a market aesthetic of beauty and body image.[46] An emphasis on the soul or mind is also seen by the movement's encouragement for intellectual development (e.g., through reading and some academic learning).[47]

Pentecostal theology is challenged by the Word of Faith's pneumacentric trichotomist view of humans because such anthropology, William Atkinson concludes, "does not have a strong biblical or theological basis"[48] and stands in contrast with the holistic anthropology testified to in the biblical texts. The iconic ontological relation between Adam and God in the Word of Faith is also lacking in a similar way: "claiming an identity of essence between the human spirit and God's Spirit . . . is scripturally unwarranted."[49] Pneumacentric trichotomist anthropology challenges Pentecostal theology because it invites a fractured view of humanity by compartmentalizing human nature, thus lowering the importance of intellectual and embodied life to effectively undercut the presence of a unique human nature and human experience.[50] The fidelity to reality in the Word of Faith worldview is thus challenged.

Historical research points to underlying influences shaping Word of Faith anthropology that stand apart from traditionally Christian sources. Non-Christian sources include forms of Platonism and Gnosticism but particularly streams of thought from New Thought metaphysics.[51]

6.2.1.3 Exalted Anthropology The move the Word of Faith does from pneumacentric ontology via iconic logic to pneumacentric anthropology results in an exalted view of humankind.[52] The Word of Faith holds that humans share by ontological rationality in the very nature of God.[53] I refer to this belief as "exalted anthropology" to differentiate Word of Faith beliefs from theologies which hold to

---

46. Winslow, "Imaged Other." E.g., Kenneth W. Hagin, *How to Be a Success in Life* (Tulsa: Faith Library Publications, 1982).

47. E.g., Hagin, *How to Be.*

48. "This anthropology does not have a strong biblical or theological basis. Its prioritisation of the immaterial over the physical cannot be justified. Furthermore, its distinction between spirit and soul, let alone its promotion of one over the other as controlling self, cannot claim support" (Atkinson, *Spiritual Death*, 141).

49. Hejzlar, *Two Paradigms*, 199.

50. McConnell, *DG*, 122; Perriman, *FHP*, 105.

51. Atkinson, *Spiritual Death*, 130–2; Atkinson, "Spirit, Soul;" McConnell, *DG*, 122; Lindholm and Broshe, *Framgångsteologin*, 33; Bowman, *Word-Faith*, 97–104; Jones and Woodbridge, *HWH*, 63–4.

52. "since both God and people are spirits, human beings exist in the same class as God" (Bowman, *Word-Faith*, 130).

53. Atkinson, *Spiritual Death*, 27–8; McConnell, *DG*, 115–16. See Section 3.4.2.4.

a high anthropology but do so based on other narratives and kinds of logic. The exalted anthropology of the Word of Faith interprets human nature ontologically according to iconic logic and elevates humans to be in equality with God and partaking of God's very nature.[54] This trajectory is evident in the following quote from Hagin (I insert comments to elucidate the development of thought): "God is a Spirit [pneumacentric ontology]. Man is made in the likeness and image of God [iconic logic], also as a spirit creature [pneumacentric anthropology]. He is in the same class of being as God [exalted anthropology]."[55] This exalted view of humans in the Word of Faith worldview leads them to embrace an optimistic view of human nature, overascribe human agency, cultivate a sense of entitlement, hold to a low functional Christology and shape the JDS doctrine. I discuss each of these five points in turn.

The Word of Faith's exalted anthropology furthers an optimistic view of human nature that affirms the believer's inner present perfection (often referred to as "righteousness") and dismisses sin from the human spirit by deferring it to the realms of soul, body, and the outside world.[56] This view of Christian perfection follows iconic logic, which expects a direct correspondence between the sign-vehicle and the object: only a perfected human spirit can serve as a sign-vehicle for the holy God. Yet, by declaring the spirit to be restored to Adam's prelapsarian state, the Word of Faith leaves no room for "the corruption of fallen human nature that remains even in the redeemed."[57] This leads to a forfeiting of any substantial criticism of the inner self and its desires in the Word of Faith, making the theology to pose no significant challenge to the human ego taking the preeminent place. The potential for spiritual discernment and unmasking human selfish motives in the Word of Faith is significantly reduced, especially issuing any prophetic critiques of the beliefs and practices formed by global consumerism that profits the human ego.[58] The influence of the competing prosperity narrative in the movement, which makes personal prosperity the believer's Task, is empowered by unbridled egocentrism that may arise out of the exalted anthropology.

54. Perriman, *FHP*, 26–9; Creflo Dollar writes, "After being born again, the real person, the spirit, is an exact duplicate of God, perfect in every way" (Creflo Dollar, "How to Experience Real Life Transformation Part 3," *Creflodollar.us.*, November 20, 2016, accessed April 7, 2021, https://www.creflodollarministries.org/Bible-Study/Study-Notes/How-to-Experience-Real-Life-Transformation-Part-3.

55. Hagin, *Human Spirit*, 9. Hagin also builds the argument in reverse: "We know that man is a spirit because he is in the same class as God. Man is made in the image and the likeness of God (Gen. 1:26). And Jesus said, 'God is a Spirit' (John 4:24)" (Hagin, *Bible Faith Study Guide*, e-book edition, "Chapter 7").

56. See Section 3.4.2.2.

57. Sarles, "Prosperity and Healing," 343. Such optimistic view of the Christian is labeled "charismatic humanism" by Farah (Farah, "Roots," 6).

58. Brandon, *Health and Wealth*, 115. See Marti, *Hollywood Faith*, 177–92; Marti, "The Adaptability," 23.

Exalted anthropology places the believer in a superclass of species—a form of super human—which finds doctrinal expression in the Word of Faith's teaching of believers as "little gods."[59] This anthropology underlies the literal interpretation of the believer being born again in an ontological sense as a child of God (hence the "very" in answer to this worldview-question).[60] Their view of humankind does not mean, however, that humans are preexistent, share in the divine attributes, are worthy of worship, or that the Word of Faith holds to either pantheism, panentheism, or polytheism.[61] But their anthropology leads Word of Faith theology to overestimate human agency in God's plan and be mesmerized with "human capacity to eclipse the physical world"[62] and to push back against any restrictions of what being a creature entails. The Word of Faith seeks ways to override anything that limits human potential, be it grounded in theology or human experience. Despite the weaknesses just discussed, the strengths of the Word of Faith's exalted anthropology are its assertions of every human's great dignity and potential.[63] It is easy to see that Word of Faith anthropology can empower believers to take personal action in life and break out of destructive and diminishing life patterns.[64]

The second point to discuss is that the exalted anthropology cultivates a sense of entitlement. Iconic semiosis, which places the believer to reflect the realities of the spiritual world by direct correspondence, coupled with the exalted anthropology, finds practical expression in the narrative Task of exercising authority in the world. The narrative position of the believer is as a literally born-again child of God enthroned with Jesus in the heavenly realm to rule in the here and now.[65] The believer's life and circumstances should, therefore, reflect the abundance and life of the spiritual world. A fundamental premise in Word of Faith theology, drawn

---

59. Jones and Woodbridge, *HWH*, 61, 63–4; MacGregor, "Recognising and Successfully Averting," 55; Atkinson, *Spiritual Death*, 130; McClymond, "Prosperity Already," 304–5; Sarles, "Prosperity and Healing," 342. Brandon, *Health and Wealth*, 116; Vondey, *Pentecostalism*, 101; Nel, *Prosperity Gospel*, Kindle edition, "Prosperity Theology's View of Christ and Humankind." Cf. DeArteaga, *Quenching the Spirit*, 222. See Bowler, *Blessed*, 18, 179. On "Übermensch" see Friedrich Nietzsche, *Thus Spoke Zarathustra* (London: Penguin, 1969).

60. See Section 3.2.6.2. See MacGregor, "Recognising and Successfully Averting."

61. Perriman, *FHP*, 117, 121; Bowman, *Word-Faith*, 129–30; Jones and Woodbridge, *HWH*, 64. Contra Walton's *homoousios* argument, (Walton, *Watch This*, 150). See Hagin, *Human Spirit*, 9.

62. "The human capacity to eclipse the physical world is indicative of one of the more conspicuous and controversial aspects of Word of Faith theology" (Walton, *Watch This*, 150).

63. "Prosperity theology correctly asserts that every human, even the poorest, is of great dignity in God's eyes" [Laura M. Hartman, *The Christian Consumer: Living Faithfully in a Fragile World* (Oxford: Oxford University Press, 2011), 70].

64. E.g., Harrison, *RR*, 51–4.

65. See Section 3.2.5.

from the Adam plot, is the ruling authority over the earth given to Adam.[66] Jesus' redemption, it is held, restored the believer to Adam's position, making health and prosperity to be the believer's rights which are available in the now. What in other Pentecostal theological contexts often are considered gifts of grace, which can be humbly requested but are distributed according to God's sovereign will, are reinterpreted in the Word of Faith as the entitlement of every believer that should be claimed by faith.[67] The believer's royal assignment and their right to blessings generate the theme of personal entitlement, which is foundational to the Word of Faith belief system.[68]

The exalted anthropology cultivates a low functional Christology in Word of Faith theology.[69] The born-again believer is imagined as being as much a son of God as Jesus was on the earth.[70] However, this equality must not be misunderstood as setting out a low Christology that compromises the divinity of Christ or ascribing divinity to humans. Charges that the Word of Faith denies the deity of Jesus are based on misreadings of their overall narrative belief structure and their explicit Christology.[71] Jesus, though fully God, is believed to be "a replica of the first Adam in his unfallen state"[72] sent for "the recovery of mankind's [*sic*] lost Edenic nature."[73] As this was accomplished in the Christ-event, Jesus' ongoing significance in Word of Faith theology is primarily as a passive Helper for the believer to implement their restored authority according to his set example.[74] The theological system thus cultivates a low functional Christology that privileges exalted anthropology above an ongoing emphasis on the uniqueness of God the Son, thus downplaying the believer's need for a dynamic and submissive relationship with him.[75]

---

66. "The fundamental premise of the Word-Faith doctrine is that Adam was the god of this world" (Bowman, *Word-Faith*, 141).

67. See, e.g., Warrington, *Healing and Suffeirng*, 38–9.

68. Mumford, *Exploring*, 123; Harrison, *RR*, 8–10, 51–4; Walton, "Blessed," 157; Bowler, *Blessed*, 20, 45; Lin, *Prosperity Gospel*, Kindle edition, "Endowed by Their Creator."

69. Bowman, *Word-Faith*, 153; "he [Hagin] has an inappropriately high anthropology at the expense of a low Christology" (Warrington, "Teaching and Praxis" 128).

70. The Word of Faith thus contains a form of radical kenoticism. See Perriman, *FHP*, 106–9.

71. Perriman, *FHP*, 109.

72. Perriman, *FHP*, 106.

73. Perriman, *FHP*, 116, see 106–10; see also Atkinson, *Spiritual Death*, 25–39.

74. Bowman, *Word-Faith*, 153; "When God made man, He gave man dominion over everything on earth. To have an idea of the kind of dominion that man would have had had he not sinned, let's look at the perfect Man, Jesus Christ" (Prince "Born Again to Have Dominion"); cf. Warrington, *Healing and Suffering*, 44–5.

75. Perriman, *FHP*, 196.

Finally, pneumacentric ontology expressed in a trichotomist anthropology also serves as the backdrop for the JDS doctrine (see Chapter 3).[76] JDS states in brief that in The Fall, human beings lost their divine nature and partook of satanic nature.[77] For this reason, Jesus had to die not just physically on the cross but also spiritually in hell. Such dual death was necessary for the ontological transformation of replacing fallen satanic nature in the believer's spirit with godlike nature. Pneumacentric trichotomist anthropology thus sets the need for Jesus' death to affect the human spirit; Jesus' bodily death could only affect bodily salvation, making spiritual death also a requirement for humanity's spiritual salvation.[78] Hence, the JDS doctrine is a soteriology framed by a pneumacentric, trichotomist anthropology.

The Word of Faith unapologetically places the human at the very center of theological attention, making a certain anthropocentrism to permeate their entire belief system.[79] The Word of Faith privileges human equality with God, leading to an almost autonomous conception of royal agency, where God and Jesus are reduced in the narrative categories from Senders to Helpers in the believer's Task of ruling and increasing.[80]

The Word of Faith's theological anthropology involves a move from the theocentrism typical of much of Pentecostal and evangelical Christianity.[81] The shift from God-centeredness to human-centeredness is problematic from a Pentecostal theological perspective. In their exalted anthropology, the Word of

---

76. Atkinson, *Spiritual Death*, 27–30, 253; McConnell, *DG*, 114–31, 123–8; Hanegraaff, *CIC*, 145–78; Perriman, *FHP*, 22–5, 110–15; Jones and Woodbridge, *HWH*, 89–92; Brandon, *Health and Wealth*, 121–8; Johansson, *Vad Ska Man Tro*, 77–82; Smail, Walker and Wright, *Love of Power*, 80–5.

77. A consequence of the image of God being imagined to be completely abolished and replaced by satanic nature is the implicit degrading of the value of the nonbeliever to less than animals (Bowman, *Word-Faith*, 145; Lindholm and Brosché, *Framgångsteologin*, 39–40). This is surely an unintended consequence and never directly stated nor implied in Word of Faith discourse, yet it speaks to obvious weaknesses in their theological anthropology.

78. E.g., "People argue that, Jesus did not die spiritually. They are fully persuaded that He only died physically. If He only died physically, then He redeemed us from physical death only. It did not affect sin. Sin is a spiritual force, any physical exercise cannot stop it. Jesus did more than die physically on the cross. He also died spiritually" (Oyedepo, *Born to Win*, e-book edition, "Chapter 2").

79. Lioy, "The Heart;" Farah, "Roots;" Sarles, "Prosperity and Healing," 342–3; McConnell, *DG*, 142–4.

80. See Section 3.4.2.1. "The autonomy the faith-teachers afford to people who are allegedly able to exercise faith and speak things into existence without the Holy Spirit commissioning them to do so on a particular occasion goes hand in hand with their overall exaggeration of the human ontological status" (Hejzlar, *Two Paradigms*, 199).

81. Morris, "Biblical and Theological," 263; Sarles, "Prosperity and Healing," 343; McConnell, *DG*, 144.

Faith "perhaps . . . makes its most dramatic and clear-cut departure from traditional Christian doctrine."[82] The exalted anthropology significantly blurs the ontological distinction between creator and creation and so crosses a line which Christian tradition has closely guarded.[83] The Word of Faith also does not fully acknowledge God's continuous and active sovereign kingship over the entire creation and the human need for continuous submission and total reliance on God.[84] God's autonomous sovereignty is reduced by the elevation of human nature; "The exaltation of man [sic] inexorably means the denigration of God."[85] Or rephrased, "what God's sovereignty lacks [in Word of Faith theology] human sovereignty supplies."[86] Having recovered Adam's authority, believers are empowered to act independently from discerning the Spirit's direction in each unique situation as long as they follow God's expressed promises.[87]

Concluding this section, the Word of Faith's theological anthropology has theological problems that undercut its potential to serve as a thoroughly Pentecostal option. However, it is important to acknowledge that a theology that views human nature positively and empowers human agency does not by default reduce God's glory. Without alleviating the tensions the Word of Faith's conception of humanity pose for Pentecostal theology, it must be recognized that theological anthropologies which ascribe humans a place of shared sovereignty with God by necessity do not reduce God's glory. Such scalelike correspondence between God's power and human power seems to arise out of a view of God as seeking to guard power within a hierarchical and closed system, where the exaltation of one must come at the lowering of the other. The picture emerging from Genesis 1 and 2 and in the Word of Faith worldview is of God taking pleasure in power-sharing with humans.[88] God's glory is in this view not lessened but rather increased by inviting humans to share (a limited) sovereignty over creation.[89] It can be argued that Word of Faith has explored other possible answers to this worldview-question ("Who are we?") to addresses a vacuum present in some Pentecostal and evangelical theologies, which underemphasize the human role in God's plan of salvation. While aiming for a more inclusive understanding of human agency, the lack of theological precision

---

82. Bowman, *Word-Faith*, 124. See also Fee, *Disease*, 15; Farah, *FTP*, 136.

83. Hejzlar, *Two Paradigms*, 171; Perriman, *FHP*, 28; Jones and Woodbridge, *HWH*, 61, 63–4; Bowman, *Word-Faith*, 129; "The only difference in nature between man [sic] and God is of degree, not of kind" (McConnell, *DG*, 116); "Although the distance between God and human beings is radically narrowed, it is still there" (Nel, *Prosperity Gospel*, Kindle edition, "Prosperity Theology's View of Christ and Humankind"). See Pinnock, *Flame of Love*, 150–1, 154.

84. Perriman, *FHP*, 105; Williams, *Christian Approaches*, 214–15.

85. Farah, "Roots," 10; da Silva, *Framgångsteologin*, 63.

86. Sarles, "Prosperity and Healing," 342.

87. See Perriman, *FHP*, 198.

88. Middleton, *Liberating Image*, 287–9.

89. Wright, *PFG*, 908.

by the Word of Faith movement makes them overstate their case at some sensitive points. Also, Word of Faith theology allows no critical stance against the shaping forces of globalized consumerism. Rather, market logic, with its commodification and hierarchical power matrix, shapes their perception of what it means to rule as a king. Nonetheless, their departure from traditional theological categories must not per default disqualify the Word of Faith from contributing to the discussion on how theological anthropology can faithfully reflect human ontology and agency as portrayed in the biblical story. It is worth exploring if the Word of Faith's emphasis on human value and royal vocation may at some points lie closer to the biblical story than other presentations that historically are considered "orthodox."[90]

6.2.2 *The Word of Faith Cosmology: Where Are We?*

The nature of the environment in which believers find themselves shapes the focus of the second question. Here I seek to probe the Word of Faith's ultimate cosmological beliefs about the nature of the world.[91] Since this setting is not a distinct aspect of the narrative analysis in Chapter 3, analyzing the movement's cosmological beliefs is an important component in addition to previous analyses. I use "cosmology," not as a synonym to worldview, but to speak of how one imagines the present constitution of the universe.[92] The answer to "Where are we?" emerging from the cumulative findings of the past chapters on the Word of Faith worldview may be stated as: *we live in a world made up of the physical and the spiritual realms, where God and Satan are active, spiritual laws causative, nothing is impossible and all God's blessings are available to be claimed by faith.* Generative to this answer is the Eden Redeemed story, where each part has direct links. Especially important is the Initial Sequence 1, which sets out the creation of the world and Adam's place in it. The symbols of faith, revelation knowledge, and optimism interconnect at various points with their view of the world. The praxis of speaking positive confession, sowing money seeds, following the charismatic leader, and extending influence into the world particularly situate the believer to perform the answer.

6.2.2.1 *Dualistic Cosmology* Out of the Word of Faith's pneumacentric ontology arises not only how the movement views human nature but also its cosmology. The Word of Faith places the physical realm in a derivative relationship to the spiritual realm in terms of both origin and causality. An important dimension of their belief that the spiritual dimension makes the really real world is how the Word of Faith ascribes the spiritual dimension as the root cause of everything significant happening in the physical world.[93] What other Christian belief systems consider

90. Cf. McConnell, *DG*, 116.
91. Walsh and Middleton, *TV*, 35.
92. See Wright, *PFG*, 483.
93. E.g., "Psychological, social, behavioral, emotional, and physical causes could be rooted out and identified as spiritual realities" (Bowler, *Blessed*, 142); "faith operated

physical entities with physical causality are in the Word of Faith's spirit-ontology and spirit-causality thought to be ultimately of spiritual essence and with spiritual roots.[94] Hence, physical experiences such as sickness and poverty are taken as problems with spiritual origins that require spiritual solutions.[95]

The Word of Faith's theological beliefs arise out of a strong emphasis on God's immanence and an expectancy of God's ongoing work in the world. The pneumacentric cosmology leads the Word of Faith, similar to Pentecostals generally, to imagine the world as enchanted, filled with the activity of God and spirits both holy and fallen.[96] As seen in the Topical Sequence 2 of Eden Redeemed, the Word of Faith carries a distinct expectation on the helping work of the Holy Spirit in the world and in the believer's personal experience.[97] These convictions foster a position of expecting spiritual realities in the forms of glossolalia, prophecies, personal Spirit-guidance, visions, miracles, and power encounters.[98] What emerges is a theology built on the Pentecostal "position of radical openness to God, and in particular, God doing something different or new."[99] The so-called rhema doctrine, which (among other things) expects an inspired and authoritative now-word, is an attempt to put in dogmatic categories this radical openness to God's actions in the world.[100] The beliefs in healing and prosperity are likewise rooted in the expectancy of God's intervention in miraculous ways. The Word of Faith's radical openness thus makes an optimistic theology, which paints the world of limitless spiritual and material resources and as full of opportunities, where anything is possible in the now.[101]

as a spiritual guarantee, drawing health and finances into the lives of people willing to suspend naturalistic explanations in favor of supernatural, Holy Spirit causality" (Bowler, *Blessed*, 177).

94. Bowler, *Blessed*, 142.

95. Perriman, *FHP*, 23; Bowler, *Blessed*, 95; Wrenn, "Consecrating Capitalism."

96. Bowler, *Blessed*, 189. "Everything on this earth—every human, every being—is dominated, ruled or influenced by spirits in the unseen world" (Hagin, *Art of Prayer*, 131). See also Allan Anderson, *Spirit-Filled World* (London: Palgrave McMillan, 2018), 13–18; Vondey, *Pentecostalism*, 29–47.

97. See Section 3.2.6.13.

98. "Across the faith movement, believers envisioned a spiritual cosmos dominated by unseen forces, divine and demonic, which steered the course of people's lives" (Bowler, *Blessed*, 158).

99. Smith, *Thinking*, 12. See Vondey, *Pentecostalism*, 47.

100. King, *Only Believe*, 203–12.

101. Cf. Vondey, *Pentecostalism*, 47. "The prosperity gospel mistakenly presupposes a world of limitless resources that can provide limitless wealth to limitless people. This thinking stands squarely against the agrarian imagination and against a primary strand of the biblical narrative. If everyone received prosperity through faith as promised, our limited ecological world would simply be unable to keep up. A limited world cannot provide a limitless economy. The prosperity gospel teaches something that the earth

Foundational to this cosmology is a particular dualism that divides reality into spiritual and physical dimensions, drawing on the polarized categories of God and Satan.[102] Leaving comments on Satan to the next section, suffice here to note that cosmic dualism makes a world that significantly downplays the possibility of any "neutral" area in human existence, as experiences ultimately originate from either of the dual categories of God or Satan. Despite the movement's dualistic cosmology, a certain holism in their worldview is equally striking. Though the spiritual and physical realms are categorically polarized, they function in symbiosis as the spiritual realm is expected to have physical consequences and vice versa. The Word of Faith, therefore, passionately refuses to read biblical promises of restored health and wealth as having only spiritual, nonmaterial significance in a disembodied afterlife.[103] Rather, foundational to Word of Faith theology is the expectation of God's work of salvation to have positive material consequences in the present. The Word of Faith thus affirms God's direct involvement in the physical realm and celebrates the goodness of material creation.

It can be argued that the Word of Faith's emphasis on the spiritual value of money and wealth in Christian discipleship constitutes a "radical break"[104] with attitudes within some forms of classical Pentecostalism that have prioritized other-worldly values while overlooking the economic dimensions for Christian living (or at times even degrading them).[105] The "absence of theological contradiction between faith and the material"[106] in the Word of Faith worldview expresses a holism that strengthens the worldview's fidelity.[107] This holistic focus makes the Word of Faith to be "most un-Gnostic"—paradoxically enough in light of the dualism in other parts of their theology that are critiqued for having gnostic tendencies (see the following text).[108]

6.2.2.2 Reductionist Goodness The cosmological dualism, which divides reality into spiritual and physical dimensions, has direct effects on how the Word of Faith views God's nature. The image of God is formed in dualistic tension with Satan, that is, God is defined in contrast to evil. The Word of Faith's polarized logic means that all categories that can be thought of as evil, insufficient, ugly, and unpleasant are reserved descriptions for Satan, leaving the opposite categories to

---

literally cannot provide. The earth is not, as industrialism assumes, an open system of endless resources, endlessly harvested. Rather, creation has its limits and humans are created to live within the laws of creation that God has sovereignly established" (Swoboda, "Prosperity or Posterity," 406).

102. Walton, *Watch This*, 151.

103. Cf. Horton, "TV Gospel," 149.

104. Heuser, "Charting African Prosperity," 3.

105. Anderson, *Introduction to Pentecostalism*, 220.

106. Chong, "Of Riches and Faith," 153.

107. Perriman, *FHP*, 115; Smith, *Thinking*, 43.

108. See Section 1.2.

define God.[109] The result is that God does not define Godself in the Word of Faith belief system.[110] Rather, Satanology shapes the Word of Faith's theology proper: God always seeks "the abundant life" for God's children because Satan always seeks "to steal, and to kill, and to destroy."[111] Suffering and failure are always a work of Satan, while God only brings prosperity, health, beauty, and success.[112] Degrees of interpretation allowing for paradox and mystery in human experience and God's action in the world are downplayed or excluded.[113]

The worldview's polarized logic makes the movement committed to mutually opposite categories, which results in a God who is without exception good, kind, abundant, and pleasant.[114] I refer to this as "reductionist goodness," by which I mean not to contrast the basic understanding of God as morally good, but that the Word of Faith's image of God is reduced to the movement's particular definition of "good." Thus, the standard Word of Faith descriptive "God is good" takes on absolute defining power in their system of belief.[115] Theological constructs and exegetical choices in the movement's discourse must consequently stand the litmus test of compatibility with a commitment to their particular understanding of the goodness of God.[116] The Word of Faith's definition of God's goodness does not show necessary signs of being informed by a broad reading of Scripture— as the movement claims—but rather draws on a theological dualism that forms

109. "It is simple. Satan is the defiler. Satan is the tormentor. Satan is the one brings sickness and disease; he is the oppressor and our adversary, the thief and the liar. . . . Therefore, anything that hurts or destroys must come from Satan" (Hagin, *God's Word*, 19).

110. Cf. "According to the Bible and Christian tradition generally, God is truly known only through himself" (Olson, *Essentials*, 92).

111. John 10:10 KJV; Hagin, *Zoe*; Perriman, *FHP*, 83–4; Nel, *Prosperity Gospel*, Kindle edition, "View of God."

112. Brandon, *Health and Wealth*, 53–4, 69; Hejzlar, *Two Paradigms*, 172, 179ff.

113. E.g., see Hagin, *Don't Blame God*. "There is no mystery behind the evil that befalls people in Prosperity Gospel Pentecostalism. Its teachings make it very clear that God only desires goodness and flourishing for his people" (Lin, *Prosperity Gospel*, Kindle edition, "Get Ready for the Harvest").

114. "God only wants the best and the most pleasant and blessed life for you that is possible" (Harrison, *RR*, 63). See Section 3.2.6.1.

115. "Faith is believing that we have a good God" (Joseph Prince Ministries, "See God as a Good Father," *Josephprince.org*, accessed June 6, 2020, https://www.josephprince.org /blog/daily-grace-inspirations/see-god-as-a-good-father *Josephprince.org*.); Copeland lists "God is good" as the most important truth for a Christian, before God's trinity (Kenneth Copeland Ministries, "10 Things Every Christian Should Know," *Kcm.org*, accessed April 7, 2021, https://www.kcm.org/believers-academy/series/10-things-every-christian-should -know).

116. Perriman, *FHP*, 83–4; Nel, *Prosperity Gospel*, Kindle edition, "View of God," "Hermeneutical Angle and Key of the Prosperity Gospel."

a distinct hermeneutic which prioritize biblical passages that seem to speak to reductionist goodness over texts that speak to the contrary.[117] In turn, their view of God constrains a theology of God's freedom to act in the world, for example, God *cannot* send sickness, poverty, or failure nor use such for pedagogical purposes (see Section 6.2.5.2).[118] Despite the Word of Faith's radical openness to God's miracles, the repertoire of possible divine actions is restricted by the commitment to reductionist goodness. The Word of Faith's image of God, therefore, stands in tension with the Bible's multifaceted characterization of God, thus challenging its internal commitment to biblical faithfulness and weakens richer Pentecostal characterizations of God as both good and holy.[119]

6.2.2.3 *Law-Governed Causality* The Word of Faith's pneumacentric cosmology and view of spirit-causality (i.e., that experiences such as poverty or sickness in the physical realm have underlying spiritual causes) interconnect with their belief in spiritual laws which govern the world.[120] That is, the influence of the spiritual realm over the physical follows stipulated and ironclad rules. Word of Faith cosmology invites believers into "a closed spiritual universe ruled by consistent spiritual laws."[121] Underneath this belief lies an iconic view of the world that holds the physical in an analogous relationship to the spiritual. Since there are physical laws governing physical life (such as the law of gravity), by iconic logic there must be spiritual laws governing the spiritual realm.[122] These laws are found in the Bible. Belief in law-governed pneumatic causality marks one of the most significant unifying theological elements in the Word of Faith movement and their entire belief system.[123]

Belief in law-governed pneumatic causality introduces a "Newtonian paradigm"[124] in theology, which perceives God and the world to function

---

117. E.g., Copeland, *Laws of Prosperity*, e-book edition, "The Rich Young Ruler."

118. Walton, "Blessed and Highly Favored," 188.

119. "What we see in our protagonists [Fred F. Bosworth, Kenneth E. Hagin, Agnes Sanford, and Francis Macnutt] is a reaction to fatalistic acceptance of sickness as God's will. While opposing this concept, however, they lean too much on the humanist side, attempting to exonerate God from any involvement in afflicting people with sickness. Nevertheless, the implied dichotomy is false. The biblical God is neither malevolent, arbitrarily dispensing evil without a promise of redemption; nor does his benevolence spare people hardship" (Hejzlar, *Two Paradigms,* 186); See Warrington, *Healing and Suffering*, 47–53.

120. See Section 3.4.2.6.

121. Bowler, *Blessed*, 186.

122. Kenneth Copeland Ministries, "Ministry Minute: How Do You Know Spiritual Laws Exist?," *Kcm.org*, accessed April 7, 2021, https://blog.kcm.org/ministry-minute-spiritual-laws-exist/; Hagin, *Biblical Keys*, 115, 118–9; Copeland, *Laws of Prosperity*, 15–21. Cf. Perriman, *FHP*, 141.

123. See Section 1.4.

124. Bowler, *Blessed*, 46.

according to "a legal spiritual system."[125] Word of Faith theology is built on a robust indexical view of the world, resulting in an "act-consequence theology."[126] But there is "an elementary category mistake" in this iconic logic, captured by Nimi Wariboko: "In the deep structure of prosperity-gospel thought, nature is well behaved and even rational, a thought that ignores the irregularity and complexity of nature."[127] Wariboko draws from quantum physics in critiquing the Word of Faith worldview. Since quantum physics challenges the concept of an absolutist system of knowledge and predictability, it challenges the Word of Faith's portrayal of the world as operating by spiritual laws.[128] Law-governed pneumatic causality also limits openness to neutral, human/creation causations (e.g., we sometimes get sick because we live in an imperfect, fallen world or we have financial lack because of unjust sociopolitical structures). The lack of fit between law-governed pneumatic causality on human experience has consequences for the worldview's fidelity to reality, which is discussed in the conclusion.

While spiritual laws' conceptual power originates in iconic logic that places the physical and spiritual worlds in direct correspondence, it is the cause-and-effect expectation inherent in indexical logic that energizes their ongoing influence in the movement's worldview-praxis. Key practices, such as speaking positive confessions and sowing money seeds, are indexical practices grounded in the ultimate belief of a law-governed pneumatic causality. The belief in spiritual laws thus functions as the theological expression of a worldview that paints the world iconically in a corresponding relationship to the really real, to be indwelt indexically through performing cause-and-effect actions.

Although belief in law-governed spiritual causality circumscribes God's character of grace (see Sections 3.2.6.6 and 5.2.3), it works as a powerful motivator

---

125. Bowler, *Blessed*, 46.

126. Farah, *FTP*, 144.

127. Wariboko, *Economics*, 94; Perriman, *FHP*, 141, 137; Bowler, *Blessed*, 186; Hejzlar, *Two Paradigms*, 128–9.

128. "Prosperity preachers in their vivid assurances and self-interested displays behave as if in their world the Heisenberg uncertainty principle does not exist. This principle of quantum physics holds that the location and momentum of an electron cannot be simultaneously known with any degree of certainty. For instance, an insurance company actuary expert can tell you the frequency of death in a given demographic segment, but she cannot tell you the specific time and place a particular individual will die. Prosperity preachers claim to have discovered, through the name-it-and-clam-it approach, both the location and momentum of prosperity–and that they can through faith determine them simultaneously. They often tell their audience the frequency of occurrence of prosperity for those who heeded their advice and also the specific place or time of prosperity (e.g., give X amount and in the next 50 days you will be swimming in wealth)" (Wariboko, *Economics*, 94). As discussed, Hagin challenged later in life the fidelity of indexical interpretations of prosperity and health. He noted how such reading simply "is not true" because it does not fit the reality of human experience (Hagin, *MT*, 199).

and serves to democratize the believer's capacity of reaching financial and healing victories. A world governed by spiritual laws affords everyone—regardless of gender, position, status, or geographical home—equal access to the laws of perpetual blessings.[129] The rise of women leaders in the Word of Faith movement has been facilitated, at least partially, by law-governed pneumatic causality, which is operative irrespective of the gender of the agent using the spiritual laws.[130] The doctrine of spiritual laws thus engender hope and empower human agency by bringing the initiative and future guaranteed result into the realm of individual human causality.[131]

Law-governed pneumatic causality generates a reductionist depiction of God's person and actions in creation. Similar to how reductionist goodness restricts God's possible actions in the world, so does spirit-causality limit the range of divine activity, that is, God cannot break spiritual laws, hence weakening "the personality and autonomy of God and restrict[s] the life in the Spirit"[132] which challenges a Pentecostal view of the world. Wariboko writes about the Word of Faith's belief in law-governed pneumatic causality: "The view of the world as well behaved and predictable is arguably not Pentecostal. The pentecostal worldview ('social imaginary') is informed by the dynamic unpredictable fluid movement of the Spirit (pneuma, wind), which simply is not predictable."[133] The Word of Faith's ultimate belief in pneumatic causality, therefore, subverts such a core Pentecostal distinctive as the freedom of the Spirit.[134]

By providing access to causative power that is not fully grounded in the believer's personal relationship with God, the Word of Faith's belief in spiritual laws invites an impersonal facet into the God-human relationship. In the end, the Word of Faith's spiritual system can—together with the teacher who masters it—come to occupy a place between the believer and God (see Section 5.2.5).[135] God is portrayed as passive and reactive, waiting to respond to the believer's initiation

---

129. Bowler, *Blessed*, 186; Bowler, "Successful Calling," 184, 198.

130. "women could also claim an authority that sprang from the nature of the prosperity gospel itself. Their theology turned on the importance of spiritual certainty, for faith functioned as a perfect law as predictable and uniform as gravity. Prosperity theology trumpeted that the laws of faith should work for women no less than for anyone else" (Bowler, "Successful Calling," 198, 184); Bowler, *Blessed*, 186.

131. Though overstated, the critical concern is still valid in terms its trajectory that Word of Faith presents "a universe out of God's control, a universe subject to laws that even God cannot change" (Bowman, *Word-Faith*, 143). See Farah, *FTP*, 134–5.

132. Perriman, *FHP*, 138.

133. Wariboko, *Economics*, 95; "Pneumatologically, care must also be taken to respect the sovereignty and freedom of the Holy Spirit and to nurture utter dependence of faith on the Spirit's leading" (Macchia, "Call for Careful Discernment," 235).

134. See Macchia, "Call for Careful Discernment," 235–6; Perriman, *FHP*, 116, 198.

135. Perriman, *FHP*, 138–9.

of a particular law.[136] A theological consequence of this is observed by Andrew Perriman: "In effect it [a reliance on spiritual laws] produces a form of deism differing from classic deism only in that it incorporates the miraculous into the system; but the God of the system is pushed into the background."[137] However, it is important to point out that the Word of Faith does not ascribe to an impersonal concept of God.[138] Rather, God is wholly personal and the power channeled through spiritual laws is mostly believed to (somehow) originate in the person of God.[139]

In the formation of spiritual laws, what in Pentecostal theology are thought to be moral principles internal to God (e.g., God blesses generosity) are externalized and translated into a legal apparatus in the Word of Faith (i.e., the law of sowing and reaping). The belief in spiritual laws follows the logic of practical instrumentality inherent in the Word of Faith belief structure.[140] The emphasis on spiritual laws has caused some to accuse the Word of Faith for encompassing magical beliefs (see Section 5.2.1.1).[141] But this critique is overstated because it is based on a selective reading of the Word of Faith beliefs and practices.[142] Law-governed pneumatic causality, coupled with a reductionist view of God's goodness, is better understood as forming a kind of determinism.[143] That is, God's actions can be caused and predicted according to spiritual laws and the fundamental presupposition of God's goodness.[144] The Word of Faith's kind of determinism thus makes God to be "both endlessly beneficent and perfectly predictable;"[145] the immediate future must be blessed for the one who lives by faith.[146] So, what in Pentecostal and evangelical systems of belief can look like false hopes and deceptive predictions, or even magical beliefs, are better understood as the theological expressions of the Word of Faith's determinism that is formed by commitments to reductionist goodness and law-governed pneumatic causality.[147]

---

136. Hejzlar, *Two Paradigms*, 129.

137. Perriman, *FHP*, 138; Cf. Bowman, *Word-Faith*, 52.

138. Atkinson, *Spiritual Death*, 25; Bowman, *Word-Faith*, 52; Hejzlar, *Two Paradigms*, 129.

139. Perriman, *FHP*, 139.

140. See Sections 3.4.2.6, 5.2.1.1, and 6.2.4.3.

141. E.g., Hunt, "Magical Moments;" Hunt and McMahon, *Beyond Seduction*, 23–34.

142. Perriman, *FHP*, 139.

143. Cf. Macchia, "Call for Careful Discernment," 235. "their [Word of Faith believers] upward mobility results from the certainty of God's goodness. Since God is good, and God is in ultimate control of the world, the spiritual and material trajectory of believers is on sure footing" (Walton, "Blessed," 188).

144. Wariboko, *Economics*, 94.

145. Coleman, *Globalisation*, 127.

146. Hejzlar, *Two Paradigms*, 129.

147. E.g., "If you will stay in faith and keep honoring God, one day you will come into what already belongs to you. It's a prepared blessing!;" "Know that your best days are ahead.

A view of suffering as a test case for Word of Faith theology uncovers the "hard" consequences of the indexical logic contained in the concept of spiritual laws, namely that the blame falls on the sufferer who has not properly worked the spiritual laws which govern God's action in the world.[148] Far from all Word of Faith believers vocalize the hard consequences of spiritual laws, many opt for a "soft" approach.[149] Hillsong exemplifies, according to Gerardi Marti, "a softer Word of Faith" orientation.[150] Yet, the difference between the hard and soft approaches resides not necessarily in different worldviews but in the degree to which one is willing to explicitly voice the (unpleasant) consequences of indexical logic.[151]

6.2.3 The Word of Faith Problem Statement: What Is Wrong?

Wright's third question is based on a presupposition that follows Christian worldview scholarship generally, that is, that all humans have a sense of something

---

Know that He is working things together for your good, and he has victory in store for your future!" (Osteen, *Wake Up*, 146, 200).

148. Olson *CT*, 161.

149. Bowler, *Blessed*, 7–8.

150. Gerardo Marti, "Foreword," in *The Hillsong Movement Examined: You Call Me Out Upon the Waters*, ed. Tanya Riches and Tom Wagner (New York: Palgrave McMillian, 2017), vii. See Gerardo Marti, "The Global Phenomenon of Hillsong Church," *Sociology of Religion* 78, no 4 (2017): 381; Bowler and Reagan, "Bigger Better;" Tanya Riches, "Next Generation Essay: The Evolving Theological Emphasis of Hillsong Worship (1996–2007)" *Australasian Pentecostal Studies* 13 (2010): 87–133.

151. Bowler, *Blessed*, 7–8, 110, 116, 118, 125. See Pauline Muir, "Sounds Mega: Musical Discourse in Black Majority Churches in London," (doctor of philosophy thesis, University of London, 2018), 139. The categories of "hard prosperity" and "soft prosperity" developed by Kate Bowler should in this light not necessarily be understood as fundamentally different theologies but rather the extent to which one is willing to press the underlying indexical logic of the Word of Faith worldview. Her division of hard and soft prosperity is best understood in terms of rhetorical emphasis rather than theological categories. This is made clear by her labeling Creflo Dollar as "soft," who by all measures embody indexical logic and repeatedly emphasize the operation of spiritual law. Or it could be argued that the "soft" approach is an indication of people who are also drawing from other worldviews, which stand in tension to, and thus limit the hard consequences of the indexical logic of the Word of Faith worldview. Bowler writes, "The theological language of the prosperity gospel was also changing. 'Hard prosperity,' a term I use to describe a heavily instrumental language of instantaneous results, was giving way to the predominance of 'soft prosperity,' a gentler and often therapeutic account of how faith turns words into material blessings. Hard prosperity ruled the 1980s, but soft prosperity was better suited for the 1990s and its therapeutic turn toward the spiritual significance of psychology" (Bowler, "Successful Calling," 194).

being amiss in the world.[152] Therefore, the question is not *if* something is wrong, but rather how to define the world's predicament. With the help of this question, I want to specify the Word of Faith's ultimate beliefs as found in their problem statement. Their reply to the question ("What is wrong?") emerging out of the cumulative findings of the past chapters may be stated as: *we humans have lost our equality with God and our ruling authority over the world and the entitled blessings. Satan's power, working with our ignorance and inaction, makes us live beneath our privileges.*

The initial narrative sequence of The Fall in the Eden Redeemed story contains the basis for this answer as it narrates Adam's loss and Satan's gain. The privileged place given the signs of faith, prosperity, health, and revelation knowledge speaks to the problem statement, as do the practices of speaking positive confessions, sowing money seeds, gaining revelation knowledge, and extending influence in the world.

6.2.3.1 High Satanology Word of Faith discourse is focused on defining the root cause of evil and human suffering (and to offer practical solutions).[153] Two areas to discuss arise from their answer, that is, the movement's high Satanology and human ignorance and inaction. I discuss each in turn.

The Word of Faith's dualistic cosmology assigns Satan a most powerful status and a major cause for the problems of the world.[154] In their enchanted world, Satan is constantly active in bringing sickness, financial lack, fear, unbelief, and failure.[155] By ascribing Satan to be literally "the god of this world,"[156] Satan is placed in an

---

152. Wright, *NTPG*, 123; Walsh and Middleton, *TV*, 35.

153. "what gives the prosperity movement breadth and depth for many is its thorough accounting for the pain of life, and for the longing we have for restoration" (Bowler, *Everything Happens*, 7); "The prosperity gospel is a theodicy, an explanation for the problem of evil. It is an answer to the questions that take our lives apart. . . . The prosperity gospel looks at the world as it is and promises a solution. It guarantees that faith will always make a way" (Bowler, *Everything Happens*, 8).

154. Farah, *FTP*, 152–7; Perriman, *FHP*, 32; McConnell, *DG*, 121, 124; Hanegraaff, *CIC*, 129–45.

155. E.g., Jerry Savelle narrates, "A short time ago he [Satan] tried to put symptoms of the flu on me. My nose and my eye started to run. I began to sneeze and ache all over. I haven't had the flu since 1969, and I'm not going to have it now. I'm redeemed from the flu! Immediately I began to confess God's Word that I'm healed by the stripes of Jesus. I rebuked Satan and refused his lying symptoms. I wasn't trying to get something I didn't have; I was keeping something I already have. I am healed. Those symptoms were an intimidation of the adversary. The thief was trying to steal one of my possessions—my health. I have health and I stand protective over what is already mine" (Savelle, *If Satan Can't Steel*, e-book edition, "He Can't Keep Your Goods").

156. Hagin, *New Thresholds*, 56. See 2 Corinthians 4:4 KJV.

opposite position to God.[157] Such dualism overlooks God's inherent distinction from creation (which in some sense includes Satan), while exaggerating the power and sphere of Satan's influence. The Word of Faith's dualism ends up (unintentionally) to promote Satan at the expense of God's unique sovereignty. Word of Faith theology, through the concept of spiritual laws, on the one hand, moves God into a somewhat (but not fully) distant relationship in the believer's daily experience, while their Satanology, on the other hand, places the believer in closer, day-to-day interaction with evil. Satan's role in the Word of Faith is thus larger than in most other Pentecostal and evangelical theologies.[158]

The underlying narrative structure of their high Satanology comes from the second initial sequence in the Eden Redeemed story, which portrays an exchange of humanity's absolute sovereignty over the earth from Adam to Satan.[159] The fall is held as an act of high treason that legally gave Satan lordship over the earth.[160] However, the basis for a belief that absolute sovereignty over the world was transferred to Satan is unsubstantiated by the biblical texts.[161] Rather than drawing on biblical exegesis, the belief draws more on their exalted anthropology together with a hierarchical and commodified view of power; if Adam in his prelapsarian state had the legal, absolute authority over the earth that somehow existed separated from the God-human relationship, it is not a far stretch to imagine a possible transaction of that authority over to Satan in The Fall.[162] Nevertheless, this view conceives of power (i.e., authority over the earth) as an impersonal commodity, which can change ownership and user.[163] Such a view of power agrees with the worldview's pragmatic and instrumental logic and an underlying market logic, yet disagrees with the biblical accounts on several key points.[164]

Regardless of its poor biblical support, Satan's sovereignty over the fallen world serves as a hinge pin in Word of Faith theology; the belief system requires an active and powerful Satan to function properly. Satan makes an apologetic tool to explain from where negative experiences originate (as "attacks") and why the

157. See Atkinson, *Spiritual Death*, 188–90.

158. Olson, *CC*, 162.

159. See Section 3.3.1.2. See also Hagin, *New Birth*, 11.

160. McConnell, *DG*, 116–17; Bowman, *Word-Faith*, 140–1; Perriman, *FHP*, 104.

161. Bowman, *Word-Faith*, 137–45; Perriman, *FHP*, 104–5; Atkinson, *Spiritual Death*, 234–5.

162. Cf. "The Creator appoints human beings as stewards and gardeners but, as it were, retains title to the earth" (Cox, *Market,* 20; see Cox, "Pentecostalism and Global Market," 392).

163. However, this also introduces an unresolved tension. The underlying rationality for Adam's authority over the earth was him sharing God's nature. Yet, Word of Faith doctrine does not address how Satan, who lacks the exalted nature of Adam, could still wield the same authority.

164. For a biblical critique of Word of Faith sataonology see Bowman, *Word-Faith*, 137–45.

promises of health and prosperity are sometimes slow or even fail to materialize.[165] Also, while one is justified for thinking that Satan's powerful role might discourage adherents, their Satanology does the reverse. Since believers regardless of social positions and geographical locations equally hold authority over Satan, Word of Faith Satanology empowers all believers into action (similar to spiritual laws). Each believer can—and must—use their faith and ruling authority to establish the victory wrought by Jesus. Satan's high place in Word of Faith theology further functions as a motivation by anxiety. Believers are invited into a world where Satan is powerful and active, while God is passive and reactive, thus making it up to each individual to do something about Satan's attacks through their restored authority.

6.2.3.2 Human Ignorance and Inaction Regardless of Satan's authoritative role, Satan is only the penultimate reason for the problems in the world; the ultimate responsibility lies with the believer.[166] The Word of Faith's exalted anthropology and law-governed pneumatic causality together form the belief system where the highest expectations and responsibility are placed on the individual. The believer is restored to Adam's position of authority, Satan is defeated, all blessings are available through Jesus' finished work and the world operates according to the cause and effect of indexical rationality (e.g., spiritual laws).[167] Hence, the only real hindrances to living in the fullness of Eden's blessings are ignorance and inaction.[168] The problem is not ignorance in a general sense, but lack of revelation knowledge, that is, spiritual knowledge of the believer's identity, their rights and privileges, and how the world operates.[169] If believers are unaware that they are meant to rule as kings and that prosperity and health are entitled to them, they will not use faith to claim their rightful inheritance, and so they will live "beneath their privileges."[170] Failure to manifest the abundant life provided by Jesus is not just a

---

165. Bowler, *Blessed*, 159; Olson, *CT*, 161–2; Ackerly, "Importing 'Faith,'" 293.

166. Farah, *FTP*, 144–5. E.g., see Hagin, *Believer's Authority*, 48.

167. See Andrew Wommack, *You've Already Got It! So Quit Trying to Get It* (Tulsa: Harrison House, 2006).

168. E.g., "God has already placed His healing power within us, and it is now under our authority. It isn't up to God to determine who receives healing; it's up to us! . . . .It's our failure to understand and use the authority we have that is keeping God's healing power from flowing as it should" [Andrew Wommack, "Faith for Healing is Based on Knowledge," *Awmi.net*, accessed April 7, 2021, https://www.awmi.net/reading/teaching-articles/spirit-s oul-and-body/].

169. "The reason the Church hasn't been dominating the earth and our circumstances as we should have, is that most of us haven't realized who we are. It hasn't been taught" (Winston, *Imitate God*, 2).

170. Harrison, *RR*, 9. E.g., "Every Spirit-filled believer has within him enough power to claim God's very best for his life! If he is living beneath his privileges, it is not because of a lack of power, but because of a failure to release that power through faith" (Hagin, *Thresholds*, 94, 87, 91).

failure of revelation knowledge but also of acting on such knowledge; ignorance (lack of revelation knowledge) makes the believer's faith inactive. Inactive faith neglects to bring into manifestation the blessings available in the spirit realm and gives Satan room to attack.[171] Not living at "God's best" is the individual's fault by not acting in faith according to revelation knowledge.[172]

6.2.4 *The Word of Faith Remedy: What Is the Solution?*

The focus of the fourth question is to explore how the Word of Faith worldview states the remedy to the aforementioned problem of the loss of human equality with God and ruling authority.[173] Their concise answer to "What is the solution?" may be stated as: *the solution to the problem of humankind is first to know our true identity and rights and then to use the faith of God to rule through health and prosperity.* The topical sequence of Redemption in the Eden Redeemed story sets out the solution to the problem, depicting Jesus' redemption of Adam's lost nature, authority, and blessings. The worldview-signs of faith, revelation knowledge, prosperity, and health inform the answer. The worldview-praxis of speaking positive confession, gaining revelation knowledge, manifesting health and prosperity, and extending influence in the world together enact the answer.

6.2.4.1 *Spiritual Activism* The Word of Faith's answer to "What is the solution?" correlates to how they defined the problem. The problem that believers are held from their ruling authority and entitled blessings by Satan's power and their ignorance and inaction, and God's passive narrative role as Helper in The Church sequence of the Eden Redeemed story, drive the activism of the Word of Faith. Since God is imagined as waiting for the believer's initial move, it places "a tremendous

171. "I want to make it crystal clear that Satan is a defeated foe! The only reason he's able to do anything is because of our own ignorance, unbelief, and fear" (Wommack, *You've Already Got It*, 112).

172. "According to Prosperity Gospel teachers, many believers experience financial hardship because they are ignorant of their own spiritual rights and the formula of faith, positive confession, and donations that are necessary to access those rights" (Walton, "Blessed and Highly Favored," 148); "We can become successful and prosperous. If we don't, we have no one to blame but ourselves, for God has provided the way whereby we can succeed" (Hagin, *Human Spirit*, 12). A note should be made on how the Word of Faith does not, in contrast to much of Pentecostalism and evangelicalism, emphasize human sinfulness and the need to gain victory over sin as part of their problem statement. The attention of the Word of Faith is rather set on the loss of their blessed position and the need to regain victory over material and external elements (i.e., sickness and poverty). In short, sin is not the most significant problem in the Word of Faith worldview.

173. See Walsh and Middleton, *TV*, 35.

onus on the individual to act in God's stead."[174] Given that, according to their pneumacentric ontology, all that is wrong with the world ultimately has spiritual roots, it follows that the remedy must also be spiritual. The Word of Faith thus offers a particular spirituality as their theodicy.[175] Spirituality must not be thought of as passive other-worldliness detached from daily life.[176] On the contrary, they offer a spiritual kind of activism. The answer to all life's problems is reduced to the basic formula: practice faith.[177]

We must remember the semiotic shift in the sign of faith, from faith *in* God to the faith *of* God (see Section 4.3.2).[178] Faith is in this second meaning transferred from the domains of personal relation to that of impersonal instrumentality. This instrumental conception of faith is, like spiritual laws, also rooted in an indexical rationality, which seeks to anchor human action and experience in an unbroken chain of cause and effect. It is in this context of a "highly objectified conception of faith"[179] that Word of Faith theology seeks to uncover faith's rightful nature and operation as an answer to the problems of the world. Faith, conceived of as power, is an instrument to be mastered and used, one that always functions without failure when applied correctly. As such, faith speaks of the practical understanding of the spiritual world which operates indexically. Performed faith makes the causative link between the otherwise separated spheres of the spiritual and physical dimensions.[180]

6.2.4.2 Spirit-Epistemology The Word of Faith focuses on acting on revelation knowledge.[181] This knowledge is spiritual illumination gained only by revelation and concerns, especially human identity, "rights and privileges"[182] and the tools available to manifest the blessing of prosperity and health and how the spiritual world functions.[183] It is vital to recognize that revelation knowledge takes two different shapes in the movement. Either knowledge is expressed in a solid shape,

174. Sarles, "Prosperity and Healing," 342.

175. Bowler, *Everything*, 8.

176. "It is not primarily a religion of contemplation or meditation but is centered on understanding how God and the spiritual world 'works' in order to live in such a way as to please him" (Harrison, *RR*, 32).

177. Lin, *Prosperity Gospel*, Kindle edition, "Formula for the Abundant Life;" "Essential to this theology is the conviction that faith is an active practice rather than a spiritual attitude" (Vondey, *Pentecostalism*, 101).

178. "faith is not merely a theocentric act of the will in which one exercises simple trust in God; rather, it is an anthropocentric spiritual force one directs toward God" (Morris, "Biblical and Theological," 250).

179. Perriman, *FHP*, 137.

180. E.g., Wommack, *You've Already Got It*, 90.

181. Farah, *FTP*, 116.

182. Harrison, *RR*, 9.

183. Harrison, *RR*, 9–10.

as intellectual facts and formulas.[184] Or revelation knowledge is expressed in a porous poetic form, consisting of metaphor, personal narrative, and visionary perspectives.[185] In both expressions, the chief source for all revelation knowledge is the Word (a preferred name for the Bible in the movement).[186] Through the biblical texts, the believer's spirit gains the revelational understanding needed to operate in the faith of God. Hence, the Word's ability to impart the necessary spiritual knowledge to practice faith is central to Word of Faith theology.[187]

As part of their cosmic dualism stands the Word of Faith's epistemological dualism, which is evident in their understanding of revelation knowledge.[188] Knowledge gained by the human spirit through revelation is cast against knowledge gained by the mind and body. This sharp division made between the spiritual and physical realms shows how the Word of Faith's "world view [*sic*] is based on a dualistic epistemology."[189] Sickness causes "lying symptoms,"[190] as knowledge of the sickness comes from the body and mind. Truth comes from the human spirit, which is the only human part that has access to the really real spiritual realm where one's healing is a forever settled matter.[191] Knowledge gained by the mind, for example, through academic theological studies, does not serve as a foundation strong enough for practicing faith. In consequence, the interpretation of biblical passages and the formation of doctrine in the Word of Faith are built on spiritual illumination rather than on knowledge gained through academic biblical exegesis, theological training, and reflection.[192]

184. E.g., Gloria Copeland, *God's Success Formula* (Fort Worth: Kenneth Copeland Publications, 1993); Hagin, *Bible Faith Study Guide*, e-book edition, "How to Write Your Own Ticket with God."

185. This loosely corresponds to Bowler's "hard" and "soft" taxonomy (Bowler, *Blessed*, 7–8).

186. McConnell, *DG*, 102.

187. "The notion that individuals can and should apply the scriptures instrumentally and attempt to 'live the promises' in them as a tool to reconstruct their lives and situations as they would have them be is a very important part of the teaching in Word of Faith Movement churches" (Harrison, *RR*, 26).

188. See Sections 3.4.2.15; 4.3.2; 5.2.2.

189. Horn, *FRTR*, 93. See Perriman, *FHP*, 34; Hanegraaff, *CIC*, 130; Mumford, *Exploring Prosperity*, 40. E.g., Hagin, *I Believe in Visions*.

190. Savelle, *If Satan Can't Steal*, e-book edition, "He Can't Keep Your Goods."

191. See Brandon, *Health and Wealth*, 38–9. Cf. Lederle who argues that sometimes a temporary "disregarding" of symptoms, rather than a denial, is a sound Pentecostal way of walking by faith (Lederle, *Theology with Spirit*, 154, see 148).

192. See Warrington, "Teaching and Praxis," 96–7, 99; Horn, *FRTR*, 25, 50, 99; Bowman, *Word-Faith*, 181. Cf. "sometimes within those circles that claim to take the Bible most seriously—often, in fact, there above all—there is a woeful refusal to do precisely that" (Wright, *NTPG*, 60).

This "spirit-epistemology" is critiqued in scholarship for having gnostic tendencies in that it ascribes unrivaled soteriological power to esoteric knowledge.[193] However, even though the polarization of spiritual and natural knowledge is problematic for Pentecostalism, the basic concept of nuggets of knowledge gained from the Holy Spirit which trump other sorts of knowledge is not foreign to Pentecostal and evangelical spirituality.[194] Hence, the Word of Faith should not be classified as "cultic" simply on their taxonomy of knowledge. An evaluation of the movement should be based on the content of their beliefs.[195] That is, criticism must center on the theology that emerges out of the compound of the Word of Faith's revelation knowledge, rather than on the idea of revelation knowledge itself.

A discernible pattern in the Word of Faith trajectory of spiritual progress is the movement from ontology ("who you are in Christ"[196]) to epistemology (revelation knowledge) expressed through orthopraxis (worldview-praxis).[197] The pneumacentric ontology of the Word of Faith requires that ultimate solutions are always spiritual; "believers do not have to overcome structural factors because the spiritual world has ultimate control over the physical world."[198] The priority awarded to the spiritual realm and to spiritual actions is repeatedly faulted by critics for not engaging systemic injustices that are socially and politically grounded.[199] Nonetheless, it is accurately noted that, in the face of their view of spirit-epistemology, the Word of Faith does carry a response to structural problems in their pedagogy.[200] The social responsibility of believers is "to prioritize teaching others about the sufficiency of spiritual laws and piety rather than prioritizing the critique of systemic structures."[201] The Word of Faith's answer of practicing active faith puts them on a pedagogical-motivational mission. Believers need first to be educated through the Word in who they are, how the spiritual world operates, and what their entitled rights are, and then be motivated to act based on their position "in Christ."[202] That is, the Word of Faith's foremost response to structural problems

---

193. See Section 5.2.2.1.

194. See King, *Only Believe,* 213–4. For an account of pentecostal epistemology see Simo Frestadius, *Pentecostal Rationality: Epistemology and Theological Hermeneutics in the Foursquare Tradition* (London: Bloomsbury T&T Clark, 2019).

195. Cf. McConnell, *DG,* 101–13.

196. Harrions, *RR,* 8–10.

197. See Bowler, *Blessed,* 18.

198. Walton, "Blessed and Highly Favored," 143.

199. See Section 5.2.2.1.

200. "One of the key distinctives of Prosperity Gospel communities is fundamentally epistemological. They believe they have received the unique knowledge that leads to prosperity and they intend to spread this message to other believers" (Walton, "Blessed and Highly Favored," 148); Bowler, *Blessed,* 98, 142.

201. Walton, "Blessed and Highly Favored," 68, 148.

202. Harrison, *RR,* 8–10.

is to bring people on the path from ontology through epistemology to orthopraxis. Chapter 5 discussed how the movement could have political motivations, arising out of their desire to extend influence in the world when their worldview is under threat. Acting on revelation knowledge can thus also include political actions, if necessary.

6.2.4.3 Practical Instrumentality Word of Faith discourse emphasizes how revelation knowledge must be implemented to be effective. The Word of Faith is a "practical theology" that "theologises on the interplay between faith and action."[203] It offers a solution-based, "how to" theology, attempting at formulating a fail-safe and predictable system based on indexical logic in which Eden's blessed life is guaranteed here and now.[204] Actions which "release faith" and manifest Eden are part of the Word of Faith worldview-praxis.

The Word of Faith's activism and pragmatic logic breed a theological rationality that converts into a theology of practical instrumentality, expressed on a spectrum from "hard" steps, keys, and formulas to "soft" practical wisdom for daily life.[205] An objectified and instrumental conception of faith (faith *of* God) and an indexical usage of words and gifts make certain identity markers of the movement.[206] This form of "applied Christianity"[207] underlies its attractiveness among Christians who are seeking a theology that "works" and addresses felt needs.[208] The Word of Faith worldview's optimism and exalted anthropology coupled with the causative logic offer hope, self-worth, and an upgraded agency.[209] However, within the pragmatic logic there is a notable current toward theological impersonality. God is fully personal in the Word of Faith, but the believer's success requires more—not less— than a relationship with God. Continuous Christian interaction with the spiritual realm, rather than a direct personal I-Thou relation with God, easily shifts to

---

203. "In its core, Prosperity Gospel theologises on the interplay between faith and action; it is practical theology, so to speak, with a strong call to enactment" (Heuser, "Charting African Prosperity," 3); Harrison, *RR*, 32, 148.

204. Perriman, *FHP*, 139; Harrison, *RR*, 28ff. "The billboard of one Word of Faith church read: 'Always wealthy, never poor. Always healthy never sick—Guaranteed'" (Olson, *CT*, 155); See Bowler, *Blessed*, 181. Cf. Salinas, *Prosperity Theology*, 82.

205. Bowler, *Blessed*, 7–8.

206. Bowler, *Blessed*, 79, 252; "The Faith Message is a *practical* and instrumental form of religion that purports to take complex points of theological debate and reduce them to elements that can and will work for any persons with enough faith to appropriate them—to name and claim them—for themselves" (Harrison, *RR*, 148, emphasis original. See also 26, 47, 90).

207. Harrison, *RR*, 32.

208. Harrison, *RR*, 31–2. See Ma, "Blessing," 274–5.

209. E.g., Harrison, *RR*, 27; Chong, "Of Riches and Faith," 148; Johnson, "The Gospel," 29; Gifford, "The Bible in Africa," 219; Bowler, *Blessed*, 232; Kay, *Pentecostalism*, 118. See also Marti, *Hollywood Faith*.

an impersonal I-It relation, mediated through objectified and instrumental categories.[210]

6.2.5 The Word of Faith View of Time: What Time Is It?

The last worldview-question highlights where the worldview adherents consider themselves to be in the succession of narrative events in their worldview-story.[211] This aspect, like the second question, was not part of the narrative analysis and hence important to examine here. I use this question to analyze the Word of Faith's eschatological orientation. Their response to "What time is it?" may be stated as: *the time to rule as kings and manifest all God's promises by faith is now.* Their answer flows from the fourth sequence in the Eden Redeemed story, which places the believer back in the fullness of Eden's authority and blessings. The signs of faith, prosperity, health, and optimism particularly point to their view of time. It is also performed in their worldview-praxis, especially in speaking positive confessions, sowing money seeds, manifesting prosperity and health, following the charismatic leader, and extending influence in the world.

6.2.5.1 Overrealized Theology of the Present In terms of the storied structure of their theology, it is imperative to recognize that "Word of Faith teaching defines salvation not primarily in eschatological terms but as the recovery of mankind's lost Edenic nature."[212] Word of Faith theology stipulates how the believer through right knowledge can use the faith of God to affect a direct correspondence between spiritual and physical reality, and so fulfill their Task of ruling as a king in this life. This makes it a substantially imminent and this-worldly theology with its focus set on the present. Hagin was unequivocal on this point: "*Now* faith is. If it's not *now*, it's not faith."[213] This overrealized theology of the present functions not as a detached eschatological perspective but is formative to the structure of Word of Faith theology and makes the hermeneutical key for their belief system.[214]

Word of Faith theologizes on the believer's present restoration to Eden's prelapsarian condition. The movement presents a form of radical restorationism that goes beyond locating believers in the primitive church to placing them in

---

210. See Section 3.4.2.2.

211. Wright, *JVG*, 467; Wright, *RSG*, 38.

212. Perriman, *FHP*, 116, 118; McClymond, "Prosperity Already," 297.

213. Hagin, *What Faith Is*, e-book edition, "Chapter 1," emphasis original; "Our trouble is that we relegate everything to the future!" (Hagin, *Beleiver's Authority*, 20); "The first thing you need to understand is faith operates in the realm of the now. God is not yesterday. God is not tomorrow. God abides in the eternal now" (Dollar, *Divine Order*, e-book edition, "Chapter 2). See McClymond, "Prosperity Already," 296–7; Morris, "Biblical and Theological," 239.

214. Horn, *FRTR*, 110.

Eden's perfection.[215] Their belief system thus repudiates classical theological anticipations of a correlation between the beginning of time (*Urzeit*) and the end of time (*Endzeit*) in favor of a direct and absolute correspondence between the beginning of time (*Urzeit*) and the present time (*Jetztzeit*).[216] Their view of time is an overrealized view of present time, as it encourages expectations of the iconic role of the believer to be realized in the immediate present. A hallmark of Word of Faith theology is its resilient emphasis on salvation's material consequences in the now: the time for the fulfillment of God's promises of health and prosperity is in this life and on this earth.[217] Because the focus is on the possibility of present and complete fulfillment of the Edenic life, the theology makes a form of "triumphalism."[218]

Previous chapters showed how the logic of global consumerism is embodied in the Word of Faith. The movement's view of time reveals another correlation with how time is understood in a world governed by market logic. There is a significant overlap between the Word of Faith's eschatology and the expectations of "instant and perpetual happiness"[219] found in the society of consumers.[220] Zygmunt Bauman observed how consumers live in a "pointillist" understanding of time, where each moment (now) provides the possibility for happiness; "the society of consumers . . . promise happiness in earthly life, and happiness here and now and in every successive 'now'; in short, an instant and perpetual happiness."[221] Such "nowist"[222] view of time in the society shaped by consumerism depends on an overrealized present: "The first principle of the religion of consumption is then this: immanent transformation. Things can and should become different, here and now."[223] Thus,

---

215. "The 'faith' which the Word of Faith movement seeks to restore is not fundamentally an attitude of eschatologically-oriented trust in the context of a fallen world. It is rather a return to the 'faith' of Adam, to the condition of an unfallen humanity" (Perriman, *FHP*, 139). See S. L. Ware, "Restorationism in Classical Pentecostalism," in *The New International Dictionary of Pentecostal and Charismatic Movements*, ed. Stanley M. Burgess and Eduard M. Van Der Maas, rev. and exp. edn. (Grand Rapids: Zondervan, 2003), e-book edition, "Restorationism in Classical Pentecostalism;" Tony Richie, "Ecumenical Theology," in *Routledge Handbook to Pentecostal Theology*, ed. Wolfgang Vondey, (London: Routledge, 2020), 378–88.

216. "*Endzeit gleicht Urzeit*" (the end of time resembles the beginning of time). I use *Jetztzeit* simply for "here-and-now" and not in reference to its use in critical theory.

217. "God's plan for us is that we rule and reign in life as kings: to rule and reign over circumstances, poverty, disease, and everything else that would hinder us . . . In the next life? No, in this life" (Hagin, *Believer's Authority*, 39); Hagin, *In Him*, 18.

218. Farah, *FTP*, 136; Vondey, *Pentecostalism*, 97.

219. Bauman, *Consuming Life*, 44.

220. Arvidsson, "Christianity and Consumer Culture," 3.

221. Bauman, *Consuming Life*, 44; Arvidsson, "Christianity and Consumer Culture," 3.

222. Bauman, *Consuming Life*, 35.

223. Arvidsson, "Christianity and Consumer Culture," 3.

the Word of Faith's view of an overrealized present fits how time is viewed in the society of consumers.

The pneumacentric trichotomist anthropology forms the context where it is possible to ascribe present perfection and total fulfillment of God's promises to the born-again human spirit.[224] That is, in their exalted anthropology, the human spirit is the space where God's promises are fully realized. The Word of Faith must, to sustain the fidelity of their beliefs, therefore, retain their particular pneumacentric view of humans as a unifying element, as all other spheres of human existence challenge the belief in total fulfillment of God's promises in the present. A pneumacentric and trichotomist division of humans serves as an apologetic element that confirms the truthfulness of the Word of Faith's eschatological claims, that is, even if no other of God's promises are completely realized, at least those pertaining to the human spirit are.

6.2.5.2 Overrealized Eschatology Foundational to their overrealized view of the present and the believer's location in time is the Word of Faith's "radical realised eschatology,"[225] which breeds triumphalist expectations of complete fulfillment of the promises of God's eschatological kingdom in the immediate present.[226] Such theology goes beyond a realized eschatology, which acknowledges an inaugurated and partial inbreaking of God's kingdom in the present to become "overrealised" in that it leaves no room for a time lag between the inauguration and consummation of the kingdom of God.[227] This so-called now-but-not-yet tension that the Word of Faith shuns is widely recognized by New Testament scholarship as the constitutive element of how the eschatological schema is presented in the biblical texts.[228] But not so in the Word of Faith worldview.[229] Instead, one of the most defining parts of their belief system is making the now-but not-yet dimension to be "almost obliterated."[230] Any argument that brings in either an irregularity in the absolute cause-and-effect system or simply a postponement in the fulfillment of God's

224. Perriman, *FHP*, 118.

225. Horn, *FRTR*, 110; Nel, *Prosperity Gospel*, Kindle edition, "The Sources of the Prosperity Message."

226. Horn, *FRTR*, 110–12; Ma, "Blessing," 277–8.

227. Farah, *FTP*, 163.

228. Fee, *Disease*, 30–4; Wright says that the now-but not-yet perspective "is one of the most obvious and significant characteristics of his [Paul's] worldview" (Wright, *PFG*, 548); Gordon Fee, *The First Epistle to the Corinthians* (Grand Rapids: Eerdmans, 1987), 172. See also Andrew Gabriel, "The Holy Spirit and Eschatology—with Implications for Ministry and the Doctrine of Spirit Baptism," *Journal of Pentecostal Theology* 25 (2016): 203–21.

229. Moo, "Divine Healing," 198, 203; Fee, *Disease*, 30–4; McConnell, *DG*, 208–11; Lindholm and Brosché, *Framgångsteologin*, 40–5; Farah, "Roots," 13; Ma, "Blessing," 277–8.

230. Farah, "Roots," 13.

promises is refused as either lack of faith or as faulty exegesis due to the corruptive influence of Satan and "religious" traditions.[231]

It is suggested that that Word of Faith's eschatology is "essentially an overreaction to the reductionism and defeatism—the 'poverty' gospel—that have characterised much Christian spirituality."[232] Perhaps, some say, an "eschatology which always sees the 'not yet' as 'already' may be no worse than one that sees the 'not yet' always as 'not yet.'"[233] However, though valid in itself, this argument is based on compartmentalizing the eschatology of the Word of Faith, and thus overlooks the larger context of their view of time and its theological implications. Overrealized eschatology easily leads to radical beliefs that are ungrounded in the biblical story and irresponsible practices which challenge the worldview's coherence and fidelity.[234] Word of Faith eschatology does not address the ethical problems of life in a now-but-not-yet-tension, and thus leaves Word of Faith adherents ill-equipped to handle suffering.[235] The global suffering caused by the Covid-19 pandemic posed a particular challenge to the Word of Faith belief system.[236] Word of Faith theology has little room to acknowledge "[t]he positive and necessary role of suffering"[237] in the Christian life, and an instrumental or pedagogical use of suffering is denied God (see Conclusion for more on suffering).[238]

231. "Everything has to do with the here and now, healing now, wealth now, prosperity now as the right and heritage of every believing Christian" (Farah, "Roots," 9).

232. Perriman, *FHP*, 135. See Anderson, *To the Ends*, 222–3; Biehl, "To Prosper," 135; Alexander, *Signs and Wonders*, 72–3. A dampening of early Pentecostal eschatological expectations of the soon coming of God's kingdom may also have contributed to a shift toward the "short-term apocalyptic vision" inherent in their overrealised eschatology (Cox, *Fire from Heaven*, 318).

233. Anderson, *Introduction to Pentecostalism*, 220.

234. Farah, *FTP*, 145, 158–64; McConnell, *DG*, 156–7; Ma, "Blessing," 277–8.

235. The Word of Faith "avoids the ethical struggles of our 'now-not-yet' life in the kingdom. It substitutes this tension for . . . triumphalist anthropology which fails to prepare believers for the inevitable moments of vulnerability and leaves them ill-equipped to deal with it in other people" (Edwards, "Ethical Dimensions," 94).

236. "Many of the principles of prosperity come unstuck in the face of misfortune, calamity and evil, and the hope is that the coronavirus has among other things exposed the areas of deficiency" (Asamoah-Gyadu, *Christianity and Faith*, Kindle edition, "Chapter 9: Charismatics and Coronavirus"). See also, J. Kwabena Asamoah-Gyadu, "Pentecostalism and Coronavirus: Reframing the Message of Health and Wealth in a Pandemic Era," *Spiritus: ORU Journal of Theology* 6, no. 1 (2021):157–74; Ukah, "Prosperity, Prophecy."

237. Anderson, *To the Ends*, 222.

238. Anderson, *Introduction to Pentecostalism*, 218; da Silva, *Framgångsteologin*, 63. See Keith Warrington, "Healing and Suffering in the Bible," *International Review of Mission* 95, no. 376/377 (January/April 2006): 154–64.

6.2.5.3 Ethereal Eschaton The Word of Faith holds to the popular view of the eschaton as the destruction of creation and a disembodied state in a spiritual heaven for the saved.[239] Yet, the eschatological convictions in the Word of Faith contain unresolved tensions that challenge the worldview's coherence. The dispensational framework for Word of Faith theology that expects a final rapturous salvation out of the material world does not fit their optimistic materialism.[240] It seems that their commitment to overrealized material eschatology is partly a deduction based on their pneumacentric ontology with the premise of their belief in the final state of believers as immaterial. Their pneumacentric ontology causes tensions with their emphasis on how Jesus' redemption was material in nature, that is, salvation is not just from immaterial sin but also sickness and poverty. But the fulfillment of such material promises of salvation cannot logically be in a disembodied heavenly eternity, which is the final goal in the Word of Faith worldview-story. So, the conclusion comes as a deduction of necessity: since the future state is spiritual in the ethereal "heaven," all of salvation's material promises *must* find their fulfillment in this present, embodied life.[241] If not fulfilled in the now, there will be no other opportunity for them to be realized. Since, in Word of Faith thinking, "the silver and gold are not all here for the devil and his crowd,"[242] it follows that the abundance must be for the believer's present life—or significant parts of Jesus' redemption would be in vain.[243]

The shift in Word of Faith theology from the traditional Christian hope of "treasures in heaven" to expectations of this-worldly blessings is significant.[244] Such optimistic materialism challenges many traditional interpretations (inclusive of traditional Pentecostal), which view salvation in purely spiritual terms and often downplays the value of material creation, or at least, its part in redemption.[245] Much traditional eschatology (often inspired by forms of Platonism) interprets the biblical promises of restored prosperity and health as referring to immaterial

239. See Section 3.3.1.5. It is striking that the Word of Faith's belief in the final immaterial state of the believer as being a saved soul in heaven is one of the only parts of traditional Christian narrative that they have adopted wholesale without any alteration.

240. See Horn, *FRTR*, 56–7.

241. The Word of Faith expectancy of an "end-time transfer of wealth" is best explained in this context. The promises of restored material abundance in especially the Old Testament prophets cannot in the Word of Faith understanding be in the eschaton, because it is only spiritual and so the promises must be fulfilled before the parousia.

242. Hagin, *Biblical Keys*, e-book edition, "Chapter 3."

243. "In this form of gospel, sacrificial poverty is not a virtue since it denies everything that Christ has won through his death, that is, prosperity for the born-again believers" (Hunt, "Winning Ways," 334).

244. "I'm more concerned about the life that now is than I am about the life that is to come" (Hagin, *Classic Sermons*, 12).

245. Perriman, *FHP*, 115; Middleton, *New Heaven*.

blessings in the afterlife. Theologians holding to such a "spiritual" interpretation of salvation are quick to judge the Word of Faith for materialistic motives that cause them to trade spiritual treasures for earthly wealth.[246] Still, it must be recognized that the Word of Faith's willingness to include (parts of) the material creation in God's drama of salvation (for some time) is a move toward a holistic eschatology of the redemption of creation. This view arguably lies closer to biblical eschatology than the narratives which portray salvation as only affecting the immaterial domains in the present and concluding with the final escape from the destruction of creation to an other-worldly existence.[247] The Word of Faith's step toward a holistic view of salvation that includes creation should be welcomed as a movement in the right direction, while at the same time recognizing that their eschatological scope, to agree with the biblical story, needs to embrace all of creation and human embodiment for a perpetual time and speak of the healing rather than the consumption of creation.[248] In fact, if Word of Faith would welcome a holistic eschatology that allows for the ultimate fulfillment of redemption's material consequences to be in the future of a renewed material cosmos and in resurrected human bodies, it would lessen their need to press an overrealized material eschatology. The Bible's holistic eschatology offers the Word of Faith a way to make their worldview more coherent as well as increasing its fidelity.

Conclusion

This chapter applied Wright's worldview-element of ultimate beliefs to the Word of Faith, using his five worldview-questions to analyze the movement's theological presuppositions. Here I note four critical insights that the analysis offers into the Word of Faith worldview which add nuance and complexity and speak to the analytical, evaluative, and comparative goals.

First, the Word of Faith has a thoroughly enchanted and supernatural view of the world. The spiritual dimension is not an additional element but makes up the very essence of what they believe about the world. This enchanted view becomes evident in their pneumacentric ontology, spirit-causality, spirit-epistemology, and spiritual activism. Hence, the Word of Faith's worldview is well described as a spirit-worldview. This is an essential yet ironic insight, considering the material emphasis of prosperity and health and how they repeatedly are being critiqued for blatant materialism. Nevertheless, the movement's ultimate beliefs require that we understand the Word of Faith as foremost a spirit-worldview which brings material consequences.

246. E.g., Hunt, *Seduction*, 223–5.
247. Anderson, *Introduction to Pentecostalism,* 219; Middleton, *New Heaven.*
248. Swoboda, "Prosperity or Posterity."

Second, the Word of Faith worldview is occupied with the possibilities of a transformed immediate future. The Word of Faith offers a settled soteriological reality, where a radical reading of Jesus' finished work makes redemption to be fully complete and all blessings presently available as the believer's rights.[249] This generates an optimistic theological outlook, characterized by the compression of the "not-yet" into the "now" in an overrealized eschatology, the sense of personal entitlement as well as the spiritual activism geared toward the appropriation of one's blessings through the instrumental use of faith.

Third, the worldview of the Word of Faith over-privileges human agency.[250] The God of the Word of Faith is limited in sovereignty, passive in action, and predictable due to reductionist goodness and spiritual laws. A dualistic cosmology, on the other hand, makes Satan powerful and active. But beyond both God and Satan stands the believer's self, whose action, empowered by the exalted anthropology and the instrumental usage of faith, is determinative for victory. As such, the worldview of the Word of Faith makes a certain form of humanism that shapes an egocentric theology.[251] Not in the sense of being necessarily egoistic (as one often seeks blessings to be a blessing to others),[252] but of taking the human ego as the ultimate starting and finishing points in theologizing.[253]

Fourth, the Word of Faith worldview is shaped by iconic and indexical rationalities to the exclusion of symbolic logic. As made clear in their pneumacentric ontology and pneumatic causality, Word of Faith parses the world in terms of like-like and cause-and-effect relationships. Word of Faith theology is systemic, interested in the absolute, causative, and predictable.[254] Their reality virtually excludes the symbolic.[255] That is, there is little room for symbolic relations between sign-vehicles and their objects, one that can only be defined by convention.[256] A theology that accommodates the dimension of symbol embraces paradox as a natural aspect of life and motivates suspension of any absolute and cause-and-effect judgments to a realm of mystery beyond

---

249. Walton, "Blessed and Highly Favored," 110; Bowler, *Blessed*, 43–4. E.g., "everything is provided for in the spiritual realm" (Hagin, *Prevailing Prayer*, 3).

250. Wrenn argues that this personal fault-finding is parallel to the logic of neoliberalism, both movements "overascribe agency to the individual" (Wrenn, "Consecrating Capitalism," 429).

251. Farah, "Roots," 6.

252. Harrison, *RR*, 69; Anderson, "Prosperity Message," 79–80.

253. Word of Faith can thus be described as "ego-theology" (Mikael Stenhammar, "Vem tar ansvar för 'egoteologin' mitt ibland oss?" *Dagen*, May 3, 2016).

254. Farah, *FTP*, 135, 144–5; "Word of Faith has superimposed . . . [a] prelapsarian model, in which there is no margin of error or unpredictability, on the New Testament description of faith" (Perriman, *FHP*, 139).

255. See Farah, *FTP*, 135–6, 152–7.

256. See Section 4.1.2.

human penetration.[257] Theological paradox is seen by the Word of Faith as a weakness and an embarrassing problem they must solve.[258] Hence, Word of Faith theology exchanges paradox and mystery for dualism and triumphalism.

257. Symbolic logic holds that each experience is unique and that no predetermined system of cause-and-effect can explain human pain. A worldview catering to symbolic logic leaves room for the unpredictable, paradox, and mystery in human experience and for God's pedagogical use of suffering; "Theology always lives within the realm of mystery" (Farah, *FTP*, 135). It calls for a vulnerable faith in God that releases human control in the recognition that suffering can only be interpreted through the illumination of the Holy Spirit, available in fullness at the eschaton.

258. Hagin, *God's Word*, 19.

CONCLUSION

Employing Wright's worldview-model, this book tested if the Word of Faith is a distinct worldview and (if so) to identify its characteristics, its essential parts, identity-carrying features, and inner logic. Of significance is how the completed worldview-analysis validates the claim that the Word of Faith is a distinct worldview. I have been able to show that the Word of Faith operates as a complex and structured worldview with a unique theological story that interrelates with a set of signs and practices which together generate a set of ultimate beliefs. Following Wright's definition of worldview, the argument of this project is confirmed. The concise picture arising from this worldview-analysis is that the Word of Faith worldview is characterized by a unique mixture of iconic logic, indexical logic, pragmatic logic, polarized logic, and market logic. This mix is narrated in the Adam plot and expressed in an instrumental use of faith made effective by words and gifts to cause a direct correspondence between present reality and Eden's perfection, imagined in ideals shaped by market consumerism and measured by attained prosperity and health.

The strength of this concise definition is that it draws together the most critical aspects revealed by Wright's elements. The worldview's narrative core is captured in the Adam plot's drive to return to Eden and the pragmatic logic and polarized logic in the Eden Redeemed story. The semiotic analysis shows the instrumental function of the faith of God, the iconic expectancy of a perfected representation of Eden, and the indexical role of prosperity and health. The analysis of praxis reveals the influence of market logic in shaping the image of Eden and the expectancy of the indexical practices of speaking positive confessions and sowing money seeds to carry causative power. The propositional analysis shows how overrealized eschatology expects fulfillment of Eden in the immediate present through faith interpreted by a pragmatic logic.

This definition allows for the variations evident in the local manifestations of the Word of Faith. I do not mean that every adaption embodies all aspects of the Word of Faith worldview brought out in this book. Nor do I deny that individuals selectively filter and absorb parts of the worldview into their mindsets. Rather, unity in the diverse expressions—which doubtless draw from a variety of worldviews— should be sought in the formative influences from the Word of Faith worldview. Claiming that commonality among a diversity of expressions is found in shared worldview-features is not to impose a foreign mold, to deny particularities, or to simplify complex phenomena. It does not mean that all Christian groups that evidence "pluralistic shades of prosperity"[1] should automatically be categorized as the Word of Faith. One overall gain from this work is that the Word of Faith's prosperity theme is interconnected with narrative, semiotic, practical, and propositional worldview-elements. Such world-perceiving framework needs to be analyzed before a group, and its prosperity emphasis can adequately be classified. Further research has to clarify what other sorts of worldviews apart from the Word of Faith also give rise to a prosperity emphasis in Pentecostal and other Christian groups. Further investigation is also required to measure the level to which specific groups are influenced by and express the worldview of the Word of Faith. Since worldviews are in a constant state of flux, later research can identify how the Word of Faith worldview continues to change. Of interest would be to examine if there are individuals and groups that have lived out of the Word of Faith worldview but now have shifted into other worldviews.[2]

Since the Word of Faith worldview is—like all worldviews—ultimately a human construct (despite the Word of Faith's claim to direct revelation), evaluating the worldview on its own terms is important. This is especially necessary since the

---

1. Yong, "Typology," 16.

2. Particularly interesting would be to investigate the changes in Ulf Ekman's worldview (or "mindset" to use Wright's term) after his leaving the Word of Faith to join Roman Catholicism (see Coleman, "From Excess to Encompassment"). See also Kate Bowler's distinction between "hard" and "soft" prosperity—which has gained usage in current studies—raises the question if these are expressions of changes in the worldview or merely a change in rhetorical representations (Bowler, *Blessed*, 7–8, 110, 116, 118, 125. See, e.g., Muir, "Sounds Mega," 139). That more research is needed is supported by her labeling Creflo Dollar as "soft," who by all measures fit the characteristics of the worldview presented here, which she would classify as "hard." Though not applicable to Dollar, it could also be argued that the "soft" approach is an indication of people who are also drawing from other worldviews, which stand in tension to, and thus limit, the hard consequences of the indexical logic of the Word of Faith worldview. Bowler writes, "The theological language of the prosperity gospel was also changing. 'Hard prosperity,' a term I use to describe a heavily instrumental language of instantaneous results, was giving way to the predominance of 'soft prosperity,' a gentler and often therapeutic account of how faith turns words into material blessings. Hard prosperity ruled the 1980s, but soft prosperity was better suited for the 1990s and its therapeutic turn toward the spiritual significance of psychology" (Bowler, "Successful Calling," 194). Inviting further studies is also what sources shape the Word of Faith worldview. Especially interesting is to examine the claim by the Lausanne Community that local Word of Faith manifestations are a result of a merger with non-Christian worldviews (other than the market worldview) [Lausanne Theology Working Group, "Statement on the Prosperity," §7]. E.g., see Lawrence Nwankwo, "'You Have Received the Spirit of power . . .' (2 Tim. 1:7) Reviewing the Prosperity Message in the Light of a Theology of Empowerment," *Journal of the European Pentecostal Theological Association* 22, no. 1 (2002): 56–77, accessed April 7, 2021, http://dx.doi.org/10.1179/jep.2002.22.1.005.

Word of Faith has suffered sharp and sometimes unjust criticism due to critics not first giving the worldview a fair hearing. To evaluate the Word of Faith worldview, I use a set of three criteria developed by the worldview scholars Brian Walsh and Richard Middleton, on whom Wright draws in developing his own worldview-model: (1) fidelity to reality, (2) internal coherence, and (3) openness to correction.[3] These criteria have shaped my analysis of the elements in the preceding chapters, and I now direct these to the cumulative findings of this book to make an initial assessment of the Word of Faith worldview as a whole. More research is needed to develop the points raised. After this, I discuss in a comparative perspective how the Word of Faith worldview relates to Pentecostalism.

External Fidelity

The first question is if the Word of Faith worldview is coherent with reality. The fidelity of the Word of Faith worldview is strengthened when it guides life and gives meaning to human experiences. But its fidelity is challenged if it either absolutizes or omits any significant part of life and the world. I have noted tensions and conflicts with reality in the worldview's elements in the previous chapters and emphasize here the most critical insights.

When fidelity speaks of how the worldview fits the adherents' subjective view of reality, the worldwide growth evidences how the Word of Faith offers many Christians a meaningful framework that makes sense of present experiences, guides their lives, and speaks to felt needs. This contribution should not be taken lightly as simply accommodating believer's selfishness and greed. The worldview's attention to material salvation and promises of empowerment for this-worldly success carries a "ring of truth"[4] for adherents living within global consumerism, more so than many other Christian options rooted in dualistic paradigms that subsumes the material under other-worldly outlooks. The worldview's optimism, exalted anthropology, and causative logic are meaningful in life and offer guidance to people needing hope, self-worth, and upgraded agency. Fidelity to subjective reality offers critical insights into what makes this "one of the most widespread manifestations of Christianity on earth today."[5]

Nevertheless, the fidelity of the Word of Faith worldview is challenged by its dualistic privileging of the spiritual realm as the really real, its approach to suffering, its characterization of the physical world as law-governed, and with infinite resources and the limited role of the believer in their social worlds. The fidelity of the Word of Faith worldview is challenged by its pneumacentric ontology, which absolutizes the spiritual realm and its overrealized view of time.

---

3. Walsh and Middleton, *TV*, 36–9. See Wright, *NTPG*, 112; Wright, *PFG*, 27.

4. J. B. Phillips, *Ring of Truth: A Translator's Testimony* (London: Hodder and Stoughton, 1967).

5. Wright, "Calling the Church Back," 193.

In the really real world of the spiritual realm, the believer is already back in Eden. All evidence to the contrary only arises out of the lesser-real realm of human material existence and experience. The worldview's dualistic epistemology that makes contradictory, experiential data communicated by the mind or the body to be taken as "lies"[6] that oppose the really real spiritual realm, challenges the fidelity of the worldview, and speaks to problems of coherence and ideological tendencies (explored in the following text). For believers to bring Eden into physical manifestation, they must subordinate the natural realm under what they already know through revelation knowledge to be real and present in the spiritual realm. Faith thus requires "corresponding action," which means that the believer speaks and acts in accordance with what they know to be true in the really real spiritual realm. This leads to a catch 22, because the believer can only attain, for example, health by speaking as if their healing is a present fact—"I *am* healed"— while all natural evidences speak of ongoing sickness.

The acid test for the Word of Faith worldview is how it handles disappointments and suffering. According to Walsh and Middleton: "any worldview, if it is to be both biblical and illuminative of what human life is really like, must be a worldview that comprehends our brokenness and suffering."[7] Suffering plays a key role in the Word of Faith worldview; the focus is set on elevating all bodily, mental, and material suffering in this life. Its unique form of theodicy is probably the worldview's greatest attraction. The outstanding promises of the Word of Faith to deliver Edenic bounty and bliss to the one who practices faith do not fit the experience of every adherent. The lack of agreement between the worldview's iconic promises and lived reality speaks to the need for increased fidelity in the worldview to handle experiences contradictory with its vision of a redeemed Eden. The worldview's parsing of the world through the lens of faith's causative power to affect a direct correspondence between present reality and Eden's perfection makes human weakness and limitations embarrassing problems to its optimistic outlook. The indexical logic that reads prosperity and health as signs of faith makes the worldview to add judgment to pain when a believer experiences prolonged suffering as their trials signify a lack of faith. The "messiness" of human experience—which is all but absolute and predictable—and the implicit paradox in human suffering contrast with the Word of Faith's law-governed causality, their image of God shaped by reductionist goodness, and their polarized logic, which favors opposed and mutually exclusive categories. Suffering is thus deterred from serving the narrative role of Helper for the believers to accomplish their Task. Symbolic interpretations and the richer biblical characterizations of suffering are excluded. For example, prosperity and health and their opposites of poverty and sickness are interpreted as "blessings" (Helpers) and "curses" (Opponents). Such radical division does not embrace the multifaceted roles prosperity/poverty and health/sickness play in Scripture and human experience. History and biography

---

6. Savelle, *If Satan Can't Steal*, e-book edition, "He Can't Keep Your Goods."

7. Walsh, *Subversive Christianity*, 10. See Olthuis, "A vision of and for Love."

are rich with examples of how these entities can play opposite roles: prosperity can be destructive and sickness can bring new vistas. Only a symbolic interpretation of suffering may be faithful to reality and the biblical texts.

Beyond suffering, the fit between the Word of Faith worldview and reality is limited by the restricted view of the believer's narrative Task of ruling the world. Because significant areas of the believers' social world, such as racism, poverty reduction, social justice, and consumerism, are left unaddressed, these challenge the worldview's comprehensive capacity. This vacuum makes the Word of Faith to draw meaning and direction from other worldviews, which often results in tensions with their own worldview and challenges to Pentecostal distinctives.

The fidelity of the Word of Faith worldview is also lessened by how it represents the physical world. The nonhuman, physical world resists full predictability and the Newtonian characterizations that arise out of the Word of Faith's commitments to law-governed pneumatic causality.

Eden Redeemed interprets the believer's narrative Task of ruling and increasing partly in terms of consuming the world and celebrating conspicuous consumption. Yet, depicting the earth as having unlimited resources ready to be extracted does not fit the reality of a finite planet. The environmental crisis, caused to a large degree by the "growthism" of global consumerism, challenges the worldview's capacity to encompass nonhuman creation in long-term and meaningful ways.

Internal Coherence

The second criteria to test the Word of Faith worldview is that of internal coherence. This aspect tests if the Word of Faith offers a coherent vision of the world or if it is fragmented or containing mutually exclusive features. Coherence is either strengthened or challenged depending on the level of internal unity or friction within the worldview-elements and in their interaction with each other. It is important to note how the Word of Faith worldview's storied structure and the often seamless interconnection between the worldview-elements form a system that communicates a sense of "clarity and coherence"[8] to its adherents. The polarized logic and a reductionist view of God's goodness deconstructs mystery and provides bold and easy solutions to complex problems.

Yet, the sense of coherence generated by the worldview is contested by the definition and role of prosperity and inclusion of market logic and practices, the characterization of God, and the ideal of biblical adherence. If suffering is the greatest challenge to the worldview's external fidelity, prosperity offers the definitive problem to its inner coherence. I noted tensions at the fundamental level of whether to define prosperity as absolute or relative. At present, this conflict is unresolved, and it has a fragmentary effect on the worldview. But a more significant

8. Walton, "Stop Worrying," 127.

tension, which is perhaps the very breaking point for the worldview's inner coherence, is the discovery made by this study that the worldview is conflicted on prosperity's role. The Eden Redeemed story's portrayal of prosperity as Helper is challenged by the competing prosperity narrative. Because the competing prosperity narrative recasts prosperity as the believer's Task in the world, it makes the worldview to be deeply conflicted. As long as the internal problems in the movement that empowers the competing prosperity narrative are unaddressed, the Word of Faith does not offer a coherent vision of the world but stands as a fractured worldview.

The worldview's relation with the market causes other problems beyond the recasting of prosperity's role. The inclusion of market logic and practices, especially its aesthetic ideals and conspicuous consumption, leads to incoherent practices, such as critiquing the fallen system of the world while at the same time promoting and profiting from the same system. An acute question for the Word of Faith is how (or if) they can make use of market practices without their worldview being shaped by the same. The present unreflective use of market logic and practices threatens the worldview from within.

The worldview's characterizations of God and faith contain incoherencies. Their ultimate belief in indexical, law-governed pneumatic causality causes tensions with their characterization of God as personal and sovereign. The incompatibility between unmerited grace and "merited" reward in the indexical logic leaves unresolved theological tensions in the image of God. The semiotic complexities discussed in Chapter 4 challenge the worldview's coherence. The sign of faith, particularly that the same sign-vehicle signifies different objects, challenges the coherences of the worldview as it makes a confusing mix of what is familiar in Christian tradition and with new, unfamiliar concepts; the worldview's emphasis on an objectified and instrumental faith *of* God stands in tension with the emphasis on a personal and relational faith *in* God.

Their explicitly stated ideal of holding the Word as the ultimate source for belief and practice causes internal conflict with a hermeneutical framework formed by Eden Redeemed and revelation knowledge mediated by spiritual experiences and charismatic leaders. Eden Redeemed is incoherent and causes frictions with the Bible's basic storyline, leading into resurrected humans in embodied life in God's restored creation. The eschatological vision of the Word of Faith, which expects the eternal life of the believer's soul in an immaterial heaven, weakens the worldview's coherence. Neither their optimistic, material soteriology nor Eden Redeemed's basic drive of placing the believer back in Eden to rule and reign find closure in their final ethereal vision.

Bringing the two criteria of fidelity and coherence together reveals how the Word of Faith worldview is caught in a conflict between the two. Prolonged sickness or poverty exposes the problem that to remain coherent the worldview has to interpret these indexically as ultimately rooted in a lack of faith, but in doing so, the worldview compromises its fidelity as reality shows a number of reasons for sickness and poverty. Encountering such problems trigger either cognitive dissonance or require heavy filtering by the adherents.

Openness to Correction

The last evaluative question tests how open for correction the Word of Faith worldview is. This probes its recognition of finitude and receptiveness for refinement and revision. The criterion arises out of a Christian rationality committed to alter its view of the world to fit reality and revelation and to accept correction from worldviews that give better expression to these dynamics. It is not shaped by relativistic ideals of all worldviews being equal in truth and value. Since the Word of Faith presents itself as the best available Christian worldview, this question is important. The Word of Faith's hegemonic power to function as a potential ideology is a cause of concern that deserves further investigations.[9] I understand "ideology" here as the totalitarian function of a worldview that does not recognize its finitude and seeks to dominate all other worldviews.

The worldview's claim to enjoy unique access to the really real spiritual realm by its revelation knowledge evidences strong reification tendencies.[10] Because the worldview's human origins are concealed, the world is presented as "that's just the way things are,"[11] with little encouragement to critical evaluation on the part of its recipients or openness for self-reflection and correction. The worldview has shown little evidence of responding to outside criticism, even when such has been well grounded.

The Word of Faith's claims to be the culmination of God's revelation to the church easily develops ideological tendencies. As noted earlier, their commitment to revelation knowledge makes the worldview to resist contradictory empirical data as mere sense knowledge that has to be subdued; to press the worldview over experienced reality is an expressed objective within the worldview. Another ideological tendency is the privileged position awarded the charismatic leader. Their position of embodying the worldview places them beyond critique; to oppose the leader is to oppose the reality which they represent. The worldview's propensity to impose itself over other worldviews is also seen in how it actively censures expressions of human experiences of suffering, fear, and failure. This censorship stifles authenticity in personal relationships and reduces the scope of human experience that the Word of Faith worldview allows to be expressed. Since Word of Faith semiosis positions economic and material well-being in an indexical relationship to faith and under the power of the believer, the worldview requires

---

9. See Perriman, *FHP*, 232–3.

10. "Reification is the apprehension of human phenomena as if they were things, that is, in non-human or possibly superhuman terms . . . the apprehension of the products of human activity as if they were something else than human products. . . . The reified world is, by definition, a dehumanized world" (Berger and Luckmann, *Social Construction*, 106). By drawing on Berger and Luckmann's concept of reification, it does not follow that all worldviews by virtue of being human constructs are by necessity disconnected from external reality or objective truth (see Naugle, *Worldview*, 178–80, 331–9).

11. Naugle, *Worldview*, 179.

that there must be a justification for their absence; there is nothing like innocent suffering, because someone must be at fault.[12] This reasoning nurtures a fault-finding mechanism to discover what is hindering the blessings from manifesting. Such a process speaks to an oppressive tendency in the Word of Faith worldview and is personally destructive. Adherents experiencing cognitive dissonance within the Word of Faith are often left with the choice of embracing the worldview even more resolutely or abandoning it altogether for a new worldview. Further work is invited to make comparative analyses of the Word of Faith worldview's hegemonic impact on other worldviews.

For the Word of Faith worldview to be a sound alternative and to be a positive power in Pentecostalism, the issues of fidelity, coherence, and openness to correction need to be further explored and addressed in the relationship to Pentecostalism.

The Word of Faith Worldview and Pentecostalism

I do not intend a full comparison between the Word of Faith and Pentecostalism but through the worldview-analysis offer conceptual tools for further exploring the relationship and point out key areas where the Word of Faith worldview strengthens and challenges Pentecostal distinctives. This is important because Pentecostal scholarship is increasingly aware that some Word of Faith features may be unique gifts of the Spirit that could propel the growth and rejuvenation of not just Pentecostalism but also global Christianity. Yet, it is equally observed that for the Word of Faith to be such a positive influence, these features must be properly revised.

In forwarding a comparative perspective on the Word of Faith, it is crucial that critics discard stereotypes and reductions for a thorough and charitable understanding of the Word of Faith worldview that acknowledges its contributions and challenges. Critics must also allow that their own worldview is potentially influenced by similar logic as the Word of Faith—only taking different and perhaps more subtle expressions. Western readers of the Word of Faith, in particular, should be aware of possible hypocrisy caused by their middle-class privileges.[13]

An important comparative question is if the Word of Faith worldview conceptually belongs within Pentecostalism. Given the historical roots and the present part of the Word of Faith *movement* in Pentecostalism (see Introduction), this question means to ask whether the Word of Faith *worldview* should be classified as Pentecostal or not. To fully answer the question requires work in defining Pentecostal worldview distinctives using the elements of Wright's worldview-model. Here I can only offer a preliminary reply based on what current scholarship points to as the characteristics of a Pentecostal worldview. There are

---

12. Perriman, *FHP*, 42.
13. Yong, "Typology," 20–1.

no findings of this worldview-analysis that contest the inclusion of the Word of Faith within a Pentecostal orientation to the world. Most of the significant features of what current scholarship say define a Pentecostal worldview are also found in the Word of Faith.[14] Yet, this response is not to say that all features of the Word of Faith's worldview sit comfortably within Pentecostalism, only that the worldview is better classified as Pentecostal in contrast to the options of non-Pentecostal or even non-Christian.

Exploring how the Word of Faith worldview contributes to Pentecostalism invites further research. Here I can only note the most significant ways that emerge from the preceding analysis: the worldview's interrogative mode, positive image of God and humans, its practice of Pentecostal enchantment and holistic soteriology. By pointing out these contributions, I do not deny that problems remain to be addressed or that Pentecostalism completely lacks these aspects without the Word of Faith. The Word of Faith contributes to Pentecostalism by engaging the world in an interrogative mode. Their hunger to see more of God's power and a Christianity that "works" generate an inquisitiveness that makes them, like a Socratic gadfly, to raise probing questions—some challenging established worldviews and become so charged for conservative scholarship as needing repeated counsel to exercise temperance.[15] An important area requiring further work is for Pentecostal scholarship to engage the questions raised by the Word of Faith worldview. Entering in dialogue with their questions ensures that the researcher does not get entangled in the Word of Faith's answers—which is the domain of much previous academic work—but to discern in their queries the potential wind of the Spirit to blow away old paradigms for fresh visions that could revitalize stagnant orthodoxy. For example, their exalted anthropology expressed through a royal, Spirit-empowered vocation within creation raises important questions on how the human royal-priestly vocation can be narrated to be more representative of God's economy of salvation.[16]

14. See Smith, *Thinking in Tongues*, 17–47.
15. E.g., Perriman, *FHP,* 117, 57, 136.
16. Among other questions the Word of Faith asks are: Did God share sovereignty over creation with Adam? Is there a spiritual dimension to the Adamic vocation? Did God intend humans to share in Godself? Is there an instrumental aspect to faith? Are there ways to presently experience more of the "not-yet"? Can human words and thoughts affect external reality? Can the Spirit give new revelation beyond what is written in the Bible? Is there an economic side to salvation? Is there a dimension of reciprocity in giving to God? Does God want prosperity for every person? How can wealth be amassed in righteous ways and be used for God's work? Is it good for a Christian to have material abundance and comfort in this life? Should Christian leaders be prosperous? It does not mean that by allowing these and other questions to be heard, their questions need to be accepted without reformulation. But when taken seriously as a starting point for theological conversations, the questions can lead into venues that enrich Pentecostalism.

Beyond their interrogative mode, the Word of Faith enriches Pentecostalism with its positive image of God and humans. The Word of Faith presents a "good" God who is lavishly generous and wants abundant life, health, and flourishing for everyone in this life. Harvey Cox concludes, "God wants people to be well fed and clothed. He wants us all to 'prosper.' . . . On this point the much maligned 'prosperity gospel' has it right."[17] Pentecostalism benefits from the emphasis on God's holistic love and care, which generates a high view of human value and potential. Believers are authorized and empowered to develop themselves and their economic, social, vocational worlds in a positive work ethic as a response to God's generous character. The economic focus of being "blessed to be a blessing" also makes the Word of Faith to exemplify substantial altruism that strengthens attitudes of generosity in Pentecostalism. The Word of Faith's positive image of God and human potential makes nothing impossible, which can generate this-worldly hope into Pentecostalism's eschatologically oriented hope. When their emphasis is on an uncompromised faith *in* God to fulfill God's promises regardless of contrary circumstances, it contributes vitality and strength to Pentecostalism.

The Word of Faith worldview, formed by pneumacentric ontology, places the believer in a thoroughly enchanted, supernaturalistic world that leaves no dimension of human life beyond the interventions of God and the spiritual realm. Their belief in the world saturated by the Spirit offers a robust contribution to Pentecostalism's enchanted worldview.[18] The Word of Faith embodies a Pentecostal enchantment in ways that exceed many other groups who self-identify as Pentecostals but are drifting away from an enchanted worldview and decreasing the practices of spiritual gifts and their expectations of God's interventions. In practicing enchantment (e.g., in speaking positive confessions, sowing money seeds, practice of the charismata, and fervent expectations of miracles), the Word of Faith draws upon and develops Pentecostalism's pragmatic approach to human need by offering hope of a transformed life through implementable steps.[19]

The Word of Faith worldview also strengthens and develops the holism of Pentecostalism's soteriology by going beyond the classical affirmation of physical healing in the atonement to include a wholly material economic dimension in salvation. In this way, the Word of Faith deconstructs the dualistic division between spiritual and material while drawing on Pentecostalism's resources to

---

17. Cox, *Market*, 70.

18. "Enchantment" is used here positively in relation to Pentecostalism following Smith (Smith, *Thinking in Tongues*, 39–41). "The central theme of the early Pentecostal worldview was the persistent emphasis upon the supernatural (charismatic) manifestations of the Spirit within the worshipping community" [Kenneth J. Archer, *A Pentecostal Hermeneutic: Spirit, Scripture and Community* (Cleveland: CPT Press, 2009), 42, see 44]. "the Word of Faith movement . . . teaches and encourages its followers to apply [its worldview] in the most mundane situations, infusing the profane with sacred significance in their lives" (Harrison, *RR*, 58).

19. Anderson, *Introduction to Pentecostalism*, 192, 203.

offer a holistic soteriology that speaks to felt material needs. For the Word of Faith to enrich Pentecostalism, however, it is of critical importance that adjustments are made to counter the influence of the competing prosperity narrative that threatens to make personal prosperity the foremost objective. Pentecostalism's full gospel motif can be significantly enriched by the Word of Faith's addition of Jesus as "provider" to the fourfold/fivefold narrative. For their current understandings of prosperity to become the new element of "Jesus the provider" in the full gospel narrative, the worldview-story must adopt the full gospel's Christocentric focus and be pruned from, among other things, its entanglement with the worldview's iconic logic, indexical logic, and market logic. Developing the theme of Jesus as provider to fit the full gospel narrative creates a platform for promising dialogue between Pentecostal theology and the Word of Faith.

Beyond strengthening Pentecostalism's identity, as this research shows, the Word of Faith worldview has flaws that challenge Pentecostal distinctives. Since these offer particularly important areas for further research, I slightly expand this discussion. I do not intend to repeat the sometimes significant theological points that place the Word of Faith in conflict with Pentecostalism noted here and in other studies, nor to gloss over the very disturbing ethical problems within parts of the movement. Without restating what was discussed under the aforementioned evaluative questions, here I examine the most critical aspects that arise from the worldview-analysis, that is, problems in the Adam plot, the dominance of iconic and indexical logic, and the influence of market logic.

Problems in the Adam Plot

Since the Adam plot shapes the Word of Faith worldview and their goal of achieving an iconic, direct correspondence with Eden in the now, weaknesses in the plot have far-reaching consequences. Deviances from the biblical story in their reading of the plot grow increasingly problematic as the story unfolds. Exactly how the Adam plot differs from the biblical accounts and challenges Pentecostal distinctives requires more research.

First, one problem for Pentecostalism is the restorationist impulse in the Adam plot. The worldview's narrative drive directed at a return to Eden challenges Pentecostal commitments to the dynamic, future-oriented role of the Spirit in God's economy of salvation. "The centrality of the Edenic model of restoration makes Pentecost something of a non-event."[20] It leads to a restrictive view of the Spirit that effectively subsumes the Spirit's role in creation, redemption, and new creation. More particularly, the Adam plot leads to a pneumatic deficiency in Eden Redeemed, which subverts a Pentecostal emphasis on the Spirit's role in birthing the world made new. The narrative structure of their worldview-story that purports an instrumentalized conception of the Spirit as Helper advances a restrictive pneumatology also in the believer's life, which stands in conflict with

20. Perriman, *FHP*, 116.

Pentecostalism's emphasis on the Spirit's freedom and human dependency on the Spirit.

Second, the reductions made in their pneumatology is countered by the Adam plot's exalted anthropology. Pentecostalism is challenged by the reading of Adam as essentially a spirit being who shared God's very nature and could operate like God. Having recovered Adam's authority, believers are empowered to act independently from discerning the Spirit's direction in each unique situation as long as they follow God's expressed promises. The Word of Faith's interpretation of Adamic authority also challenges Pentecostal paradigms of servant-leadership, the Spirit's work from below with "preferential option for the marginalized"[21] and the prophethood of all believers.

Third, Adam's dominion mandate interpreted within a vertical power matrix places Adam on top of the world as its owner. The commodified and almost autonomous conception of Adamic authority fails to fully recognize human dependence and need for submission to God's continuing ownership and sovereignty over all creation. The Adam plot makes Jesus the iconic representation of prelapsarian Adam, which challenges Pentecostal characterizations of Jesus's uniqueness and his present role as active and sovereign king, on whom the believer is continuously and ultimately dependent and whose actions cannot be fully predicted or directed. Pentecostalism is also challenged by the Adam plot's tendency to imagine aspects of the God-human relationship in impersonal terms.

Dominance of Iconic Logic and Indexical Logic

The dominance of iconic and indexical logic in the Word of Faith worldview challenges Pentecostalism. Indexical logic, involving faith and spiritual laws, places the Spirit within human control and predictability, in a passive and reactive role to human practices.

The Word of Faith's semiotic logic that demands sign-vehicles to be big according to market standards to represent God introduces an oppressive logic and a bias to those who can display such, that is, the world's rich and powerful. This kind of iconic logic thus subverts Pentecostal distinctives that holds what appears as weak and insignificant in the eyes of the world can be both beautiful and powerful in God's eyes.

Placing prosperity and health in an indexical relation to faith also challenges Pentecostalism. To read the quality of believers' faith from its projection in their economic and bodily conditions challenges Pentecostal identity formation grounded in the participation of the Spirit.[22] The symbolic deficiency in the Word of Faith worldview that comes because of the dominance of iconic and indexical

---

21. Smith, *Thinking in Tongues*, 45.

22. See Steven M. Studebaker, "Trinitarian Theology: The Spirit and the Fellowship of the Triune God," in *Routledge Handbook to Pentecostal Theology*, ed. Wolfgang Vondey (London: Routledge, 2020), 189.

logic is detrimental to Pentecostalism. A conventional, symbolic understanding of prosperity and health allows suffering to be a narrative Helper—though never God's creational intent—and so also serves God's greater soteriological purposes. Symbolic logic thus deconstructs the polarized logic that absolutizes prosperity and poverty and the indexical measuring of a believer's faith by their material standards, bodily health, and attractiveness. A symbolic reading allows prosperity and health to function as narrative Opponents, which offers the necessary critique of prosperity's potentially deceiving and destructive powers—as in the inclusion of market logic and practices.[23]

Influence of Market Logic

The iconic logic of the Word of Faith worldview challenges Pentecostalism in terms of its telos, that is, the goal-image of Eden that the movement wants to realize. Iconic logic is not by itself a challenge to Pentecostalism, which desire to relive the primitive church's pneumatic life expresses a similar logic.[24] The subversive element in the Word of Faith lies in how images and practices of market consumerism shape the telos—rather than those stemming from a "pneumatic imagination."[25] The individualistic focus on prosperity as personal abundance manifest through consumer ideals challenges Pentecostal visions of communal and creational flourishing within a holistic eschatology and prosperity's narrative role as a Helper (means) to be a blessing to the world in a thoroughly pneumatic imagination freed from self-serving desires. In the final analysis, the influence of

23. Pentecostal understandings of the cross and the creative tension between the now-but not-yet eschatological dimensions counter the symbolic deficiencies in the Word of Faith. The logic of the cross is nothing but symbolic as it embraces paradox and mystery as fundamental parts of the life of faith. When the cross is restoried into a present role in the Word of Faith worldview-story, it challenges the supremacy of iconic and indexical logic. The symbolic logic offered by the cross is a viable approach to human suffering, thus enhancing the Word of Faith's fidelity to human brokenness as well as their coherence with the biblical story in which the cross plays an irreplaceable part in the church's present experience (see Wright, *Day the Revolution Began*). Including the now-but not-yet dimension of biblical eschatology also significantly infuses symbolic logic into the Word of Faith worldview and challenges the dominance of the causative, indexical logic, and the possibility of a corresponding, iconic representation of Eden's perfection in the present while still allowing for expectancies of eschatological foretastes.

24. Frank D. Macchia, "Spirit Baptism," in *Routledge Handbook to Pentecostal Theology*, ed. Wolfgang Vondey (London: Routledge, 2020), 248.

25. See Amos Yong, *Spirit-Word-Community: Theological Hermeneutics in Trinitarian Perspective* (Eugene, Wipf and Stock, 2006); Archer, *Pentecostal Hermeneutic*, 32; "Cannot the spiritual battle at the heart of history and the human heart be defined as a conflict between true and false conceptions of the world and between alternative interpretations of the meaning of the cosmos?" (Naugle, *Worldview*, 186).

market logic and practices is a theological problem for Pentecostalism, since the market's worldview operates as a functional religion.

Frank Macchia asks whether the Word of Faith is an accommodation to the governing social and economic structures or offers a theological method of "correlation . . . that grants the biblical texts the dominant role in how believers view and engage the larger social setting."[26] As this study shows, the Word of Faith worldview is shaped by the Eden Redeemed story, which is a unique narration of the biblical story. Word of Faith discourse also explicitly critiques the fallen system of the world. An argument for economic accommodation is thus a simplification. The Word of Faith is better captured in the terms of offering its own religious faith economy rather than being simply a capitalistic religious expression. However, this faith economy, though founded in a theological story, is deeply influenced by market logic. Thus, instead of actually deconstructing the market's economic narrative and worldview, the Word of Faith's theologically constructed worldview-story establishes it. It turns out, paradoxically enough, that the Word of Faith's unique method of correlation leads to a unique form of accommodation.

The Word of Faith's iconic logic and its telos shaped by market consumerism domesticates Pentecostalism's prophetic power to confront the present powers by pneumatically imagined alternatives to current economic, racial, social, aesthetic, political, and spiritual power structures. By conforming to, and even capitalizing on, the powers of the market, the Word of Faith subverts the Pentecostal prophetic capacity of embodying the world subjunctively "as if" taken up in the Spirit's work of "material, physical, emotional, ethical, social, national and spiritual transformation and restoration"[27] in the image of God's shalom. The Word of Faith challenges Pentecostalism's ability to create spaces that embody and signify pneumatic alternatives, by accepting the assumed natural state of competitive, consumer capitalism and so surrenders to the so-called TINA doctrine, which says that "There Is No Alternative" to present economic and social power structures.[28] The Word of Faith worldview thus restricts Pentecostals to serve prophetic roles as "emancipated imaginers of alternative"[29] who first "*criticise* and dismantle the dominant worldview, and then *energise* the covenant community with an alternative worldview, an alternative imagination."[30] This can cause Pentecostalism to miss the warning that by allowing the functional religion of the market to influence its logic and telos, Pentecostalism will have "lost its original vision and may be nurturing

---

26. Macchia, "Call for Careful Discernment," 233.

27. Ma, "David Yonggi Cho," 150.

28. Zygmunt Bauman and Leonidas Donskis, *Liquid Evil* (Cambridge: Polity, 2016), 2, 5; Rieger, *No Rising*, 26; Bauman, *Consuming Life*, 65; "The underlying epistemology is . . . oriented towards buttressing the worldview of global capitalism" (Niemandt, "Prosperity Gospel," 214).

29. Walter Brueggemann, *From Judgment to Hope: A Study on the Prophets* (Louisville: Westminster John Knox Press, 2019), vii.

30. Walsh, *Subversive*, 36, emphasis original. See Ma, "Blessing," 291.

a monster that will later turn around and significantly incapacitate it."[31] The Word of Faith does not empower Pentecostalism to develop a critique of culture to make people aware of how the powers of the religion of the market "coincide with or contradict Christian values."[32]

The Word of Faith stands in a paradoxical relationship to Pentecostalism; while the movement arose within and is a significant part of Pentecostal history, the Word of Faith worldview at present both strengthens and subverts Pentecostal distinctives. Due to the problems discussed in this book, it is easy to see why the Word of Faith is said to be "Pentecostalism at its (near) worst."[33] Yet, at the same time, the Word of Faith's contributions to Pentecostalism make it perhaps also Pentecostalism at its (near) best.

31. Samuel Zalanga, "Religion, Economic Development and Cultural Change: The Contradictory Role of Pentecostal Christianity in Subsaharan Africa," *Journal of Third World Studies* 27, no. 1 (2010): 49. See Meyer, "Pentecostalism and Neo-liberal," 23.

32. Cox, "Pentecostalism and Global Market," 389, 392.

33. Bowman, *Word-Faith*, 12. See Robbins, "World Christianity," 234; Joel Robbins, "Anthropology and Theology: The Prosperity Gospel, Humanity, and the Problem of Judgment," YouTube video, 1:18:24, Posted by "The Finnish Anthropological Society," March 16, 2018, accessed April 7, 2021, https://www.youtube.com/watch?v=4jAkIng8 FOU. In this context, some Pentecostals would probably agree with the saying that "[t]he corruption of the best is the worst (*Corruptio optima pessima*)" (Taylor, *Secular Age*, 741).

BIBLIOGRAPHY

Abbott, H. Porter. *The Cambridge Introduction to Narrative*. Cambridge: Cambridge University Press, 2008.

Abbott, H. Porter. "Story, Plot, and Narration." In *The Cambridge Companion to Narrative*, edited by David Herman, 39–51. Cambridge: Cambridge University Press, 2007.

Ackerly, Glyn. "Importing Faith: The Effect of American 'Word of Faith' Culture on Contemporary English Evangelical Revivalism." Doctor of philosophy thesis, King's College, London, 2013.

Adedibu, Babatunde. *Coat of Many Colours: The Origin, Growth, Distinctiveness and Contributions of Black Majority Churches of British Christianity*. Gloucester: Wisdom Summit, 2012.

Adeleye, Femi. *Preachers of a Different Gospel*. Nairobi: Hippobooks, 2011.

Adeleye, Femi. "The Prosperity Gospel and Poverty: An Overview and Assessment." In *Prosperity Theology and the Gospel: Good News or Bad News for the Poor?*, edited by J. Daniel Salinas, 5–22. Peabody: Hendrickson, 2017.

Aechtner, Tomas. *Health, Wealth, and Power in an African Diaspora Church in Canada*. New York: Palgrave Macmillan, 2015.

Agana, Wilfred Asampambila. *"Succeed Here and in Eternity": The Prosperity Gospel in Ghana*. Bern: Peter Lang, 2016.

Akinabola, Olugbenga. "'I Will Make It': The Socio-Economic Consequences of the Prosperity Gospel on Christian Youth in Lagos, Nigeria." Doctor of philosophy thesis, Trinity International University, Deerfield, 2012.

Alexander, Paul. *Signs and Wonders: Why Pentecostalism Is the World's Fastest Growing Faith*. San Francisco: Jossey-Bass, 2009.

Anderson, Allan Heaton. *An Introduction to Pentecostalism*. 2nd edn. Cambridge: Cambridge University Press, 2014.

Anderson, Allan Heaton. "Pentecostal Approaches to Faith and Healing." *International Review of Mission* 91, no. 363 (2002): 523–34.

Anderson, Allan Heaton. "The Prosperity Message in the Eschatology of Some New Charismatic Churches." *Missionalia: Southern African Journal of Mission Studies* 15, no. 2 (August 1987): 72–83.

Anderson, Allan Heaton. *To the Ends of the Earth*. Oxford: Oxford University Press, 2013.

Anderson, Allan Heaton. "Varieties, Taxonomies, and Definitions." In *Studying Global Pentecostalism*, edited by Allan Anderson, Andre Droogers, Michael Bergunder and Cornelis van der Laan, 13–29. Berkeley: University of California Press, 2010.

Anderson, Herbert and Edward Foley. *Mighty Stories, Dangerous Rituals*. San Francisco: Jossey-Bass, 1998.

Angel, Uebert. *Praying for the Impossible*. No Place: SpiritLibrary Publications, 2012. E-book edition.

Anim, Emmanuel. "The Prosperity Gospel in Ghana and the Primal Imagination." *Pentvars Business Journal* 4, no. 2 (2010): 66–76.

Ankerberg, John and John Weldon. *The Facts on the Faith Movement*. Eugene: Harvest House, 1993.

Anthony, Chris. "The Theological Structure of Word of Faith." Paper presented at the Center for Charismatic and Pentecostal Studies, Birmingham, United Kingdom, January 2018.

Archer, Kenneth J. *A Pentecostal Hermeneutic: Spirit, Scripture and Community*. Cleveland: CPT Press, 2009.

Archer, Kenneth J. *The Gospel Revisited: Towards a Pentecostal Theology of Worship and Witness*. Euguene: Pickwick, 2011.

Aronson, Torbjorn. "Continuity in Charismata: Swedish Mission and the Growth of Neo-Pentecostal Churches in Russia." *Occasional Papers on Religion in Eastern Europe* 31, no. 1 (2012): 33–40.

Arvidsson, Adam. "Brands: A Critical Perspective." *Journal of Consumer Culture* 5, no. 2 (2005): 235–58.

Arvidsson, Adam. "Christianity and Consumer Culture." *Sociologica* 3 (2014): 1–11.

Asamoah-Gyadu, J. Kwabena. *Christianity and Faith in the COVID-19 Era: Lockdown Periods from Hosanna to Pentecost*. Accra: Step Publishers, 2020. Kindle edition.

Asamoah-Gyadu, J. Kwabena. "Christianity in Sub-Saharan Africa." In *Christianity in Sub-Saharan Africa*, edited by Kenneth R. Ross, J. Kwabena Asamoah-Gyadu and Todd M. Johnson, 19–42. Edinburgh: Edinburgh University Press, 2017.

Asamoah-Gyadu, J. Kwabena. *Contemporary Pentecostal Christianity: Interpretations from an African Context*. Oxford: Regnum, 2013.

Asamoah-Gyadu, J. Kwabena. "Did Jesus Wear Designer Robes?" *Lausanne.org*. November 1, 2019. Accessed April 7, 2021. https://www.lausanne.org/content/did-jesus-wear-designer-robes.

Asamoah-Gyadu, J. Kwabena. "God Is Big in Africa: Pentecostal Mega Churches and a Changing Religious Landscape." *Material Religion* (2019): no page numbers. DOI:10.1080/17432200.2019.1590012

Asamoah-Gyadu, J. Kwabena. "Pentecostalism and Coronavirus: Reframing the Message of Health and Wealth in a Pandemic Era." *Spiritus: ORU Journal of Theology* 6, no. 1 (2021):157–74.

Asamoah-Gyadu, J. Kwabena. "Pentecostalism and the Transformation of the African Christian Landscape." In *Pentecostalism in Africa: Presence and Impact of Pneumatic Christianity in Postcolonial Societies*, edited by Martin Lindhardt, 100–14. Leiden: Brill, 2014.

Asamoah-Gyadu, J. Kwabena. "Prosperity and Poverty in the Bible: Ghana's Experience." In *Prosperity Theology and the Gospel: Good News or Bad News for the Poor?*, edited by J. Daniel Salinas, 99–114. Peabody: Hendrickson, 2017.

Asamoah-Gyadu, J. Kwabena. *Sighs and Signs of the Spirit: Ghanaian Perspective on Pentecostalism and Renewal in Africa*. Oxford: Regnum, 2015.

Assemblies of God, General Presbytery of the. "Divine Healing: An Integral Part of the Gospel." In *Where We Stand: The Official Position Papers of the Assemblies of God*, 45–54. Springfield: Gospel Publishing House, 1994a.

Assemblies of God, General Presbytery of the. "The Believer and Positive Confession." In *Where We Stand: The Official Position Papers of the Assemblies of God*, 131–44. Springfield: Gospel Publishing House, 1994b.

Atkinson, William. "Christology." In *Routledge Handbook to Pentecostal Theology*, edited by Wolfgang Vondey, 216–25. London: Routledge, 2020.

Atkinson, William. "Spirit, Soul and Body: The Trichotomy of Kenyon, Hagin and Copeland." *Refleks* 5, no. 1 (2006): 98–118.

Atkinson, William. *The "Spiritual Death" of Jesus: A Pentecostal Investigation*. Leiden: Brill, 2012.

Attanasi, Katherine and Amos Yong, eds. *Pentecostalism and Prosperity: The Socio-Economics of the Global Charismatic Movement*. New York: Palgrave Macmillan, 2012.

Augustine, Daniela. "Pentecost and Prosperity in Eastern Europe: Between Sharing of Possessions and Accumulating Personal Wealth." In *Pentecostalism and Prosperity: The Socio-Economics of the Global Charismatic Movement*, edited by Katherine Attanasi and Amos Yong, 189–214. New York: Palgrave Macmillan, 2012.

Austin, J. L. *How to Do Things with Words*. Oxford: Clarendon Press, 1962.

Avanzini, John and Larry Huggins. *Prosperity: The Choice Is Yours*. Self-published. The Commonwealth of Christ Embassy Press, no date.

Avanzini, John. *It Is Not Working, Brother John*. Tulsa: Harrison House, 1992.

Avanzini, John. *John Avanzini Answers Your Questions on Biblical Economics*. Tulsa: Harrison House, 1992.

Avanzini, John. *Powerful Principles of Increase*. Tulsa: Harrison House, 1989.

Avanzini, John. *Rich God, Poor God*. Tulsa: Abel Press, 2001.

Bailey, Pulliam Sarah. "'A Wake-Up Call:' British Theologian N.T. Wright on the Prosperity Gospel, Climate Change and Advent." *The Washington Post*, December 5, 2019. Accessed April 7, 2021. https://www.washingtonpost.com/religion/2019/12/05/wakeup-call-british-theologian-nt-wright-prosperity-gospel-climate-change-advent/.

Bainbridge, William Sims. *The Sociology of Religious Movements*. New York: Routledge, 1997.

Bakker, Jim. *I Was Wrong*. Nashville: Thomas Nelson, 1996.

Bangura, Joseph Bosco. "The Charismatic Movement in Sierra Leone (1980–2010): A Missio-historical Analysis in View of African Culture, Prosperity Gospel and Power Theology." Doctoral thesis, Vrije Universitet, Amsterdam, 2013.

Barker, Isabelle. "Charismatic Economies: Pentecostalism, Economic Restructuring, and Social Reproduction." *New Political Science* 29, no. 4 (2007): 407–27.

Barnhart, Joe. "Prosperity Gospel: A New Folk Theology." In *Religious Television: Controversies and Conclusions*, edited by Robert Abelman and Stewart Hoover, 159–65. Norwood: Ablex, 1990.

Barron, Bruce. *The Health and Wealth Gospel*. Downers Grove: IVP, 1987.

Bartholomew, Craig and Michael Goheen. *Christian Philosophy: A Systematic and Narrative*. Grand Rapids: Baker, 2008.

Bauman, Zygmunt. *Consuming Life*. Cambridge: Polity, 2007.

Bauman, Zygmunt and Leonidas Donskis. *Liquid Evil*. Cambridge: Polity, 2016.

Beach, Lee Roy, *Narrative Thought*. Self-published, Xlibris, 2010.

Beaudoin, Tom. *Consuming Faith*. Lanham: Sheed and Ward, 2003.

Bell, Catherine. *Ritual*. Oxford: Oxford University Press, 1997.

Bell, Catherine. *Ritual Theory, Ritual Practice*. Oxford: Oxford University Press, 1992.

Bellah, Robert, Richard Madsen, William M. Sullivan, Ann Swidler, and Steven M. Tipton, *Habits of the Heart: Individualism and Commitment in American Life*. Berkeley: University of California Press, 1996.

Benson, Brue Ellis. "Structuralism." In *The Dictionary for Theological Interpretation of the Bible*, edited by Kevin J. Vanhoozer, 772–3. Grand Rapids: Baker, 2005.

Berger, Peter L. "Afterword." In *Global Pentecostalism in the 21st Century*, edited by Robert Hefner, 251–7. Bloomington: Indiana University Press, 2013.

Berger, Peter L. "Globalization and Religion." *The Hedgehog Review* 4, no. 2 (Summer 2002): 7–20.

Berger, Peter L. "Max Weber is Alive and Well, and Living in Guatemala: The Protestant Ethic Today." *The Review of Faith & International Affairs* 8, no. 4 (2010): 3–9.

Berger, Peter L. "'You Can Do It!' Two Cheers for the Prosperity Gospel." *Books & Culture*, September/October, 2008, Accessed: June 14, 2021, https://www.booksandculture.com /articles/2008/sepoct/10.14.html.

Bevir, Mark. "Narrative as a Form of Explanation." *Disputatio* 8 (November 2000): 10–18.

Bialecki, Jon, Naomi Haynes and Joel Robbins. "The Anthropology of Christianity." *Religion Compass* 2, no. 6 (2008): 1139–58.

Biehl, Michael. "To Prosper and to Be Blessed: Prosperity, Wealth and 'Life in Abundance' in Ecumenical Debate." In *Pastures of Plenty: Tracing Religio-Scapes of Prosperity Gospel in Africa and Beyond*, edited by Andreas Heuser, 131–46. Frankfurt: Peter Lang, 2015.

Van Biema, David. "Christians Wrong About Heaven, Says Bishop." *Time*, February 7, 2008. Accessed April 7, 2021. http://content.time.com/time/world/article/0,8599,17108 44,00.html.

Biemann, Asher ed. *The Martin Buber Reader*. New York: Palgrave Macmillan, 2002.

Billingsley, Scott. "The Midas Touch: Kenneth E. Hagin and the Prosperity Gospel." In *Recovering the Margins of American Religious History*, edited by Dwain Waldrep, 43–59. Tuscaloosa: University of Alabama Press, 2012.

Bjornstad, James. "What's Behind the Prosperity Gospel?." *Moody Monthly*, November 1986.

Blackburn, Simon. *Oxford Dictionary of Philosophy*. Oxford: Oxford University Press, 1996.

Blomberg, Craig. *Neither Poverty Nor Riches*. Downers Grove: IVP, 1999.

Bonzo, Matthew and Michael Stevens, ed. *After Worldview: Christian Higher Education in Postmodern Worlds*. Sioux Center: Dordt College, 2009.

Bosworth, F. F. *Christ the Healer*. Grand Rapids: Revell, 1973.

Bowler, Kate. "Blessed Bodies: Prosperity as Healing within the African-American Faith Movement." In *Global Pentecostal and Charismatic Healing*, edited by Candy Gunther Brown, 81–106. New York: Oxford University Press, 2010.

Bowler, Kate. *Blessed: A History of the American Prosperity Gospel*. New York: Oxford University Press, 2013.

Bowler, Kate. "Daily Grind: The Spiritual Workday of the American Prosperity Gospel." *Journal of Cultural Economy* 8, no. 5 (2015): 630–6.

Bowler, Kate. *Everything Happens for a Reason*. New York: Random House, 2018.

Bowler, Kate. *The Preacher's Wife: The Precarious Power of Evangelical Women Celebrities*. Princeton: Princeton University Press, 2019.

Bowler, Kate. "A Successful Calling: Women, Power, and the Rise of the American Prosperity Gospel." In *Women In Pentecostal and Charismatic Ministry: Informing Dialogue on Gender, Church, and Ministry*, edited by Margaret English de Alminana and Lois E. Olena, 184–200. Leiden: Brill, 2016.

Bowler, Kate and Wen Reagan. "Bigger, Better, Louder: The Prosperity Gospel's Impact on Contemporary Christian Worship." *Religion and American Culture: A Journal of Interpretation* 24, no. 2 (2014): 186–230.

Bowman, Robert. *The Word-Faith Controversy: Understanding the Health and Wealth Gospel*. Grand Rapids: Baker, 2001.

Bradshaw, Paul and John Melloh, ed. *Foundations in Ritual Studies*. London: SPCK, 2007.

Brandon, Andrew. *Health and Wealth: Does God Always Promise Prosperity*. Eastbourne: Kingsway, 1987.

Brekus, Catherine. "The Perils of Prosperity." In *American Christianities: A History of Dominance and Diversity*, edited by Catherine Brekus and Clark Glipin, 279–306. Chapel Hill: The University of North Carolina Press, 2011.

Brison, Karen J. "The Empire Strikes Back: Pentecostalism in Fiji." *Ethnology* 46, no. 1 (Winter 2007): 21–39.

Brogdon, Lewis. *The New Pentecostal Message? An Introduction to the Prosperity Movement*. Eugene: Cascade, 2015.

Brouwer, Steve, Paul Gifford and Susan Rose. *Exporting the American Gospel: Global Christian Fundamentalism*. New York: Routledge, 1996.

Brown, Andrew. "The Prosperity Gospel Makes a Mockery of Christianity." *The Guardian*, May 29, 2013. Accessed April 7, 2021. https://www.theguardian.com/commentisfree/andrewbrown/2013/may/29/prosperity-gospel-mockery-christianity.

Brown, Michael L. *Hyper-Grace: Exposing the Dangers of the Modern Grace Message*. Lake Mary: Charisma House, 2014.

Brueggemann, Walter. *From Judgment to Hope: A Study on the Prophets*. Louisville: Westminster John Knox Press, 2019.

Bruner, Jerome. *Actual Minds, Possible Worlds*. London: Harvard University Press, 1986.

Burgess, Richard. *Nigeria's Christian Revolution: The Civil War Revival and Its Pentecostal Progeny (1967–2006)*. Eugene: Wipf and Stock, 2008.

Burgess, Stanley. "Introduction." In *The New International Dictionary of Pentecostal and Charismatic Movements*, edited by Stanley Burgess and Eduard Van Der Maas, "Introduction." Rev. and exp. edn. Grand Rapids: Zondervan, 2003. E-book edition.

Burns, David and Jeffrey Fawcett. "The Role of Brands in a Consumer Culture." *Journal of Biblical Integration in Business* 15, no. 2 (2012): 28–42.

Byassee, Jason. "Surprised by N.T. Wright." *Christianity Today*, April 8, 2014. Accessed April 7, 2021. https://www.christianitytoday.com/ct/2014/april/surprised-by-n-t-wright.html.

Cao, Nanlai. "Urban Property and Spiritual Resource: The Prosperity Gospel Phenomenon in Coastal China." In *Pentecostalism and Prosperity: The Socio-Economics of the Global Charismatic Movement*, edited by Katherine Attanasi and Amos Yong, 151–70. New York: Palgrave Macmillan, 2012.

Capps, Charles. *Angels—Ministering Spirits*. England: Charles Capps Ministries, n.d. E-book edition.

Capps, Charles. *Authority in Three Worlds*. Tulsa: Harrison House, 1980. E-book edition.

Capps, Charles. *Faith and Confession: How to Activate the Power of God in Your Life*. England: Capps Publishing, 1987. E-book edition.

Capps, Charles. *Faith that Will Work for You*. England: Charles Capps Publishing, 1999. E-book edition.

Capps, Charles. *Seedtime and Harvest*. England: Capps Publishing, 1988. E-book edition.

Carol, Sanders, ed. *The Cambridge Companion to Saussure*. Cambridge: Cambridge University Press, 2004.

Carson, D. A. *Exegetical Fallacies*. 2nd edn. Grand Rapids: Baker Academic, 1996.

Cartledge, Mark J. *Encountering the Spirit*. London: Dartmon, Longman and Todd, 2006.

Cartledge, Mark J. "Text–Community–Spirit: The Challenges posed by Pentecostal Theological Method to Evangelical Theology." In *Spirit and Scripture: Exploring a Pneumatic Hermeneutic*. edited by Kevin L. Spawn and Archie T. Wright, 130–42. London: T&T Clark, 2012.

Cavanaugh, William. *Being Consumed: Economics and Christian Desire*. Grand Rapids: Eerdmans, 2008.

Chandler, David. *Semiotics*. 2nd edn. London: Routledge, 2007.

Charisma News. "Bishop Eddie Long Dead at 63." *Charismanews.com*. Accessed April 7, 2021. https://www.charismanews.com/us/62407-bishop-eddie-long-dead-at-63.

Charisma News. "Joel Osteen: I am Not a Prosperity Preacher." *Charismanews.com*. June 9, 2014. Accessed April 7, 2021. https://www.charismanews.com/us/44185-joel-osteen-i -am-not-a-prosperity-preacher.

Chatman, Seymour. *Story and Discourse*. Ithaca: Cornell University Press, 1978.

Chauvet, Louis-Marie. *The Sacrament*. Translated by Madeleine Beumont. Collegeville: Liturgical Press, 2001. Kindle edition.

Chesnut, Andrew. *Born Again in Brazil: The Pentecostal Boom and the Pathogens of Poverty*. New Brunswick: Rutgers, 1997.

Chesnut, Andrew. "Prosperous Prosperity: Why the Health and Wealth Gospel is Booming across the Globe." In *Pentecostalism and Prosperity: The Socio-Economics of the Global Charismatic Movement*, edited by Katherine Attanasi and Amos Yong, 215–24. New York: Palgrave Macmillan, 2012.

Cho, Paul Yonggi. *The Fourth Dimension: Volume 2*. South Plainfield: Bridge, 1983.

Chong, Terence. "Of Riches and Faith: The Prosperity Gospels of Megachurches in Singapore." In *New Religiosities, Modern Capitalism, and Moral Complexities in Southeast Asia*, edited by Juliette Koning and Gwenaël Njoto-Feillard, 147–68. Singapore: Palgrave Macmillan, 2017.

Christerson, Brad and Richard Flory. *The Rise of Network Christianity: How Independent Leaders are Changing the Religious Landscape*. Oxford: Oxford University Press, 2017.

Clavier, Mark. *Rescuing The Church from Consumerism*. London: SPCK, 2013.

Clifton, Shane. "Pentecostal Approaches to Economics." In *The Oxford Handbook of Christianity and Economics*, edited by Paul Oslington, 263–81. Oxford: Oxford University Press, 2014.

Coleman, Simon. "The Charismatic Gift." *The Journal of the Royal Anthropological Institute* 10, no. 2 (2004): 421–42.

Coleman, Simon. "From Excess to Encompassment: Repetition, Recantation, and the Trashing of Time in Swedish Christianities." *History and Anthropology* (2018): 1477–2612. Accessed April 7, 2021. https://doi.org/10.1080/02757206.2018.1541323.

Coleman, Simon. *Globalisation of Charismatic Christianity*. Cambridge: Cambridge University Press, 2000.

Coleman, Simon. "Morality, Markets, and the Gospel of Prosperity." In *Religion and the Morality of the Market*, edited by Daromir Rudnyckyj and Filippo Osella, 50–71. Cambridge: Cambridge University Press, 2017.

Coleman, Simon. "Prosperity Unbound? Debating the 'Sacrificial Economy.'" In *The Economics of Religion: Anthropological Approaches*, edited by Lionel Obadia and Donald Wood, 23–45. Bingly: Emerald, 2011.

Coleman, Simon. "Why Health and Wealth? Dimensions of Prosperity among Swedish Charismatics." In *Global Pentecostal and Charismatic Healing*, edited by Candy Gunter Brown, 47–60. Oxford: Oxford University Press, 2011.

Coleman, Simon and Martin Lindhardt. "Prosperity and Wealth." In *The Routledge Handbook of Economic Theology*, edited by Stefan Schwarzkopf. London: Routledge, 2020. Kindle edition.

Colson, Charles and Nancey Pearcy. *How Now Shall We Live*. Wheaton: Tyndale, 1999.

Comaroff, Jean and John Comaroff. "Millennial Capitalism: First Thoughts on a Second Subject." In *Millennial Capitalism and the Culture of Neoliberalism*, edited by Jean Comaroff and John Comaroff, 1–56. Durham: Duke University Press, 2001.

Comaroff, Jean and John Comaroff. "Occult Economies and the Violence of Abstraction: Notes from the South African Postcolony." *American Ethnologist* 26, no. 2 (1999): 279–303.

Comaroff, Jean and John Comaroff. "Privatizing the Millennium: New Protestant Ethics and the Spirits of Capitalism in Africa, and Elsewhere." *Africa Spectrum* 35, no. 3 (2000): 293–312.

Cook, Bernard and Gary Macy. *Christian Symbol and Practice*. Oxford: Oxford University Press, 2005.

Copeland, Gloria. *Blessed Beyond Measure: Experience the Extraordinary Goodness of God*. Forth Worth: Kenneth Copeland Ministries, 2004. E-book edition.

Copeland, Gloria. *Don't Buy the Lie*. Forth Worth: Kenneth Copeland Publications, 2013. E-book edition.

Copeland, Gloria. *God's Will Is Prosperity*. Forth Worth: Kenneth Copeland Ministries, 1978. E-book edition.

Copeland, Gloria. *Harvest of Health*. Fort Worth: Kenneth Copeland Ministries, 1992. E-book edition.

Copeland, Gloria. *Living in Heaven's Blessings Now*. Tulsa: Harrisons House, 2012. E-book edition.

Copeland, Gloria. *Live Long Finish Strong*. New York: FaithWords, 2010. E-book edition.

Copeland, Gloria. *Love: The Secret of Your Success*. Fort Worth: Kenneth Copeland Ministries, 1985. E-book edition.

Copeland, Kenneth Ministries. "Did Jesus Go to Hell?" *Kcm.com*. Accessed April 7, 2021. https://www.kcm.org/de/node/7893.

Copeland, Kenneth Ministries. "How to Develop the God Kind of Faith." *Kcm.org*. Accessed April 7, 2021. https://blog.kcm.org/develop-god-kind-of-faith/.

Copeland, Kenneth Ministries. "How to Meditate on the Word of God." *Kcm.org*. Accessed April 7, 2021. https://www.kcm.org/real-help/spiritual-growth/learn/how-meditate -the-word-god.

Copeland, Kenneth Ministries. "How to Receive Revelation Knowledge." *Kcm.org*. Accessed April 7, 2021. https://www.kcm.org/real-help/spiritual-growth/learn/how-rec eive-revelation-knowledge.

Copeland, Kenneth Ministries. "The Garden of Eden Restored." YouTube Video, 23:57. December 8, 2019. Accessed April 7, 2021. https://www.youtube.com/watch?v=t1QZ jdvClNs.

Copeland, Kenneth Ministries. "Why Do Bad Things Happen?" *Kcm.com*. Accessed April 7, 2021. https://www.kcm.org/real-help/spiritual-growth/learn/why-do-bad-things-happen.

Copeland, Kenneth Ministries. "What Does It Mean to Be Born Again?" *Kcm.org*. Accessed April 7, 2021. https://www.kcm.org/read/questions/what-does-it-mean-be- %E2%80%9Cborn-again%E2%80%9D.

Copeland, Kenneth Ministries. "10 Things Every Christian Should Know." *Kcm.org*. Accessed April 7, 2021. https://www.kcm.org/believers-academy/series/10-things- every-christian-should-know.

Copeland, Kenneth. *Blessed to be a Blessing*. Tulsa: Harrison House, 2013. E-book edition.

Copeland, Kenneth. *The Blessing of the Lord*. Tulsa: Harrison House, 2012. E-book edition.

Copeland, Kenneth. *Dream Big, Talk Big*. Forth Worth: Kenneth Copeland Ministries, 2012. E-book edition.

Copeland, Kenneth. *The Force of Faith*. Forth Worth: Kenneth Copeland Ministries, 1983. E-book edition.

Copeland, Kenneth. *The Force of Righteousness*. Tulsa: Harrison House, 2015. E-book edition.

Copeland, Kenneth. *Freedom from Fear*. Forth Worth: Kenneth Copeland Ministries, 1979. E-book edition.

Copeland, Kenneth. *Giving and Receiving*. Fort Worth: Kenneth Copeland Ministries, 1987. E-book edition.

Copeland, Kenneth. "Have God's Faith." YouTube Video, 22:00. Posted by Kenneth Copeland Ministries, November 28, 2015. Accessed April 7, 2021. https://www.you tube.com/watch?v=pAA-4My0FRk.

Copeland, Kenneth. *How You Call It Is How It Will Be*. Forth Worth: Kenneth Copeland Publications, 2010. E-book edition.

Copeland, Kenneth. *The Laws of Prosperity*. Fort Worth: Kenneth Copeland Ministries, 1974.

Copeland, Kenneth. "No Poor among You." *Believer's Voice of Victory*, October 2018.

Copeland, Kenneth. *Twitter Post*. August 28, 2018, 4:30 AM. Accessed April 7, 2021. https ://twitter.com/copelandnetwork/status/1034402721200304128?lang=en.

Copeland, Kenneth. *Walking in the Realm of the Miraculous*. Forth Worth: Kenneth Copeland Publications, 1980. E-book edition.

Copeland, Kenneth. *Your Rightstanding with God*. Tulsa: Harrison House, 1983. E-book edition.

Cotterell, Peter. *Prosperity Theology*. Leicester: Religious and Theological Studies Fellowship, 1990.

Cox, Harvey. *Fire from Heaven: The Rise of Pentecostal Spirituality and the Reshaping of Religion in the Twenty-First Century*. London: Casell, 1996.

Cox, Harvey. *The Market as God*. Cambridge: Harvard University Press, 2016.

Cox, Harvey. "Pentecostalism and Global Market Culture." In *The Globalization of Pentecostalism: A Religion Made to Travel*, edited by Murray Dempster, Byron Klaus and Douglas Peterson, 386–95. Eugene: Wipf and Stock, 1999.

Cox, John. "The Prosperity Gospel in Anthropology and Theology: The Case of Fast Money Schemes in Papua New Guinea." *St Mark's Review* 2, no. 244 (June 2018): 87–100.

Csordas, Thomas. "Ritualization of Life." In *Practicing the Faith: The Ritual Life of Pentecostal-Charismatic Christians*, edited by Martin Lindhardt, 129–51. New York: Berghahn, 2011.

da Silva, Antonio Barbosa. *Framgångsteologin—Svärmeri eller Väckelse?* Uppsala: Uppsala Universitet, 1988.

da Silva, Antonio Barbosa. "The 'Theology of Success' Movement: A Comment." *Themelios* 12 (1986): 91–2.

Danesi, Marcel. *Of Cigarettes, High Heels, and Other Interesting Things: An Introduction to Semiotics*. New York: St. Martin's Press, 1999.

Daniels III, David D. "Prosperity Gospel of Entrepreneurship in Africa and Black America: A Pragmatist Christian Innovation." In *Pastures of Plenty: Tracing Religio-Scapes of Prosperity Gospel in Africa and Beyond*, edited by Andreas Heuser, 265–78. Frankfurt: Peter Lang, 2015.

Dannenberg, Hilary. "Plot." In *Routledge Encyclopaedia of Narrative Theory*, edited by David Herman, Manferd Jahn and Marie-Laure Ryan, s.v. "Plot." London: Routledge, 2005.

Dayton, Donald. *Theological Roots of Pentecostalism*. Grand Rapids: Baker Academic, 1987.

DeArteaga, William. *Quenching the Spirit: Discover the Real Spirit Behind the Charismatic Controversy*. Lake Mary: Creation House, 1996.

DeBernardi, Jean. "Epilogue." *Culture and Religion* 3, no. 1 (2002): 125–8.

Dempster, Murray, Byron Klaus and Douglas Peterson, eds. *The Globalization of Pentecostalism: A Religion Made to Travel*. Carlisle: Regnum, 1999.

Dickow, Helga. *Religion and Attitudes Towards Life in South Africa: Pentecostals, Charismatics and Reborns*. Baden-Baden: Nomos, 2012.

Djupe, Paul and Ryan Burge. "The Prosperity Gospel of Coronavirus Response." *Politics and Religion* (2020): 1–22.

Dockery, David and Trevin Wax, eds. *CSB Worldview Study Bible*. Nashville: Holman Bible Publisher, 2018. Kindle edition.

Dollar, Creflo Ministries. "Angel Power Confession." *Creflodollarministries.org*. January 18, 2016. Accessed April 7, 2021. https://creflodollarministries.org/Daily-Confessions/Angel-Power-Confession.

Dollar, Creflo Ministries. "Becoming Established in Righteousness." *Creflodollarministries.org*. Accessed April 7, 2021. https://www.creflodollarministries.org/Daily-Confessions/Becoming-Established-in-Righteousness?returnUrl=%2FDaily-Confessions.

Dollar, Creflo Ministries. "Walk in Your Authority." *Creflodollar.us*. Accessed April 23, 2019. http://www.creflodollar.us/creflo-dollar-walk-in-your-authority/.

Dollar, Creflo. "Abundant Health on All Levels." *Creflodollarministries.org*. January 23, 2019. Accessed April 7, 2021. https://www.creflodollarministries.org/Bible-Study/Articles/Abundant-Health-on-All-Levels?returnUrl=%2FBible-Study%2FArticles%2FBe%2520Healed.

Dollar, Creflo. "The Blessings of Good Health and Long Life." *Creflodollarministries.org*. July 18, 2018. Accessed April 7, 2021. https://www.creflodollarministries.org/Bible-Study/Articles/The-Blessings-of-Good-Health-and-Long-Life?returnUrl=%2FBible-Study%2FArticles%3Fpage%3D3.

Dollar, Creflo. "Concerning Total Life Prosperity." *Creflodollarministries.org*. January 18, 2016. Accessed April 7, 2021. https://www.creflodollarministries.org/Daily-Confessions/Concerning-Total-Life-Prosperity?returnUrl=%2FDaily-Confessions.

Dollar, Creflo. *The Divine Order of Faith*. College Park: World Changers Ministries, 2001. E-book edition.

Dollar, Creflo. "2018 Grace Life Conference (Session 1)." *Creflodollarministries.org*. July 9, 2018. Accessed April 7, 2021. https://www.creflodollarministries.org/Bible-Study/Study-Notes/2018-Grace-Life-Conference-Session-1?returnUrl=%2FBible-Study%2FStudy-Notes%3Fpage%3D3.

Dollar, Creflo. "How to Experience Real Life Transformation Part 3." *Creflodollar.us*. November 20, 2016. Accessed April 7, 2021. https://www.creflodollarministries.org/Bible-Study/Study-Notes/How-to-Experience-Real-Life-Transformation-Part-3.

Dollar, Creflo. "Sunday Service." YouTube Video, 2:30:16. Creflo Dollar Ministries, May 12, 2019. Accessed June 6, 2020. https://www.youtube.com/watch?v=W8U5YuGAZZI.

Dooyeweerd, Herman. *Roots of Western Culture*, translated by John Kraay. Toronto: Wedge, 1979.

Dorch, Richard. *Integrity: How I Lost It and My Journey Back*. Green Forest: New Leaf Press, 1991.

Downs, David. "Giving for Return in the Prosperity Gospel and the New Testament." In *Prosperity Theology and the Gospel: Good News or Bad News for the Poor?*, edited by J. Daniel Salinas, 36–49. Peabody: Hendrickson, 2017.

Dronen, Tomas Sundnes. "'Now I Dress Well. Now I Work Hard' Pentecostalism, Prosperity, and Economic Development in Cameroon." In *Pastures of Plenty: Tracing*

Religio-Scapes of Prosperity Gospel in Africa and Beyond, edited by Andreas Heuser, 249–64. Frankfurt: Peter Lang, 2015.

Droogers, André. "The World of Worldviews." In *Methods for the Study of Religious Change: From Religious Studies to Worldview Studies*, edited by André Drooger and Anton van Harskamp, 13–24. Sheffield: Equinox, 2014.

Droogers, André and Anton van Harskamp, eds. *Methods for the Study of Religious Change: From Religious Studies to Worldview Studies*. Sheffield: Equinox, 2014.

Droz, Yvan and Yonathan Gez. "A God Trap: Seed Planting, Gift Logic, and the Prosperity Gospel." In *Pastures of Plenty: Tracing Religio-Scapes of Prosperity Gospel in Africa and Beyond*, edited by Andreas Heuser, 295–308. Frankfurt: Peter Lang, 2015.

Duffield, Guy and Nathaniel Van Cleave. *Foundations of Pentecostal Theology*. Los Angeles: LIFE, 1987.

Duncan-Williams, Nicolas. *Binding the Strong Man*. Self-published. Xulon, 2012. E-book edition.

Duncan-Williams, Nicolas. *Destined to Make an Impact*. Accra: Digital iNQ, 2012. E-book edition.

Duncan-Williams, Nicolas. *Prayer that Moves God*. Accra: Prayer Summit Publishing, 2015. Kindle edition.

Edwards, Joel. "Ethical Dimensions: Holiness and Fake Idols." In *Prosperity Theology and the Gospel: Good News or Bad News for the Poor?*, edited by J. Daniel Salinas, 88–98. Peabody: Hendrickson, 2017.

Ehrenreich, Barbara. *Bright Sided: How Positive Thinking Is Undermining America*. New York: Picador, 2010.

Ekman, Ulf. *Tillintetgör Djävulens Gärningar*. Uppsala: Livets Ords Förlag, 1987.

Ellington, Scott. "Pentecostalism and the Authority of Scripture." *Journal of Pentecostal Studies* 9 (1996): 16–38.

Ellington, Scott. "Scripture: Finding One's Place in God's Story." In *Routledge Handbook to Pentecostal Theology*, edited by Wolfgang Vondey, 63–72. London: Routledge, 2020.

Eltagouri, Marwa. "A Televangelist's Flu-season Advice: 'Inoculate Yourself with the Word of God.'" *The Washington Post*, February 6, 2018. Accessed April 7, 2021. https://www.washingtonpost.com/news/acts-of-faith/wp/2018/02/06/televangelist-suggests-alternate-flu-shot-inoculate-yourself-with-the-word-of-god/.

Enns, Paul. *The Moody Handbook of Theology*. Chicago: Moody, 2014.

Ericksen, Annelin. "Engaging with Theories of Neoliberalism and Prosperity." In *Going to Pentecost: An Experimental Approach to Studies in Pentecostalism*, edited by Annelin Eriksen, Ruy Llera Blanes and Michelle MacCarthy, 138–56. New York: Berghahn, 2019.

Everts, Janet Meyer and Jeffrey S. Lamp, eds. *Pentecostal Theology and the Theological Vision of N. T. Wright*. Cleveland: CPT Press, 2015.

Ewell, Rosalee Velloso. "Can We Offer a Better Theology? Banking on the Kingdom." In *Prosperity Theology and the Gospel: Good News or Bad News for the Poor?*, edited by J. Daniel Salinas, 161–6. Peabody: Hendrickson, 2017.

Eyoboka, Sam and Olayinka Latona. "RCCG Convention: Adeboye Prepares Christians to Regain Dominion." *Vanguard*, August 5, 2018. Accessed April 7, 2021. https://www.vanguardngr.com/2018/08/rccg-convention-adeboye-prepares-christians-to-regain-dominion/.

Farah, Charles. "A Critical Analysis: The 'Roots and Fruits' of Faith-Formula Theology." *Pneuma: The Journal of the Society for Pentecostal Studies* 3, no. 1 (Spring 1981): 3–21.

Farah, Charles. *From the Pinnacle of the Temple: Faith vs. Presumption*. Plainfield: Logos, 1979.

Fea, John. *Believe Me: The Evangelical Road to Donald Trump*. Grand Rapids: Eerdmans, 2018.

Fee, Gordon. *The Disease of the Health and Wealth Gospels*. Vancouver: Regent College Publishing, 2006.

Fee, Gordon. *The First Epistle to the Corinthians*. Grand Rapids: Eerdmans, 1987.

Fee, Gordon. "The 'Gospel' of Prosperity—An Alien Gospel." *The Pentecostal Evangel*, June 24, 1979, 4–8.

Félix-Jäger, Steven. "Material Visions of the Good Life: Pentecostalism, Visual Culture, and the Prosperity Gospel." *Pneuma: The Journal of the Society for Pentecostal Studies* 41, no. 2 (2019): 279–90.

Festinger, Leon, Henry Riecken and Stanley Schachter. *When Prophecy Fails*. Minneapolis: University of Minnesota Press, 1955.

Fisher, Walter. *Human Communication as Narration*. Columbia: University of South Carolina Press, 1989.

Folarin, George. "The Prosperity Gospel in Nigeria: A Re-Examination of the Concept, Its Impact, and an Evaluation." *The Asia Journal of Theology* 21, no. 1 (2007): no page numbers. Accessed April 7, 2021. http://www.pctii.org/cyberj/cyberj16/folarin.html.

Foltz, Richard. "The Religion of the Market: Reflections on a Decade of Discussion." *Worldviews* 11 (2007): 135–54.

Foster, Richard. *Money, Sex and Power*. London: Hodder and Stoughton, 2009.

Francis, Pope. *Evangelii Gaudium: The Joy of the Gospel*. Vatican: Vatican Press, 2013.

Frederick, Marla. *Between Sundays: Black Women's Everyday Struggles of Faith*. Berkeley, University of California Press, 2003.

Frederick, Marla. *Colored Television*. Stanford: Stanford University Press, 2015.

Freeman, Dena. "The Pentecostal Ethic and the Spirit of Development." In *Pentecostalism and Development: Churches, NGOs and Social Change in Africa*, edited by Dena Freeman, 1–38. London: Palgrave Macmillan, 2012.

Frei, Daniel. "'With Both Fee in the Air': The Prosperity Gospel in African Migrant Churches in Switzerland." In *Pastures of Plenty: Tracing Religio-Scapes of Prosperity Gospel in Africa and Beyond*, edited by Andreas Heuser, 335–70. Frankfurt: Peter Lang, 2015.

Frestadius, Simo. *Pentecostal Rationality: Epistemology and Theological Hermeneutics in the Foursquare Tradition*. London: Bloomsbury T&T Clark, 2019.

Freston, Paul. "Pentecostalism in Brazil: A Brief History." *Religion* 25, no. 2 (1995): 119–33.

Freston, Paul. "Prosperity Theology: A (Largely) Sociological Assessment." In *Prosperity Theology and the Gospel: Good News or Bad News for the Poor?*, edited by J. Daniel Salinas, 66–76. Peabody: Hendrickson, 2017.

Fröchtling, Drea. "Between Gutter and Gucci, Boss and *Botho*: A Relocation of 'Prosperity Gospel' by Nigerian Pentecostal Christians in Soweto, South Africa." In *Pastures of Plenty: Tracing Religio-Scapes of Prosperity Gospel in Africa and Beyond*, edited by Andreas Heuser, 325–38. Frankfurt: Peter Lang, 2015.

Gaines, Adrianne. "Billy Joe Daugherty Dies at 57." *Charisma Magazine*, November 23, 2009. Accessed April 7, 2021. https://www.charismamag.com/site-archives/570-news/featured-news/8133-billy-joe-daugherty-dies-at-57.

Gauthier, François, Linda Woodhead and Tuomas Martikainen. "Introduction: Consumerism as the Ethos of Consumer Society." In *Religion in Consumer Society: Brands, Consumers and Markets*, edited by François Gauthier and Tuomas Martikainen, 1–26. London: Routledge, 2013.

Gbote, E. Z. M and S. T. Kgatla. "Prosperity Gospel: A Missiological Assessment." *HTS Teologiese Studies/ Theological Studies* 70, no. 1 (2014): 1–10.

Geertz, Clifford. "An Inconstant Profession: The Anthropological Life in Interesting Times." *Annual Review of Anthropology* 31 (2002): 1–19.

Geertz, Clifford. *The Interpretation of Cultures*. New York: Basic Books, 1973.

Geisler, Norman and William Watkins. *Worlds Apart: A Handbook on World Views*. 2nd edn. Eugene: Wipf and Stock, 2003.

Genette, Gérard. *Narrative Discourse Revisited*. Translated by Jane E. Lewin. Ithaca: Cornell University Press, 1988.

George, Folarin. "Contemporary State of the Prosperity Gospel in Nigeria." *The Asia Journal of Theology* 21, no. 1 (2007): 69–95.

George, Pierson. "Evangelicals and Worldview Confusion." In *After Worldview: Christian Higher Education in Postmodern Worlds*, edited by J. Matthew Bonzo and Michael Stevens, 29–42. Sioux Center: Dordt College Press, 2009.

Gerber, Lynne. "Fat Christians and Fit Elites: Negotiating Class and Status in Evangelical Christian Weight-Loss Culture." *American Quarterly* 64, no. 1 (March 2012): 61–84.

Gifford, Paul. *African Christianity: Its Public Role*. Bloomington: Indiana University Press, 1998.

Gifford, Paul. "The Bible in Africa: A Novel Usage in Africa's New Churches." *Bulletin of SOAS* 71, no. 2 (2008): 203–19.

Gifford, Paul. "The Complex Provenance of Some Elements of African Pentecostal Theology." In *Between Babel and Pentecost; Transnational Pentecostalism in Africa and Latin America*, edited by Andre Corten and Ruth Marshall-Fratani, 62–79. London: Hurst, 2001.

Gifford, Paul. *Christianity, Development and Modernity in Africa*. London: C. Hurst & Co, 2015.

Gifford, Paul. "Healing in African Pentecostalism: The 'Victorious Living' of David Oyedepo." In *Global Pentecostal and Charismatic Healing*, edited by Candy Gunther Brown, 251–64. Oxford: Oxford University Press, 2011.

Gifford, Paul. *Ghana's New Christianity: Pentecostalism in a Globalizing African Economy*. Bloomington: Indiana University Press, 2004.

Gifford, Paul. "The Prosperity Theology of David Oyedepo, Found of Winner's Chapel." In *Pastures of Plenty: Tracing Religio-Scapes of Prosperity Gospel in Africa and Beyond*, edited by Andreas Heuser, 83–100. Frankfurt: Peter Lang, 2015.

Gifford, Paul. "Ritual Use of the Bible in African Pentecostalism." In *Practicing the Faith: The Ritual Life of Pentecostal-Charismatic Christians*, edited by Martin Lindhardt, 179–97. New York: Berghahn, 2011.

Gifford, Paul and Trad Nogueira-Godsey. "The Protestant Ethic and African Pentecostalism: A Case Study." *Journal for the Study of Religion* 24, no. 1 (2011): 5–22.

Gilkey, Langdon. "Symbols, Meaning, and the Divine Presence." *Theological Studies* 35, no. 2 (1974): 249–67.

Godawa, Brian. *Hollywood Worldviews*. 2nd edn. Downers Grove: IVP, 2009.

Goh, Daniel. "Grace, Megachurches, and the Christian Prince in Singapore." In *Pentecostal Megachurches in Southeast Asia*, edited by Terence Chong, 181–206. Singapore: ISEAS Publishing, 2018.

Goh, Daniel. "Hillsong and 'Megachurch' Practice: Semiotics, Spatial Logic and the Embodiment of Contemporary Evangelical Protestantism." *Material Religion* 4, no 3 (2008): 284–304.

Goheen, Michael and Craig Bartholomew. *The Drama of Scripture*. 2nd edn. Grand Rapids: Baker Academic, 2014.

Goheen, Michael and Craig Bartholomew. *Living at the Crossroads: An Introduction to Christian Worldview*. Grand Rapids: Baker, 2008.

Goheen, Michael. "The Urgency of Reading the Bible as One Story." *Theology Today* 6, no. 4 (2008): 469–83.

Gossett, Don and E. W. Kenyon. *The Power of Your Words*. New Kensington: Whitaker House, 1981. E-book edition.

Gottschall, Jonathan. *The Storytelling Animal*. New York: Mariner, 2012.

Goudzwaard, Bob. *Idols of Our Time*. Downers Grove: IVP, 1984.

Grady, Lee. *The Holy Spirit Is Not for Sale*. Grand Rapids: Chosen, 2010.

Grenz, Stanley. *Prayer: The Cry for the Kingdom*. Grand Rapids: Eerdmans, 2005.

Grenz, Stanley. *A Primer on Postmodernism*. Grand Rapids: Eerdmans, 1996.

Grenz, Stanley and Roger E. Olson. *Who Needs Theology?: An Invitation to the Study of God*. Downers Grove: IVP, 1996.

Griffioen, Sander. "The Approach to Social Theory: Hazards and Benefits." In *Stained Glass: Worldviews and Social Science*, edited by Paul Marshall, Sander Griffioen, Richard Mouw, 81–118. Lanham: University Press of America, 1989.

Grimes, Ronald. *The Craft of Ritual Studies*. Oxford: Oxford University Press, 2014.

Griswold, Wendy. *Cultures and Societies in a Changing World*. 4th edn. London: SAGE, 2014.

Groothuis, Douglas. *Christian Apologetics: A Comprehensive Case for Biblical Faith*. Downers Grove: IVP, 2011.

Gukurume, Simbarashe. "Singing Positivity: Prosperity Gospel in the Musical Discourse of Popular Youth Hip-Hop Gospel in Zimbabwe." *Muziki* 14, no. 2 (2017): 36–54.

Gunnarsson, Kent. "Den Kristna Gnosticismens Återkomst: Ett Studium av Ulf Ekmans Teologi [The Return of Christian Gnosticism: An Investigation of the Theology of Ulf Ekman]." Doctor of theology thesis, Umeå Universitet, Umeå, 2004.

Gustafson, Scott. *At the Altar of Wall Street: The Rituals, Myths, Theologies, Sacraments, and Mission of the Religion Known as the Modern Global Economy*. Grand Rapids: Eerdmans, 2015.

Habarurema, Viateur. *Christian Generosity According to 2 Corinthians 8–9: Its Exegesis, Reception, and Interpretation Today in Dialogue with the Prosperity Gospel in Sub-Saharan Africa*. Carlisle: Langham Creative Projects, 2017.

Hackworth, Jason. "Religious Neoliberalism." In *The SAGE Handbook of Neoliberalism*, edited by Damien Cahill, Melinda Cooper, Martijn Konings and David Primrose, 323–34. Los Angeles: SAGE Publishing, 2018.

Hagin, Kenneth E. *The Art of Prayer*. Tulsa: Faith Library Publications, 1992.

Hagin, Kenneth E. *A Better Covenant*. Tulsa: Faith Library Publications, 2013.

Hagin, Kenneth E. *The Bible Healing Study Course*. Tulsa: Faith Library Publications, 1999. E-book edition.

Hagin, Kenneth E. *Bible Faith Study Course*. Tulsa: Faith Library Publications, 1991. E-book edition.

Hagin, Kenneth E. *Biblical Keys to Financial Prosperity*. Tulsa: Faith Library Publications, 1995.

Hagin, Kenneth E. *Classical Sermons*. Tulsa: Faith Library Publications, 1992.

Hagin, Kenneth E. *A Commonsense Guide to Fasting*. Tulsa: Faith Library Publications, 1981.

Hagin, Kenneth E. *Concerning Spiritual Gifts*. Tulsa: Faith Library Publications, 1986.

Hagin, Kenneth E. *Don't Blame God*. Tulsa: Faith Library Publications, 1979. E-book edition.

Hagin, Kenneth E. *El Shaddai: The God Who Us More Than Enough*. Tulsa: Faith Library Publications, 2010.

Hagin, Kenneth E. *Exceedingly Growing Faith*. Tulsa: Faith Library Publications, 1983.

Hagin, Kenneth E. "Faith Brings Results." *Rhema.org*. Accessed April 7, 2021. https://www.rhema.org/index.php?option=com_content&view=article&id=1026:faith-brings-results&catid=46&Itemid=141.

Hagin, Kenneth E. *A Fresh Anointing*. Tulsa: Faith Library Publications, 1989.

Hagin, Kenneth E. *God's Word*. Tulsa: Faith Library Publications, 1996.

Hagin, Kenneth E. *Godliness Is Profitable*. Tulsa: Faith Library Publications, 1982.

Hagin, Kenneth E. *Growing up Spiritually*. Tulsa: Faith Library Publications, 1976.

Hagin, Kenneth E. *The Healing Anointing*. Tulsa: Faith Library Publications, 1997.

Hagin, Kenneth E. *Having Faith in Your Faith*. Tulsa: Faith Library Publications, 1980.

Hagin, Kenneth E. *Healing Belongs to Us*. Tulsa: Faith Library Publications, 1981.

Hagin, Kenneth E. *How to Be Led by the Spirit*. Tulsa: Faith Library Publications, 1993.

Hagin, Kenneth E. *How to Turn Your Faith Loose*. Tulsa: Faith Library Publications, 1980. E-book edition.

Hagin, Kenneth E. *The Human Spirit: Volume 2 of the Spirit, Soul, and Body Series*. 2nd edn. Tulsa: Faith Library Publications, 1985.

Hagin, Kenneth E. *I Believe in Visions*. Tulsa: Faith Library Publications, 1984.

Hagin, Kenneth E. *In Him*. Tulsa: Faith Library Publications, 1983.

Hagin, Kenneth E. *Jesus the Open Door*. Tulsa: Faith Library Publications, 1996.

Hagin, Kenneth E. *Knowing What Belongs to Us*. Tulsa: Faith Library Publications, 1989.

Hagin, Kenneth E. *Man on Three Dimensions: Volume 1 of the Spirit, Soul, and Body Series*. Tulsa: Faith Library Publications, 1979.

Hagin, Kenneth E. *The Midas Touch: A Balanced Approach to Biblical Prosperity*. Tulsa: Faith Library Publications, 2000.

Hagin, Kenneth E. *The Ministry Gifts*. Tulsa: Faith Library Publications, 1981.

Hagin, Kenneth E. *Must Christians Suffer?* Tulsa: Faith Library Publications, 1982.

Hagin, Kenneth E. *The Name of Jesus*. Tulsa: Faith Library Publications, 1984.

Hagin, Kenneth E. *The New Birth*. Tulsa: Faith Library Publications, 1975.

Hagin, Kenneth E. *New Thresholds of Faith*. Tulsa: Faith Library Publications, 1985.

Hagin, Kenneth E. *Obedience in Finances*. Tulsa: Faith Library Publications, 1983.

Hagin, Kenneth E. *The Origin and Operation of Demons*. Tulsa: Faith Library Publications, 1983.

Hagin, Kenneth E. *The Present Day Ministry of Jesus*. Tulsa: Faith Library Publications, 1980.

Hagin, Kenneth E. *Prevailing Prayer to Peace*. Tulsa: Faith Library Publications, 1985.

Hagin, Kenneth E. *The Real Faith*. Tulsa: Faith Library Publications, 1985.

Hagin, Kenneth E. *Redeemed from Poverty, Sickness and Spiritual Death*. 2nd edn. Tulsa: Faith Library Publications, 1983.

Hagin, Kenneth E. *Right and Wrong Thinking*. Tulsa: Faith Library Publications, 1986.

Hagin, Kenneth E. *Seven Things You Should Know About Divine Healing*. Tulsa: Faith Library Publications, 1979.

Hagin, Kenneth E. *The Triumphant Church*. Tulsa: Faith Library Publications, 1993.

Hagin, Kenneth E. *Understanding the Anointing*. Tulsa: Faith Library Publications, 1983.

Hagin, Kenneth E. *Welcome to God's Family*. Tulsa: Faith Library Publications, 2003.

Hagin, Kenneth E. *What Faith Is*. Tulsa: Faith Library Publications, 1983.

Hagin, Kenneth E. *What to Do When Faith Seems Weak and Victory Lost*. Tulsa: Faith Library Publications, 1979.

Hagin, Kenneth E. *Where Do We Go from Here?* Tulsa: Faith Library Publications, 1988.

Hagin, Kenneth E. *Why Do People Fall Under the Power?* Tulsa: Faith Library Publications, 1981.

Hagin, Kenneth E. *Why Tongues?* Tulsa: Faith Library Publications, 2001.

Hagin, Kenneth E. *Words*. Tulsa: Faith Library Publications, 1979.

Hagin, Kenneth E. *You Can Have What You Say*. Tulsa: Faith Library Publications, 1988.

Hagin, Kenneth E. *Your Faith in God Will Work*. Tulsa: Faith Library Publications, 1991. E-book edition.

Hagin, Kenneth E. *Zoe: The God-Kind of Life*. Tulsa: Faith Library Publications, 1981.

Hagin Jr., Kenneth W. *Another Look at Faith*. Tulsa: Faith Library Publications, 1996.

Hagin Jr., Kenneth W. "Back to the Basics." *Rhema.org*. Accessed April 7, 2021. http://www
.rhema.org/index.php?option=com_content&view=article&id=233:back-to-the-basics
&catid=45:healing&Itemid=144.

Hagin Jr., Kenneth W. *Creating the World You Want to See*. Tulsa: Rhema Bible Church, 2011. E-book edition.

Hagin Jr., Kenneth W. *How to Be a Success in Life*. Tulsa: Faith Library Publications, 1982.

Hagin Jr., Kenneth W. *How to Live Worry Free*. Tulsa: Faith Library Publications, 1996.

Hagin Jr., Kenneth W. *It's Your Move*. Tulsa: Faith Library Publications, 1994.

Hagin Jr., Kenneth W. *Overflow: Living Above Life's Limits*. Tulsa: Rhema Bible Church, 2006. E-book edition.

Hagin Jr., Kenneth W. *Staying Positive in a Negative World*. Tulsa: Faith Library Publications, 2003.

Hagin Jr., Kenneth W. *The Untapped Power of Praise*. Tulsa: Faith Library Publications, 1990.

Hanegraaff, Hank. *Christianity in Crisis*. Eugene: Harvest House, 1993.

Hanegraaff, Hank. *Christianity in Crisis: 21st Century*. Nashville: Thomas Nelson, 2009.

Harding, Susan. *The Book of Jerry Falwell: Fundamentalist Language and Politics*. Princeton: Princeton University Press, 2000.

Harrell Jr., David Edwin. *All Things Are Possible: All Things Are Possible: The Healing and Charismatic Revivals in Modern America*. Bloomington: Indiana University Press, 1975.

Harrison, Milmon. *Righteous Riches: The Word of Faith Movement in Contemporary African American Religion*. New York: Oxford University Press, 2005.

Hartman, Laura M. *The Christian Consumer: Living Faithfully in a Fragile World*. Oxford: Oxford University Press, 2011.

Harvey, David. *A Brief History of Neoliberalism*. Oxford: Oxford University Press, 2007.

Hasu, Päivi. "World Bank and Heavenly Bank in Poverty and Prosperity: The Case of Tanzanian Faith Gospel." *Review of African Political Economy* 33, no. 110 (2006): 679–92.

Haynes, Naomi. "On the Potential and Problems of Pentecostal Exchange." *American Anthropologist* 115, no. 1 (2013): 85–95.

Haynes, Naomi. "Pentecostalism and the Morality of Money: Prosperity, Inequality, and Religious Sociality on the Zambian Copperbelt." *Journal of the Royal Anthropological Institute* 18 (2012): 123–39.

Hays, Richard. *The Faith of Jesus Christ*. 2nd edn. Grand Rapids: Eerdmans, 2002.

Hedges, D. J. "Television." In *The New International Dictionary of Pentecostal and Charismatic Movements*, edited by Stanley M. Burgess and Eduard M. Van Der Maas, s.v. "Television." Rev. and exp. edn. Grand Rapids: Zondervan, 2003. E-book edition.

Hefner, Robert. "Introduction: The Unexpected Modern—Gender, Piety, and Politics in the Global Pentecostal Surge." In *Global Pentecostalism in the 21st Century*, edited by Robert Hefner, 1–36. Bloomington: Indiana University Press, 2013.

Heilig, Christoph, Thomas Hewitt and Michael Bird, eds. *God and the Faithfulness of Paul: A Critical Examination of the Pauline Theology of N. T. Wright.* Minneapolis: Fortress, 2017.

Heilig, Theresa and Christoph Heilig. "Historical Methodology." In *God and the Faithfulness of Paul: A Critical Examination of the Pauline Theology of N. T. Wright,* edited by Christoph Heilig, Thomas Hewitt and Michael Bird, 115–50. Minneapolis: Fortress, 2017.

Hejzlar, Pavel. *Two Paradigms for Divine Healing: Fred F. Bosworth, Kenneth E. Hagin, Agnes Sanford, and Francis Macnutt in Dialogue.* Leiden: Brill, 2014.

Henry, Melanie. "Wealth Without Toil." *Believer's Voice of Victory,* September 2019. Accessed April 7, 2021. https://www.kcm.org/magazines/wealth-without-toil.

Herman, David. "Actant." In *Routledge Encyclopaedia of Narrative Theory,* edited by David Herman, Manferd Jahn and Marie-Laure Ryan, s.v. "Actant." London: Routledge, 2005.

Herman, Luc and Bart Vervaeck. "Ideology." In *The Cambridge Companion to Narrative,* edited by David Herman, 217–30. Cambridge: Cambridge University Press, 2007.

Herrick, James. "Response to Albert Wolters." In *After Worldview: Christian Higher Education in Postmodern Worlds,* edited by J. Matthew Bonzo and Michael Stevens, 115–18. Sioux Center: Dordt College Press, 2009.

Heslam, Peter. "The Rise of Religion and the Future of Capitalism." *De Ethica* 2, no. 3 (2015): 53–72.

Heuser, Andreas. "Charting African Prosperity Gospel economies." *HTS Teologiese Studies/Theological Studies* 72, no. 1 (2016): 1–9.

Heuser, Andreas. "Prosperity Theology." In *Routledge Handbook to Pentecostal Theology,* edited by Wolfgang Vondey, 410–20. London: Routledge, 2020.

Heuser, Andreas. "Religio-Scapes of Prosperity Gospel: An Introduction." In *Pastures of Plenty: Tracing Religio-Scapes of Prosperity Gospel in Africa and Beyond,* edited by Andreas Heuser, 15–30. Frankfurt: Peter Lang, 2015.

Hicks, Douglas. "Prosperity, Theology, and Economy." In *Pentecostalism and Prosperity: The Socio-Economics of the Global Charismatic Movement,* edited by Katherine Attanasi and Amos Yong, 239–52. New York: Palgrave Macmillan, 2012.

Hiebert, Paul. *Transforming Worldviews: An Anthropological Understanding of How People Change.* Grand Rapids: Baker Academic, 2008.

Hill, Joanna. *Spiritual Law: The Essence of Swedenborg's Divine Providence.* Santa Fe: Rock Point, 2014.

Hill, Judith. "Theology of Prosperity." *Africa Journal of Theology* 28, no. 1 (2009): 43–55.

Hinn, Costi. *God, Greed, and the (Prosperity) Gospel.* Grand Rapids: Zondervan, 2019.

Hobson, N. M., J. J. Kim and G. MacDonald. "A Camel Through the Eye of a Needle: The Influence of the Prosperity Gospel on Financial Risk-Taking, Optimistic Bias, and Positive Emotion." *Psychology of Religion and Spirituality* (2018): no page numbers. Accessed April 7, 2021. https://doi.org/10.1037/rel0000235.

Hollinger, Dennis. "Enjoying God Forever: An Historical/Sociological Profile of the Health and Wealth Gospel." *Trinity Journal* 9, no. 2 (1988): 131–49.

Holmes, Arthur. *Contours of a World View.* Grand Rapids: Eerdmans, 1983.

Horn, J. N. *From Rags to Riches: An Analysis of the Faith Movement and Its Relation to the Classical Pentecostal Movement.* Pretoria: University of South Africa Muckleneuk, 1989.

Hornborg, Ann-Christine. *Ritualer: Teorier och Tillämpning.* Lund: Studentlitteratur, 2005.

Horton, Michael, ed. *The Agony of Deceit: What Some TV Preachers are Really Preaching.* Chicago: Moody Press, 1990.

Horton, Michael. "The Agony of Deceit." In *The Agony of Deceit: What Some TV Preachers are Really Preaching*, edited by Michael Horton, 21–31. Chicago: Moody Press, 1990.

Horton, Michael. "The TV Gospel." In *The Agony of Deceit: What Some TV Preachers are Really Preaching*, edited by Michael Horton, 123–50. Chicago: Moody Press, 1990.

Horton, Stanley ed. *Systematic Theology*, Revised edition. Springfield: Logion Press, 2007.

Hoskins, Janet. "Symbolism in Anthropology." In *International Encyclopedia of the Social & Behavioral Sciences*, edited by James D. Wright, 860–5. London: Elsevier Science, 2015.

Houston, Brian. *How to Maximize Your Life*. Castle Hill: Hillsong Music, 2013.

Hughes, Graham. *Worship as Meaning*. Cambridge: Cambridge University Press, 2010.

Hunt, David. *Beyond Seduction: A Return to Biblical Christianity*. Eugene: Harvest House, 1987.

Hunt, Dave and T. A. McMahon. *The Seduction of Christianity*. Eugene: Harvest House, 1985.

Hunt, Stephen. "Deprivation and Western Pentecostalism Revisited: Neo-Pentecostalism." *PentecoStudies* 1, no. 2 (2002): 1–29.

Hunt, Stephen. "Magical Moments: An Intellectualist Approach to the Neo-Pentecostal Faith Ministries." *Religion* 28, no. 3 (1998): 1096–151.

Jackson, Andrew. "Prosperity Gospel and the Faith Movement." *Themelios* 15, no. 1 (1989): 16–24.

Jacobsen, Douglas. *Thinking in the Spirit*. Bloomington: Indiana University Press, 2002.

Jason Hackworth, "Religious Neoliberalism." In *The SAGE Handbook of Neoliberalism*, edited by Damien Cahill, Melinda Cooper, Martijn Konings and David Primrose, 323–34. Los Angeles: SAGE Publishing, 2018.

Jenkins, Kathleen E. and Gerardo Martí. "Warrior Chicks: Youthful Aging in a Postfeminist Prosperity Discourse." *Journal for the Scientific Study of Religion* 51, no. 2 (2012): 241–56.

Jenkins, Philip. "The Case for Prosperity." *The Christian Century*, November 19, 2010. Accessed April 7, 2021. https://www.christiancentury.org/article/2010-11/case-prospe rity.

Johansen, Jørgen and Svend Larsen. *Signs in Use*. Translated by Dinda L. Gorleé and John Irons. London: Routledge, 2010.

Johansson, Hans, ed. *Vad Ska Man Tro Egentligen? Den Modernistiska Teologin, Trosförkunnelsen och den Nya Andligheten i Biblisk Prövning*. Örebro: Libris, 1989.

Johnson, Bill. *Release the Power of Jesus*. Shippensburg: Destiny Image, 2009. E-book edition.

Johnson, Bill. *When Heaven Invades Earth*. Shippensburg: Destiny Image, 2005.

Johnson, Luke Timothy. "A Historiographical Response to Wright's Jesus." In *Jesus and the Restoration of Israel: A Critical Assessment of N. T. Wright's Jesus and the Victory of God*, edited by Carey Newman, 206–24. Downers Grove: IVP, 1999.

Johnson, Luke Timothy. "Review of *The New Testament and the People of God*, by Nicholas Thomas Wright." *Journal of Biblical Literature* 113, no. 3 (1994), 536–8.

Johnson, Russell. "The Gospel and the Prosperity Gospel: Joel Osteen's Your Best Life Now Reconsidered." *Theology* 121, no. 1 (2018): 28–34.

Jones, David. "The Errors of the Prosperity Gospel." *Marks Journal* 9 (2014): 34–7.

Jones, David and Russel Woodbridge. *Health, Wealth & Happiness: Has the Prosperity Gospel Overshadowed the Gospel of Christ?* Grand Rapids: Kregel, 2010.

Kahl, Werner. "'Jesus Become Poor so that We Might Become Rich': A Critical Review of the Use of Biblical Reference Texts among Prosperity Preachers in Ghana." In *Pastures of Plenty: Tracing Religio-Scapes of Prosperity Gospel in Africa and Beyond*, edited by Andreas Heuser, 101–16. Frankfurt: Peter Lang, 2015.

Kahl, Werner. "Prosperity-Preaching in West-Africa: An Evaluation of a Contemporary Ideology from a New Testament Perspective." *Ghana Bulletin of Theology* 2 (2007): 21–42.

Kaiser Jr., Walter. "The Old Testament Promise of Material Blessings and the Contemporary Believer." *Trinity Journal* 9 (1988): 151–70.

Kalu, Ogbu. *African Pentecostalism: An Introduction*. Oxford: Oxford University Press, 2008.

Kärkkäinen, Veli-Matti. "Pneumatologies in Systematic Theologies." In *Studying Global Pentecostalism*, edited by Allan Anderson, Andre Droogers, Michael Bergunder and Cornelis van der Laan, 223–44. Berkeley: University of California, 2010.

Kathrine Wiegele. "The Prosperity Gospel Among Filipino Catholic Charismatics." In *Pentecostalism and Prosperity: The Socio-Economics of the Global Charismatic Movement*, edited by Katherine Attanasi and Amos Yong, 171–88. New York: Palgrave Macmillan, 2012.

Kavanaugh, John. *Following Christ in a Consumer Society*. Maryknoll: Orbis, 2006.

Kay, William. *Pentecostalism*. London: SPCK, 2009.

Kay, William. *Pentecostalism: A Very Short Introduction*. Oxford: Oxford University Press, 2011.

Kay, William. "Review of The Globalisation of Charismatic Christianity, by Simon Coleman." *Journal of Ecclesiastical History* 53, no. 2 (2002): 427–8.

Keane, Webb. "On Semiotic Ideology." *Signs and Society* 6, no. 1 (Winter 2018): 64–87.

Keener, Craig. *Spirit Hermeneutics: Reading Scripture in Light of Pentecost*. Grand Rapids: Eerdmans, 2016.

Kenyon, E. W. *Advanced Bible Course*. Lynnwood: Kenyon's Gospel Publishing Society, 1998.

Kenyon, E. W. *The Bible in the Light of Our Redemption*. Lynnwood: Kenyon's Gospel Publishing Society, 1989.

Kenyon, E. W. *The Father and His Family*. Lynnwood: Kenyon's Gospel Publishing Society, 1998.

Kenyon, E. W. *Two Kinds of Faith*. Lynnwood: Kenyon's Gospel Publishing Society, 1989.

Kenyon, E. W. *What Happened from the Cross to the Throne*. Lynnwood: Kenyon's Gospel Publishing Society, 1993.

Kenyon, E. W. and Don Gossett. *The Power of Your Words*. New Kensington: Whitaker, 1981.

Kim, Sung-Gun. "The Heavenly Touch Ministry in the Age of Millennial Capitalism: A Phenomenological Perspective." *Nova Religio* 15, no. 3 (February 2012): 51–64.

King, Paul. *Only Believe: Examining the Origin and Development of Classic and Contemporary Word of Faith Theologies*. Tulsa: Word and Spirit, 2008.

King, Paul and Jacques Theron. "The 'Classic Faith' Roots of the Modern 'Word of Faith' Movement." *Studia Historiae Ecclesiasticae* 32, no. 1 (2006): 309–34.

Kinnebrew, James. "The Charismatic Doctrine of Positive Confession: A Historical, Exegetical, and Theological Critique." Doctor of theology thesis, Mid-America Baptist Theological Seminary, Cordova, 1980.

Klaver, Miranda. "Pentecostal Pastorpreneurs and the Global Circulation of Authoritative Aesthetic Styles." *Culture and Religion* 16, no. 2 (2015): 146–59.

Klein, Naomi. *No Logo*. New York: Picador, 2002.

Klink III, Edward and Darian Lockett. *Understanding Biblical Theology: A Comparison of Theory and Practice*. Grand Rapids: Zondervan, 2012.

Kluttz, Jeff. *Apostasy! The Word-Faith Doctrinal Deception*. Self-published. Returningking
.com, 2011. Kindle edition.

Knight III, Henry. "God's Faithfulness and God's Freedom: A Comparison of
Contemporary Theologies of Healing." *Journal of Pentecostal Theology* 2 (1999):
65–89.

Koch, Bradley. "Penny-Pinching for Prosperity: The Prosperity Gospel and Monetary
Giving Habits." Paper presented at the Annual Meeting of the American Sociological
Association, August 2010 Atlanta.

Koch, Bradley. "The Prosperity Gospel and Economic Prosperity: Race, Class, Giving, and
Voting." Doctor of philosophy thesis, Indiana University, Bloomington, 2009.

Koch, Bradley. "Who Are the Prosperity Gospel Adherents?" *Journal of Ideology* 36 (2014):
1–46.

Köhrsen, Jens. "Pentecostal Improvement Strategies: A Comparative Reading on African
and South American Pentecostalism." In *Pastures of Plenty: Tracing Religio-Scapes of
Prosperity Gospel in Africa and Beyond*, edited by Andreas Heuser, 49–64. Frankfurt:
Peter Lang, 2015.

Koning, Juliette. "Beyond the Prosperity Gospel: Moral Identity Work and Organizational
Cultures in Pentecostal-Charismatic Churches in Indonesia." In *New Religiosities,
Modern Capitalism, and Moral Complexities in Southeast Asia*, edited by Juliette
Koning and Gwenaël Njoto-Feillard, 17–38. Singapore: Palgrave Macmillan, 2017.

Krabbendam, Henry. "Scripture-Twisting." In *The Agony of Deceit: What Some TV
Preachers are Really Preaching*, edited by Michael Horton, 63–88. Chicago: Moody
Press, 1990.

Kraft, Charles. *Christianity with Power*. Ann Arbor: Servant Books, 1989.

Kreinath, Jens. "Semiotics." In *Theorizing Rituals: Issues, Topics, Approaches, Concepts*,
edited by Jens Kreinath, Jan Snoek and Michael Stausberg, 429–70. Leiden: Brill, 2006.

Kuhrt, Stephen. *Tom Wright for Everyone*. London: SPCK, 2011.

Land, Steven J. *Pentecostal Spirituality: A Passion for the Kingdom*. Sheffield: Sheffield
Academic Press, 1993.

Landrus, Heather. "Hearing 3 John 2 in the Voices of History." *Journal of Pentecostal
Theology* 11, no. 1 (2002): 70–88.

Larsen, David. "The Gospel of Greed Versus the Gospel of the Grace of God." *Trinity
Journal* 9 (1988): 211–20.

Larson, Martin. *New Thought or A Modern Religious Approach: The Philosophy of Health,
Happiness, and Prosperity*. New York: Philosophical Library, 1985.

Lausanne Movement. "The Cape Town Commitment: A Confession of Faith and a Call to
Action." 2011. Accessed April 7, 2021. https://www.lausanne.org/content/ctc/ctcommit
ment.

Lausanne Theology Working Group. "A Statement on the Prosperity Gospel." January 16,
2010. Accessed April 7, 2021. https://www.lausanne.org/content/a-statement-on-the
-prosperity-gospel.

Lauterbach, Karen. *Christianity, Wealth, and Spiritual Power in Ghana*. New York: Palgrave
Macmillan, 2017.

Lauterbach, Karen. "Fakery and Wealth in African Charismatic Christianity: Moving
Beyond the Prosperity Gospel as Script." In *Faith in African Lived Christianity: Bridging
Anthropological and Theological Perspectives*, edited by Karen Lauterbach and Mika
Vähäkangas, 111–32. Leiden: Brill, 2020.

Lederle, Henry. *Theology with Spirit: The Future of the Pentecostal and Charismatic
Movements in the 21st Century*. Tulsa: Word and Spirit, 2010.

Lee, Edgar. "The Role of the Bible in Shaping a Christian Worldview." In *Elements of a Christian Worldview*, edited by Michael Palmer, 79–106. Springfield: Logion, 1998.

Lee, Shayne. *T. D. Jakes: America's New Preacher*. New York: New York University Press, 2005.

Lee, Shayne and Phillip Luke Sinitiere. *Holy Mavericks: Evangelical Innovators and the Spiritual Marketplace*. New York: New York University Press, 2009.

Lewison, Elsie. "Pentecostal Power and the Holy Spirit of Capitalism: Re-Imagining Modernity in the Charismatic Cosmology." *Symposia* 3, no. 1 (2011): 31–54.

Lie, Geir. "E. W. Kenyon: Cult Founder or Evangelical Minister?" *Journal of the European Pentecostal Theological Association* 16 (1996): 71–86.

Lie, Geir. *E.W. Kenyon: Cult Founder or Evangelical Minister*. Oslo: Refleks, 2003.

Lifeway Research. "Churchgoers Views—Prosperity." 2018. Accessed April 7, 2021. http://lifewayresearch.com/wp-content/uploads/2018/07/American-Churchgoers-Prosperity-2017.pdf.

Lin, Tony Tian-Ren. *Prosperity Gospel Latinos and Their American Dream*. Chapel Hill: The University of North Carolina Press, 2020. Kindle edition.

Lin, Tony Tian-Ren. "The Gospel of the American Dream." *The Hedgehog Review* 15, no. 2 (Summer 2013): 34–43.

Lindhardt, Martin. "Are Blessings for Sale?: Ritual Exchange, Witchcraft Allegations, and the De-alienation of Money in Tanzanian Prosperity Ministries." In *Pastures of Plenty: Tracing Religio-Scapes of Prosperity Gospel in Africa and Beyond*, edited by Andreas Heuser, 309–22. Frankfurt: Peter Lang, 2015.

Lindhardt, Martin. "Introduction." In *Practicing the Faith: The Ritual Life of Pentecostal-Charismatic Christians*, edited by Martin Lindhardt, 1–48. New York: Berghahn, 2011.

Lindhardt, Martin. "More Than Just Money: The Faith Gospel and Occult Economies in Contemporary Tanzania." *Nova Religio* 13, no. 1 (2009): 41–67.

Lindholm, Hans and Fredrik Broshe. *Varför Är Trosförkunnelsen Farlig?* Uppsala: EFS Förlaget, 1986.

Lindsley, Art. "Settling for Mud Pies." In *The Agony of Deceit: What Some TV Preachers are Really Preaching*, edited by Michael Horton, 49–60. Chicago: Moody Press, 1990.

Lindstrom, Lamot. "Cargo Cults." In *International Encyclopedia of the Social and Behavioural Sciences*, edited by James D. Wright, 139–44. 2nd revised edition. London: Elsevier Science, 2015.

Lovett, Leonard. "Positive Confession Theology." In *The New International Dictionary of Pentecostal and Charismatic Movements*, edited by Stanley M. Burgess and Eduard M. Van Der Maas, s.v. "Positive Confession Theology." Rev. and exp. edn. Grand Rapids: Zondervan, 2003. E-book edition.

LoveWorld Television Ministry. "Watch Your LoveWorld Praise-A-Thon with Pastor Chris & Pastor Benny Hinn Day 3." YouTube Video, 38:14. December 11, 2019. Accessed June 6, 2020. https://www.youtube.com/watch?v=BW9c2DOXnwM.

Luce, Edward. "A Preacher for Trump's America: Joel Osteen and the Prosperity Gospel." *Financial Times*, April 18, 2019. Accessed April 7, 2021. https://www.ft.com/content/3990ce66-60a6-11e9-b285-3acd5d43599e.

Ma, Wonsuk. "Blessing in Pentecostal Theology and Mission." In *Pentecostal Mission and Global Christianity*, edited by Wonsuk Ma, Veli-Matti Kärkkäinen and J. Kwabena Asamoah-Gyadu, 272–91. Oxford: Regnum Books International, 2014.

Ma, Wonsuk. "David Yonggi Cho's Theology of Blessing: Basis, Legitimacy, and Limitations." *Evangelical Review of Theology* 35, no. 2 (2011): 140–59.

MacArthur, John. *Charismatic Chaos*. Grand Rapids: Zondervan, 1992.

MacArthur, John. *Strange Fire*. Nashville: Thomas Nelson, 2013.

Macchia, Frank D. *Baptized in the Spirit: A Global Pentecostal Theology*. Grand Rapids: Zondervan, 2009.

Macchia, Frank D. "A Call for Careful Discernment: A Theological Response to Prosperity Preaching." In *Pentecostalism and Prosperity: The Socio-Economics of the Global Charismatic Movement*, edited by Katherine Attanasi and Amos Yong, 225–38. New York: Palgrave Macmillan, 2012.

Macchia, Frank D. "The Spirit and God's Return to Indwell a People." In *God and the Faithfulness of Paul: A Critical Examination of the Pauline Theology of N. T. Wright*, edited by Christoph Heilig, Thomas Hewitt and Michael Bird, 632–44. Minneapolis: Fortress, 2017.

Macchia, Frank D. "Spirit Baptism." In *Routledge Handbook to Pentecostal Theology*, edited by Wolfgang Vondey, 247–56. London: Routledge, 2020.

Machado, Daisy. "Capitalism, Immigration, and the Prosperity Gospel." *Anglican Theological Review* 92, no. 4 (2010): 723–30.

MacGregor, Kirk R. "Recognizing and Successfully Averting the Word-Faith Threat to Evangelicalism." *Christian Apologetics Journal* 6, no. 1 (2007): 53–70.

MacTavish, Ron. "Pentecostal Profits: The Prosperity Gospel in the Global South." Master of arts thesis, University of Lethbridge, 1999.

Maddox, Marion. "Prosper, Consume and Be Saved." *Critical Research on Religion* 1, no. 1 (2013): 108–15.

Magliato, Joe. *The Wallstreet Gospel*. Eugene: Harvest House, 1981.

Maldonado, Guillermo. *The Kingdom of Power*. New Kensington: Whitaker House, 2013. E-book edition.

Maltese, Giovanni. "An Activist-Holiness Hagin? A Case Study of Prosperity Theology in the Philippines." In *Pastures of Plenty: Tracing Religio-Scapes of Prosperity Gospel in Africa and Beyond*, edited by Andreas Heuser, 65–80. Frankfurt: Peter Lang, 2015.

Maritz, Daniel and Henk Stoker. "Does the Christian Worldview Provide a Place for the Law of Attraction? (Part 1): An Apologetic Evaluation of the Roots of this Doctrine." *Verbum et Ecclesia* 37, no. 1 (2016): no page numbers. Accessed April 7, 2021. http://dx.doi.org/10.4102/ve.v37i1.1571.

Maritz, Daniel and Henk Stoker. "Does the Christian Worldview Provide a Place for the Law of Attraction? (Part 2): An Apologetic Evaluation of the Way the Bible Is Used in Promoting This Idea." *Verbum et Ecclesia* 37, no. 1 (2016): no page numbers. Accessed April 7, 2021. http://dx.doi.org/10.4102/ve.v37i1.1570.

Marshall-Fratani, Ruth. "Mediating the Global and Local in Nigerian Pentecostalism." In *Between Babel and Pentecost*, edited by André Corten and Ruth Marshall-Fratani, 80–105. Bloomington: Indiana University Press, 2001.

Marti, Gerardo. "The Adaptability of Pentecostalism: The Fit Between Prosperity Theology and Globalized Individualization in a Los Angeles Church." *Pneuma: The Journal of the Society for Pentecostal Studies* 34, no. 1 (2012): 5–25.

Marti, Gerardo. "Foreword." In *The Hillsong Movement Examined: You Call Me Out Upon the Waters*, edited by Tanya Riches and Tom Wagner, v–x. New York: Palgrave Macmillan, 2017.

Marti, Gerardo. "'I Determine My Harvest:' Risky Careers and Spirit-Guided Prosperity in Los Angeles." In *Pentecostalism and Prosperity: The Socio-Economics of the Global Charismatic Movement*, edited by Katherine Attanasi and Amos Yong, 131–50. New York: Palgrave Macmillan, 2012.

Marti, Gerardo. *Hollywood Faith: Holiness, Prosperity, and Ambition in a Los Angeles Church*. New Jersey: Rutgers University Press, 2008.

Martin, Bernice. "New Mutations of the Protestant Ethic among Latin American Pentecostals." *Religion* 25 (1995): 101–17.

Martin, Lee Roy. "Longing for God: Psalm 63 and Pentecostal Spirituality." *Journal of Pentecostal Theology* 22, no. 1 (2013): 54–76.

Maton, Karl. "Habitus." In *Pierre Bourdieu: Key Concepts*, edited by Michael Grenfell, 47–64. London: Routledge, 2014.

Matta, Judith. *The Born Again Jesus of the Word-Faith Teaching*. Bellevue: Spirit of Truth, 1987.

Mauss, Marcel. *The Gift: The Form and Reason for Exchange in Archaic Societies*. New York: Routledge, 2002.

Maxwell, David. "'Delivered from the Spirit of Poverty?': Pentecostalism, Prosperity and Modernity in Zimbabwe." *Journal of Religion in Africa* 28, no. 3 (1998): 350–73.

Maxwell, David. "Social Mobility and Politics in African Pentecostal Modernity." In *Global Pentecostalism in the 21st Century*, edited by Robert Hefner, 91–114. Bloomington: Indiana University Press, 2013.

Mbamalu, Abiola. "'Prosperity a Part of the Atonement': An Interpretation of 2 Corinthians 8:9." *Verbum et Ecclesia* 36, no. 1 (2015): 1–8.

McCauley, John. "Africa's New Big Man Rule? Pentecostalism and Patronage in Ghana." *African Affairs* 112, no. 446 (January 2013): 1–21.

McCauley, John. "Pentecostals and Politics: Redefining Big Man Rule in Africa." In *Pentecostalism in Africa: Presence and Impact of Pneumatic Christianity in Postcolonial Societies*, edited by Martin Lindhardt, 322–44. Leiden: Brill, 2014.

McClymond, Michael. "Prosperity Already and Not Yet: An Eschatological Interpretation of the Health-and-Wealth Emphasis in the North American Pentecostal-Charismatic Movement." In *Perspectives in Pentecostal Eschatologies*, edited by Peter Althouse and Robby Waddell, 293–312. Cambridge: James Clarke, 2012.

McConnell, D. R. *A Different Gospel: A Bold and Revealing Look at the Biblical and Historical Basis of the Word of Faith Movement*. Updated edition. Peabody: Hendrickson, 1995.

Mcfadden, Cynthia and Mary Marsh. "How Joyce Meyer Built a Worldwide Following." *ABC News*, April 13, 2010. Accessed April 7, 2021. https://abcnews.go.com/Nightline/joyce-meyer-transparent-evangelist/story?id=10355887.

McGee, Paula. "The Wal-Martization of African American Religion: T.D. Jakes and Woman Thou Art Loosed." Doctor of philosophy thesis, Claremont Graduate University, Claremont, 2012.

McGowman, Andrew. "Ecclesiology as Ethnology." In *God and the Faithfulness of Paul: A Critical Examination of the Pauline Theology of N. T. Wright*, edited by Christoph Heilig, Thomas Hewitt and Michael Bird, 584–85. Minneapolis: Fortress, 2017.

McGrath, Alister E. *Christianity's Dangerous Idea: The Protestant Revolution: History from the Sixteenth Century to the Twenty-First*. New York: HarperCollins, 2007.

McGrath, Alister E. *Christian Theology: An Introduction*. 5th edn. Chichester: Wiley-Blackwell, 2011.

McGrath, Alister E. *Evangelicalism and the Future of Christianity*. Downers Grove: InterVarsity, 1995.

McGrath, Alister E. *Heresy: A History of Defending the Truth*. London: SPCK, 2009.

McGrath, Alister E. *Narrative Apologetics: Sharing the Relevance, Joy, and Wonder of the Christian Faith*. Grand Rapids: BakerBooks, 2019.

McGrath, Alister E. "Narratives of Significance." In *Theologically Engaged Anthropology*, edited by J. Dereck Lemons, 123–39. Oxford: Oxford University Press, 2018.

McGrath, Alister E. "Reality, Symbol and History." In *Jesus and the Restoration of Israel: A Critical Assessment of N. T. Wright's Jesus and the Victory of God*, edited by Carey Newman, 159–79. Downers Grove: IVP, 1999.

McGrath, Alister E. *Re-Imagining Nature: The Promise of a Christian Natural Theology*. Chichester: John Wiley and Sons, 2017.

McIntrye, Joe. *E. W. Kenyon and His Message of Faith: The True Story*. Lake Mary: Charisma House, 1997.

Medina, Erron and Jayeel Cornelio. "The Prosperity Ethic: Neoliberal Christianity and the Rise of the New Prosperity Gospel in the Philippines." *Pneuma: The Journal of the Society for Pentecostal Studies* 43, no. 1 (2021): 72–93.

Meeks, Gina. "Hillsong NYC's Carl Lentz Dubbed 'Apostle of Cool' By Secular Men's Mag." *Charisma News*, September 26, 2013. Accessed April 7, 2021. https://www.charisma news.com/us/41154-hillsong-nyc-s-carl-lentz-dubbed-apostle-of-cool-by-secular-me n-s-mag.

Meister Butler, Susie. "Presents of God: The Marketing of the American Prosperity Gospel." Doctor of philosophy thesis, University of Pittsburgh, Pittsburgh, 2014.

Melton, J. Gordon. "The Prosperity Gospel in Texas: The Case of Kenneth Copeland." Paper presented to the 47th Annual Meeting of the Society for Pentecostal Studies, Cleveland, Tennessee, March, 2018.

Menzies, William and Robert Menzies. *Spirit and Power*. Grand Rapids: Zondervan, 2000.

Merrell, Floyd. "Charles Sanders Peirce's Concept of the Sign." In *The Routledge Companion to Semiotics and Linguistics*, edited by Paul Cobley, 28–39. London: Routledge, 2001.

Meyer, Birgit. "Christianity in Africa: From African Independent to Pentecostal-Charismatic Churches." *Annual Review of Anthropology* 33 (2004): 447–74.

Meyer, Birgit. "Commodities and the Power of Prayer: Pentecostalist Attitudes Towards Consumption in Contemporary Ghana." *Development and Change* 29 (1998): 751–76.

Meyer, Birgit. "'Delivered from the Powers of Darkness': Confessions of Satanic Riches in Christian Ghana." *Africa: Journal of the International African Institute* 65, no. 2 (1995): 236–55.

Meyer, Birgit. "'Make a Complete Break with the Past.' Memory and Post-Colonial Modernity in Ghanaian Pentecostalist Discourse." *Journal of Religion in Africa* 28, no. 3 (1998): 316–49.

Meyer, Birgit. "Pentecostalism and Globalization." In *Studying Global Pentecostalism*, edited by Allan Anderson, Andre Droogers, Michael Bergunder and Cornelis van der Laan , 113–32. Berkeley: University of California Press, 2010.

Meyer, Birgit. "Pentecostalism and Neo-Liberal Capitalism: Faith, Prosperity and Vision in African Pentecostal-Charismatic Churches." *Journal for the Study of Religion* 20, no. 2 (2007): 5–26.

Meyer, Birgit. "Religious Sensations: Why Media, Aesthetics and Power Matter in the Study of Contemporary Religion." Presentation, Vrije Universiteit, Amsterdam, 2006. Accessed April 7, 2021. https://www.researchgate.net/publication/241889837_Reli gious_Sensations_Why_Media_Aesthetics_and_Power_Matter_in_the_Study_of _Contemporary_Religion.

Meyer, Joyce. *Battlefield of the Mind*. New York: FaithWords, 2012. E-book edition.

Meyer, Joyce. *Enjoying Where You Are on the Way to Where You Are Going*. New York: FaithWords, 2012. E-book edition.

Meyer, Joyce. *Expect a Move of God in Your Life . . . Suddenly!* New York: Warner Books, 2003. E-book edition.

Meyer, Joyce. *How to Succeed at Being Yourself*. New York: Warner Faith, 1999. E-book edition.

Meyer, Joyce. *In Pursuit of Peace*. New York: Warner Faith, 2004. E-book edition.

Meyer, Joyce. *Jesus: Name Above All Names*. New York: Warner, 2000. E-book edition.

Meyer, Joyce. *The Most Important Decision You Ever Make*. Tulsa: Harrison House, 1996. E-book edition.

Meyer, Joyce. "Strong in Spirit." *Joycemeyer.org*. Accessed April 7, 2021. https://joycemeyer.org/everydayanswers/ea-teachings/strong-in-spirit.

Meyer, Joyce. *Victory in Your Mind, Mouth, Moods and Attitudes*. Fenton: Joyce Meyer Ministries, 2013. E-book edition.

Meyer, Joyce Ministries. "Exercise Your Authority." *Joycemeyer.org*. Accessed April 7, 2021. https://www.joycemeyer.org/everydayanswers/ea-teachings/exercise-your-authority.

Micheelsen, Arun. "'I Don't Do Systems': An Interview with Clifford Geertz." *Method & Theory in the Study of Religion* 14, no. 1 (2002): 2–20.

Middleton, Richard. *A New Heaven and New Earth: Reclaiming Biblical Eschatology*. Grand Rapids: Baker, 2014.

Middleton, Richard. "A New Heaven and a New Earth: The Case for a Holistic Reading of the Biblical Story of Redemption." *Journal for Christian Theological Research* 6, no. 4 (2006): 73–97.

Middleton, Richard and Brian Walsh. *Truth Is Stranger than It Used to Be*. Downers Grove: IVP, 1995.

Millennium Magazine. "Pastor Paula White: Taking Ownership." *Millmag.org*. May 19, 2020. Accessed April 7, 2021. https://www.millmag.org/pastor-paula-white-taking-ownership-2/.

Miller, Christine and Nathan Carlin. "Joel Osteen as Cultural Selfobject: Meeting the Needs of the Group Self and Its Individual Members in and from the Largest Church in America." *Pastoral Psychology* 59 (2010): 27–51.

Miller, David W. "Wealth Creation as Integrated with Faith." Presentation, Muslim, Christian, and Jewish Views on the Creation of Wealth, Notre Dame, April 23–24, 2007.

Miller, Donald. "Introduction: Pentecostalism as Global Phenomenon." In *Spirit and Power: The Growth and Global Impact of Pentecostalism*, edited by Donald Miller, Kimon Sargeant and Richard Flory, 1–24. New York: Oxford University Press, 2013.

Miller, Donald and Tetsunao Yamamori. *Global Pentecostalism: The New Face of Christian Social Engagement*. Berkeley: University of California Press, 2007.

Miller, Vincent. *Consuming Religion*. New York: Continuum, 2003.

Minkov, Michael. *Cross-Cultural Analysis*. New York: SAGE, 2013.

Mitchem, Stephanie. *Name It and Claim It?: Prosperity Preaching in the Black Church*. Cleveland: Pilgrim, 2007.

Mombi, George. "Impact of the Prosperity Gospel in the Assemblies of God Churches of Papua New Guinea." *Melanesian Journal of Theology* 25, no. 1 (2009): 32–58.

Moo, Douglas. "Divine Healing in the Health and Wealth Gospel." *Trinity Journal* 9 (1988): 191–209.

Moore, Keith. *God's Will to Heal*. Branson: Moore Life Ministries, 2013.

Mora, Cristina. "Marketing the 'Health and Wealth Gospel' Across National Borders; Evidence from Brazil and the United States." *Poetics* 36 (2008): 404–20.

Moreton, Bethany. *To Serve God and Wal-Mart: The Making of Christian Free Enterprise.* Cambridge: Harvard University Press, 2009.

Morran E. S. and L. Schlemmer. *Faith for The Fearful?: An Investigation Into New Churches in The Greater Durban Area.* Durban: Centre for Applied Social Sciences University of Natal Durban, 1984.

Morris, Russell. "A Biblical and Theological Analysis of Specific Tenets of Word of Faith Theology: Pastoral Implications for The Church of God." Doctor of philosophy thesis, South African Theological Seminary, 2012.

Mumford, Debra. *Exploring Prosperity Preaching: Biblical Health, Wealth and Wisdom.* Valley Forge: Judson Press, 2012.

Mumford, Debra. "Prosperity Gospel and African American Prophetic Preaching." *Review and Expositor* 109 (2012): 365–85.

Mundey, Peter. "The Prosperity Gospel and the Spirit of Consumerism According to Joel Osteen." *Pneuma: The Journal of the Society for Pentecostal Studies* 39, no. 3 (2017): 318–41.

Munroe, Myles. *Applying the Kingdom.* Shippensburg: Destiny Image, 2007. E-book edition.

Munroe, Myles. *The Purpose and Power of Authority.* New Kensington: Whitaker House, 2011. E-book edition.

Munyon, Timothy. "The Creation of the Universe and Humankind." In *Systematic Theology*, edited by Stanley Horton, 215–54. Revised edition. Springfield: Logion, 2007.

Murdock, Mike. *The Craziest Thing God Ever Told Me.* Fort Worth: The Wisdom Center, 2002.

Nash, Ronald. *Faith and Reason: Searching for a Rational Faith.* Grand Rapids: Zondervan, 1988.

Nash, Ronald. *Worldview in Conflict.* Grand Rapids: Zondervan, 1992.

Naugle, David. "Narrative and Life: The Central Role of Stories in Human Experience." Paper Presented at Friday Symposium, Dallas Baptist University, February 5, 1999. Accessed April 7, 2021. https://www3.dbu.edu/Naugle/pdf/narrative_and_life.pdf.

Naugle, David. *Worldview: The History of a Concept.* Grand Rapids: Eerdmans, 2002.

Naugle, David. "Worldview: History, Theology, Implications." In *After Worldview: Christian Higher Education in Postmodern Worlds*, edited by J. Matthew Bonzo and Michael Stevens, 5–26. Sioux Center: Dordt College Press, 2009.

Nel, Marius. *The Prosperity Gospel in Africa: An African Pentecostal Hermeneutical Consideration.* Eugene: Wipf and Stock, 2020.

Nelson, Robert. "Economics and Environmentalism: Belief Systems at Odds." *The Independent Review* 17, no. 1 (Summer 2012): 5–17.

Nelson, Robert. "Economics as Religion." In *Economics and Religion: Are They Distinct?*, edited by Geoffrey Brennan and A.M.C. Waterman, 227–36. New York: Springer, 1994.

Nelson, Robert. "The Secular Religion of Progress." *The New Atlantis* 39 (Summer 2013): 38–50.

Neuman, Terris. "Cultic Origins of Word-Faith Theology within the Charismatic Movement." *Pneuma: The Journal of the Society for Pentecostal Studies* 12, no. 1 (1990): 32–55.

Newman, Carey ed. *Jesus and the Restoration of Israel: A Critical Assessment of N. T. Wright's Jesus and the Victory of God.* Downers Grove: IVP, 1999.

Newport, John. *The New Age Movement and the Biblical Worldview: Conflict and Dialogue.* Grand Rapids: Eerdmans, 1998.

Niemandt, Nelus. "The Prosperity Gospel, the Decolonisation of Theology, and the Abduction of Missionary Imagination." *Missionalia* 45, no. 3 (2017): 203–19.

Nietzsche, Friedrich. *Thus Spoke Zarathustra*, translated by R. J. Hollingdale. London: Penguin, 1969.

Nolivos, Eloy. "Capitalism and Pentecostalism in Latin America: Trajectories of Prosperity and Development." In *Pentecostalism and Prosperity: The Socio-Economics of the Global Charismatic Movement*, edited by Katherine Attanasi and Amos Yong, 87–106. New York: Palgrave Macmillan, 2012.

Nöth, Winfred. *Handbook of Semiotics.* Bloomington: Indiana University Press, 1990.

Nwankwo, Lawrence. "'You Have Received the Spirit of power . . .' (2 Tim. 1:7) Reviewing the Prosperity Message in the Light of a Theology of Empowerment." *Journal of the European Pentecostal Theological Association* 22, no. 1 (2002): 56–77. Accessed April 7, 2021. http://dx.doi.org/10.1179/jep.2002.22.1.005.

O'Neill, Patrick. "Narrative Structure." In *Routledge Encyclopaedia of Narrative Theory*, edited by David Herman, Manferd Jahn and Marie-Laure Ryan, s.v. "Narrative Structure." London: Routledge, 2005.

Obadare, Ebenezer. "'Raising Righteous Billionaires': The Prosperity Gospel Reconsidered." *HTS Teologiese Studies/Theological Studies* 72, no. 4 (2016): 1–8. Accessed April 7, 2021. http://dx.doi.org/10.4102/hts.v72i4.3571.

Oliverio, L. William Jr. *Theological Hermeneutics in the Classical Pentecostal Tradition: A Typological Account.* Leiden: Brill, 2012.

Olson, Roger E. *Counterfeit Christianity.* Nashville: Abingdon, 2015.

Olson, Roger E. *The Essentials of Christian Thought.* Grand Rapids: Zondervan, 2017.

Olson, Roger E. *The Mosaic of Christian Belief.* Downers Grove: IVP Academic, 2002.

Olson, Roger E. *Reformed and Always Reforming: The Postconservative Approach to Evangelical Theology.* Grand Rapids: Baker Academic, 2007.

Olson, Roger E. *The SCM Press A–Z of Evangelical Theology.* London: SCM Press, 2005.

Olthuis, James. "On Worldviews." In *Stained Glass: Worldviews and Social Science*, edited by Paul Marshall, Sander Griffioen, Richard Mouw, 26–40. Lanham: University Press of America, 1989.

Olthuis, James. "Where There Is Love, There Is Vision: Witnessing in/under/through Worldviews." In *After Worldview: Christian Higher Education in Postmodern Worlds*, edited by Matthew Bonzo and Michael Stevens, 81–94. Sioux Center: Dordt College, 2009.

Ortner, Sherry. "On Key Symbols." *American Anthropologist* 75 (1973): 1338–46.

Oro, Ari Pedro and Pablo Semán. "Brazilian Pentecostalism Crosses National Boarders." In *Between Babel and Pentecost: Transnational Pentecostalism in African and Latin America*, edited by André Corten and Ruth Marshall-Fratani, 181–95. London: Hurst, 2001.

Osborn, T. L. *Healing the Sick.* Tulsa: Harrison House, 1992.

Osborn, T. L. *The Good Life.* Tulsa: Harrison House, 1994.

Osborne, Grant. *The Hermeneutical Spiral.* Downers Grove: IVP, 1991.

Osteen, Joel and Victoria Osteen. *Wake Up to Hope Devotional.* New York: FaithWords, 2016.

Osteen, John. *Unravelling the Mystery of the Blood Covenant.* Houston: John Osteen Publications, 1988.

Osteen, Victoria. "Keeping Dominion." *Joel and Victoria's Blog*, Joel Osteen Ministries. September 29, 2015. Accessed April 7, 2021. https://www.joelosteen.com/Pages/Blog.aspx?blogid=10587.

Otieno, Maura Michael, Conrad Mbewe, Ken Mbugua, John Piper and Wayne Grudem. *Prosperity? Seeking the True Gospel*. Nairobi: Africa Christian Textbooks, 2015.

Oyakhilome, Chris. *How to Make Your Faith Work*. Essex: LoveWorld, 2005. E-book edition.

Oyedepo, David. *Anointing for Breakthrough*. Lagos: Dominion Publishing House, 2017. E-book edition.

Oyedepo, David. *Born to Win*. Lagos: Dominion Publishing House, 1993. E-book edition.

Oyedepo, David. *Releasing the Supernatural*. Lagos: Dominion Publishing House, 1995. E-book edition.

Palmer, Michael ed. *Elements of a Christian Worldview*. Springfield: Logion, 1998.

Parry, Robin. "Narrative Criticism." In *The Dictionary for Theological Interpretation of the Bible*, edited by Kevin J. Vanhoozer, 528–31. Grand Rapids: Baker, 2005.

Pasicka, Malgorzata. "Mundane Transcendence? Conceptualisations of Faith in Prosperity Theology." In *Cognitive Linguistics in Action: From Theory to Application and Back*, edited by Elzbieta Tabakowska, Michal Choinski and Lukas Wiraszka, 371–86. Berlin: De Gruyter Mouton, 2010.

Peale, Norman Vincent. *The Power of Positive Thinking*. New York: Prentice-Hall, 1952.

Pearcey, Nancy. *Total Truth: Liberating Christianity from Its Cultural Captivity*. Wheaton: Crossway, 2004.

Peck, Jamie. "Preface: Naming Neoliberalism." In *The SAGE Handbook of Neoliberalism*, edited by Damien Cahill, Melinda Cooper, Martijn Konings and David Primrose, xxii–xxiv. Los Angeles: SAGE Publishing, 2018.

Perriman, Andrew, ed. *Faith, Health and Prosperity: A Report on 'Word of Faith' and 'Positive Confession' Theologies by ACUTE (the Evangelical Alliance Commission on Unity and Truth among Evangelicals)*. Carlisle: Paternoster, 2003.

Perrin, Nicholas and Richard Hays, eds. *Jesus, Paul and the People of God: A Theological Dialogue with N. T. Wright*. London: SPCK, 2011.

Peter, C. B. "The Church's Response to Poverty: A Jungian Appraisal of the 'Prosperity Gospel' Phenomenon." *Ogbomoso Journal of Theology* 14 (2009): 137–47.

Peters, Justin. "Clouds without Water: A Biblical Critique of the Word of Faith Movement. Exposing the False Prosperity Gospel." *DVD*. Edmond: Justin Peters Ministries, 2016.

Pew Research Center. *Religion in Latin America: Widespread Change in a Historically Catholic Region*. Washington: Pew Research Center, 2014.

Pew Research Center. *Spirit and Power: A 10-Country Survey of Pentecostals*. Washington: Pew Research Center, 2007.

Pew Research Center. *What Americans Know About Religion*. Washington: Pew Research Center, 2019.

Phillips, J. B. *Ring of Truth: A Translator's Testimony*. London: Hodder and Stoughton, 1967.

Pinnock, Clark. *Flame of Love: A Theology of the Holy Spirit*. Grand Rapids: IVP Academic, 1996.

Piper, John. *The Future of Justification: A Response to N. T. Wright*. Wheaton: Crossway, 2007.

Piper, John. "Prosperity Preaching: Deceitful and Deadly." *Marks Journal* 9 (2014): 50–2.

Pool, Jeff. *God's Wounds*. Eugene: Pickwick, 2009.

Poole, Eve. *Buying God: Consumerism and Theology*. London: SPCK, 2018.

Posel, Deborah and Ilana van Wyk. "Thinking with Veblen: Case Studies from Africa's Past and Present." In *Conspicuous Consumption in Africa*, edited by Deborah Posel and Ilana van Wyk, 1–24. Johannesburg: Wits University Press, 2019.

Premawardhana, Devaka. "Transformational Tithing: Sacrifice and Reciprocity in a Neo-Pentecostal Church." *Nova Religio* 15, no. 4 (2012): 85–109.

Price, Fred K. C. *Faith, Foolishness or Presumption*. Tulsa: Harrison House, 1979.

Prince, Joseph Ministries. "Declare God's Word Over Your Situation." *Josephprince.org*. Accessed June 6, 2020. https://www.josephprince.org/blog/daily-grace-inspirations/declare-gods-word-over-your-situation.

Prince, Joseph. "Born Again to Have Dominion." *Daily Grace (blog)*, Joseph Prince Ministries. Accessed June 6, 2020. https://www.josephprince.org/blog/daily-grace-inspirations/born-again-to-have-dominion.

Prince, Joseph. *Destined to Reign*. Tulsa: Harrison House, 2010. E-book edition.

Prince, Joseph. *Grace Revolution*. New York: FaithWords, 2015. E-book edition.

Prince, Joseph. *Healing and Wholeness through the Holy Communion*. Singapore: Joseph Prince Teaching Resources, 2006.

Prince, Joseph. "Jesus' Authority has been Given to Us." *Daily Grace (blog)*, Joseph Prince Ministries. Accessed June 6, 2020. https://www.josephprince.org/blog/daily-grace-inspirations/jesus-authority-has-been-given-to-us.

Prince, Joseph. *The Power of Right Believing*. New York: FaithWords, 2013.

Prince, Joseph. *Unmerited Favor*. Lake Mary: Charisma House, 2011.

Puckett, Kent. "Narrative Theory's *Longue Durée*." In *The Cambridge Companion to Narrative Theory*, edited by Matthew Garrett, 13–28. Cambridge: Cambridge University Press, 2018.

Pugh, Ben. *Bold Faith: A Closer Look at the Five Key Ideas of Charismatic Christianity*. Eugene: Wipf and Stock, 2017.

Quentin J. Schultze. *Televangelism and American Culture*. Grand Rapids: Baker, 1991.

Quentin J. Schultze. "TV and Evangelism: Unequally Yoked?" In *The Agony of Deceit: What Some TV Preachers are Really Preaching*, edited by Michael Horton, 185–204. Chicago: Moody Press, 1990.

Rabens, Volker. "The Faithfulness of God and Its Effects on Faithful Living." In *God and the Faithfulness of Paul: A Critical Examination of the Pauline Theology of N. T. Wright*, edited by Christoph Heilig, Thomas Hewitt and Michael Bird, 555–82. Minneapolis: Fortress, 2017.

Rakow, Katja. "Religious Branding and the Quest to Meet Consumer Needs." In *Religion and the Marketplace in the United States*, edited by Jan Stievermann, Philip Goff and Detlef Junker, 216–33. Oxford: Oxford University Press, 2015.

Ramm, Bernard. *Protestant Bible Interpretation: A Textbook on Hermeneutics*. 3rd edn. Grand Rapids: Baker Academic, 1970.

Rappaport, Roy A. *Ritual and Religion in the Making of Humanity*. Cambridge: Cambridge University Press, 1999.

Reed, David. "The Prosperity Gospel and Money—Plundering the Devil's Den?" *Canadian Journal of Pentecostal-Charismatic Christianity* 10 (2019): 50–68.

Rey, Jeanne. "Missing Prosperity: Economies of Blessings in Ghana and the Diaspora." In *Pastures of Plenty: Tracing Religio-Scapes of Prosperity Gospel in Africa and Beyond*, edited by Andreas Heuser, 339–54. Frankfurt: Peter Lang, 2015.

Riches, Tanya. "Next Generation Essay: The Evolving Theological Emphasis of Hillsong Worship (1996–2007)." *Australasian Pentecostal Studies* 13 (2010): 87–133.

Richie, Tony. "Ecumenical Theology." In *Routledge Handbook to Pentecostal Theology*, edited by Wolfgang Vondey, 378–88. London: Routledge, 2020.

Rieger, Joerg. "Christianity, Capitalism, and Desire: Can Religion Still Make a Difference?" *Union Seminary Quarterly Review* 64, no. 1 (2013): 1–13.

Rieger, Joerg. "Divine Power, Donald Trump, and How the 2016 Presidential Elections Challenge Common Religious Assumptions." *Huffpost*, October 18, 2016. Accessed April 7, 2021. https://www.huffpost.com/entry/divine-power-donald-trump_b_124880 82.

Rieger, Joerg. *Jesus vs. Caesar: For People Tired of Serving the Wrong God*. Nashville: Abingdon, 2018.

Rieger, Joerg. *No Rising Tide: Theology, Economics and the Future*. Philadelphia: Fortress, 2009.

Robbins, Joel. "Anthropology and Theology: The Prosperity Gospel, Humanity, and the Problem of Judgment." YouTube Video, 1:18:24. Posted by "The Finnish Anthropological Society" March 16, 2018. Accessed April 7, 2021. https://www.you tube.com/watch?v=4jAkIng8FOU.

Robbins, Joel. "Pentecostal Networks and the Spirit of Globalization." *Social Analysis* 53, no. 1 (Spring 2009): 55–66.

Robbins, Joel. "Ritual Communication and Linguistic Ideology." *Current Anthropology* 42, no. 5 (December 2001): 591–614.

Robbins, Joel. "The Globalization of Pentecostal and Charismatic Christianity." *Annual Review of Anthropology* 33 (2004): 117–43.

Robbins, Joel. "The Obvious Aspects of Pentecostalism: Ritual and Pentecostal Globalization." In *Practicing the Faith*, edited by Martin Lindhardt, 49–67. New York, Berghahn, 2011.

Robbins, Joel. "World Christianity and the Reorganization of Disciplines." In *Theologically Engaged Anthropology*, edited by J. Derrick Lemons, 226–43. Oxford: Oxford University Press, 2018.

Robinson, Andrew. *God and the World of Signs*. Leiden: Brill, 2010.

Rosin, Hanna. "Did Christianity Cause the Crash?" *The Atlantic*, December 2009. Accessed April 7, 2021. https://www.theatlantic.com/magazine/archive/2009/12/did -christianity-cause-the-crash/307764/.

Ryan, Marie-Laure. "Narrative." In *Routledge Encyclopaedia of Narrative Theory*, edited by David Herman, Manferd Jahn and Marie-Laure Ryan, s.v. "Narrative." London: Routledge, 2005.

Ryan, Marie-Laure. "Toward a Definition of Narrative." In *The Cambridge Companion to Narrative*, edited by David Herman, 22–35. Cambridge: Cambridge University Press, 2007.

Ryken, Leland. *Words of Delight*. 2nd edn. Grand Rapids: Eerdmans, 1992.

Salinas, J. Daniel, ed. *Prosperity Theology and the Gospel: Good News or Bad News for the Poor?* Peabody: Hendrickson, 2017.

Salinas, J. Daniel. "Mainline Churches and Prosperity Theology in Latin America." In *Prosperity Theology and the Gospel: Good News or Bad News for the Poor?*, edited by J. Daniel Salinas, 115–22. Peabody: Hendrickson, 2017.

Samuel, Joy T. "The Pneumatic Experiences of the Indian Neocharismatics." Doctor of philosophy thesis, University of Birmingham, UK, 2017.

Samuel, Vinay. "A Biblical Ethical Assessment of Prosperity Teaching and the Blessing Movement." In *Prosperity Theology and the Gospel: Good News or Bad News for the Poor?*, edited by J. Daniel Salinas, 77–87. Peabody: Hendrickson, 2017.

Sánchez-Walsh, Arlene. "Santidad, Salvación, Sanidad, Liberación: The Word of Faith Movement among Twenty-First-Century Latina/o Pentecostals." In *Global Pentecostal and Charismatic Healing*, edited by Candy Gunter Brown, 151–68. Oxford: Oxford University Press, 2011.

Sánchez-Walsh, Arlene. *Pentecostals in America*. New York: Columbia University Press, 2018.

Sandmel, Samuel. "Parallelomania." *Journal of Biblical Literature* 81 (1962): 1–13.

Sannes, Kjell Olav. *Det Guddommeliggjorte Menneske og den Menneskeliggjorte Gud*. Oslo: Refleks-Publishing, 2005.

Saracco, J. Norberto. "Prosperity Theology." In *Dictionary of Mission Theology*, edited by John Corrie, 322–6. Nottingham: IVP, 2007.

Sarles, K. L. "Prosperity and Healing: Is It Promised to the Believer? A Theological Evaluation." *Bibliotheca Sacra*, 143 (1986): 329–52.

Savelle, Jerry. *Take Charge of Your Financial Destiny*. Crowley: Jerry Savelle Ministries, 1998.

Savelle, Jerry. *If Satan Can't Steal Your Joy . . . He Can't Keep Your Goods*. Revised edition. Tulsa: Harrison House, 2002. E-book edition.

Savelle, Jerry. *The Nature of Faith*. Crowley: Jerry Savelle Ministries, 2012.

Savelle, Jerry. *A Right Mental Attitude*. Tulsa: Harrison House, 1993.

Savelle, Jerry. *The Spirit of Might*. Tulsa: Harrison House, 1982. E-book edition.

Savelle, Jerry. *Turning Your Adversary into Victory*. Tulsa: Harrison House, 1994. E-book edition.

Savelle, Jerry. *Victory and Success are Yours*. Tulsa: Harrison House, 1982. E-book edition.

Savelle, Jerry. *Why God Wants You to Prosper*. Crowley: Jerry Savelle Ministries, 2014.

Schaeffer, Francis. *How Should We Then Live?* Wheaton: Crossway, 2005.

Schieman, Scott and Jong Hyun Jung. "'Practical Divine Influence': Socioeconomic Status and Belief in the Prosperity Gospel." *Journal for the Scientific Study of Religion* 51, no. 4 (2012): 738–56.

Schilbrack, Kevin, "Religion, Models of, and Reality: Are We Through with Geertz?" *Journal of the American Academy of Religion* 73, no. 2 (2005): 429–52.

Searle, John. *Speech Acts*. Cambridge: Cambridge University Press, 1969.

Sebeok, Thomas. *Signs: An Introduction to Semiotics*. 2nd edn. Toronto: University of Toronto Press, 2001.

Sedgwick, Peter. *The Market Economy and Christian Ethics*. Cambridge: Cambridge University Press, 1999.

Senapatiratne, Timothy. "A Pneumatological Addition to N. T. Wright's Hermeneutic Done in the Pentecostal Tradition." In *Pentecostal Theology and the Theological Vision of N. T. Wright*, edited by Janet Meyer Everts and Jeffrey S. Lamp, 141–78. Cleveland: CPT Press, 2015.

Shepperd, J. W. "Sociology of World Pentecostalism." In *The New International Dictionary of Pentecostal and Charismatic Movements*, edited by Stanley M. Burgess and Eduard M. Van Der Maas, s.v. "Sociology of World Pentecostalism." Rev. and exp. edn. Grand Rapids: Zondervan, 2003. E-book edition.

Short, T. L. "The Development of Peirce's Theory of Signs." In *The Cambridge Companion to Peirce*, edited by Cheryl Misak, 214–22. Cambridge: Cambridge University Press, 2009.

Shuttleworth, Abigail. "On Earth as It Is in Heaven: A Study of The Healing Praxis of Bill Johnson." Doctor of philosophy thesis, University of Birmingham, UK, 2015.

Simmons, Dale. "Hagin: Heretic or Herald of God? A Theological and Historical Analysis of Kenneth E. Hagin's Claim to Be a Prophet." Master of arts thesis, Oral Roberts University, Tulsa, 1985.

Simmons, Dale. "The Postbellum Pursuit of Peace, Power, and Plenty: As Seen in the Writings of Essek William Kenyon." Doctor of philosophy thesis, Drew University, Madison, 1990.

Sims, Bryan. "Evangelical Worldview Analysis: A Critical Assessment and Proposal." Doctor of philosophy thesis, The Southern Baptist Theological Seminary, Louisville, 2006.

Sinitiere, Philip Luke. *Salvation with a Smile: Joel Osteen, Lakewood Church, and American Christianity*. New York: New York University Press, 2015.

Sire, James. *Naming the Elephant: Worldview as a Concept*. 2nd edn. Downers Grove: IVP, 2015.

Sire, James. *Scripture Twisting: 20 Ways Cults Misread the Bible*. Downers Grove: InterVarsity Press. 1980.

Sire, James. *The Universe Next Door*, 5th edn. Downers Grove: IVP, 2009.

Smail, Tom, Andrew Walker and Nigel Wright. *The Love of Power or the Power of Love: A Careful Assessment of the Problems Within the Charismatic and Word-of-Faith Movements*. Minneapolis, Bethany House, 1994.

Smart, Ninian. "The Philosophy of Worldviews—That Is, the Philosophy of Religion Transformed." *Neue Zeitschrift für Systematische Theologie und Religionsphilosophie* 23, no. 1 (1981): 212–24.

Smart, Ninian. *The World's Religions*. Cambridge: Cambridge University Press, 1989.

Smietana, Bob. "Most Churchgoers Say God Wants Them to Prosper Financially." *Lifeway Research*. July 31, 2018. Accessed April 7, 2021. https://lifewayresearch.com/2018/07/31/most-churchgoers-say-god-wants-them-to-prosper-financially/.

Smith, Adam. *The Wealth of Nations Books I–III*. London: Penguin, [1776] 1999.

Smith, Christian. *Moral, Believing Animals*. Oxford: Oxford University Press, 2009.

Smith, James K. A. "Abundance for All." *Catapult* 8, no. 10 (2009): no page numbers. Accessed April 7, 2021. http://www.catapultmagazine.com/life-abundant/feature/abundance-for-all/.

Smith, James K. A. *Awaiting the King: Reforming Public Theology*. Grand Rapids: Baker Academic, 2017.

Smith, James K. A. *Desiring Kingdom: Worship, Worldview, and Cultural Formation*. Grand Rapids: Baker, 2009.

Smith, James K. A. *Imagining the Kingdom: How Worship Works*. Grand Rapids: Baker Academic, 2013.

Smith, James K. A. *The Devil Reads Derrida and Other Essays on the University, the Church, Politics and the Arts*. Grand Rapids: Eerdmans, 2009.

Smith, James K. A. *Thinking in Tongues: Pentecostal Contributions to Christian Philosophy*. Grand Rapids: Eerdmans, 2010.

Snodgrass, Klyne. "Exegesis." In *Dictionary for Theological Interpretation of the Bible*, edited by Kevin Vanhoozer, 203–6. Grand Rapids: Baker, 2007.

Souders, Michael. "A God of Wealth: Religion, Modernity, and the Rhetoric of the Christian Prosperity Gospel." Doctor of philosophy thesis, University of Kansas, 2011.

Steffen, Tom. *Worldview-based Storying: Making the Case for Worldview-based Storying*. Richmond: Orality Resources International, 2018. Kindle edition.

Stenhammar, Mikael. "Vem Tar Ansvar för 'Egoteologin' Mitt ibland Oss?" *Dagen*, May 3, 2016.

Stephenson, Barry. *Ritual: A Very Short Introduction*. Oxford: Oxford University Press, 2015.

Steuernagel, Valdir. Foreword to *Prosperity Theology and the Gospel: Good News or Bad News for the Poor?*, edited by J. Daniel Salinas, ix–xi. Peabody: Hendrickson, 2017.

Steuernagel, Valdir and Micon Steuernagel. "Historical Overview: Cape Town and Our Mission." In *Prosperity Theology and the Gospel: Good News or Bad News for the Poor?*, edited by J. Daniel Salinas, 53–65. Peabody: Hendrickson, 2017.

Stewart-Mill, Dag. *Steps to the Anointing*. London: Parchment House, 2008. Kindle edition.

Stewart, Robert. "N. T. Wright's Hermeneutic: Part 2—The Historical Jesus." *Churchman* (Autumn 2003): 235–66.

Stott, John. *Issues Facing Christians Today*. 4th edn. Grand Rapids: Zondervan, 2006.

Strawn, Bernt. "Epilogue: The Triumph of Life." In *The Bible and the Pursuit of Happiness*, edited by Bernt Strawn, 287–322. New York: Oxford University Press, 2012.

Stronstad, Roger. *The Prophethood of All Believers*. Irving: ICI University Press, 1998.

Studebaker, Steven M. *From Pentecost to the Triune God*. Grand Rapids: Eerdmans, 2012.

Studebaker, Steven M. "Trinitarian Theology: The Spirit and the Fellowship of the Triune God." In *Routledge Handbook to Pentecostal Theology*, edited by Wolfgang Vondey, 185–94. London: Routledge, 2020.

Sullivan, Katie Rose and Helen Delaney. "A Femininity That 'Giveth And Taketh Away': The Prosperity Gospel and Postfeminism in the Neoliberal Economy." *Human Relations* 70, no. 7 (2017): 836–59.

Swaggart, Jimmy. "Hyper-Faith: The New Gnosticism? Part I." *The Evangelist* 48, no. 8 (2014): 12–15.

Swaggart, Jimmy. "Hyper-Faith: The New Gnosticism? Part II." *The Evangelist* 48, no. 9 (2014): 12–15.

Swaggart, Jimmy. "Hyper-Faith: The New Gnosticism? Part III." *The Evangelist* 48, no. 10 (2014): 10–15.

Swoboda, A. J. "Posterity or Prosperity? Critiquing and Refiguring Prosperity Theologies in an Ecological Age." *Pneuma: The Journal of the Society for Pentecostal Studies* 37, no. 3 (2015): 394–411.

Tabb, Brian. *Suffering in Ancient Worldview: Luke, Seneca and 4 Maccabees in Dialogue*. London: Bloomsbury, 2017.

Tambiah, S. J. *A Performative Approach to Ritual*. Oxford: Oxford University Press, 1979.

Tanner, Kathryn. *Theories of Culture*. Minneapolis: Fortress, 1997.

Tawa, Anderson, Michael Clark and David Naugle. *An Introduction to Christian Worldview*. Downers Grove: Apollos, 2017.

Taylor, Charles. *Modern Social Imaginaries*. Durham: Duke University Press, 2004.

Taylor, Charles. *A Secular Age*. Cambridge: Belknap Press, 2007.

Tejedo, Joel. "Asian Perspectives on Prosperity Theology, Simplicity and Poverty." In *Prosperity Theology and the Gospel: Good News or Bad News for the Poor?*, edited by J. Daniel Salinas, 136–47. Peabody: Hendrickson, 2017.

Thiessen, Elmer John. "Educating Our Desires for God's Kingdom." *International Journal of Christianity & Education* 14, no. 1 (2010): 47–53.

Thomson, Leroy. "I AM a Commander Over Unlimited Prosperity #PR19." YouTube Video, 0:20:19. LeroyThomson TV, November 7, 2019. Accessed June 6, 2020. https://www.youtube.com/watch?v=W_sPgQmzdow.

Thomson, Leroy. *Money Cometh! to the Body of Christ*. Darrow: Ever Increasing Word Ministries, 1997.

Tillich, Paul. "The Religious Symbol." *Daedalus* 87, no. 3 (1958): 3–21.

Tillich, Paul. *Ultimate Concern*. London: SCM, 1965.

Togarasei, Lovemore. "The Pentecostal Gospel of Prosperity in African Contexts of Poverty: An Appraisal." *Exchange* 40 (2011): 336–50.

Ughaerumba, Chidiebere. "Pastorpreneurship in Southern Nigeria and Weber's Protestant Ethic: Insights for National Development." *International Journal of Advanced Research* 4, no. 8 (2016): 1931–41.

Ukah, Asonzeh. "God, Wealth, and the Spirit of Investment." In *Religious Activism in the Global Economy: Promoting, Reforming, or Resisting Neoliberal Globalization?*, edited by Sabine Dreher and Peter J. Smith, 73–90. Lanham, MD: Rowman & Littlefield International, 2016.

Ukah, Asonzeh. "Prophets for Profit: Pentecostal Authority and Fiscal Accountability among Nigerian Churches in South Africa." In *Alternative Voices: A Plurality Approach for Religious Studies*, edited by Afe Adogame, Magnus Echtler and Oliver Freiberger, 134–59. Göttingen: Vandenhoek and Ruprecht, 2013.

Ukah, Asonzeh. "The Redeemed Christian Church of God (RCCG), Nigeria. Local Identities and Global Processes in African Pentecostalism." Doctoral thesis, University of Bayreuth, Bayreuth, 2003.

Ukah, Asonzeh. "Review of *Pentecostalism and Prosperity: The Socio-Economics of the Global Charismatic Movement*." *Pneuma: The Journal of the Society for Pentecostal Studies* 35 (2013): 147–8.

Ukah, Asonzeh. "Prosperity, Prophecy and the Covid-19 Pandemic: The Healing Economy of African Pentecostalism." *Pneuma: The Journal of the Society for Pentecostal Studies* 42, no. 3–4 (2020): 430–59.

Vähäkangas, Mika. "The Prosperity Gospel in the African Diaspora: Unethical Theology or Gospel in Context?." *Exchange* 44, no. 4 (2015): 353–80.

van Dijk, Rijk. "Pentecostalism and Post-Development: Exploring Religion as a Developmental Ideology in Ghanaian Migrant Communities." In *Pentecostalism and Development: Churches, NGOs and Social Change in Africa*, edited by Dena Freeman, 87–109. London: Palgrave Macmillan, 2012.

van Dijk, Rijk. "The Pentecostal Gift: Ghanaian Charismatic Churches and the Moral Innocence of the Global Economy." In *Modernity on a Shoestring: Dimensions of Globalization, Consumption and Development in Africa and Beyond*, edited by Richard Fardon, Wim M. J. van Binsbergen and Rijk van Dijk. Leiden: Eidos, 1999.

Veblen, Thorsten. *Theory of the Leisure Class*. New York: Penguin, 1995.

von Sinner, Rudolf. "'Struggling with Africa': Theology of Prosperity in and from Brazil." In *Pastures of Plenty: Tracing Religio-Scapes of Prosperity Gospel in Africa and Beyond*, edited by Andreas Heuser, 117–30. Frankfurt: Peter Lang, 2015.

Vondey, Wolfgang. *Beyond Pentecostalism*. Grand Rapids: Eerdmans, 2010.

Vondey, Wolfgang. "Conclusion: Christianity and Renewal—A Plea for Interdisciplinarity." In *The Holy Spirit and the Christian Life*, edited by Wolfgang Vondey, 217–26. New York: Palgrave Macmillan, 2014.

Vondey, Wolfgang. *Pentecostal Theology: Living the Full Gospel*. London: Bloomsbury T&T Clark, 2017.

Vondey, Wolfgang. *Pentecostalism: A Guide for the Perplexed*. London: Bloomsbury, 2013.

Vondey, Wolfgang and Chris Green. "Between This and That: Reality and Sacramentality in the Pentecostal Worldview." *Journal of Pentecostal Theology* 19, no. 2 (2010): 243–64.

Vreeland, Derek. "Reconstructing Word of Faith Theology: A Defence, Analysis and Refinement of the Theology of the Word of Faith Movement." Paper presented at the 30th Annual Meeting of the Society for Pentecostal Studies, Oral Roberts University, Tulsa, Oklahoma, March 2001.

Vreeland, Derek. *Through the Eyes of N. T. Wright: A Reader's Guide to Paul and the Faithfulness of God*. Self-published. Doctrina Press, 2015.

Wacker, Grant. *Heaven Below: Early Pentecostals and American Culture*. Cambridge: Harvard University Press, 2003.

Walsh, Brian. "From Housing to Homemaking: Worldviews and the Shaping of Home." Paper presented at Adequate and Affordable Housing for All International Conference, University of Toronto, June 2004.

Walsh, Brian. "Transformation: Dynamic Worldview or Repressive Ideology?" *Journal of Education and Christian Belief* 4, no. 2 (2000): 101–14.

Walsh, Brian. *Subversive Christianity*, 2nd edn. Eugene: Wipf and Stock, 2014.

Walsh, Brian and Richard Middleton. *The Transforming Vision: Shaping a Christian World View*. Downers Grove: IVP, 1984.

Walton, Johnathan L. "Stop Worrying and Start Sowing! A Phenomenological Account of the Ethics of 'Divine Investment.'" In *Pentecostalism and Prosperity: The Socio-Economics of the Global Charismatic Movement*, edited by Katherine Attanasi and Amos Yong, 107–30. New York: Palgrave Macmillan, 2012.

Walton, Johnathan L. *Watch This! The Ethics and Aesthetics of Black Televangelism*. New York: New York University Press, 2009.

Walton, Nathan Ivan. "Blessed and Highly Favored: The Theological Anthropology of the Prosperity Gospel." Doctor of philosophy thesis, University of Virginia, 2018.

Ward, W. R. *Early Evangelicalism: A Global Intellectual History 1670–1789*. Cambridge: Cambridge University Press, 2006.

Wariboko, Nimi. *Economics in Spirit and Truth: A Moral Philosophy of Finance*. New York: Palgrave MacMillan, 2014.

Wariboko, Nimi. "Pentecostal Paradigms of National Economic Prosperity in Africa." In *Pentecostalism and Prosperity: The Socio-Economics of the Global Charismatic Movement*, edited by Katherine Attanasi and Amos Yong, 35–62. New York: Palgrave Macmillan, 2012.

Warrington, Keith. "Healing and Kenneth Hagin." *Asian Journal of Pentecostal Studies* 3, no. 1 (2000): 119–38.

Warrington, Keith. *Healing and Suffering: Biblical and Pastoral Reflections*. Carlisle: Paternoster Press, 2005.

Warrington, Keith. "Healing and Suffering in the Bible." *International Review of Mission* 95, no. 376/377 (January/April 2006): 154–64.

Warrington, Keith. "The Teaching and Praxis Concerning Supernatural Healing of British Pentecostals, of John Wimber and Kenneth Hagin in the Light of an Analysis of the Healing Ministry of Jesus as Recorded in the Gospels." Doctor of philosophy thesis, King's College London, 1999.

Warrington, Keith. "The Use of the Name (of Jesus) in Healing and Exorcism with Special Reference to the Teachings of Kenneth Hagin." *The Journal of the European Pentecostal Theological Association* 17 (1997): 16–36.

Weaver, Mary Jo and David Brakke. *Introduction to Christianity*. 4th edn. Belmont: Wadsworth, 2009.

Wheeler, Sondra. *Wealth as Peril and Obligation*. Grand Rapids: Eerdmans, 1995.

White, Joel R. "N. T. Wright's Narrative Approach." In *God and the Faithfulness of Paul: A Critical Examination of the Pauline Theology of N. T. Wright*, edited by Christoph Heilig, Thomas Hewitt and Michael Bird, 181–204. Minneapolis: Fortress, 2017.

Wiegele, Kathrine. *Investing in Miracles: El Shaddai and the Transformation of Popular Catholicism in the Philippines*. Honolulu: University of Hawaii, 2004.

Wiegele, Kathrine. "Politics, Education, and Civic Participation: Catholic Charismatic Modernities in the Philippines." In *Global Pentecostalism in the 21st Century*, edited by Robert Hefner, 223–50. Bloomington: Indiana University Press, 2013.

Wilkens, Steven. *Beyond Bumper Sticker Ethics: An Introduction to Theories of Right and Wrong*. Grand Rapids: IVP, 2011.

Wilkens, Steven and Mark Sanford. *Hidden Worldviews: Eight Cultural Studies That Shape Our Lives*. Downers Gove: IVP, 2009.

Williams, David. "Anselm and Hagin: Ontological Argument and Prosperity Cult." *Koers* 57, no. 2 (1992): 227–39.

Williams, David. *Christian Approaches to Poverty*. Lincoln: iUniverse, 2001.

Williams, Joseph. *Spirit Cure: A History of Pentecostal Healing*. Oxford: Oxford University Press, 2013.

Williams, Patrick. "Ideology and Narrative." In *Routledge Encyclopedia of Narrative Theory*, edited by David Herman, Manfred Jahn and Marie-Laure Ryan, s.v. "Ideology and Narrative." London: Routledge, 2010.

Williams, Tammy. "Is There a Doctor in the House?" In *Practicing Theology*, edited by Miroslav Volf and Dorothy Bass, 94–121. Grand Rapids: Eerdmans, 2002.

Winston, Bill. *Imitate God and Get Results*. Oak Park: Bill Winston Ministries, 2005.

Winston, Bill Ministries. "According to Heaven's Economy." *Bwm.org*. December 2012. Accessed April 7, 2021. http://lwccportal.com/ebooks/ebook/pl122012/files/assets/dow nloads/publication.pdf.

Wishemeyer, Oda. "N. T. Wright and Biblical Hermeneutics." In *God and the Faithfulness of Paul: A Critical Examination of the Pauline Theology of N. T. Wright*, edited by Christoph Heilig, Thomas Hewitt and Michael Bird, 73–100. Minneapolis: Fortress, 2017.

Witherington, Ben. *Jesus and Money*. London: SPCK, 2010.

Withrow, Lisa. "Success and the Prosperity Gospel: From Commodification to Transformation." *Journal of Religious Leadership* 6, no. 2 (2007): 15–41.

Wolters, Albert. "Appropriating *Weltanschauung*: On Jerusalem's Speaking the Language of Athens." In *After Worldview: Christian Higher Education in Postmodern Worlds*, edited by Matthew Bonzo and Michael Stevens, 101–14. Sioux Center: Dordt College, 2009.

Wolters, Albert. *Creation Regained*. 2nd edn. Grand Rapids: Eerdmans, 2005.

Wolters, Albert. "Worldview." In *The Dictionary for Theological Interpretation of the Bible*, edited by Kevin J. Vanhoozer, 854–6. Grand Rapids: Baker, 2005.

Wolterstorff, Nicholas. *Reason within the Bounds of Religion*. 2nd edn. Grand Rapids: Eerdmans, 1984.

Wommack, Andrew Ministries. "Effects of Praise." *Awmi.org*. Accessed April 7, 2021. https ://www.awmi.net/reading/teaching-articles/effects_praise/.

Wommack, Andrew Ministries. "Faith of God." *Awmi.net*. Accessed April 7, 2021. https:// www.awmi.net/reading/teaching-articles/faith_god/.

Wommack, Andrew Ministries. "Power of Faith-Filled Words." *Awmi.org*. Accessed April 7, 2021. https://www.awmi.net/reading/teaching-articles/power_faith/.

Wommack, Andrew Ministries. "The Holy Spirit." *Awmi.org*. Accessed April 7, 2021. https ://www.awmi.net/reading/teaching-articles/holy_spirit/.

Wommack, Andrew Ministries. "It's Not a Faith Problem, It's Your Unbelief." YouTube Video, 1:18. Living Word Christian Center, July 27, 2016. Accessed April 7, 2021. https ://www.youtube.com/watch?v=lq6YjjxUY5s.

Wommack, Andrew Ministries. "Revelation Knowledge." *Awmi.net*. Accessed April 7, 2021. https://www.awmi.net/reading/teaching-articles/revelation_knowledge/.

Wommack, Andrew Ministries. "Staying Positive in a Negative World." *Awmi.net.*
Accessed April 7, 2021. https://www.awmi.net/reading/teaching-articles/stay_positive/.
Wommack, Andrew Ministries. "Spirit, Soul and Body." *Awmi.org.* Accessed April 7, 2021.
https://www.awmi.net/reading/teaching-articles/spirit-soul-and-body/.
Wommack, Andrew Ministries. "You Already God It!" *Awmi.org.* Accessed April 7, 2021.
https://www.awmi.net/reading/teaching-articles/already_got/.
Wommack, Andrew Ministries. "The War Is Over." *Awmi.org.* Accessed April 7, 2021.
https://www.awmi.net/reading/teaching-articles/war_over/.
Wommack, Andrew. *The Believer's Authority*. Tulsa: Harrison House, 2009. E-book edition.
Wommack, Andrew. *Financial Stewardship: Experience the Freedom of Turning Your Finances Over to God*. Tulsa: Harrison House, 2012. E-book edition.
Wommack, Andrew. *Spirit, Soul and Body*. Tulsa: Harrison House, 2010. E-book edition.
Wommack, Andrew. *You've Already Got It! So Quit Trying to Get It*. Tulsa: Harrison House, 2006. E-book edition.
Woodbridge, Russell. "The Prosperity Gospel in North America." In *Prosperity Theology and the Gospel: Good News or Bad News for the Poor?*, edited by J. Daniel Salinas, 151–7. Peabody: Hendrickson, 2017.
Wrenn, Mary V. "Consecrating Capitalism: The United States Prosperity Gospel and Neoliberalism." *Journal of Economic Issues* 53, no. 2 (2019): 425–32.
Wright, Christopher. "Calling the Church Back to Humility, Integrity and Simplicity." In *Prosperity Theology and the Gospel: Good News or Bad News for the Poor?*, edited by J. Daniel Salinas, 187–98. Peabody: Hendrickson, 2017.
Wright, Christopher. *The Mission of God*. Downers Grove: IVP Academic, 2006.
Wright, N. T. *After You Believe: Why Christian Character Matters*. New York: HarperCollins, 2010.
Wright, N. T. "The Challenge of Dialogue: A Partial and Preliminary Response." In *God and the Faithfulness of Paul: A Critical Examination of the Pauline Theology of N. T. Wright*, edited by Christoph Heilig, Thomas Hewitt and Michael Bird, 711–70. Minneapolis: Fortress, 2017.
Wright, N. T. *The Climax of the Covenant: Christ and the Law in Pauline Theology*. Minneapolis: Fortress Press, 1993.
Wright, N. T. *The Day the Revolution Began*. London: SPCK, 2016.
Wright, N. T. *Jesus and the Victory of God*. London: SPCK, 1996.
Wright, N. T. *Justification: God's Plan and Paul's Vision*. London: SPCK, 2009.
Wright, N. T. *The New Testament and the People of God*. London: SPCK, 1992.
Wright, N. T. *Paul and the Faithfulness of God*. Minneapolis: Fortress Press, 2013.
Wright, N. T. *Paul: Fresh Perspectives*. London: SPCK, 2005.
Wright, N. T. *The Paul Debate*. London: SPCK, 2016.
Wright, N. T. *The Resurrection of the Son of God*. London: SPCK, 2003.
Wright, N. T. *Scripture and the Authority of God*. New York: HarperOne, 2005.
Wright, N. T. "The Word and the Wind: A Response." In *Pentecostal Theology and the Theological Vision of N. T. Wright*, edited by Janet Meyer Everts and Jeffrey S. Lamp, 141–78. Cleveland: CPT Press, 2015.
Wuthnow, Robert. *American Mythos*. Princeton: Princeton University Press, 2006.
Wuthnow, Robert. *God and Mammon in America*. New York: The Free Press, 1994.
Yelle, Robert. "The Peircean Icon and the Study of Religion: A Brief Overview." *Material Religion* 12, no. 2 (2016): 241–3.

Yip, Jeaney and Susan Ainsworth. "'We Aim to Provide Excellent Service to Everyone Who Comes to Church!': Marketing Mega-Churches in Singapore." *Social Compass* 60, no. 4 (2013): 503–16.

Yong, Amos. *In the Days of Caesar: Pentecostalism and Political Theology*. Grand Rapids: Eerdmans, 2010.

Yong, Amos. *The Spirit Poured Out on All Flesh: Pentecostalism and the Possibility of Global Theology*. Grand Rapids: Baker, 2005.

Yong, Amos. *Spirit-Word-Community*. Eugene: Wipf and Stock, 2002.

Amos. "To See or Not to See: A Review Essay of Michael Palmer's *Elements of a Christian Worldview*." *Pneuma: The Journal of the Society for Pentecostal Studies* 21, no. 2 (1991): 305–27.

Yong, Amos. "A Typology of Prosperity Theology." In *Pentecostalism and Prosperity: The Socio-Economics of the Global Charismatic Movement*, edited by Katherine Attanasi and Amos Yong, 15–34. New York: Palgrave Macmillan, 2012.

Zalanga, Samuel. "Religion, Economic Development and Cultural Change: The Contradictory Role of Pentecostal Christianity in Subsaharan Africa." *Journal of Third World Studies* 27, no. 1 (2010): 43–62.

Zaprometova, Olga. "From Persecution to 'Prosperity.'" *Journal of the European Pentecostal Theological Association* 38, no. 2 (2018): 2–12.

INDEX

Jesus died spiritually   30, 69, 136, 137, 258; *see also* dual death
justice   193; *see also* social justice

kenotic Christology   98
Kenyon connection   35
kingdom of God   212, 238, 259, 279

language   151, 202, 204
Latin America   1
liturgy   199, 206, 210, 212, 217
logic   12, 14, 29, 33, 50, 52, 53, 55, 60, 93, 94, 102, 108, 113, 114, 124, 137, 140, 143, 150, 159, 178, 179, 185, 187, 188, 195, 196, 198, 200, 202, 207, 212, 215, 216, 220, 222, 224–6, 229, 230, 232, 233, 237, 241, 242, 250–5, 260, 262–5, 267, 268, 270, 276, 278, 283, 285, 287–90, 292, 295, 297, 298; *see also* market logic; polarized logic; pragmatic logic

magic   51, 203, 267
market   44, 45, 51, 52, 56, 71, 186, 209, 212–15, 220, 223, 225–7, 231–3, 235, 237, 242, 251, 254, 260, 270, 278, 285, 289, 290, 295–8
market logic   212, 215, 243, 251, 270, 278, 285, 290, 295, 297, 298
Marxist critical economic theory   43
materialism   52, 221, 281, 282
media   45, 185, 206, 207, 229, 234, 238; *see also* social media; television
medicine   203, 218
meditation   206
megachurch   99–101, 151, 196, 234
mega mindset   237
metanarrative   81
metaphysics   36, 37, 39, 126, 166, 172, 209, 252, 254
mind   36, 127, 156, 206, 208, 209, 247, 254, 274
mindset   74, 103, 179, 285; *see also* worldview
miracle   52, 164, 261, 264, 294
missions   193
modernism   70, 83
money   1, 9, 49, 52, 53, 55, 130, 142, 170, 193, 197, 210, 212–15, 218, 223,

226, 229, 232, 236, 239, 242, 260, 262, 265, 269, 277, 285, 294; *see also* wealth
movement; *see* Word of Faith, as movement
music   235; *see also* song
mystery   158, 177, 188, 263, 283, 289

name it and claim it   6, 198
name of Jesus   121, 134
narrative   87
narrative categories   113
narrative entities   113
narrative gap   114, 115, 126, 128, 140, 203
narrative tension   126, 131
narrative themes   93, 113, 118, 119, 121, 124, 136, 140, 239
narrative vacuum   136, 239
nationalism   121
negative confession   201, 204, 242
neoliberalism   41
New Age   24, 69, 71
new birth; *see* born-again; salvation
New Thought   36, 38, 39, 69, 126, 172, 209, 254

occult economics   51, 52, 172
ontology; *see* pneumacentric ontology
opponents, narrative category of   109–12, 136, 140, 141, 218, 288, 297
optimism   57, 145, 158, 162, 167, 179–82, 184, 185, 188, 196, 201, 218, 260, 276, 277, 287
overrealized eschatology   279, 282, 283, 285
overrealized theology of the present   277, 279

panentheism   256
pantheism   256
paradox   124, 158, 177, 188, 263, 283, 288
Peirce, C. S.   148; *see also* semiotics
Pelagianism   24
Pentecostalism   1, 8–12, 14, 21, 26–9, 32, 39–41, 47, 52, 59, 60, 72, 76, 80, 98, 113, 171, 190, 213, 226, 227, 237, 250, 262, 275, 287, 292–9; *see also* full gospel